D0372693

What's the Harm?

*Does Legalizing Same-Sex Marriage Really
Harm Individuals, Families or Society?*

**Edited by
Lynn D. Wardle**

University Press of America,® Inc.
Lanham · Boulder · New York · Toronto · Plymouth, UK

Copyright © 2008 by
University Press of America,® Inc.
4501 Forbes Boulevard
Suite 200
Lanham, Maryland 20706
UPA Acquisitions Department (301) 459-3366

Estover Road
Plymouth PL6 7PY
United Kingdom

Library of Congress Control Number: 2008932453

ISBN-13: 978-0-7618-4316-0 (paperback : alk. paper)
ISBN-10: 0-7618-4316-7 (paperback : alk. paper)
eISBN-13: 978-0-7618-4317-7
eISBN-10: 0-7618-4317-5

TABLE OF CONTENTS

ACKNOWLEDGEMENTS

It is appropriate that this book contains at the very beginning an expression of appreciation for the many persons whose efforts have made publication of this book possible. First, the authors or co-authors of each of the nineteen chapters made sacrifices and invested limited personal and professional assets to research, write, revise and refine the papers that through their patient persistence are published as chapters in this anthology.

The wonderful work of Marcene Mason, Genevieve Beck, and Karen Sandstrom, fifth floor secretaries at the J. Reuben Clark Law School at Brigham Young University, was indispensable. They all made editing changes repeatedly, with great skill and good will, and Karen formatted and reformatted the papers to perfection. Likewise, the work of my student research assistant, Malisa Whiting King was very helpful in bringing the editorial work to completion. Scott Loveless of the World Family Policy Center did a wonderful, effective, final, quick proof-reading for us.

The professional work of the editors and production staff at University Press of America is greatly appreciated. Samantha M. Kirk was particularly encouraging and helpful in arranging for publication, and Alison Syring provided excellent and timely editorial review.

The institutional support of Brigham Young University through the J. Reuben Clark Law School and its Marriage and Family Law Research Project, as well as the support and encouragement of the Marriage Law Project of the Columbus Law School at The Catholic University of America also are greatly appreciated. Those two great academic institutions sponsored an academic Symposium which led to this book. Sponsoring academic symposia where difficult issues and unpopular aspects of controversial public policy dilemmas can be addressed in the most thoughtful, open, and respectful way by scholars and experts in many disciplines, and the pursuit of excellence in the consideration of such issues encouraged, is in the highest and best tradition of all great universities.

Finally, it is important to acknowledge the unidentified supporters, our family members and friends, upon whose good will the authors have imposed while writing this book. Their patience and encouragement also (especially) made this book possible. We hope the resulting product is of such high quality and excellence that it merits the burdens borne by our families and friends. It is for them that we have written these chapters. It is to them that we dedicate this book.

Lynn D. Wardle
Provo, Utah
May 2008

PREFACE:
"WHAT'S THE HARM?" AND WHY IT MATTERS

Lynn D. Wardle
Brigham Young University

Provo, Utah
May 2008

Perhaps the most decisive question in the debate about whether same-sex marriage should be legalized is – "what's the harm?" As a participant in debates, panel discussions, conferences, symposia, presentations, and lectures about same-sex marriage at dozens of law schools in the United States over the past decade, representing the position that same-sex marriage should not be legalized, the question that I am most frequently asked is some variation that question. Law students, professors, and staff repeatedly ask: "How will legalizing same-sex marriage harm me or my family?" "How will society be hurt if we allow same-sex couples to marry?" "If there is any harm, isn't it really "victimless" harm incurred, if at all, only by the two consenting adults?" "Same-sex marriage became legal in The Netherlands in 2001, and Massachusetts legalized same-sex marriage in 2004, and the sky has not fallen in those places – so *what's the harm?*"

In a tolerant, liberty-loving, democratic society, this is a very important question. America has warmly embraced John Stuart Mill's "harm principle" – that the individual ought to be free from government restriction and able to do whatever he or she wants unless it harms someone else.[1] That utilitarian concept actually builds upon centuries of earlier political and philosophical work (including writings of Jefferson, Montesquieu, and Locke) that laid the foundation for a government designed to protect and preserve individual liberty.[2] It is undeniable that the contemporary concept of "autonomy" differs in some significant respects from the meaning and connotation associated with the term "liberty" in 1787-89, when the Founders of the American Constitution and Bill of Rights, were creating the documents and structures and fundamental principles of the government of the United States.[3] Nonetheless, today, in the dawn of the twenty-first century, Americans have come to value and expect nearly complete individual autonomy, privacy and freedom from government restraint in their adult, consensual, personal, intimate, family, and sexual lives. The recent mainstream social acceptance of homosexual relations is the latest manifestation of this personal autonomy principle.[4]

Of course, there are many other important questions in the debate over legalizing same-sex marriage. The consequentialist or utilitarian approaches that underlie the "what's the harm" question are not the only, or necessarily the most important perspectives. One might see the issue as having greater symbolic than consequentialist significance. Or one might view the same-sex or conjugal marriage issue as a matter of fundamental rights or basic human values with overriding intrinsic merit separate and apart from any measurable material effects, harmful or beneficial. However, American pragmatism focuses on the fruits of the behavior rather than on the motive for or metaphysical merit of it. Our generation seems to assume that there are connections between symbols and substance, and that the protection of basic human rights and fundamental values is not only good in itself, but produces good consequences, making for a better society.

Most Americans today take the live-and-let-live approach to legal policies regarding marriage and family relations. Thus, it is not surprising that the decisive question in the minds of many people who are considering whether same-sex marriage should be legalized is: *"What's the harm?"* So it is important to consider whether and how legalizing same-sex marriage will or might reasonably be expected to cause harm to society, to the institution of marriage, to families, as well as to specific individual members of society (children and adults).

This anthology contains an interdisciplinary collection of perspectives on the question of harm – whether *legalizing* same-sex marriage will or does cause harm to society, and whether the *denial* of same-sex marriage causes harm to society; what are the societal, familial, individual, and jurisprudential harms of legalizing (or of prohibiting) same sex marriage? The authors wrestle with the "what's the harm" question from a variety of perspectives reflecting the disciplines of law, political science, business, psychology, anthropology, sociology, family studies, and other fields of study. They present a variety of conclusions, from opposing same-sex marriage to advocating same-sex marriage, from claiming same-sex marriage harms society and individuals to arguing that denial of same-sex marriage harms society and individuals. The chapters illustrate the wide range of harms asserted to result from the refusal to allow same-sex marriage, as well as the broad range of the detriments that may flow from, or that are predicted to follow, the legalization of same-sex marriage.

There are four Parts in the book. Each part begins with one essay arguing that legalizing same-sex marriage does or will cause harm, and one essay arguing that legalizing same-sex marriage does not and will not cause harm but that denial of marriage to same-sex couples causes harm. Following those two chapters the other chapters in each Part address the "what's the harm" question, asserting diverse disciplinary perspectives supporting one side or the other, or taking a different, intermediate position. The chapters range in perspective from Mark Strasser's comprehensive review of the harms resulting from denial of gay marriage and point-by-point refutation of the arguments against same-sex marriage, to Vince Samar's carefully-presented claim that denial of same-sex marriage violates basic international human rights, to Dale Carpenter's principled arguments that conservative opposition to same-sex marriage is causing unconservative harms to society, to Martha Bailey's analysis of the importance of accommodating change in society and marriage law. In between, Allan Carlson, for example, gives a moderate assessment of whether legalizing same-sex unions in Sweden undermined marriage there; he disputes that legalization of gay marriage caused the disintegration of marriage there (arguing that decades of earlier policies leveling marriage and other relationships did most of the damage), but he suggests that legalization of same-sex unions furthers the erosion. On the "harm" side are articles that vary in approach from the thorough historical work of Charles Reid, to the powerful political theory analysis of Seana Sugrue, to the deep philosophical analysis of Scott FitzGibbon, to the contemporary ethical analysis of Marianne Jennings, to the exhaustive review of empirical studies by Jason Carroll, David Dollahite, and Dean Byrd, to the challenging review of psychological theory by Dr. Gantt, to the detailed legal analysis of Roger Severino of the religious liberty harm-implications, to Charles Russo's very knowledgeable assessment of the evolving detrimental impact on public education, to mention just a few examples.

It is important to note that most of the potential harms identified are neither immediate nor dramatic. Rather, the most profound harms from legalizing same-sex marraige are likely to be much more subtle and longitudinal, like the harm that followed the adoption of "divorce-on-demand" laws and social mores in the 1970s (short term depression, then return to functionality, but long-lasting personal, social, and intrafamilial harms, especially for children), or the harm from smoking cigarettes (first addiction, then, after years of indulging the habit, often lung cancer and emphysema for the smokers, and sometimes for those who live or work with them), or the harm to a community that comes from the failure to regularly maintain roads, water pipes, and sewage systems (decay, disintegration and degeneration until eventually the roads are dangerously potholed, the water is undrinkable, and the sewage system fails). The most severe harms from legalizing same-sex marriage appear to be longitudinal, inter-generation, and inflicted upon the infrastructure – the social, moral, familial, relational, political and conceptual architecture – of the community. On the other hand, it is clear that same-sex couples and parents are real and exist in large numbers in America. Thus, the detriment of denial of marital legal status is urged by advocates of same-sex marriage in urgent terms.

It is also important to mention that children are singled out in several of the papers as the most vulnerable victims of most of the serious potential harms that may come from redefining marriage because marriage is the basic foundation of the most secure, happiest families, and the family is the key socializing environment and system that shapes children's lives, values, and expectations. Part of the predicted detrimental effect upon children is the consequence of the longitudinal nature of the harm – the harms emerge and build over time and are not fully realized for a generation, until today's children have become (or are becoming) adults. But the particular impact on children also may result from the effect that changing the meaning of marriage may have upon the morality and institutional integrity of marriage, and upon the linkage between marriage, procreation, and parenting. On the other hand, several authors emphasize the value of the evolving nature of marriage, and the greater harms that may flow from the refusal to legalize same-sex marriage because alternative solutions may erode and reshape the institution of marriage as well.

Thus, this book presents many sides and many perspectives on the same-sex marriage debate. A high-quality collection of very thoughtful papers by knowledgeable experts presenting the "potential harms" arguments pro- and con- clearly needed, if not long overdue.

We believe that this advocative anthology, presenting perspectives about harm caused by the denial or legalization of same-sex marriage, makes at least three very important contributions to the public discourse and to the literature. First, in at least a small but a very important way, it contributes some balance and contrasting perspectives to the intellectual discourse and scholarly literature. It will improve the completeness, honesty and fairness of the academic discussion of one of the most profound social issues of this generation. Second, the comprehensive, interdisciplinary positions presented in this volume will broaden and edify the general public consideration of the same-sex marriage public policy issue. It will improve the public discourse about what could well be the most critical social policy issue of our time. Third, by providing some of the missing arguments and presenting some generally-unheard information about potential harms on both sides of the debate, the authors hope that this book will help to answer the question that lies at the very core of the academic, public and political debate over whether same-sex marriage should be legalized. Thus, we hope that this book will increase general understanding of what we can expect to see and what we should prepare to cope with in those societies where same-sex marriage and equivalent relations have been or will be legalized.

Notes

1. "[T]he only purpose for which power can be rightfully exercised over any member of a civilised community, against his will, is to prevent harm to others." John Stuart Mill, On Liberty 10-11 (David Spitz ed., W.W. Norton & Co. 1975) (1859). *See also id.* at 154; John Stuart Mill, *A Few Words on Non-Intervention*, in 3 Dissertations and Discussions: Political, Philosophical, and Historical 238, 258-60 (1882).
2. *See generally* John Locke, *Second Treatise of Government* in Two Treatises of Government (Peter Laslett ed., Cambridge University Press 1960) (1690); Charles de Secondat (Baron de Montesquieu), The Spirit of the Laws (1755); Declaration of Independence (1776) (Thomas Jefferson, chief author). *See further* Abraham Lincoln, *The Gettysburg Address* (1863), available at Abraham Lincoln Online, http://showcase.netins.net/web/creative/lincoln/speeches/gettysburg.htm (seen 13 February 2007) ("government of the people, by the people and for the people" declaration by Mill's contemporary, Lincoln).
3. *See generally* Lynn D. Wardle, *Lessons from the Bill of Rights About Constitutional Protection for Marriage*, 38 Loy. Univ.-Chi. L. J. 279, 302 (2007) ("In the founding generation, liberty was not the same as unfettered autonomy. Liberty was not the right to do whatever one wanted to do. Rather, as Marci Hamilton has explained, it was the right to

act as one chooses within the limits of the commonwealth—to do whatever one wanted that did not harm the common good.").

4. *See generally* Lawrence v. Texas, 539 U.S. 558, (2003) ("Liberty protects the person from unwarranted government intrusions into a dwelling or other private places. . . . [T]here are other spheres of our lives and existence . . . where the State should not be a dominant presence. Freedom extends beyond spatial bounds. Liberty presumes an autonomy of self that includes . . . certain intimate conduct." *Id.* at ("When sexuality finds overt expression in intimate conduct with another person, the conduct can be but one element in a personal bond that is more enduring.") *Id.* ("These matters, involving the most intimate and personal choices a person may make in a lifetime, choice central to personal dignity and autonomy, are central to the liberty protected by the Fourteenth Amendment. At the heart of liberty is the right to define one's own concept of existence, of meaning, of the universe, and of the mystery of human life.")(quoted from *Planned Parenthood v. Casey,* 505 U.S. 833 (1992)). The warm reception of the *Lawrence* decision in academic and professional circles (law reviews), and the by public generally (in popular media) attests to the widespread acceptance of the general principle of adult sexual autonomy.

PART I
DOES LEGALIZING SAME-SEX MARRIAGE HARM FAMILIES AND CHILDREARING?

CHAPTER 1
CONJUGAL MARRIAGE FOSTERS HEALTHY HUMAN AND SOCIETAL DEVELOPMENT

A. Dean Byrd
University of Utah

"Conjugal society is made by a voluntary compact between man and woman; and tho' it consists chiefly in such a communion and right to one another's bodies and is necessary to its chief end, procreation; yet it draws with it mutual support and assistance, and a communion of interests too, as necessary not only to write their care and affection, but also necessary to their common off-spring, who have a right to be nourished, and maintained by them, till they are able to provide for themselves."[1]
—John Locke

I.   Introduction

Locke's view reflects the important benefits marriage provides to a good society, including permanency, sexual complementarity and mutual fidelity. Marriage from time immemorial has contributed to the healthy development of both men and women and provides an optimal environ for child rearing, all of which have added to the betterment of society. The benefits of this family structure find extensive support in the scientific literature. Other family structures do not provide similar benefits and may, indeed, cause harm.

II.   The Benefits of Conjugal Marriage

A.   Traditional Marriage Benefits Both Men and Women

The well-being of adults is an important consideration in marriage. Men and women who marry benefit financially, emotionally, physically and socially from this unique institution.

Married men and women, when compared to unmarried men and women, are more likely to be financially stable, to accumulate assets, and to own a home.[2] This conclusion holds true even when the comparison group is cohabiting adults.[3] The income of men who are married is 10 to 40% more than that of single men with similar professional/educational background and experience.[4]

Women who are married do not experience a similar financial advantage over women who are not, primarily because most women combine marriage with motherhood, which tends to depress the earnings of married women.[5] However, women from disadvantaged backgrounds are less likely to fall into poverty if they marry and the marriage stays intact.[6]

Marriage is protective of the emotional and physical health of men and women. Adults who are married have greater longevity, less disease and illness, increased happiness and lower levels of mental illness, especially depression and substance abuse, than do both single and cohabiting adults.[7] Married men and women are more likely to encourage their spouses to seek medical screenings and health care than do cohabiting partners.[8] Adult maturity and fidelity correlates with marriage and provides a source of motivation for both men and women to avoid risky health behaviors, such as heavy alcohol and drug use, as well as promiscuous sexual behaviors.[9] In addition, the financial stability associated with marriage enables men and women to afford better health care.[10] The social and emotional support that emerges from marriage reduces the consequences of stressors and the associated stress hormones, like cortisol, that often cause both physical and mental illnesses.[11]

Replicated studies have arrived at the same conclusion: marriage-related gains are translated into increased life expectancy and overall better health for men.[12] Women also experience gains, but the marriage benefits differ for women depending upon marital quality. The benefits for women are associated with the quality of the marriage: marriages that are poor in quality are associated with psychological distress in women, while good quality marriages provide women with important psychological and physical boosts.[13]

Marriage plays an important social function in turning men toward the good of family and society. Married men, for example, are less likely to commit crime.[14] However, it is not marriage, the institution, that civilizes men, but rather the gender complementarity afforded by marriage that has the civilizing effect.[15] That is, it is not marriage *per se* that civilizes men but rather the influence of women in the marriage relationship. Married men tend to be less sexually promiscuous, more faithful and less likely to abuse alcohol than single men.[16] They are more frequent church attenders, spend more time with relatives than with friends and work longer hours.[17] One researcher concluded that only 4% of married men had been unfaithful during the past year compared to 16% of cohabiting men and 37% of men who were presently in an ongoing relationship with a woman.[18]

In his longitudinal research, Nock concluded that these effects were the direct result of marriage, not an artifact of selection. In his research, Nock tracked men longitudinally from being single as they transitioned into marriage and post marriage. He concluded that men's behavior actually underwent a change after marriage which included working harder in their place of employment, frequenting bars less often, attending church more often and spending more time with relatives.[19] For men, it appears that marriage is a rite of passage that transitions them fully into the adult world of responsibility and self-control.[20]

The gender specific characteristics accorded by biology also support the importance of marriage in lowering testosterone levels in men. [21] Research on men, marriage and testosterone concludes that married men, particularly married men with children, have lower levels of testosterone than single men. [22] Also, cohabiting men have lower testosterone levels than do single men. [23] Testosterone levels in men are moderated by secure, stable, permanent procreative relationships.[24] According to the literature on testosterone, this decrease in testosterone levels is associated with marriage and makes men less inclined to risky, aggressive behavior.[25]

Women are uniquely benefited by marriage as well. In 1994, a Department of Justice report concluded that single and divorced women were four times more likely to be victimized by violent crime than married women.[26] Married women were significantly less likely to be abused by a partner than women in a cohabiting intimate relationship.[27] The data from one study found that 4% of married couples compared to 13% of cohabiting couples had arguments that resulted in domestic violence. [28] Researchers suggest that infidelity is higher in cohabiting couples than in married couples, and that infidelity invites serious marital conflict.[29] Marriage, it appears, provides a safe harbor for woman.

B.   Dual Gender Parenting and Child-rearing

The research supporting the importance of dual gender parenting and child-rearing is extensive and clear in its singular conclusion: all variables considered, children are best served when reared in a home with a married mother and father.[30] Mothers and fathers contribute in gender specific and in gender complementary ways to the healthy development of children. Children reap unique developmental benefits when reared in a home with a married, reasonably harmonious union of their own biological mother and father. A Child Trends research brief provided the following scholarly summary:

> Research clearly demonstrates that family structure matters for children, and the family structure that helps children the most is a family headed by two biological parents in a low-conflict marriage…There is thus value for children in promoting strong, stable marriages between biological parents.[31]

Children raised in homes with both mothers and fathers navigate the developmental stages more easily, are more solid and secure in their sense of self and in their sense of gender identity, perform better in the school system, have fewer social and emotional problems and become better functioning adults. The plethora of studies which span decades supports the conclusion that gender-linked differences in child-rearing are protective for children.[32] From her research, Baumrind concluded that children of dual-gender parents are more competent, function better with fewer problems in living.[33] Her later research focused on the complementary nature of the expressive parenting of mothers and the instrumental parenting of fathers.[34] Greenberger noted that the essential contributions to the optimal development of children are not only gender specific but also gender complementary and virtually impossible for a mother or father to do alone.[35] Children learn about male and female differences through parental modeling. The parental, mother-father relationship provides children with a model of marriage, the most meaningful, enduring relationship that the vast majority of individuals will have during their lives.

The complementary contributions of mothers and fathers are readily observable in their gender specific parenting styles. The parenting style of mothers is most often seen as flexible, warm and sympathetic while fathers' styles are more directive, consistent and predictable. Rossi supported this observation with research which concluded that mothers could better read an infant's facial expressions, respond with tactile gentleness and soothe with the use of voice.[36] Fathers, on the other hand, were less involved in caretaking and engaged in more overt play.[37] Such complementary contributions appear critical for later development. Male and female differences are readily observed in the characteristics of physicality associated with mothering and fathering. Mothers use touch to calm, soothe and to bring comfort to children. When mothers reach for children, they frequently bring them to their breasts to provide safety, warmth and security. Fathers' touch is most often described as playful and stimulating, bringing with it a sense of excitement to the child. This rough and tumble play (RTP) is characterized by holding the child at arm's length in front of them, making eye contact, tossing the infant in the air and holding the child in such a way to have the child look over the father's shoulder. Shapiro notes that these "daddy holds" emphasize a sense of freedom for the child.[38]

Rohner and Veneziano conducted an analysis of more than a 100 studies on the role of fathers in child development and concluded that not only did a nurturing father play a critical role in a child's well-being but in some cases father love was a stronger factor in a child's well-being than mother love.[39] The researchers summarized: "Overall, father love appears to be as heavily implicated as mother love in offspring's psychological well-being."[40]

Clarke-Stewart also investigated differences in how mothers and fathers play with children.[41] She noted that mothers tended to play at the child's level, and are more likely to provide opportunities to direct the play, allowing the child to proceed at his or her own pace. On the other hand, fathers' play was more instructional. RTP was much more noticeable, focusing clearly on acceptable/non-acceptable behaviors. RTP does not correlate with aggression and violence, but rather is associated with self-control. Through RTP, children quickly learn that physical violence such as biting and kicking are not acceptable. In RTP, children learn from their fathers how to manage emotionally-charged situations in the context of play and how to recognize and respond appropriately to an array of emotions.[42]

Stress resilience is another area where fathers' contributions are noticeable. The research conducted by Marissa Diener at the University of Utah is particularly poignant.[43] She demonstrated that infants (12 months old) who had close relationships with their fathers were more stress resistant than those who did not have close relationships with their fathers. These babies who had secure father relationships used more coping strategies. Diener concluded: "there may be something unique to fathers that provides children with different opportunities to regulate their emotions."[44]

Discipline is another area where differences between mothers and fathers emerge quite prominently. Fathers more frequently rely on firmness, principles, and rules. Mothers rely more on responding, negotiating, and adjusting toward the children's moods as well as to the context. Mothers place much more emphasis on intuition in trying to understand children's needs and the emotions of the moment.[45] Gilligan attributes these characteristics to innate differences between men and women: men stress fairness, justice and duty based on rules and principles whereas women are more inclined to focus on understanding, sympathy, care and helping.[46]

Another area of considerable research is the investment of fathers in their biological children. Wilson concluded that children of married, biological parents received a greater investment from their fathers than children of cohabitants. These differences persisted after controlling for socioeconomic factors.[47]

The children of unmarried or divorced parents are at risk for emotional, behavioral and health problems. They are more likely to be abused by their own parents, by step-parents or parents' boyfriends/girlfriends. Children of unmarried or divorced parents have lower academic achievement, poorer school attendance and more discipline problems when compared to children of married parents. These academically-related problems are associated with a greater use of remedial and special needs resources. In addition, these children are more apt to encounter trouble with the law such as committing crimes, abusing drugs, and spending time in incarceration. They are more likely to have difficulty in forming their own stable families.[48]

The consequences of father absence has been well-documented. Blankenhorn concluded that father hunger is the primary cause of the declining well-being of children in our society and is associated with social problems such as teenage pregnancy, child abuse, and domestic violence against women.[49] Masser, a psychiatrist at Northside Hospital in Atlanta, Georgia, noted that an increasing number of children who seek psychiatric care are suffering from father hunger.[50]

Golombok, Tasker & Murray found that "children in father absent families perceive themselves to be less cognitively competent and less physically competent than children in father-present families, with no differences between children in lesbian and single heterosexual families."[51] Most of the research on gay parenting compares children in some fatherless families to children in other fatherless families. Such studies cannot be reasonably used to contradict extensive social science research which concludes that family structure indeed matters, and the intact, married biological family structure is the most protective of child well-being.[52]

Although there is more research to support the ill effects of father hunger in children, the consequences of mother hunger are beginning to emerge in case studies. This is partially explained because of the historical preference for mothers to be the primary caretakers of their children even when divorce occurs. The Eisold report provides evidence that mother hunger may indeed emerge when a child is deprived of a mother or mother figure. In the article titled "Recreating Mother," a male child was conceived by a surrogate mother for two homosexual men.[53] They had arranged an artificial insemination with a woman who agreed to relinquish her parental rights in return for medical care and financial compensation. The child, Nick, was cared for by a hired nanny and began attending school when he was two years old. When Nick was 2½ years old, the nanny was abruptly terminated, another nanny was hired and subsequently fired, and a third nanny was hired. The homosexual couple adopted a second child. At 4½ years old, Nick's behavioral problems resulted in a referral to a female child psychologist, a fourth mother substitute. Because Nick lived in a world where mothers were hired and fired, he fantasized about buying a new mother. Eisold questioned, "How do we explain why this child, the son of a male couple, seemed to need to construct a woman—'mother'—with whom he could play the role of a loving boy/man? How did such an idea enter his mind? What inspired his intensity on the subject?" Eisold sees some normal, innate developmental forces at work in a boy who has no mother: if he has none, he will need to make one. [54]

Biller's extensive research on parent-child interaction yields the following conclusion: mothers and fathers are not interchangeable.[55] His research concludes that:

- Paternal and maternal differences are stimulating for the infant as they provide contrasting images via differences in mothers' and fathers' dress, their movements, even voices. Because of these differences, infants may prefer mothers when they want to be consoled or soothed and fathers when they want stimulation.
- These differences are important sources of complementary learning for children.
- Where there are strong parental attachments, infants are at a decided developmental advantage compared to those infants who only had close maternal relationships.
- Fathers who are involved with their children stimulated them to explore and investigate whereas mothers focused on pre-structured and predictable activities.
- Parental relationships seem particularly important for boys during the second year of the child's life, as boys become more father-focused. Unlike boys, girls do not seem to have this consistent focus during this developmental period.[56]

Biller's research demonstrates clearly the importance of mothers and fathers to the healthy development of children, not only in the unique paternal and maternal contributions, but in the complementary nature of those contributions. The following conclusion aptly summarizes his research:

> Infants who have two positively involved parents tend to be more curious and eager to explore than those who do not have a close relationship with their fathers....Well-fathered infants are more secure and trusting in branching out in their explorations, and they may be

somewhat more advanced in crawling, climbing and manipulating objects.[57]

Extensive research spanning decades yields an overwhelming abundance of data supporting the importance of both mothers and fathers to the healthy development of children. Recent evidence, not only supportive but compellingly, demonstrates that a society concerned with optimal child development is most benefited by traditional marriage and married, dual-gender parenting.

III.   What's the Harm? Same-Sex Marriage and Societal Harm

The scientific data clearly demonstrates than traditional marriage offers a protection for men, women and children. Such families have unique benefits not found in other family structures. Not all family structures are equally as healthful or helpful for individuals, especially children. Society is harmed when the family structures within it are harmed.

A.   Social and Individual Impacts

Unlike the benefits society reaps from traditional marriage, the benefits of same-sex marriage accrue primarily to a few individuals at the expense of society. Gay marriage advocates are fond of pointing out that civil marriage confers more than 1049 automatic federal and additional state protections, benefits and responsibilities, according to the Federal Government's General Accounting Office. If these governmentally-bestowed benefits and responsibilities are indeed the core of marriage, then this package should be equally available to all citizens, including homosexual couples. It follows, however, that making them available to homosexual couples means that these benefits should also be available to any grouping of individuals, of any size or combinations of genders, of any degree of permanence.[58]

Ironically, as feminist scholar Martha Fineman observed, the protections of same-sex marriage would actually exclude non-sexual arrangements for those who seek the protections that marriage offers, such as a sister caring for an ill brother or sister, single parents with children, or close neighbors and friends who would benefit from the protections of marriage.[59] Yet, permitting same-sex couples to call their sexual arrangements "marriage" while excluding non-sexual arrangements from marriage is incongruous considering that The Supreme Judicial Court of Massachusetts has declared that procreation as the ground that explains and justifies marriage may not be privileged, nor is consummation a necessary ingredient defining marriage.[60] But by this reasoning, the Court opens itself to arguments that marriage should be open to uncles and nieces or fathers and daughters who happen to be sterile and intimate. Or to the man who is willing to have a vasectomy in order to marry his mother. Or even to the marriage of a father and a son.[61]

A significant number of influential voices on the gay left reject the idea of same-sex marriage, suggesting that marriage itself is oppressive. They tolerate same-sex marriage only as a transitional moment toward the eventual abolition of marriage."[62] The lawyer activist Nan Hunter laid out this view when she wrote, "the impact of gay and lesbian marriage will be to dismantle the legal structure of gender in every marriage." According to her, this arrangement has "the potential to expose and denaturalize the historical construction of gender at the heart of marriage."[63] For Hunter and those who share her views, there is really no motivation to shore up marriage as an institution. For them, discrediting of marriage is simply an interim step to its disintegration.[64]

The concept of sexual orientation itself is noticeably absent in recent discussions about same-sex marriage. Homosexuality, unlike gender and race, is a self-attribution. According to social constructionism, the philosophy underlying queer theory, homosexuality is a construct, not a biological reality. Those who hold this view suggest that the distinction between gay and straight is giving way to a new, liberated concept of sexual fluidity. Lisa Diamond, in an article in the *Monitor on Psychology,* concluded from her research that "sexual identity is far from fixed who are not exclusively heterosexual."[65] Schechter supports this fluidity in her research on women who, after ten years in a lesbian relationship, are now in heterosexual relationships lasting more than a year.[66]

Further, a recent issue of the *Advocate* decries the use of the term "gay," preferring to replace it with the terms queer, fluid, open or questioning.[67] Matt Foreman, Executive Director of the National Gay and Lesbian Task Force, in response to the fluidity of homosexuality, makes this comment: "We as a movement can take pride that we opened this door for young people to be much more fluid about sexuality, gender, gender roles, orientation and sexual behavior than any other generation in history. That's what the gay movement has contributed to society, and that's a tremendously good thing."[68]

But what is the impact of this fluidity on children? While there is a paucity of research on same-sex couples and child-rearing, the literature on the impact of changes in parental sexual orientation and children is non-existent. The greater issue is whether or not gender is important and whether or not gender matters for children.

A distinguished group of 33 neuroscientists, pediatricians, and social scientists recently reviewed the evidence on gender as a basic reality. They concluded that boys and girls differ in a number of distinct areas such as selection of playmates, toy preference, fantasy play, rough and tumble play, activity level and aggression. Though some of these differences are likely related to environment, others are biologically primed and established pre-natally. They noted that as early as 18-24 months of age that children begin to make sense of their sexual embodiment. As children search for meaning, the relationship with both mothers and fathers assist in understanding the same-sex-as-me parent and the opposite-sex-as-me parent.[69] They summarized their findings succinctly:

> Gender also runs deeper, near to the core of human identity and social meaning—in part because it is biologically primed and connected to differences in brain structure and function, in part because it is also deeply implicated in the transition to adulthood.[70]

From the Stacey research it is quite clear that parenting can derail biological priming. And gender nonconformity, an observable consequence of parenting by lesbian couples, appears consequential of this derailing.[71]

Simply, gendered differences in response to father absence/father presence is sufficient affirmation that gender is important. In fact, sexual orientation itself assumes that gender exists and that it is important for human relationships. If gender is important to adult romantic relationships, one must also assume that it also has significance in the hungry love a child feels for his or her parents.[72] Many people are capable of loving and caring for a child who is not biologically related to them. Nonetheless, over the broad sweep of history, the phenomenon of kin altruism suggests that creating social connections between children and their biological parents has value for children. Kin altruism basically refers a mutual process between biological parents and their offspring. Natural parents bond with their children because they recognize them as an extension of themselves, a continuation to be valued, preserved and protected. Biological children perceive this bodily connection from those who gave them life and attach their parents accordingly.[73]

Same-sex marriage harms men, women, children, and society. It undercuts the idea that procreation is intrinsically connected to marriage. It undermines the idea that children need both a mother and a father, further weakening the societal norm that men should take responsibility for the children they beget.

Same-sex marriage harms women because it increases transactional procreation.[74] Like transactional sex, transactional procreation exploits, demeans and devalues women. Because same-sex male couples can not procreate, it is likely that men will contract for reproductive services. Children become commodities or trophies, products for bargains.[75] James warns, " If we imagine that every relationship is simply contractual, and can be broken at will—at a price to be paid for the renunciation of the contract—we find ourselves in a position where the bedrock of certainty of which contracts depend melts away."[76]

Same-sex relationships are different from opposite-sex relationships in ways that are harmful both to society and to the individuals themselves. Same-sex relationships are less permanent, and its participants are less monogamous. Those engaged in homosexual relationships are at greater risk for mental illness and physical disease. Although the reasons for these differences are not clear, efforts need to be made to seek answers and solutions. Bailey notes that the sociopolitical environment should not preclude the seeking of such answers.[77]

B.   Mental Health Data on Homosexuality

Research clearly demonstrates that homosexual practices place individuals at risk for some forms of mental disorders such as anxiety, depression, suicidality and multiple disorders. The studies have repeatedly shown that the risks for mental illnesses remain even in societies where there is a greater acceptance of homosexuality.

Herrel, Goldberg, True, Ramakrishnan, Lyons, Eisen offered the following conclusion from their research: "same gender sexual orientation is significantly associated with each of the suicidality measures...the substantial increased life-time risk of suicidal behaviors in homosexual men is unlikely due to substance abuse or other psychiatric co-morbidity."[78]

Ferguson, Horwood, and Beautrais reached the following conclusion: "Gay, lesbian and bisexual young people were at increased risks of major depres-sion...generalized anxiety disorder...conduct disorder...nicotine depen-dence...multiple disorders...suicidal ideation...suicide attempts."[79]

Commentators Bailey, Remafedi and Friedman reviewed this research, seeking to discover reasons for these significant differences. They all concluded that there was little doubt that there is a strong association between homosexual practices and mental illness.[80] Bailey in particular offered the following hypo-theses for consideration:

- The increased depression and suicidality among homosexual in-dividuals are consequential to society's negative views of treat-ment of this group.
- Because homosexuality represents a deviation from normal hete-rosexual development, it represents a developmental error, ren-dering homosexual individuals vulnerable to mental illness.
- The increased psychopathologies in homosexual people is a life-style consequence such as the risk factors associated with recep-tive anal sex and promiscuity. [81]

Bailey's first hypothesis is quite unlikely because the study was replicated in The Netherlands, arguably the most gay-affirming society in the world, with similar, more robust results. The researchers, Sandfort, de Graaf, Bijl and Schnabel summarized their research which was conducted in The Netherlands:

> Homosexual men had a much larger chance of having 12-month and lifetime bipolar disorders, and a higher chance of having a lifetime major depression...the greatest differences were found in obsessive-compulsive disorder and agoraphobia. The 12-month prevalences of agoraphobia, simple phobia and obsessive-compulsive disorder were higher in homosexual men than in heterosexual men. [82]

Researchers have concluded that lesbians have a much higher rate of sub-stance abuse disorders during their lifetime as well as a higher prevalence of mood disorders. [83] Suicidal attempts are significantly higher among lesbians.[84]

There are higher rates of sexual molestation reported in the history of ho-mosexuals than in the history of heterosexuals. Using a non-clinical population, Tomeo, Templer, Anderson, and Kotler found that 46% of gay men and 22% of lesbians were sexually abused as children compared to 7% of heterosexual men and 1% of heterosexual women.[85] Particularly intriguing was the finding that 68% of the men and 38% of the women did not self-identify as gay or lesbian until after the molestation.[86]

Significantly higher rates of domestic violence have also been found in ho-mosexual relationships. Waldner-Haugrud, Gratch, and Magruder concluded from their sample of 283 participants that 47.5 % of the lesbians and 29.7% of the gay men had been victimized by a gay partner.[87] Lockhart found that 90% of lesbians had been recipients of one or more acts of violence in the 12 months preceding the study.[88] Lie and Gentlewarrior concluded that more than 50% of the lesbians in their study had been abused by a partner.[89] Island and Letellier noted that the incidence of domestic violence among gay men almost doubled that of the heterosexual population.[90] Bradford, Ryan, Rothblum in their national survey of lesbians found that 75% of the 2000 respondents had received psychological care, a large number for depression.[91] These researchers noted that among this sample there was high prevalence of life events and behaviors related to mental illness which included physical, sexual, alcohol, and drug abuse. Twenty percent of this sample had attempted suicide during the past year and more than a third of the sample had been depressed.[92]

C.   Medical Health Data on Homosexuality

Public health and medical researchers have produced morbidity and mortality data for those engaged in homosexual practices. From their research in a major urban area in Canada, Hogg and Strathdee offered the following summary:

> In a major Canadian centre, life expectancy at age 20 for gay and bisexual men is 8 to 20 years less than for all men. If the same pattern of mortality were to continue, we estimate that nearly half of gay and bisexual men currently aged 20 years will not reach their 65th birthday. Under even the most liberal assumptions, gay and bisexual men in this urban centre are now experiencing a life expectancy similar to that experienced by all men in Canada in the year 1871.[93]

The AIDS epidemic is driven overwhelmingly by behavior, with homosexual behavior as the primary means of transmission in the United States. Of the twenty-four categories of AIDS transmission listed by the U. S. Department of Health and Human Services, male homosexuality occupies the first space.[94] Of the 402,722 cumulative AIDS cases reported through 2004, 55% involved the single mode of exposure of men who had sex with men.[95] By including all modes of exposure that involved male homosexual behavior, the sole or potential cause of more than seventy percent of all AIDS cases that have been reported in the United States from the first case through 2004 is male homosexual behavior.[96]

Extensive medical evidence supports greater rates of medical disease among homosexuals.[97] For example, the rate of anal cancer infection is 10 times the rate of heterosexual males.[98] Other medical conditions where there is an overrepresentation among homosexual males include damaged sphincter tissue leading to incontinence, hemorrhoids and anal fissures, anorectal trauma, retained foreign bodies, rectosigmoid tears, allergic proctitis, and penile edema.[99] A study of cancer incidence among male registered homosexual partners in Denmark likewise showed an elevated risk of cancer compared to cancer incidence among the general population.[100] Lesbians have higher rates of hepatitis B & C, bacterial vaginosis, heavy cigarette smoking, intravenous drug use and abuse of alcohol.[101]

The June 2003 issue of *The American Journal of Public Health* focused on health risks associated with homosexual practices.[102] The journal's editor summarized, "Having struggled to come to terms with the catastrophic HIV epidemic among MSM (men who have sex with men) in the 1980s by addressing the pointed issues of sexuality and heterosexism, are we set to backslide a mere 20 years later as HIV incidence rates move steadily upward, especially among MSM."[103]

D.   *Homosexual Relationships Differ from Heterosexual Relationships*

Homosexual relationships differ in significant ways from heterosexual relationships. Promiscuity is not a myth among gay men. Rotello, a gay author, noted "Gay liberation was founded...on a sexual brotherhood of promiscuity and any abandonment of that promiscuity would amount to a communal betrayal of gargantuan proportions."[104] In fact, there is a significant portion of the gay community who question whether or not adapting to marriage is a betrayal of those who fought at Stonewall. In a recent article in *The New York Times* (July 30, 2006), gay activists, such as Bill Dobbs, question whether or not monogamy is normal and questioned why gay men and lesbians are buying into an institution [marriage] they see as rooted in oppression.[105] There are those gay activists who are strongly opposed to marriage, which they view as a way of narrowing of sexual opportunity, noting that in France "...adultery is actually an equal opportunity. Women have almost as much adultery[sic] relationships as men."[106]

Prior to the AIDS epidemic, Bell and Weinburg reported that 28% of homosexual men had more than 1000 life time partners.[107] Subsequent to the AIDS epidemic, homosexual men averaged four partners per month instead of six partners.[108] CDC reported that between 1994 and 1997, the percentage of gay men reporting multiple partners increased from 23.6 percent to 33.3 percent, with the largest increase in men under 25 years of age.[109] In another CDC report, 30 percent of all gay black men were HIV positive.[110] Sternberg reported that 46% of study participants had unprotected anal sex during the previous month, and less than 30 percent realized that they were infected.[111]

While promiscuity among lesbians is less extreme, an Australian study revealed that lesbians were 4.5 times more likely to have had more than 50 lifetime male partners than heterosexual women.[112]

Homosexual relationships are significantly less sexually monogamous than heterosexual relationships. Michael, Gagnon, Laumann, and Kolata concluded that the vast majority of heterosexual couples were monogamous while the marriage was intact.[113] Ninety-four percent of married couples and 75% of cohabiting couples had only one sexual partner in the previous 12 months.[114]

McWhirter and Mattison studied 156 couples who had been in homosexual relationship from 1 to 37 years. Of these couples, only seven had been able to maintain sexual fidelity, and of these seven couples, none had been together for more than 5 years.[115] The authors suggest a different standard for homosexuals couples: fidelity without monogamy.[116]

A more recent study published in the journal AIDS found that gay "marital" relationships in The Netherlands lasted 1½ years on the average and had a mean of eight partners per year outside those relationships.[117]

Bailey references the preeminence of sexuality, the relatively short typical duration and the sexual infidelity in homosexual relationships, and concludes "Gay men will always have many more sex partners than straight people do. Those who are attached will be less sexually monogamous. Although some gay male relationships will be for life, these will be fewer than among heterosexual couples."[118] Further, Bailey notes, "Gay men who are promiscuous are expressing an essentially masculine trait. They are doing what most heterosexual men would do if they could. They are in this way just like heterosexual men, except they don't have women to constrain them"[119]

This lack of monogamy and relational stability in gay male relationships finds significant support in the research. These characteristics of homosexual relationships alone fail the primary purpose of marriage. Same-sex marriage advocates downplay the importance of fidelity in their definition of marriage. Surveys conducted of men who entered same-sex unions in Vermont indicate that 50% of them do not value sexual fidelity.[120] Judith Stacey, a leading advocate of gay marriage, suggests that "perhaps some might dare to question the dyadic limitations of Western marriages and seek some of the benefits of extended family life through small group marriages."[121] Indeed, the recent pages of the *Advocate*, the mainstream gay publication, suggest that such arrangements are already occurring. Greg Hernandez, the author of "Big Gay Love," focuses on groups who consider themselves engaged in a marriage. One member of a trio concludes, "We're as married as we could be...we all have rings and have a day we celebrate our anniversary."[122] A man from another trio states, "There were definitely ups and downs...because Richard and Reid had already been together. But the initial adjustment is over. No regrets."[123] In fact, soon after same-sex marriage advocates suffered a defeat in Washington State, a group of 250 academics and celebrities including Cornell West, Gloria Steinem, Rabbi Michael Lerner, Judith Stacy, Nan Hunter and Armistead Maupin signed the manifesto, "Beyond Same-Sex Marriage, A New Strategic Vision for All Our Families and Relationships," which petitions for legal rights and privileges of marriage for all arrangements, like extended families living in one household and friends in long term, care-giving relationships. [124]

Much of the public discourse about same-sex marriage has downplayed the differences between homosexual couples and heterosexual couples. The notion that there are no differences between homosexual couples and heterosexual couples lacks basis in the scientific literature. In fact, these differences should and must be considered when focusing on the institution of marriage and when considering the best interest of children.

E.   Same-sex Couples and Child-rearing

The gay rights movement, with its push for the recognition of same-sex marriage, has forced the issue of parenting by same-sex couples to center stage. Advocacy groups argue that there are no differences between children raised by same-sex parents and those raised by opposite-sex parents. Though the advocacy seems to be illogical and at odds with the significant number of well-conducted studies, attempts continue to blur the lines between men and women.

The studies on same-sex parenting are quite limited and quite limiting. They are basically restricted to children who were conceived in a heterosexual relationship whose mothers later divorced and self-identified as lesbians. It is these children who were compared to divorced, heterosexual, mother-headed families. A better comparison would have been with children in intact families because the research is clear that children in single parent families are at risk for a variety of difficulties including juvenile criminal offenses, mental illness and poverty. The logical conclusion is that children from both of these family forms are at risk for a number of problems.

Studies of children raised by male couples are virtually non-existent. The few available studies are either anecdotal in nature or so plagued by methodological flaws as to make them simply invalid from a scientific perspective.

In their excellent review of the existing studies on children raised by homosexual couples (primarily lesbian couples), Lerner and Nagai reached the following conclusion:

> The claim has been made that homosexual parents raise children as effectively as married biological parents. A detailed analysis of the methodologies of the 49 studies, which are put forward to support this claim, shows that they suffer from severe methodological flaws. In addition to their methodological flaws, none of the studies deals adequately with the problem of affirming the null hypothesis, of adequate sample size, and of spurious correlation. [125]

Williams arrived at similar conclusions to those of Lerner and Nagai, but actually went further in his re-analyses of some of the major studies whose authors reported no differences between children raised in lesbian and heterosexual families.[126] In reviewing both the Golombok, Spencer, and Rutter research[127] and the Golombok and Tasker research,[128] Williams noted that the authors ignored a follow-up study that found that the children of lesbian parents were more likely to have considered and actually engaged in homosexual relationships. In reviewing other studies, Williams found similar omissions. For example, Huggins noted a difference in the variability of self-esteem between children of homosexual and heterosexual parents but did not test for significance. [129] Upon a re-analysis of the data, Williams discovered the difference to be significant. Lewis recorded differences in social and emotional difficulties in the lives of children of homosexual parents but left such data unreported. Patterson also observed and left unreported similar data in her research.[130]

Patterson's research, which has been repeatedly cited by the American Psychological Association to support gay rights, has come under significant criticism not only because of methodological flaws but because of substantial misrepresentation and selection bias. In fact, her research and subsequent testimony were excluded from a Florida court because of the use of herself and friends as subjects and her unwillingness to comply with a court order to provide documentation, even when requested by her own side in the conflict.[131]

More recently, Wainwright and Patterson reported research on adolescents with lesbian parents/ heterosexual parents and the relationship to delinquency, victimization and substance abuse.[132] Their conclusion that adolescents raised by lesbian couples do not differ from those raised by heterosexual couples, and subsequently their findings "provide no warrant for legal or policy discrimination" find little support in their own study.[133] First of all, no parents in their study were asked about their sexual identities. Secondly, their conclusion that adolescents whose parents had good relationships with them reported less delinquent behavior and substance abuse is not a novel finding. It is interesting that Wainwright and Patterson either did not address or did not find differences on other measures such as sexual behaviors (they only reported sex behavior under the influence of alcohol). In order to make a case for policy, the authors would need to replicate with much larger sample sizes, directly ascertain the sexual identities of the parents and follow these adolescents into adulthood. Stacey and Biblarz accurately highlighted the importance of longitudinal studies noting, "Thus far, no work has compared children's long-term achievements in education, occupation, income, and other domains of life."[134]

Nock, a sociologist at the University of Virginia, reviewed all of the available studies on parenting by same-sex couples and concluded, "Through this analysis I draw my conclusion that 1) All of the articles I reviewed contained at least one fatal flaw of design or execution; and 2) Not a single one of those studies was conducting according to general accepted standards of scientific research.[135]

Even the activist, Charlotte Patterson, conceded the following:

1. No research used nationally represented samples.
2. There were limited outcome measures, most of which were unrelated to standards of child well-being used by family sociologists.
3. There were few longitudinal studies which followed children of same-sex couples into adulthood.
4. Virtually all of the studies compared single lesbian mothers to single heterosexual mothers rather than comparing single lesbian mothers to married heterosexual mothers.[136]

The Stacey and Biblarz meta-analysis repudiated over 20 years of research which claimed to show no difference between children raised by homosexual parents and those raised by heterosexual parents.[137] This research clearly demonstrated that lesbian mothers had a feminizing effect on their sons and a masculinizing effect on their daughters. Boys raised by lesbian mothers behaved in less traditionally masculine ways, and girls, particularly "adolescent and young girls raised by lesbian mothers, appear to have been more sexually adventurous and less chaste."[138]

The most reputable scientists would agree that the research on children raised by same-sex couples is in its infancy. However, in spite of the many flaws in the very limited pool of rigorous studies such as small sample size, selection bias, and lack of longitudinal data, there appears to be an emerging theme: children raised by same-sex couples exhibit poor outcomes not so dissimilar to those raised by divorced heterosexual parents. The comparison groups in most of the studies have been children in divorced households headed by a lesbians or gay men or children in divorced households headed by heterosexual divorced parents. Children in both of these groups are at higher risks for certain kinds of problems than are children raised in an intact family headed by a mother and father who are married.[139] In addition, children raised by a lesbian couples may be at risk for unique problems associated with gender non-conformity.

In summary, the available research supports the following: children raised in homes headed by gay men and lesbians do not resemble their peers raised in homes with a married mother and father. And given the historical and prevailing legal and psychological standard, the best interest of the child, one can reasonably conclude that based upon this standard, the optimal health, well-being and best interest of a child is not best served by support of motherless or fatherless family structures. The placement of children in such settings begins a slippery slope filled with potential harms for children that society simply cannot afford to take.

IV.   Conclusion

Traditional marriage has supported societies for millennia. Historical and current research clearly demonstrates that both adults and children benefit from this family structure. Differences emerge when comparisons are made between same-sex couples and opposite-sex couples. Same-sex relationships are less permanent and less monogamous. Homosexual practices place its participants at risk for mental illness and physical disease. Emerging research suggests potential risks for children raised by lesbian parents including gender non-conformity. The rejection of gender roles thus appears to be unhealthy.

Same-sex marriage essentially redefines marriage, discounts gender realities, and rejects the historic relationship between marriage and kin altruism. It dispenses with the principle that individuals who give birth to children should be the ones to raise those children. Same-sex marriage is adult-centered, where the rights of adults take center stage and the best interests of children are considered only superficially.

The battle of beliefs which is at the base of same-sex v. opposite-sex marriage was articulated by Morse, who summarizes, "I claim the sexual urge is a natural engine of sociability, which solidifies the relationship between spouses and brings children into being. Others claim that human sexuality is a private recreational good, with neither intrinsic moral or social significance. I claim that the hormone oxytocin floods a woman's body during sex and tends to attach her to her sex partner, quite apart from her wishes or our cultural norms. Others claim that women and men alike can engage in uncommitted sex will no ill effects. I claim that children have the best life chances when they are raised by married, biological parents. Others believe children are so adaptable that having unmarried parents presents no significant problems. Some people believe marriage is a special case of free association of individuals. I say the details of this form of free association are so distinctive as to make marriage a unique social institution that deserves to be defended on its own terms, and not a special case of something else." [140]

The Goodridge Court viewed marriage as a legal construct with its importance for children and society consisting of the legal benefits and responsibilities the law dispenses along with a marriage license. However, this view is not consistent with the social science evidence we have on the effects of family structure on child well-being. If the legal benefits of the social status of marriage played a critical role in protecting child well-being, we would expect children who live with remarried parents to do better than children who remain with an unmarried parent. In fact, children in remarried families do no better (or worse) on the average than children raised by single mothers. As noted in the Child Trends research, it is not marriage that protects children's well-being, but the intact, married, reasonably harmonious union of the child's own biological mother and father. [141]

Children born within a marriage are far more likely to be socialized, outgoing and able to form permanent relationships of their own than children born out-of-wedlock. Children of married parents find a place in society already prepared for them, furnished by a regime of parental sacrifice, and protected by social norms. Taking away marriage exposes children to the risk of coming into the world as strangers, a condition in which they may remain for the rest of their lives. [142]

Brown and Marquardt conclude that "...there is a persistent core value that is widely cherished and protected around the world. This is the importance of the people who give life to the infant also being, as nearly as possible, the ones who care for it. This principle is based on the widely held assumption that people who conceive a child, when they recognize their relation to it, will on the average be the most invested in its nurture and well-being. It is also based on the observation that, when other things are equal, children themselves want—indeed, often long—to be raised by those who gave life to them." [143]

On July 6, 2006, the New York Court of Appeals issued a 4-2 decision determining that the state's marriage law limiting marriage to only a man and a woman is constitutional. [144] The New York court concluded, " Heterosexual intercourse has a natural tendency to lead to the birth of children" and "homosexual intercourse does not," noting that the legislature "could find that an important function of marriage is to create more stability and permanence in the relationships that cause children to be born" by offering an inducement to opposite couples to marry. The same considerations do not apply to same-sex couples because they cannot have children without intending to do so." [145]

The New York Court is correct. Gender matters. Family structure matters. Conjugal marriage fosters healthy human and societal development. Traditional marriage benefits both men and women, is protective for children, all of which contributes to the good society.

Notes

1. Locke, J. (1980). *Second treatise of government*, Hackett Publishing, c. VII, s. 78, p. 43.
2. Wilcox, W. B. et al. (2005). *Why marriage matters: Twenty-six conclusions from the social sciences.* 2d ed. New York: Institute for American Values.
3. *Id.*
4. *Id.*
5. Budig, M.J. & England, P. (2001). The wage penalty for motherhood. *American Sociological Review* 66:204-225.
6. Wilcox, W. B. et al. (2005).
7. Waite, L. & Gallagher, M. (2000). The Case for Marriage. New York: Doubleday.
8. *Id.*
9. *Id.*
10. *Id.*
11. *Id.*
12. Wilcox, W. B. et al. 2005. *Why Marriage Matters, Second Edition: Twenty-six Conclusions from the Social Sciences.* New York: Institute for American Values. Lorraine Blackman, Obie Clayton, Norval Glenn, Linda Malone-Colon, and Alex Roberts, 2005. *The Consequences of Marriage for African Americans: A Comprehensive Literature Review*: New York: Institute for American Values.
13. Wilcox, W. B. et al. (2005).
14. Nock, S. (1998). "The Consequences of Premarital Fatherhood," *American Sociological Review,* 63: 250-263.
15. Bailey, J. M. (2003). The man who would be queen. Washington, D. C.: Joseph Henry Press, p. 100.
16. Waite, L. & Gallagher, M, 2000.
17. Nock, S., 1998.
18. Waite, L. & Gallagher, M.. (2000).
19. Nock, S. (2005). "Marriage as a Public Issue." *The Future of Children* 15: 13-32.
20. The Witherspoon Institute. (2006). *Marriage and the public good: Ten principles.* Princeton, June: p. 21.
21. Wilcox. W. B. et al (2005)
22. *Id.*
23. *Id.*
24. *Id.*
25. Dabbs, J. (2000*). Heroes, rogues, and lovers: Testosterone and behavior.* New York: McGraw-Hill.
26. Waite, L. & Gallagher, M., (2000), p. 152.
27. *Id.*
28. Waite, L. & Gallagher, M., (2000), p. 155
29. *Id.*
30. Popenoe, D. 1996. *Life without father.* New York: Mark Kessler Books, The Free Press, p. 176.

31. Moore, K.A. et al. (2002). Marriage from a child's perspective: How does family structure affect children and what can we do about it? *Child Trends Research Brief* (Washington D.C.: Child Trends)(June)

32. Cabrera, et al. (2000) "Fatherhood in the Twenty-First Century", 71 Child Development, 127, p. 130.\\

33. Baumrind, D. (1982) Are androgynous individuals more effective persons and parents? Child Development, 53, 44-75.

34. Baumrind, D. (1991). The influence of parenting style on adolescent competence and substance use. *Journal of Adolescence*, 11(11), 59-95.

35. Greenberger, E. (1984). Defining psychosocial maturity in adolescence. In P. Karoly & J.J. Steffans, (Eds.) *Adolescent behavior disorders: foundations and temporary concerns.* Lexington, MA: Lexington Books.

36. Rossi, A.S. (1987) Parenthood in transition: From lineage to child to self-orientation. In J.B. Lancaster, J. Altman, A.S. Rossi, and L.R. Sherrod, eds., *Parenting across the life span:Biosocial dimensions.* New York: Aldene de Gruyter, 31-81.

37. Yogman, M.W. (1982) Development of the father-infant relationship. In H.E. Fitzgerald, B.M. Lester and M.W. Yogman, eds. *Theory and research in behavioral pediatrics.* New York: Plenum Press.

38. Shapiro, J.L. (1994). Letting dads be dads. *Parents*, June, 165, 168.

39. Rohner, R. P. & Veneziano, R.A (2001). "The importance of father love: history and contemporary evidence," *Review of General Psychology 5.4, 382-405.*

40. Id at 405.

41. Clark-Stewart, K.A. (1980). The father's contribution to children's cognitive and social development in early childhood. In F.A. Pedersen, ed., *The father-infant relationship: observational studies in the family setting.* New York: Praeger.

42. Cromwell, N.A. & Leper, E.M. (Eds.) (1994) *American fathers and public policy*, Washington, D.C.: National Academy Press.

43. Diener, M.L., Mangelsdorf, S.C., McHale, J.L & Frosch, C.A. (2002). *Infancy,* 3(2), 153-174.

44. Broughton, A.E. (2002). U. study says dads are important, too. *Salt Lake Tribune,* April 5:A1.

45. Harris, K. M. et al. (1998) "Paternal Involvement with Adolescents in Intact Families: The Influence of Fathers Over the Life Course", 35 *Demography* 201, pp. 201-216.

46. Gilligan, C. (1994). *In a different voice.* Cambridge, MA. Harvard University Press.

47. Wilson, R.F. (2002) Book review, 35 Fam. L.Q. 833, 863 (reviewing June Carbone, *From Partners to Parents: The Second Revolution Family Law* (2003))

48. Garfunkel I. & McLanahan. S.S. (1986). *Single mothers and their children.* Washington, D.C.: Urban Institute Press, pp 30-31.

49. Blankenhorn, D. (1995). *Fatherless America: Confronting our most urgent social problem.* New York: Basic.

50. Masser, A. (1989). Boys' father hunger: The missing father syndrome. *Medical Aspects of Human Sexuality*, 23(1), 44-50.

51. Golombok, S., Tasker, F., & Murray, C. (1997). Children raised in fatherless families from infancy: Family relationships and the socioeconomic development of children of lesbian and single heterosexual mothers. *Journal of Child Psychology and Psychiatry* 38:783-791, 788.

52. Spaht, K.S. (2006). The Current Crisis in Marriage Law, Its Orign, and Its Impact. In Robert P. George & Jean Bethke Elshtain *The meaning of marriage: Family, state, market, & morals*. Dallas: Spence Publishing Co., p 216.

53. Eisold, B., (1998) Recreating mother: The consolidation of 'heterosexual' gender identification in the young son of homosexual men. *American J. of Orthopsychiatry* 68:3:433-442.

54. Id.

55. Biller, H. (1993). *Fathers and families: Paternal factors in child development*. Westport, CT: Auburn House.

56. *Id.* at 12-14.

57. *Id.* at 16.

58. Fineman, M. *The Neutered Mother and the Sexual Family*, p. 229.

59. Fineman's most mature theory of dependency can be found in her recent book, *The autonomy myth: A theory of dependency* (2004). New York: The New Press.

60. Goodridge v. Dept. of Public Health, 798 N. E. 2d 941 (Mass. 2003).

61. Hadley A. 2006. The Family and the Laws, in Robert P. George & Jean Bethke Elshtain (ed.) The Meaning of Marriage. Dallas: Spence Publishing Company, 129-130.

62. Warner, *The trouble with normal*, pp 88-89.

63. Hadley, A. 126.

64. Id.

65. Diamond, L. (2000) Sexual identity is far from fixed in women who aren't exclusively heterosexual, *Monitor on Psychology*, vol 31, no.3, p 15.

66. Schecter, E. (2004) Labels may oversimplify women's sexual identity, experiences. *Monitor on Psychology*, vol 35, no. 9, p. 28.

67. Vary, A.B., (2006, June 20) Is gay over? *Advocate*, pp. 98-102.

68. Id., at pp. 98-99

69. Commission on Children at Risk. (2003). *Hardwired to connect: The new scientific case for authoritative communities*. New York: Institute for American Values, p 23.

70. Commission on Children at Risk, (2003). *Hardwired to connect: The new scientific case for authoritative communities*. YMCA, Dartmouth Medical School, Institute for American Values, pp. 23-25.

71. Stacey, J. & Biblarz, T. (2001) How does sexual orientation of parents matter? American Sociological Review, 66 (2), pp. 159-183.

72. Gallagher, M. (2006) (How) Does Marriage Protect Child Well-being? In Robert P. George & Jean Bethke Elstain (ed.) The Meaning of Marriage. Dallas: Spence Publishing Company, 211.

73. Browning, D. & Marquardt, E. (2006). What about the Children? In Robert P. George and Jean Bethke Elshtain (ed.) The Meaning of Marriage, Dallas: Spence Publishing Company, p. 36.

74. Williams, C. S. (2005, December 12). *Women, Equality and the Federal Marriage Amendment*.

75. *Id.*

76. James, H. (2006) Changing Dynamics of the Family in Robert P. George & Jean Bethke Elshtain, *The Meaning of Marriage*. Dallas, Spence Publishing Company, 73.

77. Bailey, J. M. (1999). Homosexuality and mental illness. *Archives of General Psychiatry*, 56, 884.

78. Herrell, R. Goldberg, J. True, W.R., Ramakrishnan, V., Lyons, M. Eisen, D. et al. (1999). Sexual orientation and suicidality. *Archives of General Psychiatry*, 56, 867.

79. Ferguson, D.M., Horwood, J.L. & Beautrais, A.L. (1999). Is sexual orientation related to mental health problems and suicidality in young people? *Archives of General Psychiatry*, 876.

80. Bailey, J. M. (1999). Homosexuality and mental illness. *Archives of General Psychiatry*, 56, 883-884. Remafedi, G. (1999). Suicide and sexual orientation. *Archives of General Psychiatry*, 565, 885-886. Friedman, R. C. (1999). Homosexuality, psychopathology, and suicidality. *Archives of General Psychiatry*, 56, 887-888.

81. Bailey, J. M., p. 884.

82. Sandfort, T.G. de Graaf, R. Bijl, R.V. & Schnabel, P. (2001). Same-sex behavior and psychiatric disorder. *Archives of General Psychiatry*, 58, 87.

83. Healthwatch. Study: " Lesbian, bisexual women take more health risks than gay men. *The Washington Advocate*, December, 2002.

84. *Id.*

85. Tomeo, M.E. et al. (2001). Comparative data of childhood and adolescence molestation in heterosexual and homosexual persons. *Archives of Sexual Behavior*, 30(5), 535-541.

86. *Id.*

87. Waldner-Haugrud, L.K., Gratch, L.V. & Magruder, B. (1997). Victimization and perpetration rates of violence in gay and lesbian relationship: Gender issues explored. *Violence and Victims*, 12(2), 173-185.

88. Lockhart, L.L., (1994). Letting out the secret: violence in lesbian relationships. *Journal of Interpersonal Violence*, 9, 469-492.

89. Lie, G.Y. & Gentlewarrior, S. (1991). Intimate violence in lesbian relationships; discussion of survey findings and practice implications. *Journal of Social Service Research*, 15, 41-59.

90. Island, D. & Letellier, P. (1991). *Men who beat the men who love them: Battered gay men and domestic violence.* New York: Haworth Press.

91. Bradford, J., Ryan, C., & Rothblum, R.C. (Eds.), 1994. National Lesbian Health Care Survey: Implications for mental health care. *Journal of Consulting and Clinical Psychology*, 62(2), 228-242.

92. *Id.*

93. R. S. Hogg. & S. A. Strathdee (1997). " Modeling the impact of HIV disease on mortality in gay and bisexual men." *International Journal of Epidemiology*, 26(3), 657.

94. 2004 HIV/Aids Surveillance Report, Center for Disease Control and Prevention, Vol. 16, at 32, Table 17.

95. *Id.*

96. *Id.*

97. Diggs, J. R., The health risks of gay sex, Corporate Resource Council, 1-16.

98. *Id* at 4.

99. *Id.*

100. Frisch, M. et al., (2003). Cancer in a population-based Cohort of men and women in registered homosexual partnerships, *Am. J. Epidemiology* 157(11).

101. Diggs, *supra* note 97.

102. 93,6.

103. Nothbridge, M. E. (2003). HIV Returns, American Journal of Public Health, 93 (6), 860.

104. Rotello, G. (1997). *Sexual ecology: AIDS and the destiny of gay men.* New York: Penguin Group.

105. Hartocollis, A. For some gays, a right they can forsake. (2006, July 30) *New York Times*, 9,2.

106. *Id.*

107. Bell, A.P. & Weinberg, M. S. (1978). *Homosexualities: a study of diversity among men and women.* New York: Simon & Schuster.

108. McKusick, L. (1985). Reported changes in sexual behavior of men at risk for AIDS, San Francisco, 1982-84—The AIDS behavioral research project. *Public Health Reports,* 100, 6, 622-629.

109. Center for Disease Control (1999). Resurgent bacterial sexually transmitted disease among men who have sex with men—King County, Washington, 1997-1999. *Morbidity and Mortality Weekly Report,* 48(35), 773-777, September 10.

110. Sternberg, S. (2003). 1 in 3 young gay black men are HIV positive, USA Today, February 6.

111. *Id.*

112. Price, J. et al. (1996). Perceptions of cervical cancer and pap smear screening behavior by women's sexual orientation. *Journal of Community Health,* 2(2), 89-105.

113. Michael, R., Gagnon, J.H. Laumann, E.O. & Kolata, G. (1994). *Sex in America: A definitive survey.* Boston: Little, Brown, and Company.

114. *Id.*

115. McWhirter, D.P. & Mattison, A. M. (1984). *The male couple: How relationships develop.* Englewood Cliffs, N.J.: Prentice Hall, Inc.

116. Id.

117. Xiridou, M. et al. (2003). The contribution of steady and casual partnerships to the incidence of HIV infection among homosexual men in Amsterdam. *AIDS,* 17 (7), 1029-1038.

118. Bailey, J.M. (2003), Id.

119. *Id.* at 87.

120. Rothblum, E. & Solomon, S. (2003). *Civil Unions in the State of Vermont: A Report on the First Year.* University of Vermont Department of Psychology.

121. Stacey, J. (1998) Gay and lesbian families: Queer like us. *In All Our Families: New Policies for a New Century,* edited by M.A. Mason, A. Skolnick, and S.D. Sugarman. New York: Oxford University Press, pp 117, 128-129.

122. Hernandez, G. (2000, June 6) Big gay love, *The Advocate,* 37-42.

123. Hernandez, G. , Id.

124. Hartocollis, *Id.*

125. Lerner, R. & Nagai, A.K. (2000). Out of nothing comes nothing: Homosexual and heterosexual marriage not shown to be equivalent for raising children," paper presented at the Revitalizing the Institution of Marriage for the 21st Century conference, Brigham Young University, March, Provo, UT, p.1

126. Williams, R. N. (2000) A critique of the research on same-sex parenting. In D.C. Dollahite, ed. *Strengthening Our Families,* Salt Lake City, Utah: Bookcraft, 325-355.

127. Golombok, S., Spencer, A. & Rutter, M. (1983). Children in lesbian and single-parent households: psychosexual and psychiatric appraisal. *Journal of Child Psychology and Psychiatry,* 24, 551-572. *Sociological Review,* 66(2), 159-183.

128. Golombok, S. & Tasker, F. (1996). Do parents influence the sexual orientation of their children? Finding from a longitudinal study of lesbian families? *Developmental Psychology,* 32, 3-11.

129. Williams, R.N. (2000), Id.

130. Patterson, C.J. (1995). Families of the lesbian baby boom: Parent's division of labor and children's adjustment. *Developmental Psychology,* 31-115-123.

131. JUNE AMER, Petitioner, v. Floyd P. Johnson, District Administrator, District X, Florida Department of Health and Rehabilitative Services, Respondent, 17th Judicial Circuit in and for Broward County, Case No. 92-14370 (11). July 27, 1997.

132. Wainwright, J. & Patterson, C. (2006). *Journal of Family Psychology,* 20,3,526-530.

133. Id at 529.

134. Stacy, J. & Biblarz, T.J. (2001). (How) does the sexual orientation of parents matter? *American Sociological Review,*66 (2), 172.

135. Nock Affidavit ¶3. Halpern v. Attorney General of Canada, No. 684/00 (Ont. Sup. Ct. of Justice) (copies available from the Institute for Marriage and Public Policy: info@imapp.org).

136. Patterson, C.J. et al. (2000). Children of Lesbian and Gay Parents: Research, Law and Policy in Bette L. Bottoms et al., eds., *Children and the Law: Social Science and Policy* 10-11.

137. Stacy, J. & Biblarz. T.J. Id, at 159-183.

138. *Id.* at 171.

139. Parke, M. (2003). "Are married parents really better for children?" *Center for Law and Social Policy, Policy Brief,* May: 1.

140. Morse, J.R. (2006). Why unilateral divorce has no place in a free society. In Robert P. George & Jean Betheke Elshtain, The Meaning of Marriage. Dallas: Spence Publishing Company, 78.

141. Gallagher, M. p. 204

142. Scruton, R, (2006), Sacrilege and Sacrament, in Robert P. George & Jean Bethke Elshtain (ed.). The Meaning of Marriage, Dallas: Spence Publishing Company, 6.

143. Browning, D. & Marquardt, E. (2006), Id..

144. Hernandez v. Robles, 2006 WL 1835429 (N.Y. 2006)

145. *Id.*

CHAPTER 2

THE ALLEGED HARMS OF RECOGNIZING SAME-SEX MAR-
RIAGE

Mark Strasser[1]
Capital University School of Law

I. Introduction

Commentators allege that the recognition of same-sex marriage will have
dire consequences for children in particular and for society as a whole. Yet, the
arguments offered to establish these claims often involve non sequiturs or the
use of implicit assumptions that, when made explicit, undermine the plausibility
and persuasiveness of the conclusions reached. Arguments to the contrary notwithstanding, affording civil marriage rights to same-sex couples would benefit
them, their dependents, and society as a whole, and, ironically, some of the arguments offered to preclude same-sex couples from marrying may well contribute to the tarnishing of the institution that same-sex marriage opponents allegedly wish to protect, namely, marriage. By implicitly if not explicitly supporting the gender roles and stereotypes that many women currently reject and by
bemoaning the disappearance of a bygone era that preceded the advancement of
women's rights, same-sex marriage opponents may be unwittingly contributing
to the decline in the perceived value of marriage. By treating marriage as another weapon to be used in the culture wars and suggesting that access to the institution should be a matter resolved at the ballot box, same-sex marriage opponents contribute to the perception that marriage is like other benefits to be conferred at the discretion of the legislature. In short, while same-sex marriage opponents have successfully delayed the recognition of same-sex marriage in many
states, their efforts may be exacting a heavy toll by cheapening the value of the
institution that they claim to hold dear and damaging their own credibility on
this matter in particular and on social matters more generally.

II. The Benefits of Same-Sex Marriage

Same-sex and different-sex couples wish to marry for many of the same
reasons. They wish to express their love for and commitment to their partners,
and to provide for each other, their children, and any other dependents that they
might have. In addition, marriage may have religious significance as a civilly

recognized relationship embodying a sacred commitment. As a practical matter, individuals with a same-sex orientation, like individuals with a different-sex orientation, may wish to have access to the multitude of benefits that accompany marriage. Thus, same-sex and different-sex couples are much more similar than many commentators seem to appreciate.

A.   Marriage and Children

Commentators sometimes suggest that same-sex marriages should not be recognized because children do best when they are raised by their happily married, biological parents.[2] Yet, this kind of analysis is misconceived from the start, and then only compounds the errors as the argument is developed. It determines who are optimal parents based on contested claims concerning which attitudes are best for children to have, and often relies on studies that do not even attempt to gauge the efficacy of parenting by same-sex couples. Further, even were the claims about which parents are optimal correct, that would not have advanced the discussion at hand, since that statistic would not even be relevant to determine who should adopt, much less who should be permitted to wed.

First, consider how commentators establish that children do best in homes with their biological parents. Some compare (1) children who are raised by their biological parents in low-conflict homes with (2) children who are raised in single-parent homes, noting that the children in the first group tend to do better than the children in the second group. However, were same-sex couples permitted to marry, the children whom they would be raising would be growing up in a two-parent home, so it is not at all clear why the fact that children do less well in single-parent homes would be a reason to preclude same-sex couples from marrying. On the contrary, given that children seem to do better in two-parent than single-parent homes whether the two parents are of the same or different sexes,[3] one would think that this statistic would be used to justify rather than undercut the need to permit same-sex couples to marry. If recognizing such marriages would make it more likely that a given child would be raised by two parents rather than just one, and if the real interest were to improve the lot of children, one would expect that these commentators would be supporters rather than detractors of the recognition of same-sex marriage. It is at the very least surprising that commentators recognize the importance of stability for children and that people who marry are more likely to stay together than are people who do not, but nonetheless do not want to confer the benefits of that stability on the children of lesbian and gay couples.

Some commentators compare children raised by parents of different sexes with children raised by parents of the same sex. While children thrive in both contexts, some differences have been noted in the literature. For example, same-sex marriage opponents sometimes note that children may be less likely to adhere to traditional gender roles when raised by two parents of the same sex, as if that provides a reason to reject same-sex marriage. Yet, many parents would be pleased were their children less likely to conform to gender stereotypes so that, for example, their daughters would not be deterred from excelling in occupations traditionally performed by men, so it is hardly clear that this difference establishes that children are better off when raised by different-sex parents. So, too, it has been reported that children raised by parents of the same sex are more likely to be tolerant than are children raised by parents of different sexes, as if this provides yet another reason that same-sex marriages should not be permitted. Again, however, many parents would be pleased were their children more tolerant than they otherwise would have been, so it is not at all clear that the children would be better off were they raised by parents of different sexes rather than by parents of the same sex.

Recent constitutional jurisprudence suggests that states should not rely on or promote "overbroad generalizations about the different talents, capacities, or preferences of males and females."[4] Yet, this jurisprudence suggests that parents are doing something less desirable if they are teaching their children to conform to traditional roles so that, for example, their daughters are less willing to pursue careers that are not in line with gender stereotypes. Or, to put this another way, parents should be praised when their encouragement of their children allows them to pursue employment options which years ago might not have been thought appropriate for someone of that sex.

In this country, tolerance is promoted both as a constitutional good and as a matter of good public policy. Yet, this suggests that same-sex parents should be praised rather than pilloried if their parenting practices help their children to be more rather than less tolerant.

The claim here is not that children raised by same-sex parents are better on average than children raised by different-sex parents. Rather, the claims are that children can and do thrive in both contexts, and that some of the differences noted in the literature do not establish that children are better off when raised by parents of different sexes.

Some commentators have noted that fathers and mothers tend to play with their children differently, with mothers acting in ways that are more nurturing and fathers acting in ways that promote more independence. Yet, before this is trumpeted as establishing that therefore parenting by different-sex parents is superior, at least two points might be noted. First, that there are these differences does not establish that these different ways of parenting are best for children. Second, it has been noted that in families with same-sex parents, the parents sometimes adopt differing roles, one being more nurturing and the other acting in ways that would promote more independence.[5] The claim here is not that all same-sex parents adopt these differing roles (whether consciously or subconsciously), but merely that even were it true that these differing ways of interacting with children were better for children, that would not establish the superiority of having different-sex parents raising the children. Were the claims about the catastrophic effects of having children raised by same-sex parents true, we would expect that children would do much less well than they in fact do in such households.

Suppose that it could be established beyond question that children fare best when raised by their biological parents in a low-conflict home. What implications would this have for whether same-sex couples should be able to marry?

As an initial point, it is not even clear why this comparison is being offered. It is not as if flourishing children are being taken out of their homes where they had been living with their biological parents and are then being placed into homes headed by same-sex couples. Rather, children who are adopted by same-sex couples might well have had as an alternative the prospect of having *no* parents to provide a home in which they might thrive. Even in those cases in which the child might have been adopted by someone else, that adopter would presumably *not* have been the child's biological parent.

Suppose that the issue at hand were not who should be allowed to wed but, instead, who should be permitted to adopt a particular child. Even were that the relevant question, it would be at best unhelpful to suggest that the child would be best off with her biological parents in a low-conflict home. That simply would not be an option for this particular child—she would be available for adoption precisely because she could not live with her biological parent or parents for whatever reasons.

Who should be able to adopt the child? That would depend upon a variety of factors. Certainly, someone who was not a fit parent should not be able to adopt, but that would not as a general matter preclude members of the LGBT (lesbian, gay, bisexual, transgender) community from adopting.[6] As to whether a particular individual or couple would be best for a child, this is a matter which would be decided case by case. Thus, there are two distinct reasons that it should not be assumed that members of a different-sex couple would necessarily be better parents for a child than members of a same-sex couple. First, some commentators have suggested that same-sex couples as a general matter might be better than different-sex couples as *adoptive* parents.[7] Second, regardless of who would be better as an adoptive parent as a general matter, the important determination involves establishing who among the available would-be adopters would provide the best home for this child. Given that the biological parents would not be among these potential adopters, it would at best be unhelpful to note that the child would have been most likely to flourish with her biological parents. Such a point would play no role in deciding who should adopt and certainly should play no role in deciding who should be able to marry. Thus, the point trumpeted by so many same-sex marriage opponents is surprisingly unconnected to the thesis that they intend to support.

Suppose that a theorist were to argue that because children do best when raised by their biological parents in a low-conflict home,[8] there should be no adoption. Such a proposal would be rejected out of hand, because critics would point out that there are many children in need of placement for whom living with their biological parents simply is not an option. Thus, critics might say, it is all well and good to point out that children do best with their biological parents but that point is simply irrelevant when that is not an option. Adoption is an option created by the law to help alleviate some of the difficulties created when children cannot live with their biological parents.

Not only is the children-do-best-with-their-biological-parents argument a non sequitur in the context of public policy decision-making with respect to both adoption and marriage, but it can be dangerously misleading, precisely because it is not clear which factors are doing the work to enable children to thrive when they are being raised by their biological parents. Is it because the low-conflict home is thought to be stable?[9] Then, all else being equal, it would be best to place the child in a stable home. Is the better outcome due to the fact that both parents are biologically related to the child? Then, all else being equal, it might be better to place the child in a home of someone biologically related to the child.[10] Is the outcome better for a child in a low-conflict home because such a home might at least be correlated with individuals who are comfortable economically? Then, all else being equal, it might be preferable to place the child with someone who is financially comfortable.[11] Doubtless there are a number of other possible factors which might help explain why children do better in some homes than in others.

To make matters even more complicated, it is likely that there are several factors each of which is positively correlated with successful outcomes for children. Discovering that a particular factor all else being equal would improve the likelihood of success for a child would not establish whether to favor one home that does best with respect to Factor A rather than another home that does best with respect to Factor B, when both Factors A and B have been correlated with successful child-rearing. It goes without saying that it would rarely be the case that all else would be equal in a given case. One potential adoptive parent might be better off financially while another could offer a more stable home while still another might involve an individual who is biologically related to the child. The point here is that even were children to do best when raised by their biological parents in a low-conflict home, one would not know what implications that would have in a case involving a child in need of placement. Such a finding certainly does not somehow suggest that same-sex couples should not be allowed to marry and, indeed, may well offer support for the opposite conclusion.

Sometimes, children are already living in a home with a parent and his or her same-sex partner. The child might have been produced through the use of advanced reproductive techniques or may have been the product of a previous relationship or may have been adopted by one of the adults in the home. Assuming that the child does not have another legal parent outside the home, e.g., because the rights of the biological parents were terminated or because the child was produced using the egg or sperm of an anonymous donor, then at least one issue involving this child is whether the state will permit her to have two legal parents rather than only one.

Depending upon the jurisdiction, a parent's non-marital partner may be able to establish a legal relationship with the child that she is helping to raise. Thus, suppose that Ann makes use of artificial insemination to conceive a child, Bernard. Suppose further than Ann is raising Bernard with her partner, Nancy. In some but not all jurisdictions, Nancy will be able to adopt Bernard so that both adults will have a legally recognized relationship with the child. Permitting the parent's non-marital partner to adopt can have a number of benefits for the child, e.g., he will be eligible to be covered under Nancy's employer-provided insurance policy. However, in some jurisdictions, a non-marital partner is not allowed to adopt unless the parent is willing to surrender her own parental rights. Thus, in some jurisdictions, unless Nancy and Ann were married or Ann was willing to surrender her own parental rights, Nancy would not be permitted to establish a legal relationship with Bernard, and Bernard would be unable to avail himself of various financial benefits to which he would have been entitled had he been recognized as Nancy's child.

Recognition of Nancy's relationship with Bernard might be important for non-financial reasons as well. Nancy might be more willing to invest in her relationship with Bernard if that relationship were accorded legal protection. Further, recognition would provide protection for that relationship should the relationship between Nancy and Ann end. Suppose, for example, that Nancy and Ann were raising Bernard together and that Ann were in a fatal automobile accident. If Nancy had no parental rights, then she might be viewed as a legal stranger to Bernard and he might instead be placed with someone whom he had never met or only knew casually. This car accident would have robbed him of the only parents he had ever known, even though only one of his parents had died in the accident. Or, suppose that after raising Bernard for several years, Ann and Nancy were to break up. Ann might refuse to permit Nancy to see Bernard, even though it would have been better for him to have maintained contact with both of the people who had been raising him since infancy. If Nancy's parental rights had been recognized by the state, Ann would not have been able to preclude her from seeing him.

An individual reading some of the discussions in the literature regarding whether same-sex couples should be permitted to marry might assume that only optimal parents are allowed to marry. Otherwise, it would seem rather strange that same-sex adults can be precluded from marrying because they, allegedly, would not be optimal parents, whereas other individuals are permitted to marry even though they will not be optimal parents. Yet, as a general matter, we do not impose an optimal-parent requirement on those seeking to marry. Indeed, we do not even impose an optimal parent requirement on those seeking to adopt. Nor would anyone think of proposing such a standard were this not a discussion of same-sex marriage or LGBT parenting. That this criterion is suggested *only* in the context of LGBT parenting or marriage suggests that this criterion is not really embraced as the appropriate consideration to determine who may marry or adopt but, instead, is being used as a makeweight to justify the imposition of a burden on members of the LGBT community.

Consider the implications of the adoption of such a standard for adoption or marriage. Presumably, the optimal parent is not only patient, empathic, loving, and nurturing but also has ample funds to spend on a child. Does this mean that individuals who are not wealthy cannot be good parents? Of course not. But optimality is not merely about those who are good or even great parents. Instead, it is about those who would be the *best* parents. Few parents could meet such an exacting standard even were there consensus about what such a parent would be like.

It would be absurd to say that only optimal parents can adopt, precisely because children can flourish even if adopted by non-optimal parents and because children who would thereby be precluded from being adopted would grow up in circumstances much less preferable than would have obtained had they been adopted by less than optimal parents. Would anyone really suggest that because a would-be parent with somewhat more limited means might be non-optimal, that individual should therefore be statutorily barred from adopting? The same point might be made about marriage. Would anyone really suggest that because a would-be parent with somewhat more limited means might be non-optimal, that individual should therefore be statutorily barred from marrying?[12]

Permitting same-sex couples to marry might well induce more couples to adopt children, thereby providing those children with the opportunity to flourish in a loving home rather than remain unadopted. Of course, permitting same-sex couples to marry would not only provide more potential homes for children in need of placement; it would also likely result in more children being produced.[13] Thus, it may well be that same-sex couples who married would be more likely to make the financial and emotional investment sometimes required when making use of advanced reproductive techniques.

Children are created in a variety of ways, including surrogacy and in vitro fertilization. Yet, these advanced reproductive techniques can be quite expensive.[14] The same point might be made about adoption.[15] A same-sex married couple might well view their marriage as both a symbolic and legal commitment, and this acknowledged commitment might be the deciding factor when the couple was considering whether to adopt a child or whether to produce a child through the use of advanced reproductive techniques. Thus, permitting same-sex couples to marry might increase the number of stable, two-parent homes in which children were being raised, both because some of the children already in the world might be more likely to be adopted and because affording marriage rights might increase the likelihood that same-sex couples would make use of non-coital techniques by which to have children.

Certainly, different issues might be thought implicated when one is talking about adopting a child in need of placement on the one hand or bringing a child into the world by making use of advanced reproductive techniques on the other. But a discussion of *optimal* parents is out of place in either context. Needless to say, many, many fewer children would be brought into this world if individuals were precluded from having children unless it could be established that they would be optimal parents.

B.   *Marriage Promotes the Ability to Take Care of One's Partner or Older Dependents*

Marriage affords to individuals themselves and society as a whole a host of benefits whether or not the couple has or will have children. At least one point that might be considered when discussing the benefits of marriage is that with the changing demographics of our country, dependents other than children should also be considered in a discussion of the potential nurturing benefits of marriage. Thus, the population of the United States is aging.[16] More and more adults are acting as caregivers for their own parents.[17] An adult child may want or have to quit her job or work fewer hours in order to take on that role.[18] However, without some of the benefits afforded by marriage, e.g., being covered under a marital partner's insurance policy or the increased security afforded by a formalized commitment, it may simply be impossible for an adult to stop work to take care of an aging parent, even though the adult child's doing so would benefit the aging parent, the adult child, and society itself.

So, too, legal recognition of the relationship between the partners might facilitate their taking care of each other, both because of the availability of insurance and because the legal commitment might make the individuals more willing to invest in their own relationship. Commentators have suggested that one of the differences between cohabiting different-sex couples and married different-sex couples is their relative willingness to invest in their relationship.[19] The same point has been made about the partners' willingness to invest in the children whom they are raising.[20] Indeed, as a related point, some have noted that extended family members are more likely to aid married than cohabiting couples, which might make such couples more able to remain together during difficult financial times.[21] Presumably, we would see similar patterns among same-sex couples, i.e., that married individual would invest more in their relationships and each other than would cohabiting individuals and, perhaps, that extended family would be more willing to extend financial help to married than to cohabiting same-sex couples. But all of this speaks to why it would be a good investment for society to permit same-sex marriages, and why same-sex couples might indeed benefit themselves and society were they to marry.

C.   Current Challenges Faced by Marriage

Many commentators have noted with dismay some of the difficulties that they see facing marriage today. The number of children being born out of wedlock continues to rise--it has recently been suggested that over one third of children are born to an unmarried parent.[22] There continues to be a high rate of divorce in the United States, and for the first time in the country's history, fewer that 50% of American households are headed by married couples.[23] In addition, many individuals seem not to place as high a value on marriage as did members of previous generations.

While no one factor explains the changing attitudes toward marriage, some suggest that economics plays an important role. Thus, some argue that women in previous generations had relatively few employment options and would sometimes marry to achieve economic security. However, because there are increased economic opportunities for women now, many women may feel less of a need to marry. Of course, women still seek marital partners for non-economic reasons, e.g., the desire to have a partner with whom to share one's life.[24] Further, it may well be both easier and more rewarding to raise a child with a partner. Thus, there are ample non-financial reasons to marry. That said, however, it might be noted that the growing acceptance of individuals' having children out of wedlock may make it easier for "single mothers by choice" to have children,[25] especially if those women are able to provide for themselves and their children economically. That more women are doing this may itself lead to further acceptance of parenthood by single adults, making this even less of a factor in inducing individuals or couples to marry.

That there are growing numbers of single women who are choosing to have children and that growing numbers of women are delaying marriage or choosing not to marry are noteworthy trends, and it may be important to figure out why this is happening. It may be, for example, that these trends reflect an increased unwillingness on the part of women who are able to provide for themselves (and, perhaps, their children) to take on traditional gender roles. Ironically, if that is so, then some of the arguments used by same-sex marriage opponents may well make marriage less attractive to those who do not wish to take on traditional gender roles in a marriage.

D.   Same-Sex Marriage Opponents and Gender Equality

Some commentators suggest that precluding same-sex couples from marrying somehow affirms gender equality, because such a limitation makes it necessary that both sexes be part of the marriage. [26] Yet, a few points might be made about such an argument. It might be noted, for example, that commentators do not offer an analogous argument with respect to race and religion by suggesting that the law should preclude individuals of the same race or religion from marrying as a way of affirming racial and religious equality. Presumably, these theorists believe in the importance of racial and religious equality, so it may be noteworthy that they do not think it necessary for marriage to be limited along such lines to promote equality.

Historically, we have not had laws requiring that individuals of different races marry but, instead, prohibiting their marrying.[27] Some same-sex marriage opponents have suggested that the reason that such laws were offensive is that they promoted the supremacy of one race over another.[28] While those laws were offensive for that reason, they were offensive for other reasons as well.

Suppose that a state were to pass a law precluding individuals from marrying outside of their races. Suppose further there was no implicit privileging of one race over another. Would that make such laws acceptable or even permissible? One would think that those who only find interracial marriage laws offensive because of their privileging one race over another would not object to laws that precluded intermarriage but did not in addition suggest anything about the races themselves. After all, such laws might be said to classify among the races equally, just as same-sex marriage bans are allegedly not imposing greater burdens on either sex but instead imposing the burdens equally.[29] If, indeed, same-sex marriage bans are permissible as long as they do not involve an "attempt to stigmatize one gender as inferior and untouchable,"[30] one would expect that these commentators would take an analogous position with respect to interracial marriage bans.

Yet, interracial marriage bans are offensive whether or not they impose greater burdens on race rather than on another and even if they do not implicitly privilege one race over another.[31] Marriage simply should not be denied on such a basis, and commentators are doing themselves and others a disservice when suggesting that the only objectionable feature of interracial marriage bans was that they privileged one race over another.

Same-sex marriage opponents who discuss the interracial marriage bans that once existed suggest that the abolition of such bans sufficed to promote attitudes of racial equality. Yet, one must wonder why it is necessary to prohibit same-sex marriage to promote gender equality when it suffices to permit interracial marriage to promote racial equality.

Suppose that a theorist had argued that the state's willingness to recognize different-race marriages would somehow impugn same-race marriages and that this was a reason that such mixed marriages should be prohibited. Such an argument would be rejected for both theoretical and practical reasons. First, that the state recognizes different-race marriages does not establish or even imply that the state disapproves of same-race marriages. Second, just because the state permits different-race couples to marry does not make it likely that most individuals would therefore marry someone of a different race. Rather what would happen is that some would marry someone of another race but that most would marry someone of the same race.[32] So, too, the recognition of same-sex marriage would not establish or even imply that the state disapproves of different-sex marriage, and the recognition of same-sex marriage would not result in a huge number of individuals forsaking their different-sex partners so that they could marry same-sex partners instead. Indeed, if Massachusetts is any guide of what will likely happen after other states recognize same-sex marriage, there will be no cataclysmic effect and, indeed, society will continue much as it did before.[33]

Suppose that we bracket that the argument that same-sex marriage bans promote gender equality would, if applied in other contexts, yield results that these commentators would never accept. Let us instead examine why those promoting same-sex marriage bans might not be viewed as promoting gender equality.

When commentators note that our country is advancing in terms of gender equality, they are often discussing a growing acceptance of women performing a variety of roles in society and a growing disinclination to assign women fixed gender roles or a subordinate position in the family. Insofar as those opposing same-sex marriage are doing so because they want to reinforce fixed notions of the roles of women,[34] they may well not only be undermining the well-being of both women and men,[35] but they may be making marriage less attractive to those who do not wish to play those assigned roles. Ironically, some of the rhetoric allegedly justifying the refusal to permit same-sex couples to marry may well contribute to the decrease in the perceived desirability of marriage and to the tendency among some women to either delay marriage or to avoid the institution entirely.

E.   Same-Sex Marriage and Religious Freedom

Some commentators have suggested that recognition of same-sex marriage would somehow infringe on religious freedom[36] or, perhaps, thwart God's Plan.[37] First, the same argument might have been offered to justify the refusal to recognize interracial marriages, since some groups believed such unions against God's Will.[38] Second, various religious groups recognize same-sex unions,[39] so it is not as if the recognition of such unions is anti-religious. On the contrary, there is a disagreement among religions about whether to recognize same-sex unions. Yet, given that the state's recognizing such unions would not entail that religious groups would have to recognize them,[40] one might have expected that those in favor of religious liberty would have supported state recognition of same-sex unions. Indeed, the refusal to recognize such marriages *might* have Establishment or Free Exercise Clause implications,[41] although it is not argued here that the state must recognize all unions that are religiously celebrated. Rather, the claims are that is at best misleading to imply that the same-sex marriage debate is between the religious and the areligious and that the state interests articulated in favor of same-sex marriage bans should be examined more closely, given that extremely important associational and religious rights are at issue.

Marriage provides numerous benefits to the individuals themselves, even if they do not have parents or children in need of care.[42] These benefits may be physical, mental, financial, and sexual.[43] Their existence is explained in a number of ways, for example, that the increased security afforded by marriage allows individuals to invest in the relationship in ways that will benefit both members of the couple. Yet, all kinds of couples can benefit from the security afforded by marriage.

Some commentators suggest the same-sex couples would not benefit from marriage,[44] implying that gay and lesbian lifestyles simply are not marital. Yet, the difficulties with such an argument should be clear. Members of the LGBT community are like other members of the population, and they vary greatly in their attitudes and practices. For this very reason, it would be misleading to cite a study of gay men in urban southern California as if they would represent gay men nationally. Indeed, suppose that a particular study revealed that a high percentage of heterosexual individuals surveyed in Los Angeles seemed overly concerned about their appearance or, perhaps, that a high percentage of married individuals surveyed in Los Angeles had committed adultery. What would one conclude about national policy based on these results?

What effect would marriage have on same-sex couples? This is unclear. Precisely because members of the LGBT community are like other people, it would seem likely to affect different people in different ways. Claims to the contrary notwithstanding, many members of the LGBT community value monogamy and fidelity.[45] Indeed, recent reports suggest that same-sex couples who marry or celebrate civil unions are *more* likely to stay together than are comparable different-sex couples.[46] Given that many states refuse to recognize same-sex relationships and that many of these relationships are continuing notwithstanding the lack of the kinds of state support that is offered to marriages, the characterization of members of the LGBT community as being incapable of having committed, monogamous relationships is simply inaccurate.

Certainly, some members of the LGBT community believe that monogamy is not a worthy goal. However, it is simply unclear how many believe that or whether these attitudes might change if these individuals were afforded the right to marry, especially for those couples who had married and were raising children. In any event, recognition of marriage rights would likely induce some same-sex couples to stay together longer than they otherwise would have, thereby helping them and any dependents who were in their care.

Some of the discussions regarding whether same-sex marriage should be recognized have an other-worldly feel to them, if only because there does not seem to be an appreciation of the relatively high incidence of divorce and adultery among different-sex married couples.[47] That said, however, it is of course true that some same-sex couples who marry will divorce, just as is true of different-sex couples. Yet, the high probability that some same-sex couples will divorce is not a reason to refuse to permit such marriages for two distinct kinds of reasons.

First, recognizing same-sex marriage will provide to same-sex couples some of the benefits that married different-sex couples receive, including societal support for their staying together. It seems reasonable to expect that this support would positively correlate with the length of time that couples would stay together. However, a cautionary note should be offered. Those who are in the limelight because they are in the forefront of the battle to secure same-sex marriage rights may well face pressures that they otherwise would not have, and it would be unsurprising if those pressures might sometimes result in an earlier break-up than would otherwise have occurred. But those pressures would not be a result of marriage per se but rather the accompanying publicity (and the feeling of being under a microscope) to which individuals in the public eye are subjected. For example, the fact that some of the named parties in *Goodridge v. Department of Public Health*[48] have split[49] may be due in no small part to all of the publicity accompanying their struggle. In any event, it might be noted that same-sex couples who have had their relationships recognized by the state have been splitting up at a lower rate than have comparable different-sex couples.[50]

For those same-sex couples who do split up, it is important that there is a formal mechanism in law to help sort out support and property issues. Just as it is important for the state to provide a means whereby a fair and equitable distribution of assets can occur should a different-sex marital relationship dissolve, the same point should be made about same-sex marital relationships.

F.   On the Use of the Courts to Vindicate Marriage Rights

One somewhat surprising argument that has recently been offered is that same-sex couples should not seek to have their right to marry vindicated through the courts. These commentators imply that it is somehow anti-democratic to seek protection from the courts when legislatures are unwilling to afford recognition to the rights to which many individuals feel entitled.[51] Yet, there is reason to doubt that many of these commentators are worried about the preservation of the ability of the electorate to have its will represented. For example, some support a Federal Marriage Amendment, which would preclude state legislatures or electorates from recognizing same-sex marriage. Passage of such an amendment would hardly promote the autonomy of individual state legislatures or electorates.

By the same token, there is something antidemocratic about some of the recent state constitutional amendments precluding same-same couples from marrying. Presumably, one of the reasons that they were passed has nothing to do with the fear that the legislature was about to pass legislation recognizing same-sex marriages. Rather, at least one of the purposes behind passing these amendments was to tie the hands of future legislatures that might be tempted to afford marriage rights to same-sex couples.[52]

The point here should not be misunderstood. Marriage amendments can be repealed, and thus it would be false to suggest that the marriage amendments that have been passed recently have tied the hands of legislatures and electorates forever. Rather, these amendments make it more difficult and more costly for marriage equality to be achieved.

Needless to say, Richard Loving and Mildred Jeter might have waited a very long time before their marriage could be recognized in Virginia had they believed that it was anti-democratic of them to seek vindication of their marriage rights in the courts. For example, the Alabama electorate removed an admittedly unenforceable anti-miscegenation provision from that state's constitution in the year 2000.[53]

Further, it will not do to say that what the Lovings did was acceptable because, after all, they were merely seeking to vindicate their right to marry rather than effect a fundamental change in the marriage law. They were seeking to modify a provision that had been part of the Virginia code for centuries.[54]

Same-sex couples have the same needs as do different-sex couples. They have children and parents in need of their care. Both society and the individuals themselves will benefit from society's supporting the stability and longevity of same-sex relationships.

Marriage is of fundamental importance,[55] and it should not be characterized as simply another benefit to be conferred at a legislature's discretion. A brief review of the historical treatment of interracial marriages should be enough to illustrate why something as important as marriage should not simply be a matter of popular will. Ironically, by suggesting that same-sex couples are acting inappropriately when seeking to vindicate marriage rights in the courts, same-sex marriage opponents devalue marriage, implying that it is like other benefits appropriately subject to legislative discretion and largesse. This is exactly the wrong message to send, and it is both surprising and disheartening that some same-sex marriage opponents have taken this tack.

III.   Conclusion

Marriage helps provide a setting in which children can thrive. This is a reason that same-sex couples should be permitted to marry. They already have children who would benefit from the increased stability afforded by marriage, and the recognition of same-sex unions would likely mean that even more children would thereby benefit.

Recognition of same-sex marriage might benefit other dependents too, e.g., elderly parents who were in need of care. Because recognition of such unions might include insurance benefits, an individual might be able to stop working outside of the home to take care of a parent without worrying that doing so would result in the loss of insurance.

Even if one brackets the benefits that would accrue to the same-sex couple's dependents, same-sex marriages should still be recognized, because doing so would benefit the individuals themselves and society as a whole. When the individuals themselves are happier, they can be more productive, which benefits society as a whole. Further, when individuals take care of each other, which might be even more likely were the relationships legally recognized, the state may not be forced to bear costs that it otherwise would have been forced to bear.

One disturbing aspect of the same-sex marriage debate is that same-sex marriage opponents too often offer arguments which are non sequiturs or which would not be offered in any other context. For example, it simply makes no sense to suggest that same-sex couples should not be allowed to marry because children do best with their biological parents. Such an argument does not even make sense in the context of adoption, and it makes even less sense in the context of marriage.

Whether or not same-sex couples are permitted to marry, they will continue to have children. Further, whether or not such marriages are recognized, there will continue to be children in need of adoption placement. The refusal to recognize same-sex marriage does not bolster marriage, although it does imposed an undeserved burden on an unpopular minority.

Some of the arguments offered by commentators are especially implausible. For example, the claim that gender quality is promoted by refusing to recognize same-sex marriage simply is not credible. Were it plausible, one might expect it to be offered in other contexts. That few if any of the commentators would suggest the enactment of intra-racial or intra-religious marriage bans as a way of promoting racial or religious equality suggests that this rationale should not be taken seriously. Recognizing same-sex marriage would not somehow imply that the state disapproves of different-sex marriage, just as the recognition of interracial marriage does not somehow signal the disapproval of intra-racial marriage. It is not demeaning to either sex that same-sex couples can marry, just as it is not demeaning to different races or religions than same-race or same-religion couples can marry.

Yet, the gender equality argument offered by same-sex marriage opponents may mask something that that they do not seem to appreciate, namely, that it may well be that one of the reasons that marriage may seem to be in trouble is that proponents of traditional marriage seem to extol traditional gender roles and stereotypes. Given that workplace demographics have changed dramatically, it may well be that those who seek to promote marriage are doing themselves and society as a whole a disservice by suggesting a return to the "good old days." For those women for whom the good old days do not look particularly good, such descriptions may well make marriage seem less rather than more desirable.

Same-sex couples have many of the same needs and desires as do different-sex couples. They want to provide for themselves and their families. They wish to enjoy the tangible and symbolic benefits that access to marriage may bring.

It is of course true that some same-sex married couples will divorce, just as is true of different-sex couples. Yet, even in cases where the relationship dissolves, legal recognition of the relationship is important to help assure that the parties are treated equitably.

When same-sex marriage opponents do their utmost to prevent same-sex couples from enjoying the benefits of marriage notwithstanding that many of the same individual and societal interests would be served by recognizing those marriages, same-sex marriage opponents are doing marriage a disservice in yet another respect. It then becomes yet another tool by which to impose undeserved burdens. But using marriage in this way tarnishes rather than protects it. Ironically, by using specious reasoning (and thereby implicitly suggesting that the real reasons cannot stand the light of day), by extolling a period in our history during which women were not viewed as equals, and by refusing to permit the needs of same-sex couples and their families to be met, same-sex marriage opponents may be doing more harm to the institution that they allegedly venerate than the recognition of same-sex marriage ever could.

Notes

1. Trustees Professor of Law, Capital University School of Law.

2. See, for example, George W. Dent, Jr., "How Does Same-Sex Marriage Threaten You?" 59 Rutgers L. Rev. 233, 243 (2007).

3. See Mary Becker, Family Law in the Secular State and Restrictions on Same-Sex Marriage: Two Are Better than One, 2001 U. Ill. L. Rev. 1, 52.

4. U.S. v. Virginia, 518 U.S. 515, 533 (1996).

5. See Donald J. Cantor, Elizabeth Cantor, James C. Black & Campbell D. Barrett, Same-Sex Marriage: The Legal and Psychological Evolution in America 64 (Middletown, CT: Wesleyan University Press, 2006).

6. See Mary L. Bonauto, Civil Marriage as a Locus of Civil Rights Struggles, 30 Hum. Rts. Q 3, 7 (2003) (noting that various medical and psychiatric associations support adoptions by members of the LGBT community and that children raised by same-sex couples are healthy according to the relevant measures of child development).

7. See Heather F. Latham, Desperately Clinging to the Cleavers: What Family Law Courts are Doing About Homosexual Parents, and What Some are Refusing to See, 29 L. & Psychol. Rev. 223, 235 (2005) ("Social work experts even indicate that many of the differences between homosexual and heterosexual parents actually serve to make homosexual parents more suitable for foster care and adoption than some of their heterosexual counterparts.")

8. For the suggestion that this is the optimal child-raising arrangement, see W. Bradford Wilcox & Robin Fretwell Wilson, *Bringing Up Baby: Adoption, Marriage, and the Best Interests of the Child*, 14 Wm. & Mary Bill Rts. J. 883, 892 (2006).

9. *Cf.* Lynn D. Wardle, *Form and Substance In Parentage Law*, 15 Wm. & Mary Bill Rts. J. 203, 244-45 (2006) ("instability in the home is a cause of detriment for children").

10. For the suggestion that biology should not trump all other factors, see Wilcox and Wilson, supra note 8, at 895 ("the research to date indicates that children raised in adopted two-parent homes do better than children raised in single-parent, biologically related homes").

11. *Cf.* John D. Athey, Student Work, *The Ramifications of West Virginia's Codified Child Custody Law: A Departure from* Garska v. Mccoy, 106 W. Va. L. Rev. 389, 398 (2004) ("all other factors being equal, homes marred by poverty or limited educational opportunities might not be in the children's best interests").

12. *Cf.* Zablocki v. Redhail, 434 U.S. 374 (1978) (striking down Wisconsin law limiting the marriage options of poor non-custodial parents). Of course, even the Wisconsin law was not as broad as the law being discussed here, since the Wisconsin law would "merely" have limited the marriage options of non-custodial parents who were or would be unable to pay their existing child support obligations.

13. *See* Reproductive Science Center of New England, *Doctors Note Increase in Same-Sex Couples Using IVF to Start Families*, Obesity, Fitness & Wellness Wk. 2864, 12/22/07, 2007 WLNR 24683327 (noting that now that same-sex marriage has been recognized in Massachusetts, there has been a significant increase in the use of assisted reproductive technologies by same-sex couples).

14. Marnie W. Mueller, *Financing High-Tech Reproductive Medical Expenditures*, 6 Stan. L. & Pol'y Rev. 113, 113 (1995) ("advanced reproductive techniques . . . are quite expensive").

15. *See* J. Blake Byrd, Anne Kelley Russell, Vanessa Kinney, Elizabeth Marie Dulong, Rick Behring, Jr., *Constitutional Law*, 29 U. Ark. Little Rock L. Rev. 809, 840 (2007) (discussing "the cumbersome and expensive reality of the adoption process").

16. *See* David Barnhizer, *Waking From Sustainability's "Impossible Dream": The Decisionmaking Realities of Business and Government*, 18 Geo. Int'l Envtl. L. Rev. 595, 626 (2006) ("The United States . . . has a rapidly aging and increasingly expensive population.").

17. *Cf.* Lynne Marie Kohm & Britney N. Brigner, *Women and Assisted Suicide: Exposing the Gender Vulnerability to Acquiescent Death*, 4 Cardozo Women's L.J. 241, 261 (1998) (noting that "the burden of caring for the frail elderly (mostly women) will fall more heavily upon their grown children").

18. *Cf.* Timothy Stoltzfus Jost & Sandra J. Tanenbaum, *Selling Cost Containment*, 19 Am. J.L. & Med. 95, 118 (1993) (discussing individuals who "long to quit jobs to take care of an aging parent").

19. *See* Margaret F. Brinig & Steven L. Nock, *Marry Me, Bill: Should Cohabitation Be the (Legal) Default Option?* 64 La. L. Rev. 403, 426 (2004) ("the partners invest less in each other or in the relationship than they do if married").

20. Wilcox and Wilson, *supra* note 8, at 884 ("marriage matters to how children flourish and to the extent to which their parents are willing to invest in them").

21. Kathleen Mullan Harris, *Family Structure, Poverty And Family Well-Being: An Overview Of Panel 2*, 10 Employee Rts & Employment Pol'y J. 45, 54 (2006) ("a family that has resources to help out will be less likely to share those resources with a cohabiting couple than with a married couple").

22. *See* Michael Dobbs, *The Fact Checker: Same-Sex Marriage*, Wash. Post (Bus. Sec.), 10/3/07, 2007 WLNR 19385976 ("According to the latest data from the National Center for Health Statistics, 36.8 percent of children born in the United States in 2005 were born out of wedlock.").

23. *See* Ryan White, *Fiancé finds himself flat-footed*, Portland Oregonian E01, 12/14/06, 2006 WLNR 21811317 ("for the first time in the history of the United States, the percentage of households headed by married couples has dipped below 50 percent").

24. *See* Linda C. McClain, The Place of Families Fostering Capacity, Equality and Responsibility 146 (Cambridge: Harvard University Press, 2006) (discussing a report where over 90% of the never-married singles surveyed said that it was important for their future spouse to be their soul mate).

25. *See* Bernie D. Jones, *Single Motherhood by Choice, Libertarian Feminism, and the Uniform Parentage Act*, 12 Tex. J. Women & L. 419, 420 (2003) ("[B]irths are on the rise amongst older single women. Within this group are those who call themselves 'single mothers by choice,' women who have chosen motherhood when the traditional option of marriage and family seemed impossible.").

26. *See*, for example, Richard F. Duncan, *From* Loving *to* Romer: *Homosexual Marriage and Moral Discernment*, 12 BYU J. Pub. L. 239, 243 (1998) ("by requiring participation by one person of each gender, conventional marriage laws affirm the concept of gender equality"); Dent, *supra* note 2, at 239 ("traditional marriage promotes equality of women").

27. *See* Loving v. Virginia, 388 U.S. 1, 6 n.5 (1967) (listing the states banning interracial marriage in 1967). The Court noted that over the previous fifteen years, fourteen states had repealed their interracial marriage bans. *See id.* n.5.

28. Duncan, *supra* note 26, at 243 ("Anti-miscegenation laws endorsed the invidious doctrine of White Supremacy")

29. *See id.* at 241.

30. *Id.* at 243.

31. *See Loving*, 388 U.S. at 11 n.11 ("we find the racial classifications in these statutes repugnant to the Fourteenth Amendment, even assuming an even-handed state purpose to protect the 'integrity' of all races").

32. A separate question is whether the state should care whether individuals are marrying inside or outside of their race, however defined. The point here is merely that many intra-racial marriages were celebrated even after the recognition of interracial marriage. See John DeWitt Gregory & Joanna L. Grossman, *The Legacy of Loving*, 51 How. L.J. 15, 49 (2007) ("the rates of intermarriage between blacks and whites remain relatively low after *Loving*").

33. *See* Jack B. Harrison, *The Future of Same-Sex Marriage after* Lawrence v. Texas *and the Election of 2004*, 30 U. Dayton L. Rev. 313, 324 (2005).

34. *Cf.* Linda C. McClain, *The "Male Problematic" and the Problems of Family Law: A Response to Don Browning's "Critical Familism,"* 56 Emory L.J. 1407, 1422 (2007) (discussing "religious conceptions of family that embrace gender hierarchy or a fixed vision of sex roles (such as women as sexual gatekeepers or men as 'head of household'").

35. *See* Linda C. McClain, *Some ABCs of Feminist Sex Education (in Light of the Sexuality Critique of Legal Feminism)*, 15 Colum. J. Gender & L. 63, 69 (2006) ("Rigid gender role expectations harm both females and males.").

36. *See* Teresa Stanton Collett, *Constitutional Confusion: The Case for the Minnesota Marriage Amendment*, 33 Wm. Mitchell L. Rev. 1029, 1054 (2007) ("While proponents of same-sex unions disavow any intention of demanding that religious bodies rec-

ognize or participate in solemnizing these unions, defenders of traditional marriage have cause to worry."); *see also* Helen M. Alvaré, *The Moral Reasoning of Family Law: The Case of Same-Sex Marriage*, 38 Loy. U. Chi. L.J. 349, 371-72 (2007). Charles Russo goes much farther when suggesting that many same-sex marriage proponents are simply anti-religious bigots. *See* Charles J. Russo, *Same-Sex Marriage and Public School Curricula: Preserving Parental Rights To Direct the Education of Their Children*, 32 U. Dayton L. Rev. 361, 365-66 (2007).

37. *See* Toni Lester, J.D., Ph.D., *Adam And Steve vs. Adam And Eve: Will The New Supreme Court Grant Gays the Right to Marry?* 14 Am. U.J. Gender Soc. Pol'y & L. 253, 272 (2006) (noting that the official position statement of the Southern Baptist Convention states, "We affirm God's plan for marriage and sexual intimacy--one man, and one woman, for life. Homosexuality is not a 'valid alternative lifestyle.' The Bible condemns it as sin.").

38. *See Loving*, 388 U.S. at 3

> He [the *Loving* trial judge] stated in an opinion that:
>
> 'Almighty God created the races white, black, yellow, malay and red, and he placed them on separate continents. And but for the interference with his arrangement there would be no cause for such marriages. The fact that he separated the races shows that he did not intend for the races to mix.'

See also Adele M. Morrison, *Same-Sex Loving: Subverting White Supremacy through Same-Sex Marriage*, 13 Mich. J. Race & L. 177, 208 (2007) (noting parallels in the views of those opposing same-sex marriage and those opposing interracial marriage).

39. *See* Hon. Irwin Cotler, *Marriage in Canada--Evolution or Revolution?* 44 Fam. Ct. Rev. 60, 68 (2006) ("Some religious groups, including some within the Christian, Jewish, and other religious communities, do not agree with the perspective put forward by others and wish to have the ability to celebrate legal marriages between same-sex partners.").

40. *See* Harrison, *supra* note 33, at 336 ("Recognition of same-sex civil marriages will never result in any religious organization being forced by the state to conduct gay marriages against its religious belief.").

41. *See* Joseph William Singer, *Same Sex Marriage, Full Faith and Credit, and the Evasion of Obligation*, 1 Stan. J. Civ. Rts. & Civ. Liberties 1, 24 (2005) ("if the government interest is in establishing a particular religious definition of marriage (given that some religions celebrate-in both senses of the word-same sex marriages), then asserting this moral interest to justify nonrecognition would seem to be prohibited by the Establishment Clause"); Wilson Huhn, *Ohio Issue 1 Is Unconstitutional*, 28 N.C. Cent. L.J. 1, 9 (2005)

> The recognition of same-sex marriage will . . . reinforce the free exercise of religion in that many same-sex couples presently participate in religious weddings even though the government does not recognize the legal validity of their marriage. The legal recognition of same-sex marriage will accommodate their religious beliefs.

42. *See* Nicholas Bala, *The Debates about Same-Sex Marriage in Canada and the United States: Controversy over the Evolution of a Fundamental Social Institution*, 20 BYU J. Pub. L. 195, 221 (2006) (discussing the "psychological, social, economic, and legal benefits of marriage").

43. *See* Levi R. Smylie, Book Note, *Strengthening Our Families: An In-Depth Look at the Proclamation on the Family*, 6 J. L. & Fam. Stud. 375, 377 (2004).

44. *See*, for example, Dent, *supra* note 2, at 252.

45. *See* Tobin A. Sparling, *All in the Family: Recognizing the Unifying Potential of Same-Sex Marriage*, 10 L. & Sex. 187, 203 (2001) ("many gay people do [live in committed monogamous relationships] and many of their relationships have endured far longer than the average heterosexual marriage").

46. *See* Paul Maley, *I Do, More or Less*, Australian, 12/13/07, at 13, 2007 WLNR 24526559.

47. Rates of adultery are notoriously difficult to establish. Estimates range from 20% to 70%. *See* Elizabeth F. Emens, *Monogamy's Law: Compulsory Monogamy and Polyamorous Existence*, 29 N.Y.U. Rev. L. & Soc. Change 277, 299 (2004). To make matters more complicated, these statistics are based on individuals admitting that they have committed adultery, and it may well be that some of the low estimates understate the prevalence of adultery because individuals are simply unwilling to admit that they have had an affair. *See id.*

48. 798 N.E.2d 941 (Mass. 2003).

49. *See* Wyatt Buchanan, *The Battle over Same-Sex Marriage: Couple split up, drop names from state court case*, S.F. Chron. B1, 11/13/06, 2006 WLNR 19669619 (discussing "the July breakup of Julie and Hillary Goodridge in Massachusetts").

50. *See id.*
> But the nation's divorce rate hovers between 40 and 50 percent while same-sex couples in officially sanctioned relationships appear to be separating at a much lower rate. In Vermont, which became the first state to enact civil unions five years ago, 113 of 8,109 couples have terminated them, about 1.4 percent.

51. *Cf.* Lynn D. Wardle, *The Proposed Federal Marriage Amendment and the Risks to Federalism in Family Law*, 2 U. St. Thomas L.J. 137, 159 (2004) ("judicial elitists who will impose their own private preference for gay marriage upon the people by anti-democratic judicial interpretation").

52. *Cf.* Steve Sheppard, *Intelligible, Honest, and Impartial Democracy: Making Laws at the Arkansas Ballot Box, or Why Jim Hannah and Ray Thornton Were Right about* May v. Daniels, 2005 Ark. L. Notes 123, 130 (2005) (noting that "the amendment would preclude the legislature from future recognition of gay marriages").

53. *See* Mary LaFrance, Book Review, *Politics, Gay Rights and the Light at the End of the Rainbow*, 1 Nev. L.J. 441, 449 n.26 (2001).

54. *See* Barbara K. Kopytoff & A. Leon Higginbotham, Jr., *Racial Purity and Interracial Sex in the Law of Colonial and Antebellum Virginia*, 77 Geo. L.J. 1967, 2021 (1989) (noting that interracial marriage was first outlawed in Virginia in 1691).

55. *See Zablocki*, 434 U.S. at 378.

CHAPTER 3
"WHO'S MY DADDY?"
HOW THE LEGALIZATION OF SAME-SEX PARTNERSHIPS
WOULD FURTHER THE RISE OF AMBIGUOUS FATHERHOOD
IN AMERICA

Jason S. Carroll, Ph.D., and David C. Dollahite, Ph.D.
Brigham Young University

I.   Introduction: The Rise of Ambiguous Fatherhood

At the dawn of the 21st century, an examination of fatherhood in American family life reveals that its status may be best captured in the classic Charles Dickens line from his *Tale of Two Cities*— "it was the best of times, it was the worst of times." Similar to other aspects of family well-being in the United States (e.g., economic prosperity), father-child relationships today are marked by two contrasting trends that lead to strikingly divergent life experiences for men and their children. On the one hand, many American children are growing up with high levels of connection to their fathers as they benefit from a culture that has historically high expectations for men's involvement in the everyday lives of their children. The last generation has witnessed the widespread acceptance of the ideal of fathers as equal co-parents in nurturing and caring for children.[1] The emergence of this ideal has been supported by an increased social recognition that "children need and deserve active, involved fathers throughout their childhood and adolescence."[2] Furthermore, these cultural ideals have been bolstered by a sizeable body of scientific evidence documenting that multiple aspects of children's well-being are positively influenced by high levels of father involvement.[3]

However, despite increased norms for father involvement, the last generation has also witnessed the rise of ambiguous fatherhood in America. Many of the historical supports that have traditionally preserved men's involvement in their children's lives have been eroding for contemporary families. Historically high rates of non-marital cohabitation, out-of-wedlock childbirth, and marital divorce[4] have dramatically altered the landscape of fathering, leaving unprecedented numbers of children growing up with uncertain or non-existent relationships with their fathers. While these demographic trends have changed family life in general within the United States, these contextual changes have been particularly grim for father-child relationships, which have been found to be more sensitive than mother-child relationships to contextual forces and supports.[5]

It is within this "tale of two cities" context of father-child relationships in America that some are proposing that we alter the culture of fatherhood even further by legalizing same-sex partnerships and granting these unions the status of marriage, including legally supported parenting. While the current "culture wars"[6] over so-called same-sex marriage rarely center on discussions of children's developmental needs and how such a course of action would impact our collective culture of parenting, these issues are at the heart of the matter. Some key questions that must be addressed include: "Can we alter the legal definition of marriage without subsequently changing our understanding of father-child relationships and the nature of parenting within our culture?" "How will the widespread legalization of same-sex partnerships influence our culture of parenting and, therefore, the well-being of children in our society?" "Will the legalization of same-sex partnerships further erode the foundation of fathering in this country?" These questions deserve serious consideration in any discussion of public policy that has the potential to radically alter the legal definition and meaning of marriage, and therefore parenthood and childhood in our society.

A.   Purpose of this Paper

The purpose of this paper is to address the potential harmful impact on father-child relationships of changing the legal definition of marriage to include same-sex couples. Efforts to confer the legal status of marriage on same-sex couples are only the latest, and perhaps most problematic, in a series of cultural trends that weaken father-child relationships. In particular, we examine the consequences for father-child relationships of changing the legal definition of marriage within a framework of generative fathering, which emphasizes the developmental needs of children and the ethical responsibility fathers have to create and maintain relationships that foster those needs. We review the contextual factors that have been found to sustain this type of responsible, child-centered fathering (i.e., committed marriage, shared residential involvement, and legal paternity based in kin altruism). Drawing from this discussion, we detail how the legalization of same-sex partnerships (together with other societal trends) threatens to increase the number of children raised in settings of what we call *ambiguous fatherhood*—with detrimental developmental outcomes for children and fathers. Although we believe women and mothers would also be negatively influenced by these changes, we confine our analysis to fathers and children. The central thesis of this paper is that the legalization of same-sex partnerships not only poses a threat to children raised by same-sex couples, but will also have predictable negative consequences for all men and fathers (and their children) in America, regardless of an individual's expressed sexual orientation.

B.   Accurately Framing the Debate

Before proceeding with our analysis and commentary, it is essential to accurately frame the debate to legalize same-sex partnerships. We feel that there are a number of issues and questions that are central to the current debate over so-called same-sex marriage that have become nearly invisible in public discourse on the matter. In this section, we briefly articulate some of these issues and explain some foundational assumptions that influence how we frame and approach this topic.

C.   The Social Ecology of Fatherhood

First, we are both family scholars and researchers who view fathering with a systemic lens. We view the father-child relationship as one defined by reciprocal influence and interconnection. Only a systems approach to fathering that views the welfare of fathers and their children as intertwined and interdependent can fully capture the nature of these relationships in men's and children's lives. Additionally, fathers and their children are inter-generationally connected. Simply put, today's boys will be tomorrow's fathers. Because of this systemic approach to fathering, we examine the negative impacts of legalizing same-sex partnerships for both fathers and children, recognizing that a negative impact to one will also harm the other.

D.   The Nature of Homosexual Orientation

Second, we concur with Browning and Marquardt, who have noted that the question of the nature of sexual orientation has nearly vanished from the contemporary discussion of legalizing same-sex partnerships, yet assumptions about the concept are constantly being made by all sides in the controversy.[7] As Browning and Marquardt[8] point out, some advance an "essentialistic" definition of orientation,[9] which holds that sexual orientation is a given, perhaps biologically determined, inclination that cannot be changed short of serious damage to the psyche and personhood of the people with such feelings. This view is strikingly different from another pervasive perspective—the "social constructionist" view that holds that human sexuality is plastic and flexible. According to this view, one learns to think of oneself as gay or lesbian depending on the social context, opportunities, and language systems available to read one's sexual feelings.[10]

While it is not our intention here to get entangled in an assessment of the contradictory evidence from the social, psychological, and biological sciences on the nature and causes of sexual orientation, we do want to make a few points on the matter that are relevant to the role of law in changing the definition of marriage. First, homosexual orientation is a self-attribution. As Browning and Marquardt point out, in contrast to race or gender, "homosexuality is a definition that people place on their own subjective feelings, often struggling to read them correctly and even changing their self-definitions several times throughout the lifecycle."[11] Furthermore, the gay community itself is quite conflicted about the concept of orientation, with many holding the constructionist view and advocating for society to move beyond the distinction between gay and straight, forming a new, liberated, fluid bisexuality.[12] Acknowledging these debates within the homosexual community is relevant to an accurate understanding of what is happening to marriage now and what could happen in the near future. The central question here is: what exactly is being asked for by those who advocate for the legalization of same-sex partnerships? Is the legalization of so-called same-sex marriage the final destination or is it merely a stepping stone towards a complete reorganization of how we are to understand sexuality in adult relationships? Out of fairness to children, we must not act as if these debates do not exist.

E.   *Extending vs. Redefining Marriage*

Third, connected to the question of the nature of sexual orientation, we are persuaded that the current cultural debate about so-called same-sex marriage is frequently misconstrued as a decision about whether or not to "expand" or "extend" the definition of marriage to include individuals of the same gender. This argument rests on the assumption that the basic nature of marriage would remain largely unchanged by the legalization of same-sex partnerships and that all this policy change would do is extend the benefits of marriage to a wider segment of society. In fact, the very term "same-sex marriage" infers that same-sex coupling is merely a "type of marriage" and should be appropriately recognized and labeled as such. We believe that this extension-of-marriage hypothesis is fundamentally flawed in that it fails to recognize how the legalization of same-sex partnerships would signify a radical change in how marriage is collectively understood and the social purposes for why it exists. Although rarely featured within the mainstream media, a significant number of influential voices on the gay left reject what they see as the oppressive notions of traditional marriage and advocate for alternative definitions of marriage that disavow the ethos of monogamy and other central elements of traditional marriage.[13]

At its core, the legalization of same-sex partnerships really is about changing the essence of what marriage is in our society. In short, it is about abandoning a collective morality of marriage that is based in long-standing social norms and standards and replacing it with a personally defined approach to marriage that emphasizes individual freedom and self-definition.[14] We agree with Browning and Marquardt who noted that when properly framed, the same-sex marriage question has become "should marriage be seen primarily as an interpersonal 'close relationship' between consenting adults, with considerations such as material dependency, the conception of children, and child-rearing responsibilities being viewed as contingent and incidental?"[15] Our analysis here explores the ramifications of retreating from the shared morals and standards that have upheld marriage and fathering and the negative consequences for men and children in a world of self-defined marriage where many fathers would become at best peripheral and at worst dispensable.

F.   *Toward a Self Definition of Parenthood?*

Fourth, we are persuaded by recent arguments that forces of modernization are introducing into society a variety of separations and disjunctions into the complex range of goods that the institution of marriage legally and religiously has intended to integrate.[16] One of the more notable of these forces is the modernizing effects of reproductive technology. Reliable contraception, legal abortion, artificial insemination, in vitro fertilization, and surrogacy all interject new separations into the historically marital integration of sexuality, love, childbirth, socialization of children, and mutual dependency. Although many of the advances in reproductive technology can be used within the institution of marriage to enhance its integration with childbearing, many are increasingly being used outside of marriage. In framing our analysis, we have little doubt that these advances will be used more and more to promote childbirth by singles and same-sex couples. Furthermore, "the legalization of same-sex relationships will likely spur demands for greater legal and social support for same-sex couples to have access to reproductive technologies, since only by using these technologies can they have their 'own' children."[17]

With this view, we frame our analysis here in terms of how the legalization of same-sex marriage would not only alter the meaning and function of marriage, but would also usher in a new, self-determined definition of parenthood. In short, we believe that a central question in the so-called same-sex marriage debate is whether or not we collectively and legally want to promote a culture of parenting founded on parents' rights or one grounded in children's needs.[18] From our vantage point, just because a parent desires something does not mean a child needs it. Therefore, we frame our discussion around the risks of a self-defined parenting ideal for children raised by gay or lesbian parents and to father-child relationships across society.

G.   *Innovation vs. Integration*

There is one final issue worth mentioning here before we proceed. Our efforts in this chapter have been to integrate several lines of thinking into the beginnings of a focused line of thought around the potential impact of legalizing same-sex partnerships on father-child relationships. Our emphasis, therefore, has been on integration rather than innovation of thought. Because of this, we have generously incorporated ideas expressed by other authors at various points throughout the essay. While we reference these authors where appropriate throughout the manuscript, we also wanted to make note of a handful of sources that have been particularly influential to the thinking articulated here. These "core sources" include Dollahite, Hawkins, and Brotherson's "*Conceptual Ethic of Generative Fathering*,"[19] Doherty and colleagues' "*Responsible Fathering Framework*,"[20] Browning and Marquardt's "*Liberal Cautions on Same-Sex Marriage*,"[21] and Marquardt's report: "*The Revolution in Parenthood: The Emerging Global Clash Between Adult Rights and Children's Needs*."[22]

II.   A Conceptual Ethic of Generative Fathering

In order to assess the potential harm to father-child relationships of legalizing same-sex partnerships, a standard is needed of what good fathering is and why it matters in the lives of children. In legal circles, definitions of fathering form a central dimension of the "best interests of the child" principle that guides legal decision making to protect the rights and needs of children. This section discusses a conceptual framework of generative fathering that was developed to provide a coherent framework for understanding fathers' responsibility to children and how fathering meets children's needs. The framework is grounded in decades of theory and research on good fathering[23] and has resulted in numerous published research studies.[24]

A.   Needs of the Next Generation

Dollahite and his colleagues[25] proposed a conceptual ethic of generative fathering that emphasizes meeting children's deep and abiding, though varied and changing, needs. This approach "places fathering on the firm foundation of the needs of the next generation rather than on the shifting sands of societal role expectations, the fragile fault line of adult gender relations, or the engulfing quagmire of expressive individualism."[26] The conceptual ethic is grounded in fathers' personal desires and moral responsibility to strive to meet the needs of children that emerge from fundamental and universal challenges of the human condition.

B.   A Generative Conceptual Ethic

Generative fathering is defined as fathering that meets the needs of children by working to create and maintain a developing ethical relationship with them. The generative approach assumes that fathers are under the obligation of an ethical call from their child and communities to meet their child's needs and that the needs of the next generation are usually preeminent over the needs of adults. The generative fathering perspective conceives good fathering as generative work, rather than as a social role embedded in a changing sociohistorical context. The core idea of generative fathering is that all children have inherent needs that must be met and that fathers have an ethical responsibility to work toward meeting those needs. This framework is consistent with Ruddick's critique of contemporary thinking about fathering in which she argues that social scientists view fathering as a "role determined by cultural demands [rather] than a kind of work determined by children's needs"[27] Thus the framework suggests that children's needs, rather than adults' rights, should be the fundamental orienting principle of public policy regarding marriage, parenting, and father-child relationships. It also suggests that it is in the best interests of children to have these needs fulfilled by both their fathers and mothers.

C. The Generative Fathering Conceptual Framework

Table 3.1 summarizes the main ideas underlying the generative fathering conceptual framework. The ideas integrate and build on each other. Careful exploration of Table 3.1 gives a snapshot of the major ideas and can be helpful for lawyers, judges, and policy makers considering how generative fathering reflects the best interests of children at various ages.

The framework is based on two central ideas: (a) the human context creates needs in the next generation that fathers have the ethical responsibility and capability to meet, and (b) both fathers and children benefit and grow from this work. Four types of linked concepts presented in the conceptual ethic are found in the columns labeled: (a) challenges of the human condition, (b) attendant needs of the next generation, (c) types of generative work and father's capabilities and responsibilities, and (d) desired results of generative fathering for fathers and children.

All the human challenges (such as dependency, scarcity, change, stress, perplexity, isolation, and obligation), attendant needs, types of generative work, and desired results of generative work are present at all stages of the life cycle. Thus all these issues are always present, but different challenges, needs, and types of work take center stage at different times in the child's development.

Generative fathering must be tailored to situations, contexts, developmental stages, persons, types of interests and abilities of father and child, and many other factors as well. The concepts in the model are intended to be broad enough to include all these diversities. The seven sets of concepts outlined in Table 3.1 do not exhaust all the challenges, needs, types of generative work, capabilities, responsibilities, and desired results of good fathering that are important for fathers and children. But these seven are critical, and together they form a coherent set of ideas that suggests important areas to attend to in policy involving children. Relevant to the major thesis of this chapter, for a father to be able to best meet his child's needs as outlined in this framework, he must be clearly and consistently involved with his child to the fullest extent possible throughout the child's life.

III. Contextual Factors That Promote Generative Fathering

For some time now, scholars have recognized the importance of responsible fathering in the lives of both men and children and have conducted numerous studies to identify what contextual factors best promote generative associations between fathers and children. In a landmark report to the U.S. Department of Health and Human Services, which was later published in a highly regarded peer-reviewed journal, Doherty, Kouneski, & Erickson summarized this body of research and integrated it into a contextually sensitive model for responsible fathering. In their report, the authors acknowledged that the term *responsible fathering* reflects an explicit value advocacy approach to scholars' current work on fathering and suggests that there is a desired set of norms for evaluating fathers' behaviors. They further note that "the term conveys a moral meaning

Table 3.1 GENERATIVE FATHERING CONCEPTUAL FRAMEWORK

	A Challenges of the Human Condition	B Attendant Needs of the Next Generation	C Types of Generative Work: Fathers Capabilities and Responsibilities	D Desired Results of Generative Fathering
1	DEPENDENCY Vulnerability & Uncertainty (infancy)	SECURITY & CONTINUITY	ETHICAL WORK Commit pledge to ensure child's well- being Continue be an enduring presence in child's life	INVOLVED Fathers SECURE Children
2	SCARCITY Necessities & Aspirations (early childhood)	RESOURCES & OPPORTUNITIES	STEWARDSHIP WORK Consecrate dedicate material resources to child Create provide possibilities for child to achieve	RESPONSIBLE Fathers CONFIDENT Children
3	CHANGE Development & Transformation (play age)	ATTENTION & ACCOMMODATION	DEVELOPMENT WORK Care respond to child's needs & wants Change adapt in response to child's needs	RESPONSIVE Fathers PURPOSEFUL Children
4	STRESS Tension & Demands (school age)	RELAXATION & CAPABILITIES	RECREATION WORK Cooperate relax & play together on child's level Challenge extend child's skills & coping abilities	PLAYFUL Fathers JOYFUL Children
5	PERPLEXITY Apprehension & Confusion (adolescence)	ENCOURAGEMENT & MEANING	SPIRITUAL WORK Confirm affirm belief & confidence in child Counsel guide, teach, advise, impart meaning	FAITHFUL Fathers PEACEFUL Children
6	ISOLATION Aloneness & Misunderstanding (young adult- hood)	INTIMACY & EMPATHY	RELATIONAL WORK Commune share love, thoughts, feelings with child Comfort express empathy & understanding to child	LOVING Fathers CARING Children
7	OBLIGATION Complexities & Burdens (adulthood)	WISDOM & SUPPORT	MENTORING WORK Consult impart insights & suggestions when asked Contribute sustain & support generative work	GENERATIVE Fathers GENERATIVE Children

(right or wrong) because it suggests that some fathering could be judged irresponsible."[28] Similar to the generative fathering framework that guides our analysis here, Doherty and colleagues note that this moral imperative in fathering stems from the long-standing recognition of "children's needs for predictability, nurturance, and appropriate limit setting from fathers and mothers, as well as for economic security and a cooperative, preferably loving relationship between their parents."[29]

From their extensive review of the fathering literature, Doherty and colleagues drew two major conclusions.[30] First, they noted that fathering is more sensitive than mothering to contextual forces. Because of this, father-child relationship quality is remarkably dependent upon the social, legal, and relational factors that surround the relationships and create either barriers or bridges for generative interactions between men and their children. The second major conclusion drawn from their review is that research on responsible fathering has identified several key contextual factors that form the ecology of fathering and consequentially shape the nature and quality of father-child relationships. These factors include: (1) a quality marriage between a child's parents, (2) residential involvement of fathers and children, and (3) biological certainty in the parent-child relationship. Because the legalization of same-sex partnerships would have widespread impact on each of these aspects that promote responsible fathering, we discuss them here. The following summary draws heavily from Doherty and colleagues' review.[31]

A.   The Quality of Marriage between a Child's Parents.

A number of studies have shown that the quality of father-child relations both inside and outside of marriage is more highly correlated with the quality of the co-parental relationship than is true for the mother-child relationship.[32] For this reason, scholars have noted that fathering is strongly connected to marriage for the vast majority of men. As Furstenberg and Cherlin have asserted, for many men, marriage and parenthood are a "package."[33] Or one might say "that in American culture, a woman is a mother all of her life, but a man is a father if he has a wife."[34] Doherty and colleagues concluded, "the research strongly indicates that substantial barriers exist for men's fathering outside of a caring, committed, collaborative marriage and that the promotion of these kinds of enduring marital partnerships may be the most important contribution to responsible fathering in our society."[35]

As a society, we are typically aware of the negative health consequences of distressed marriages, but we are often unaware that married people tend to have better physical and emotional health than single people, at least in part because they are married.[36] The social support provided by a spouse, combined with the economic resources produced by the marriage, facilitate both the production and maintenance of health. The specialization, economies of scale, and insurance functions of marriage all increase the economic well-being of family members, and the increase is typically quite substantial. Furthermore, over the past 20 years, a body of research has developed on how changes in patterns of family structure affect children. Most researchers now agree that together these studies support the notion that, on average, children do best when raised by their two married, biological parents who have low-conflict relationships.[37] In particular, children raised by their own married parents do better across a range of outcomes than children who grow up in other living arrangements.

B.   Residential Involvement

Given that a conceptual ethic of generative fathering focuses on the quality of father-child interactions, the perspective assumes the need for quantity of involvement and father presence in a child's life. However, contemporary family life often does not facilitate a high quantity of father involvement for many children; as research highlights, a major determinant of father presence versus father absence is whether or not men share a residence with a child. To date, the two major structural threats to fathers' residential presence with their children in modern society are nonmarital childbearing and divorce.

In terms of percentages of all births in the United States, nonmarital births have risen from 4% of births in 1940 to 33% in 2002.[38] In over 90% of cases, children born outside of marriage reside with their mothers. A growing body of research has shown that if fathers do not live with the mother and child, their presence in the child's life is frequently marginal and, even when active for a while, tends to be fragile over time.[39]

Although the number of non-marital births has risen dramatically, an even greater number of children (more than 10 million) live with a single parent subsequent to divorce.[40] In about 90% of cases, these children reside with their mothers. Research has documented a declining presence of noncustodial fathers over the years after a divorce. In general, although father involvement after divorce seems to be increasing and some fathers are quite involved with their children after divorce, the predominant pattern among noncustodial fathers is one of gradual withdrawal from their children's lives.[41]

While these patterns of declining child involvement among non-residential fathers are in part explained by men who relinquish involvement, a number of structural and relationship barriers confront men who try to stay involved with their children. A number of studies have documented how mothers and grandmothers serve as gatekeepers of a father's presence in a child's life.[42] This type of gatekeeping becomes particularly salient in situations marked by conflict in the co-parental relationship. Research also shows that co-parental conflict involving non-residential fathers has negative consequences for child outcomes[43] and father payment of child support[44].

C.   Legal Paternity, Biological Certainty, Kin Altruism, and Boundary Ambiguity

Establishing legal paternity is at the core of responsible and generative fathering. With legal paternity comes a variety of economic, social, and psychological benefits to the child and some degree of protection of the father's rights.[45] As traditionally defined, legal paternity has been attached, as nearly as possible, to the naturally defined paternity that arises when a father biologically conceives a child. This connection is important in that in addition to social and economic goods, legal paternity serves to strengthen the natural ties between fathers and their biological children and to provide children with the intangible but important benefit of knowing their biological heritage and having a clearer sense of social identity.[46] Browning and Marquardt contend that the bond between natural parents and their biological children has been a core aspect of the meaning of marriage in Western societies, and represents one of the principal and most radical ways that the legalization of same-sex partnerships would alter our collective definition of marriage.[47] The following summary relies heavily on their arguments.

Our current understanding of legal paternity is based in Western culture's long-standing support of what evolutionary psychologists today call "kin altruism." The term *kin altruism* is used to describe the bond between biological parents and children and emerges from evolutionary psychology, which has long recognized a genetic predisposition for each of us to invest ourselves more in those individuals to whom we are biologically related—those individuals who carry our genes.[48] Kin altruism refers to the care natural parents are inclined to give to their children because they labored to give them birth and have come to recognize them as part of themselves that should be preserved and extended. This perspective also implies a reciprocal identification of children with natural parents because of this labor and because children perceive the bodily continuity of those who give them life.

Kin altruism is a persistent core value that is widely cherished and protected around the world. There has been a long-standing preference for people who give life to an infant to also be , to the fullest extent possible, the ones who care for it. This principle is based on the widely held assumption that those who conceive a child, when they recognize their relation to it, will nearly always be the people most invested in its nurturance and well-being. It is also based on the observation that, when other things are equal, children want—indeed, often long—to be raised by those who gave them life.

Research evidence also supports the notion that, on average, parenting based in kin altruism differs from non-biological parenting on several key aspects related to child well-being. For example, studies on childhood abuse have found that children in homes with stepparents were much more likely to be abused than children who lived with both biological parents.[49] In fact, after years of research in the area, Daly and Wilson[50] concluded that having a stepparent is the most powerful risk factor for severe child mistreatment. Also a review of studies on child sexual abuse found that two of the leading risk factors for children reporting that they have experienced abuse during their childhood were that the child lived without one of his or her biological parents and the child reported having a stepfather.[51] More recently, using a United States national-level database of over 400,000 homicides, Weeks-Shackelford & Shackelford found that stepparents commit filicide at higher rates than do genetic parents.[52] These findings supported previous theoretical work that proposed a "biosocial theory of child mistreatment and homicide"[53] which contends that parental commitments are seen as more readily and more profoundly established with one's own offspring than in cases where parent-offspring relationships are non-biological.

Another line of scholarship that supports a continued emphasis on kin altruism in our definitions of marriage and parenting lies in family stress theory and the concept of boundary ambiguity. Within this view, families are viewed as a system, made up of subsystems, each of which is surrounded by a semipermeable boundary, which is actually a set of processes influencing who is included within that subsystem and how they interact with those outside of it.[54] Accordingly, unclear boundaries can create dysfunction in family processes and interactions. Broadly defined, family boundary ambiguity is "a state in which family members are uncertain in their perception about who is in or out of the family and who is performing what roles and tasks within the family system."[55] Boss has suggested that boundaries include both physical and psychological phenomena which serve to foster a sense of group and individual identity that differentiates the members of a family from one another and from other groups.[56] In settings where biological certainty is questioned or where relational complexity (i.e., non-marital cohabitation, non-marital childbearing, divorce) challenges boundary clarity, the potential for ambiguity in the father-child relationships is present and poses a threat to generative fathering.

One of the most studied areas in the boundary ambiguity literature is that of divorced families and the experiences of loss and ambiguity associated with the dissolution of marriage. Associated with this are several studies investigating family change that results when individuals re-marry and enter into stepfamily situations. In general, these studies have substantiated the premise that families experiencing divorce and remarriage have an increased potential for high boundary ambiguity.[57] Associated with boundary ambiguities related to divorce, several studies have investigated boundary changes associated with remarriage and stepfamily situations. These studies have shown that boundary ambiguity is more prevalent in stepfamilies than original two-parent families[58] and that the structure and complexity of stepfamily arrangements (e.g., nonresident children, shared biological children) influence the level of boundary ambiguity in stepfamilies.[59]

IV.   What's the Harm? The Furtherance of Ambiguous Fatherhood

The purpose of this volume and our analysis here is to investigate the potential harm that would almost certainly come to children and families if same-sex partnerships were legally sanctioned. Our focus here is particularly on the negative impact of this type of change on father-child relationships. To this point, we have discussed several grounding perspectives that frame the core issues of this discussion, namely:

1. A change in the definition of marriage will inherently alter the definition of parenthood in our society.

2. Our collective and legal definitions of fatherhood should be based on the generative needs of children. Simply put, our primary concern should be children's needs, not adults' rights or desires.

3. The overwhelming conclusion of more than two decades of social science research on father-child relationships is that father involvement is extremely sensitive to contextual factors. In particular, research shows that for most men, marriage and fatherhood are a package deal. Thus, fathering outside of the context of a committed marriage relationship that involves shared residential living with a child is a fragile arrangement at best for fostering generative father-child relationships.

4. As a social institution, marriage has traditionally been defined so as to provide a natural mechanism to provide for the widely held cultural ideal that children are entitled to birth within the bonds of matrimony and to be raised by the father and mother who gave them life. This persistent core value of kin altruism is at the center of our society's definition of marriage and parenthood.

Grounded in these perspectives, it is our contention that providing legal sanction of same-sex partnerships would increase the number of children raised in settings of ambiguous fatherhood; thus exposing a greater number of children to the risks of poor or non-existent father involvement. This negative impact is likely to occur in both direct and indirect ways.

A.   Legalizing Same-Sex Partnerships Will Directly Further the Rise of Ambiguous Fatherhood

All of the contextual supports of responsible fathering (i.e., marriage to the child's mother, residential involvement, legal paternity based in kin altruism, clear boundaries in the father-child relationship) share the common factor that they contribute to the degree of certainty or ambiguity in the father-child relationship. When a child is raised in a setting with a biological father who is in a collaborative and committed marriage, ambiguity is very low; thus fostering an environment that is optimal in supporting generative fathering. However, the absence of any of these factors creates an environment that constrains generative responsibility in the lives of men and exposes children to a non-generative context. Children raised by same-sex couples will inherently experience ambiguous father-child relationships due to the fact that they, by definition, lack a marriage between a child's two biological parents. In short, same-sex parenting requires the intentional disregard for kin altruism as the entitlement of children and the best environment to foster the best interests of children.

All forms of same-sex parenting are inherently non-kin altruistic. In the common situation where a child is the biological offspring of a previous hetero-

sexual relationship, only one of the adults in the household is biologically related to the child. Lesbian couples who "become" parents through anonymous
or outside sperm donation intentionally bring a child into a father-absent home.
Even if the couple intends for the "third-party father" to be involved in the
child's life, this form of non-marital, non-residential, non-legal paternity has
proven to be an unreliable and unrealistic approach to fostering generative fathering in a child's life. The ambiguity of two-gay men "becoming" fathers
through surrogacy reverses the ambiguity and now intentionally brings children
into mother-absent homes. It also increases ambiguity because the child now has
two "fathers." These types of ambiguous-mother homes challenge even further
society's long-standing norms about children's needs and rights; overwhelming
such ideals with an emphasis on adults' wants. Given the known negative effects
of boundary ambiguity on family functioning,[60] these types of situations create a
sort of genetic boundary ambiguity that creates complexity that often over-
whelms generative associations between men and their children.

The legalization of same-sex partnerships would further divide the integration of natural parenthood from social or self-defined parenthood. Figure 3.1
portrays how this division leads to four potential parenting contexts for father-
child and mother-child relationships. Where parents are both biologically and
personally defined as a child's parent (quadrant I) this forms a non-ambiguous
parenting context. In settings where a parent is not a biological parent to a child,
but defines oneself as a parent (quadrant II) (e.g., a step- or adopted parent) or
where a biological parent does not define himself or herself as a child's parent
(e.g., a father who does not establish paternity nor remain involved in a child's
life) are inherently ambiguous parenthood settings. Finally, an adult who does
not biologically conceive a child and does not define himself or herself as a
child's parent resides in a "non-parenthood" setting. Biological parents who
define themselves as their child's parents experience a unique personal, social,
and legal recognition of their parental status.

B.   Triad Parenting

Only two-biological parent homes have the ability to have both parents in a
child's life that fit the criteria of quadrant I in Figure 3.1 (i.e., both biologically
defined and self-defined as a child's parent). In every case, same-sex partnerships who "become" parents will inherently have at least one partner who resides in a setting of ambiguous parenthood (quadrant II) and another "biological
parent" who also resides in ambiguous parenthood (quadrant III). In fact, every
same-sex partnership that brings a child into the world is by definition a parenting triad—in that one partner substitutes for one of the child's biological parents. Is the world of same-sex parenting one where children are intentionally
brought into the world to be raised by three or more parents? Clearly this would
represent a new definition of parenting than what currently exists. Furthermore,
same-sex partners cannot have equal claim on a child due to the fact that at best
only one of the partners can actually be the child's biological parent.

While these distinctions may be disregarded by committed same-sex couples as merely semantically created differences, cases involving the dissolution of the relationships and resultant complexities in legal standing in relation to the child (i.e., *Goodrich v. Goodrich*) reveal that the biological parent and

---

Figure 3.1 Definitions of Parenthood and Settings of Parenthood.

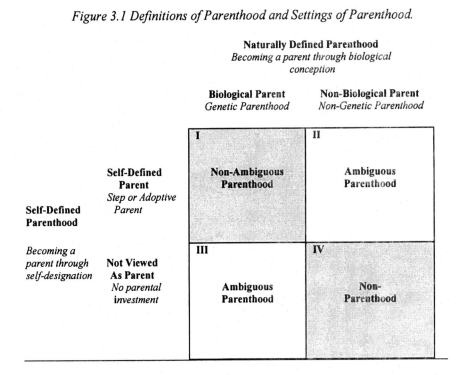

non-biological parent do not stand on equal legal footing. This difference in parental certainty creates incongruence in same-sex parenting—potentially disrupting co-parental dynamics and limiting the degree that non-biological same-sex parents invest in and commit to children. Furthermore, given the well-documented evidence showing that children who live with a non-biological parent are much more likely to be abused than children who live with both of their biological parents,[61] these distinctions may have direct implications for the collective wellbeing of children. There is no evidence to suggest that children living with a non-biological, homosexual parent would experience, on average, lower rates of abuse than children living with a non-biological, heterosexual parent.

Unfortunately, our society is already experiencing the consequences of a rise in generatively ambiguous contexts for fathering. As we mentioned earlier, increases in divorce and out-of-wedlock childbirths have eroded the certainty of fathering. Some point to these trends as evidence that same-sex parenting is no more ambiguous than these situations and that such forms of father-child relationships are becoming normative and that two-biological parent homes are less of an ideal for children in the modern era. Of course, legal adoption permits the possibility of legal paternity between men and children who are not biologically related. However, to date, this mechanism exists legally and socially to address the needs of children who due to *unintentional* circumstances are separated from their biological parents. Providing for the relatively small number of children who are with us and by no fault of their own are separated from their biological parents is quite different from providing legal and social encouragement for establishing ambiguous parent-child relationships from the start. Providing legal standing to same-sex partnerships will deepen and give legal sanction to the existing cultural trends we have seen with all the attendant harm to children that social science research has demonstrated.

C.   Legalizing Same-Sex Partnerships Will Indirectly Further the Rise of Ambiguous Fatherhood

We believe the evidence suggests that the legalization of same-sex partnerships poses a threat to children intentionally raised in the non-kin altruistic ambiguous context of gay parenting. Further, we believe that changing the definition of marriage will also further the rise of ambiguous fatherhood in heterosexual families. If same-sex partnerships are legalized, various social institutions in a variety of public settings (e.g., educational, political, judicial) would be required to advocate the equality of all legally-recognized arrangements for the rearing of children, even though a large body of social science research belies this idea. Altering the legal definition of marriage would further erode the societal recognition that fathers matter to children. As this occurs, two primary mechanisms will increase the ambiguity of fatherhood for children, men and society. First, the rise of a "self-defined parenting paradigm" that equates single mothers and lesbian couples with two biological parents in meeting the developmental needs of children threatens to further disenfranchise men from family life and weakens social norms discouraging divorce and non-marital childbearing.

Until the current generation, the widely held (and now empirically supported) belief that children needed their fathers was a central tenet in social norms encouraging men to work through marital troubles with their wives and to demonstrate responsibility in sexual relationships outside of marriage. For the sake of inclusiveness, our society has retreated from the ideal of father-mother parenting. Such a stance has allowed us to recognize collectively the strengths of many single-parent and step-parent families and not merely assume the virtue of a two-parent biological family in all cases. However, this approach has paradoxically lessened the norms that encourage and foster two-parent biological families. This retreat from the ideal may be particularly devastating for men who, according to research, are more reliant on such social and relationship supports to foster their healthy involvement in family life and parenting.

A second way that the legalization of same-sex partnerships would further the rise of ambiguous fatherhood is that it would support a retreat from fatherhood altogether among some American men. One aspect of a self-defined parenting ideology in society is the option of not being a parent at all. If fathering is not a cultural ideal, the potential exists for an increase in men who live outside marriage and parenthood altogether. Given the data on the negative social consequences of communities that have a large number of unmarried men (e.g., higher rates of crime and other anti-social behavior), we should resist movement toward a parenting culture that would suggest that men can be viewed as "sperm donors" whose only essential "parenting role" is conception and then women can do it alone, either as single parents or as a lesbian couple. The loss of a cultural ideal for men to become responsible fathers could lead to increased numbers of men and children who live in non-generative contexts.

In summary, the legalization of same-sex marriage will increase ambiguous fatherhood at a number of levels in our society (see Table 3.2). For children, such an arrangement places them in at-risk developmental settings and increases their likelihood of having ambiguous relationships with their father and other men. For men, such a culture is potentially harmful because more men will be exposed to the risk factors associated with living in ambiguous fatherhood or non-generative lifestyles. In addition, men will miss out on the documented benefits of married life.[62] A lack of clear societal norms for men and fathers erodes clarity in social processes. Furthermore, such cultural and legal ambiguity will almost certainly increase the involvement of the legal system in family life as the court system will be called upon increasingly to clarify family boundaries. Perhaps this explains why countries and states that have legalized same-sex partnerships more frequently embrace and practice more socialized forms of government.

Table 3.2 Levels of Ambiguous Fatherhood

Children: "*Who's my Daddy?*"
- At-risk developmental setting
- Ambiguous relations with father & other men

Men: "*Am I the Daddy?*"
- Less paternal responsibility in ambiguous fatherhood or non-generative lifestyles
- Fewer men receiving the benefits of marriage

Couples: "*Who's the Daddy?*"
- Within-couple ambiguity about who the child's father is
- Within-couple inequality in the event of dissolution of partnership

Society: "*What's a Daddy?*"
- Lack of clear social norms for men and fathers
- Increased involvement of the legal system in family life; attempts to legally clarify family boundaries

V.   Conclusion

We conclude with a metaphor that we believe captures the dilemma we now face. In several ways generative fathering can be viewed, both individually and collectively, as a protective tent in children's lives. The nurturing presence of a father shelters children from a host of risk factors and social threats. Within the protection of this tent, children find the environment that is most likely to promote healthy outcomes and optimal development. Likewise, fathers' efforts to provide this type of environment for their children and families have focused their energies in a way that meets their own generative needs (to procreate and nurture) and gives a deeper sense of meaning and purpose in life. At a societal level, the tent of generative fathering serves as a sort of social institution that assists in socializing the rising generation, regulating men's sexual behaviors, and protecting both men and their children from anti-social and even criminal lifestyles.

Carrying the metaphor a step further, we can liken the poles supporting the tent of generative fathering to the social and relational supports that foster and sustain generative fathering. The center pole of the tent is a committed and collaborative marriage between fathers and the mothers of their children. This focal pole of marriage provides for the central support that encourages the mutual investments of both fathers and mothers in their biological children. Marriage also props up generative fathering by providing for shared residential involvement with their children, thus encouraging quality father involvement in children's lives. Connected to this center pole of marriage are the corded stakes of cultural norms and social practices that anchor and sustain marriage as a critical institution in our society. These include cultural ideals of child-centeredness, kin altruism, and optimal parenting, as well as societal expectations and practices patterns pertaining to marital childbirth, sexual monogamy, and the critical application of divorce. The deeper these stakes are driven, the more firm a foundation marriage has in society, thus sustaining the overall tent of generative fathering.

What is the condition of the collective tent of generative fathering for American families at the beginning of the 21st century? Without a doubt, the tent is not in optimal condition. Many of the stakes that should be anchoring the center pole of marriage have come loose and some parts of the tent are flapping in the wind. Historically high rates of non-marital cohabitation, out-of-wedlock childbirth, and marital divorce have left many children on the perimeter of the tent exposed and unsheltered as they live in father-absent or ambiguous fatherhood conditions. Some children at the center of the tent continue to enjoy the shelter of generative fathering in their lives, but even these children are at risk for divorce, which would push them to the outer boundaries of the tent. With so many of the traditional stakes of marriage pulling loose, some have begun to question the need for such a tent. Bolstering such views are the high number of resilient children who succeed with little or no "father shelter" in their lives, often due to the laudable efforts of their mothers and various "father figures." However, such accepting rhetoric ignores the high number of children who succumb to the elements, so to speak, as they experience the pile-up effects of not having an active and involved father in their lives.

At this time, when the tent of generative fathering is in a vulnerable condition, the idea to change the legal definition of marriage is proposed. Proponents of such action point to the shabby condition of the tent in current form and ask how the inclusion of same-gender couples into our definition of marriage could do any harm to the social institution of marriage. The legalization of same-sex partnerships however, presents an irreconcilable dilemma for society as it considers the collective tent of generative fathering. While same-sex couples are asking to be included within the tent, they are simultaneously proposing a course of action that will severely damage or remove the center pole of marriage between biological parents. The legal definition of marriage is the center pole. If the legal definition of marriage is changed, then the legal weight added to our society's collective definition of marriage will be lost. Marriage will be left as a cultural and personal issue only, leaving only religious institutions and a few others to try to hold up the tent of generative fathering.

Responsible fathering is already eroding in our culture, but if the center pole (marriage between a man and woman) is removed, we will have little chance of collectively re-driving the stakes that have already come loose due to our society's devaluing of marriage and the meaning of fathers in children's lives.

Historically and today, our legal definition of marriage has represented and reinforced our collective recognition that married two-parent families are uniquely suited to the best interests of children. The primary implication of our analysis is that the social institution of marriage is already weakened enough from cohabitation, out-of wedlock childbirth, and divorce. We need to maintain the definition of marriage as being between a man and a woman as we seek to reverse or reduce these cultural trends. Our collective foundation of fatherhood needs to be grounded in strong legal and social expectations for marriage and fatherhood. To do otherwise ignores the developmental needs and ethical rights of children to be raised, as often as possible, by those who gave them life.

Notes

1. E. H. Pleck & J. H. Pleck, *Fatherhood ideals in the United States: Historical dimensions,* in M. E. Lamb (Ed.), *The role of the father in child development* (3rd Ed., Wiley 1997).

2. W. J. Doherty, E. F. Kouneski & M. F. Erickson, *Responsible fathering: An overview and conceptual framework* 60 J. Marriage Fam. 277, 279 (1998).

3. R. D. Day & M. E. Lamb, *Conceptualizing and measuring father involvement* (Lawrence Erlbaum Associates 2004).

4. S. McLanahan, *Diverging destinies: How children are faring under the second demographic transition,* 41 Demography 607 (2004).

5. Doherty et al., *supra* n. 2.

6. D. Browning, *From culture wars to common ground: Religion and the American family debate* (John Knox 2000).

7. D. Browning & E. Marquardt, *Liberal cautions on same-sex marriage* (Witherspoon Institute, Princeton University, Dec, 2004).

8. Browning et al., *supra* n. 7.

9. R. Posner, *Sex and reason* (Harvard University Press 1992), J. Rauch, *Gay marriage: Why it is good for gays, good for straights, and good for America* (Henry Holt & Company 2004).

10. D. Greenberg, *The construction of homosexuality* (The University of Chicago Press 1988).

11. Browning & Marquardt, *supra* n. 7, at 11.

12. R. Goldstein, *The attack queers: Liberal society and the gay right* (Verso 2002); R. F. Oswald, L. B. Blume & S. R. Marks, *Decentering heteronomativity: A model for family studies,* in V. L. Bengston, A. C. Acock, K. R. Allen, P. Dilworth-Anderson & D. M. Klein (Eds.), *Sourcebook of Family Theory and Research,* 263, 243, 165, (Sage Publications 2005); M. Warner, *The trouble with normal: sex, politics, and the ethics of queer life* (Harvard University Press 1999).

13. Goldstein, *supra* n. 12, Warner, *supra* n. 12.

14. S. Kurtz, *The libertarian question: Incest, homosexuality, and adultery,* National Review Online (April 30, 2003).

15. Browning & Marquardt, *supra* n. 7, at 3.

16. D. Browning, *Marriage and modernization: How globalization threatens marriage and what to do about it* (Wm. B. Eerdmans 2003); Browning et al., *supra* n. 7

17. Browning & Marquardt, *supra* n. 7, at 2.

18. E. Marquardt, *The Revolution in Parenthood: The Emerging Global Clash Between Adult Rights and Children's Needs* (Institute for American Values 2006); S. Sugrue, *Canadian marriage police: A tragedy for children,* Report, The Institute of marriage and Family (2006).

19. D. C. Dollahite, A. J. Hawkins & S. E. Brotherson, *Fatherwork: A conceptual ethic of fathering as generative work,* in A. J. Hawkins & D. C. Dollahite (Eds.), *Generative fathering: beyond deficit perspectives* 17 (Sage 1997).

20. Doherty et al., *supra* n. 2.

21. Browning & Marquardt, *supra* n. 7.

22. Marquardt, *supra* n. 18.

23. Doherty et al., *supra* n. 2; E. H. Erickson, *The life cycle completed,* (Norton 1982), J. Snarey, *How fathers care for the next generation: A four decade study* (Harvard University Press 1993).

24. See, S. E. Brotherson, D. C. Dollahite & A. J. Hawkins, *Generative fathering and the dynamics of connection between fathers and their children,* 3 Fathering 1 (2005); D. C. Dollahite, *Fathering for eternity: Generative spirituality in Latter-day Saint fathers with children with special needs,* 44 Review Religious Research 237 (2003); L. D. Marks & D. C. Dollahite, *Religion, relationships, and responsible fathering in Latter-day Saint families of children with special needs,* 18(5) J. Soc. Personal Relationships 625 (2001).

25. D. C. Dollahite & A. J. Hawkins, *A conceptual ethic of generative fathering* 7 J. Men's Studies 109 (1998); Dollahite et al., *supra* n. 19.

26. Dollahite et al. *supra* n. 19, at 34.

27. S. Ruddick, *Maternal thinking: toward a politics of peace* (Beacon 1989), at 42.

28. Doherty et al., *supra* n. 2, at 278.

29. Doherty et al., *supra* n. 2, at 279.

30. Doherty et al., *supra* n. 2.

31. Doherty et al., *supra* n. 2.

32. J. Belsky & B. L. Volling, *Mothering, fathering, and marital interaction in the family triad during infancy,* in P.W. Berman & F.A. Pederson (Eds.), *Men's transitions to parenthood: Longitudinal studies of early family experience* 37 (Erlbaum 1987); M. J. Cox, M. T. Own, J. M. Lewis & V. K. Henderson, *Marriage, adult adjustment, and early parenting,* 60 Child Dev. 1015 (1989).

33. F. S. Furstenburg & A. J. Cherlin, *Divided families: What happens to children when parents part?* (Harvard University Press 1991).

34. Doherty et al., *supra* n. 2, at 286.

35. Doherty et al., *supra* n. 2, at 290.

36. J. Mirowsky & C. Ross, *Social causes of psychological distress* (Aldine De Gruyter 2003); L. J. Waite & M. Gallagher, *The case for marriage: Why married people are happier, healthier and better off financially* (Doubleday 2000).

37. M. Parke, *Are married parents really better for children? What research says about the effects of family structure on child well-being,* Center for Law and Social Policy (CLASP) (Policy Brief No. 3 May 2003).

38. B. Downs, *Fertility of American Women: June 2002,* Current Population Reports, P20-548. U.S. Census Bureau, Washington, DC. (2003).

39. F. S. Furnstenburg Jr. & K. M. Harris, *When and why fathers matter: Impacts of father involvement on the children of adolescent mothers,* in R. I. Lerman & T. J. Ooms (Eds.), *Young unwed fathers: Changing roles and emerging principles* (Temple University Press 1993); R. I. Lerman, *A national profile of young unwed fathers,* in R. I. Lerman & T. J. Ooms (Eds.), *Young unwed fathers: Changing roles and emerging policies* (Temple University Press 1993).

40. U.S. Bureau of the Census, 2005.

41. P. R. Amato & S. J. Rejac, *Contact with non-residence parents, interpersonal conflict, and children's behavior,* 15 J. Fam. Issues 191 (1994); J. A. Seltzer, *Relationships between fathers and children who live apart: The father's role after separation,* 53 J. of Marriage and Fam. 79 (1991).

42. W. D. Allen & W. J. Doherty, *The responsibilities of fatherhood as perceived by African American teenage fathers. Families and Society,* 77 J. Contemporary Human Services 142 (1996); E. Wattenburg, *Paternity actions and young fathers,* in R. I. Lerman & T. J. Ooms (Eds.), *Young unwed fathers: Changing roles and emerging policies* (Temple University Press 1993).

43. Amato & Rejac, *supra* n. 41.

44. U.S. Census Bureau, 1995.

45. Doherty et al, *supra* n. 2.

46. Wattenburg, *supra* n. 42.

47. Browning & Marquardt, *supra* n. 7.

48. M. Daly & M. Wilson, *The evolutionary Psychology of Marriage and Divorce,* in L. J. Waite (Ed..), *The Ties That Bind* 91 (Aldine De Gruyter 2000).

49. M. Wilson, M. Daly & S. J. Weghorst, *Household composition and the risk of child abuse and neglet,* 12 J. Biosocial Sci. 333 (1980); M. Daly & M. Wilson, *Child abuse and other risks of not living with both parents,* 6 Ethology and Sociobiology 197 (1985).

50. M. Daly & M. Wilson, *Violence against stepchildren,* 5 Current Directions Psychol. Sci. 77, pp (1986).

51. D. Finkelhor & L. Baron, *Risk factors for childhood sexual abuse,* 1 J. Interpersonal Violence 43 (1986).

52. V. A. Weekes-Shackelford & T. K. Sackelford, *Methods of filicide: Stepparents and genetic parents kill differently,* 19 Violence Victims 75 (2004).

53. M. Daly & M. Wilson, *Discriminative parental solicitude: A biological perspective,* 42 J. Fam. Marriage 277 (1980).

54. M. P. Nichols & R. C. Schwartz, *Family therapy: Concepts and methods* (Allyn & Bacon 1995).

55. P. Boss & J. Greenberg, *Family boundary ambiguity: A new variable in family stress theory,* 23(4) Fam. Process 535, 536 (1984).

56. P. Boss, *Normative family stress: Family boundary changes across the lifespan,* 29 Family Relations 445 (1980).

57. C. Buehler & K. Pasley, *Family Boudary Ambiguity, Marital Status, and Child Adjustment,* 20(3) J. Early Adolescence 281 (2000); Marquardt, *supra* n. 18, A. Taanila, E. Liatninen, I. Moilanen & M. Jarvelin, *Effects of family interaction on the child's behavior in single-parent or reconstructed families,* 41 Fam. Process 693 (2002).

58. S. D. Stewart, *Boundary ambiguity in stepfamilies,* 26 J. Fam. Issues 1002 (2005).

59. C. Hobart, *The Family System in Remarriage: An Explanatory Study,* 50 J. Marriage Fam. 649 (1988); K. Pasley, *Family ambiguity perception of adult stepfamily members,* in K. Pasley & M. Ihinger-Tallman (Eds.), *Remarriage and step-parenting: Current research and theory* (Guilford Press 1987); K. Pasley & M. Ihinger-Tallman, *Boundary ambiguity in remarriage: Does degree of ambiguity influence marital adjustment?,* 38 Fam. Rel. 46 (1989); M. Rosenberg & J. Guttmann, *Structural boundaries of single-parent families and children's adjustment,* 36(1-2) J. Divorce & Remarriage 83 (2001); Stewart, *supra* n. 58.

60. J. S. Carroll, C.D. Olson & N. Buckmiller, *Family Boundary Ambiguity: A 20-year Review of Theory, Research, and Measurement,* 56 Family Relations 210 (2007).

61. Daly & Wilson, *supra* n. 49.

62. Waite & Gallegar, *supra* n. 36.

CHAPTER 4
UNINTENDED CONSEQUENCES: THE FLAWS IN "IT DOESN'T AFFECT ANYONE BUT US" ARGUMENT IN FAVOR OF LEGALIZING SAME-SEX MARRIAGE

Marianne M. Jennings
Arizona State University

"Just tell me, who's Daddy?"
David Letterman to Melissa Etheridge and Julie Cypher on their children[1]
"Why should my marriage bother you?"[2]

This paper examines the often advanced argument that there is no impact beyond the couples themselves when same-sex marriage is sanctioned, that the legalization of same-sex marriage is a benign act. This emotional reaction, often clothed in the sanctity of accusations of bigotry, manages to reduce what should be a broad and lengthy public policy discussion about a proposed revolution in family structure to accusations and emotional stalemates. The societal impact of legalized same-sex marriages has not been properly nor intellectually explored. Debate has been stifled even as evidence on the long-term and consequential effects of changes in the definition of marriage continues to appear.

There are three critical components of the unintended consequences of same-sex marriage that should be the focus of discussion and debate: (1) History indicates that public policies, programs, and legislation that have affected or addressed family issues, and were often enacted with good intentions and noble goals, have not only failed, but have introduced a responsive form of iatrogenic public policy that finds us addressing the unintended consequences of the goodness believed to be inherent in the initial public policy change. (2) Legalization of same-sex marriage on a state-by-state basis will produce conflicts of law and require the invocation, interpretation, and application of constitutional provisions including full faith and credit and freedom of religion with resulting definitional and legal confusion. (3) Finally, same-sex marriage would end the exclusive sanction of procreation capability as the province of marriage thereby reducing the number of marriages and affecting the stability of the home environment and the family structure.

I.   A Poor Track Record On Public Policy Decisions Related to Family

A brief look at public policy decisions related to the family demonstrates that the unanticipated and unintended consequences of such decisions often require correction by additional changes in public policy and laws. Those corrections cannot be implemented immediately, with effects of corrective action neither seen nor felt for decades. Generations are negatively affected before the u-turn on the initial flawed policy can be made.

For example, the Johnson Administration's goal of "The Great Society," one intended to provide income, housing, and food for families was grounded in the same notions and tempting appeal of fairness, equality, and compassion. Those same notions and emotions surround, indeed engulf and consume, the debate on same-sex marriage. As a result of the emotional appeal of "The Great Society," and the dismissive approach to those who raised questions and issues with labels of "opposed to helping the poor," the country undertook massive social program reforms to afford relief in the form of housing, food, and income assistance, or, in some cases, full economic support. Instead of lending a helping hand or even a hand up, the programs had the unintended consequences of creating dependence and inculcating in generations a sense of entitlement and an inability to understand or embrace self-sufficiency. However, aside from the destruction of work ethic, self-esteem, and personal responsibility, there was a secondary, but also unintended, effect. The impact of the welfare system was the destruction of the family unit with a rise in births to single parents and a continuing cycle of welfare dependence. Just the creation of government-subsidized housing proved problematic. Intended as a measure to prevent homelessness, the subsidization facilitated fragmented families. Governmental support and subsidies became the substitute for, at that time, the wage-earner father. Without the responsibility, family disintegration occurred, and continued across generations. Today, the grandchildren of those who were beneficiaries of well intentioned government assistance programs have an out-of-wedlock birth rate of almost 40%.[3]

Yet another tragic consequence of the government housing program was "the projects," public housing with high crime rates, high levels of drug use and abuse. Government-subsidized housing became a central repository for fragmented families, with a resulting culture in which undisciplined youth had free reign. Unfortunately, the harm to the young people who grew up in these social experiments was already complete, with multigenerational effects from their crime rate and continuing lack of family structure, the social model that existed in this housing. The social Utopia of government-subsidized housing projects proved elusive because of a breakdown in natural order. After generations of young people were raised in these projects, the social experiment was abandoned in favor of Section 8 housing in which the government-assisted were mainstreamed into communities where traditional family structure was intact.[4]

Other Great Society welfare programs had an impact on family structure. Because of the government income and food stamp subsidies, fathers (again, the primary wage earners at the time) were dismissed from their critical roles in raising children. The subsidies enabled women to raise children without the presence of fathers. What began with the good intention of lifting families from poverty resulted in the abandonment of families by fathers. The ripple effect of the lost fathers again produced higher crime rates. James Q. Wilson has documented that "being born to an unmarried mother is by far the most significant factor disposing children to a life of crime—more significant than IQ, race, culture, or education."[5] In 1970, 11% of births were outside marriage. The Great Society had just taken hold and would continue until welfare reform was implemented in 1996. By 2001, the number of births to unwed mothers had still grown to 33%.[6] In 2006, the percentage of children born to single minority mothers was 70% (as noted above). The impact of this decline in the presence of fathers in the home, an effect of the beneficent public policies, served to spawn iatrogenic programs undertaken to remedy the increase in crime, the unintended consequences of the impact of the public policy changes on family structure. When Rudy Giuliani served as New York City's mayor he inherited prisons in which 70% of New York state's long-term prisoners and 75% of adolescents charged with murder grew up without a father. His plan for remedying the problem was a foster parent and adoption program to encourage couples to give troubled children a stable home. He said, at the time of his announcement, "I guess the social program would be called fatherhood."[7] Reversing the trends required a return to family structure.

The liberalization of the legal requirements for divorce is another example of public policy shifts made with the compassionate goal of allowing people to walk away from poor choices or unhappiness in marriage. The era of no-fault divorce was with the comfort of "it doesn't really hurt anyone." Another's divorce had no effect. Yet, hindsight from this perch of three decades of experience with this seemingly innocuous change, reveals its true impact social fabric. The ease of walking away, as in the case of the lost fathers in the welfare system, produced, once again, the fatherless children. The negative impact of divorce on children has become an unassailable proposition in the sociological and anthropological literature, as well documented by other participants in this conference.

So profound has been the impact that even those who sponsored and initiated the principle of no-fault divorce now understand the unintended consequences. Katherine Spaht helped bring no-fault divorce to Louisiana in the 1980s, something that was called the "walk-away divorce." By the end of the 1990s, Ms. Spaht was a key advocate for covenant marriage in Louisiana, a form of marriage that gave each spouse what was tantamount to "a right to marriage" that could not be taken away unilaterally.[8] Within a decade, even a vocal advocate with an untrained sociological eye saw the negative effects of this shift to "more compassionate" divorces.

Shifts in public policy that affect family structure have, historically, proved ineffectual, indeed, damaging. The social experiments related to family have yet to render a victory. But, with the public policy programs and changes in marital status, there is not just the effect of a decline in traditional family structure.

There are also unintended and nonconsenting participants in these social experiments. There are, in addition to the affected adults, children who spend their formative years in a stilted and tainted view of the role and importance of marriage. Their perception of marriage is one of marginalized value. Children between the ages of 8 and 18 reflect a disturbing ambivalence toward marriage. While 32% see marriage as very important, 33% see it as somewhat important and 19% see it as not important. Only 16% believe that marriage is extremely important.[9] One of the difficulties opponents to the legalization of same-sex marriage face is clearing the initial hurdle for making the case that marriage itself matters. The social experiments and generations influenced by the lack of family structure have set the stage for same-sex marriage. Those who have lived only in the era of no-fault and the Great Society and its aftermath have difficulty understanding the unique role that heterosexual marriage plays in a society because such structure has not been the norm during their formative years. The children of these programs have a "whatever" view toward an institution that has not served them well. Participants in today's public policy question on the definition of marriage have little information on the capability or role of traditional marriage and family structure.

When the importance of marriage is raised as an argument against expanding its definition, the emotional response is that heterosexuals have not done what could be called a crackerjack job with marriage as an institution. That heterosexuals have faltered in the marital state is not an argument for same-sex marriage. Their imperfection is an argument for leaving marriage in its status quo. Marriage is a delicate institution that requires work, nurturing, and exclusivity of public sanction. Removing that exclusivity not only raises questions about survival of the species; it raises questions as to whether the institution will exist at all. This further step from the norm of civilizations will not solve the decline in perceived value of marriage. Nor will it stop the steady destruction of the social fabric.

II.   The Conflicts of Law and Full-Faith-and-Credit-Confusion From Grappling with State-By-State Sanctions or Prohibitions on Same-Sex Marriage

If same-sex marriage legalization is relegated to the state level, one consequence is the application of the full faith and credit clause to such unions in order to allow same-sex couples interstate mobility without loss of rights.[10] However, honoring that constitutional provision requires states in which same-sex marriages are not legalized to honor their existence. State rights, traditionally exclusive in matters of marriage, are thus usurped. This constitutional coup will take hold despite recent state referenda on same-sex marriages that indicate a clear public sentiment against their legalization.[11]

If one constitutional issue is solved, another is created. Conflicts in constitutional rights would only exacerbate the problems if legalization were undertaken at the federal level.[12] The recent Massachusetts decision that required adoption agencies to place children with same-sex couples forced the Catholic Church to withdraw from its adoption work because of its inability to compromise religious beliefs. The result of such a decision is a mandate from the state to religious organizations to sanction a union that runs contrary to the organization's religious tenets and foundation. The real impact is that churches and other religious groups lose their freedom of religion to grant rights to another group. Such a deprivation of rights at the expense of others cannot be found in any interpretation or historical backdrop to the U.S. Constitution. Such a new precedent of loss of rights in favor of emotional and media-active groups is a quicksand foundation for constitutional law. Another argument to be considered is that the result of such federal usurpation is a form of religious discrimination, a clear foundation of the Bill of Rights and the founding of this country. Denying religious groups their ecclesiastical freedom has proven to be a sticky business, in a litigation sense. Further, the practical effect of such precedent would preclude churches from participating in basic social services and other activities in which they play a critical role in the improvement of the fabric of society. Few could dispute that such elimination of ecclesiastical social service operates to society's benefit.

One additional impact of this tenuous prohibition on religious activities will be its First Amendment consequences. Religious opposition to same-sex marriage will see its last days, as evidenced by the treatment of those who have joined in the discussion with a view contra to same-sex marriage. Fully a decade ago, California Superior Court Judge John Farrell was dealt a "violation of judicial ethics" blow when his fellow judges learned that he was a parent volunteer in the Boy Scouts in San Fernando. Ethics rules exist now that prohibit judges from belonging to organizations that discriminate on the basis of sexual orientation.[13] Religiously grounded opposition to same-sex marriage will now result in the deprivation of freedom of association, freedom of speech, and even economic survival as jobs hang in the balance depending upon religious affiliation.

III.   The Societal Impact of Recognizing Same-Sex Marriage

The impact of same-sex unions on the social fabric is neither resolved nor limited. The impact of the social programs previously discussed provides a type of preview for what awaits in the event the centuries-old structure of marriage is overturned. Stable, parenthood-focused marriages have an impact on the social fabric and require social support to survive.[14] One clear impact of the decline in marriages has been a decline in birth rates, a trend that will perhaps reach exponential levels with same-sex marriages. Anatomy dictates that the means for procreating in same-sex couples are limited and not quite as efficient as procreation in heterosexual couples. The National Marriage Project data reveal the following declining structure of the U.S. household:

YEAR	PERCENTAGE OF U.S. HOUSEHOLDS WITH AT LEAST ONE CHILD UNDER 18
1960	48.7%
1970	42.2%
1980	38.4%

1990	34.6%
2000	32.8%
2010 (projected)	28.0%[15]

One obvious result of the decline in birth rates is the resulting decline in global population growth. The U.N. world population estimate for 2050 has been decreasing. In 2004, the figure was one-half billion less than the population growth estimate in 2002.[16]

Even if the population/procreation argument were dismissed, there remains the question of whether children raised by same-sex couples do indeed experience, as is often touted, the same atmosphere and opportunities as children raised by heterosexual couples. While studies have claimed that the children of gay and lesbian couples experience no detrimental effects, the issue is not resolved. Further, much of the science behind the research cited to support same-sex marriage is unsound.[17] Social scientists have cited 49 studies in support of same-sex couples raising children that suffer from severe methodological flaws, limited sample size, spurious non-correlation, and difficulty in affirming the null hypothesis.[18] Contra studies have concluded that the impacts on the children of same-sex parents include lower self-esteem, sexual promiscuity in the female children of lesbian couples, emotional difficulties, social difficulties, and departures from heterosexual norms.[19] Assuming *arguendo* that the science is not yet definitive, the earlier discussion of the dramatically low success rate of public policy changes in family structure at least requires a wait-and-see pause prior to the expansion of marriage beyond its present structure.

While the slippery slope argument is often trivialized and recited in rote fashion, its basic premise should not be dismissed. "To endure (tolerance), to pity (compassion), to embrace (affirmation): This sequence of change in attitude and judgment has been used by the gay and lesbian movement with notable success."[20] Already afoot in the legal literature is a discussion that the reintroduction of polygamy as a means of ensuring a true democracy. Professor Alyssa Rower's piece entitled, "The Legality of Polygamy: Using the Due Process Clause of the Fourteenth Amendment"[21] and Professor Samantha Slark's "Are Anti-Polygamy Laws an Unconstitutional Infringement on the Liberty Interests of Consenting Adults?"[22] are two examples of trends in further liberalization of the concept of marriage. This school of thought has arrived before the same-sex marriage debate is resolved. Professor Chesire Calhoun has touted multipartner unions and noted carefully in his scholarship that such polygamous relationships would be open to gays and lesbians.[23] Professor Nancy Rosenblum has argued that legalized polygamy would create "subversive counterpatriarchal forms of group sex and domestic life" and, thereby, be a means of achieving true democracy.[24] Professor Angela Campbell of McGill University has recommended in her report to the Canadian government that the country decriminalize polygamy.[25] Placing this literature in historical context and extrapolating trends tells us that the camel-and-tent metaphor applies. In 1987, the first law review articles on same-sex marriage made their way into the legal literature.[26] By 1996, we had *Romer v. Evans.*[27]

Sanctioned same-sex marriages necessarily introduce a host of legal complications. There will no longer be, as in heterosexual marriages, a mother and a father, responsible for the rearing of children. There will be a birth mother, a donor, a biological father, a biological mother, and, in addition, the two souls who run the household and care for the children, one of whom may also play one of the previous roles. One minister noted the difficulty he had in sorting through what he referred to as a "truple" in his congregation. A truple consists of three men in one relationship who are committed to each other.[28] How does one sort through the rights of a truple? The family structure most likely to produce a well adjusted human being has two, and that combination has proven a challenge, as surely the divorce and family court activity can attest. Multiply those rights, concerns, personalities, and disagreements by two or three and the potential for haggling and confusion about rights, custody, and responsibilities becomes an exponential function. Settling the adults' differences and hedonistic demands will take its toll on the children.

Some of the other unintended consequences will have demographic and multigenerational impact. For example, it now appears that marriage provides a longer life. In what seems to be an unassailable proposition, one scholar described the relationship between life span and traditional marriage as follows, "The relationship between marriage and death rates has now reached the status of a truism, having been observed across numerous societies and various social and demographic groups."[29]

The recognition of same-sex marriage in parity with marriage requires that societal distinctions fall. Evidence of the current impact of legal parity vis-à-vis homosexuality can be found in the judicial battering of the Boy Scouts of America for its simple credo on morality and prohibition on homosexual males as leaders. If society has afforded equal standing in marriage, sheer judicial constancy mandates equal treatment in other aspects of life.

Without the stability of monogamous parenthood and its pedestal sanctioning for survival of the species, the activities of unstable cohabitation increase. The liberal family laws in the Netherlands have produced a host of social problems. Same-sex marriage was approved legislatively in Holland in 2000. Since that passage, out-of-wedlock births have crept up 8%, from 25% to 33%, the highest rate of increase since 1970.[30] More broadly, there has been the effect on the stability of children who have suffered from the casual relationships of cohabitation, and, ironically, an increase in the need for welfare support for increasingly fluid family relationships.[31] Sociologists have observed that the liberalization of the definition of marriage has the effect of trivializing the institution with commitment waning..[32] The result returns us to the impact of the social programs discussed earlier.

IV.   Conclusion and Thoughts

The sheer emotion of the debate on the legalization of same-sex marriage has precluded rational consideration of its likely and ominous, albeit unintended, consequences. Those consequences are neither simple nor limited and deserve both research and deliberation. Unique to this proposed change in family structure is a remarkable impact on the rights and status of those who, through religious affiliation, find themselves silenced as mandated rights favorable to one group deprive a less-favored group of another set of rights. Those who advocate same-sex marriage have yet to address the legal consequences of such recognition. Beyond that discussion, however, there remain more relevant issues including how society will teach and transmit morality to children or whether it will address the societal harms evident in countries that have embraced the "whatever" marriage. The debate requires a shift from its emotional and ad hominem approach to one of meaningful discussion of all public policy implications.

Notes

1. Jancee Dunn, *Melissa's Secret,* ROLLING STONE, January 17, 2000, at www.rollingstone.com.

2. A standard response during discussions between advocates and opponents of same-sex marriage.

3. USA TODAY, Nov. 21, 2006, at 1A.

4. Marianne M. Jennings, "My Neighborhood Ruined, Thanks to HUD," WALL STREET J., June 19, 1997, A18.

5. Roger Scruton, *The Moral Birds and Bees,* NATIONAL REVIEW, Nov. 15, 2003, 37, at 39.

6. Urban Institute and Centers for Disease Control and Prevention's National Vital Statistics Report, as reported in *Births Outside Marriage,* USA TODAY, March 5, 2004, at 1A.

7. Deroy Murdock, *Ready for Rudy,* AMERICAN SPECTATOR, Sept. 2006, 18, at 21.

8. La. Code Civ. Proc. Ann. art. 102, 103 (West 1999); La. Rev. Stat. Ann. §§ 9:224(C),:225(A)(3),:234,:245 (A)(1),:272-75,: 307-09 (West 2000). Spaht, a lawyer, worked to draft the covenant marriage legislation, despite having served since 1981 as a public policy expert on the Louisiana Commission on Marriage, a commission that created the no-fault legislation. Katherine Shaw Spaht, *What's Become of Louisiana Covenant Marriage Through the Eyes of Social Scientists,* 47 LOY. L. REV. 709, 720-21 (2001).

9. Cristiane Nascimento and Marcy E. Mullins, *How Young Americans Value Marriage,* USA TODAY, March 4, 2003, at 1D.

10. U.S. Const. art. IV, sec. 1.

11. The states with laws that do not permit same-sex marriage: Alaska, Alabama, Arizona, Arkansas, Flordia, Louisiana, Montana, Idaho, Utah, Nevada, Oregon, Kentucky, Indiana, Illinois, Minnesota, North Dakota, South Dakota, North Carolina, South Carolina, Oklahoma, Texas, Kansas, Colorado, Wisconsin, Ohio, Indiana, West Virginia, Pennsylvania, Rhode Island, Virginia, Mississippi, Louisiana, Missouri, Maine, Vermont, New Hampshire, and Hawaii. States where courts have ruled to uphold a ban on gay marriage: Washington, Nebraska, Tennessee, Georgia, New York, and Connecticut. States that recognize gay marriage: Massachusetts. States with court challenges to gay marriage pending: California, Iowa, New Jersey, Delaware, and Maryland. Elisabeth Salemme, *The State of Gay Marriage,* TIME, Aug.7, 2007, at 17,

12. Lynn D. Wardle, The *Proposed Federal Marriage Amendment and the Risks to Federalism in Family Law,* 2 U. ST. THOMAS L.J. 137 (2004).

13. Alan Abrahamson, *Boy Scout Issues Splits State's Judges,* LOS ANGELES TIMES, February 8, 1995, at B-1.

14. Both the legislative and judicial branches have recognized the unique role of marriage in civilization's survival. Joshua K. Baker, *Status, Benefits, and Recognition: Current Controversies in the Marriage Debate,* 18 BYU J. PUB. L. 569, 621-22 (2004)

15. The State of Our Unions 2006, The National Marriage Project, calculated from U.S. Census Data, as reported in Christopher Caldwell, "Childproof," *New York Times Magazine,* August 13, 2006, at 13.

16. Jeff Louderback, *World's Population Increases Leveling Off,* NEWSMAX, February 2004, at 64.

17. R. Faberman, *Council Actions Include Gay-Marriage Resolution,"* 35 MONITOR ON PSYCHOLOGY 9, at 24. Noting that the American Psychological Association's support of same-sex marriage was grounded in research indicating no difference in child-rearing in same-sex couple homes.

18. A. Dean Byrd, *When Activism Masquerades As Science: Potential Consequences of Recent APA Resolutions,* 13 NARTH BULLETIN 10 (2004).

19. *Id.,* citing the work of J. Stacy and T.J. Biblarz, *Does Sexual Orientation of Parents Matter?* 66 AMERICAN SOCIOLOGICAL REVIEW 159, at 174.

20. The Ramsey Colloquium, *Morality and Homosexuality,* WALL STREET J., February 24, 1994, at A18.

21. 38 FAMILY L.Q. 711 (2004).

22. 6 J. L. & FAMILY STUDIES 451 (2004).

23. CHESIRE CALHOUN, FEMINISM, THE FAMILY, AND THE POLITICS OF THE CLOSET: LESBIAN AND GAY DISPLACEMENT 83, 83-87 (2000); Chesire Calhoun, Sexuality Injustice, 9 NOTRE DAME J. L. ETHICS & PUB. POL'Y 241, 254 (1995)

24. Nancy L. Rosenblum, Democratic Sex: Reynolds v. U.S., Sexual Relations, and Community, in Sex, Preference, and Family: Essays on Law and Nature 63, 63 (David M. Estlund & Martha C. Nussbaum eds. 1997); Nancy L. Rosenblum, Membership and Morals: The Personal Uses of Pluralism in America 15 (1998).

25. Stanley Kurtz, *You Can't Have Both,* WEEKLY STANDARD, June 5, 2006, 18, at 24.

26. The gay rights movement in the United States can be traced back to Greenwich Village in 1969. However, the legal literature took hold at the time the Bowers v. Hardwick case was edging its way to the U.S. Supreme Court, a case in which Georgia's sodomy statute was upheld. 479 U.S. 186 (1986). The literature between 1969 and 1986 focused on individual rights, not specifically addressing marriage.

27. 517 U.S. 620 (1996).

28. The minister was the Rev. Dee Dale of the Metropolitan Community Church, and his anecdote was described in SUZANNE SHERMAN, ed., LESBIAN AND GAY MARRIAGE: PRIVATE COMMITMENTS, PUBLIC CEREMONIES (1992).

29. Lee A. Lillard and Linda J. Waite, *'Til Death Do Us Part': Marital Disruption and Mortality,"* 100 AMERICAN J. OF SOCIOLOGY 1131, AT 1156 (1995).

30. Stanley Kurtz, *Going Dutch?* WEEKLY STANDARD, May 31, 2004, 26, at 27.

31. Katherine Shaw Spaht, *For the Sake of the Children: Recapturing the Meaning of Marriage,* 73 NOTRE DAME L. REV. 1547, 1559-60 (1998).

32. *Id.* The effect in Sweden, with its authorization of same-sex partnerships is similar.

CHAPTER 5
WHAT'S THE HARM TO WOMEN AND CHILDREN?
A PROSPECTIVE ANALYSIS

Lynne Marie Kohm[*]
Regent University

The sexual revolution heralded newfound individual freedoms, which pre-cipitated rising rates of divorce, unmarried cohabitation, the decline of marriage, and widespread acceptance of homosexuality.[2] This article will examine the devastating impact these trends have had on women and children, and will show that even in the short time same sex unions have been recognized they are con-tinuing and magnifying these damaging results.

This impact is evident in statistics and academic studies; however it is most vividly illustrated through the lives of real women and children who are trying to survive in the wake of the extended sexual revolution and its fallout. Two of the starkest examples involve prototypical same sex couples whose legal battles for state recognition of their relationships lasted longer than the unions them-selves.

Massachusetts same sex couple, Julie and Hillary Goodridge, were very vocal about their commitment to one another as they lent their names to the court case that ultimately led to the state's recognition of same sex marriage.[3] They insisted that they were as committed as any heterosexual couple.[4] Unfortu-nately, they were right. Their union fared as well as half of the heterosexual American couples whose marriages end in separation and divorce.[5] The Goo-dridge marriage lasted less than two years. The couple announced their separa-tion in July of 2006, after less than 22 months of marriage.[6] "Julie Goodridge, 49, and Hillary Goodridge, 50, were married on May 17, 2004, the first day that same-sex couples were permitted to wed in Massachusetts under the terms of Goodridge v. Department of Public Health.... The Goodridges declined to comment Friday on the split. The couple has a 10-year-old daughter, Annie."[7] As this article will explain, statistics indicate that Annie Goodridge will now face significantly increased challenges, as both a child of divorce and of a same sex union.

Carolyn Conrad and Kathleen Peterson of Brattleboro, Vermont are another groundbreaking same-sex couple whose battle to have their relationship legally recognized[8] had more permanence than the relationship itself. Theirs was the first legally recognized same-sex union in the country and it officially ended on August 23, 2006.[9] The two women entered into a civil union shortly after midnight on July 1, 2000, the day Vermont's first-in-the-nation law went into effect; but Conrad filed to end the union in October 2005, and dissolution was granted in August of 2006.[10]

Same sex marriages have been legal in Massachusetts for two years, and at the time of publication, at least 45 of the couples who married during that time have already divorced.[11] Statistics indicate that this trend toward dissolution is likely to intensify. Same sex marriage advocates justifiably counter that the institution has not existed long enough to allow for longitudinal studies that can provide reliable insight into the negative or positive effects of same sex marriage. However, reports out of Canada, where same sex marriage has been legal since 2003, indicate that the impact of recognizing such unions is overwhelmingly negative for children and for marriage overall.

In addition to the statistically proven negative impacts same sex marriage has had on children, the phenomenon has also detrimentally impacted marriage and society overall because of the ways in which it has changed the national dialogue about marriage. As this chapter will further explain, historically, marriage has been considered, and has been legally regarded and protected, as a sacred and socially indispensable institution. Same sex marriage advocates have realized tremendous, albeit tragic, success in changing the emphasis of the discourse on marriage from protecting it as a sacred institution foundational to society to redefining the institution itself to accommodate and validate personal preferences. The political impact of these changes has led to social policies that prioritize temporal, personal feelings of happiness and acceptance over protecting the fundamental institution upon which society is based. These changes also prioritize adult autonomy over protecting vulnerable members of society, generally women and children, that marriage policies have traditionally sought to protect.

This destructive reprioritization is clear in the contrast between two Canadian studies on the social impact of same sex marriage. Canada's Institute of Marriage and Family issued a report discussing the effects of sanctioning same sex marriage and other marriage "reforms" such as no fault divorce and affording legal rights to unmarried cohabitating couples; they have called it "a tragedy for children."[12]

> Marriage reformers are quite right to argue that marriage has suffered since the advent of the sexual revolution in the late 1960s, but this is no reason to accept a trend that has been harmful for children. Same-sex marriage, like prior marriage reforms, will also harm children by further weakening the normative connection between marriage and procreation.[13]

In contrast, however, the University of Calgary issued a report published by the Canadian Journal of Human Sexuality proffering research indicating that same sex marriage is a permanent societal change.[14] The study declares that "we know little about how these couples construct their relationships within the new context of marriage," and mainly researched homosexual couples' experiences of being in a same-sex marriage.[15] This study detailed the feelings of those involved in the research, showing how they felt marriage validated their relation-ships.[16] It did not detail the societal or long-term effects of these relationships.

The study that examined the impact same sex marriage had on children and families indicates in no uncertain terms that it is a socially destructive phenome-non. However, the study that focuses on the feelings of those involved in the relationships indicates that same sex marriage is a wonderful construct. Basing social policy, especially policy governing an institution as essential as marriage, on personal politics rather than social responsibility is dangerous, but the rhetor-ic surrounding same sex marriage advocacy does just that.

The second danger same sex marriage advocates have interjected into the national political discourse on marriage is that their rhetoric on marriage, like that of marriage "reformers" before them, focuses disproportionately on divorce and the "benefits" of divorce, rather than working to strengthen the institution of marriage. This underlying premise became explicit following the Goodridge separation when several mainstream media outlets and same sex marriage advo-cates cited the fact that the relationship ended as proof of its normalcy, "They are so normal in fact, that Julie and Hillary Goodridge, the lesbian couple who lent their name to the groundbreaking case, have announced their amicable sepa-ration..."[17] Comments surrounding the Goodridge divorce also indicated that the couple's divorce underscored the necessity of allowing same sex marriage.

Herein lays the problem. Instead of working to strengthen the institution of marriage, same sex advocates seek only to provide greater access to failure by seeking to secure marriage and thereby divorce benefits for their constituents. This chapter considers same-sex relationships and will reveal why the incidence of divorce is likely to continue to be higher among same sex couples than hete-rosexual couples. Statistical indicators reveal that couples who cohabit before marriage yield a much higher rate of divorce than those who do not cohabit prior to marriage. The greater incidence of premarital cohabitation among same sex couples will yield a very high divorce rate.

Section I will discuss how the institution of marriage uniquely benefits so-ciety, specifically with regard to the social interests in protecting vulnerable family members. Section II will examine the ways in which those social benefits of marriage may be diminished or even eliminated, resulting in further harms to women and children if same-sex marriage is legalized. It will also discuss why and how that harm will come about, examining the evidence that supports the prediction of harm. This section shows very clearly the immensely harmful ef-fects cohabitation and divorce have on children. It will also show how same sex relationships, even those that have been civilly formalized, will inevitably ma-nifest similar negative effects for women and children as have unmarried coha-bitation and divorce. Section III will anticipate and respond to counter-arguments.

Do same sex partnerships provide the benefits marriage provides for women and children? Statistics indicate that same sex relationships are relatively unsta-ble, even when formally recognized. Further, the likelihood of premarital coha-bitation and other destabilizing factors indicate that same sex couples are likely to have even higher divorce rates than heterosexual couples. This chapter projects that their dissolutions will generate similar negative effects that are associated with divorce among heterosexual couples. If same sex marriages are even more likely to end in divorce than heterosexual marriages, sanctioning same sex marriage will exponentially multiply the number of divorces, thus multiplying the impact of divorce on society overall. The burden will fall disproportionately, however, on women and children. The impact of divorce will be compounded with the other negative impacts of same sex relationships. And therein lies the misnomer of marriage benefits sought by same sex couples—these are not marriage benefits, but the benefits of divorce.[18]

What's the harm? This article clarifies that harm from same sex relationships will mirror, if not magnify, the harms associated with divorce and cohabitation that are already overwhelming society. Same sex unions will not protect women or children. Rather they will bring further harm—and that harm is likely to grow.

I.   The institution of marriage uniquely benefits society, and it benefits women in particular

The institution of marriage has uniquely benefited society, specifically in protecting vulnerable family members like women and children. In fact, marriage and family law is fundamentally oriented towards creating and protecting the next generation.[19] Eighty percent of women and seventy percent of men believe that marriage is "extremely important" and even higher percentages "believe that marriage is for a lifetime."[20] Beyond opinions, studies have indicated that, "good family life ... encourages self-sacrificing love" toward others and discourages "rampant individualism."[21]

Marriage is a powerful aspect of the law, intentionally influencing social norms with legal rules to foster a basic intrinsic good rather than a functional instrumental good.[22] The law cannot regulate happiness; it can only incentivize behavior that enhances the stability and welfare of its citizens. More than a private emotional relationship, marriage is a social good. "Marriage is an important social good associated with an impressively broad array of positive outcomes for children and adults alike..."[23]

The benefits marriage affords to individuals, though they are profound, are dwarfed by the benefits marriage provides to a society as a whole.

> [B]ecause of its unique qualities among adult human relationships, and due to the specific external social expectations associated with it, marriage like no other relationship, offers us constant, even relentless opportunities to build and strengthen these virtues. Marriage brings ever-changing mutual dependencies—physically, emotionally, and financially—requiring each spouse to learn to give and to take, to sacrifice, and to receive sacrificial gifts. Lived, according to social hopes and ideals, therefore, marriage is an important source of and witness to, virtues widely desired in America society and beyond.[24]

Marriage imposes legal restrictions that take away rights individuals might otherwise have, and those restrictions are designed to protect the most vulnerable parties to that marriage.

> "Wives, for example, typically invest in the family by restricting their own work force participation, if only long enough to take care of small children. Studies show such differences still persisting in this liberated age, and even among women and men with postgraduate degrees from Harvard and Yale. In the absence of marriage laws, a husband could dump his wife at will and she could lose decades of investment in their relationship. Marriage laws seek to recoup some of that investment for her through alimony when divorce occurs."[25]

These facts will not change when the parties to the marriage are of the same sex. Inevitably, one partner, or at times both, will somehow restrict their work force participation to prioritize childrearing, which will result in a dependence on the other partner. It is unlikely, even in a same sex relationship, that such restriction for childrearing will be equally distributed, thereby precluding any dependence on the other who is less restricted economically by childbearing and rearing.. Generally, one partner will experience decreased financial worth and marketability for the sake of prioritizing child care and other domestic responsibilities. Recouping that investment for the dependent partner will continue to be a major part of the process of dissolution. The harm will be most likely to grow with each new relationship entered into and dissolved. Women have traditionally relied on the promises of marriage, particularly when investing in that relationship to care for children. Marriage provides security, support and stability for women and the children they care for.

This promise of security provides essential social benefits. Thirteen of the top family life scholars issued a report on the importance of marriage. Based on decades of research, it is a definitive report on the financial, emotional, and physical impact marriage has on men, women, children and society, and the findings are striking.[26] This report and its twenty-one findings are now widely agreed upon and "based on a steadily accumulating and by now very large body of social science evidence about the consequences of marriage and its absence."[27] Science is finally revealing, and government is acting upon, what societies have known, relied upon and founded nations upon for as long as history has been recorded: Marriage is a very good thing.

> Despite changing attitudes toward sex and gender roles, the substance of the marriage vow as Americans understand it has changed surprisingly little. Marriage is, above all, seen as a permanent union, which includes the promise of sexual union, of financial union, and of mutual support. ...
> The promise of permanence is integral to marriage's transformative power. People who expect to be part of a couple for their entire lives—unless something awful happens—organize their lives differently from people who are less certain their relationship will last. The marriage contract, because it is long-term, encourages husbands

and wives to make decisions jointly and to function as part of a team. Each spouse expects to be able to count on the other to be there and to fulfill his or her responsibilities. This expectation of a long-term working relationship between husband and wife leads to substantial changes in their behavior... [28]

One of the most important publications on this subject is *The Case for Marriage* by Linda J. Waite and Maggie Gallagher, two social scientists writing from differing political perspectives yet agreeing on one thing: the data suggest marriage is very important to every area of life.[29] "Marriage is an important social good associated with an impressively broad array of positive outcomes for children and adults alike..."[30]

Declines in marriage and parenthood for men have led to social problems such as crime and substance abuse.[31] Studies indicate that when men avoid marriage or delay it, they continue with some of the antisocial and destructive behaviors that are more common among single men.[32] Taking on the role of husband, rather than that of boyfriend or father, seems to be the key.[33] "Having children by itself does not work the same transformation in men's lives."[34] Marriage makes life better for the women and children involved. "[F]or most people at most times, marital roles lead men and women to act in responsible ways."[35]

The medical power of marriage is astounding. Married women tend to be far healthier than their unmarried counterparts.[36] "Compared to married people, the nonmarried...have higher rates of mortality than the married: about 50% higher among women and 250% higher among men.[37] In fact, Waite and Gallagher stat that being unmarried can actually be a greater risk to one's life than having heart disease or cancer.[38] Studies of hospital surgery patients reveal that patients who are married do not pile up hospital charges, but recover more quickly than those who are not married, who do pile up bigger hospital charges and longer hospital stays. This is of certain concern to employers who pay for employee health insurance, life insurance, and other health related employee benefits. Marital status is the most powerful predictor of mental health and an individual's psychological well being.[39]

Many of these benefits appear to flow from marital longevity and even more from marital permanence. These health benefits and satisfaction levels decrease significantly after divorce, even with subsequent marriages. For those with second and third marriages, the satisfaction and health benefits brought on by marriage are increasingly lessened.[40] In fact, Linda Waite declares that if you want a long and healthy life, stay married.[41] "Marriage is a public promise to stay together for life."[42] Length of marriage seems to accrue health benefits to the point of extending length of life of the individuals who participate in it. "The strong relationship between marriage and mortality has been observed across numerous societies and among various social and demographic groups.... Marriage not only preserves life, but it protects health."[43]

Marriage is not just one arrangement among many. Rather, it is a crucial building block of "social order that makes a special contribution to civil society that justifies [a] distinctive honor or status."[44] Who is eligible for entry into the relationship of marriage is a legal issue.[45] Marriage-like relationships, particularly same sex partnerships, have received significant attention in courts and in voting booths, and judges and society overall continue to recognize the uniqueness of marriage as opposed to same sex partnerships.[46] "...[A] prudent and wise society ought to afford superior moral and legal status to heterosexual marriage and family because it serves an important purpose. To make all relationships morally normative is ... wrong in terms of the right ordering of society."[47]

Marriage is generally viewed as a set apart, special, legally protected and stabilizing relationship from which benefits of critical importance arise. "...[T]here are important psychological benefits from predictability with marriage, providing insurance that encourages a commitment by both parties."[48] This commitment is found only in marriage.

> Marriage is not an arbitrary construct; it is an 'honorable estate' based on the different, complementary nature of men and women— and how they refine, support, encourage, and complete one another. To insist that we maintain this traditional understanding of marriage is not an attempt to put others down. It is simply an acknowledgment and celebration of our most precious and important social act.[49]

The law recognizes marriage because it produces good results— individually and socially. Marriage is good for women's health, longevity, responsibility and stability.[50] These benefits of marriage to women are lost in same sex relationships, even when sanctioned by the law in some way.

II.   Evidence to support the prediction of harm

There are many known effects the breakdown of marriage has on women, individually and overall. As of yet, it is too early to study what effect redefining marriage to include same sex couples will have on women, but there are already many studies that show the negative effects that marriage redefinition has had on children.

Families take on many different configurations. Among them are 1) never married with children, 2) divorced with children, 3) widowed with children, 4) unmarried cohabitation with children, 5) unmarried cohabitation without children, 6) same sex partners without children, 7) same sex partners with children, 8) married without children, 9) married with children. These choices show how diverse living situations can be for women and children.

Patterns 1, 2, and 3 include only one parent figure in the household, and that parent is most likely the mother.[51] Studies consistently show that children experience dramatic harm from these patterns of fatherlessness.[52] Studies also consistently show that major detriments occur to children with a parent who cohabits.[53] Studies have overwhelming shown that a child thrives when he or she grows up in a home headed by dual-gender parents married to each other.[54] This is true of pattern 9, and brings benefits to women as well.[55]

Pattern 7 reflects those children with same sex parents. Children in such family structures are forced to grow up without a mother or a father in every instance. This pattern presents an immediate detriment to children because the child grows up being intentionally deprived of either a father or a mother. This also automatically violates the most basic tenet of family law, working to preserve the best interests of a child. This is clearly harmful to a child.

These negative effects on children have been apparent before.

> "At the time that divorce reforms were being passed, it was fashionable among intellectuals to contend that the best interest of adults also serve the best interests of children. This formerly conventional wisdom has proven to be gravely mistaken, as the belief that mothers and fathers don't matter to children in determining parenthood is apt to prove to be."[56]

A most radical view offered by some legal academics would abolish marriage as a sanctioned legal institution to accomplish the objective of treating all family forms equally.[57] For children, however, the law is not so concerned with treating family forms alike as it is with accomplishing the legal standard for children—determining the best interests of the child. The bottom line in achieving the best interests of a child is to provide for that child to be raised by a mother and a father married to each other. By nature same sex parents preclude the very best interests of a child.

> The argument that traditional marriage is discriminatory begs the question of whether marriage ought to be simply companionate, or whether it makes sense to preserve child-centered marriage norms. If the best interest of children is the standard by which marriage reforms are to be assessed, same-sex marriage cannot be justified.[58]

The gay community recognizes that the average homosexual lifestyle is more undomesticated than the average heterosexual lifestyle.[59] Same sex relationships advocates clarify and advance that by their very nature homosexual relationships are generally sexually open.[60] This fact lends to the inherent instability of gay and lesbian relationships. Therefore, even if same sex couples pledge fidelity via marriage the nature of homosexuality is not one of sexual loyalty. This can extend to the exchange of partners over a short period.

Basing any relationship on sexual encounters may generally lead to cohabitation of partners. Cohabitation is a critical factor in the success or failure of a relationship. "[U]nmarried cohabitations overall are less stable than marriages."[61] Premarital cohabitation increases the likelihood of marital failure.

> The probability of a first marriage ending in separation or divorce within 5 years is 20 percent, but the probability of a premarital cohabitation breaking up within 5 years is 49 percent. After 10 years, the probability of a first marriage ending is 33 percent, compared with 62 percent for cohabitations.[62]

The Calgary study revealed that cohabitation precedes same sex marriage,[63] and the participants' relationships sometimes "developed following a sexual encounter."[64] Relationships based on sexual encounters inherently lead to instability. By analogy, a same sex relationship will be very likely to follow the results current research already reveals about cohabitation. This is a major reason why same sex relationships, even those that lead to marriage, lose the benefits marriage has to offer.

If cohabitation increases the likelihood of divorce, and homosexual couples cohabit prior to marriage, homosexual couples will logically be more likely to divorce. Therefore, the negative effects of divorce are also likely to follow and be magnified in the expansion of marriage to same sex relationships.

Marriage of same sex partners does not seem to lessen the instability these relationships foster. By their very nature homosexual relationships have a strong sexual dimension between the partners prior to any personal commitment toward the relationship. If the sexual dimension turns into a relationship, this quite often leads to cohabitation. Trends already seen from cohabitation are likely quite good predictors of the negative effects of same sex relationships. These tend to disproportionately harm women, as women's same sex sexual encounters generally lead to some sort of relationship. The same sex relationship phenomenon more clearly tracks cohabitation and the exchange of partners over a short period than it does marriage, losing the benefits marriage has to offer to same sex couples.

Sociological studies indicate that there are vast differences between the relational security and other benefits that cohabitation and marriage provide.[65] Often considered an alternative family arrangement, cohabitation is one of several family structures that has become more common in American society.[66] One reason why many in same sex partnerships pursue the legal right to marry is that marriage provides a relational security second to none. The question becomes whether the negative effects of cohabitation or the positive benefits of marriage appear in those same sex relationships sanctioned by marriage. Same sex marriage has not been available long enough in Massachusetts to gather strong statistical evidence or comparisons. However, the statistics indicating the volatility of same sex relationships in general and the detrimental impacts of cohabitation combined with the anecdotal evidence from the lives of some of the movements' greatest proponents present very negative implications for same sex marriage. Sadly, the instability statistics of cohabitation, rather than the benefits marriage, are apparent in the Goodridge separation in Massachusetts. The same comparisons can be made with civil unions, and are shown by example in the Conrad-Peterson dissolution in Vermont. It is too early to conclude that these examples show that same sex partnerships are inherently unstable, but they do follow the pattern, and therefore present quite accurate pictures of expectations and predictors.

We already know that women have not benefited from the sexual revolution and the feminism that helped to fuel it as predicted. The sexual revolution has not helped further pay equity for women,[67] nor has it brought any greater economic security to women as they still comprise the majority of citizens under the poverty line,[68] the majority of impoverished single parents,[69] and the majority of impoverished seniors.[70] There is a significant disparity between women with children and women without children.[71] For women who marry and later divorce, poverty rates exceed those of never-married women.[72]

> ...[T]he main benefit of marriage for women, traditionally one of economic support from men, has eroded as the economic position of men, especially young men with limited education or work skills, has declined relative to women's over the past two decades. The implication...is that rising female headship results from the blurring of traditional gender and economic roles.[73]

Because of the correlation between cohabitation and same sex marriage, the effects of cohabitation on women and children are equally important to the discussion of same sex unions .

Statistics indicate that cohabitation increases domestic violence, which victimizes women and children.[74] A study of relationship violence among same sex couples revealed "that 47.5% of lesbians and 29.7% of gays have been victimized by a same sex partner."[75] This means that nearly 1 in 2 lesbians is victimized by her partner. Other studies have also documented domestic violence among homosexual partners.[76] It is estimated that battery occurs in 50 percent of gay male couples,[77] some of which may be related to sexual coercion.[78] These statistics show that a same sex marriage may not be a safe place for a woman or a child. Negative effects of cohabitation combined with these facts of violence among same sex couples set an unstable foundation for the relationships of the women involved in them and the children dependent upon them.

Nonmarital cohabitation is also "one of the most robust predictors of marital dissolution that has appeared in the literature."[79] In direct contrast, children raised by dual-gendered married parents are healthier on average than children in other family forms,[80] and have sharply lower rates of substance abuse.[81] Children raised outside a marital home are more likely to divorce, become unwed parents themselves,[82] and experience significantly elevated risks of child abuse.[83] "In recent years, this scholarly consensus on the importance of marriage for child well-being has broadened and deepened, extending across ideological lines to become the conventional wisdom among mainstream child welfare organizations."[84] The statistics, however, show that many children are not born and raised in intact marital families. Births to cohabiting women now account for thirty-nine percent of all births to unmarried women.[85] This means that from birth more than one in every three children is likely to be raised in a cohabiting household, or by a single (cohabiting) parent. That fact presents a significant measure of instability for those children from the outset.

Cohabitation also creates economic hardships that impact children. 34% of American children between the ages of 1 year and 17 will spend at least 1 year below the poverty line; 18% will experience extreme poverty; and children living in non-married households have the greatest occurrence of poverty at 81%.[86] "Over the past 25 years, one of the most apparent and disturbing aspects of American society has been its exceedingly high rate of poverty among children."[87] Children of divorce have a greater likelihood of cohabitation, being twice to three times as likely to cohabit and to cohabit earlier.[88]

The negative effects of divorce upon women and children are well documented. In the age of fault-based divorce, family law "favored women (and children) by making divorce difficult to obtain and by requiring extended support for the wife and children in the event of divorce, in the belief that wives were less able to take care of themselves economically than were husbands."[89] Women have lost that advantage with the tremendous rise of no-fault divorce, a direct result of the sexual revolution. Divorce affects more than economics. It also dramatically affects personal well-being. A study examining the well-being of once-married, divorced and remarried individuals found that "being remarried, or divorced, increases stress relative to being in an intact first marriage."[90] The negative implications of divorce for mental health are apparent,[91] and greater psychological well-being is reported for married mothers than for cohabiting or single mothers.[92] On a universal scale however, divorce has produced devastating results for adults and children alike.[93]

The past forty years have brought no greater custody assurances to women, as the fight for legal equality has forced courts toward a primary caretaker standard based on gender equality, where the bygone tender years presumption worked in favor of women in custody disputes.[94] Family social researcher Judith Wallerstein completed a landmark study on divorce and she concluded that there are no positive effects of divorce on children.[95]

These negative effects of divorce and cohabitation will be similar, if not more devastating, for same sex couples. It is likely they will be more pronounced because homosexual relationships are necessarily based on pre-marital sexual encounters, leading virtually every same sex marriage to be a cohabiting relationship before marriage. Treating domestic partnerships, same sex or heterosexual, as equal to marriages furthermore encourages people to cohabite rather than marry.[96] Waite and Gallagher suggest there is a sharp distinction between marriage and cohabitation,[97] and that the lines are not as blurred as legislation may seem to indicate. The costs of cohabitation are surprisingly similar to those of divorce.

> The prime difference between marriage and cohabitation in contemporary American culture has to do with time horizons and commitment. What makes marriage unique among emotional and financial relationships is the vow of permanence. With marriage, partners publicly promise each other that neither one will be alone any longer: Whatever else happens in life, someone will care about and take care of you. Even spouses who choose divorce hang on with surprising persistence, to the ideal of marital permanence, preferring to see their own marriages as 'a lie' rather than to reimagine marriage as a less than permanent union. Eighty-one percent of divorce and separated Americans still believe marriage should be for life.
>
> Cohabitation, by contrast, is seen by partners and society as a temporary arrangement. The majority of cohabitors either break up or marry within two years.[98]

That two-year trend is apparent in the Goodridge separation in Massachusetts and in the Conrad-Peterson dissolution in Vermont. Each of these relationships was based first on a sexual relationship, changed to cohabitation, then to a legally sanctioned union, and each union ended in a very short time.

Profound negative effects of cohabitation will inure to the children of same sex partnerships as well. When sexual freedom takes priority over motherhood, a child's best interests cannot be compatible with unrestrained adult autonomy. With sexual progressiveness has come a dramatic rise in cohabitation that affects children.[99] It is estimated that 2.2 million U.S children live in families headed by cohabiting couples.[100] Economic resources lag among children whose parents are cohabiting.[101] Although some are better off financially than children with single mothers, generally their economic resources lag far behind those children with married parents.[102]

The intergenerational effects of cohabitation will likely be similarly apparent in the children of same sex relationships. Children of cohabiting parents find themselves in cohabiting relationships at a rate of 18% more than children raised in intact marital families.[103] "Conversely the continued presence of a married father in the home strongly predicts the happy marriage of the child,"[104] but the marital status of men has dropped from 70% in 1960 to 42% in 1995,[105] making the trends for children having stable fathers all the more disturbing. With same sex parents, children with two mothers will be fatherless. Their parents, even if they are married, will have a higher rate of breaking up because they most likely cohabited prior to marriage.

These considerations are disturbing. Yet, proponents of same sex marriage will argue from fairness and equality and a desire for recognition of a loving commitment. These arguments—presented and answered in the next section— serve to illustrate that same sex unions have only served to further weaken the institution of marriage.

III.   Counter-arguments and responses

Critics of the positions this chapter takes will have several arguments to make. Some of these arguments can be set forth and addressed immediately. They will ultimately show that women and children are harmed when same sex unions are sanctioned by law.

1. Proponents of same sex partnerships argue that those partnerships are more stable when recognized in marriage. Answer: Statistical indicators and anecdotal examples of even the strongest proponents of same sex marriage indicate that marriage does not necessarily enhance the stability of same sex relationships. In the case of the Goodridge divorce, obvious concerns are apparent, in that the legal union was very short lived, was based initially on a sexual relationship, and the marriage was preceded by cohabitation. Observers expressed concern for the Goodridge family, especially the daughter, noting that research points to instability in many homosexual relationships.[106]

2. Same sex marriage proponents will argue that just because a marriage ends in divorce is no reason to limit it. Answer: Minimum requirements for marriage entry are designed to protect the vulnerable parties, namely women and

children, who become part of it. Divorce protections are no reason to enter into any marriage.

3. Proponents of same sex marriages argue that legally recognized marriage for homosexual couples will provide the same things for children that marriage does. Answer: No they won't. Every child needs a mother and a father. Children thrive when they have a father and a mother married to each other. Same sex unions require the intentional detriment of a father or a mother to a child; this renders the best interests of the child an impossibility from the outset.

4. Same sex marriage proponents believe that one of their strongest arguments is that legal equality is of utmost importance and is being denied to homosexual couples. Answer: Equality is available to all citizens. Those similarly situated must be treated the same. All those who wish to marry must meet minimum requirements set forth by that society as valued in protecting those most vulnerable. Protecting the vulnerable is an equally important societal objective.

5. Homosexual advocates argue that the fight for same sex marriage is about recognizing love and commitment. Answer: Law does not regulate love, and never has. Rather, the law holds accountable reliance on a promised contract, and requires that broken promises be accounted for to protect the most vulnerable members of that marriage. Generally, these are women and the children.

6. Same sex marriage proponents will argue that the law should not restrict individuals from marrying just because they will follow the established negative patterns toward divorce. Equal protection in dissolution should be provided regardless. Answer: The future of any society rests on the furtherance of future generations. Any law, be it no-fault divorce or same sex marriage, that works to break down that society is not beneficial, and harms the entire social structure.

IV.   Conclusion

All of the same sex couples referred to in this piece have been women. The marriage partners and the children are all females who will suffer harm from the dissolution of their families. Trends in cohabitation and divorce have had devastating results on women and children, and same sex relationships will follow and magnify these trends. They do not promise any greater benefits to women and children. Rather, it promises more harm.

This picture is portrayed clearly in the lives of women and children who are trying to survive in the wake of the extended sexual revolution and all that has come with it. This picture is being colored in with the lives of real people, like Annie Goodridge and her two moms who have now split up. Like these women in Massachusetts, Canadians are starting to see the results of same sex marriage legislation, and they have called it a tragedy for children. Companionate marriage is not child-centered marriage. Rather, it brings major societal harm. "All agree that marriage is a fundamental institution, but few are willing to acknowledge the implications of what it means for a fundamental institution of society to be gutted of its constitutive norms."[107] Same sex marriage will bring that harm to societies that embrace it and do not "anticipate the long-range implications of the erosion of traditional marriage."[108]

So what's the harm if same sex relationships are legally recognized as marriages or civil unions or partnerships? The harm is in the instability of those relationships, and the dissolutions that will inevitably follow. With each successive relationship and dissolution, all benefits of marriage are lost and all harm of divorce or cohabitation is magnified.

Indeed, the benefits have been lost and the harm has been magnified already in the highest profile cases in Massachusetts and Vermont, each lasting very brief periods of time. All the women are harmed by lost investment in the relationship. Those who are always most harmed are the children. The brokenness of individuals, the dilution of the institution of marriage, and the weakening of the purpose and objectives of this most basic institution of humankind harms society. These negative trends harm not only society, but individual women and children as well. Women and children indeed will continue to be harmed by these trends, which will clearly be further exacerbated by the expansion of marriage to same sex unions.

Notes

---

* John Brown McCarty Professor of Family Law, Regent University School of Law; J.D. Syracuse; BA Albany. My gratitude is extended to Colleen M. Holmes for her brilliant editing and insight, to William Catoe for superb research assistance on this project, and to Rena Campbell for her priceless technical expertise. Most importantly, my deepest gratitude is extended to Professor Lynn D. Wardle for his tireless, priceless, pivotal and culturally crucial work on this project.

2. The law manifested many of the freedoms associated or brought forth from what is heralded as the sexual revolution, such as freedom to use contraception regardless of marital status (*Eisenstadt v. Griswold*, 405 U.S. 438 (1965))(extending the privacy of contraceptive use to unmarried individuals) which has in turn grown cohabitation rates; the fundamental rights aspects of divorce (*Boddie v. Connecticut*, 401 U.S. 371 (1971)(holding that the right to adjust the fundamental relationship of marriage is constitutionally protected to the point of fee waiver for indigent divorce petitioners); abortion (*Roe v. Wade*, 410 U.S. 113 (1973)(holding abortion as a fundamental right) and more recently other freedoms of sexuality (*Lawrence v. Texas*, 539 U.S. 558 (2003))(extending privacy to the protection of consensual sodomy).

3. Goodridge v. Dept. of Pub. Health, 440 Mass. 309 (2003).

4. "They told the world that their relationship was like any other and that's why they should be allowed to marry. Now, friends say, they are showing once again that they are just like any other couple: Two years after getting married, Julie and Hillary Goodridge, lead plaintiffs in the state's landmark gay marriage case, are splitting." *After 2 years, same-sex marriage icons split up*, Boston.com (July 21, 2006), available at http://www.boston.com/news/local/massachusetts/articles/2006/07/21/after_2_years_same... [hereinafter AFTER 2 YEARS]

5. Rose M. Kreider and Jason M. Fields, *Number, Timing, and Duration of Marriages and Divorces: 1996*, U.S. Census Bureau, Household Economic Studies, Feb. 2002, at 1 [hereinafter U.S. CENSUS BUREAU]. "Nearly half of recent first marriages may end in divorce." *Id*. Some reports appear to show a rate of divorce at somewhere between 43% and 50% over the past five years. *Divorce Rate: It's Not as High as You Think*, NEW YORK TIMES, April 2005; *See also* Matthew Bramlett and William Mosher, *First mar-*

riage dissolution, divorce, and remarriage: United States, ADVANCE DATA FROM VITAL
AND HEALTH STATISTICS, No. 323 (Hyattsville, MD, National Center for Health Statistics,
2:1).

6. *Perspectives*, NEWSWEEK, July 31, 2006, at 21; also available at 2006 WLNR
12758821. "The Goodridges' breakup was first reported ... in Bay Windows, New England's major newspaper for homosexuals. The paper said a breakup had been rumored for
months, but the women had worked to time release of the news in the best way to protect
their daughter." Cheryl Wetzstein, *Gay 'Marriage' First Couple splits up on Massachusetts*, THE WASHINGTON TIMES, July 21, 2006, at
http://www.washingtontimes.com/national/20060721-111920-1539r.htm. From these
facts, it appears this marriage remained happy much less than 22 months.

7. Elizabeth Mehren, *Couple in same-sex marriage suit separate, Lesbian partners
were among the first to wed in Massachusetts after landmark court ruling*, BUFFALO
NEWS, July 22, 2006, at A1; also available at 2006 WLNR 12660000. "The 4-3 landmark
decision by the Massachusetts Supreme Judicial Court revolutionized the concept of marriage as Massachusetts became the first state to extend marriage rights to gay and lesbian
couples." *Id.* Amicably separated, the couple has not yet filed for divorce. *Id.*

8. Baker v. Vermont, 170 Vt. 194 (1999).

9. *First civil union ends*, THE BARRE MONTPELIER TIMES ARGUS, (Aug. 24, 2006) also available at www.timesargus.com/vermont/news&information.

10. *Id.* Perhaps equally disturbing is the forthright disclosure for divorce made by
the Vermont Freedom to Marry Task Force leader on this occasion. "Beth Robinson,
chairwoman of the Vermont Freedom to Marry Task Force, said the union's end shows
that the law is working the way it was intended to. 'One of the goals was to create a mechanism to protect people in a relationship and create a mechanism to help people dissolve relationships,' she said." *Id.*

11. "A 2006 Boston Globe survey said 7,300 same-sex couples have 'married' and
45 have formally ended their union." Wetzstein, *supra* note 5. Similar information on
Vermont civil dissolutions was not obtainable.

12. Seana Sugrue, *Canadian Marriage Policy: A Tragedy for Children*, REPORT,
INSTITUTE FOR MARRIAGE AND FAMILY CANADA, May 31, 2006 [hereinafter CANADIAN
REPORT].

13. *Id.* at 4. The Report argues that Canada's policies 1)shift the focus from being
duty-driven and child-centered to one that accommodates "antinomian hedonism among
adults;" 2) render parenthood a matter of choice rather than obligation, encouraging the
commodification of children; and 3) invite greater state intrusions into family life over
time. *Id.* at 2-3. "As same-sex couples cannot procreate themselves, if they are to become
parents, a mother-child and/or father-child bond must be severed. Hence, the corollary of
the expectation that same-sex couples ought to be able to be parents is societal acceptance
of biological parents forsaking responsibility toward their children." *Id.* at 4. The Report
cites the opinion in *Halpern v. Canada*, 2003 Can. L. II 26403, the landmark case establishing same sex marriage in Canada, and quite effectively demonstrates how nearly everything the opinion stated as reasons for declaring legal same sex unions are based on the
near complete sacrifice of children for adult desires. *See id.*

14. Kevin G. Alderson, *A Phenomenological Investigation of Same-Sex Marriage*,
13 CANADIAN J. HUMAN SEXUALITY 107 (2004).

15. *Id.* at 108. The study used a very small, self-selected group (some of whom requested to be part of the research) rather than a random sample of couples. The researchers noted the limitation of this methodology. *See id* at 121.

"Furthermore, given that political activists have a huge investment in their cause, it is possible that their responses to questions were influenced by their need to present same-sex marriage in an overly favourable light. This possibility is offset to some extent, however, in that the responses from the nine couples who were not activists did not differ appreciably compared to the activists in their motives to marry and in their descriptions of their relationships." *Id.*

16. *Id.* Additionally, the average age of the participants was much older than a random sample of marriage partners would likely be. "This research appears to be the first phenomenological study of same-sex marriage conducted in either Canada or the U.S. …[I]ts results must be considered cautiously…" *Id.* at 121.

17. After 2 years, *supra* note 3.

18. This is apparent in domestic partnership and same sex marriage claims generally when advocates of these relationships claim they are denied the benefits of marriage. By way of example is the Hawaii case that was the first to really focus on rights of same sex partners, *Baehr v. Miike*, 852 P.2d 44 (Haw. 1993). The opinion in that case at page 59 is instructive because the litany of marital rights sought by the claimants reads much more like a list of benefits of divorce. "The applicant couples correctly contend that the DOH's refusal to allow them to marry on the basis that they are members of the same sex deprives them of access to a multiplicity of rights and benefits that are contingent upon that status. Although it is unnecessary in this opinion to engage in an encyclopedia recitation of all of them, a number of the most salient marital rights and benefits are worthy of note. They include: … (3) control, division, acquisition, and disposition of community property… (4) rights relating to dower, curtsey, and inheritance…(5) rights to notice, protection, benefits…(6) award of child custody and support payments in divorce proceedings…(7) the right to spousal support …(8) the right to enter into premarital agreements…(9) the right to change name… (10) the right to file a nonsupport action…(11) post divorce rights relating to support and property division…(12) the benefit of the spousal privilege and confidential marital communications (13) the benefit of the exemption of real property from attachment or execution…" 852 P.2d at 59.

19. *See generally*, John Witte, Jr., *The Goods and Goals of Marriage*, 76 NOTRE DAME L. REV. 1019 (2001).

20. Helen M. Alvare, *Saying "Yes" Before Saying "I Do": Premarital Sex and Cohabitation as a Piece of the Divorce Puzzle*, 18 N.D.J.L. ETHICS & PUB. POL'Y 7, n.25 (2004(citing Arland Thornton & Linda Young-DeMarco, *Four Decades of Trends in Attitudes Toward Family Issues in the United States: The 1960s Through the 1990s*, 63 J. MARRIAGE & FAM. 1009, 1018, 1020 (2001).

21. *Id.*

22. *See generally* June Carbone, *Back to the Future: The Perils and Promise of a Backward-Looking Jurisprudence*, in RECONCEIVING THE FAMILY: CRITICAL REFLECTIONS ON THE AMERICAN LAW INSTITUTE'S PRINCIPLES OF THE LAW OF FAMILY DISSOLUTION (Robin Fretwell Wilson, ed. Cambridge University Press)(2006).

23. WILLIAM J. DOUGHERTY, ET AL., WHY MARRIAGE MATTERS: TWENTY-ONE CONCLUSIONS FROM THE SOCIAL SCIENCES 6 (2002).

24. *Id.*

25. Thomas Sowell, *Gays are not "entitled" to marriage*, THE VIRGINIAN-PILOT, Aug. 21, 2006, at B9.

26. Mary Schwarz, Press Release, Institute for American Values, available at www.americanvalues.org,, Feb. 14, 2002.

27. *Id.*

28. Dougherty, *supra* note 22, at 24-25, discussing the power of the vow and the permanence of marriage.

29. *See generally* LINDA J. WAITE AND MAGGIE GALLAGHER, THE CASE FOR MARRIAGE 103 (Broadway Books 2000). In their preface and introduction, the authors explain their differing perspectives and views, yet also discuss the importance of working together on this book, and the critical nature of their research.

30. Dougherty, *supra* note 22, at 6.

31. George A. Akerlof, *Men without Children*, 108 THE ECONOMIC J. 287-309 (1998).

32. *Id.* "...[M]en settle down when they get married: if they fail to get married they fail to settle down." *Id.*

33. Steven L. Nock, *The Consequences of Premarital Fatherhood*, 63 AM. SOCIOLOGICAL REV. 250-263 (1998).

34. *Id.* at 255.

35. *Id.*, at 23, discussing the public side of the marriage bargain.

36. Lee A. Lillard and Linda J. Waite, *'Til Death Do Us Part: Marital Disruption and Mortality*, 100 AM. J. SOCIOLOGY 1131-56 (1995). Health is also better for married men. *Id. See also* Don S. Browning, *The Language of Health Versus the Language of Religion: Competing Models of Marriage for the Twenty-First Century*, in MARRIAGE MYTHS AND REVITALIZING MARRIAGE, IN REVITALIZING THE INSTITUTION OF MARRIAGE FOR THE TWENTY-FIRST CENTURY 30-33, Alan J. Hawkins, et. al eds. (Praeger Publishing 2002), discussing marriage as the road to health. Married people "have better psychological and physical health, live longer, have fewer heart attacks, have more satisfying sex, and accumulate more wealth. This is true for both men and women, although marriage is slightly better for men than women." *Id.* at 31. Professor Harold Morowitz of Yale University discovered evidence that divorce seemed to be about as dangerous to a man's health as picking up a pack-a-day cigarette habit. GLENN STANTON, WHY MARRIAGE MATTERS: REASONS TO BELIEVE IN MARRIAGE IN A POST-MODERN SOCIETY 81 (1997), *citing* Harold J. Morowitz, Hiding in the Hammond Report," 10 HOSPITAL PRACTICE 35, 39 (1975).

37. Catherine E. Ross, John Mirowsky, and Karen Goldsteen, *The Impact of the Family on Health: Decade in Review*, 52 J. MARRIAGE & FAM. 1061 (1990),

38. Waite, *supra* note 28, at 48. *See also* Browning, *supra* note 35, at 32. "The health argument is important and has a place in the total cultural task of deepening and reformulating our understanding of marriage." *Id.* at 31.

39. Walter R. Gove, Michael Hughes, and Carolyn Briggs Style, *Does Marriage Have Positive Effects on the Psychological Well-Being of the Individual?* 24 J. HEALTH & SOC. BEHAVIOR 122 (1983)(finding that marital status was the most powerful predictor of the mental health variables considered in this study).

40. Anne E. Barrett, *Marital Trajectories and Mental Health*, 41 J. HEALTH AND SOC. BEHAVIOR 451 (December 2000)(finding that the number of prior losses in marriage (by divorce or widowhood) moderates the health enhancing effect of marriage even in those individuals currently married).

41. Carla Garnett, *The Case for Wedded Bliss, Want a Long, Healthy Life? Get, Stay Married, Says Waite*, NIH Record, Jan. 4, 2005, available at http://www.nih.gov.eres.regent.edu:2048/nihrecord/01_04_2005/story01.htm.

42. *Id.* at 2.

43. Waite, *supra* note 28, at 49. Waite and Gallagher extensively discuss the health benefits of marriage and marriage's power to heal, the risky behavior and wild lives of

single men, the virtues of nagging and the medical consequences of meaninglessness. *Id.* at 49-64.

44. John Leo, *Marriage on the rocks*, U.S. NEWS & WORLD REPORT, Dec. 16, 2002, at 47. Leo states these comments in the negative in a tongue-in-cheek rhetorical style to demonstrate the war on marriage that the ALI promotes in their recent proposals. "At a time when efforts to bolster marriage are gaining some traction, the elites are telling us marriage is defunct and almost any kind of short-term, self-serving relationship will do. Can these people be taken seriously?" *Id.*

45. *See* HARRY D. KRAUSE, FAMILY LAW 58-109 (1998) outlining the requirements for legal entry into marriage; they are 1) one at a time 2) unrelated by blood or affinity 3) of minimum age and 4) of different sexes; *See also* CARL SCHNEIDER AND MARGARET F. BRINING, AN INVITATION TO FAMILY LAW 10-18 (2000) also outlining the legal requirements for entry into marriage; *See also generally* Lynne Marie Kohm, *A Reply to "Principles and Prejudice": Marriage and the Realization that Principles Win Over Political Will*, 22 J. CONT. L. 293 (1996).

46. More than twenty states have amended their constitutions (by voter referendum upheld judicially) to describe that marriage is a legally sanctioned relationship only between a man and a women. Numerous cases have been decided to uphold this definition in various states, such as New York, in *Hernandez v. Robles*, 2006 WL 1835429 (N.Y. July 6, 2006), and Washington, in *Anderson v. King County*, 138 P.3d 963 (Wash. 2006). For further comprehensive information and updates on all the states, see the Coalition for Traditional Values' listing of state legislation at www.Stateline.org and the Alliance Defense Fund record of Defense of Marriage Act state legislation and ensuing litigation at www.domawatch.org.

47. Charles Colson, "Family Matters," BREAKPOINT, Dec. 4, 2002, at 1; *available at* http://www.breakpoint.org/Breakpoint/ChannelRoot/FeaturesGroup/BreakPointComment arie.

48. Allen M. Parkman, *Good Incentives Lead to Good Marriages*," in MARRIAGE MYTHS AND REVITALIZING MARRIAGE, IN REVITALIZING THE INSTITUTION OF MARRIAGE FOR THE TWENTY-FIRST CENTURY 74, Alan J. Hawkins, et. al eds. (Praeger Publishing 2002).

49. William J. Bennett, "Gay Marriage: Not a Very Good Idea," THE WASHINGTON POST, May 21, 1996, at 1. *See also* WILLIAM J. BENNETT, BROKEN HEARTH 101-38 (2003).

50 Professor, attorney and social researcher Camille Williams has argued "that the norm of heterosexual marriage is a necessary—albeit not a sufficient—condition for social equality for women." Camille S. Williams, *Women, Equality, and the Federal Marriage Amendment*, (forthcoming 2006) (manuscript on file with the author).

51. Statistics reveal that one parent is more likely to be the mother. "Since 1970, the percentage of children living in mother-only families has increased from 11 percent to 24 percent in 1997 and was at 23 percent in 2004. ... [During that same period] children living in father-only families increased from 1 percent to 5 percent. The percentage living without either parent remained fairly constant at about 3-4 percent." *Family Structures,* Child Trends DataBank, at www.childtrendsdatabank.org, relying on statistical research from 1970 to 2004 gathered from numerous federal agencies and embodied in a graph entitled "Living Arrangements of Children, 1970-2004."

52. See generally DAVID POPENOE, LIFE WITHOUT FATHER (The Free Press, 1996); See also Michael G. Myers, *Polygamist Eye for the Monogamist Guy: Homosexual Sodomy... Gay Marriage... Is Polygamy Next?* 42 HOUS. L. REV. 1451 (2006) noting that 72.2% of the U.S. Population believes that fatherlessness is the most significant family or

social problem facing America, citing the national Center for Fathering, Fathering America Poll (Jan. 1999). *See also* Krista Taylor, Book note on Jeffrey M. Leving, Keith A. Durham, Ph.D. FATHER'S RIGHTS: HARD HITTING AND FAIR ADVICE FOR EVERY FATHER INVOLVED IN A CUSTODY DISPUTE (1997), 8 J. L. & FAM. STUD. 167 (2006).

> "...[S]o many societal problems can be attributed to the lack of a father's presence in a child's life.
>
> Statistics reveal the serious effect that a father's absence can have on the lives of his children. For example, fatherless children are twice as likely to drop out of school as those living with both parents; fatherless children are eleven times more likely to exhibit violent behavior; fatherless children consistently score lower than normal on math and reading tests; daughters of single parents are 164% more likely to become pregnant before marriage, 53% more likely to marry as teenagers, and 92% more likely to dissolve their own marriages; there is a high correlation between fatherlessness and violence among young men against women; and a daughter's vulnerability to rape and sexual abuse increases by 900% with the absence of a biological father. ...
>
> A father's involvement in his child's life is essential to both the child and to society at large. Fatherlessness has been declared "the most destructive trend of our generation..." *Id.*

53. Social science studies find a very significant correlation between cohabitation and child abuse. Robert E. Rector, Patrick F. Fagan, Kirk A. Johnson, *Marriage: Still the Safest Place for Women and Children*, 1732 HERITAGE FOUNDATION BACKGROUNDER 2-3 (2004), cited in familyfacts.org (July 21, 2006) available at http://www.familyfacts.org.eres.regent.edu:2048/finding=7349.

54. *See* Robert Coombs, Marital Status and Personal Well-Being: A Literature review," 40 FAM. RELATIONS 97-102 (1997); Linda Waite, Does Marriage Matter? 32 DEMOGRAPHY 483-507 (1995); Lois Verbrugge and Donald Balaban, *Patterns of Change, Disability and Well-Being*, 27 MEDICAL CARE S128-S147 (1989); I.M. Joung, et al., *Differences in Self-Reported Morbidity by Marital Status and by Living Arrangement*, 23 INT'L J. EPIDEMIOLOGY 91-97 (1994); Leslie Carbone, *For Better or For Worse*? PHIL. INQ., June 5, 1999, *available at* www.frd.org/get/ar99g2.cfm (Nov. 22, 2002)(stating that children residing in homes with cohabiting couples have more behavior problems); Harold Morowitz, *Hiding in the Hammond Report*, HOSPITAL PRACTICE 39 (August 1975); James Goodwin, et al., *The Effect of Marital Status on Stage, Treatment, and Survival of Cancer Patients*, 258 J. AM. MED. ASSOC. 3152-3130 (1997); Benjamin Malzberg, "Marital Status in Relation to the Prevalence of Mental Disease," 10 PSYCHIATRIC Q. 245-261 (1936); David Williams, et al., *Marital Status and Psychiatric Disorders Among Blacks and Whites*, 33 J. HEALTH & SOC. BEHAVIOR 140-157 (1992); Catherine Malkin and Michael Lamb, *Child Maltreatment: A Test of the Sociobiological Theory*, 25 J. OF COMP. FAM. STUDIES 121-133 (1994); Steven Stack and J. Ross Eshleman, *Marital Status and Happiness: A 17 Nation Study*, 60 J. MARRIAGE & FAM. 527-536 (1998); ROBERT T. MICHAEL, ET AL., SEX IN AMERICA: A DEFINITIVE SURVEY (Little Brown Co., 1994); Randy Page and Galen Cole, *Demographic Predictors of Self-Reported Loneliness in Adults*, 68 PSYCHOLOGICAL REP. 939-945 (1991); Jan Stets, *Cohabiting and Marital Aggression: The Role of Social Isolation*, 53 J. MARRIAGE & FAM. 669-680 (1991); Criminal Victimization in the United States, 1992, U.S. Dept. of Justice, Office of Justice Programs, Bureau of Justice Statistics (March 1994) P.31, NCJ-145125; RONALD ANGEL AND JACQUELINE ANGEL, PAINFUL INHERITANCE: HEALTH AND THE NEW GENERATION OF FATHERLESS

FAMILIES 139, 148 (Madison Univ. of Wisc. Press 1993); Richard Rogers, *Marriage, Sex, and Mortality*, 57 J. MARRIAGE & FAM. 515-26 (1995); Popenoe, *supra* note 54.

In fact, the research is overwhelming that a child is more likely to be abused by mother's partner to whom she is not married. *Id.* SARA MCLANAHAN AND GARY SANDEFUR, GROWING UP WITH A SINGLE PARENT: WHAT HELPS (Harv. U. Press 1994); Deborah Dawson, *Family Structure and Children's Health and Well-Being: Data from the 1988 National Health Interview Survey on Child Health*, 53 J. MARRIAGE & FAM. 573-84 (1991); MICHAEL GOTTFREDSON AND TRAVIS HIRSCHI, A GENERAL THEORY OF CRIME 103 (Stanford U. Press 1990); Richard Koestner, et al., *The Family Origins of Emphatic Concern: A twenty-6 year Longitudinal Study*, 58 J. PERSONALITY & SOC. PSYCH. 709-717 (1990); E. Mavis Hetherington, *Effects of Father Absence on Personality Development in Adolescent Daughters*, 7 DEV. PSYCH. 313-326 (1972); IRWIN GARFINKEL AND SARA MCLANAHAN, SINGLE MOTHER'S AND THEIR CHILDREN: A NEW AMERICAN DILEMMA 30-31 (Wash. DC: Urban Inst. Press 1986); DAVID ELLWOOD, POOR SUPPORT: POVERTY IN THE AMERICAN FAMILY 46 (Basic Books 1988); Ronald J. Angel and Jacqueline Wombey, *Single Motherhood and Children's Health*, 29 J. HEALTH AND SOC. BEHAVIOR 38-52 (1988); L. Remez, *Children Who Don't Live With Both Parents Face Behavioral Problems*, FAM. PLANNING PERSPECTIVES (Jan/Feb 1992); JUDITH WALLERSTEIN AND SANDRA BLAKESLEE, SECOND CHANCES: MEN AND WOMEN A DECADE AFTER DIVORCE (Ticknor & Fields 1990); Nicholas Zill, Donna Morrison and Mary Jo Coiro, *Long-term Effects of Parental Divorce on Parent-Child Relationships, Adjustment, and Achievement in Young Adulthood*, 7 J. FAM. PSYCH. 91-103 (1993).

55. "Married mothers are less likely to suffer abuse than never-married mothers. In fact, even when the very high rates of abuse of separated and divorce mothers are added into the statistic, the rates of abuse among ever-married mothers are still the lowest of all—lower than the never married and than the cohabiting mothers. Among mothers who are currently or even have been married, the rate they are abused is 38.5 per 1,000 mothers. Among mothers who have never been married the rate is 81 per 1,000 mothers." *Id.*

56. Canadian Report, *supra* note 10, at 2, citing numerous studies.

57. *See* Martha Ertman, *Reconstructing Marriage: An InterSEXional Approach*, 75 DENV. U. L. REV. 1215 (1998); MARTHA FINEMAN, THE NEUTERED MOTHER, THE SEXUAL FAMILY, AND OTHER TWENTIETH CENTURY TRAGEDIES (1995).

58. Canadian Report, *supra* note 10, at 5.

59. *See* MARSHALL KIRK AND HUNTER MADSEN, AFTER THE BALL 280-347 (1990). It is not unfair to surmise that this gap widens when the same comparison is made between the average homosexual lifestyle and heterosexuals who are married to each other due to the stability cited herein that surrounds marriage generally.

60. ANDREW SULLIVAN, VIRTUALLY NORMAL 202-03 (2003), stating that heterosexuals will have to develop a greater "understanding of the need for extramarital outlets between two men than between a man and a woman...The truth is, homosexuals are not entirely normal; and to flatten their varied and complicated lives into a single, moralistic model is to miss what is essential and exhilarating about their otherness."

61. *Cohabitation, Marriage, Divorce, and Remarriage in the United Sates*, Series Report 23, Number 22 (PHS), at http://www.cdc.gov/nchs/data/series/sr_23/sr23_022 .pdf.

62. *Id.*

63. Alderson, *supra* note 12, at 114, 118. The study also found that participants felt marriage "symbolized monogamy for most of them." *Id.*

64. *Id.* at 116. "'Oh, it was love at first sight, it better have been love at first sight! It was sex at first sight.' (Sheldon, age 55)." *Id.*

65. David Popenoe & Barbara Dafoe Whitehead, *Should We Live Together? What Young Adults Need to Know about Cohabitation Before Marriage: a Comprehensive Review of Recent Research* (Rutgers University National Marriage Project 2d ed. 2002) *available at* http://marriage.rutgers.edu/Publications/swlt2pdf (March 31, 2004).

66. *See e.g.* Jay D. Teachman, et al., *The Changing Demography of America's Families*, 62 J. MARRIAGE & THE FAM. 1234 (Nov. 2000).

67. Women still only earn 76% of what men earn. See *White House Focuses on Gap in Gender Pay*, ATLANTA J. & ATLANTA CONST., Apr. 8, 1999, at A14, available in 1999 WL 3761237; *The Gender Wage Ratio: Women's and Men's Earnings*, Institute for Women's Policy Research, www.iwpr.org (August 2005) stating that women earned 76.5 percent as much as men in 2004.

68. Karen Laing, *Doing the Right Thing: Cohabiting Parents, Separation and Child Contact*, 20 INT'L J. L. POL'Y & FAM. 169 (2006)(noting increase in poverty levels for women and children).

69. *See* Maria Foscarinis, *Realizing Domestic Social Justice Through International Human Rights, Advocating for the Human Right to Housing: Notes from the United States*, 30 N.Y.U. REV. L. & SOC. CHANGE 447 (2006)(noting the concern for disproportionate numbers of single parent families headed by women who live below the poverty line, and that one in four children under six therefore live in poverty); *See also generally* Tanisha L. Jackson, *TANF and its Implications on the Autonomy of Indigent Single Mothers*, 11 WM. & MARY J. WOMEN & L. 153 (Fall, 2004); Taylor Flynn, *What Does Oakley Tell Us About the Failures of Constitutional Decision-Making?* 26 W. NEW ENG. L. REV. 1 (2004)(noting a disproportionate number of single parents living in poverty are women).

Furthermore, divorced women comprise the majority of impoverished single parents. *See* Harriet Shaklee, *Divorce and Children: What Hurts, What Helps?*, at http://www.agls.uidaho.edu/ccc/CCC% 20Families/Research/divorce.htm. (visited Mar. 17, 2003)(noting that after a divorce, the mother and child normally receive half of the former family income although it costs more to raise a child in a one-parent household than in a two-parent household). *See generally* Jim McKeever, *2000 Census: East Syracuse Is Splitsville--They Live Happily Ever After in Pompey, Says the Tally of Marriages, Divorces*, POST-STANDARD (Syracuse, NY), June 18, 2002, at A1 (reporting that after divorce many women become single parents and fall below the poverty level).

70. "Older women have a higher poverty rate (12.5%) than older men (7.3%) in 2003... The highest poverty rates (40.8%) were experienced by older Hispanic women who lived alone." *A Profile of Older Americans: 2004*, Administration on Aging, U.S. Department of Health and Human Services, at 11 (based on data from Current Population Survey, Annual Social and Economic Supplement, "Income, Poverty, and Health Insurance Coverage in the United Sates: 2003, at 60, August 2004, U.S. Bureau of the Census).

71. *See generally* Jane Waldfogel, *Understanding the "Family Gap" in Pay for Women with Children*, 12 J. ECONOMIC PERSPECTIVES 137 (Winter 1998).

72. Daniel T. Lichter, Deborah Roempke Graefe, J. Brian Brown, *Is Marriage a Panacea? Union Formation Among Economically Disadvantaged Unwed Mothers*, Social Problems, 50 Caliber 60, Feb. 2003, available at http://caliber.ucpress.net/doi/abs /10.1525/sp.2003.50.1.60.

73. Daniel T. Lichter, Diane K. McLaughlin, and David C. Ribar, *Welfare and the Rise in Female-Headed Families*, 103 AM. J. SOCIOLOGY 112, at 115 (July 1997)(referring to a broad microeconomic study by Becker in 1981).

74. A woman's risk of being abused is elevated for women who cohabit. *See generally* Judy A. Van Wyk, Michael L. Benson, Greer L. Fox, and Alfred DeMaris, *Detangling Individual-, Partner-, and Community-Level Correlates of Partner Violence*, 49 CRIME AND DELINQUENCY 412 (July 2003). A Swedish study proved that children who live in single parent homes are at a greater risk for health disadvantages compared to children in two-parent households. Gunilla Ringback Weitoft, Anders Hjern, Bengt Haglund, and Mans Rosen, *Mortality, Severe Morbidity, and Injury in Children Living with Single Parents in Sweden: A Population-Based Study*, 361 THE LANCET 289 (Jan. 2003). That risk increases with cohabitation. *Id.*

75. Lisa K. Waldner-Haugrud, Linda Vaden Gratch & Brian Magruder, *Victimization and Perpetration Rates of Violence in Gay and Lesbian Relationships: Gender Issues Explored*, 12 VIOLENCE & VICTIMS 173 (1997).

76. Reported rates of abuse in lesbian couples ranged from 30% to 75% depending on definition of violence, timeframe and sampling techniques. *Id.* at 173-75, citing P.A. Brand & A.H. Kidd, *Frequency of physical aggression in heterosexual and female homosexual dyads*, 59 PSYCHOLOGICAL REPORTS 1307 (1986)(30% report being abused in lesbian relationships); M.J. Bologna, C.K.Waterman & L. J. Dawson, *Violence in gay male and lesbian relationships: Implications for practitioner and policymakers*, paper presented at Third National Conference for Family Violence Researchers, Durham, NH (July 1987)(50% of lesbians in relationships abused); R. Schlit, G. Lie & M. Montagne, *Substance use as a correlated of violence intimate lesbian relationships*, 19 J. HOMOSEXUALITY 51 (1990)(38% lesbian partner abuse); G. Lie & S. Gentlewarrior, *Intimate violence in lesbian relationships: Discussion of survey findings and practice implications*, 15 J . SOCIAL SERV. RES. 41 (1991)(52% lesbian abuse). *See also* Mark A. Yarhouse, *When Clients Seek Treatment for Same-Sex Attraction: Ethical Issues in the 'Right to Choose' Debate*, 35 PSYCHOTHERAPY 248, 250 (1998).

77. David Island and Patrick Letellier, *Men Who Beat the Men Who Love Them*, National Lesbian & Gay Domestic Violence Network Newsletter, cited at Culture and Family Institute, Concerned Women for America, Mar. 12, 2003, at http://www.cultureandfamily.org/articledisplay.asp?id=3521&department=CFI.

78. *See* D. Duncan, *Prevalence of sexual assault victimization among heterosexual and gay/lesbian university students*, 66 PSYCHOLOGICAL REPS. 65 (1990)(reporting that approximately 31& of lesbians had sex against their will compared to 18% of heterosexual women. Approximately 12% of gay men were forced to have sex compared to 4% of heterosexual men.)

79. Alvare, *supra* note 18, at 28 (citing Jay Teachman, *Premarital Sex, Cohabitation, and the Risk of Subsequent Marital Dissolution among Women*, 65 J. MARRIAGE & FAM. 444, 445 (2003).

80. *Id.* at 11-12.

81. *Id.* at 12-13. Marriage also reduces child poverty, and boys from intact married homes are less likely to commit crimes. *Id.* at 9, 15-16.

82. *Id.* at 8.

83. *Id.* at 17.

84. *See generally* Maggie Gallagher and Joshua K. Baker, *Do Moms and Dads Matter? Evidence From the Social Sciences on Family Structure and the Best Interests of the Child*, 4 MARGINS 161 (2004).

85. Larry L. Bumpass and Hsien-Hen Lu, *Trends in Cohabitation and Implications for Children's Family Contacts in the United States*, 54 POPULATION STUD. 29 (2000).

86. Mark R. Rank, Thomas A. Hirschl, *The Economic Risk of Childhood in America: Estimating the Probability of Poverty Across the Formative Years*, 61 J. MARRIAGE & FAM. 1058, 1059-67 (Nov. 1999).

87. *Id.* at 1058.

88. *The Effects of Divorce on America*, HERITAGE FOUNDATION, *at* http://www.heritage.org/liobrary/backgrounder/bg1373html, at 626.

89. MARY ANN MASON, FROM FATHER'S PROPERTY TO CHILDREN'S RIGHTS 124 (1994).

90. Helen R. Weingarten, *Marital Status and Well-being: A National Study Comparing First-married, Currently Divorced, and Remarried Adults*, J. MARRIAGE AND THE FAM. 653, 659 (August 1985).

91. Megan M. Sweeney and Allan V. Horwitz, *Infidelity, Initiation, and the Emotional Climate of Divorce: Are There Implications for Mental Health?* 42 J. HEALTH & SOC. BEHAVIOR 293 (2001). Reduced depression is found when divorce is initiated by individuals with unfaithful spouses, but divorce is associated with increased depression when there is an absence of spousal infidelity. *Id.* These results seem to indicate that marriage is good if it is long term, and divorce is worse if initiated for a reason other than infidelity.

92. Stacy R. Aronson, Aletha C. Huston, *The Mother-Infant Relationship in Single, Cohabiting, and Married Families: A Case for Marriage?* 18 J. FAM. PSYCH. 5 (2004).

93. Lynn D. Wardle, *Parental Infidelity and the "no-Harm" Rule in Custody Litigation*, 52 CATH. U.L. REV. 81, 124 (2002) (CITING JUDITH S. WALLERSTEIN & JOAN B. KELLY, SURVIVING THE BREAKUP: HOW CHILDREN AND PARENTS COPE WITH DIVORCE (1980); JUDITH S. WALLERSTEIN & SANDRA BLAKESLEE, SECOND CHANCES: MEN, WOMEN, AND CHILDREN A DECADE AFTER DIVORCE (1989)).

94. Mason, *supra* note 92, at 171. Men and third parties prevail in a high percentage of cases, as many judges view the best case scenario for children in the event of divorce to be joint custody. Many feminist legal theory scholars claim the mother-child dyad is the most critically significant relationship in the family (*see e.g.* Fineman, *supra* note 60), arguing for a presumption for mother custody under at least a tender years concept. See *Judging the Best Interests of the Child: Judges' Accounts of the Tender Years Doctrine*, 38 LAW & SOC'Y REV. 769 (Dec. 2004)(showing statistics that report the persistence of a maternal preference among family court judges). "Contrary to feminist theory, however, gender is not linked to care-oriented values." Hong Xiao, *Class, Gender, and parental Values in the 1990s*, 14 GENDER & SOCIETY 785 (Dec. 2000).

95. JUDITH WALLERSTEIN ET AL., THE UNEXPECTED LEGACY OF DIVORCE: A TWENTY-FIVE YEAR LANDMARK STUDY (Hyperion 2000).

96. Linda J. Waite, Foreword, *Marriage Myths and Revitalizing Marriage*, in REVITALIZING THE INSTITUTION OF MARRIAGE FOR THE TWENTY-FIRST CENTURY ix, Alan J. Hawkins, et. al eds. (Praeger Publishing 2002) ("Cohabiting couples get most of the same economies of scale as married couples. But cohabiting couples almost always marry or split up within a few years, economies of scale notwithstanding.")

Without domestic partnerships, however, we find two extremes: cohabitants have little to no rights on one extreme; or they have duties imposed upon and imputed to them as if they are married, when they have chosen not to marry. Cynthia Grant Bowman, *Legal Treatment of Cohabitation in the United States*, 26 LAW & POL'Y 119 (Jan.2004).

97. Waite, *supra* note 28, at 37. "Cohabitation is not 'just like marriage' but rather an emerging social lifestyle with a different set of social meanings, which generally serves different purposes. Contemporary cohabitations do not take on the protective coloration of marriage but flaunt their differences." *Id.*

98. *Id.* at 37-38, citing DENNIS K. ORTHNER, THE FAMILY IN TRANSITION 93-118.

99. In the United States, unmarried cohabitation has been on the rise since 1960. At that time, only 500,000 people lived together outside of marriage. By 1995 that number had grown exponentially to 4 million. Couples cohabiting with children were at 250,000 on 1960 whereas that number in 1995 appeared to peak at just under 2.5 million. PAUL AMATO AND ALAN BOOTH, A GENERATION AT RISK 112 (1997). A slight drop in couples with children cohabiting occurred in 1995 when that figure dropped from around 2.4 million to approximately 2.3 million. *Id.*

100. S. Edwards, *Economic Resources Lag Among Children Whose Parents are Co-habiting*, 29 FAM. PLANNING PERSPECTIVES 143 (May-June 1997).

101. *Id.*

102. *Id.*

103. *The Effects of Divorce on America, supra* note 91.

104. *Id.* at 23.

105. *Id.*

106. Wetzstein, *supra* note 5. "Of course, we don't take any pleasure in the sadness of any individual or couple, and I don't believe one couple's experience necessarily proves anything,' said Peter Sprigg of the Family Research Council. But there is research indicating that homosexual relationships are less likely to be monogamous or lifelong than heterosexual relationships, he said. 'I think it demonstrates again why we are so concerned for children in inherently unstable relationships," said Jan LaRue of Concerned Women for America. Recent court decisions have recognized that homosexual unions 'are not the equivalent of heterosexual marriage' and 'it's better for children to be in stable, heterosexual marriage with a mom and a dad,' she said." *Id.*

107. Canadian Report, *supra* note 10, at 7. "The demise of child-centered marriage is thus not only a tragedy for children; it is a tragedy for all Canadians." *Id.* at 11.

108. *Id.* at 7.

CHAPTER 6
SAME-SEX MARRIAGE AND THE RIGHTS OF THE CHILD

Louis DeSerres[1]
Preserve Marriage—Protect Children's Rights (Canada)

I.   Introduction

Is there a more natural, self-evident and fundamental birth right for a child than to have both a mother and a father and to be raised by them?

For the first time in over 150 years, the fight for human rights, which has led to the abolition of slavery, the emancipation of women and civil rights for African-Americans, is now in the process of moving backwards. With same-sex marriage we are now taking away the fundamental rights of our most vulnerable citizens, children. How can this be?

This paper takes inspiration from the debates in France and in Canada surrounding same-sex marriage. Both countries reached fundamentally different conclusions. The rationale and directions taken by both countries illustrate two different models to same-sex marriage and same-sex parenting. How could two mature countries reach such different conclusions?

France has been at the forefront of the worldwide movement to recognize the rights of the child. It signed the 1989 U.N. Convention on the Rights of the Child [2] and has actively sought to abide by its principles. By 1994, France set out child centered rules and regulations with regards to medically assisted reproduction, including a prohibition on surrogacy. [3] After lengthy discussions, further amendments were added in 2004, including elevating human cloning to the status of a crime against humanity.[4]

Since then, confronted with pressing demands to legalize same-sex marriage, it established a Parliamentary commission that studied the issue for a year and submitted its report early in 2006.[5] In its conclusions, the Commission reiterated France's rejection of same-sex marriage as well as adoption and access to medically assisted reproduction for same-sex couples, explaining that "the child now has rights and the aspirations of adults can no longer be systematically placed ahead of respect for these rights." [6]

Canada legalized same-sex marriage in 2005 [7] following several provincial court of appeals rulings. These rulings relied on implied equality guarantees contained in its Charter of Rights and Freedoms. While the Charter does not mention sexual orientation in its equality provisions, Canada's Supreme Court had chosen to include it in 1995.[8] Over the years, adult homosexual rights have increased in weight to the point where they now trump children's rights and best interests. What is striking about Canada is that, while it is a signatory to the Convention on the Rights of the Child [9], it has chosen, particularly during the debates on same-sex marriage, to ignore its essential features, leading to same-sex legislation that most probably violates at least two articles of the Convention:

> Article 3: "In all actions concerning children, whether undertaken by public or private social welfare institutions, courts of law, administrative authorities or legislative bodies, the best interests of the child shall be a primary consideration." [10]
> Article 7: Each child "shall have, as far as possible, the right to know and be cared for by his or her parents". France refers to these as filiative rights. [11]

Same-sex marriage is part of a larger set of issues directly affecting children, namely adoption and medically assisted reproduction. One cannot separate these issues. As French parliamentarians discovered from their travels to various countries, "the countries that have made marriage accessible to same-sex couples have all authorized adoption by such couples and developed systems of assisted conception – even surrogate gestation – to enable such couples to have children." [12]

II.   The Rights of the Child

The history of constitutional law "is the story of the extension of constitutional rights and protections to people once ignored or excluded." [13]

Rights are often based on the notion that their denial or absence is harmful. For example, the Canadian Charter of Rights and Freedoms states that "Everyone has the right to life, liberty and security of the person and the right not to be deprived thereof except in accordance with the principles of fundamental justice."[14]

Thus, one way to measure the validity of restricting marriage to heterosexual couples is to examine the harm to children when heterosexual (dual gender) marriage is replaced by same-sex (genderless) marriage.[15] Heterosexual marriage offers a multitude of unique benefits to children, all of which are lost when marriage loses its dual gendered nature.

Heterosexual marriage (and the parenting that flows from it)[16] protects the rights of children in fourteen ways.

Heterosexual marriage provides that a child will know and be raised by his own parents.[17] Every child has a double origin, being created from both a father and a mother. Nature does not create fatherless or motherless children.[18] Yet same-sex marriage, in conjunction with new reproductive technologies, endorses and institutionalizes the creation of fatherless or motherless children. This occurs because the right to marry has traditionally included the right to found a family.[19] Same-sex marriage confers a right to reproduction on same-sex couples, even though they cannot naturally reproduce. Thus, when two men, desiring to create a child, rely on the services of a surrogate mother, the child is taken away from his mother at birth and is given a second father instead. When two women want to create a child, they often rely on an anonymous biological father (anonymous sperm donor) who has no interest in the child and who, for all practical purposes, does not exist for the child.

Since the legalization of same-sex marriage in Canada, visible evidence of this is now showing up on birth certificates, the core document providing the child with his or her legally recognized identity. Some Canadian children now have two mothers listed on their birth certificates and no father, while others may have two fathers listed with no mother.[20] Such birth certificates deny part of the child's identity dealing with his dual gender biological origin. They also reflect the permanent separation between the child and at least one of his or her biological parents.

When asked by a Canadian legislator about same-sex-marriage: "surely with this piece of legislation we're not throwing away anything. Aren't we extending rights [for gays and lesbians]?" Margaret Somerville, Professor of Law at the McGill Center for Medicine, Ethics and Law answered: "No, you're absolutely throwing away a child's right to a mother and a father."[21] The child's right to both his mother and father is best protected by heterosexual marriage.

Research demonstrates conclusively that heterosexual marriage serves children's best interests.[22] For example, as the foundation of the procreative process, the complementary characteristics of mothers and fathers have been and continue to be well documented. The presence of both mother and father also provides an example, a pattern, for the next generation.

There is no such evidence for same-sex marriage.

The French National Assembly Commission was presented with:

> a list of studies on children brought up by persons of the same sex. The conclusion, based on these studies, was that there were no negative effects on children. These studies' scientific basis and the representativeness of the population samples studied were widely criticized and disputed at the hearings... the lack of objectivity in this area is blatant.[23]

Furthermore, there is no data as yet concerning the long term well being of children conceived with donor sperm, a donor egg, or a surrogate mother, or combinations thereof.

It is incumbent upon legislators to ensure that children are protected. For example, we require that drug companies, relying on sound science, prove the safety of new drugs before approving them. We recall baby strollers when even just a small number of children get hurt. In its Report on the Family and the Rights of Children, The French National Assembly Commission endorses the statement of an expert witness: "Ultimately, while there is absolutely no reason to doubt the emotional and childrearing qualities of homosexual parents, at the same time we do not yet know all the effects on the formation of the adopted child's psychological identity. As long as doubt persists, however slight, is it not in the child's best interests to apply the precautionary principle to adoption, as to other areas?"[24]

Heterosexual marriage provides the child with a natural network of care and support from his immediate and extended biological family including parents, brothers and sisters, aunts and uncles, grandparents, etc. In a world where increasing numbers of parents, even biological parents, already "divorce" from their own children and abandon their responsibilities, France nevertheless favors the permanent nature of biological filiation over fleeting emotions and unstable relationships.[25]

Same-sex marriage denies these benefits for the child. It is not grounded on biological ties and seeks to replace them. William Eskridge explains that same-sex marriage…

> involves the reconfiguration of family, de-emphasizing blood, gender, and kinship ties and emphasizing the value of interpersonal commitment. In our legal culture the linchpin of family law has been the marriage between a man and a woman who have children through procreative sex. Gay experience with 'families we choose' delinks family from gender, blood, and kinship. Gay families of choice are relatively ungendered, raise children that are biologically unrelated to one or both parents, and often form no more than a shadowy connection between the larger kinship groups.[26]

Heterosexual marriage sets the foundation for the child to have the same biological, legal and care giving parents.[27] While it is true that most but not all marriages produce this result, same-sex marriage does not and cannot.

At its foundation, same-sex marriage is based on a gender imbalance (two women and no man, or two men and no woman) and the absence of at least one biological parent. These structural flaws have important consequences. Thus, to create a child, a third party of the opposite sex is required. This third party progenitor is often anonymous right from conception (anonymous sperm donor) or later, disappears after the birth of the child (surrogate mother). When this happens, the child is also deprived of his right to know and be raised by both his progenitor parents (see point 1).

This biological imbalance can also be the source of numerous tensions and conflicts that are not likely to benefit the child: the biological parent might feel more "legitimate"; the non biological parent may feel unequal because of his/her lack of biological bond with the child; the child may sense a greater affinity with his biological parent rather than his non-biological parent; the non-marital biological parent, when he/she is known, may find him/herself in competition with the non-biological married parent; he or she may challenge his/her "non-parent" status; in a reconstituted family, the non-biological married partner may seek for recognition as a third parent. In simple terms, legally involving increasing numbers of adults multiplies opportunities for conflict and can greatly magnify the complexity of these conflicts,[28] not to mention the deleterious consequences on children.[29]

The existence and/or inclusion of third parties resulting from this imbalance can even lead to legal recognition, potentially complicating the life of the child.[30] In early 2008, a court in Ontario recognized the non-biological lesbian spouse as a third parent for a child born from her partner and another man and ordered this third parent to be listed on the child's birth certificate. In this case, all three adults were in agreement. This will not always be the case.

There are also subtle but significant differences between male and female same-sex reproduction and their consequences on children. When two women decide to have a child, one of them is usually the biological mother, carrying the child through pregnancy. But when two men want a child, they must rely on a surrogate mother. France does not allow surrogates.[31] When asked to reconsider, the recent National Assembly report maintained the prohibition because "without it, the door would be open to abuses of all sorts and even to situations like those that can arise in California, where the birth of a child can involve up to five people: a sperm donor, an ovocyte donor, a gestatrix and an intended parent couple."[32] Taking a child away from the mother that nurtured him for nine months denies the bond that grows between mother and child during pregnancy and creates an emotional discontinuity for the child, weakening his sense of security.

There is another critically important reason relating to the dignity and worth of the child. While procreation within man-woman marriage clearly sets who the child's parents are, along with their parental responsibilities towards the child, the multiplication of potential parents introduces the very real possibility of parents opting in or opting out of their parental responsibilities without any objective consideration for the needs or rights of the child.[33]

For example, in Quebec, when two married lesbians have a child, they are automatically recognized as "mother" and "father" on the child's birth certificate. But before the child is even conceived, the intended parents get to choose what kind of father their child will have, if any. If they opt for an anonymous sperm donor, the father will simply not exist for the child. If they opt for in vitro fertilization from a male acquaintance, the child might get to know his biological father (there is no guarantee), but his biological father has no legally recognized filiation or responsibility towards the child. If they opt for sexual intercourse, then the male progenitor has the additional option to claim his paternity up to one year after the birth of the child.[34] Thus, during the child's first year of existence, the male progenitor, for any reason whatsoever and at his total discretion, may opt out of any responsibility towards the child. And finally, if the male progenitor exercises his paternity rights, the child will have three parents, recognized by law.

All these options are at the complete discretion of the intended parents, without rational consideration for the needs and rights of the child. This "a la carte" parenting is demeaning towards the dignity and worth of the child, creates tensions, encourages irresponsibility, fragments parental roles and is discriminatory, in that the lesbian mothers may choose to deny the child the male figure that his father represents.

In man-woman marriage, there is no such opting out. By default, the child has his two biological parents with well defined, clearly recognized and socially reinforced responsibilities. Biology, legal filiation and care-giving responsibilities unite for the greater benefit of the child.

Heterosexual marriage greatly reduces the risk that a child or his constituent parts will become commodities deprived of human dignity. Same-sex marriage increases those risks as it creates a new market for assisted reproduction, adding to the demand for sperm, eggs, surrogate mothers and adopted children. This can easily lead to the commoditization of human life where some of the participants have little regard for the rights of children. This is similar to the bygone era when slaves were traded as property.

In France, surrogacy is viewed as an assault on human dignity, turning both the mother's gestational capacity and the child's bonds of filiation into objects that can be traded outside socially controlled processes like adoption. This creates a situation where filiation can be brokered between individuals, without regards to the rights or best interests of the child.[35]

In Canada, giving eggs is legal but selling them is strictly forbidden by law and subject to substantial penalties. Increasing demand and the government's failure to enforce its own regulations is allowing an illegal market to flourish. Early in 2006, a Montreal investigative reporter revealed that he had located six women offering eggs for free but who, over the course of discussions, ended up demanding payments of up to $10,000.[36]

Indications of an increase in demand can be clearly seen in the U.S., where discussion of gay rights, same-sex marriage, civil unions and the militancy of gay activists have had an impact on the homosexual population's perceptions about having children. Between 2002 and 2006, the proportion of lesbians wanting to have children has gone from 18% to two thirds while the proportion for gay men has increased from 5% to one third. According to those conducting the survey, "People are saying they're more comfortable with their sexuality, that they have a right to a life partner. And along with that -- if they have a loving home -- why not a child?" [37]

Infertility drives the demand for sperm, ova and surrogacy. While only a minority of heterosexual couples is infertile, with same-sex couples, the proportion is 100%.[38]

Heterosexual marriage provides the child with a multi-generational sense of identity. At its first level, part of the child's identity derives from his biological parents. Such factors as likeness, personality, talents and abilities, personal history, all contribute to the child's identity. But his sense of identity goes much further. In testimony to Canadian parliamentarians, Margaret Somerville explained: "In conclusion, children and their descendants who don't know their genetic origin cannot sense themselves as embedded in a web of people past, present, and in the future through whom they can trace the thread of life's passage down the generations to them. As far as we know, humans are the only animals where experiencing a genetic relationship is integral to their sense of themselves. We do know the effect of eliminating this experience--which we do know through reproductive technologies and adoption--is harmful to children, to biological parents, to families, and to society.

"Same-sex marriage puts in jeopardy the rights of children to know and experience their genetic heritage in their lives and withdraws society's recognition of its importance to them, their wider family, and society itself. Finally, same-sex marriage also opens up the wider, unprecedented question of what is ethically required in terms of respect for the mode of transmission of human life."[39]

She adds: "There are obligations on society not to create genetic orphans, which is what we would be doing. I think we have to recognize a right to natural genetic origins and genetic identity. We have to recognize the full scope of the harms we do and the ethical problems, and first we have to be activated by a principle that's called non-maleficence--first do no harm."[40]

A child born from heterosexual parents has access to his own genetic heritage (DNA) for medical and identification purposes. Genetic research for medical purposes is expanding rapidly. Its uses are also extending into other non-medical areas. For example, DNA testing is increasingly used to establish paternity or prove family relationships.[41] Within heterosexual marriage (and parenting), access to parents' DNA is usually easily obtained and immediate, even in most cases of parental breakup. But for the majority of children born within same-sex unions, this is not the case. Some jurisdictions have laws requiring that DNA samples of anonymous sperm donors be kept, but accessing these samples can be complex. In Quebec, for example, a court order is required and can be granted only when there is a risk of "serious harm", and then the DNA is only made available, confidentially, to the treating physician.[42] What happens if these records are lost? What about costs and timeliness? What if the child has moved to a different jurisdiction?

Constitutionally defining marriage between one man and one woman strengthens the judicial protection accorded to children; without it, children are inadequately protected. Absent a marriage amendment defining marriage as only between one man and one woman in its constitution, Massachusetts' court ruling stated that "the Commonwealth... has failed to identify any constitutionally adequate reason for denying civil marriage to same-sex couples."[43] It is interesting to note that had the Commonwealth raised the issue of children's bonding rights as a constitutional issue, the courts would have been hard pressed to ignore them, and might have ruled differently.

A brief history of how same-sex marriage was adopted in Canada illustrates how children are inadequately protected. The Canadian Charter of Rights and Freedoms (a constitutional document) was adopted in 1982 to protect individual rights and minorities. Children, the most vulnerable group in society, were ignored.[44] This was not an omission by design or malevolence, but simply because it was considered a given that children would always benefit from the protection of the law. Later, sexual orientation was added by the courts to the list of groups needing protection (1995).[45] When judges ruled that gays and lesbians were discriminated against because they were prevented from marrying a person of the same gender, they focused only on adults' implied Charter rights, leaving children voiceless. Today, sexual orientation, which was specifically excluded from the Charter by its framers, now trumps the rights of the child.

Just before submitting legislation legalizing same-sex marriage, the Canadian government asked the Supreme Court of Canada to answer four questions.[46] In its response, while the Supreme Court ruled that same-sex marriage did not violate the Charter, it refused to rule whether man-woman marriage violated the Charter. It also completely ignored children.

Unless a child's right to a father and a mother is affirmed by legislators, same-sex marriage will erase it. It is interesting to note that even Canada's Prime Minister, when introducing legislation to legalize same-sex marriage, said in its support: "If we do not protect a right, then we deny it."[47] He, like many adults, obviously had not thought about children!

Allowing same-sex marriage to prevail creates a precedent for further erosion of children's rights. After various provincial courts of appeal in Canada had ordered same-sex marriage, Canada's Parliament adopted national same-sex marriage legislation that now applied to all provinces and territories.[48] This legislation simply reaffirmed court decisions by judges who did not have the tools required to adequately defend the rights of all children when confronted with equality claims on the part of a small number of adults. Not only that, but cognizant of certain inherent potential contradictions in the new law, the bonding rights of all Canadian children and their natural parents were diluted, as will be seen later in point number 10.

In the U.K., after the British government had approved same-sex civil unions that virtually replicate same-sex marriage except in name only, the British health Minister later announced that the government will replace the "need for a father" with the "need for a family" in IVF cases before the end of 2006.[49] This new measure, still under discussion in 2008, would strip the child of his right to a father.

Heterosexual marriage protects the filiative rights of all children. Same-sex marriage legislation jeopardizes them for all children. The reason is quite straightforward. Since both partners in a same-sex marriage cannot both be the biological parents of their children, the biologically-based parental filiation must be replaced with another parental concept. After the courts imposed same-sex marriage in Canada, Parliament adopted formal legislation making it applicable across Canada and changed the definition of parent from (biological) parent to legal parent for all children. According to the Institute for the Study of Marriage, Law and Culture, this erasure of the biological link to the child's parent affects all children, not just those in same-sex relationships.[50] [51]

Whether this is done explicitly or not, unhinging filiation from its biological mooring is leading to new and more fragile concepts like psychological parenting that could affect any child. In a recent U.K. court case, two young girls were removed from their biological mother and given to her former lesbian partner. The judge concluded by saying that "We have moved into a world where norms that seemed safe 20 or more years ago no longer run. ... But in the eyes of the child, the natural parent may be a non-biological parent who, by virtue of long settled care, has become the child's psychological parent." [52]

Legally defining heterosexual marriage is an absolutely essential first step in protecting the bonding rights and best interests of the child. This is particularly important in countries where adults pursue their human rights challenges to the detriment of the rights of children. As was seen in Massachusetts, Canada and even in the U.K., failure to constitutionally affirm heterosexual marriage jeopardizes the bonding rights of all children.

Adoption of marriage laws but preferably constitutional amendments would contribute to protecting children's bonding rights. Furthermore, a preamble to a constitutional amendment would reinforce these rights by highlighting that heterosexual marriage is the only institution that can guarantee the right of the child to know and be raised by his/her natural parents. Interestingly, France's Civil Code "already contains all the elements of a definition of marriage, which are clearly and consistently applied by all jurisdictions, even though the Code does not provide a definition as such." [53] In Canada and in Massachusetts, that is clearly not the case.

Heterosexual marriage laws alone are insufficient to ensure adequate protection for children's bonding rights and best interests. In addition to marriage laws, these rights need to be affirmed in the context of other laws on adoption and assisted reproduction.

For instance, France refuses to legalize adoption by same sex couples because it is a back door to circumventing laws meant to protect the filiative rights of children. Same-sex couples could circumvent French prohibitions against medically assisted reproduction by traveling to another country, coming back with a child, and then having the non-biological parent adopt the child. Therefore, unless the state adopts a coherent and comprehensive set of laws, children will not be adequately protected. [54]

The absence of restrictions on same-sex adoptions and medically assisted reproduction for same-sex couples can also lead to near automatic legalization of same-sex marriage. This is essentially what happened in Quebec when judges imposed same-sex marriage after highlighting that Quebec's civil unions resembled marriage in almost every feature.

Heterosexual marriage provides a simple and understandable set of norms. France explains: "Family law, particularly with regard to filiation, has in some countries undergone profound reforms that have radically altered family configurations. In this connection, Quebec, which the Mission visited, has been especially imaginative in putting in place a system of filiation that achieves an unrivalled complexity."[55] Rather, France believes that laws should not simply validate changing mores but should set norms in order to "enable individuals to grow on the basis of stable, certain and comprehensible criteria."[56] Same-sex marriage would create the need to open up simple adoption, which the French report rejects "since this might lead to a proliferation of bonds of filiation for the child and open the door to distortion and abuse."[57] This would also produce "confusing points of reference for children."

Heterosexual marriage naturally protects children from potential discrimination because of the sex of their parents. Two kinds of discrimination are involved. The first, which the law prohibits, is external and involves the behavior of "others", while the second is internal and based on the child's observation that his parents are different and the feelings that this difference generates. When same-sex couples decide to have a child, either naturally through a willing third party, through medically assisted reproduction or adoption, they create a new minority, their own children, who are prevented from having both a mother and a father. They then turn around and ask that their children be protected from potential discrimination because of their unique family situation. Who is discriminating here?

The January 25, 2006 Report on the Family and the Rights of Children to the French National Assembly approaches the issue from a wider precautionary perspective: "the defense of the interests of children, who everyone agrees are the foundation of any society's future, unarguably justifies the legislator's total attention to the conditions under which children are born and raised."[58] The report later adds: "the legislator's first duty is to ensure that as children face changing family structures, they are fully taken into consideration and do not suffer as a result of situations imposed on them by adults. The interests of the child must outweigh the exercise of freedom by adults. Thus, the legislator's response should be made primarily in the area of affirming the rights of the child, whatever life choices are made by the parents."[59] In other words, adults are free to adopt the lifestyle of their choice, but society is not required to acquiesce by granting same-sex marriage if these choices harm the interests and rights of children. This does not constitute discrimination.[60]

As for asking for social acceptance of same-sex marriage (and parenting),[61] this would require all of society to be transformed, an uncertain proposition at best, including mandating changes in the teaching of the doctrines of many churches as well as denying issues imposed by nature itself. This would violate existing freedom of religion protections.[62] Freedom of speech would also have to be curtailed, a truly dangerous and odious proposition in our free and open societies.

III.   Can The Harm Be Undone?

When slavery was abolished, all slaves – who up to that time had been treated as mere property – became free men and women. When women obtained the right to vote, the discrimination ended with the very next election. For children of same-sex parents, the situation is radically different. Even if a legislature, after having legalized same-sex marriage in the first place, then returns to marriage defined as exclusively between one man and one woman, not a single child born fatherless or motherless within a same-sex marriage will get his missing parent back. The same applies with other non-marriage arrangements allowing the creation of fatherless or motherless children.

For children, only prevention will protect their rights. How can the State protect children? Can it prevent the harm? In the Goodridge case, the justices refer to the "formidable regulatory authority" of the Commonwealth.[63] On the issuance of marriage licenses, the State sets minimum qualifications and exercises gate keeping functions. The Legislature has the power to enact rules to regulate conduct, to the extent that such laws are "necessary to secure the health, safety, good order, comfort, or general welfare of the community."[64]

The State has the authority and the resources to regulate the means whereby children can enter into a family in most situations that require the involvement of third parties like adoption and medically assisted reproduction.

Adoption is a regulated process that on the precautionary principle. If there is a reasonable probability that the best interests of the child will not be served by would-be parents, the application is rejected and the search for suitable parents continues.

With regards to surrogate motherhood, most jurisdictions have laws providing some form of regulation. In some jurisdictions, surrogacy is not recognized; it is "absolutely null".[65] With regards to sperm donation, the process of regulating the sperm banks and their use is well within the State's prerogatives. In both these cases, the medical profession plays a pivotal role, and the medical profession falls under the State's authority to regulate.

The law also acts as a teacher. When the State officially endorses same-sex or genderless marriage by legalizing it, it expresses a preference for adults over the child. When it affirms man-woman marriage, it recognizes the importance of the child. This teaching effect also finds expression in school curriculum, in the media, and in the culture generally.

If the State has not legislated and exercised its control over the definition of marriage, adoption, surrogacy, sperm and ova donation with a view to protect the child's bonding rights, it is either unaware or has ignored whole classes of children. Most importantly, the State, as guarantor of rights, should not be complicit in their violation.

IV.   Conflict of rights

In this conflict of rights between adults and children, whose rights should prevail? International human rights conventions suggest that children should be given preference.[66] Yet, these conventions have little legal weight in countries like Canada until they are enshrined into the laws of the country. From a family law perspective, the answer is clear: the best interests of the child must prevail. But family law is gradually being overtaken by adults who have a clear advantage and are busy setting new constitutional precedents.[67]

In Canada and in Massachusetts, the children who will be born within families formed by same-sex partners after they marry were ignored after adults convinced the courts that marriage is not necessarily procreative.[68] This paper makes the case that children have a vital interest in marriage and reproductive issues, and that this interest cannot be ignored.

A.   Classes of individuals and nature of the harm

How many adults are being harmed by the prohibition against marrying a same-sex partner versus how many children will be harmed by allowing same-sex marriage? One could surmise that there are more same-sex partners than there are children of same-sex partners, and that numbers warrant giving preference to adults. But as has been seen, there are multiple classes of children that are adversely affected. And there are also adults.

First, there is the class of children born within families composed of two same gender partners who are deprived of either a father or a mother from birth.[69] For these children, this deprivation is fundamental and multi-faceted. It is also permanent. Replacing the missing biological parent with an unrelated same-sex parent, without any possible consent on the part of the child, clearly does not constitute a remedy for the child. The harm cannot be reversed. Once the child is born fatherless or motherless, he will never get his missing parent back.[70]

The second group comprises children born and raised in one family structure who later find themselves raised by two same gender parents.[71] There is ongoing debate about whether these children are harmed by same gender parenting. Proponents of same-sex marriage claim that there is no harm and demand same-sex marriage for their children's benefit. Opponents stress that the research showing there is no harm from same gender parenting is flawed and cannot be relied upon.[72] Whatever the outcome of this scientific debate, a fundamental problem remains: while same-sex marriage might bring some benefits to these children, it is clearly harmful to the first class of children intentionally created without a father or a mother. This is important because it is impossible to separate these two classes of children with a single marriage definition as there is no legal difference between a marriage and a remarriage.[73] To claim that same-sex marriage will beneficial for this second group of children is only possible if one ignores the harms to the first group of children described previously.

Third, we find all other natural children, whose filiative bonds to their parents have been weakened because the definition of parent has changed from biological to legal parent. The permanent biological bond is being replaced with a weaker and modifiable legal filiation that is subject to change, inviting greater interference by the State and the courts. This in turn affects all other children.

Fourth, we find all natural parents' being harmed because their exclusive biological bonds with their own children have been similarly weakened by the redefinition of a parent,[74] creating the potential for competing parental challenges and greater intrusion by the State and the courts.

B.   Adult advantage over children

As can readily be seen, adults are overwhelmingly advantaged in this conflict of rights. Contrast the many court challenges brought about by adults seeking to affirm their "equality" rights in numerous jurisdictions in different countries with the number (probably zero) of cases brought about by children who want to preserve their bonding rights to their mother and father.

From an ethical point of view, the child should be protected and his rights and interests should be given preference over those of adults. This is society's moral and ethical obligation.

Because a child is not a mature agent capable of self representation, the struggle to safeguard his bonding rights must be accomplished by proxy. This is important for two reasons. First, it is only as children become adults and are sufficiently autonomous that they can initiate action to affirm their rights. Nevertheless, by then, it is too late as most of the harm has already occurred. The second reason is that the affirmation of the bonding rights of the child must find its expression before the child is even conceived. The required action is prevention.

V.   Conclusion

As has been shown, heterosexual or dual gender marriage, by uniting the biological, legal and care giving dimensions of parenting, makes it possible for the child to know and be raised by both his mother and father within an easy to understand and generally stable family structure that has been proven to serve the child's best interests; heterosexual marriage also provides the child with a multigenerational sense of identity and a natural network of care and support from his or her immediate and extended biological family as well as access to biologically significant family genetic heritage (DNA).

Heterosexual marriage is essential in strengthening the largely reciprocal filiative rights of all children with their parents. Even with heterosexual marriage, these bonding rights can still be diluted and even denied by certain uses of medically assisted reproduction and adoption. From the moment of conception, heterosexual marriage also greatly reduces the risk that children or their constituent parts will become tradable commodities deprived of human dignity. Finally, heterosexual marriage protects children from potential external and internal discrimination.[75]

Taken together, these benefits illustrate the many dimensions of the child's bonding rights which heterosexual marriage is able to protect with relative ease. Same-sex marriage, mostly as a result of structural considerations, does not and in most cases cannot provide any of these benefits to the child.

Many societies protect the rights of the child by giving preference to the best interests of the child and applying the precautionary principle. When adults appeal to the constitution to advance their own rights, the rights of the child can be weakened and even disappear. To restore the rightful place of the child, efforts need to be deployed along two major themes.

First, research is needed in order to further bring out, explore, expand, substantiate and affirm the bonding rights of the child. This needs to occur in our universities, in our public discourse, within legal circles and our legislative assemblies.

Second, children need proxies to affirm and defend their bonding rights in courts of law and in legislatures.[76] The child's bonding rights need to be affirmed in three areas: marriage, assisted reproduction and adoption. Courts and legislatures need to recognize the child's constitutional bonding rights and cease being complicit in violating the rights of the child. In this manner, at least future children can receive the protection society owes them.

Notes

1. B.A., M.B.A. Co-Founder, Preserve Marriage – Protect Children's Rights Www.Preservemarriage.Ca.; Fellow, Canadian Center for Policy Studies. He lives in Montréal, Canada.

2. Convention on the Rights of the Child, United Nations, 1989, http://www.ohchr .org/english/law/crc.htm.

3. In applying the principles of the Convention, France's laws and regulations have effect from the moment of conception. Yet, within the international children's rights community, some have interpreted the Convention to apply only to the child after birth. This is incorrect, as explained by Bruce Abramson: "The original working draft of the Convention expressly limited rights 'from the moment of birth.' But this limitation was promptly removed. And according to the *travaux préliminaries*, one of the reasons for removing it was to give CRC coverage 'from the moment of conception' onwards." Abramson, Bruce, Violence Against Babies: Protection or Pre- and Post-natal Children Under the Framework of the Convention on the Rights of the Child, World Family Policy Center (2006), p. v.

4. The law, part of the "code de la santé publique", is concerned with respect for the human body. It was adopted on July 29, 1994 (law number 94-653) and amended on August 6, 2004 (law number 2004-800).

5. Rapport sur la famille et les droits de l'enfant, Assemblée Nationale, Paris, (25 janvier 2006). 453 pages.

6. French Report on the Family and the Rights of Children, edited English translation, p. 17, available at http://www.preservemarriage.ca/docs/France_ Report_on_the_Family_Edited.pdf. A 2 page summary of the report is also available in English at http://www.preservemarriage.ca/docs/France - summary.pdf

7. The Civil Marriage Act received Royal Assent on July 20, 2005.

8. Supreme Court of Canada, Egan c. Canada, [1995].

9 .The Convention on the Rights of the Child is not self-executing in Canada, as is the case in most countries.

10. Convention on the Rights of the Child, United Nations, 1989, Art. 3.

11. Ibid.

12. French Report on the Family and the Rights of Children, edited English translation, p. 68.

13. United States v. Virginia, 518 U.S. 515, 557 (1996), as quoted in Goodridge, Supreme Judicial Court, Massachusetts, November, 2004, p. 55.

14. Canadian Charter of Rights and Freedoms, Section 7.

15. Same-sex or genderless marriage is not an extension of marriage, but a redefinition where the gender ceases to be a requirement. Marriage can only be genderless or gendered, not both at the same time. See Monte Neil Stewart, Marriage Facts, Harvard Journal of Law & Public Policy, (Winter 2008).

16. "Man-woman marriage is the indispensable foundation for married mother-father child-rearing." While parenting exists without marriage, the institution of marriage confers significant additional benefits for the child, parents and society." See Monte Neil Stewart, Marriage Facts, Harvard Journal of Law & Public Policy, (Winter 2008), p. 352.

17. Monte Stewart suggests a lengthier but more accurate formulation: Marriage is "Society's best and probably only effective means to make real the right of a child to know and be brought up by his or her biological parents with exceptions justified only in the bests interests of the child, not those of any adult.", Monte Stewart, Eliding in Washington and California, Gonzaga Law Review, v. 42, number 3 (2007) p. 504.

18. A key argument made in defense of equality rights for gays and lesbians is that they were born that way. In all fairness, if this scientifically unresolved claim based on Nature is to be accepted, (see www.mygenes.co.nz), then the child's uncontested dual gender biological origin must also be accepted. It is also a deeply personal characteristic that cannot be changed.

19. Universal Declaration of Human Rights, Art. 16.1, United Nations. http://www.unhchr.ch/udhr/lang/eng.htm

20. For example, in Québec's Civil Code, art. 115, the biological mother is listed first, with the second parent being identified as Father or Mother. The law also allows the listing of two fathers without reference to a mother. In Ontario and Nova Scotia, the second same-gender parent can be listed as "other parent" and in British Columbia as "co-parent", thus confirming the absence of either a father or a mother.

21. Justice Committee hearings on Bill C-38, Canadian Parliament, June 2, 2005. See   http://cmte.parl.gc.ca/Content/HOC/committee/381/cc38/evidence/ev1900398 /cc38ev10-e.htm#Int-1315978

22. See "Do Mothers and Fathers Matter, The Social Science Evidence on Marriage and Child Well-Being ", Maggie Gallagher & Joshua K. Baker, iMAPP Policy Brief, February 27, 2004. and "Gender Complementarity and Child-rearing: Where Tradition and Science Agree", A. Dean Byrd, NARTH, Journal of Law and Family Studies, University of Utah, Volume 6 Number 2.

23. French Report on the Family and the Rights of Children, edited English translation, p. 88. Similarly, an American researcher explains: "But the biggest problem by far is that the vast majority of these studies compare single lesbian mothers to single heterosexual mothers—in other words, they compare children in one kind of fatherless family with children in another kind of fatherless family." Steven Nock, as quoted in The Revolution in Parenthood, The Emerging Global Clash Between Adult Rights and Children's Needs, Institute For American Values, 2006, pp. 21-22.

24. French Report on the Family and the Rights of Children, edited English translation, p. 88.

25. Ibid.

26. William N. Eskridge Jr. "Gaylaw: Challenging Apartheid in the Closet", Cambridge: Harvard University Press (1999) p. 11

27. David Blankenhorn writes that "In all or nearly all of human societies, marriage is a socially approved sexual intercourse between a man and a woman, conceived both as a personal relationship and as an institution, primarily such that any children resulting from the union are – and are endorsed by the society to be – emotionally, morally, practically, and legally affiliated with both parents." The Future of Marriage, Encounter Books, New York (2007) p.91

28. The opportunity for conflict increases faster than the number of adults. When a child has two parents, there is only one pair of adults (AB). Add a third parent and you triple the number of adult pairs (AB, AC, BC).

29. A recent court case in Québec illustrates how complicated these situations can become. Two married lesbians asked a male homosexual friend to inseminate one of them. A child was born and given a birth certificate with two mothers and no father. Shortly thereafter, the natural mother sought for divorce. The non-biological "mother" sued to be recognized as the child's mother with visitation rights. The natural mother strongly opposes this. To complicate matters, the man who sired the child also sued for recognition as the biological father with visiting rights.

30. While same-sex marriage is fairly recent and will lead to more such court cases, un-married same-sex parenting is already providing a glimpse of the future. See Elizabeth

Marquardt, The Revolution in Parenthood, The Emerging Global Clash Between Adult Rights and Children's Needs

31. Civil Code in the chapter devoted to « Respect for the human body », Title I, Book 1, law of July 29,1994.

32. French Report on the Family and the Rights of Children, edited English translation, p. 112.

33. see Marquardt, Elizabeth, The Revolution in Parenthood, The Emerging Global Clash Between Adult Rights and Children's Needs; and Sugrue, Seana, Canadian Marriage Policy – A Tragedy For Children, IMFC Review, Spring/Summer 2006

34. Québec Civil Code, Art. 538.

35. As one expert explained, "In reality, this type of maternity undermines two essential values that protect human dignity: first, the unavailability of the human body, more specifically, the unavailability of a woman's capacity for procreation; second, the unavailability of filiation. To accept such maternities is to place in trade, even at no charge, the gestational capacity of the mother. It means allowing the transfer of bonds of filiation outside what have hitherto been controlled processes – socially controlled in the case of adoption. It means introducing into the law of filiation, which is now granted by an outside authority, the possibility of contracted filiation. We would thus be moving away from institutional filiation and towards brokered filiation." French Report on the Family and the Rights of Children, edited English translation, p. 111.

36. Journal de Montréal, February 25, 2006. Nouveau marché noir – des québécoises vendent leurs ovules.

37. San Francisco Chronicle, April 25, 2006: More same-sex couples want kids, Survey looks at trends among homosexuals, http://www.sfgate.com/cgi-bin/article.cgi?f=/c/a/2006/04/25/BAG06IEGDN1.DTL

38. While one infertile individual renders the heterosexual couple infertile, a same-sex couple is functionally infertile, regardless of the fertility of either individual.

39. Margaret Somerville, Legislative Committee on Bill C-38, 38th Parliament, Thursday, June 2, 2005

40. Ibid.

41. To facilitate family reunification, France will allow some prospective immigrants, on an experimental basis, to prove their family relationships through DNA tests paid for by the French government. Loi no 2007-1631 du 20 novembre 2007 relative à la maîtrise de l'immigration, à l'intégration et à l'asile, Art. 13. Use of DNA in immigration cases also exists in other European countries.

42. Québec Civil Code, Art. 542

43. GOODRIDGE - SJC-08860 - Massachusetts Supreme Judicial Council, November 2004.

44. The only reference to children in the Charter relates to linguistic education rights, not a very useful reference in this matter.

45. Supreme Court of Canada, Egan c. Canada, [1995]

46. Supreme Court of Canada ,Reference re Same-Sex Marriage, Dec. 9, 2004

47. Address by Prime Minister Paul Martin on Bill C-38 (The Civil Marriage Act), House of Commons, Canada, February 16, 2005

48. Bowing to partisan political pressure, the federal government refused to appeal decisions by provincial courts of appeal in Ontario and British Columbia mandating same-sex marriage to the Supreme Court of Canada. Since the S.C. later refused to rule on this same question when asked by the federal government, one will never know if the dual gender requirement for marriage is constitutional in Canada.

49. IVF 'need for a father' rule may go, BBC News Channel, July 13, 2006, see http://news.bbc.co.uk/1/hi/health/5175640.stm. See also Playing God, bbc.co.uk Health http://www.bbc.co.uk/health/fertility/bigissues_playinggod1.shtml .

50. Adolphe, Jane, Bill C-38: Redefining Parenthood and Ignoring children, The Institute for the Study of Marriage, Law and Culture, March 7, 2005. Also, David Blankenhorn similarly addresses public meaning: "Changing a public meaning is a collective event. If the child's current right to her two natural parents goes down completely, as the proponents of the new rights claim insist that it must, then that right as a societal promise will no longer pertain to any child." The Future of Marriage, p. 199.

51. In another example, after legalizing same-sex marriage, Spain sought to change references to father and mother on all new birth certificates with the mention Progenitor A and Progenitor B. (The Revolution in Parenthood, p. 5.) It eventually backed down in the face of significant popular opposition.

52. Court rules mother must give children to lesbian ex-partner, The Guardian, April 7, 2006. That court decision was later reversed. www.guardian.co.uk/uk_news/story/0,,1748756,00.html

53. French Report on the Family and the Rights of Children, edited English translation, p. 78

54. Even France's largely coherent child centered set of laws can't fully protect children from competing interpretations. In 1998, a lesbian woman submitted an application to adopt, as a single person (which French law allows for singles over the age of 28). French courts ruled against the adoption. In January 2008, the European Court ruled that France had discriminated against her because French courts appeared to have been motivated by her sexual orientation when they referred to "the absence of a paternal image" and the nature of her partner's commitment to the adoption. See http://www.iht.com/articles/ap/2008/01/22/europe/EU-GEN-France-Lesbian-Adoption.php. When France's Parliamentary commission debated the issue of adoptions by singles, the arguments were all centered on the child. In its conclusion, it stated: "Adoption by a single person does not involve only unmarried persons, but also a spouse who adopts a child alone, a widow or widower, or a divorced person. It was instituted in order to give children, particularly those no longer young and those with a disability, an additional chance of being adopted, for example, by a caregiver who had taken care of them for years. It also allows for adoption by someone close to the child or related by marriage in the event of the death of the child's parents or his or her abandonment. Frédérique Granet pointed out that adoption by a single person could be in the child's interests and that a judge's assessment of the desirability of adoption for the child offers an adequate guarantee. Like almost all of those heard from, including the Minister of Justice and the Minister responsible for the family, the Mission believes that the child's interests justify maintaining this type of adoption [adoption by a single person]." French Report on the Family and the Rights of Children, edited English translation, pp. 88-90.

55. Ibid. p. 41.

56. Ibid. p. 18.

57. Ibid. pp. 128-129

58. Ibid. p. 25

59. Ibid. p. 48.

60. "Given the filiation aspects of marriage, the difference between the situations of homosexual and heterosexual couples may thus justify differential treatment that does not, in itself, constitute discrimination." Ibid. p. 76.

61. "But it is primarily in the interests of the child that Janice Peyré speaks for adopted children: 'As much as adoptive parents are open to the idea of extending adop-

tion – legally and transparently – to homosexuals, adolescents or adults who have been adopted express genuine reservations. They attest to a private feeling of being different when they grew up – a feeling accompanied by a very deeply experienced desire for normalcy. In their view, having homosexual parents would simply add to the sense of difference and the curiosity that adoption already engenders. In certain cases and in certain communities, it might even lead to rejection.' She therefore feels that 'bringing an adopted child into a society in which he or she will have the same rights and the same place as other children – as the Hague Convention provides – requires that the child be received into pre-existing family structures, already recognized as such, and not serve as an instrument for obtaining recognition of new family structures.'" Ibid. pp. 86-87

62. See Severino, Roger, Or for Poorer? How Same-Sex Marriage Threatens Religious Liberty, Harvard Journal of Law & Public Policy, Vol. 30, pp. 941-982.

63. GOODRIDGE - SJC-08860 - Massachusetts Supreme Judicial Council, November 2004, p. 4.

64. Ibid., p. 19

65. Quebec Civil Code, art. 541; France Title I, Book 1, law of July 29,1994.

66. For example, see the U.N. Convention on the Rights of the Child.

67. Two recent Ontario court cases illustrate how constitutional issues are being used to override family law. The first case was a challenge by a lesbian couple to have both partners listed on a child's birth certificate conceived through artificial insemination. The judge relied on equality arguments to strike down existing birth registry provisions allowing only the listing of a father and a mother. Globe and Mail, Two mothers should be allowed on birth document, judge says. June 6, 2007 http://www.mccarthyco.ca /documents/2.pdf .

The second case concerns a request to have three parents recognized on a birth certificate. A lesbian had a child with a man. Both are recognized as (biological) parents on the birth certificate. After the child's birth, the lesbian partner asked to be recognized as a second mother for the child but was turned down by the lower court on the grounds that the law can only recognize two parents for a child. The plaintiff, with the help of a constitutional lawyer, appealed on the basis that her same-sex relationship required assisted reproduction and that her rights should be recognized, thereby moving the issue beyond family law. Rejecting these equality arguments on technical grounds, the Ontario Court of Appeals (the same court that had mandated same-sex marriage in Ontario a few years earlier) nevertheless ruled that, in the best interests of the child, the child would now have three legally recognized parents. (National Post, Ruling may redefine family, January 3, 2007) http://www.canada.com/nationalpost/news/story.html?id=f0d64498-3fbb-43cc-940e-b2fc29e30736&k=94330

68. The argument was based on the narrow notion that marriage is strictly a close relationship between adults. In addition, the claim was made that since not all marriages are procreative and that procreation is not an obligation in marriage, therefore procreation is not an issue. This logic is deeply flawed, for if the focus shifts from the adults to the child, it is abundantly clear that every child has an interest in the marriage of his parents. The fact that some don't marry, or marry a same gender partner, doesn't change its importance.

69. Some might say, let's make sure that the child's second biological parent is both known and takes part in the upbringing of the child, thus providing the child with three parents. The difficulty here is obvious. If one were to assume that this was best for the child, it is highly unlikely that all same gender couples would readily accept such an arrangement as a precondition to marrying, particularly given the purposeful exclusion of an opposite gender partner that led to the same-sex marriage in the first place.

70. There are increasing pressures in many parts of the world to allow children born from anonymous sperm donors to eventually know the identity of their biological progenitor and to make contact, usually when they reach majority, and subject to the willingness of the donor. But given that the biological donor had no interest in becoming a parent to the child, it will be difficult for a number of children to accept that they were not wanted by one of the persons who gave them life and could feel rejected. This is probably even more evident for children born of surrogates who find themselves without a mother.

71. Most of the studies used to support same-sex marriage that claim that children are not harmed concern this class of children.

72. See footnote 23. It would be inappropriate to extrapolate these results to the first class of children for a number of reasons. First, there is evidence that differences were under reported in a number of studies and that a large number of studies suffer from important scientific flaws making their conclusions questionable. Second, there are many fundamental differences between children born and raised parts of their lives by both their biological parents and later by same gender parents, and children deprived from birth of a father or a mother being raised by two same gender parents.

73. One way to resolve this problem is to allow civil unions, like France's PACs for example. PACS require a lesser commitment than marriage and, to protect the child's rights, they do not entitle access to assisted reproduction or adoption. (See French Report on the Family and the Rights of Children, edited English translation). These civil unions, different from marriage, were rejected by proponents of same-sex marriage in Canada. They nevertheless offer an intermediate solution for same-sex couple who already have children.

74. When dealing with the bonding rights of the child, one cannot escape the observation that these bonds are largely reciprocal between the child and the parents. Therefore, if the child is separated from his parent, the parent is also separated from his child. Because of the child's dependency and vulnerability, parents also have responsibilities attached to their bonding rights. Parental rights thus include both bonding rights and parental responsibilities.

75. The first, which the law prohibits, is external and involves the behavior of "others", while the second is internal and based on the child's observation that his parents are different and the feelings that this difference generates.

76. For example, in Canada, an individual has one year from the time the discrimination occurred to file a complaint with a human rights tribunal (this may or may not be the appropriate venue). How can a child file a complaint to the effect that he was deprived at birth of a father or a mother do so before he reaches age one? Beyond timeliness, this isn't even desirable as this would pit the child against his own parents.

PART II
DOES LEGALIZING SAME-SEX MARRIAGE HARM RESPONSIBLE
SEXUAL BEHAVIOR AND PROCREATION?

CHAPTER 7
THE PRINCIPLES OF JUSTICE IN PROCREATIVE
AFFILIATIONS

Scott FitzGibbon[1]
Boston College

"Make thee another self, for love of me."
—Shakespeare, Sonnet X[2]
"The basic principles of justice are to live honorably, not to harm any other person, and to render each his due."
—Justinian, Digest[3]

I.   Introduction

If you procreate at all, you should try to do it well. If you and another person procreate together, you should try for a good relationship. Goodness in procreation and goodness in a procreative relationship are the subjects of this paper. More specifically, *justice* in procreation is the subject. Justice makes special demands on those who procreate. It applies to the associations they establish to conduct the projects of procreation.

The usual instance of an association for the projects of procreation is an exclusive and aspirationally permanent affiliation between a man and a woman. In our day, various other arrangements are proposed, notably uncommitted cohabitational connections, arrangements between persons of the same sex, polygamy, polyandry, and "polyamorous" relationships involving shifting populations of various types. To assess such proposals wisely, to determine what is just in the matter of structuring associations for procreation, and to sustain sound procreative associations, are the great problematics of our age.

What criteria should be applied? Findings from the social sciences are suggestive but sketchy. No comprehensive standards have emerged for determining when an associational structure is appropriate and just for the projects of procreation. This paper proposes such standards.

Applying the standards here proposed leads to the conclusion that marriage between a man and a woman can be procreatively just. The structure and elements of marriage are wise ones—its foundation in an oath of fidelity and in a certain unique kind of love; its commitments to permanence and exclusivity. None of the other forms fills the bill.[4]

Forms which fail to fill the bill should not in all cases be prohibited or condemned. Plainly some procreatively oriented affiliations which fall short in one
way or another deserve some measure of recognition. Sometimes exigencies
preclude the optimal choice; no one would abolish orphanages or foster care.
Sometimes optimal arrangements are supplemented with more limited ones; no
one thinks it is wrong to hire a nanny. This paper proposes a set of criteria which
identify the most appropriate form for a basic procreative affiliation.

This paper proposes that fully procreatively just affiliations—the ones
which satisfy the criteria developed here—deserve special support and recognition. It proposes that procreative justice requires such recognition. This paper
proposes that it is unjust to conflate and revise the usual categories so as to confuse procreatively just affiliations with other forms. It discusses the harm that
ensues.

II.   Procreation

"Procreation" refers in part to "making" or "producing," but goes beyond
those terms. You make pies, you make mistakes, but you do not procreate them.
Perhaps this is because procreation involves producing living things. Still, a
scientist has not procreated when he colonizes bacteria. Procreation involves
replication; reproduction of life; the making of something which resembles the
maker. It involves developing and extending the maker into a new generation
(and into generations thereafter). Only the sheep can procreate a sheep. The
scientist can procreate humans.

Procreation is not just a matter of biology: it includes the development of
the mind and heart and spirit as well. It means doing your part in commencing
the existence of another human being and bringing him along towards responsible adulthood. It means fostering his full personal development, including development of the capacity himself to procreate some day.

It involves some degree of participation, in other words, in the procreation
of subsequent generations as well. It aims at offspring who may themselves pursue the projects of their parents and who may extend the line on into posterity. It
is thus one of the great goods of life and a central element of human flourishing.
It enters the procreator in the procession of "illustrious men whose good works
have not been forgotten":

> "In their descendants they find
> a rich inheritance, their posterity.
> Their descendants stand by the commandments
> And, thanks to them, so do their children's children."[5]

III.   Justice

Justice is the most fundamental social virtue. It involves all that is requisite
in conduct affecting another person. Thus, in the most fundamental sense, justice
involves understanding that another person *is* another person; a person comparable to oneself; a person who is, like oneself, entitled to decent treatment. The

radically unjust person never gets this idea. The basically just person does get it. He accepts the demands of commutativity and reciprocity in human relations.

Justice involves three basic principles. The first is not to harm. Subject to excuses such as duress and impossibility, you act unjustly if you damage someone in an important way. Underlying this requirement lies the insight, grasped by the just man and not by the radically unjust one, that harm is a bad thing in a general way so that everyone, not only he himself, deserves to be free of it.

The second principle of justice is to "render each his due." This requires, of some people in some situations, that they act affirmatively to assist or protect. Justice for a lifeguard, for example, involves more than not drowning people. He should rescue the distressed swimmer. Perhaps he has implicitly promised to do so; perhaps society has appointed him to a sort of office which requires him to do it; swimmers have probably relied upon him. No one else, perhaps, can swim so well or foresee so accurately the struggles of the drowning man. Other instances can readily be adduced. A trustee is obliged to assist the beneficiaries and an executor to protect the estate. After a shipwreck, the only man with extra food should feed the survivors and the only man with knowledge of the native language should teach the others. The just person accepts—as a self-indulgent or self-involved person will not—that another person's concerns have a traction on his own life, drawing him into a course of assistance, service, and sometimes even self-sacrifice.

A third aspect relates justice to practices of honor and the recognition of duty, office, and merit. It is just to honor the honorable and unjust to disgrace them; just to accredit what is creditable and not confuse it with the irrelevant or disgraceful; just to recognize someone for who he is and not to assign him to an order which is not his own. Bad social ideology violates these requirements. A communist or a fascist is unjust in this way. He thinks stereotypically, ignores individuality, places people in meretricious categories ("bourgeois," "Aryan"), and assigns unjustified opprobrium and unmerited praise. The just person "gets the idea" of honor and dishonor and accepts the importance of recognizing things as what they really are. A person who is hostile to clear distinctions and anxious to avoid becoming "judgmental" will not be just in this way.

In all these ways the just man not only acts but also thinks and perhaps even feels as he should. As Aristotle observes, we would not call someone fully just who did the just thing but only under compulsion.[6] Nor would we call someone just who did the just thing but only in order to satisfy his needs, or only as a consequence of his emotions. We would not call a parent just, for example, who performed the duties of parenthood only out of a "need for belongingness"[7] or a "dyadic intention toward a ... dependent growing out of a feeling toward that dependent,"[8] conforming to a theory from the social sciences which proposes that "[w]hat the parent does is to feel."[9] A fully just person acts as he does owing to his appreciation of the good of justice.

IV.   Justice In Affiliations Involving Procreativity

A.   Justice between Procreator and Procreated.

Consider how the requirements of justice may apply in the case of a baby or a child. His vulnerability to harm is extensive. His "due" may be great, as his circumstances bear comparison with the inexperienced swimmer and the castaway who needs food and shelter and successful integration into the indigenous society.

Consider how the requirements of justice may apply to you, as his procreator. You may be lifeguard, trustee, and estate executor rolled into one. You may be food owner, language teacher, cultural guide and social intermediary, from the affiliations of the household on outwards into the wider world. You are his link to the affiliational chain of his ancestors. You are a major determinant of how he in later life will appraise honor and dishonor and, apportion praise or blame.. If you are a just person, you must accept that this state of affairs has a traction on your own life.

B.   Justice among Procreators.

Affiliations among those who work together on the basic projects of procreation (here, "procreative affiliations") pay the rent and buy the groceries; more important still, they furnish examples to the offspring. Children develop morally through a process of modeling:

> "A young child is able to latch onto the moral kind, bravery, or lying, by grasping central paradigms of that kind . . . . Moral development is . . . something much more complicated than simple concept displacement. It is: enlarging the stock of paradigms . . . developing better and better definitions of whatever it is that these paradigms exemplify; appreciating better the relation between straightforward instances of the kind and close relatives; and learning to adjudicate competing claims from different moral kinds . . . ."[10]

Children's well-being—and much of what they do in later life—is thus affected intensely by the character of the affiliations around them. "Research clearly demonstrates" what common sense would in any case suggest: "family structure matters for children."[11] Doing justice to offspring thus requires procreators to establish well ordered relationships with one another.

This section proposes seven requirements for justice in structuring procreative affiliations.[12] The first two requirements respond to the offspring's good in general. The next four respond to the offspring's good as regards his affiliative future, looking to the day when he himself will form friendships and other important associations. The final requirement looks to his procreative future. Procreative affiliations which fulfill these requirements are here called "Procreatively Just Affiliations."

What sort of house is suitable for raising a child? A house may be a metaphor for a household.

The First Requirement. A procreatively appropriate house is not built on sand and will not collapse in a windstorm. It gives the offspring his "due" in the sense that it affords what its residents need from a house: shelter from the rain, warmth in winter, and facilities for cooking. The metaphor illustrates one aspect of the procreative affiliation: it is a "tasked" association. It aims at instrumental goods. Whereas other sorts of association might be arranged *ad libitem,* or as an exercise in risk, adventure, and the recurrent temptation of fate—like Zelda and Scott Fitzgerald during their early years together—procreative affiliations are dedicated to supplying an offspring's necessities. They should pay the rent, for example, and supply the food. These points can be summed up as the first requirement of justice for procreative affiliations: *they should be well ordered towards supplying an offspring's practical needs.*

The Second Requirement. More abstractly: perhaps a house ought to be in a sense "honorable" in that it should it convey true and not disordered implications about the residents and their appropriate roles. It should not be a slave quarters nor, in a republic, should it be a palace. It should be human-sized, with human-sized rooms and hallways, well suited to balanced, person-to-person, on-the-level relationships. Fascist architecture, complete with monstrous stairsteps and cavernous hallways filled with heroic sculpture would be procreativity inappropriate. So also would the temporary shelters of Woodstock.

Applying similar criteria: the affiliations of the house*hold* should be "honorable," in the sense that they should conform to a reasonable order of honor, merit, and demerit, and reflect a reasonable recognition of office and role. Honor implies not just one affiliation but an affiliational system. In a household or any such system, people who do their part should be acknowledged as doing their part and people who stand as pillars of the household establishment should not be confused with those whose involvement is sporadic and self-serving.

Married couples recognize this aspect of procreative justice when they promise to "love, *honor* and cherish" one another and when they set their shoulders to the tasks of maintaining a household. A husband would violate this requirement of procreative justice by bringing girlfriends in to live and demanding that they be treated with respect. A polyamorous affiliation—one whose members are celebrated for amorous amenability rather than respected for procreative dedication—would be procreatively unjust under this criterion.

The first two requirements of procreative justice might be satisfied by colleagues whose associations were deeply chilly. People who cared little about one another's well-being and perhaps even disliked one another could perform the practical tasks of a household and treat one another with grudging respect. This suggests a search for further requirements.

Suppose two sculptors undertake to carve a statue out of some mythological material which has a sort of life of its own. It gradually changes shape in response to variations in its environment such as wind and light and it changes responsively to the characters and personalities, beliefs, intentions, and motives of the sculptors themselves. If they dislike sculpting and are disappointed with the statue it becomes less attractive. If they determine to destroy it, it shrivels up. If they dislike *one another,* and each plans to harm the other, the statue, similarly, acquires a malevolent aspect. Suppose further that this statue will spring up some day and take on life-like characteristics like Pinocchio, and that its character and conduct as well as its outward form will reflect the influences of the sculptors. If the sculptors are malicious or insensitive, the statue may become that way as well. If they are unfriendly to one another, the statue's capacity to befriend will be affected.

The metaphor illuminates another aspect of the procreative affiliation: it is a model.[13] Affiliational character is formed by the close affiliations of early life Children's affiliational well-being: their own marriages and friendships in later life—are intensely affected by the affiliational order of their upbringing.. [14] Judith Wallerstein reports:

> "A central finding of my research is that children identify not only with their mother and father as separate individuals but with the relationship between them. They carry the template of this relationship into adulthood and use it to seek the image of their new family. "[15]

Were progeny not involved, there might be little objection to conducting an association largely with an eye to generating tumultuous raw material for semi-autobiographical fiction (as may have been the case with Zelda and Scott Fitzgerald).[16] But where offspring are involved, the procreative affiliation should be conducted with a mind to the example presented. It should model successful affiliation, not only by way of efficiency in performing tasks, but also by way of the noninstrumental goods. It should model those elements which make affiliation good for its own sake, and establish it as a basic dimension of human life.

Benevolence and knowledge are fundamental elements of affiliation. You would certainly not be friends if you wished one another ill; you would certainly not be friends if you did not even know one another; and you would not be *good* friends unless each of you cared quite a bit for the well-being of the other[17] nor unless you knew one another *well.* Friendship involves shared benevolence and knowledge; benevolence leading on to discourse: "sharing discussion and thought," as Aristotle observes.[18] Thoroughgoing friendship involves benevolence as to a fulsome range of the friends' projects and knowledge as to much of their actions and plans. Exercising their benevolence and deepening their knowledge, friends participate together, as Aristotle observes, in much of life.[19]

These two virtues can, therefore, be identified as the objects of the third and fourth requirements of procreative justice: *procreators should model the virtues of benevolence and knowledge and their integration into an affiliation.* Procreative affiliates should wish each other well and act well towards one another. They should know one another, and they should aspire to know one another well.

Married couples recognize these requirements of procreative affiliation when they promise to love and cherish one another. Studies establish the importance of benevolence and knowledge within marriage when they report the adverse effects on marriage of practices such as defensiveness and stonewalling.[20]

An association could not be fully procreatively just if it were based, as some modern writers recommend, on emotion rather than cognition,[21] nor if it were attempted by people who were too selfish, narcissistic, confabulatory or delusional to understand one another well (as may have been the case with Zelda and Scott Fitzgerald).[22] Such a couple would be likely to transmit their cognitive deficiencies on to the parent-child affiliation and thence into the next generation. "I was an imaginary daughter," wrote Scottie Fitzgerald, "as fictional as one of his early heroines."[23] One of Scottie's own kids later said much the same thing about himself: "We were characters in our mother's novel".[24]

Fidelity is a fundamental component of affiliation. Steadiness grounds affiliational benevolence, which is more than a matter of "random acts of kindness," as the bumper sticker puts it. True friends stand by you "through thick and thin." Steadiness is a cornerstone of affiliational knowledge, which is not a matter of episodic insights and brief glimpses of the truth. Knowledge between true friends is, rather, hard-headed and clear-eyed, informed by an honest and extensive exchange of views, and not occluded by the shifting clouds of self-indulged romanticism. This virtue can, then, be identified as the object of the fifth requirement of procreative justice: *procreators should model the virtue of fidelity and its integration into an affiliation.*

The traction of this requirement helps explain the intention, generally to be found among couples who marry, that their relationship be permanent rather than dissoluble upon the completion or frustration of the practical projects of maintaining a household.[25] The virtues of constancy help to explain the sense, commonly to be found among married couples, that their relationship finds expression even in the ordinary tasks of household life: the "irreplaceable daily fidelities."[26] A short-term affiliation—a "marriage" planned in advance to expire after a term of years—would be procreatively unjust; and so also would be an affiliation whose members were prepared to split up, even though they had not set a date: a readiness to terminate the relationship or to minimize its obligations upon the occurrence of eventualities such as discomfort or dissatisfaction.

Procreators should not only act with consistency, they should "think consistent" in order to model consistency and stability of mind to their offspring. Fully procreatively just affiliations are founded on fully committed intentions. A contingent intention to betray or desert will affect the offspring even if it is never acted upon.

Cohabitating couples omit the commitment to permanence[27] and in other ways minimize obligations and so fail to satisfy this requirement. A study by Joanna Reed finds:

> "[M]ost cohabiting parents begin cohabiting in response to a pregnancy but do not believe they should stay in a relationship because of shared children. They view cohabitation as a practical response to parenthood that allows them to coparent and share expenses yet avoid the greater expectations of commitment, relationship quality, and more traditional and scripted family roles they associate with marriage."[28]

As Linda Waite and Maggie Gallagher put it, "For many cohabitors, the idea of relatively easy exit with no well-defined responsibilities constitutes co-habitation's biggest attraction. * * * * [L]lesser commitment to one's partner extends through all aspects of life, including sexual fidelity." [29]

Studies indicate that cohabitation adversely implicates the offspring's own affiliational and procreative future. [30]

A further requirement relates to the connection between affiliations and the societies around them. The affiliations which the offspring later forms will not subsist in isolation but will intersect with many others, including those of ex-tended family, neighborhood, region, and nation. Man flourishes best when he participates in a general social order. This suggests a sixth requirement: *procreators should model a successful relationship between their affiliation and the society in which it is embedded.* It is not unjust to be a hermit, but it would be procreatively unjust to raise a family in a hermitage. [31]

Uncritical conformity is not the ticket; and certainly where procreators find themselves surrounded by a social order which is seriously unjust this criterion will not demand that they conform to its unjust practices. The successful relationship with society identified by this sixth requirement should involve critical reciprocity; and where a social order has become thoroughly depraved, procreators may find it impossible to satisfy the sixth requirement of procreative justice. A corollary thesis to that proposed in this article for procreators can therefore be identified for societies: they themselves must be procreatively just. [32]

Married couples comply with the sixth requirement of procreative justice by exemplifying successful integration into the extended family (showing how to be a good in-law, uncle, and aunt, for example) and into the social order of neighborhood, region and nation (manifesting, for example, good manners and social discretion). [33]

The sculptors' little Pinocchio would be headed for disaster if he turned into a real boy, grew up, and started down the usual road towards procreating himself. Little in the affiliation of the sculptors prepares him for that project. This suggests the seventh requirement of procreative justice: *the affiliation of procreators should model successful procreative affiliation.* It should, in other words, model the fulfillment of the first six requirements of procreative justice as applied, not just in any context, but specifically in the procreative role which the offspring is likely to assume.

The offspring, as soon as he reaches his early teenage years, is likely to start thinking and acting in ways which lead to biological procreation. Sooner than he expects, he may find that he has begotten a child and is charged with responsibility for its upbringing. He is likely to find himself affiliated with a partner in these projects. [34] These circumstances will present him with a special problematic, and with the opportunity to participate in special goods.

The Special Problematic. Procreators are pulled in two directions: on the one hand by the urgent demands of erotic love, on the other by the requirements of procreative justice. *Eros,* in its primitive forms, can be the enemy of procreative justice. It is a sort of love, [35] but sometimes the love "of the wolf for the sheep," [36] characterized by "irrational desire" [37] reaching to the point of "furor and agony" and leading on, when it miscarries, to aggression and destruction. *Eros* can delight in conquest and humiliation,[38] whereas justice entails "getting it" that the other person should be treated as one would wish to be treated oneself. *Eros* may chafe under the bonds of obligation,[39] whereas justice involves respecting the call of duty. *Eros* can be unstable, whereas procreative justice calls for fidelity. *Eros* may seek additional partners, whereas procreative justice calls for exclusivity. *Eros* may rejoice in the illicit and lead on to concealment, withdrawal from society,[40] and antipathy to convention and law, whereas procreative justice requires the couple to establish a fulsome and worthwhile relationship with extended family, neighborhood, village, and nation. *Eros* can lead to shame, whereas procreative justice deserves honor. *Eros* can lead to a loss of self-possession and the debasing of the character, as Pinocchio discovered when he realized that he and his friends were turning into donkeys.[41]

The erotic man, Plato emphasizes in the *Republic*, may throw off the discipline of reason in favor of a mentality of dreams.[42] [He may be swayed by sensations and emotions, whereas justice requires a steady and clear-headed dedication to the other person's good. He may experience a "blurring of form" and suffer the "forgetting of form,"[43] whereas justice calls for focusing on relevant distinctions. After he has lived a life governed by pleasure for a while, the erotic man may develop an antipathy to drawing certain important distinctions:

> "[I]f someone says that there are some pleasures belonging to fine and good desires and some belonging to bad desires, and that the ones must be practiced and honored and the others checked and enslaved . . . . [he] throws his head back and says that all are alike and must be honored equally."[44]

The Special Goods. From resolution of the special problematic can emerge a unique two-stranded affiliation between the procreators. Their benevolence derives an intensity from its erotic roots. They give themselves to one another physically, and in unique psychological ways as well.[45]

Their mutual knowledge is unique. Procreative affiliates can "know" in the biblical, carnal sense.[46] They may experience the heightened, rhapsodic awareness which emerges during courtship. They draw one another into unfamiliar territory:

> "Heterosexual union is imbued with the sense that your partner's sexual nature is strange to you, a territory into which you intrude without prior knowledge and in which the other and not the self is the only reliable guide. This experience has profound repercussions for our sense of the danger and the mystery of sexual union."[47]

The couple awakens from the dreamy eroticism of Plato's *Republic* and opens their eyes to very real projects calling for very clear thought.

The procreators are benevolent by procreating: each gives the gift of procreation to the other. They *know* one another better by procreating: each knows the other in the capacity of procreator and, eventually, through the eyes of their offspring. They confirm their fidelity through commitment to the offspring.

They extend their affiliational benevolence and knowledge and fidelity on into future generations.

> "In their descendants they find
> a rich inheritance, their posterity.
> Their descendants stand by the commandments
> And, thanks to them, so do their children's children."[48]

The Special Temptation of Meretricious Alternatives. Offspring may be enticed to fall into one or another destructive alternative to the procreatively just affiliation.

Cohabitation, for example, is one frequent outcome. Whereas most people today aspire to be married[49] and predict (correctly) that the formation of a stable marriage can be fulfilling and beneficial,[50] many people also think (incorrectly) that cohabitation and out-of-wedlock childbirth are promising alternatives. Notoriously, people do cohabit in increased numbers (and have increasingly begotten children outside of wedlock).[51] Studies establish that cohabitation is associated with deleterious outcomes for those who practice it, compared to marriage,[52] including an increased probability of relational breakdown[53] and an increased probability of divorce if later the couple does marry.[54]

Cohabitation is bad for the offspring.[55] Its instability means an unstable home for the children. "Fully three-quarters of children born to cohabiting couples are likely to see their parents split up before they reach age sixteen, whereas only about a third of children born to married parents face a similar fate."[56] The deleterious effects which ensue for the offspring include effects on their procreative futures.[57]

Another frequent outcome may be "marriage lite:" that is, wedded relationships in which the couple adopts a casual or tentative attitude towards their marriage, considering it to be "glued together" only by the prospect of continued "emotional gratification"[58] and regarding it as subject to termination when gratification subsides.[59] The "liteness" of this kind of relationship likely entails a failure fully to satisfy several of the requirements of procreative justice, as it involves a diminution in the fidelity and mutual knowledge and benevolence of the spouses.

When divorce ensues, as it often does, the offspring are liable to incur many adverse effects.[60] Paul Amato finds that "[c]ompared to children with continuously married parents, children with divorced parents continued to score significantly lower on measures of academic achievement, conduct, psychological adjustment, self-concept and social relations"[61] and that they

> "tend to obtain less education, earn less income, have more troubled marriages, have weaker ties with parents, and report more symptoms of psychological distress. * * * [They] are more likely to drop out of high school, less likely to attend college, more likely to be unemployed, and [they are] more likely to experience economic hardship as adults . . . ."[62]

They are often raised by single parents or by reconstituted couples, preponderantly by their biological mother, alone or with her new partner.

> "[D]ivorced single mothers, compared with continuously married mothers, tend to show less warmth toward their children, engage in harsher punishment, and monitor their children less effectively . . . . With respect to fathers, postdivorce visitation arrangements make it difficult for noncustodial fathers to maintain close ties with their children. As a result, many fathers visit their children infrequently and gradually disengage from their children's lives."[63]
> "A large body of social scientific evidence now shows that the risk of physical or sexual abuse rises dramatically when children are cared for in the home by adults unrelated to them, with children being especially at risk when left at home with their mothers' boyfriends."[64]

Adverse effects ensue for the offsprings' *procreative* futures:

> "Research has consistently suggested that marital discord and divorce are transmitted across generations. Compared with spouses with continuously married parents, spouses with divorced parents tend to report less marital satisfaction . . . engage in {* *} more conflict. . ., and think about divorce more often. . . . Similarly, parental divorce is associated with a greater likelihood of seeing one's own marriage end in divorce. . . . ."[65]

The adverse effects are passed on to future generations:

> "Grandparents' decisions to divorce predict less education, greater marital discord, and weaker ties with parents two generations later. . . .These findings are particularly striking when we consider that the great majority of grandchildren were not yet born when these divorces occurred. . . . [F]amily problems can persist across generations, with divorce (and perhaps other family problems correlated with divorce) in one generation resulting in lower educational attainment and problematic family relationships in the second generation, and these outcomes in turn becoming the causes of similar problems in the third generation. . . . Parents who fight frequently or divorce may increase the risk of a variety of problems, not only for their children, but also for their children's children."[66]

The Special Importance of a Good Model. Few of the basic problems of life, least of all this one, are amenable to solution solely through the perusal of books and articles. The most prominent media of our own age present, in any case, a highly distorted set of impressions, tending to degrade the erotic and to disconnect close personal affiliations from the requirements of justice.[67] The same may be true of sex-education programs in the schools:

> "[They] impart knowledge without substance or meaning. Love, affection, and tenderness are not part of the educational portrayal of sex. [Kay

Hymowitz] describes an AIDS prevention program that issued flashcards
to students who were supposed to arrange them in the correct order (an
example of the 'robotization' of sex. The one labeled 'Talk with Partner'
was to go first. Another card of equal size to be placed last said, 'Throw
condom out.'"[68]

An offspring—today's offspring more than those of earlier eras—therefore
needs a worthwhile model from an early age and for a long time. It his "due." A
procreative affiliation is therefore fully just only when it models a solution to the
great problem of integrating erotic and responsible love, and only when it provides a guide to participation in the special procreative goods.

Marriage. Marriage between a man and a woman uniquely satisfies this requirement.[69] As one authority puts it:

> "Children learn about male-female relationships through the modeling of
> their parents. Parental relationships provide children with a model of
> marriage—the most meaningful relationship that the vast majority of in-
> dividuals will have during their lifetimes."[70]

Marriage between a man and a woman uniquely involves procreative *eros*
and its integration into the projects of procreative justice. Well conducted, marriage exemplifies a loving relationship between a man and a woman which is
free of the giddiness, embarrassment and shame which afflicts many of the episodic alliances of adolescence. Well conducted, marriage exemplifies the avoidance of adultery and the practice of periodic abstinence. (Where else but from a
good father can a young man find an example, seldom available among his pals,
of a man he admires and loves steering away from attractive women and curbing
his sexual appetites for the sake of a family?). Well conducted, marriage exemplifies the sacrificial character of pregnancy and honors the sacrality of the newly born.

V.   Same-Sex Affiliations

Same-sex affiliations are not procreatively just under the criteria set forth
above. This is the case even in the instance of those same-sex affiliations which
most nearly resemble traditional marriage.

A.   The First Six Requirements.

Same-sex affiliations are likely to fail to satisfy some of the first six requirements. They may fall short because same-sex couples lack the biological
incentives which spur on biological parents. "[P]eople who conceive a child . . .
will . . . be the most invested in its nurture"[71] and especially so people who conceive a child who will some day procreate as they have done..

Furthermore, if homosexual conduct is wrongful and homosexual inclinations are disordered, as many thinkers throughout history have maintained and
as many religious bodies such as Orthodox Judaism, Catholicism and Islam have

taught, it follows that affiliations which include homosexual practices and stimulate homosexual inclinations are deleterious to the parties morally and spiritually. If same-sex affiliations are unstable, as findings from the social sciences indicate,[72] or in other ways deleterious,[73] then a same-sex affiliation may be harmful in practical ways as well. Affiliates who sustain associations which are bad for both of them cannot be entirely beneficent towards one another. Their affiliations fail to satisfy the third requirement of procreative justice.

Social orders may reasonably refuse full recognition to affiliations which are bad for their members. American society refuses it to same-sex affiliations.[74] Under these circumstances, same-sex affiliations violate the sixth requirement of procreative justice.

B.   The Seventh Requirement.

Same-sex relationships always fail to satisfy the seventh requirement of procreative justice. They either leave *eros* aside altogether or they involve *eros* in a special way, divergent from the form it will take for the great majority of the offspring and thus unsuccessful as their model for the great problematic of procreative responsibility. Such associations cannot model the erotic benevolence unique to men and women, nor can they exemplify the inter-gender knowledge which men and women uniquely share. They do not recapitulate and ramify themselves, generation after generation.[75]

VI.   The Injustice ff Recognizing Same-Sex Affiliations As Marriages

When a legal or governmental authority identifies same-sex affiliations as marriages, it acts unjustly, contravening all three of the basic principles of justice.

It does harm insofar as people follow its guidance. (Part Seven discusses the extent to which that may occur.). It deprives people of their due when an authority or leader, charged with responsibilities comparable to that of a lifeguard, a trustee or a guardian, misleads those who rely on him. It falls short as regards the third aspect of justice by treating as the same things that are different, and by conflating procreatively just affiliations with associations which fall short of fulfilling the requirements of procreative justice.

VII.   How Extensive May Be The Harm—Ensuing Upon Legal Recognition Of Same-Sex Marriage

When a leading legal authority mandates that same-sex associations be treated like marriages, the consequences are extensive. The full ramifications must take generations to unfold, but some shorter-term consequences can be identified by considering developments in Massachusetts (and in those few foreign jurisdictions whose legal institutions have, as in Massachusetts, mandated legal recognition of same-sex marriage).[76]

A.   Legal Recognition of Same-Sex Marriage Encourages Social Recognition of Same-Sex Marriage.

Legal recognition of same-sex marriage encourages social promotion of same-sex marriage in prominent universities. Here is one instance from Massachusetts:

> "Last weekend, on the Fourth of July, Cambridge saw one of its most prominent lesbian couples marry at Memorial Church in Harvard Yard. Professor Diana Eck, of Harvard Divinity School, and her partner, the Reverend Dorothy Austin, who ministers at the famed church, wed amid a crowd of well-wishers that included Supreme Judicial Court chief justice Margaret Marshall. And not only did the brides purposely choose Independence Day for their nuptials, the ceremony's final hymn was "America" ("My Country 'Tis of Thee")."[77]

Legal recognition of same-sex marriage encourages the promotion of same-sex relationships by public school teachers and administrators. A few months after the Massachusetts same-sex marriage decision, Thomas W. Payzant, Superintendent of the Boston Public Schools,[78] issued a memorandum to the Boston School System announcing that "[t]his is a historic moment in our Commonwealth and in our country" and that the decision "continues to have, a profound impact on our civil life and discourse" which "filters through our society and our schools."[79] Superintendent Payzant's memorandum establishes a "zero-tolerance policy":

> "Administrators, teachers, parents and students are reminded that no action or speech will be tolerated that results in harassment, discrimination, bias or intimidation toward any member of our community for any reason, including his/her sexual orientation or perceived sexual orientation. We urge school staff to report and act promptly on any incidents that may create a climate of intolerance in our schools. Such incidents will be considered a serious violation of the BPS Code of Discipline . . . and will result in discipline up to and including expulsion of the responsible student or termination of the offending employee."

After this, a teacher would take her career into her hands by encouraging an examination of the cons as well as the pros of same-sex marriage.[80]

A further development has been the introduction of vivid and sometimes graphic presentation of various sexual practices, as indicated in the following interview on National Public Radio program of an eighth-grade teacher in Brookline, Massachusetts:

"[Teacher] In my mind, I know that, 'OK, this is legal now.' If somebody wants to challenge me, I'll say, 'Give me a break. It's legal now.'

"SMITH: And, [she] says, teaching about homosexuality is also more important now. She says the debate around gay marriage is prompting kids to ask a lot more questions, like what is gay sex, which [she] answers thoroughly and explicitly with a chart.

"[Teacher]: And on the side, I'm going to draw some different activities, like kissing and hugging, and different kinds of intercourse. All right?

"SMITH: [She] asks her students to fill in the chart with yeses and nos.

"[Teacher]: All right. So can a woman and a woman kiss and hug? Yes. Can a woman and a woman have vaginal intercourse, and they will all say no. And I'll say, 'Hold it. Of course, they can. They can use a sex toy . . . [A]nd we talk—and we discuss that."[81]

The effect of the Massachusetts same-sex marriage decision has been to encourage the indoctrination of public school students in the merits of same-sex relationships; and in other jurisdictions, similar pressures have been felt:

"In the wake of Canada's legalization of same-sex marriage, a human-rights complaint has been filed in British Columbia alleging the absence of pro-homosexual instruction in public schools is a denial of equal treatment. . . [Petitioner] wants [the curriculum] changed to include: 'Queer history and historical figures, the presences of positive queer role models . . . the contributions made by queers to various epochs, societies and civilizations, and legal issues relating to [lesbian, gay, bisexual, transgendered] people, same-sex marriage and adoption.'"[82]

B.   *Legal Recognition of Same-Sex Marriage Can be Predicted to Lead on to Degradation of Beliefs and Practices as to Heterosexual Marriage and the Family.*

The Massachusetts same-sex marriage decision and others like it project what might almost be called a theory of marriage, or at least a certain "take" on how to think about that institution and what it means. That "profound impact on our civil life and discourse" to which Superintendent Payzant portentously referred[83] would include an impact not only on practice but on thought and belief as well.

The marital morality of the Massachusetts and other same-sex marriage authorities displays several important features. The first might be called "positivism": the view that things all come down to the mandates of the State. The Massachusetts court announced:

"[T]he terms of marriage—who may marry and what obligations, benefits, and liabilities attach to civil marriage—are set by the Commonwealth."[84]

"[T]he government creates civil marriage."[85]

Statements like these close the door firmly on the nonpositive roots of the institution of marriage and on nonpositive, extra-state authorities for defining and understanding it; sources widely relied on in judicial authorities until recent decades, namely custom, nature, tradition, and religion. Indeed, statements in some same-sex marriage cases bluntly excoriate the marital beliefs of the citizenry. "[L]ike it or not," a Hawaii court announced, "constitutional law may mandate ... that customs change."[86] "[R]ooted in persistent prejudices," concludes the Massachusetts court.[87] "[F]undamentally repugnant," states an Ontario court.[88]

The second feature of the same-sex marriage authorities might be called "deconstruction." This feature arises from the circumstance that Massachusetts has adopted no comprehensive definition of marriage, either as a matter of the common law or as a matter of statute; people have generally understood what marriage meant through custom, tradition, religion, and morality. The Supreme Judicial Court's same-sex marriage decision called everything into question, put everything up for litigation and challenge, and closed the door on the most obvious bases for reaching a solution. Marriage is something defined by the state, we are told; but then the state does not define it.[89]

A third feature of some judicial authorities in this area is a derogatory attitude towards moral normativity. The Massachusetts court, in its same-sex marriage decision, court referred to the desirability of "defin[ing] the liberty of all, not . . . mandat[ing] our own moral code."[90] Justice O'Connor's concurring opinion in *Laurence v. Texas* seeks "other reasons . . . to promote the institution of marriage beyond mere moral disapproval of an excluded group" (turning, instead, to "state interest").[91] Note that this third feature is not merely an extension of the first: it seems to be not only social morals, or religious morals, or objective ethical morals which are to be avoided, but even positive, legal moralizing ("our own" moral order). Fixed standards of conduct are to be generally suspect, it seems, and subject to derogation when they conflict—as they almost always do—with liberty very broadly defined as ""the right to define one's own concept of existence, of meaning, of the universe, and of the mystery of human life."[92] Law and morality survive only in those (undefined and shifting) circumstances in which it serves the "interests" of the state.

The fourth feature, inevitably, is confusion and the possibility of infinite malleability in the meaning and conduct of marriage, both socially and as a matter of law. "[C]ivil marriage," the Massachusetts court announced in its same-sex marriage opinion, "is an evolving paradigm."[93]

In Toronto recently, two heterosexual men, still heterosexual, each still interested in finding a woman to love, decided to take advantage of that jurisdiction's same-sex marriage law and marry one another. (For the tax advantage, they said). They have been advised by counsel that they are eligible to do so.[94] Same-sex marriage authorities say little or nothing about the purposes and activities which couples need to perform or intend.

Not only same-sex marriage but also heterosexual marriage and the terms which define the traditional family tumble into this post-modern void. The barriers between marriage and cohabitation collapse. The furthest extension to date may appear in a recent provision in Ontario where the legislature, under the prodding of a judicial mandate to revise marriage-related terminology in its statutes, redefined "spouse" to include people who are not married. *See* Bill 56 (2004), amending the Employment Standards Act to make the term "spouse" include:"either of two persons who . . . live together in a conjugal relationship outside marriage." [95]

Your spouse might be someone you are *not* married to? The ultimate social consequence of the same-sex marriage authorities may be the destruction of the sense of the ridiculous.

The trajectory leads on to the recognition of all sorts of "pair-bonded" structures—including those intended to be temporary rather than permanent. It implies the "nonjudgmental" attitude recommended by a sociologist:

> "[Policy makers] could attempt to create policies to support and help people in whatever type of social structures they create, giving equal credence and respect to divorced and married people, cohabiting and married couples, to children born out of wedlock and children born to married couples, and to married and unmarried parents.
> "The implication of the emerging pair-bonded paradigm for social policy makers is that social policies need to support people as they enter into, reside within, and move to whatever pair-bond structures fit their needs and goals. . . . Social policies must be   based on   respect for people's right to choose . . . to live . . . within any particular pair-bond structure." [96]

And there seems to be no reason why only *pairs* should be supported and recognized. Polygamy—the absurdity to which same-sex marriage advocates resisted being reduced in argument even two or three years ago[97]—has recently come to be treated by leading authorities as eligible for legal recognition. A respected Boston columnist sees it on the horizon.[98] The head of the ACLU now favors its protection.[99]

As legal authorities and social policy makers lose their grasp on any coherent and common understanding of marriage, that institution forfeits its definitive status as a matter of general opinion and social practice as well. Marriage becomes harder and harder to distinguish from nonmarital cohabitation. Custom, tradition, and religion may be ruled out as determinative and the slight definitive language in the same-sex marriage authorities is unhelpful.[100] Both kinds of relationship are based on "choice." The most vivid example is afforded by the Ontario amendment, quoted above, which makes one of the Ontario statutes define "spouse" to include people who are not married. In Denmark, where same-sex marriage provisions have been in place for many years, cohabitation is now a "normatively accepted option."[101]

IX.   Conclusion

Marriage in its traditional form is, structurally, a procreatively just affiliation. Cohabitation and same-sex relationships are not. Legal recognition of

same-sex relationships as marriage can be predicted to ramify in its consequences, encouraging educational and social promotion of same-sex affiliations.
It can also lead to the degradation of opposite-sex marriage, with predictable
adverse consequences for the future, including the procreative future, of subsequent generations.

Notes

1. J.D., Harvard. B.C.L., Oxford. Member of the Massachusetts Bar.
2. Line 13 (in the original this line ends with a comma).
3. THE DIGEST OF JUSTINIAN Book I, 10 (vol. 1 of the edition edited by Theo-
dor Mommsen, Paul Krueger & Alan Watson, 1985) The quotation above revises this
translation, which is, in fuller context: "Justice is a steady and enduring will to render
unto everyone his right. 1. The basic principles of right are: to live honorably, not to harm
any other person, to render to each his own."
4. Owing to space limitations, only passing attention can be paid to forms other than
marriage, cohabitation, and same-sex associations.
5. ECCLESIASTICUS 44 10-13 (NEW JERUSALEM BIBLE, 1985 ed., at 1141).
6. NICOMACHEAN ETHICS 1144a 12-18 *in* II THE COMPLETE WORKS OF
ARISTOTLE: THE REVISED OXFORD TRANSLATION 1729 at 1807 (Jonathan
Barnes, ed., W. D. Ross, trans. (rev. by J.O. Urmson), 1984)(hereinafter referred to as
"Aristotle, *Nicomachean Ethics*") .
7. *See* Catrin Finkenauer & Wim Meeus, *How (Pro-)Social Is the Caring Motive?*,
11 PSYCHOLOGICAL INQUIRY 100, 101 (2000)(available on jstor)(an "important
motive for caregiving may be found in the human need for belongingness . . . .").
8. David C. Bell & Alan J. Richard, *Caregiving: The Forgotten Element in Attachment*, 11 PSYCHOLOGICAL INQUIRY 69, 79 (2000)(available on jstor).
9. *Id.* at 75.
10. Gareth B. Matthews, *Concept Formation and Moral Development*, in PHILO-
SOPHICAL PERSPECTIVES ON DEVELOPMENTAL PSYCHOLOGY 175, 185
(James Russell ed., 1987). *See generally* A. Bandura, *Social Cognitive Theory: An Agentic Perspective*, 52 ANN. REV. PSYCHOLOGY 1 (2001).Lawrence J. Walker, Karl H.
Hennig & Tobias Krettenauer, *Parent and Peer Contexts for Children's Moral Reasoning
Development*, 71 CHILD DEVELOPMENT 1033, 1047 (2000) (available on
jstor)(reporting that both parents and peers "have a role to play.").
11. Kristin Anderson Moore, Susan M. Jekielek & Carol Emig, *Marriage from a
Child's Perspective: How Does Family Structure Affect Children, and What Can We Do
About It?*, CHILD TRENDS (June, 2002):

> "[R]esearch clearly demonstrates that family structure matters for child-
> ren, and the family structure that helps children the most is a family
> headed by two biological parents in a low-conflict marriage. Children in
> single-parent families, children born to unmarried mothers, and children
> in stepfamilies or cohabiting relationships face higher risks of poor out-
> comes than do children in intact families headed by two biological par-
> ents. Parental divorce is also linked to a range of poorer academic and
> behavioral outcomes among children."

12. Specifically, it proposes these standards for what might be called "primary" procreative affiliations. These standards are not proposed to be applied in their entirety to the
nanny or the wet nurse.

13. *See* JOHN SNAREY, HOW FATHERS CARE FOR THE NEXT GENERA-
TION: A FOUR-DECADE STUDY 276-80 (1993)(reviewing the studies which demonstrate the impact of fathering—including the father's sharing of parenting with the mother—on the offspring's own parenting practices). *See generally* ANDREW J. CHERLIN,
PUBLIC AND PRIVATE FAMILIES : AN INTRODUCTION 309 (4th ed.,
2005)(concluding, after a review of the literature, that "it is better for children to be
raised by two parents than one."), Paul R. Amato, *The Impact of Family Formation
Change on the Cognitive, Social, and Emotional Well-Being of the Next Generation*, 15
MARRIAGE & CHILD WELLBEING 75, 90 (2005)(available on jstor):
> "Research clearly demonstrates that children growing up with two conti-
> nuously married parents are less likely to experience a wide range of
> cognitive, emotional, and social problems, not only during childhood, but
> also during adulthood. Although it is not possible to demonstrate that
> family structure is the cause of these differences, studies that have used a
> variety of sophisticated statistical methods . . . suggest that this is the
> case."

See Lynn D. Wardle, *Children and the Future of Marriage*, 17 REGENT U. L.
REV. 279 (2005)(reviewing several studies and stating (at page 288) that "[o]n average,
children of married parents are physically and mentally healthier, better educated, and
later in life, enjoy more career success than children in other family settings.").

14. *See* Paul R. Amato, *The Impact of Family Formation Change on the Cognitive,
Social, and Emotional Well-Being of the Next Generation*, 15 MARRIAGE AND CHILD
WELLBEING 75, 85 (2005)(available on jstor):
> "Another benefit of a positive co-parental relationship is the modelling of
> interpersonal skills, such as showing respect, communicating clearly, and
> resolving disputes through negotiation and compromise. Children who
> learn these skills by observing their parents have positive relationships
> with peers and, later, with intimate partners."

See Paul R. Amato & Jacob Cheadle, *The Long Reach of Divorce: Divorce and
Child Well-Being Across Three Generations*, 67 J. MARRIAGE & FAMILY 191 (2005);
Lynn D. Wardle, *Children and the Future of Marriage*, 17 REGENT U. L. REV. 279,
299-302 (2005).

15. JUDITH WALLERSTEIN, JULIA LEWIS & SANDRA BLAKESLEE, THE
UNEXPECTED LEGACY OF DIVORCE: A 25 YEAR LANDMARK STUDY xxix
(2002). .

16. *See* SALLY CLINE, ZELDA FITZGERALD: HER VOICE IN PARADISE 111
(2002)("Zelda and Scott . . . achieved their stories by obsessively mining their own lives
and each other's for material and created their fiction almost entirely from personal experience.").

17. *See* Aristotle, *Nicomachean Ethics*, *supra* n. 17, 1155b 31—1156a 5 (page 1826
in the Ross translation):
> "To a friend we say we ought to wish what is good for his sake. . . .
> goodwill when it is reciprocal being friendship. * * * To be friends,
> [people] ... must be mutually recognized as bearing goodwill and wish-
> ing well to each other . . . . "

18. *Id.* 1170b 11-12 (page 1850 in the Ross translation)(emphasis omitted)..

19. *See id.* 1170b 10-13 (page 1850 in the Ross translation)(a friend "needs . . . to be
conscious of the existence of his friend . . . and this will be realized in their living together and sharing in discussion and thought; for this is what living together would seem to
mean in the case of man, and not, as in the case of cattle, feeding in the same place.").

20. Notably John Mordecai Guttman & Robert Wayne Levenson, *The Timing of Divorce: Predicting When a Couple Will Divorce Over a 14-Year Period*, 62 J. MARRIAGE & FAMILY 737 (2000)(available on jstor); John M. Gottman, James Coan, Sybil Carrere & Catherine Swanson, *Predicting Marital Happiness and Stability from Newlywed Interactions*, 60 J. MARRIAGE & FAMILY 5 (1998)(available on jstor).

21. *See generally* E.J. GRAFF, WHAT IS MARRIAGE FOR? 251 (1999)("Western marriage today is a home for the heart: entering, furnishing, and exiting that home is your business alone. Today's marriage—from whatever angle you look—is justified by the happiness of the pair." "Our society has endorsed" the conclusion that the purpose of marriage is "the refreshing of the individual spirit.").

22. *See* SALLY CLINE, ZELDA FITZGERALD: HER VOICE IN PARADISE 152 (2002)("Hemingway recalls Scott telling several versions . . . [of an episode involving] Zelda falling in love with a French aviator. The later versions, according to Hemingway, were less sad and seemed to be created as useful fictional material.").

23. ELEANOR LANAHAN, SCOTTIE THE DAUGHTER OF . . .: THE LIFE OF FRANCES SCOTT FITZGERALD LANAHAN SMITH 98 (1995).

24. *Id.* at 255.

25. *See generally* Lynn Wardle, *The Morality of Marriage and the Transformative Power of Inclusion* (in this volume); Scott FitzGibbon, *Marriage and the Good of Obligation*, 47 AM. J. JUR. 41 (2002).

26. Pope Benedict XVI, address to men and women religious, Vatican City, December 10, 2005, *in* L'OSSERVATORE ROMANO (English language edition) , December 21, 2005, at 3 (discussing not marriage but rather the fidelities of religious life).

27. More than half of cohabitors separate within five years. Larry Bumpass & Hwien-Hen Lu, *Trends in Cohabitation and Implications for Children's Family Contexts in the United States,* 54 POPULATION STUDIES 29, 33 (2000)(available on jstor). "[C]ohabitors who don't marry typically have a series of relationships. Half of all cohabiting relationships last a year or less, and only 1 out of 10 lasts as long as five years . . . .". ANDREW J. CHERLIN, PUBLIC AND PRIVATE FAMILIES : AN INTRODUCTION 248 (4th ed., 2005). *See* .Harry Benson, "The conflation of marriage and cohabitation in government statistics—a denial of difference rendered untenable by an analysis of outcomes" (Bristol Family Trust, September, 2006, available at www.bcft.co.uk/Family%20breakdown%20in%20the%20UK.pdf (accessed September 23, 2006)("The odds of a cohabiting couple with a young child splitting up are more than twice that of a married couple of equivalent age, income, education, ethnic group and benefits.").

28 Joanna M. Reed, *Not Crossing the "'Extra Line": How Cohabitors with Children View their Unions,* 68 J. MARRIAGE & FAMILY 1117 (2006). .

29. THE CASE FOR MARRIAGE: WHY MARRIED PEOPLE ARE HAPPIER, HEALTHIER AND BETTER OFF FINANCIALLY 38 (2000). *See* Anne-Marie Ambert, *Cohabitation and Marriage: How Are they Related?* 13 *et seq.* (Ottawa, Ontario: The Vanier Institute of the Family, September, 2005), available at http://www.vifamily.ca/library/cft/cohabitation.pdf (accessed February 18, 2007)(reviewing the literature establishing that "cohabitors are less faithful to their partners sexually").

30. Section IV B 6 *infra*

31. *See generally* Scott FitzGibbon, The Seduction of Lydia Bennet and the Jurisprudence of the Juristic Society, in FAMILY LAW: BALANCING INTERESTS AND PURSUING PRIORITIES 64 (Lynn D. Wardle & Camille S. Williams, eds., 2007); Scott FitzGibbon, The Seduction of Lydia Bennet:

Toward a General Theory of Society, Marriage, and the Family, 4 AVE MA-
RIA L. REV. 581 (2006).

32. *See generally* Lynn D. Wardle, *Parenthood and the Limits of Adult Autonomy,*
24 ST. LOUIS U. PUB. L. REV. 169, 172 (2005)("the root paradigm of responsible parenthood—individual and social commitment to children and to posterity—is deeply
rooted in Western and other societies . . . .")..

33. *See generally* DAVID MATZKO MCCARTHY, SEX AND LOVE IN THE
HOME: A THEOLOGY OF THE HOUSEHOLD (2001).

34. *See* Barbara Dafoe Whitehead & David Popenoe, The State of Our Unions: The
Social Health of Marriage in America 2006. Essay: Life Without Children (National Marriage Project, 2006), available on line at http://marriage.rutgers.edu/Publications/
SOOU/TEXTSOOU2006.htm (accessed July 15, 2006) (82% of teenage girls and 77%
of teenage boys said that having a good marriage and family life was "extremely important" to them; 84.5 % of girls and 77% of boys expect to marry (or are already married)).

35. For general discussion of types of love see Lynn D. Wardle, *All You Need is
Love?*, 14 S. CAL. REV. L. & WOMEN'S STUDIES 51 (2004).

36. I. CESLAS SPICQ, O.P., THEOLOGICAL LEXICON OF THE NEW TES-
TAMENT 9 (James D. Ernst, trans. & ed., 1994)("the desire of the wolf for the sheep.").
See Socrates, in Plato, Phaedrus 241 d: "As wolves love lambs so lovers love their loves."
I THE DIALOGUES OF PLATO 246 (B. Jowett trans., 1892).

37. Thus the definition which Socrates places in the mouth of a persuading lover of a
boy:

> "[T]he irrational desire which overcomes the tendency of opinion towards
> right, and is led away to the enjoyment of beauty, and especially of per-
> sonal beauty, by the desires which are her own kindred—that supreme
> desire, I say, which by leading conquers and by the force of passion is
> reinforced, from this very force, receiving a name, is called love."

Phaedrus at 238 b-c, in I THE DIALOGUES OF PLATO 243 (B. Jowett trans.,
1892). A valuable discussion of this passage and of *eros* generally is presented in A.W.
PRICE, LOVE AND FRIENDSHIP IN PLATO AND ARISTOTLE 61 *et seq.* (1989).
See Encyclical Letter Deus Caritas Est *of the Supreme Pontiff Benedict XVI to the Bishops, Priests, and Deacons, Men and Women Religious, and all the Lay Faithful on
Christian   Love   (December   25,   2005),   available   at
http://www.vatican.va/holy_father/benedict_xvi/encyclicals/documents/hf_ben-
xvi_enc_20051225_deus-caritas-est_en.html (accessed February 2, 2007)("[t]hat love
between man and woman which is neither planned nor willed, but somehow imposes
itself upon human beings, was called eros by the ancient Greeks." (paragraph 3); "The
Greeks—not unlike other cultures—considered eros principally as a kind of intoxication,
the overpowering of reason by a 'divine madness' which tears man away from his finite
existence and enables him, in the very process of being overwhelmed by divine power, to
experience supreme happiness." (paragraph 4)).

38. "[T]o him who has a mind diseased anything is agreeable which is not opposed
to him, but that which is equal or superior is hateful to him, and therefore the lover will
not brook any superiority or equality on the part of his beloved; he is always employed in
reducing him to inferiority." Socrates, in Plato, *Phaedrus* 238 e—239 a, I THE DIALO-
GUES OF PLATO 243-44 (B. Jowett trans., 1892).

39. *See* THE REPUBLIC OF PLATO 574 e (Alan Bloom, trans., 2d ed., 1968, at
255)(hereinafter referred to as "Plato, *Republic*")(describing the man dominated by *eros,*
which "lives like a tyrant within him in all anarchy and lawlessness," so that he will
"stick at no terrible murder, food, or deed.").

40. This is an aspect of what Roger Scruton calls "Tristanism": "His desire * * * has divorced itself from all social norms, all forms of companionship, besides this one, of bodily union in the 'act of darkness.'" ROGER SCRUTON, SEXUAL DESIRE: A MORAL PHILOSOPHY OF THE EROTIC 171 (1986).

41. *See generally* HAROLD B. SEGEL, PINOCCHIO'S PROGENY: PUPPETS, MARIONETTES, AUTOMATONS, AND ROBOTS IN MODERNIST AND AVANT-GARDE DRAMA (1995)(observing that puppets and marionettes were used as a metaphor by the modernist movement for the helplessness of man under the influence of various powerful forces, including *eros*).

42. "[W]hat he had rarely been in dreams, he became continuously while awake." Plato, *Republic supra* n. 39, 574 e (Alan Bloom, trans., at 255). *See* TERENCE IRWIN, PLATO'S ETHICS 664-71 (1995) for a discussion of Plato on knowledge and dreaminess.

43. *See* Arlene Saxonhouse, *Democracy, Equality, and* Eidê : *A Radical View from Book 8 of Plato's* Republic, 92 AM. POL. SCIENCE REV. 272, 280 (1998).

44. Plato, *Republic, supra* n. 39, 561 b-c. The above is a medley of the Bloom translation, *supra*, at 239 and the translation in Arlene Saxonhouse, *op. cit.* at 280.

45. *See generally Encyclical Letter* Deus Caritas Est *of the Supreme Pontiff Benedict XVI to the Bishops, Priests, and Deacons, Men and Women Religious, and all the Lay Faithful on Christian Love* (December 25, 2005), available at http://www.vatican.va/holy_father/benedict_xvi/encyclicals/documents/hf_ben-xvi_enc_20051225_deus-caritas-est_en.html (accessed February 2, 2007)(acknowledging the irrational and destructive potentialities of *eros* but emphasizing its capacity for integration with the agapic. *E.g.:* " Even if eros is at first mainly covetous and ascending, a fascination for the great promise of happiness, in drawing near to the other, it is less and less concerned with itself, increasingly seeks the happiness of the other, is concerned more and more with the beloved, bestows itself and wants to 'be there for' the other. The element of agape thus enters into this love, for otherwise eros is impoverished and even loses its own nature.")(paragraph 7). *Cf.* MAGGIE GALLAGHER, THE ABOLITION OF MARRIAGE: HOW WE DESTROY LASTING LOVE 259-63 (1996)(presenting a high account of *eros*, culminating in the conclusion (at 263) that "[m]arriage is the incarnation of eros, the body of love. It is the psalms and the Song of Songs and it is the Crucifixion, or at least it is our aspiration to all of these things."); MAGGIE GALLAGHER, ENEMIES OF EROS: HOW THE SEXUAL REVOLUTION IS KILLING FAMILY, MARRIAGE AND SEX AND WHAT WE CAN DO ABOUT IT (1989).

46. *See generally* JOHN PAUL II, THE THEOLOGY OF THE BODY: HUMAN LOVE IN THE DIVINE PLAN 99 (1997)("'To know' *(jadaq)* in biblical language does not mean only a purely intellectual knowledge, but also concrete knowledge, such as the experience of suffering (cf Is 533), of sin (Wis 3:13), of war and peace (Jgs 3:1; Is 59:8). From this experience moral judgment also springs: 'knowledge of good and evil' (2:9-17).").

47. Roger Scruton, *Sacrilege and Sacrament,* in THE MEANING OF MARRIAGE: FAMILY, STATE, MARKET, AND MORALS 3, 26 (Robert P. George & Jean Bethke Elshtain, eds., 2006). Scruton adds: "Marriage has grown up around the idea of sexual difference and all that sexual difference means." *Id.*

48. ECCLESIASTICUS 44 10-13 (NEW JERUSALEM BIBLE, 1985 ed., at 1141).

49. *See* n. 34, *supra.*

50. See LINDA J. WAITE & MAGGIE GALLAGHER, THE CASE FOR MARRIAGE: WHY MARRIED PEOPLE ARE HAPPIER, HEALTHIER, AND BETTER OFF FINANCIALLY (2000); Anne-Marie Ambert, *Cohabitation and Marriage: How*

Are they Related? 18 *et seq.* (Ottawa, Ontario: The Vanier Institute of the Family, September, 2005), available at http://www.vifamily.ca/library/cft/cohabitation.pdf (accessed February 18, 2007)(reviewing the literature finding a correlation between marriage and various elements of well being; and concluding that this correlation is not only a product of a selection effect but also arises because marriage produces such benefits.).

51. *See* Lynn D. Wardle, *Children and the Future of Marriage,* 17 REGENT U. L. REV. 279, 285-86 (2005)("The number of unmarried couples has increased by over 300 percent in the last twenty years. * * * By 2000, one-third of all children born in the United States were born out of wedlock.); Larry Bumpass & Hwien-Hen Lu, *Trends in Cohabitation and Implications for Children's Family Contexts in the United States,*. 54 POPULATION STUDIES 29 (2000)(available on jstor)("[c]ohabitation has grown from a rare and deviant behaviour to the majority experience among cohorts of marriageable age" (at 29), that "many unmarried births occur in two-parent cohabiting families" (at 30) and that the trend is upwards (at 34-35)).

52. Studies are analyzed and their implications described in DAVID POPENOE & BARBARA DAFOE WHITEHEAD, SHOULD WE LIVE TOGETHER? WHAT YOUNG ADULTS NEED TO KNOW ABOUT COHABITATION BEFORE MARRIAGE (2d ed., 2002), available at http://marriage@rutgers.edu and in LINDA J. WAITE & MAGGIE GALLAGHER, THE CASE FOR MARRIAGE: WHY MARRIED PEOPLE ARE HAPPIER, HEALTHIER, AND BETTER OFF FINANCIALLY ch. 5 (2000).

53. *See* notes 52 and 54.

54. See See NICHOLAS H. WOLFINGER, UNDERSTANDING THE DIVORCE CYCLE: THE CHILDREN OF DIVORCE IN THEIR OWN MARRIAGES 68 (2005)("Both premarital childbirth and premarital cohabitation are strong predictors of divorce."); Anne-Marie Ambert, Cohabitation and Marriage: How Are they Related? 9 (Ottawa, Ontario: The Vanier Institute of the Family, September, 2005), available at http://www.vifamily.ca/library/cft/cohabitation.pdf (accessed February 18, 2007)("cohabitation before marriage seems to raise the risk of divorce later on.").
Ambert further observes:

> "[T]here is some evidence to the effect that the experience of a less secure, committed, and even faithful cohabitation shapes subsequent marital behaviour . . . . Some couples continue to live their marriage through the perspective of the insecurity, lack of pooling of resources, low commitment level, and even lack of fidelity of their prior cohabitation. Others simply learn to accept the temporary nature of relationships . . . .".

55. *See* Susan L. Brown, *Family Structure Transitions and Adolescent Well-being,* 43 DEMOGRAPHY 447 (2006):

> "[C]ohabitation is often associated with poorer outcomes [for adolescents]. Moving out of a cohabiting stepfamily into a single-mother family was not harmful and was actually associated with improvements in school engagement. Moving into a cohabiting stepfamily from a single-mother family decreased adolescent well-being, and this impact was greater than that experienced by those who moved into a married stepfamily. Stable cohabiting stepfamilies were associated with lower levels of well-being than stable married stepfamilies."

See Robin Wilson, *Evaluating Marriage: Does Marriage Matter to the Nurturing of Children?,* 42(3) SAN DIEGO L. REV. 847 (2005)(available at www. Law. Umaryland. Edu/faculty_publications.a_sp?facultynum=280); Anne-Marie Ambert, *op. cit.* (reviewing the literature on the effects of cohabitation on children and noting poorer performance in school, more behavioral problems, and, when the mother cohabits with a man who is not the father, increased risk of general neglect and physical and sexual abuse); Susan L. Brown, *Family Structure and Child Well-Being: The Significance of Parental Cohabitation*, 66 J. MARRIAGE & FAM. 351 (2004)("Children living in two-biological-parent cohabiting families experience worse outcomes, on average, than those residing with two biological married parents."). *But see* Wendy D. Manning & Susan Brown, *Children's Economic Well-Being in Married and Cohabiting Parent Families*, 68 J. MARRIAGE & FAMILY 345 (2006):

> "Our findings suggest that children can potentially benefit [economically] from living with a cohabiting partner whose resources are shared with family members. Although children living with married rather than cohabiting parents fare better in terms of material well-being, this advantage is accounted for by race and ethnic group and parents' education."

(abstract). Earlier studies are described in JAMES Q. WILSON, THE MARRIAGE PROBLEM: HOW OUR CULTURE HAS WEAKENED FAMILIES 6-7 (2002).

56. DAVID POPENOE & BARBARA DAFOE WHITEHEAD, SHOULD WE LIVE TOGETHER? WHAT YOUNG ADULTS NEED TO KNOW ABOUT COHABITATION BEFORE MARRIAGE 8 (2002). *See* Larry Bumpass & Hwien-Hen Lu, *Trends in Cohabitation and Implications for Children's Family Contexts in the United States*, 54 POPULATION STUDIES 29, 38 (2000)(available on jstor)("Children born to cohabiting parents . . . may spend about a quarter of their childhood years with a single-parent family, a quarter with a cohabiting parent, and less than half with married parents. . . . * * * Children born to married parents spend the vast majority (84 per cent) of their childhood in two-parent families.).

57. *See* Larry Bumpass & Hwien-Hen Lu, *op. cit.*, at 35 ("Parents who shared a cohabiting family with their children are likely to find it difficult to argue effectively that their children should abstain from either unmarried sex or cohabitation"—"yet another feedback loop in the inter-generational aspects of the declining significance of marriage."); Lawrence L. Wu & Brian C. Martinson, *Family Structure and the Risk of a Premarital Birth*, 58 AM. SOCIOLOGICAL REV. 210 (1993)(available on jstor) (discussing the "widely replicated finding . . . that a woman who grows up in a nonintact family is more likely to bear a child before marrying . . . ."(page 210))

58. *See* MAGGIE GALLAGHER, THE ABOLITION OF MARRIAGE: HOW WE DESTROY LASTING LOVE 259 (1996), *quoting* FRANK F. FURSTENBERG, JR. & ANDREW J. CHERLIN, DIVIDED FAMILIES: WHAT HAPPENS TO CHILDREN WHEN PARENTS PART 6 (1991).(""emotional gratification has become the *sine qua non* of married life. It is the main glue that holds couples together.").

59. Authorities noting the high divorce rate and also attitudes towards marriage are reviewed in NICHOLAS H. WOLFINGER, UNDERSTANDING THE DIVORCE CYCLE: THE CHILDREN OF DIVORCE IN THEIR OWN MARRIAGES 76-81 (2005) and in Lynn D. Wardle, *Is Marriage Obsolete?*, 10 MICH. J. GENDER & L. 189 (2003).

60. In addition to the works cited in the next several notes *infra*, see ELIZABETH MARQUARDT, BETWEEN TWO WORLDS: THE INNER LIVES OF CHILDREN OF DIVORCE (2005); Gordon E. Finley & Seth J. Schwartz, *Father Involvement and Long-Term Young Adult Outcomes: The Differential Contributions of Divorce and Gender*, 45 FAMILY COURT REV. 573 (2007)(finding, among offspring of divorce, high levels of regret as to insufficient father involvement); Paul R. Amato, *The Impact of Family Formation Change on the Cognitive, Social, and Emotional Well-Being of the Next Generation*, 15 MARRIAGE & CHILD WELLBEING 75, 90 (2005)(available on jstor):

"Research clearly demonstrates that children growing up with two continuously married parents are less likely to experience a wide range of
cognitive, emotional, and social problems, not only during childhood, but
also during adulthood. Although it is not possible to demonstrate that
family structure is the cause of these differences, studies that have used a
variety of sophisticated statistical methods . . . suggest that this is the
case."

See Lynn D. Wardle, *Children and the Future of Marriage*, 17 REGENT U. L.
REV. 279 (2005)(reviewing several studies and stating (at 288) that "[o]n average, children of married parents are physically and mentally healthier, better educated, and later in
life, enjoy more career success than children in other family settings."); Anne-Marie Ambert, *Cohabitation and Marriage: How Are they Related?* 20 (Ottawa, Ontario: The
Vanier   Institute   of   the   Family,   September,   2005),   available   at
http://www.vifamily.ca/library/cft/cohabitation.pdf (accessed February 18, 2007):

"I have reviewed the impact on children of divorce and of living on one-
parent families . . . . The conclusion of these various reviews is that children benefit unequivocally from their parents' marriage . . . . * * * Children are far better off on all dimensions when they live with their original
two parents—provided that these . . . parents are reasonably warm and
monitoring and do not engage in conjugal abuse and conflict in front of
their offspring . . . . "

See generally ANDREW J. CHERLIN, PUBLIC AND PRIVATE FAMILIES: AN
INTRODUCTION 430 (4th ed., 2005)(concluding after a review of the literature that
"the majority of offspring who experienced parental divorce probably would have been
better off if their parents had stayed together.")

61. Paul R. Amato, *Children of Divorce in the 1990's: An Update of the Amato &
Keith (1991) Meta-Analysis*, 15 J. FAM. PSYCHOL. 355 (2001).

62. Paul R. Amato & Jacob .Cheadle, *The Long Reach of Divorce: Divorce and
Child Well-Being Across Three Generations*, 67 J. MARRIAGE & FAMILY 191 (2005).

63 *Id.*

64. *The Future of Family Law: Law and the Marriage Crisis in North America* 39
(Dan Cere, Principal Investigator, 2005). *See generally* Marcia J. Carlson, *Family Structure, Father Involvement, and Adolescent Behavioral Outcomes*, 68 J. MARRIAGE &
FAMILY   137   (2006),   available   online   at   http://www.blackwell-
synergy.com/doi/full/10.111.j.1741-3737.2006.00239.x :

"Extensive research has shown that living apart from one's biological father is associated with a greater risk of adverse outcomes for children and
adolescents, regardless of race, education, or mothers' remarriage . . . . *
* * Compared to children living with two married biological parents,
children living apart from their fathers are, on average, more likely to be
suspended or expelled from school . . . more likely to engage in delinquent activities . . . more likely to experience depression or anxiety . .
.and more likely to report externalizing and internalizing behavioral problems . . . . "

See generally Laura Hamilton, Simon Cheng & Brian Powell, *Adoptive Parents,
Adaptive Parents: Evaluating the Importance of Biological Ties for Parental Investment*,
72   AM.   SOCIOLOGICAL   REV.95   (2007),   available   at
http://www.asanet.org/galleries/default-file/Feb07ASRAdoption.pdf (accessed February
15, 2007)(examining parental investment in the care of a sample of first-graders and con-

cluding that two-biological-parent and two-adoptive-parent families invest "at significantly higher levels in most resources than other types of families.").

65. Paul R. Amato & Jacob Cheadle, The Long Reach of Divorce: Divorce and Child Well-Being Across Three Generations, 67 J. MARRIAGE & FAMILY 191 (2005), available at www.blackwell-synergy.com See NICHOLAS H. WOLFINGER, UNDERSTANDING THE DIVORCE CYCLE: THE CHILDREN OF DIVORCE IN THEIR OWN MARRIAGES (2005)(passim: see especially page 74: "Parental divorce increases the chances of offspring divorce by at least 40 percent . . . ."); JUDITH WALLERSTEIN, JULIA LEWIS, & SANDRA BLAKESLEE, THE UNEXPECTED LEGACY OF DIVORCE: A 25 YEAR LANDMARK STUDY xxix (2000):

> "Contrary to what we have long thought, the major impact of divorce does not occur during childhood or adolescence. Rather, it rises in adulthood as serious romantic relationships move center stage. When it comes time to choose a life mate and build a new family, the effects of divorce crescendo. A central finding of my research is that children identify not only with their mother and father as separate individuals but with the relationship between them. They carry the template of this relationship into adulthood and use it to seek the image of their new family. The absence of a good image negatively influences their search for love, intimacy, and commitment. Anxiety leads many into making bad choices in relationships, giving up hastily when problems arise, or avoiding relationships altogether."

See ANDREW J. CHERLIN, PUBLIC AND PRIVATE FAMILIES: AN INTRODUCTION (4th ed., 2005)(reporting that "[a] number of studies show that persons whose parents divorced while they were growing up are more likely than others to become divorced themselves . . . ." (at 415); offering some criticisms of the Wallerstein study but accepting that "her basic point that the effects of divorce can sometimes last into adulthood . . . is valid" (at 429); and reporting findings that people whose parents divorced "seemed just as happy with their marriages" but "were more likely to think that their marriages were in trouble" and among those who reported their marriages as less than very happy "more likely to argue frequently and to shout or hit while arguing" (at 430)); Larry Bumpass & Hwien-Hen Lu, *Trends in Cohabitation and Implications for Children's Family Contexts in the United States,*. 54 POPULATION STUDIES 29 (2000)(available on jstor)(reviewing the literature and reporting that " [c]hildren from single-parent families are more likely . . . to enter sexual activity earlier and have premarital births . . . to cohabit . . . and to marry early and experience the disruption of their own marriages . . . ." (at pages 29-30)). Stephanie Staal, reporting her own experience and those of other offspring of divorced parents, reports "fear of intimacy" and notes that "[w]ithout a healthy model of intimacy as reference, we may internalize a skewed picture of marriage that we unwittingly recreate through our own behavior and in our choice of partner." STEPHANIE STAAL, THE LOVE THEY LOST: LIVING WITH THE LEGACY OF OUR PARENTS' DIVORCE 20, 177 (2000). She reports, among the offspring of divorce, widespread "apprehension about having children of their own [and a fear that] . . . they would pass down a legacy of divorce to their children." *Id.* at 226. *See generally* Karin Grossmann, Klaus E. Grossmann & Heinz Kindler, *Early Care and the Roots of Attachment and Partnership Representations, ,*in ATTACHMENT FROM INFANCY TO ADULTHOOD: THE MAJOR LONGITUDINAL STUDIES 98, 126 (Klaus E. Grossmann, Karin Grossmann & Everett Waters, eds., 2005)("Mothers' as well as fathers' sensitive supportiveness, acceptance of the child, and appropriate challenging behaviors . . . were powerful predictors of . . . close relationships in young adulthood.").

66. Paul R. Amato & Jacob Cheadle, *op. cit.* ("Conclusion").

67. *See* Roger Scruton, *Sacrilege and Sacrament,* in THE MEANING OF MARRIAGE: FAMILY, STATE, MARKET, AND MORALS 3, 16 (Robert P. George & Jean Bethke Elshtain, eds., 2006):

> "There is a picture of human sexuality propagated by the media, by popular culture, and by much sex education in our schools, which tries both to discount the difference between us and the other animals and also to remove every hint of the forbidden, the dangerous, and the sacred. It is a picture that makes no place for shame, save as a lingering disability, and which describes the experience of sex as a kind of bodily sensation. Sexual initiation, according to this picture, means learning to overcome guilt and shame, to put aside our hesitations, and to enjoy what is described in the literature as 'good sex.' The function of sex education in schools . . . is to rescue children from the commitments that have been attached to desire by displaying sex as a matter of cost-free pleasure."

68. Mark Daims, *Book Review: Liberation's Children: Parents and Kids in a Postmodern Age,* 4 HUMAN NATURE REV. 44 (2004).

69. *See* Sandra L. Hofferth, *Residential Father Family Type and Child Well-Being: Investment Versus Selection,* 43 DEMOGRAPHY 53 (2006) *abstract available at* http://muse.jhu.edu/cgi-bin/access.cgi?uri=/journals/demography/v043/43.1hofferth.html (accessed Nov. 26, 2006)("Children in all family types except the married-biological-parent family showed higher levels of behavioral problems."); Kristin Anderson Moore, Susan M. Jekielek & Carol Emig, *Marriage from a Child's Perspective: How Does Family Structure Affect Children, and What Can We Do About It?,* CHILD TRENDS (June, 2002) (quoted in section IV B, *supra*); Dean Lillard & Jennifer Gerner, *Getting to the Ivy League: How Family Composition Affects College Choice,* 70 J. HIGHER ED. 706 (1999), available at www.jstor.org.proxy.bc.edu (*accessed* October 9, 2006)(students who lived with both biological parents were more likely to apply to, be admitted to, and to attend a four-year college and a great deal more likely to attend a selective college). *See also* ANDREW J. CHERLIN, PUBLIC AND PRIVATE FAMILIES : AN INTRODUCTION 309 (4th ed., 2005)(concluding, after a review of the literature, that "it is better for children to be raised by two parents than one.").

70. A. Dean Byrd, *Gender Complementarity and Child-reading: Where Tradition and Science Agree,* 6 J. L. & FAMILY STUDIES No. 2.

71. Don Browning & Elizabeth Marquardt, *What About the Children? Liberal Cautions on Same-Sex Marriage,* in THE MEANING OF MARRIAGE: FAMILY, STATE, MARKET, AND MORALS 29, 36 (Robert P. George & Jean Bethke Elshtain, eds., 2006)(referring to the quoted proposition as a "widely held assumption" and apparently embracing it. The authors also there note "the observation that . . . children themselves want—indeed, often *long*—to be raised by those who gave them life."). *But see* Laura Hamilton, Simon Cheng & Brian Powell, *Adoptive Parents, Adaptive Parents: Evaluating the Importance of Biological Ties for Parental Investment,* 72 AMERICAN SOCIOLOGICAL REV. 95 (2007), available at http://www.asanet.org/galleries/default-file/Feb07ASRAdoption.pdf (accessed February 15, 2007)(examining parental investment in the care of a sample of first-graders and concluding that "two-adoptive-parent families invest at similar levels as two-biological parent families" and "at significantly higher levels in most resources than other types of families.")

72. *See* George A. Rekers, *An Empirically Supported Rational Basis for Prohibiting Adoption, Foster Parenting, and Contested Child Custody by Any Person Residing in a Household that Includes a Homosexually-Behaving Member,* 18 ST. THOMAS L. REV.

325, 342 (2005)("Homosexual partner relationships are *significantly and substantially less stable and more short-lived* on the average compared to a marriage of a man and a woman." (emphasis in original); Gunnar Andersson, Turid Noack, Ane Seierstad & Harald Weedon-Fekjaer, *The Demographics of Same-Sex Marriages in Norway and Sweden*, 43 DEMOGRAPHY 79 (2006), abstract available at http://muse.jhu.edu/journals/demography/toc/dem43.1.html (accessed January 26, 2007)("divorce-risk levels are considerably higher in same-sex marriages."(abstract)).

73. Risky to the health, for example, as is likely the case where the relationship involves sex. See Lynn D. Wardle, The Biological Causes and Consequences of Homosexual Behavior and Their Relevance for Family Law Policies, 56 DEPAUL L. REV. 997 1017 (2007)(reviewing social science literature and concluding that "[h]omosexual behavior significantly increases the risk of serious health effects. Homosexual sex is, by definition, risky sex.").

74. *See* George A. Rekers, *An Empirically Supported Rational Basis for Prohibiting Adoption, Foster Parenting, and Contested Child Custody by Any Person Residing in a Household that Includes a Homosexually-Behaving Member*, 18 ST. THOMAS L. REV. 325, 359-62 (2005)(reviewing the literature establishing that the public generally disapproves of homosexual conduct, homosexual marriage, and homosexual adoption).

75. For reviews of the literature on lesbian and gay parenting as regards its general effects on children, see William Meezan & Jonathan Rauch, *Gay Marriage, Same-Sex Parenting, and America's Children*, 15 MARRIAGE AND CHILD WELL-BEING 97 (2005)(available on jstor)("After considering the methodological problems . . . that have bedeviled this literature, . . . the authors find that the children who have been studied are doing about as well a children normally do. What the research does not yet show is whether the children studied are typical of the general population of children raised by gay and lesbian couples." (at 97); Walter R. Schumm, *Empirical and Theoretical Perspectives from Social Science on Gay Marriage and Child Custody Issues*, 18 ST. THOMAS L. REV. 425 (2005); Fiona Tasker, *Lesbian Mothers, Gay Fathers, and Their Children: A Review*, 26 DEV. & BEHAV. PEDIATRICS 224 (2005); ; Lynn D. Wardle, *Children and the Future of Marriage*, 17 REGENT U. L. REV. 279, 292-95 (2005) Lynn D. Wardle, *Adult Sexuality, the Best Interest of Children, and Placement Liability of Foster-Care and Adoption Agencies*, 6 J. L. & FAM. STUD. 59, 97-99 (2004). *Cf.* iNanette Gartrell, Carla Rodas, Amalia Deck, Heidi Payer & Amy Banks, *Interviews with Ten-Year-Old Children*, 70(4) AM. J. ORTHOPSYCHIATRY (2005)(asserting that "in social and psychological development, the children [of lesbian parents] were comparable to children raised in heterosexual families" based on a "self-selected" sample of seventy-eight mothers; data on the well-being of the children consisted almost entirely of statements made by the mothers.).

Studies from the social sciences are inconclusive as to the effects of same-sex parenting on the procreative future of the child. Such studies and their limitations are discussed in ANDREW J. CHERLIN, PUBLIC AND PRIVATE FAMILIES: AN INTRODUCTION 313-14 (4th ed., 2005) and in Judith Stacey & Timothy J. Biblarz, *(How) Does Sexual Orientation of Parents Matter?*, 66 AM. SOC. REV. 159 (2001). Narrative accounts of adverse effects on sexuality and gender identity are presented in Lynn D. Wardle: *The "Inner Lives" of Children in Lesbigay Adoption: Narratives and Other Concerns*, 18 ST. THOMAS L. REV. 511 (2006).

76. This Part Six considers developments in the social order, leaving aside the (likely extensive) further legal developments. .Marriage is the axle upon which the entirety of family law pivots, so its definition is likely to affect doctrines pertinent to visitation rights and custody, for example. Hundred of doctrines outside of family law which refer to mar-

riage and the family are likely to be affected as well. Marital status has been identified as implicated in more than a thousand federal laws. *See* Letter from GAO Associate General Counsel Barry Bedrick to the Hon. Henry Hyde dated January 31, 1997, GAO/OGC-97-16; GAO-04-353R, Defense of Marriage Act ; letter from GAO Associate General Counsel Dayna K. Shah to the Hon. Bill Frist, dated Jan. 23, 2004.

77. Michael Bronski, "Altar Ego: Why some queer political activists are raising questions about the limits and long-term worth of same-sex marriage," BOSTON PHOENIX, July 16-22, 2004, available at http://www.bostonphoenix.com/boston/news_features/other_stories/multi-page/documents/03979297.asp.

78. Thomas Payzant has subsequently been given an appointment at Harvard. *See* "Thomas Payzant Named HGSE Senior Lecturer" (article dated April 26, 2006 on the web cite of the Harvard Graduate School of Education, www.gse.harvard.edu/news_events/features/2006/04/26_payzant.html (accessed September 9, 2006).

79. Memorandum dated May 13, 2004 (first paragraph).

80. The way the memorandum is drafted, she violates the rules even if she has no bias; all she need do is say something that causes someone else to develop bias. If the teacher says nothing at all, she still may have to worry about an obligation to blow the whistle if one of her students says something unpleasant ("report and act promptly on any incidents that may create a climate of intolerance"). And as to advising a student about concerns in his social life, the mind boggles. He better not exhibit bias in the way he conducts it.

81. *All Things Considered,* September 13, 2004.

82. "Brave New Schools: Complaint demands 'pro-gay' studies for kids: Canada's legalization of same-sex marriage prompts case," article in © 2005 WorldNetDaily.com http://worldnetdaily.com/news/article.asp?ARTICLE_ID=42529 (Posted January 25, 2005). (The bracketed material is included, bracketed, in the original.).

83. Memorandum from Thomas W. Payzant, Superintendent, Boston Public Schools dated May 13, 2004 paragraph one.

84. Goodridge v. Department of Public Health, 440 Mass. 309, 321, 798 N.E.2d 941, 954 (2003).

85. *Id.*

86. Baehr v. Lewin, 74 Haw. 530, 570 (1993).

87. Goodridge v. Department of Public Health, 440 Mass. 309, 341, 798 N.E.2d 941, 968 (2003).

88. Halpern v. Canada, 215 D.L.R. (4th) 223 (Can.), par. 243 ("Any justification based upon the belief that heterosexual relationships are superior to same-sex relationships would be rejected as being 'fundamentally repugnant . . . .'").

89. There is some language in *Goodridge* which aims at a definition: "the voluntary union of two persons as spouses, to the exclusion of all others." Goodridge v. Department of Public Health, 440 MASS. 309, 343, 798 N.E.2d 941, 969 (2003). This impossibly vague language—leaving aside the use of the term "spouses," which is in this context a redundancy—would make a two-person law partnership or hiking trip into a marriage.

90. *Id.,* 798 N.E. 2d at 948, *quoting* Laurence v. Texas, 123 S. Ct. 2472, 2480 (2003).

91. 539 U.S. 558, 123 S. Ct. 2472, 2487-88 (2003).

92. Planned Parenthood v. Casey, 505 U.S. 833, 851 (1992), *quoted in* Laurence v. Texas, 123 S. Ct. 2472, 2481 (2003).

93. Goodridge v. Department of Public Health, 440 Mass. 309, 339, 798 N.E.2d 941, 967 (2003).

94. Lesley Wright, "Wedding Cashers," TORONTO SUN, August 6, 2005.

95. Bill 56 (2004)(emphasis added). The text is available on line at http://www.ontla.on.ca/documents/Bills/38_Parliament/Session1/b056ra_e.htm. The Explanatory Note identifies this bill as having been enacted.

96. William M. Pinsof, *The death of "till death us do part": the transformation of pair-bonding in the 20th century*, 41 FAMILY PROCESS 135 (2002). The author is identified as "President of the Family Institute at Northwestern University and Director of Northwestern's Center for Applied Psychology and Family Studies."

97. "Advocates of same-sex marriage, who held their own State House briefing yesterday, dismissed the argument [that SSM leads to the recognition of polygamy] by their opponents as 'an old myth' that has little to do with fundamental rights of people. Carol Rose of the American Civil Liberties Union of Massachusetts said homosexuality is about 'who they are,' while multiple marriage 'isn't about who you are.'" Raphael Lewis, "Opponents Warn Lawmakers that Polygamy Will be Next," BOSTON GLOBE, February 10, 2004 http://www.boston.com/news/local/massachusetts/articles/2004/02/10/opponents_warn_l awmakers_that_polygamy_will_be_next/ (accessed October 9, 2005).

98. Jeff Jacoby, "Is Legal Polygamy Next?" BOSTON GLOBE, January 5, 2004.

99. *See* Crystal Paul-Laughinhouse, "Leader of ACLU talks on agenda," YALE DAILY NEWS http://yaledailynews.com/article.asp?AID=27865:

> "In response to a student's question about gay marriage, bigamy and polygamy in certain communities, Strossen [the President of the ACLU] said the ACLU is actively fighting to defend freedom of choice in marriage and partnerships. 'We have defended the right for individuals to engage in polygamy,' Strossen said. 'We defend the freedom of choice for mature, consenting individuals.'"

100. *See* note 89, *supra.*

101. Cecilie Whehner, Mia Kambskard & Peter Abrahamson, *Demography of the Family: The Case of Denmark*, http://www.york.ac.uk/inst/spru/research/ nordic/denmdemo.pdf.

CHAPTER 8
DWELLING AMONG US

Martha Bailey[1]
Queen's University

Same-sex marriage has been available in some Canadian provinces since 2003, after various provincial appellate courts ruled that the exclusion of same-sex couples from marriage violated the *Charter of Rights and Freedoms*. In 2005 Canada's Parliament enacted the *Civil Marriage Act*, which opened up civil marriage to same-sex couples across the country.[2] Opponents of this reform argued strenuously that changing the traditional definition of marriage would result in great harm to Canadian society. These opponents had a final chance to make their arguments after the election in early 2006 of a Conservative government that promised to revisit the issue. On 7 December 2006, Parliament, on a free vote and by a margin of 175 to 123, defeated the following motion: "That this House call on the government to introduce legislation to restore the traditional definition of marriage without affecting civil unions and while respecting existing same-sex marriages."[3] Prime Minister Harper immediately announced that the issue was settled and that his government would not reopen the matter even if it were to win a majority government in the next election.[4]

The Prime Minister's acknowledgement that this was a losing political battle was a blow to his socially conservative supporters, many of whom vowed to continue the fight. The statement of one Catholic Bishop captured the heartfelt moral concern of those advocating for the traditional definition of marriage:

> What a terrible irony it is to witness our country sinking ever deeper into the morass of moral chaos and confusion as we ignore the sane order established by God for the good of creation. Rather than protecting this institution, so critical to the health and stability of society, our government denatures marriage and the family. The unique and irreplaceable contribution to the common good of society that men and women make when they enter into marriage, and especially when they beget and educate children, is no longer treasured or protected by those who make our laws.[5]

Despite the resolve of the Bishop and other social conservatives, the general consensus is that the same-sex marriage issue will not be reopened in the foreseeable future. The Enlightenment model of marriage, with terms set not by God or nature but by the parties themselves, in accordance with the evolving norms of civil society,[6] has long been embedded in Canadian law and remains so.

The majority of Canadians, including myself, have not found the arguments that same-sex marriage is harmful to society convincing. More persuasive in Canada have been the arguments that exclusion of same-sex couples from marriage is harmful. What has struck me in particular are the harms or problems arising from excluding same-sex relationships not just from marriage but from any family regulation. This exclusion is maintained in some Western states, even while the West in general has moved to decriminalize homosexual conduct, to prohibit discrimination on the basis of sexual orientation, and to extend marriage, or at least the benefits and burdens of marriage, to same-sex couples. States that maintain a policy of exclusion do so in the knowledge that other Western states have adopted a more inclusive and welcoming policy to same-sex couples. Same-sex couples that reside in states that exclude them from the family law regime know that they would be included under the laws of other states. It is this dynamic that seems particularly harmful to a society.

Some extreme opponents of same-sex relationships have cast homosexuality as a non-indigenous practice of an invasive external group.[7] It is not homosexuality, however, but rather the legal construction of same-sex relationships as families that is the *external* threat. Given the historical record, it is at least probable that same-sex relationships have always existed everywhere.[8] What does vary across time and place is the legal treatment of such relationships. The law has constructed same-sex relationships as accepted or even expected associations, as criminal activity, as pathological behaviour,[9] and, more recently, as families. Although it may not be possible to deny the existence of homosexuality within a territory, it is within the power of the state to exclude same-sex relationships from the family law regime.

The problem for states opposed to recognition is the impossibility of stemming the flow of news about legal reforms going on elsewhere. Popular culture and modern information technology have efficiently circulated around the world stories and information about the expansion of the family law regime to include same-sex relationships.[10] The stories have caught the attention of the general public, not just the small circle of legal specialists who regularly follow legal developments in other countries. In jurisdictions that have not introduced such reforms, the general public is aware that same-sex marriage is now available in some states. As a result, some residents of states that do not recognize their relationships as families are travelling elsewhere to be married.

Movement between countries with different legal constructions of the family raises questions about the portability of the "goods" connected to particular constructions of the family. What is the nature of the goods on offer from marriage? What are parties seeking and what can states offer? Marriage confers spousal status and the incidents of marriage.[11] The "incidents" of marriage are the "special rights, duties, privileges or incapacities"[12] that flow from the status of marriage. Parties cannot confer a status on themselves. Rather, status is a classification conferred by law "whenever a person occupies a position of which the creation, continuance or relinquishment and the incidents are a matter of sufficient social or public concern."[13] In recent years there has been an unbundling the incidents of marriage from the status of marriage in many Western countries, and in Canada in particular. Parties may contract out of some of the incidents of marriage,[14] and parties who are not married may choose or have thrust upon them the incidents of marriage.[15] Parties to a foreign marriage may find that their home state does not recognize their marriage or does not confer on them all of the incidents of marriage. Thus, while some parties seek to obtain the incidents of marriage by getting married, others already have, do not want, or cannot hope to have the incidents of marriage.

Parties may also be seeking from marriage the symbolic sanction, or blessing, of the state, and this may be more important to the parties than any legal consequences flowing from the marriage. Justice L'Heureux-Dubé made this point in her dissenting opinion in *Egan v. Canada*: "Official state recognition of the legitimacy and acceptance in society of a particular type of status or relationship in society of a particular type of status or relationship may be of greater value and importance to those affected than any pecuniary gain flowing from that recognition."[16] The symbolic value of marriage has been emphasized by same-sex marriage advocates who reject civil unions as "marriage-lite" and take the view that "the 'm' word" must be available to same-sex couples.[17] Provincial appellate courts have accepted the argument that civil unions are at best a "separate but equal" institution inconsistent with the constitutional imperative of equality. Thus, the courts have endorsed the constitutional right of same-sex couples to the symbolic value of marriage as a public and legal celebration of a relationship.[18]

Parties may also seek from marriage the opportunity to convey information to each other or to the world about the nature of their relationship. Robert Rowthorn and Michael Trebilcock have written about marriage as a signal in this sense.[19] Trebilcock focuses on marriage as a signal that may improve "the search and sorting process in the market for partners."[20] He makes the point that if marriage is well-defined in contrast to cohabitation or other forms of relationship, then a willingness or unwillingness to marry efficiently signals to potential partners the signaller's relationship preferences. Rowthorn, like Trebilcock, sees willingness to marry as a signal to potential partners, but Rowthorn also sees marriage as having a broader signalling function and is more definite than Trebilcock about the content of the marriage signal:

> When a person offers to marry another person, or accepts such an offer, this is normally taken as an indication of commitment and of desire for an enduring relationship. When a person is married, this normally signifies that he or she is in a committed relationship and is not sexually available to outsiders. The fact that a person is married may be an indication to potential employers or the government about his or her personal characteristics such as health, reliability, or ambition. The fact that a couple is married may be a good indicator of the likely stability of their relationship.[21]

Rowthorn and Trebilcock agree that marriage is a less effective signal when no-fault divorce is easily available, marriage is largely assimilated to unmarried cohabitation, and parties enjoy considerable freedom to contract out of the incidents of marriage. In such a legal context—which precisely describes that of Canada—marriage is less efficient at signalling a particular relationship preference, commitment, or stability.

The hypothesis that parties marry for reasons other than the legal incidents of marriage was confirmed in the qualitative empirical study conducted by John Eekelaar and Mavis Maclean.[22] Only a small percentage of the subjects interviewed cited pragmatic reasons for getting married instead of cohabiting outside of marriage. Many gave "conventional" reasons for getting married. Marriage was seen as a way of adhering to religious doctrine, following parental wishes or living by society's rules. Many of the subjects gave "internal" reasons for marriage. Some valued marriage simply for its symbolic value, seeing it as important "in so far as it demonstrated, usually to the outside world, a state of affairs already reached by the parties."[23] For others, marriage "was more than merely a public display undertaken mostly for others, but assumed a more personal nature, and provided in itself an added impetus for, or source of, further commitment."[24] Still others saw marriage as "a framework within which the partners consciously strive to achieve a still deeper commitment,"[25] which often is seen to occur on the birth of a child.

The goods that parties seek from marriage, then, are not simply legal status and the legal incidents of marriage. But the non-legal goods offered by marriage hinge, at least to some extent, on marriage's legal nature. For example, the value of marriage as a signal to one's partner or to third parties of the committed nature of the relationship is lessened if the marriage is not legally binding and gives rise to no legal obligations. So regardless of the nature of the goods one seeks from marriage, the portability of marital status and the legal incidents of marriages is an issue.

In jurisdictions with a public policy against same-sex unions, it will be much more difficult for residents who have traveled to Canada or elsewhere for legal sanction of their unions to achieve recognition of in their home state. However, even in the case of an explicit public policy, there may be at least some erosion of the legal wall intended to protect the jurisdiction from a foreign same-sex union. Some incidents of marriage may be extended, e.g., the power to consent to medical treatment for an incapacitated partner. In order to protect against encroachments by relatively liberal marriage rules in other states, many US states have enacted "mini-DOMA" laws [26] that explicitly prohibit recognition. Whether these laws offer perfect protection remains to be seen.

Beyond their intended effects, mini-DOMAs also communicate disapprobation to Canada and other states that allow same-sex marriage, a disapprobation so serious as to outweigh the general principle of comity. As well, mini-DOMAs communicate to disapprobation to the same-sex couples within the borders of the state.

A state's rules on who may marry and what foreign marriages will be recognized signal particular social policies and attitudes. Opening up civil marriage to same-sex couples signals that Canada is a "gay-friendly" place that values freedom of choice, diversity, equality, separation of church and state, and protection of human rights. These are qualities that may make Canada more competitive in the market for tourism and immigrants. Canada's same-sex marriage law in and of itself boosted tourism, because many couples, particularly from the US, came to Canada to celebrate their marriage.

All Canadian provinces facilitate "tourist" marriages. Quebec, Canada's one civil law province, has distinct rules. Jeffrey Talpis writes:

> In Quebec, there is no issuance of a marriage licence and it is the person performing the ceremony, known as the "officiant," who must verify whether or not the parties have the right to marry each other. Thus, if under the law of the ante-domicile of either party, same-sex marriage is not legal, the officiant is supposed to refuse to perform the marriage ceremony. In practice, however, such ceremonies are being performed. ... [27]

The common law provinces do maintain licencing requirements. In order to get married in Ontario, e.g., parties must comply with the formal licencing requirements of Ontario's *Marriage Act*[28] and the common law and federal laws on capacity to marry. But Ontario (like the other provinces) permits tourist marriages of visitors unconnected to the province, and does not undertake any inquiry into whether the parties have capacity to marry under their domiciliary law.[29] And US couples have take advantage of Canada's liberal rules. But apart from tourism directly connected with same-sex weddings, Canada's same-sex marriage law may boost to tourism more generally by signally a cluster of values and attitudes that potential tourists find appealing.

As well, Canada's law may assist it in the global competition for highly skilled immigrants.[30] The "institutionalized inclusiveness" signalled by Canada's marriage rules might give it an edge in this competition.[31] A state that refuses to permit same-sex marriage or even to extend recognition to foreign same-sex marriages is signalling of a cluster of social values that are attractive to some and repellent to others. To the extent that the opening up of civil marriage to same-sex couples is connected to tolerance and modernity, a state that enacts laws to block recognition of the same-sex family may suffer in regard to attracting immigrants and tourists who value these qualities. And they may lose residents who prefer to live in a more hospitable state.

On the other hand, a different block of tourists, immigrants and residents may well share the state's disapprobation of same-sex relationships. Bishop Wingle, who so movingly expressed his concern that Canada was sinking into a "morass of moral chaos and confusion"[32] may well prefer to relocate to, or at least to spend his leisure time, in a state that supports the traditional definition of marriage. But there will not be a perfect sorting process. The Balkanization of the West into "gay-friendly" and "gay-hostile" legal units will not be complete, with all those who share a state's values remaining and all those who don't leaving. Inevitably, there will be those who support same-sex marriage living in states that do not permit or recognize it and those who opposite it living it states where it is allowed.

It may be that opponents of same-sex marriage who live in a gay-friendly state will be negatively effected. But they are fully recognized citizens, even though their views on marriage have not held sway. Of greater concern to me are same-sex couples that reside in a gay-hostile state. Not only are their views on marriage rejected, but their experience as a family is ignored or considered in a negative light.

Consider those same-sex couples who identify themselves as a family and who may have done all they could to signal their commitment to being a family, e.g., by getting married in Canada. If they are not regarded as a family by their home state, how does this affect the couple, their family and their friends? Though dwelling among their fellow residents, they are not fully accepted as citizens. Their allegiance to the state that does not recognize their experience of family is weakened, and their loyalty or affection for the state that "blessed" their union is strengthened. The presence of a fifth column or legally invisible group of same-sex couples may undermine social cohesion. The satisfaction that opponents of same-sex marriage receive from mini-DOMAs requires a focus on positive laws that maintain the traditional definition of marriage and refusal to look at the lived reality of citizens. This creates a partial view of the nature of the society. All societies must accept that there is an underworld of deviants and criminals that want to hide their activities from public view. But to effectively force a group that wants the sunlight into a shadow society surely is self-deluding and, yes, harmful.

The mini-DOMA laws and constitutional amendments to prevent "activist" courts from ruling in favour of same-sex marriage strike me as shutting the door on same-sex families in a very decisive way. Perhaps there could be a more nu-anced and careful response to this divisive issue. We do not all hold the same values, but we can agree on much, particularly on the importance of healthy human flourishing, tolerance and mutual respect. "Genuine pluralism is built out of plurality when the differences are debated rather than ignored and a unity begins to be discerned in human affairs—what John Courtney Murray called 'the unity of orderly conversation.'"[33]

Notes

1. Professor Martha Bailey, LL.B. (U. of Toronto), LL.M. (Queen's U.), D.Phil. (Oxford U.) Teaches Family Law, Conflict of Laws and Comparative Legal Traditions in the Faculty of Law of Queen's University in Canada.

2. *Civil Marriage Act*, S.C. 2005, c. 33. Federal statutes are available online at <http://laws.justice.gc.ca/en>. Note that prior to this enactment, civil marriage was avail-able to same-sex couples in some provinces pursuant to court rulings that the traditional definition of marriage was unconstitutional.

3. 39th Parliament, 1st Session, Edited Hansard, No. 093, 7 December 2006.

4. Gloria Galloway, "Same_sex marriage file closed for good, PM says" (8 Decem-ber 2006) *Globe & Mail*.

5. John_Henry Westen, "Bishop Wingle: Canada 'Sinking Ever Deeper Into the Morass of Moral Chaos' Criticizes Politicians for Failing to Protect the 'Authentic' and 'Sane' Definition of Marriage," LifeSite (11 December 2006), online at <http://www.lifesite.net/ldn/2006/dec/06121104.html>.

6. John Witte Jr., *God's Joust, God's Justice: Law and Religion in the Western Tradition* (Grand Rapids: Eerdmans, 2006) at 306-308.

7. Carl F. Stychin, in "Same-sex Relationships and the Globalization of Human Rights Discourse" (2004) 49 McGill L.J. 951 at 956 writes that Robert Mugabe "skilfully used a discourse of colonial contamination to shore up the post-colonial state, wherein homosexuality is attributed to the white colonizer, and homosexual relations were the means he used to exploit and contaminate the colonized sexually."

8. Theodore Zeldin, *An Intimate History of Humanity* (New York: HarperCollins, 1994)

9. Ibid. at 121-26 John Boswell, *Same-sex Unions in Premodern Europe* (NY: Random House, 1994).

10. See, e.g., Tom Maurstad's piece on same-sex marriages in *The Simpsons*, "Gay in cartoon land" (20 February 2005) The National Post B1, where he writes: "Now that the world has been pop-culturalized, the yet-I'm-gay-ness of real people is old news."

11. The Supreme Court of Canada has recently emphasized that marriage signals acceptance of the incidents of marriage: *Attorney General of Nova Scotia* v. *Walsh*, [2002] 4 S.C.R. 325.

12. *Canada (A.G.)* v. *Canard*, [1976] 1 S.C.R. 170.

13. R.H. Graveson, *Status in the Common Law* (London: U of London, Athlone Press, 1953) at 2.

14. *Hartshorne v. Hartshorne*, 2004 SCC 22.

15. Winifred Holland, "Intimate Relationships in the New Millennium: The Assimilation of Marriage and Cohabitation?" (2000) 17 Canadian Journal of Family Law 114.

16. *Egan v. Canada*, [1995] 2 S.C.R. 513 at para. 86.

17. Justice Sosman, dissenting in *In re Opinions of the Justices to the Senate*, 440 Mass. 1201, 802 N.E.2d 565 (2004), in which the majority rejected civil unions as a constitutional alternative to same-sex marriage, stated at 1211: " There is, from the *amici* on one side, an implacable determination to retain some distinction, however trivial, between the institution created for same-sex couples and the institution that is available to opposite-sex couples. And, from the *amici* on the other side, there is an equally implacable determination that no distinction, no matter how meaningless, be tolerated. As a result, we have a pitched battle over who gets to use the 'm' word."

18. One of the parties to the same-sex marriage challenge in Quebec was quoted in the decision of the Superior Court of Quebec as responding to the introduction of civil unions in Quebec by saying: "Oh, we will continue to fight. I'll continue to fight for the right to marry René, yes. That has never changed. Marriage is the gold standard in social respectability and recognition of relationships. And I want my relationship to him, this twenty_nine (29) thirty (30) years, we have lived, to be recognized fully. True equality is choice. And if I have to have my choice, my choice is marriage which is the same as any other citizen in Canada has": *Hendricks v. Quebec*, [2002] R.J.Q. 2506 at para. 18. See also Bruce MacDougall, "The Celebration of Same_Sex Marriage" (2000_2001) 32 Ottawa L. Rev. 235 for extensive analysis of the importance of the symbolic celebration of same-sex couples by the state through the institution of marriage.

19. Robert Rowthorn, "Marriage as a Signal," in Anthony W. Dnes & Robert Rowthorn, *The Law and Economics of Marriage and Divorce*, eds., (Cambridge: Cambridge

UP, 2002) 132-156. Michael J. Trebilcock, "Marriage as a Signal," in F.H. Buckley, ed., The Fall and Rise of Freedom of Contract (Durham: Duke UP, 1999) 245-255.

20. Trebilcock, *ibid.* at 255.

21. Rowthorn, *supra* note 17 at 137. Perhaps one reason that Trebilcock is less assertive about the content of the marriage signal is that he is operating within the Canadian constitutional law framework, in which discrimination on the basis of marital status is prohibited: *Miron v. Trudel* (1995), 13 R.F.L. (4th) 1 (S.C.C.). Parties who attempt to signal their personal characteristics to potential employers by indicating their marital status are inviting discrimination on the basis of marital status.

22. John Eekelaar and Mavis Maclean, "Marriage and Moral Bases of Personal Relationships" (2004) 31 J. of L. & Soc. 510.

23. *Ibid.* at 521.

24. *Ibid.*

25. *Ibid.*

26. The United States enacted the *Defense of Marriage Act*, 110 Stat 2419 (1996) ("DOMA"), s. 3(a) of which defines "marriage" for purposes of federal law as "only a legal union between one man" and "spouse" as "a person of the opposite sex who is a husband or a wife." Section 2(a) of DOMA provides that: "No state, territory, or possession of the United States, or Indian tribe, shall be required to give effect to any public act, record, or judicial proceeding of any other State, territory, possession, or tribe respecting a relationship between persons of the same sex that is treated as a marriage under the laws of such other State, territory, possession, or tribe, or a right or claim arising from such relationship." After this federal legislation was enacted, many states enacted mini-DOMA laws. After the passage of DOMA, 38 US states passed "mini-DOMA" laws. See, e.g., Alabama Stat. Sec. 30-1-19(e), e.g., provides: "The state of Alabama shall not recognize as valid any marriage of parties of the same sex that occurred or was alleged to have occurred as a result of the law of any jurisdiction regardless of whether a marriage license was issued."

27. Jeffray Talpis describes the availability of "tourist" marriages in Quebec in "Same-sex Canadian Marriages Are Not Necessarily Recognized Abroad" (22 September 2006) 26: 19 *The Lawyers Weekly.*

28. *Marriage Act*, R.S.O. 1990, c. M.3.

29. The rules regarding solemnization of marriages in Ontario are set out in the province's *Marriage Act*, R.S.O. 1990, c. M.3.

30. Catherine Dauvergne, Evaluating Canada's New Immigration and Refugee Protection Act in its Global Context" (2003) 41 Alberta Law Review 725; Richard G. Harris, "Labour Mobility and the Global Competition for Skills: Dilemmas and Options," Government of Canada Skills Research Initiative Working Paper Series, Working Paper 2004 D-02.

31. The phrase "institutionalized inclusiveness" was used by Alex Markels, in "After Election Day, A Vote to Leave" (21 November 2004) The New York Times, an article on the increase in emigration from the USA, to describe the quality that attracted a same-sex couple to Canada. One member of the couple was quoted as saying of their reception in Canada that "It was the first time in my life that someone treated my relationship like something completely normal!"

32. *Supra*, note 5.

33. George Weigel, "Roman Catholicism in the Age of John Paul II" in Peter L.Berger, ed., *The Desecularization of the World: Resurgent Religion and World Politics* (Grand Rapids: Eerdmans, 1999) 19 at 34.

CHAPTER 9
MEANING, MORALITY, AND SEXUAL ATTRACTION: QUESTIONING THE REDUCTIVE AND DETERMINISTIC ASSUMPTIONS OF BIOLOGISM AND SOCIAL CONSTRUCTIONISM

Edwin E. Gantt and Emily Reynolds
Brigham Young University

I.   Introduction

In recent decades, the research and theorizing of scholars in the social and biological sciences has begun to exert an enormous influence beyond the walls of the laboratories and libraries typically home to such rarefied academic pursuits. Increasingly, the technical and highly specialized thinking of these scholars is giving shape and direction to ideological debates taking place in larger cultural, legal, and political arenas. In particular, the work of Neo-Darwinian evolutionary theorists and postmodern social constructionists has begun to contribute in profound ways to the emergent conceptual topography of contemporary political and legal discussions regarding the viability, constitutionality, and desirability of same-sex marriage.[1] Indeed, the widespread promotion and acceptance of ideas that were, for the most part, formulated only as hypotheses in the social and biological sciences has begun to not only define the grounds of contemporary political and legal debate, but also to dictate the terms and conceptual language within which questions of human sexuality and social relationships can be addressed.[2] As we will show, the conceptual framework that is being imported from the social and biological sciences is undergirded by reductionistic and deterministic assumptions that, if taken seriously, provide neither the conceptual grounds nor the vocabulary for discussing or understanding the important moral questions that inhere in all human relationships, and in particular in marital and family relationships.

It should be noted at the outset that this paper does not seek to address the question of the constitutionality of same-sex marriage or even the cultural or social desirability of same-sex marriage. Rather, it will address some of the problematic conceptual and practical implications of adopting either "essentialist" or "constructionist" theories of sexual attraction and gender[3] in addressing those questions. We will explore the basic conceptual features of theories of sexual attraction that derive their philosophical grounding from

Darwinian evolutionary theory and contemporary evolutionary psychology, on the one hand, and from one or another form of postmodernist sociology or social constructionism, on the other. The analysis which follows will show that despite their obviously divergent explanations regarding the specific origins of human sexuality and social behavior, both are committed to an essentially deterministic explanatory framework that denies the possibility that moral agency plays any substantive role in either the etiology or the expression of human sexuality. It will be argued, further, that without moral agency the social relations which foster and give context to sexual intimacy cease to exist as genuinely meaningful phenomena. The richness of sexual intimacy is reduced to sexual attraction, which is simply the necessitated byproduct of mechanical biochemical reactions, impersonal socio-cultural forces, or some complex combination of the two. From there the door is open to understanding all other human social relationships—especially those such as marriage that are reliant in important ways on sexual intimacy for their meaning and context—as merely epiphenomenal in nature, empty behavioral categories bereft of genuine moral or human significance. The ultimate harm in such theorizing is that it leads us inexorably to adopt and endorse nihilism and moral relativism, both of which are fundamentally toxic to the possibility of marriage, family, and civilization.

II.   The Evolutionary Psychology of Attraction

We now turn to theories of attraction as they have developed in evolutionary psychology. According to Darwinian theory, sexual selection takes two basic forms: same-sex competition and mate preference. In the first of these forms, members of the same sex (usually males) compete with one another for the opportunity to gain increased sexual access to available members of the opposite sex. The classic example is that of two male deer charging one another and locking horns as a demonstration of strength and virility. The various characteristics—both physical (e.g., strength) and psychological (e.g., intelligence)—possessed by the winners of these intrasexual competitions are then passed on to future generations of the species because "the victors are able to mate more often and hence pass on more genes."[4] In the second form of sexual selection, however, the emphasis is on the choosing of a mate based on one's individual preferences for certain qualities or attributes exhibited by that potential mate. Such qualities are passed on to future generations because the animals possessing them are more frequently chosen as mates than those who do not possess such qualities. For example, "since peahens prefer peacocks with plumage that flashes and glitters, dull-feathered males get left in the evolutionary dust."[5]

Clearly central to the evolutionary account of sexual behavior is the notion of reproductive success. Indeed, as the evolutionary psychologist David Buss has stated, "differential reproduction is the engine that drives the evolutionary process."[6] Likewise, recognizing the importance of the concept of reproductive success to any evolutionary account of behavior, evolutionary theorist Helen Fisher has gone so far as to suggest that "mating is the single most important act of any individual of any sexually reproducing species."[7] In order to facilitate successful mating, evolutionary theorists maintain that "attraction and attachment are emotions as primitive and universal as fear, anger, and surprise, which are (at least in part) psychopharmacological events arising from arousal circuits located primarily in the limbic system and surrounding regions of avian and mammalian brains."[8] Sexual attraction, it is held, evolved in the various species in order to initiate mating and to sustain male-female associations long enough to ensure both reproductive success and the long-term survival of resulting offspring.

Over the course of millennia of evolutionary history, and with the evolution of a sophisticated cerebral cortex in the first hominids, "our ancestors began to build on this core of primitive emotions associated with reproduction, eventually developing complex romantic feelings and elaborate traditions to celebrate and curb what European cultures would come to call romantic love."[9] And, while most evolutionary theorists admit that cultural forces play a role in the particulars of sexual attraction (e.g., whom we find attractive and how we court one another), sexual attraction is at root a matter of neurophysiology and genetic disposition. Ultimately, the emotions that surround sexual arousal and sexual attraction originate in the chemistry and physiology of the body and "evolved long ago to direct the ebb and flow of our primary reproductive strategy, serial monogamy."[10]

Given this perspective on the nature and origins of sexual attraction, then, it is no surprise that evolutionary thinkers have identified homosexuality as a "paradox."[11] Indeed, one recent book by Louis Berman is entitled *The Puzzle: Exploring the Evolutionary Puzzle of Male Homosexuality*.[12] It is worth noting in this context that the word "puzzle" appears not once but twice in the book's title. Obviously, the problem for an evolutionary account of homosexuality grounded in the assumption that current behaviors arise primarily out of past reproductive successes is that, as Potts and Short so succinctly put it: "[H]omosexual behavior is the antithesis of reproductive success."[13] Thus, the occurrence of homosexual behavior throughout human history and in most, if not all, human cultures[14] presents a legitimate challenge to evolutionary explanations of human sexual attraction. A number of strategies have been adopted to reconcile the theory with the empirical reality of same-sex attraction and homosexual behavior.

Perhaps the most common attempt to account for homosexuality is the evolutionary concept of kin selection.[15] In essence, the kin-selection hypothesis proposes that because homosexuals forgo reproduction they are thereby freed up to assist in the rearing of the offspring of close relatives. Presumably, this results not only in a reduction of the labor demands and child-care burdens of those close relatives, thereby increasing both their probability of survival and likelihood of further reproductive opportunity, but also increases the likelihood that any offspring in question (e.g., nieces, nephews, and cousins) will reach physical and reproductive maturity.[16] As Stein explains:

> Given the extra attention family members of gay men and lesbians
> would get, these family members would have increased reproductive

> success and more copies of their genes would get out into the gene
> pool. Included in their genes would be the genes that underlie the
> desire for people of the same sex-gender in their lesbian and gay
> family members. This way the genes that lead to homosexuality
> would get passed on to future generations, not (primarily) through the
> offspring of lesbians and gay men, but through their family
> members.[17]

Thus, although homosexual males and females are not likely to engage in directly effective forms of reproduction themselves, they nonetheless contribute to the overall genetic fitness of their larger family group by helping to ensure that the genetic characteristics of that family group survive in subsequent generations.

A similar version of this theory involves what is known as "group selection" rather than kin selection. In this account, rather than being inclined to assist in matters of child care, gay men and lesbians are more likely (by genetic predisposition) to devote their energies to activities that have cultural and aesthetic qualities and benefits. Although there would seem to be no direct or obvious reproductive benefit to the community or larger social group in having its homosexual members engage in artistic and literary endeavors, the group selection argument maintains that people in the larger community benefit from the artistic pursuits of homosexuals by having better, more productive lives. "It serves the community," Stein suggests, "to have some lesbians and gay men who can focus their time on projects that benefit the entire community rather than devote their time to child rearing."[18]

A third popular attempt to account for homosexual attraction by means of evolutionary theory can be found in the evolutionary psychological theory of "parental manipulation."[19] In the parental manipulation hypothesis, it is proposed that parents "subconsciously determine that it would be better for them, in terms of getting a larger number of copies of their genes into subsequent generations, if their family focused its reproductive and survival resources on the offspring of certain of their children but not others."[20] Parents would then go on to raise certain of their children in such a way that those children later become homosexual while the others would not. By way of example, Ruse asks us to "suppose that a parent has four children, each potentially having two children. But if one of the children is turned towards a homosexual helper role, the other three children will each have three children. Biological features aimed at achieving such an end would be favored by selection."[21]

A fourth (and increasingly popular) strategy for addressing the question of the evolutionary origins and maintenance of homosexual behavior is the theory of "piggyback traits."[22] This approach claims that the genes responsible for producing homosexual tendencies and desires are associated with other traits (physical, psychological, or both) that increase the likelihood of reproductive success. In short, homosexuality is a trait that piggybacks on other traits. Thus, "genes for homosexuality are retained in the gene pool not for intrinsic reasons (as suggested by kin and group selection stories), but for coincidental ones."[23]

The analogy upon which this model is based is found in the genetic sequencing that provides for immunity to malaria. Although the genetic sequence that provides for immunity to malaria has the effect of increasing the chance that its possessor will develop sickle-cell anemia, in environments where malaria is prominent, the advantages of immunity are worth the risk of sickle-cell anemia. In the case of homosexuality then:

> [T]here might be a gene for psychological mechanisms that produce men who are especially appealing to heterosexual women as mates such as 'sensitive' heterosexuals. If this gene were in some way associated with psychological mechanisms that led to male homosexuality and if being a sensitive heterosexual were selectively advantageous, then male homosexuality would remain in the gene pool because it rides piggyback on sensitive heterosexuality.[24]

Obviously, one of the most persuasive features of this "piggyback traits" approach is that it seems to promise a more straightforward connection with recognized genetic and epidemiological findings than previous hypotheses or models.

Despite the abundance of hypotheses offered by evolutionary psychologists and sociobiologists to account for the persistence of homosexual behavior in the face of the reproductive imperative at the core of theory of natural selection, there is as yet no real consensus regarding which, if any, of these various hypotheses is correct—or even on the right track. In fact, as numerous critics have noted, there is little persuasive evidence that the evolutionary models for the emergence of *heterosexual* behavior—upon which the above mentioned speculations about the origins of homosexual behavior are based—are either conceptually coherent or empirically justified.[25] Thus, one lengthy review of the current state of theory and research on the origins of homosexuality concluded that "proposed evolutionary accounts of human sexual orientation do not confirm any aspect of the emerging research program."[26] Ultimately, then, as geneticist and animal biologist Anne Innis Dagg has pointed out, "Darwinian psychology, despite its vast efforts and often bizarre hypotheses, has been able shed little light on the issue of sexual orientation."[27]

III.   *The Social Construction of Homosexuality*

Social constructionists also offer a wide array of hypotheses offered to account for the widespread occurrence of homosexual behavior through time and across extremely disparate cultures. In contrast to evolutionary accounts of the origins and nature of homosexuality, social constructionist accounts assume that sexual orientation does not exist as a "natural kind," that is, as an independent metaphysical entity or naturally occurring state. Rather, from the social constructionist perspective, sexual orientation is merely a "social human kind."[28] In other words, sexual orientation is a "cultural invention, a social construction, and a self-presentation we enact in certain settings, with certain people."[29] For example, Bohan notes that for the social constructionist, gender (like homosexuality), "is not resident in the person but exists in those interactions that are socially constructed as gendered."[30] From such a perspective, "relationality or morality is a quality of interactions not of individuals, and it is not essentially connected with sex" and what it means to term a particular interaction masculine or feminine, heterosexual or homosexual, "is socially agreed upon and is reproduced by the very process of participating in that transaction."[31] Indeed, according to Davis and Gergen, "The social constructionist position implies that any type of description of the nature of reality is dependent upon the historical and cultural location of that description."[32] Thus, sexual orientation, for the social constructionist, is not so much something essential that we are or have (e.g., in the biochemistry of our brains or the intricacies of our genes), but rather it is something we do, with others, in particular cultural and social contexts. And, as such, our sexual attractions, behaviors, and relationships derive their existence and their meaning fundamentally from the particular social arrangements, cultural contexts, and sexual traditions that give rise to them as viable possibilities in the first place.

One consequence of this perspective is that terms such as sexual orientation, heterosexuality, and homosexuality become conceptually elastic, depending entirely on contingent social relations and historical happenstance for their meaning and identity. Indeed, social constructionists are fond of pointing out that the term "homosexual" is of relatively recent origin—having first been coined only in the late nineteenth century—and has demonstrably changed in meaning since that time.[33] Of course, this is not to say that social constructionists would deny that "there were people in Attic Greece who had sex with people of the same sex-gender—they even admit that there were people who had sex *primarily* with people of the same sex-gender—but they deny that this entails that there were homosexuals in our sense of the term in Attic Greece" (italics in the original).[34] By way of example, Marecek, Crawford, and Popp draw attention to the intimate friendships enjoyed by many women in 19th century North America in which they "spent weeks at each others' homes, slept in the same beds, and exchanged passionate and tender letters describing the joys of perfect love and the agonies of parting."[35] However, these authors argue that while these passionate relationships clearly involved romance, attachment, and some physical intimacy, it is emphatically not the case that these women were "really" lesbians because "imputing the definitions, meanings, terms, and concerns of our day to the past is an error."[36]

The problem, then, for the social constructionist, is our tendency to uncritically apply our culturally bound and dictated concepts and terms to the actions and experiences of people living in other cultures or at other times. For the application of our concept of homosexuality to another culture's practices to be legitimate, then, would require persuasive evidence that the people of that culture shared our concept in essential ways. This requirement, however, social constructionists argue, is both practically and theoretically impossible to achieve given the powerful limitations of history, language, and custom—both our own and that of any other culture we might wish to understand. For example, Marecek, et al. argue that:

This way of accounting for sexuality is not universal; rather, it is specific to our time and place. The idea that one's erotic attractions, sexual activities, or emotional attachments necessarily confer a social identity is similarly an account limited to particular cultural contexts.[37]

Thus it comes as no surprise when social constructionists maintain that "there is good reason to think that few, if any, people in any cultures before the mid-1800s had sexual orientations."[38] Such a claim is the direct result of social constructionism's rejection of the concept of sexual orientation as a deep-seated or enduring inclination, or, indeed, as any real *thing* at all.

For the social constructionist, then, sexual attraction and identity are fundamentally matters of social and political context, mere reflections of the various behavioral and experiential possibilities granted by the values and core assumptions, as well as institutionalized power relations, of a given culture or sub-culture. Thus the principle explanatory focus is on the manifold ways in which human action and identity is the product of the impersonal sociohistorical forces and conditions that give form and expression to our existence. Sexual attraction (homosexual, heterosexual, or otherwise) and sexual behavior represent a sort of social discourse into which we have been invited by the others around and before us, and in which we are enmeshed always and already by virtue of the cultural and linguistic conditions of our existence as human beings. While the individual person may make little contribution to and have almost no control over the sexual attractions he or she experiences, in the social constructionist view particular cultures and social groups enjoy a great deal of flexibility in the construction and expression of sexuality and sexual relationships.

Ultimately, social constructionist accounts of sexual attraction suffer from the same basic problems that beset the various evolutionary accounts described above. That is to say, despite the extensive research being conducted, multitudes of examples and counter-examples being offered, and the voluminous number of works being published, there is as yet no genuine agreement as to the conceptual coherence or empirical viability of the entire social constructionist enterprise.[39] Indeed, it is hard to imagine any such consensus being reached in the social scientific community given the radically different epistemological and metaphysical starting points being taken by those committed to an evolutionary and biological account of sexuality versus those committed to a sociological and constructionist account. Even the most cursory survey of the literature of this debate reveals vast disagreement concerning not only how various research findings are to be interpreted, but even more deeply whether or not competing research programs are even legitimately scientific in nature in the first place.

Nonetheless, even were some consensus to be reached and the social constructionist agenda adopted, persistent epistemological questions would remain regarding the inherently vicious circularity of any social constructionist claims regarding what sexual attraction is or is not in various cultures and was or was not at various times. That is to say, if the basic premises of social constructionism are true, then any pronouncement by a social constructionist regarding the socially constructed nature of human sexuality is itself merely a byproduct of the contingent social forces that happen to construct such beliefs and interpretive frameworks in that particular social constructionist. While perhaps not a necessarily self-refuting position to take, it most certainly would seem to be a self-stultifying one, and, as such, of questionable intellectual worth as a means of scientific or philosophic advancement.

IV.   What They Have In Common

A.   Shared Reductionism

Social constructionist and evolutionary theories clearly have very different starting points and widely divergent vocabularies for addressing questions surrounding human sexuality. They are, however, woven from a common theoretical thread and it is a thread that has far-reaching intellectual, social, and moral implications, especially for our understanding of the meaning and nature of marriage. That thread is fundamental reductionism and its conceptual companion necessary determinism.[40] In the analysis that follows, it will be shown that any conceptualization of sexual attraction—indeed, any conceptualization of human nature generally—that grounds itself in fundamentally reductive and deterministic assumptions leads inescapably to nihilism and moral relativism.

In the social sciences, fundamental reductionism and necessary determinism have long been thought to be the essential requirements of any genuinely scientific theory or explanation. For example, in their examination of reductionism in contemporary science and psychology, Bem and Looren de Jong state that "In a sense, the business of science is reduction"[41] and, in his discussion of psychology's status as a science, Hergenhahn maintains that "All sciences assume determinism."[42] Echoing these sentiments, Heiman proposes that what distinguishes genuinely scientific theories and explanations from non-scientific or pseudo-scientific ones is that they assume "nature is *lawful, deterministic,* and *understandable*" (italics in the original).[43] Although many scholars dispute the necessity of the relationship between reductionism, determinism, and scientific explanation,[44] it is nonetheless very much the case that reductive and deterministic accounts of human behavior, feelings, and social interactions are rampant in the mainstream of social science research and theorizing.

At its most basic conceptual level, fundamental reductionism is the notion that complex events or things are best thought of as a mere instances or manifestations of some simpler events or things. As Slife and Williams point out, "reductionism is a claim that X is really Y. And because Y (the thing or process that explains X) is taken to be simpler than X, reductionism amounts to a claim that X is really just Y."[45] Reductionism, then, dictates that we should be skeptical of what we observe and experience and focus our scholarly attention, instead, on what is presumably going on "behind" or "beneath" the phenomena we are investigating. Thus, as Slife and Williams further note, "one of the primary purposes of experimentation and other empirical methods is to uncover, by a process of inference, hidden concepts or structures behind observable events."[46] Such "hidden concepts or structures," once identified, are then thought to be ultimately responsible for—i.e., necessarily determinative of—the existence and particular occurrence of whatever phenomenon was under investigation in the first place. Once a given set of causal conditions are in place, the events that follow do so necessarily and cannot genuinely be otherwise than they are, given the particular and efficiently causal nature of the underlying processes presumed to produce them.

In the case of evolutionary explanations of sexual attraction, it is assumed that operating somewhere beneath or behind the complex desires and emotions of particular persons in particular relations are some more basic, naturally selected biological processes or genetic conditions that are responsible for producing the person's complex and nuanced emotional experiences. Indeed, as one author sympathetic to evolutionary theory has written:

> Beneath the thoughts and feelings and temperamental differences marriage counselors spend their time sensitively assessing are the stratagems of the genes—cold hard equations composed of simple variables: social status, age of spouse, number of children, their ages, outside romantic opportunities, and so on.[47]

In other words, despite the experiential subtleties and cultural complexities of human relationships and attractions, evolutionary theory proposes that such things are "really just" genes working out their chances for survival and, as such, are not the sort of things over which real human beings have any real control—despite how they might actually experience such feelings or attractions. The question of moral agency and the intentional involvement of the person in his or her attractions or feelings are simply ruled out of bounds at the outset by the presumption of causal necessity.

Although approaching the matter from a different avenue, social constructionist theories, too, engage in this same sort of fundamentally reductionistic and deterministic explanation of sexual attraction and behavior. In the constructionist version of sexual attraction, persons are subject to the powerful social forces, cultural traditions, and discourse-narratives that have constructed their desires and their identity for them. Indeed, for many constructionists and postmodern sociologists, an important concept in their approach to re-vision human nature and deconstruct the enlightenment hegemony has been the notion of "the death of the subject," the elimination of "an autonomous and intentional agent."[48] In other words, rather than persons being conceived of as active participants in the constitution of their social and moral worlds, they are instead held to be thoroughly constructed by those worlds, little more than the site or locus at which powerful cultural and political forces converge to shape identity.[49] For example, Burr asserts that "masculinity/femininity, hetero-/homosexual, sane/insane, black/white, working-/middle-class and so on—these may be seen as socially bestowed identities rather than essences of the person . . .."[50] Likewise, Delamater and Hyde claim that "sexuality is created by culture"[51] and that "reality is socially constructed, and therefore phenomena such as homosexuality are social constructions, the product of a particular culture, its language, and institutions."[52]

On the constructionist view, sexuality and sexual intimacy are "really just" manifestations of more basic, underlying cultural, linguistic, and institutional social practices. And, though feelings or attraction may be subjectively experienced as real by particular persons, in the constructionist scheme such feelings have no significant ontological status in their own right and they are not genuinely within our intentional control or agentive participation. Rather, our sexual relationships become simply the happenstance individual expressions of historical, cultural, and political forces of which we are only dimly if ever aware.

Ironically, then, while constructionists often dispute evolutionary and biological accounts of attraction that rely solely on genetic or neurological factors, constructionists clearly share with evolutionary thinkers a desire to explain morally complex and personally meaningful experiences in fundamentally reductive and necessarily deterministic terms that deny the possibility of moral agency or genuine meaning of any sort.

B.   Evolution or Construction: Pro or Con?

It should not surprise us, then, that it is possible for both advocates and opponents of same-sex marriages to invoke evolutionary and constructionist theories in support of their arguments for or against the constitutionality and desirability of same-sex marriages.[53] This is because, as we have seen, the theories themselves provide no grounds for making moral judgments. Therefore, as a practical matter, one can adopt a position in favor of legalizing same-sex marriage and then invoke either a biologically based evolutionary account of sexual attraction or a sociologically based constructionist account as a way of claiming "scientific" support for legalization. Likewise, one could adopt an evolutionary or a social constructionist explanatory approach and then argue against the legality or desirability of same-sex marriages. For example, a social constructionist argument could be made that homosexuality is a more or less elastic term whose meaning is ultimately determined by contingent historical, political, and cultural forces, and, therefore, same-sex marriages are either (a) simply one of many equally viable and desirable ways in which we manage our social relationships or (b) inappropriate social arrangements given the institutional social fabric and traditions of a culture deeply indebted to and shaped by heterosexual norms and ideals. Similarly, one could adopt an evolutionary approach to the issue of same-sex marriage and argue that because sexual attraction is fundamentally the product of naturally selected genetic tendencies, same-sex marital relationships are (a) legitimate because they provide a net-gain for the species as a whole by contributing in various ancillary ways to the reproductive success rates of heterosexual families in the kin group, or (b) are illegitimate because they ultimately serve only to nurture evolutionarily inefficient and biologically maladaptive forms of behavior.

Given these possibilities, then, it would seem misguided to cast either evolutionary or social constructionist theories as exclusively "Pro" or "Con" in relation to contemporary debates about same-sex marriage. Since either or both can be (and have been) employed to support positions on either side of the debate, the theories themselves would appear to be politically neutral. That these theories enjoy some measure of political neutrality does not mean, however, that they are value neutral in any way, or that they are not laden with problematic assumptions that can have significant harmful impact in the political and cultural arena.

V.   So What's the Harm?

All of this, then, brings us to the central concern of this paper: What's the harm in embracing the reductive and deterministic theories of evolutionary psychology and social constructionism currently being proposed to explain human sexual attraction? In other words, what intellectually and culturally problematic implications might there be for our understanding of ourselves and our relationships if the theoretical and explanatory framework of the sort of social science thinking discussed above is taken seriously? As many scholars have noted, it is impossible to avoid making assumptions in the course of scientific research and theory-construction.[54] These scholars have also noted that the most dangerous assumptions are not necessarily those that are hidden or go unnoticed because they are so widely taken-for-granted, but rather those that can have far-reaching moral implications and whose moral impact often goes unrecognized and unappreciated until after significant (and often irreversible) cultural changes have taken place.

The first principle implication of fundamentally reductive and necessarily deterministic accounts of the origins and nature of human sexual attraction is nihilism. Once human sexual intimacy is stripped of its relational, agentive, and moral quality and explained as merely the necessitated byproduct of fundamentally non-relational, non-agentive, and non-moral conditions, states, or processes, our sexual relationships can no longer be held to be genuinely meaningful in nature. This is not to say that persons would not experience their sexuality as meaningful in nature, only that once a reductive and deterministic account is adopted to explain attraction, any experiential meaning is rendered suspect, merely a subjective matter and, thus, in an important sense, not really real. As numerous scholars have shown, meaning in human behavior and experience requires genuine possibility.[55] That is, for an event (behavioral or emotional) to be considered genuinely meaningful it must be genuinely possible for that event to have been otherwise than it in fact was. Events that are necessarily determined to be as they are and which cannot, therefore, be in anyway otherwise than they are have no genuine meaning. Such events simply are.

For example, consider the day-long motion of blades of grass that slowly and mechanically bend and change position relative to the location of the sun as it moves across the sky. As a necessarily determined event this phenomenon is simply is what it is, and, as such, has no inherent meaningfulness. Granted, a careful golfer might well ascribe various meanings to the "lean of the grass" while preparing to make an important putt, but this ascription of meaning is merely subjective in nature and, as such, does not reflect any real meaning in the events of the natural world. Of course, if the golfer's subjective experience of meaning is itself just the byproduct of underlying mechanical processes or conditions, then it too lacks genuine meaning and is an event ontologically indistinguishable from that taking place in the grass. Only if there is the genuine possibility that a given event could be otherwise than it is does it make sense to consider that event as being capable of sustaining genuine (as opposed to merely subjective) meaning.

Thus, in the case of sexual relationships, only if persons are in some fundamental sense capable of experiencing their sexuality otherwise than they do, only if they are genuinely capable of being in relationships otherwise than they are, will it be possible for there to be any genuine meaning in those attractions and relationships. Insofar as contemporary evolutionary and constructionist theories embrace reductive and deterministic accounts of attraction, they deny the possibility that human sexual desire can be otherwise than it is, thus making it impossible to understand human sexuality in any way that does not rob it of its inherent meaningfulness. Insofar as social scientific theories of sexual attraction deny the possibility of human agency in their accounts of sexual relationships and desires, they cannot help but embrace a dangerous and virulent form of intellectual and cultural nihilism. Once the conceptual door is shut on the possibility of agency in our social science accounts of human relationships, the door to nihilism is the only one left open.

Parasitic on this embrace of nihilism is the problem of moral relativism. If human desires and sexual relationships—as well as the social and moral relationships that both give rise to and context for those desires—are nothing more than the necessitated outcomes of underlying causal conditions or processes, then not only does it no longer make sense to ascribe meaning to those desires, it is no longer legitimate to make distinctions of moral worth among those desires. If one's desires and sexual attractions are not the sort of thing in which one has any active participation—if they are just experiences thrust upon us by forces outside of awareness or control—then it becomes impossible to claim that any particular attractions we might experience are in any way morally superior to any other attractions that we might happen to have. As with the question of meaning, the question of moral distinctions is bound up with the possibility of possibility. We condemn all sorts of criminals, for example, because there were alternatives to their criminal activity. They chose crime rather than honesty, charity, or self-control. In fact, if it can be shown that the accused was in some sense unable to entertain alternatives, as in cases of severe mental disorder, we do not hold them accountable for their crimes.

Likewise, if the sexual desires we experience cannot be otherwise than they are, and the determination of how they are is something in which we do not participate in fundamental or meaningful ways, then these desires are neither good nor bad nor indifferent in nature. They simply are what they are and it would be as illegitimate to consider them worthy of either moral praise or condemnation as it would be illegitimate to consider the reflexive eye blink accompanying a sneeze to be worthy of our moral praise or blame.

Given this state of affairs, then, the next conceptual step is a short one. Once events as basic to human existence as sexual attraction and desire are reduced to the status of mere byproduct—whether or evolutionary selection or cultural production—it follows all too easily to assume that any other human behavior or relationship is also merely a causal byproduct in nature. Here the danger of nihilism and moral relativism is perhaps most clearly brought into relief. Against the backdrop of deterministic explanatory strategies, our understanding of the nature and meaning of marital and family relationships becomes morally relativised and nihilistic. Marriage comes to be seen as little more than one of many avenues through which individuals experiencing causally necessary sexual attractions can seek gratification of their desires. After all, or so the social scientific story would go, marriage, in and of itself, does not mean anything and no form of marriage is in any way morally superior to any other. Traditional families, one could argue, are only one of many possible and equally desirable forms of relationship and if some people prefer other ways of involving themselves in relationships, those other ways are valid simply by virtue of the fact that they exist and some people just happen to prefer them.

Perhaps in these examples it is becoming clear that, although moral relativism seems to be the position that no grounds exist for finding any human action morally superior to any other human action, in practical terms this only cuts in one direction. Things that are not right or wrong, but simply are as they are, must be accepted, which, for practical purposes, serves the same function as saying they are right. To rail against, or try to prohibit, what is unavoidably and necessarily the case is simply irrational. If, therefore, homosexuality and/or same-sex marriage have emerged as cultural phenomena over which moral questions are being raised, then any appeal to the fundamentally deterministic theories of evolutionary psychology or social constructionism can only make nonsense of such questions, concluding as they do that what is must be as it is and, therefore, no real moral distinctions can or ought to be made.

In order for meaning and moral significance to be maintained in any accounts (scientific or otherwise) of sexual relationships (homosexual, heterosexual, or otherwise) and social relationships, such accounts must assume from the outset that sexuality and its context of social relationships are fundamentally the expressions of embodied moral agents. This is not necessarily to say that all sexual behaviors are a matter of conscious deliberative choice, decided through some process of detached reflection. Rather, it is to say that moral agency—while certainly incumbent to the possibility of conscious deliberative choice—is much more deeply a matter of the entirety of one's way of being in relation with others in concrete moral and physical contexts. Further, all such moral and physical contexts are both constitutive of and constituted by fundamentally agentic beings capable of genuinely social relations. A central implication of this view is that at the most basic level of analysis one cannot meaningfully separate the moral and the physical context of lived-experience. Therefore, persons must always be understood as embodied moral agents in meaningful relational worlds. Ultimately, only within such a conceptual framework will the moral reality and the attendant moral implications of the various expressions of human sexuality be susceptible to fruitful analysis and dialogue, and not only within the social sciences but also within the larger cultural and political world of which they are an integral part.

Notes

1. See, e.g., L. A. Berman, *The puzzle: Exploring the evolutionary puzzle of male homosexuality* (Godot Press 2003); R. N. Lancaster, *The trouble with Nature: Sex in science and popular culture* (University of California Press 2003); A. Sullivan, *Same-sex marriage: Pro and Con: A Reader* (Vintage Books 2004); L. D. Wardle, M. Strasser, W. C. Duncan & D. O. Coolidge (Eds.), *Marriage and same-sex unions: A debate* (Praeger Publishers 2003).

2. E. Stein, *The mismeasure of desire: The science, theory, and ethics of sexual orientation* (Oxford University Press 1999).

3. J. D. Delamater & J. S. Hyde, Essentialism v. Social Constructionism in the study of human sexuality. *The Journal of Sex Research, 35(1)* 10-18 (1998).

4. D. M. Buss, *Evolutionary psychology: The new science of the mind* (Allyn and Bacon 1999).

5. Buss, supra n. 4

6. Buss, supra n. 4, at 97

7. H. Fisher, *The nature of romantic love,* in B. D. Slife (Ed.), *Taking Sides: Cashing Views on Controversial Psychological Issues* 86, 86 (12th ed., McGraw-Hill/Dushkin 2002).

8. Fisher, supra n. 7, at 87.

9. Fisher, supra n. 7, at 87.

10. Fisher, supra n. 7, at 92.

11. R. C. Kirkpatrick, The evolution of human homosexual behavior. *Current Anthropology, 41(3)* 385-413 (2000).

12. Berman, supra n. 1.

13. M. Potts & R. Short, *Ever Since Adam and Eve: The evolution of human sexuality* (Cambridge University Press 1999), at 74.

14. See, e.g., M. B. Duberman, M. Vicinus & G. Chauncey, *Hidden from history: Reclaiming the gay and lesbian past* (Penguin 1989).

15. R. Dawkins, *The selfish gene* (Oxford University Press 1976); E. O. Wilson, *On human nature* (Harvard University Press 1978).

16. Wilson, supra n. 15.

17. Stein, supra n. 2, at 183-184.

18. Stein, supra n. 2, at 184.

19. e.g., M. Ruse, *Homosexuality: A philosophical inquiry* (Basil Blackwood 1988).

20. Stein, supra n. 2, at 233.

21. Ruse, supra n. 19, at 136.

22. J. McKnight, *Straight science? Homosexuality, evolution, and adaptation* (Routledge 1997).

23. Stein, supra n. 2, at 184.

24. Stein, supra n. 2, at 184.

25. See, e.g., A. I. Dagg, *"Love of Shopping" is not a gene: Problems with Darwinian psychology* (Black Rose Books 2005); A. O'Hear, *Beyond evolution:Human nature and the limits of evolutionary explanation* (Clarendon Press 1997); Stein, supra n. 2.

26. Stein, supra n. 2, at 189.

27. Dagg, supra n. 25, at 139.

28. Stein, supra n. 2, at 97.

29. R. A. Lippa, *Gender, nature, and nurture* (2nd ed., Lawrence Erlbaum Associates 2005), at 115.

30. J. S. Bohan, *Regarding gender: essentialism, social constructionism, and feminist psychology,* in M. M Gergen and S. N. Davis (eds.), *Toward a new psychology of gender* 31, 33 (Routledge 1997).

31. Bohan, supra n. 30, at 33.

32. S. N. Davis & M. M. Gergen, *Toward a new psychology of gender: Opening conversations,* in M. M. Gergen and S. N. Davis (Eds.), *Toward a new psychology of gender* 1, 6 (Routledge 1997).

33. D. F. Greenberg, *The construction of homosexuality* (The University of Chicago Press 1988).

34. Stein, supra n. 2, at 97.

35. J. Marecek, M. Crawford & D. Popp, *On the construction of gender, sex, and sexualities,* in A.H. Eagly, A. E. Beall & R. J. Sternberg (eds.), *The psychology of gender* (2nd ed., The Guildorf Press 2004), at 208.

36. Mareck, et al., supra n. 35, at 208.

37. Mareck, et al., supra n. 35, at 209.

38. Stein, supra n. 2, at 97.

39. E. J. Capaldi & R. W. Proctor, *Contextualism in psychological research? A critical Review* (Sage Publications 1999); I. Hacking, *The social construction of what?* (Harvard University Press 1999).

40. B. D. Slife & R. N. Williams, *What's behind the research? Discovering hidden assumptions in the behavioral science* (Sage Publications 1995).

41. S. Bem & H. Looren de Jong, *Theoretical issues in psychology: An introduction* (Sage Publications 1997), at 32.

42. B. R. Hergenhahn, *An introduction to the history of psychology* (4th ed., Wadsworth Publishing 2001), at 7.

43. G. W. Heiman, *Research methods in psychology* (3rd ed., Houghton Mifflin Company 2002), at 4.

44. See, e.g., Slife & Williams, supra n. 40, R. Trigg, *Understanding social science* (2nd ed., Basil Blackwell 2001).

45. Slife & Williams, supra n. 40, at 128.

46. Slife & Williams, supra n. 40, at 129.

47. Wilson, supra n. 16, at 75

48. L. Lovlie, *Postmodernism and subjectivity,* in S. Kvale (Eds.), *Psychology and postmodernism,* 120 (Sage Publications 1992).

49. V. Burr, *Social constructionism* (Routledge 1995).

50. V. Burr(1995), at 30.
51. Delamater & Hyde, supra n. 3, at 14.
52. Delamater & Hyde, supra n. 3, at 16.
53. See, e.g., Sullivan, supra n. 1.
54. See, e.g., Slife & Williams, supra n. 40; Trigg, supra n. 44
55. See, e.g., Slife & Williams, supra n. 40.

CHAPTER 10
SEXUAL VIRTUE, SEXUAL VICE, AND THE REQUIREMENTS OF THE GOOD SOCIETY: LESSONS FROM ANCIENT ROME[1]

Dr. Charles J. Reid, Jr.
University of St. Thomas

I.   Introduction

In this paper, I consider the sexual ethics of classical Rome in the period between the Battle of Actium (27 BC)—which represented the final triumph of Octavius (the future Emperor Augustus) over Marc Antony and Cleopatra and has thus customarily served as the dividing line between Empire and Republic—and the reign of the Emperor Trajan (98-117), under whose aegis the empire reached perhaps the zenith of what it would attain. The popular image of the sexual ethics of this period is one of unrestrained sexual freedom—we might even call it libertinism. One need only think of the stories found in the pages of Petronius' *Satyricon*—which portrays Roman life as an unbridled celebration of excess—to conclude that the Romans joyfully abandoned themselves to all sorts of appetites. Vulgarity and sexual excess seemed to have been the order of the day. In our own day, of course, Hollywood has made ample use of this sort of imagery, thus cementing in the popular imagination the perception that perhaps there really was no sexual ethic in Rome, that the good life was the hedonistic life, given over to the pursuit of pleasure with no sense of consequences.

The purpose of this paper is to get beneath some of these stereotypes. It is the thesis of this paper that the Romans, in fact, had a deep sense of sexual right and wrong, and that depictions of sexual excess—such as in Petronius's *Satyricon*—were deeply offensive to these moral sensibilities. In proposing this subject for investigation, we need to be sensitive to what we mean by certain basic terms. The word "Roman," which I have used two or three times in the opening paragraphs, is simply too broad to serve as a useful analytical tool without further qualification. Roman society, like American society, was rich, complex, and diverse. It was honeycombed with a wide variety of competing belief-systems and values. Petronius's *Satyricon* probably captured well the value system of some members of Rome's *nouveau riche*.

But there were also critics of this sort of licentiousness. My concern is with these critics and their perception of the harm that accrued to society when traditional Roman virtues—and in the context of this forum I mean primarily the virtues of self-restraint and control over the passions—disappears. The critics I shall consider include the leading Roman historians who were either near contemporaries of the events and personages they were describing or at least had access to the ancient sources. From Livy, to Suetonius, to Tacitus, the first century AD, from Augustus to Trajan, is an especially well-documented period of time.

These historians told nothing less than the story of the rise and consolidation of imperial Rome. What is not always appreciated, however, is that these historians did not wish only to document but to judge. They had strong moral commitments and they wished to determine—not only to satisfy their own curiosity but for the good of society—whether the ancient Roman virtues were still vital. They wanted to give examples of virtuous conduct and vice-ridden conduct so that their audience might profit from an awareness of good and evil and the rewards and punishments that accompanied each. These men, in short, were, for the most part, strict moralists, who condemned the excesses they witnessed and despaired for the future of Rome. They had a clear moral code and a keen appreciation of the grave dangers that threatened society when that code was violated.

To answer the question, "what is the harm?" as the Romans might have understood it, requires us to examine the main elements of this moral code. It was a code that demanded, most fundamentally, control of one's passions and respect for the traditional duties of hearth and home. The Roman who failed to control his passions or who rejected the responsibilities of family life, in turn, exposed himself to the risk of leading a disordered life. The Roman historians discussed below expended substantial energy in explaining the implications of such disorder for society at large and concluded that the great harm that accrued from rejecting this moral code was tyranny—the abuse of one's duties and consequent neglect of the public good. The Roman historians did not sharply differentiate between other-regarding or self-regarding acts, as we might, or between public roles and private life; one's private and public behavior blended into each other, the one shaping and influencing the other. And the tyrant was one who stepped outside the boundaries of this moral order to the great harm of those whose lives he happened to touch.

II.   Livy and the Rape of Lucretia

"When a few days had gone by, Sextus Tarquinius,
without letting Collatinus know, took a single
attendant and went to Collatia. Being kindly
welcomed, for no one suspected his purpose, he
was brought after dinner to a guest-chamber.
Burning with passion, he waited till it seemed to
him that all about him was secure and everybody
fast asleep; then, drawing his sword, he came to
the sleeping Lucretia. Holding the woman down
with his left hand on her breast, he said, 'Be
still, Lucretia! I am Sextus Tarquinius. My
sword is in my hand. Utter a sound, and you die!
In affright, the woman started out of her sleep.

No help was in sight, but only imminent death.
Then Tarquinius began to declare his love, to
plead, to mingle threats with prayers, to bring
every resource to bear upon her woman's heart.
When he found her obdurate and not to be moved
even by fear of death, he went farther and
threatened her with disgrace, saying that when she
was dead he would kill her slave and lay him naked
by her side, that she might be said to have been
put to death in adultery with a man of base
condition. At this dreadful prospect her resolute
modesty was overcome as if with force, by his
victorious lust; and Tarquinius departed, exulting
in his conquest of a woman's honour. Lucretia,
grieving at her great disaster, dispatched the
same message to her father in Rome and to her
husband at Ardea: that they should each take a
trusty friend and come; that they must do this and
do it quickly, for a frightful thing had happened.
Spurius Lucretius came with Publius Valerius,
Volesus's son. Collatinus brought Lucius Junius
Brutus, with whom he chanced to be returning to
Rome when he was met by the messenger from his
wife. Lucretia they found sitting sadly in her
chamber. The entrance of her friends brought the
tears to her eyes, and to her husband's question,
'Is it all well?' she replied: 'Far from it; for
what can be well with a woman when she has lost
her honor? The print of a strange man,
Collatinus, is in your bed. Yet my body only has
been violated; my heart is guiltless, as death
shall be my witness. But pledge your right hands
and your words that the adulterer (*adultero*) shall
not go unpunished. Sextus Tarquinius is he that
last night returned hostility for hospitality, and
armed with force brought ruin on me, and on
himself no less—if you are men—when he
worked his pleasure with me.' They gave their
pledges, every man in turn. They seek to comfort
her, sick at heart as she is, by diverting the
blame from her who was forced to the doer of the
wrong. They tell her it is the mind that sins,
not the body; and that where purpose has been
wanting there is no guilt. 'It is for you to
determine,' she answers, 'what is due for him; for
my own part, though I acquit myself of the sin, I
do not absolve myself from punishment; not in time
to come shall ever unchaste women live through the
example of Lucretia.' Taking a knife which she
had concealed beneath her dress, she plunged it
into her heart, and sinking forward upon the
wound, died as she fell. The wail for the dead

was raised by her husband and her father."[2]

Thus the Roman historian Titus Livy (ca. 59 B.C-17 A.D.) recorded the rape and suicide of Lucretia. Livy's account is not the only surviving version of this incident, purported to be the *casus belli* that led to the overthrow of the Roman monarchy in 510 B.C,[3] although Livy's is the most important for our purposes. To appreciate the connection of Livy's recounting of Lucretia's rape to our theme, it is important to set his work in its historical context, to understand his motives in calling this tragedy to mind, and to see how this story has resonated over the intervening centuries until our own age. Indeed, the Rape of Lucretia, it will be seen, forms a kind of paradigm of the relationship of private virtue and public good that will resonate loudly throughout the history of the West. And, of course, it equally demonstrates the kind of public evil that arises from private vice.

To appreciate these points, one should begin with the context. I shall speak first of the context in which Livy placed this story. The time was the later sixth-century B.C.—more precisely, the year before legend has it the Roman monarchy was overthrown, in 510 BC. Sextus Tarquinius, who perpetrated the Rape depicted in Livy's story, was the reputed son of Lucius Tarquinius Superbus ("The Proud" or "The Haughty"), the last king of Rome. (I have used words like "legend" and "reputed" here because most of what survives about the Roman monarchy is legendary, intended not to be taken as literally true but to be understood as establishing certain abiding principles of good citizenship or good morals).

Sextus was prompted to act as he did, it seems, by Lucretia's own modesty. The proximate cause that lay behind the Rape, as Livy tells the story, was a wager among a group of young Roman aristocrats. They had tired of the dull routine of serving in a Roman army that had surrounded and lain siege to a neighboring town and began to boast, after too much drinking one night, about the chastity and loyalty of their wives.[4] Tarquinius Collatinus, Lucretia's husband, urged them to saddle up their horses and ride to Rome (only a few hours' distance) to check on their wives in order to see exactly what their womenfolk were up to.[5] The winner would be the husband whose wife was engaged in the most modest activity when surprised unawares. That woman was Lucretia, who was engaged in the traditional wifely chore of spinning cloth.[6] The very sight of such propriety aroused in Sextus a "wicked desire to take her in forcible sexual outrage" (*per vim stuprandae capit*).[7] Purity, in this case, was defeated by sexual vice, but Sextus's crime was so offensive to good order that his father's dynasty was forcibly overthrown by Collatinus and his collaborator, Lucius Junius Brutus.[8]

If this is one side of the context we should consider, another aspect that must be taken into account are the political circumstances of Livy's own day. Livy wrote his history at the height of the literary revival that occurred during the long span of the Emperor Augustus's rule and his work was part of a general effort to glorify and romanticize the Roman past.[9] Augustus himself sought to restore what he understood to be the purity and virtue of the Roman past through the promulgation of several decrees that collectively aimed at the promotion of fruitful marriage. The sexual promiscuity and the childlessness of his own age caused Augustus to fret mightily about the future well-being of the imperial elites and his intention was to revive Rome by reviving the traditional Roman family.[10]

In this context, one should notice the offense Livy attributed to Sextus Tarquinius. Although Roman lawyers of Livy's day certainly possessed a concept of rape—understood not only as a crime against the man who possessed authority over the woman, but also a crime of violence against the woman herself[11]—Livy did not charge Sextus with rape. Livy, rather, used forms of the Latin words for "adulterer" (*adultero*) and "sexually outrageous conduct" (*stuprandae/stuprum*) to describe Sextus's misdeeds.

Adultery and *stuprum*, in fact, had become in Livy's own day, special targets of the Roman authorities. The Emperor Augustus, as part of his effort to revitalize Roman family life, sought to reconceptualize adultery. Where once prosecution for adultery was solely the prerogative of the aggrieved family, Augustus now declared it to be an offense against the state and entrusted its prosecution to public officials where family members proved reluctant to bring charges.[12] The Augustan-era laws went so far as to require a man to divorce a wife caught in adultery: "If a man failed to divorce and prosecute a wife he knew to be adulterous, he could be charged with pimping."[13] In using the word *adultero* in connection with Sextus Tarquinius's crime and in connecting the crime to the fall of the monarchy itself, Livy can be read as endorsing—perhaps even extolling—the elevation of adultery from a purely personal failing to the level of a great public wrong that offended against the general welfare of state and society.

While adultery was a precisely-defined offense that involved extra-marital relations between two persons at least one of whom was married to a third party, the word *stuprum* was more vague and remains today almost untranslateable. The Oxford Latin Dictionary offers as its first definition of the word, "Dishonour, shame," even apart from any sexual connotations.[14] This general understanding no doubt colored the word's legal usage in ways that probably cannot be fully appreciated today. Regarding its specifically legal significance, Adolf Berger's *Encyclopedic Dictionary of Roman Law* gives as a definition "[i]llicit intercourse with an unmarried woman or widow" and distinguishes *stuprum* from adultery by pointing out that while at least one party had to be married in an adulterous relationship, this was not true with *stuprum*.[15] The Augustan-age statutes on *stuprum*, however, were more comprehensive and less precise than this seemingly neat distinction: "The basic statute on sexual offenses, the *Lex Iulia de adulteriis* (18 B.C.) was vague and sweeping in its definition of illicit sexual unions; under its terms all sexual copulation, save for marital intercourse, might have been classed as *stuprum*."[16] Augustus, the historical consensus teaches, "certainly expressed a moral aim" through the promulgation of this legislation.[17]

A monarchy whose crown prince would engage in such gross misconduct, Livy implied, had lost its legitimacy and was worthy of being overthrown. This supposition concerning Livy's political purposes in recounting the Rape of

Lucretia coheres with what we know of his views on the virtues required to support the Roman state and on the larger purposes his history was intended to serve.

We know Livy's intentions, first, from what he declared them to be in the prefaces that periodically adorn the various segments into which his historical project was divided. Livy's undertaking, it can be fairly said, was grandly ambitious: he sought to recount in 142 books nothing less than the story of Rome from its humble beginnings to its emergence as a world power and its ultimate triumph over all its adversaries. Regrettably, only small portions of this larger enterprise survive—books one through ten detailing the early history of Rome and books 21 to 45, discussing the Punic Wars of the second and third century, BC, and a few other incidents of similar historical provenance.

Book One, introducing the history as a whole, and Book Two, introducing the founding of the Roman Republic, are each preceded by prefaces. In his preface to Book One, Livy conceded that the story he told of the old monarchy was highly embellished and was "decorated with poetic license."[18] His purpose was to ensure that Rome was given a founding myth worthy of its great accomplishments.[19] But, Livy went on, he also wished to describe the "good conduct" (*mores*) and the "discipline" (*disciplina*) of the age and to show the steady decay that these qualities had undergone in the course of Roman history until his own age, when vices became equally unbearable and incurable.[20] From the chronicle he had prepared, Livy hoped his audience would draw "lessons" *(exempli)* that he intended to engrave as if placed upon bright and luminous monuments (*monumentis*) that will pass from generation to generation and so stand as reminders of the virtuous conduct that is demanded of Romans.[21]

In his preface to Book Two, then, Livy distinguished between the tyranny that Rome experienced under Tarquinius Superbus's rule and the liberty that Romans had achieved for themselves with the overthrow of the monarchy.[22] This was not, however, a liberty to engage in licentiousness, Livy stressed, but the kind of liberty enjoyed when the ideal of the rule of law exercises greater suasion over society than the arbitrary rule of men.[23] And this newly-won liberty, Livy went on, might only be enjoyed by people with the judgment and discipline to use it wisely. The Romans who rejected the monarchy, Livy was pleased to report, were no longer crude and unlettered shepherds who might be easily aroused by the passionate outbursts of demagogues, but sturdy and virtuous men, capable of displaying love for homeland and for their wives and children.[24] His implicit wish was that Romans might always retain this virtuous independence of mind.

Livy's intentions in writing his historical epic have been the subject of several recent book-length studies. Jane Chaplin has called attention to the notion of "exemplary" history, drawing on Livy's explicitly-declared intention in the preface of Book One to impart lessons (*exempli*) to his readers.[25] And while Chaplin is certainly correct in observing that one should be cautious in accepting Lucretia as an *exemplum* because her particular act is not subsequently imitated by others,[26] it is also true that Livy's larger point—that sexual chastity is important to the integrity not only of the private realm but also of the public—is probably the lesson that Livy intended to convey.

Mary Jaeger, for her part, has seen in the word *monumentis* a main key to understanding Livy's purpose.[27] Indeed, the very title of Livy's work—*Ab urbe condita* (literally, "From the Founding of the City")—was intended to evoke the notion of an enduring monument, calling to mind not only the great accomplishments of the past but the contemporary lessons that ought to be derived from these feats.[28] In this sense, Jaeger sees Livy's work as both "moral" and "didactic" in its attempt to recommend certain courses of conduct and to condemn others.[29]

Less wedded to a close reading of particular words and phrases of the Livian prefaces in order to divine intent, the Italian classicist Lidia Storono Mazzolani has stressed the importance of virtue to the overall structure of *Ab urbe condita.* "In Livy's work," Storoni Mazzolani has written, "there is no catalogue of virtues, but each episode illustrates an unequivocal concept of duty."[30] "The characters in his epic are meant to serve as a reminder for contemporary men of the duties incumbent on the ideal soldier and the ideal citizen, who confronted with cosmopolitan concepts and the relativity of all principles, had lost their bearings."[31] And in this context, Storoni Mazzolani reminded her readers, the Rape of Lucretia "was important only because it marked the beginning of the Republic."[32] Sextus Tarquinius's unrestrained appetites marked him out as a tyrant who had to be overthrown and, at a deeper level, signified the potential tyranny of all monarchies—a point that Livy could not make directly given the political climate in which he lived.[33] It signified, finally if only implicitly, that a higher standard of sexual morality was to be expected in a flourishing republic—governance of one's private passions, it might be said, was a necessary precondition of political self-governance, while lack of self-control and disregard of one's familial duties threatened the fabric of the entire society.

An older preoccupation of historians that has now faded from view was the effort to determine whether Livy's work was intended to support or to criticize the imperial ambitions of Caesar Augustus.[34] Scholars have more recently adopted a more sophisticated analysis, seeing in Livy elements that both looked fondly backward to the simple virtues of the Republican past and toward his own time, making peace with, if not always actually endorsing the principate brought into being by Augustus's final triumph over his rivals.[35] But whether one sees Livy as a nostalgic memoirist of the Republican past, an apologist for the new Augustan order, or the representative of a more nuanced synthesis of old and new, there is no mistaking his commitment to virtue—including preeminently the virtues of home and family—as indispensable elements of the good society.

And, finally, this is the way in which Livy's work—including in particular his account of the Rape of Lucretia—has been received and interpreted by succeeding generations. Humanist and Christian writers alike all made generous use of Livy's account in order to frame moral questions of pressing concern for their own age. Concerning Niccoló Machiavelli's treatment of the Rape of Lucretia, a modern commentator has noted that to an even greater extent than

Livy, Machiavelli sought "the politicization of virtue."[36] Indeed, Machiavelli should be understood "[as trying] to demonstrate the necessity of making private morality answer to public necessity, rather than vice versa."[37] The Rape of Lucretia, for Machiavelli, thus became an ideal vehicle for making the case that in a republic the public good depended upon a healthy private morality. Jean-Jacques Rousseau, for his part, referenced the Rape of Lucretia in several of his works. And these retellings by Rousseau were intended to have a political effect: "[A]n allegory for the loss and potential rebirth of the republic."[38]

William Shakespeare, similarly, in an epic poem published in 1594, explored both the public and private dimensions of Sextus Tarquinius's act. "Rome herself," Shakespeare wrote, "doth stand disgraced."[39] Not only Collatinus in his private capacity as husband, but the entire polity of Rome was offended by Sextus's act of abuse and Lucretia's sanguinary vindication of her defiled honor. A modern writer has thus written about Shakespeare's sonnet:

> "*The Rape of Lucrece*, like *Measure for Measure*,
> is much concerned with the idea of *government*,
> in both the moral and political senses of that
> term. Through the skilful use of analogy and
> metaphor, Shakespeare constantly brings together
> in our minds the ideas of public and private
> governance, prompting us to see these ideas as
> necessarily and intimately connected. People
> should be able to govern their instincts (it is
> implied) in the same way that kings should be
> able to govern the state."[40]

Benjamin Britten, in his opera "The Rape of Lucretia," with libretto by Ronald Duncan, perhaps draws the closest relationship between Sextus's unrestrained appetites and tyranny. First performed in 1946, one year after the defeat of the Axis powers in World War II, the opera sought to Christianize Livy's story. The suffering of Lucretia, her family, and her friends, Britten's opera stressed, would only finally be redeemed in Christ. In a sense, Britten, a devoted though sometimes conflicted member of the Church of England, baptized Lucretia and her company of ancient Romans. But if anything, this dramatic move only heightened the political impact of the Rape by imbuing Sextus's crime and Lucretia's suicide with a Christian moral sensibility: "All tyrants fall through tyranny," the male chorus sang at the opening of Act II, and the implication was clear: Sextus's ungovernable lust was not a private crime, but a grave breach of public order and God's law that would bring down the royal household itself.

III.   Tacitus and the Moral Purity of the Germans

Active nearly a century after Livy, Cornelius Tacitus (ca. 56-after 120 AD) was likely a member of a provincial family of some standing who had risen through a variety of skills to a position of political prominence in Rome.[41]

Regarding his own political career, Tacitus wrote: "'I must not deny that my public career was launched by Vespasian, promoted by Titus, and still further advanced by Domitian.'"[42] To acknowledge Domitian as a patron must have been difficult for Tacitus: Domitian, the younger son of Vespasian and the brother of the Emperor Titus, had been a bloody-minded tyrant who was finally murdered in the year 96 AD in a plot engineered by his estranged wife and members of his bodyguard.[43] Tacitus must have felt deeply ambivalent at having to acknowledge this paternity. He had survived the Domitian persecutions, perhaps even aided and abetted them, yet Domitian had come to represent, for Tacitus and for others, "the personified crime of tyranny."[44]

Chastened, perhaps even hardened by these experiences, Tacitus set as his goal in writing history the passing of judgment on the virtues and vices of the past: "the most important duty of historians," Tacitus wrote, "is to ensure that virtue is recorded, and that the wicked in word and deed are forced to fear the condemnation of posterity."[45] Tacitus saw in the men of senatorial rank a collapse of all political courage. He followed his description of the duty of the historian with an account of the way in which the Senate under the Emperor Tiberius regularly engaged in acts of sycophancy and self-abasement.[46] Tiberius's response to the fawning obsequiousness he witnessed all around him was contempt: He was fond of mocking the Senate in Greek, "These men are ready for slavery!"[47] In pursuing his historical enterprise he wished to understand the roots of this collapse of courage.

Tacitus was quick to condemn not only the public and political failings of the Senatorial order, but also their sexual and marital conduct. He was unafraid, albeit a century after the fact, to denounce the marital infidelities of Julia, the wife of Tiberius and daughter of Augustus.[48] And Tacitus was unsparing in his criticism of Tiberius's daughter-in-law, Livia Julia, for her sexual trysts with Sejanus—an affair that ended badly when Sejanus attempted the overthrow of Tiberius's government.[49] In these and other similar depictions of the marital misconduct of the ruling class, Tacitus sought to draw a close connection between private immorality and public malfeasance. The collapse of virtue thus had dimensions that were simultaneously public and private and that embraced not only exalted affairs of state but extended even to the intimacies of the household. This interpretation of Tacitus receives strong support not only in his accounts of the sexual entanglements and intrigues of the Roman elites but also by a careful reading of the implicit contrast he drew between the life of a debased Roman nobility and the simple Germanic folk living north and east of the Roman frontier.

Roman contact with Germanic peoples commenced in the first century BC. Twice during his time in Gaul, in the middle 50s, B.C., Julius Caesar crossed the Rhine River and there encountered a strange collection of peoples.[50] Roman observers came to call these people, who lived beyond the Rhine, in an area bounded by the Danube River to the South, the Vistula River to the East, and "the seas in the north," Germans.[51] In the Augustan era, Rome harbored the ambition that she might conquer at least some portions of Germany and create a *provincia Germania* beyond the Rhine, but these dreams were crushed in A.D.

9, when the Roman general Quinctilius Varus suffered one of the most humiliating losses in the annals of Roman military history—three legions destroyed and the Roman adventure on the eastern bank of the Rhine repulsed at the Battle of Teutoberg Forest.[52] Seven years later, the new Emperor Tiberius halted Roman efforts to expand beyond the Rhine, preferring instead to use that river as a natural boundary for the northeastern corner of the Empire.

Although the Romans effectively lost interest in the conquest of Germany, this did not mean that they lost interest in contact with them or in trying to understand who the Germans were. Traders moved back and forth between Roman Gaul and the Germanic peoples beyond the Rhine, while Germans might enter the Empire in search of econimic opportunity.[53] Sensing the importance of these contacts and appreciating the importance of learning more about an indomitable people to the empire's north, Tacitus sought to explain to the Roman reading public what was known of the Germans. His work on the subject, popularly known as the *Germania*, was composed in the year A.D. 98. The emperor Nerva had just died and the new Emperor, Trajan, was then on the banks of the Rhine River, ostensibly to settle the German issue which had eluded his predecessors.[54] Tacitus himself was worried about the enduring threat the Germans posed to the Empire: for two hundred and ten years, he observed, the Roman people had been at intermittent war with the Germans and had failed utterly to subdue them.[55] It was therefore good, Tacitus averred, to understand why it was that the Germans were such a formidable foe.

The "liberty of the Germans," Tacitus warned, was a more serious enemy than the kingdom of the Parthians, on the empire's eastern flank.[56] Opening his work by deliberately calling to mind the opening passage of Julius Caesar's *Gallic Wars* ("All Gaul is divided in three parts"), Tacitus declared Germany to be "undivided" (*Germania omnis*).[57] Tacitus's work would be at least as much admonition to take lessons from this indivisible and free people as it would be an ethnographic study of a strange culture's very different mores and folkways.

Tacitus drew implicit contrasts between the complexity and subtlety of Roman life and the simpler virtues that the Germans had mastered. The Germans, for the most part, placed little value on gold or silver and treated the silver vases presented to their chieftains as so much base metal.[58] Their military commanders (*duces*), Tacitus wrote, were chosen for their "virtue" (*ex virtute*), by which was clearly meant the whole array of qualities that made a military leader great—courage, to be sure, but also a kind of great-heartedness.[59] This clearly is the significance of Tacitus's assertion that commanders might lead their men only by "example" (*exemplo*) and never by compulsion (*imperio*).[60] A general was never permitted to punish his men, whether by killing, imprisoning, or even by flogging or hitting them.[61] In elucidating these limitations, Tacitus was hearkening back to the simple martial virtues that had shaped the old Roman army—the citizen army that is described in the early Roman sources elected its own military tribunes and even provided the basic political structure for the nascent Roman state.[62]

Germanic *libertas*, Tacitus made clear, was not an unalloyed good thing. When asked to assemble, the Germans, far from acting promptly, consume a second and then a third day, in deliberate delay. This practice, Tacitus denounced as a "defect of their liberty" (*illud ex libertate vitium*).[63] Germans also tended to be simultaneously fractious and indolent—dividing and diminishing their strength through recurrent tribal warfare while growing torpid and lazy when there was no war to be fought.[64] On the other hand, the kings who are called upon to address the assembly are listened to only on the basis of their "age," their "noble status," their "glory in battle," or their "command of speech."[65] These leaders thus enjoy only "the authority to persuade," and do not possess the "power to command."[66] This is the sort of liberty, Tacitus implied, that Romans once enjoyed and should now fear in the Germans.[67]

The backbone of Germanic society—indeed, the backbone of Germanic liberty itself—Tacitus stressed, was the family. Indeed, Tacitus's treatment of Germanic chastity and sound marital practice might be productively read as a sustained albeit oblique denunciation of practices current among the Roman elites of Tacitus's own age. A wedding among the Germans, Tacitus noticed, was commemorated with gifts. But these were not the gifts commonly exchanged in Roman ceremonies: the husband will present his wife with livestock—some horses, maybe, or a team of oxen.[68] He might also give her some martial implements—a sword or a shield.[69] In exchange, the wife will present her new husband with "some weapons" (*armorum aliquid*).[70]

Tacitus did not stop at describing the gifts that were exchanged but offered also to explain their symbolism: by these tokens, the wife was not permitted to think of herself as freed from the concerns of virtue (*extra virtutem cognitationes*) or from the vagaries of war.[71] She should share equally in the hardships—and in the joys—of an undivided common life. This exchange and the symbolism behind it stood in potent contrast with the comparison Tacitus drew to the practice at Rome, where faddish, feminine trifles were sought and given by the prospective bride and groom and by their families.[72]

Adultery, Tacitus continued, was extremely rare in Germanic culture. Modesty was enforced both by social expectations and by the absence of the many luxuries Romans had become accustomed to.[73] Among the Germans, Tacitus noted, there were no public spectacles nor were there dinner parties "corrupted" (*corruptae*) by "irritations" (*irritationes*)—by which Tacitus meant undue arousal to the commission of adultery and other sexual indiscretions.[74] The passing of secret notes from men to women and back again—in Tacitus's mind apparently a common Roman dinner-table amusement—was unknown to the Germans.[75] Dangerous liaisons were not possible absent these furtive means of communication. Chastity, furthermore, was regarded seriously among the Germans; indeed, they did not laughingly dismiss sexual failings as nothing more than the temper of the times (*nec corrumpere et corrumpi saeculum vocatur*).[76] There were even Germanic tribes, Tacitus asserted, where second marriage was unheard of, especially among women. In these tribes, the women live by the motto, "one husband . . . one body, and one life" (*unum . . . maritum . . . unum corpus unamque vitam*).[77] Herbert Benario in his commentary on the *Germania* called attention to the force of the Latin construction Tacitus employed here: "The tricolon *unum, unum, unamque* makes the husband as integral to the woman as her body and life."[78]

Tacitus went on: The Germans did not frustrate the procreation of children. They did not set a limit on the number of children they would welcome into the home, nor would they kill undesired children—practices that they regarded as disgraceful.[79] This was because in Germany "good customs" mattered more than "good laws" elsewhere (*boni mores . . . bonae leges*).[80] Again, Benario's commentary is worth consulting:

> "Innate character and behavior are more potent
> than laws; compelled behavior is unreliable. . . .
> the state is not effective in its attempts to
> transform society. [Tacitus] may have had in mind
> the Augustan legislation on marriage and proper
> behavior."[81]

Scholars have often noted that Tacitus actually did very little research prior to writing the *Germania*. As one scholar has described the work: "The essay is largely a reworking of former works, particularly the Elder Pliny's book on the German wars, and on occasion in some matters Tacitus failed to update his sources."[82] As ethnography, judged even by the standards of Tacitus's own day, the *Germania* had its share of deficiencies. But this casualness with sources and this reliance on secondary and sometimes outdated sources can be explained even if not excused, if one bears in mind that Tacitus's intention was not merely to present a dispassionate account of Germanic folkways but, more importantly, to convey to the Roman reading public a subtle but insistent admonition to reform their own corrupt ways.

Thus one can compare Tacitus's description of chastity, divorce, adultery, and the importance of children among the Germans to the common practices of the Roman elites of his day. Chastity, in first-century Rome, was enforced by the prohibitions against *stuprum*—that multi-faceted word meaning both dishonor and sexual misconduct.[83] A whole series of words was used by the Romans to describe and encourage the sort of behavior that was expected—principally but not exclusively on the part of women. *Fides* ("fidelity", "loyalty"); *reverentia* (a kind of awe-filled respect); and *obsequium* (devotion that sometimes but not always veered into blind obedience), were among the main elements of the standard vocabulary.[84] The Roman sources, however, tell us also that these lofty standards were frequently honored only in their breach. Augustan-age poetry stands as compelling testimony to the liberties that might be taken. Large quantities of such poetry remain—some of it romantic, much of it scatological.[85] Juvenal and Martial and the "Silver-Age" successors to the Augustan writers were probably even quicker to call attention to the strong disconnection between, on the one hand, the moral code recommended by writers like Tacitus and legislatively decreed by the emperors, and, on the other, the ways in which Romans led their daily lives.[86]

Divorce, too, had become a regular feature of the Roman landscape of the latter first century AD. Roman writers believed that divorce did not exist in their earliest Republic; the first divorce, it was commonly said, was that of Carvilius

Ruga, around the year 230 B.C.[87] Fault-based divorce arose soon thereafter, but by the time one arrives at the first century, AD, divorce was possible at the will of either party, even in the absence of adequate notice being delivered to the other spouse.[88] How frequently did divorce occur? Susan Treggiari posed that question but found the evidence inadequate to supply a statistically valid sample.[89] Certainly, however, the Roman writers of the age considered the frequency of divorce to be one of the grave social problems plaguing their time.[90]

Child-birth and child-rearing, finally, was often eschewed by the Roman upper classes. When a pregnancy was unwanted, furthermore, exposure was often used to dispatch the unfortunate child. The younger Seneca recommended that "weak and deformed" children should be put to death in the same way that rabid dogs or sickly sheep are killed.[91] Cicero used the exposure of infants as a metaphor to describe how quickly an unwanted political office was created in the early Republic and then assigned to oblivion.[92] Such a metaphor must have carried force only because of the daily reality of exposure. Classical Roman law took for granted the legitimacy of exposure when applied to infants.[93] As I wrote in a different context: "Exposure, it seems, was practiced as a form of birth control throughout much of the Greco-Roman world."[94]

These social practices—the violation of traditional ideals, the perceived rise of a divorce culture at variance with an older, purer, more pristine commitment to monogamy, and the disposability of life itself in the form of exposure and infanticide—helped to shape and inform Tacitus's treatment of the morality of Germanic marriage customs. In his selective editing and in the emphasis he placed on particular Germanic practices, Tacitus held up a mirror on life at Rome. He even drew practical public and political consequences from Germanic custom. Because of their attachment to their wives, because of their commitments to their children, the first loyalty of every German warrior ran not to some artificial conglomeration of men (*conglobatio*) brought together for the occasion, but to family and near relations (*familiae et propinquitates*).[95] Stirred to defend hearth and home from hostile forces, the Germanic warrior will fight all the more fiercely because he hears calling to him the voices of his woman and his children.[96] In this sense and in others, the family can be said to be the foundation-stone of Germanic freedom. Obliquely, indirectly, perhaps even ironically, Tacitus presumed to challenge the morals of his age.

IV.   The Emperor Nero: The Perfect Tyrant

There is probably no Roman emperor better known in the popular imagination for his misdeeds than the Emperor Nero (born in A.D. 37, he ruled as emperor from 54 to 68). One should consider the reputation that has come down through the ages and then reflect on the means by which it was acquired. Within Christianity, there was an early tradition that associated Nero with the Anti-Christ. Indeed, the Apostle John, the author of the Book of *Revelations*, probably intended this comparison. The "mark of the beast" described in the Book of *Revelations* "is probably an allusion to coins with the image, name, and insignia of the emperor on them."[97] And the number "666," also used of the beast, was probably a reference to Nero's name, which in Greek and Hebrew can be given a numeric value based on counting systems then in use.[98] Nero's reputation as the incarnation of evil remained undiminished throughout the middle ages. There persisted through ancient and medieval times the myth of *Nero redivivus*—the belief that Nero would return again to usher onto the world stage a period of particularly awful diabolical misrule.[99] And the writers of the high middle ages, such as the Abbot Adso (ca. 950), in his treatise on the Antichrist, understood Nero to be a prototype of the wicked ruler who will govern the earth at the end of days.[100]

If Nero was held in enduring and powerful odium by Christian writers, the same could also be said about the non-Christian Roman writers whose works constitute the principal primary source material for his reign. Suetonius, not as perceptive or ironic as Tacitus to be sure, but nevertheless an important source for the Emperor Nero's life,[101] summarized his person and his reign as a catalogue of disasters. Nero's very body was somehow not fit; Suetonius wrote that "it was stained and it smelled" (*maculoso et fetido*).[102] But Nero never lost his capacity for vice. Even though he engaged in the grossest forms of *luxuriae*, he was able to maintain good health.[103] (*Luxuria* is another intricately complex Latin term that carries both the sense of sexual excess and a generally un-Roman abandonment to material comforts and pleasures).[104] Nero sought immortality but had no idea how to achieve it; he thus found himself even renaming the months of the year to correspond to his name.[105] He was a man who, in short, aspired to things that could not be achieved and thus lived outside the normal bounds of human sensibility.

Cassius Dio (164-after 229) wrote at a much later date but had similar things to say.[106] Merging a discussion of Nero's private misconduct and his public misrule, Dio recorded that he threw himself headlong into banqueting, drinking, and womanizing while neglecting affairs of state.[107] When told that he should listen to and respect his advisors, he reminded them that he was Caesar, not they.[108] He soon lost control, not only of his private passions, but of good government, with unfortunate consequences: "[H]e brought great disgrace upon the whole Roman race and committed many outrages against the Romans themselves. Innumerable acts of violence and outrage, of robbery and murder, were committed by the emperor himself and by those who at one time or another had influence with him."[109]

The chorus to the play *Octavia*, once attributed to the younger Seneca (one of those court advisors whom Nero first listened to and then spurned), but now attributed to an anonymous imitator of Seneca's,[110] proposed the briefest but probably the most compelling summary of Nero's character:

> "He has the heart of a tyrant.
> He hates those born of better blood.
> He despises gods and men simultaneously."[111]

The playwright's choice of words is significant—the tyrant is one who despises gods and men; in short, the tyrant is one who attacks the natural order, finding both the life of this world and of the divine order itself as unsuited to his ambitions. The tyrant attacks this order and wishes to surpass it, but will ultimately be frustrated in his goals. Octavia's prayer at the close of this play reinforces this theme. When faced with execution at the emperor's command, Octavia, Nero's first wife, prayed to the gods of heaven to bear witness to the crime and kill the wild tyrant Nero.[112] Thus invoked, the gods, ultimately promise to restore the order that the tyrant has disrupted. Of this much the audience, which would have seen the play only after Nero's death, would be assured.

In the final part of this paper, I should like to explore this point more closely. What does it mean for an individual to violate the laws of God and man as Nero did? Can it be said that marital and sexual misconduct constitute evidence of tyranny? Implicated in this, of course, is the larger question—what is the harm, both to the parties involved and to the larger society?

The three major sources for the life of Nero are Tacitus's *Annales*, which remains incomplete in the form that survives, breaking off its narrative late in Nero's reign; Suetonius's *Lives of the Caesars*; and Cassius Dio's *Roman History*. Edward Champlin has recently reviewed each of these men's motives in writing.[113] None of these three authors was an eye-witness to Nero's reign; all of them brought to bear the sensibilities and prejudices of the senatorial oligarchy and probably relied on sources now lost to modern readers that shared the same world-view; and all of them made the evidence fit the case they sought to prove, i.e., that Nero was not only a tyrant but the paradigm of all tyranny.[114]

Champlin's work is an important undertaking. He acknowledges that Nero was "a bad man and a bad ruler."[115] But he also wishes to uncover, as a good historian should, "[a] reality [that] was more complex."[116] My own purpose differs from the focus of Champlin's work. Champlin wishes to look behind the perceived biases of Tacitus, Suetonius, and Dio, to recover an accurate portrayal of Nero as he really was. I would like, on the other hand, not so much to recover the true measure of Nero's reign, as to retrieve an accurate understanding of the thought processes and presuppositions that shaped the editorial process that one of these sources—Tacitus—employed in his account of Nero's imperial tenure. Standing behind his work, it is clear, was a model of what tyranny should look like. And the tyrant, according to that model, was one who lacked control over his passions, destroyed the natural bonds of the family, and inverted the expectations of the divine and natural order.

As Tacitus recounts the years of his misrule, Nero was a tyrant not only in the ways in which he dealt with enemies but more especially in the ways he treated family, friends, and advisors. His mother Agrippina was thuggish in her own right—she was implicated in the murder of the Emperor Claudius and was entirely capable of repeating her brutish acts if her son should ever turn against her.[117] But Nero was seen as overstepping the bounds not only of government but of filial devotion and of natural instinct itself when he finally arranged her murder in the year 59.[118] He dealt in similarly harsh terms with Brittanicus, his younger brother by adoption, whom he had poisoned.[119] His advisors, the philosopher Seneca and the epicure Petronius, were induced to commit suicide after falling into Nero's disfavor,[120] while Sextus Afranius Burrus, the chief of the praetorian guard, died in mysterious circumstances on his way to prison.[121] And, of course, Nero went on to even more extreme depredations, the most obscene probably being his treatment of Christians following the Great Fire in Rome.[122]

These acts of public misconduct had their analogues, in Tacitus's account, in Nero's private life. He hated his wife Octavia and even in the first year of his reign he became involved with another woman—Acte, a freedwoman socially far beneath an emperor.[123] He simultaneously took up with young men to engage in escapades and "ambiguous secrets."[124] (Tacitus's expression—*ambigua secreta*—captures neatly the covert sexual double life that Nero sought for himself even as a teen-aged emperor).

As Tacitus tells it, Nero maintained these patterns throughout his reign. He became involved with the beautiful noble-born Poppaea Sabina and arranged eventually to marry her (it would be her third marriage and his second).[125] He also continued to inhabit a sexual demimonde. He went about Rome dressed as a slave surrounded by a retinue of ruffians so as to visit brothels and get drunk on the local wine.[126] A certain nobleman, not knowing it was Nero who was causing the ruckus, resisted violent attack and was forced to commit suicide for his troubles.[127] Nero spent time "hanging out" (*ventitabat*) under the Mulvian Bridge, famous for its nightly lecheries, where he engaged in further improprieties.[128] Nero founded the "Juvenile Games," and held stage performances that featured various improper roles.[129] The "ancestral morality" (*patrios mores*), Tacitus wrote, was subverted by this "lasciviousness" (*lasciviam*).[130] The games Nero established were nothing more than "contests in vices" (*certamina vitiorum*).[131]

This context helps to understand Tacitus's account of the mock marriage that Nero staged with a freedman named Pythagoras. According to Tacitus, the year was A.D. 64 and the circumstances involved a particularly extravagant "dinner cruise" on the *Stagnum Agrippae*,[132] hosted by Nero and arranged by Tigellinus, who had once been Agrippina's lover and who was now a major facilitator of Nero's excesses.[133] Tigellinus had constructed in the *Stagnum* a large raft that was in turn given its locomotion by a series of smaller rowboats that would tow it around the pool.[134] The oarsmen assigned the task of rowing were themselves *exoleti*—a term that Champlin translates as "male prostitutes."[135] Banquet tables were set up on the larger craft, where the guests might dine while being entertained by wild animals and birds.[136] Lining one shore of the *Stagnum* were brothels staffed by women of "noble status" (*inlustribus feminis*), while on the other side of the *Stagnum* naked female prostitutes were visible.[137] Several days after this feast, Nero staged what was for Tacitus the most outrageous act of all. "Polluted by every licit and illicit act," Tacitus recorded, Nero had left no outrage unaccomplished save one: he went through a mock marriage with a freedman named Pythagoras, one of the "contaminated herd" of oarsmen.[138]

John Boswell has wished to see in this ceremony evidence of widespread acceptance of same-sex marriage in the ancient Roman world.[139] Although

Boswell quoted Tacitus' Latin in a footnote, he failed to translate the text or to alert his readers to the intense disapproval that is apparent to any reader of Latin.[140] Tacitus's description of this event as a kind of final culmination of outrageous conduct and his use of the expression *contaminatorum grege*, which I have translated as "contaminated herd" above,[141] should give some sense of what Tacitus really thought of this ceremony.

Tacitus sustained his disapproval throughout his description of the ceremony. It was done "in the manner of a marriage" (*in modum sollemnium coniugiorum*).[142] Tacitus's point seems clear enough and his choice of the words *in modum* seems to confirm it: the ceremony was not a marriage, but something done in imitation of marriage. It was, in other words, a mockery, but it was also truly a spectacle: the emperor was dressed in a wedding veil, a dowry was established, and the wedding couch (*genialis torus*) was brought forward.[143] Everything, in sum, was done to give this ceremony the appearance of marriage (*cuncta denique spectata*).[144]

Tacitus's narrative structure strengthens the force of his condemnation. The sentence describing the false marriage is the final sentence of chapter thirty-seven of Book XV. The very next word, the opening word of chapter thirty-eight is *sequitur*, "There followed."[145] The noun that follows this choice of verbs is *clades*—"disaster."[146] A cause-and-effect is suggested by this choice of words and by the word order of the sentence, even if it is not directly stated. And what was it that Tacitus signalled with his use of *sequitur*? What followed Nero's final outrage? What was the disaster that befell Rome? It was the Great Fire at Rome. This was, Tacitus asserted, the most violent and destructive fire that Rome had ever experienced.[147] In its aftermath, as we have reviewed above, Nero would stage the first mass executions of Christians as a way of deflecting attention away from his misrule.[148] Tacitus was too careful a narrator to make the connection between the fire and Nero's outrageous personal conduct too explicit; but he was too ferocious an ironist and too stern a moralist to let such an opportunity pass entirely unnoticed.[149]

At the beginning of this section I posed some questions: They are worth reiterating here: What does it mean for an individual to violate the laws of God and man? Does this count as tyranny? Do sexual and marital misconduct suffice as evidence of tyranny? What was the harm, in short, and how should the harm be repaired?

We should begin with the observation that Nero was considered the personification of tyranny. And one manifestation of this tyranny was defiance of the proper order of things: this point is made most comprehensively in Tacitus. Nero sought to confound the natural order. As Tacitus put it in his compressed Latin style, Nero sought to "pollute himself with every licit and illicit act."[150]

Defiance of the natural order, furthermore, was not only a matter of external acts. It embraced a personal loss of self-control that suggested one had failed to develop one's character adequately. It was commonly believed, in the world that Livy and Tacitus inhabited, that the individual possessed the capacity to choose whether to pursue goodness or wickedness: One might choose a life led in accord in with the virtues, or a life of self-destruction and vice.

And the failure to conform one's behavior to the natural order, the refusal to be virtuous, the choice to follow a path of hedonistic self-destruction, could well represent the choice to pursue tyranny. One might be tyrannical in one's dealings with hierarchical subordinates—one might, for instance, mistreat one's slaves or one's clients. And at a grander scale, of course, one might abuse one's public responsibilities. The tyrant was one who subverted the *ordo mundi*—the order of the world—and there were many ways in which this might be done, but the common denominator was a life of excess—something outside the mean of virtuous behavior.

Again, one does well to advert to Tacitus. Nero's misrule eventually led to a revolt which led to the emperor's overthrow and suicide. A contest opened up between rival claimants, one of whom was Galba, an aging (he was probably 71 years old) but still vigorous Roman governor of Hispania Tarraconensis, who was among the first to revolt against Nero and who marched upon and seized Rome in the fall of A.D. 68. Tacitus had him deliver a speech explaining why it was necessary that Nero should fall. Two words placed in Galba's mouth by Tacitus require attention: *immanitas* and *luxuria*.[151] The tyrant was one who was savage and inhumane (*immanitas*) and one who led a life of wanton excess (*luxuria*).

And Nero was the perfect tyrant. He had committed matricide; he killed friends, advisors, spouses, and relatives. His *immanitas* was beyond question. His *luxuria* was also without parallel. It has been Nero's *luxuria* and the public harm that that thereby accrued that has been the focus of the last part of this paper.[152] And the public harm that resulted from Nero's vices was profound: as our discussion of the structural relationship of Tacitus's account of Nero's mock marriage to Pythagoras and the subsequent Great Fire of Rome suggests, disaster follows such defiance of the natural order.

V.   Conclusion

This paper has sought to answer the question, "What is the harm" by a close consideration of the ways in which the ancient Roman historians—men like Livy, Tacitus, Suetonius, and Cassius Dio—might have approached this question. I have looked specifically at three examples drawn from the writings of these thinkers. Three examples were chosen for consideration: The Rape of Lucretia; the life of the Germans in contrast with Roman mores; and the tyrannical life of the emperor Nero. In each of these examples, the authors were concerned to make the case that grave public harms can flow from private acts. Sextus Tarquinius's rape of the modest and upright Lucretia resulted in the overthrow of the monarchy. Germanic virtue—including marital and sexual virtue—presented a grave threat to Roman life. And the Emperor Nero, finally, found himself overthrown and forced to commit suicide in the face of a revolt against his *luxuria*. The disaster that Tacitus described as following the banquet of Tigellinus and Nero's sham marriage to Pythagoras was nothing less than the final collapse of the regime itself.

These examples were chosen to demonstrate that Roman historians and moralists had a very different answer to the question "what is the harm?" to the one commonly heard today. Living in a world bequeathed to us by John Stuart Mill, we must contend with the famous distinction between self-regarding and other-regarding acts. Other-regarding acts might properly be regulated by the state, according to Mill, but self-regarding acts cannot be. And among the self-regarding acts with which Mill was most concerned were the consensual sexual relations of adults. He believed that the state should have very little to do with regulating the private sexual morality of its citizens. To the question, "what is the harm?" Mill would reply that there is no harm, that what is private and consensual cannot result in cognizable harm to others.

This paper, it is hoped, opens the door to a very different way of answering this question. In the mind of Livy, Tacitus, and the other sources considered in this paper, there was no clear boundary line between merely private vices and public conduct. Viciousness in one's personal life translated seamlessly into public wrong-doing while virtue was a habit that required daily attention and careful cultivation. In the mind of the Roman writers, it seems clear, the harm of a disordered personal life could be very large indeed, extending even to the destruction of men and the fall of governments.

Notes

1. I would like to acknowledge the many helpful and insightful conversations I enjoyed with Robert Delahunty on the subjects of Tacitus, virtue, vice, and the abuse of power.

2. Titus Livy, *Ab urbe condita*, I.58. (I am here following the translation of B.O. Foster, found in vol. I of the Loeb Library edition, published in Cambridge, Massachusetts and London, 1961, pp. 201, 203.

3. Ovid, Plutarch, and Dionysius of Halicarnassus are among the classical writers whose reports of this incident remain extant. Standing behind this relatively large group of classical sources is the question whether the story is a fabrication from whole cloth or whether it represents the embellishment of some actual incident in the Roman past. There is no need to deal with this question in this paper, concerned as it is with Roman conceptions of private sexuality and public harm. For a discussion of the various extant accounts of the Rape of Lucretia, see Ian Donaldson, *The Rapes of Lucretia: A Myth and Its Transformations* (Oxford: Clarendon Press, 1982), pp. 5-6.

4. *Ab urbe condita*, I. 56, 6-7.

5. *Id.*, I.56.7.

6. *Id.*, I.56.9-10.

7. *Id.*, I.56.10. The translation here is my own.

8. Brutus was the one, according to Livy, who pulled the knife from Lucretia's breast and swore on her blood—an oath he asked Collatinus and others to repeat—to avenge her death by bringing down the king and the entire royal family. *Id.*, 57.1. Through his soaring oratory, directed specifically at Sextus's sexual outrages, Brutus was able to rouse the Roman crowd to his side and to aid in the expulsion of the monarchy. *Id.*, 59.8-9. Tarquinius Superbus and his offspring—including Sextus—were consequently forced into exile. *Id.*, 60.1-2.

9. One needs to be careful, however, in suggesting that Livy was an actual supporter of the Augustan regime. Augustus was recorded as describing Livy as a *pompeianus*—a

supporter of the republican Pompey in the civil wars that climaxed, after many years of struggle, in Augustus's triumph. Augustus, however, also counted Livy as among his friends. One scholar who has analyzed the relationship of the emperor and the historian has concluded that "[Livy] was anything but the emperor's panegyrist and propagandist, his message being: Romans will not tolerate unmitigated monarchy." Hans Peterson, "Livy and Augustus," *Transactions of the American Philological Association* 92 (1961), pp. 440, 452.

10. I have reviewed Augustus's program of marital and familial renewal in Charles J. Reid, Jr., "Perspectives on Institutional Change," a paper presented at a Canadian conference on marriage and the family held at Banff, Alberta, in May, 2005. In that paper, I discussed specifically Augustus's promulgation of two laws, the *Lex Iulia de maritandis ordinandibus* and the *Lex Iulia et Poppia Poppaea*, which simultaneously established a series of incentives for the Roman upper classes to marry and to have children and imposed a series of penalties on those who evaded the terms of the law. Enforcement, which was entrusted in part to informers, made the decrees odious to many members of the Roman elites.

11. Thus an excerpt from the commentary of Marcianus, found in Justinian's *Digest*, condemns as worthy of death all those who rape a woman, whether single or married. *Digest* 48.6.5.2. Book 48, title 6 of the *Digest*, in which this text is found, is entitled "*Ad Legem Iuliam De Vi Publica*," ("On the Julian Law Concerning Public Force"). Diana Moses proposes that this title has an early provenance, probably dating to Julius Caesar's time (a time well before Livy) and was concerned with the enormity of violence that was the result of the civil wars. See Diana C. Moses, "Livy's Lucretia and the Validity of Coerced Consent in Roman Law," in Angeliki Laiou, ed., *Consent and Coercion to Sex and Marriage in Ancient and Medieval Societies* (Washington, DC: Dumbarton Oaks Research Library, 1993), pp. 39, 50, and note 45 (reviewing the primary and secondary authorities on this title).

In his classic commentary on the first five books of Livy, R.M. Ogilvie noted that at several points in his account of the rape, Livy intended to recall elements of Roman law, although Ogilvie also criticizes the author for conveying ideas that "are merely the expression of contemporary legal opinion . . . ." R.M. Ogilvie, *A Commentary on Livy: Books 1-5* (Oxford: At the Clarendon Press, 1965), p. 225. In Livy's defense, it can be observed that his concern here—and elsewhere—was with using Roman historical *exempla* as a means of distinguishing between virtuous and vicious conduct *in his own day*. Indeed, it is this polemical agenda that makes Livy of such interest for a paper such as this.

12. Beth Severy, *Augustus and the Family at the Birth of the Roman Empire* (New York: Routledge, 2003), pp. 50-51.

13. *Id.*, p. 55.

14. P.G.W. Clarke, *Oxford Latin Dictionary* (Oxford: At the Clarendon Press, 1982), p. 1832.

15. Adolf Berger, *Encyclopedic Dictionary of Roman Law* (Philadelphia: Transactions of the American Philosophical Society, 1953), p. 719.

16. James A. Brundage, *Law, Sex, and Christian Society in Medieval Europe* (Chicago: University of Chicago Press, 1987), pp. 29-30. Brundage goes on: "The penalties prescribed for *stuprum* in the *Lex Iulia* were severe; they included loss of half of one's property for persons who were classified as *honesti*; *humiles*, on the other hand, might be sentenced upon conviction to corporal punishment and exile." *Id.*, p. 30.

17. Olivia F. Robinson, *The Criminal Law of Ancient Rome* (Baltimore: The Johns Hopkins University Press, 1995), p. 58.

18. *Ab urbe condita*, I.pr.6. "Decorated with poetic license" is my translation of the

phrase *poeticis . . . decora fabulis.*

19. *Id.,* I.pr.7.

20. *Id.* I.pr.9.

21. *Id.,* I.pr. 10.

22. *Id.,* II.pr.1.

23. *Id.* (*legum potentiora quam hominum*).

24. *Id.,* II.pr.4-5.

25. Jane F. Chaplin, *Livy's Exemplary History* (Oxford: Oxford University Press, 2000), p. 3.

26. *Id.* p. 1 (noting that most readers "justifiably" conclude that Livy intended Lucretia to serve as an *exemplum* but also expressing the reservation that "no one ever takes her as a model of conduct"). *Id.*

27. Mary Jaeger, *Livy's Written Rome* (Ann Arbor: The University of Michigan Press, 1997), p. 10.

28. *Id.,* pp. 8-9 The title, Jaeger notes, following earlier scholarship, "has spatial as well as temporal significance"). *Id.,* p. 9.

29. *Id.,* p. 11. Scott Feldherr has also written instructively on the political effects of the Rape of Lucretia, seeing her ritualized suicide as the decisive step that ensured the downfall of the monarchy. Scott Feldherr, *Spectacle and Society in Livy's History* (Berkeley: University of California Press, 1998), pp. 194-204.

30. Lidia Storoni Mazzolani, *Empire Without End* (New York: Harcourt, Brace, Jovanovich, 1976), p. 113.

31. *Id.*

32. *Id.*

33. Livy returned to this theme in Book Three of *Ab urbe condita,* in his account of the plebeian girl Verginia, who was sexually dishonored by the *decemvir* Appius Claudius and subsequently killed by her father to spare her further humiliation and possible degradation to slavery.

34. See, for instance, P.G. Walsh, *Livy* (Oxford: At the Clarendon Press, 1974), pp. 5-6 (criticizing this older approach and pronouncing it happily and of favor).

35. As with so much else, Sir Ronald Syme might be taken as an early and important spokesman for a balanced and sophisticated treatment of Livy. Calling attention in particular to Livy's moralizing, Sir Ronald noted: "All in all, Livy, the prince and glory of Augustan letters, should perhaps be claimed as the last of the Republican writers." Ronald Syme, "Livy and Augustus," *Harvard Studies in Classical Philology* 64 (1959), pp. 27, 53.

In this assessment, one sees the tension that exists in Livy's work between the order and stability represented by the new regime and his own nostalgic embrace of the ancient ideals. This was, perhaps, not all that different from the tension that existed in the Augustan project itself—concentrate power in the hands of a single ruler the better to ensure order, but rekindle the old republican ideals, especially those concerning marriage and the family, in order to replenish the ranks of the elite.

36. Melissa Mathes, *The Rape of Lucretia and the Founding of Republics: Readings in Livy, Machiavelli, and Rousseau* (University Park, PA: The Pennsylvania State University Press, 2000), p. 82.

37. *Id.*

38. *Id.,* p. 106.

39. William Shakespeare, "The Rape of Lucrece," line 1833.

40. Donaldson, *The Rapes of Lucretia, supra,* p. 116.

41. Tactitus's family probably originated in the province of Gallia Narbonensis, which today comprises the south of France. Donald R. Dudley, *The World of Tacitus*

(Boston: Little, Brown, and Company, 1968), p. 15. Other theories put the ancestry of his family in Spain. Whatever his ultimate place of origin, Tacitus was an outsider when seen from the perspective of the insular Roman nobility—a man who, although politically accomplished himself and capable of rising to the highest circles, nevertheless did not belong to one of the old aristocratic families with ancient roots in Rome.

42. *Id.*, p. 13 (quoting Tacitus, *Histories*, 1.1.30.

43. Max Cary and H.H. Scullard, *A History of Rome Down to the Age of Constantine*, 3d edition (New York: St. Martin's Press, 1975), p. 424.

44. Clarence W. Mandell, *Tacitus: The Man and His Work* (New Haven, CT: Yale University Press, 1957), p. 142.

45. Tacitus, *Annales*, 3.65.1 (the translation is my own).

46. *Id.*

47. *Id.*

48. *Annales* 6.51.

49. John Jackson's translation of Tacitus's account of this tryst captures well the tone of Tacitus's Latin: "And she, the grand-niece of Augustus, the daughter-in-law of Tiberius, the mother of Drusus defiled herself, her ancestry, and her posterity, with a market-town adulterer, in order to change an honoured estate in the present for the expectation of a criminal and doubtful future." Tacitus, *Annales*, 4.3, in volume 3 of the Loeb Classical Library edition of Tacitus (Cambridge, MA: Harvard University Press, 1958), p. 7.

Patrick Sinclair's study of Tacitus's depiction of Livia Julia is helpful for the way in which it makes clear that Tacitus actually used—and inverted—the Latin phraseology of Livy's Rape of Lucretia in order to present Livia Julia as an "inversion of morality." Patrick Sinclair, "Tacitus' Presentation of Livia Julia, Wife of Tiberius' Son Drusus," *American Journal of Philology* 111 (1990), pp. 238, 239.

50. Herwig Wolfram, *The Roman Empire and Its Germanic Peoples*, Thomas Dunlap, tr. (Berkeley, CA: University of California Press, 1997), p. 6.

51. *Id.*, p. 3.

52. *The Cambridge Ancient History*, 2d ed. (Cambridge, UK: Cambridge University Press, 1996), vol. X, p. 110. Cf. Fergus M. Bordewich, "The Ambush That Changed History," *Smithsonian Magazine*, September, 2005.

53. Olwen Brogan, "Trade Between the Roman Empire and the Free-Born Germans," *Journal of Roman Studies* 26 (1936), pp. 195-222; and Dina P. Dobson, "Roman Influence in the North," *Greece and Rome* 5 (1936), pp. 73-89.

54. Sir Ronald Syme, *Tacitus* (Oxford: At the Clarendon Press, 1963), vol. I, pp. 46-47; and Herbert Benario, *An Introduction to Tacitus* (Athens, GA: University of Georgia Press, 1975), pp. 30-35.

55. Syme, *Tacitus*, *supra*, vol. I, p. 47.

56. *Germania*, 37.

57. *Id.* ch. 1. *Germania omnis* are the opening words of the text. Cf. Tacitus, *Dialogus, Agricola, Germania*, William H. Peterson, tr. (Cambridge, MA: Harvard University Press, 1953) (Loeb Classical Library), pp. 264-265, footnote one (making explicit reference to Tacitus's allusion to Caesar's *Gallic Wars*).

58. *Germania*, 5.

59. *Id.*, ch. 7.

60. *Id.*

61. *Id.* Tacitus noted that this task belonged solely to the priests in time of war. *Id.*

62. See generally G.V. Sumner, "The Legion and the Centuriate Organization," *Journal of Roman Studies* 60 (1970), pp. 67-78.

63. *Germania*, ch. 11.

64. *Id.*, chs. 14-15. It was Tacitus's fond hope that the Germans kept up this general lack of unity for in it, he understood, lay Rome's best chance for survival. Bryan Ward-Perkins, *The Fall of Rome and the End of Civilization* (New York: Oxford University Press, 2005), pp. 49-50.

65. *Germania*, ch. 11.

66. *Id.*

67. One commentator has observed that "[t]he *Germania*, which describes the virtues of a free people, is interspersed with comments which underline their moral superiority over the Romans." W. Liebeschuetz, "The Theme of Liberty in the *Agricola* of Tacitus." *Classical Quarterly* 16 (n.s., 1966), pp. 126, 138.

68. *Germania*, ch. 18.

69. *Id.*

70. *Id.*

71. *Id.*

72. *Id.*

73. *Id.*, ch. 19.

74. *Id.*

75. *Id.*

76. *Id.*

77. *Id.*

78. Herbert W. Benario, *Tacitus: Germany* (Warminster, England: Aris and Phillips, Ltd., 1999), p. 86.

79. *Germania*, ch. 19.

80. *Id.*

81. Benario, *Tacitus: Germany, supra*, p. 86.

82. M.A. Fitzsimons, "The Mind of Tacitus," *Review of Politics* 38 (1976), pp. 473, 478.

83. *Supra*, pp. —.

84. Susan Treggiari, *Roman Marriage: Iusti Coniuges from the Time of Cicero to the Time of Ulpian* (Oxford: At the Clarendon Press, 19910, pp. 237-238. Treggiari provides the list of words; I have added my own commentary on their definitions in the above parentheticals.

85. Jasper Griffins, "Augustan Poetry and the Life of Luxury," *Journal of Roman Studies* 66 (1976), pp. 87-105 (making the case that the many sexual acts and attitudes described in the Augustan poets probably reflected actual social realities, including the interests and actions of the poets themselves).

86. An insightful article on this point is Susanna H. Braund, "Juvenal—Misogynist or Misogamist?" *Journal of Roman Studies* 82 (1992), pp. 71-86.

87. Alan Watson, "The Divorce of Carvilius Ruga," *Tijdschrift voor Rechtsgeschiedenis* 33 (1965), pp. 38-50.

88. Susan Treggiari, "Divorce Roman Style: How Easy and How Frequent Was It?" in Beryl Rawson, ed., *Marriage, Divorce, and Children in Ancient Rome* (Oxford: Oxford University Press, 1991), pp. 7, 37.

89. *Id.*, pp. 42-45.

90. Thus Seneca wrote: "What woman today is shamed by divorce when certain famous and noble matrons compute their ages not by the number of consuls but by the number of their husbands?" Seneca, *De Beneficiis*, 3.16.2.

91. Seneca, *De Ira*, I.15.2.

92. Cicero, *De Legibus*, 3.19.

93. W.W. Buckland, *A Text-Book of Roman Law*, 3d ed., rev. by Peter Stein (Cambridge, UK: Cambridge University Press, 1963), p. 103.

94. Charles J. Reid, Jr., *Power Over the Body, Equality in the Family: Rights and Domestic Relations in Medieval Canon Law* (Grand Rapids, MI: William Eerdmans, 2004), p. 70.

95. *Germania*, ch. 7.

96. *Id.*

97. Adela Yarbro Collins, "The Apocalypse (Revelation)," in Raymond E. Brown, Joseph Fitzmyer, and Roland E. Murphy, eds., *The New Jerome Biblical Commentary* (Upper Saddle River, NJ: Prentice Hall, 1990), p. 1009.

98. *Id.* Other Jewish and Christian "apocalypses"—which did not attain canonical status—also made steady reference to Nero as the Anti-Christ. See Gregory C. Jenks, *The Origins and Early Development of the Antichrist Myth* (Berlin: Walter de Gruyter, 1991), pp. 257-306 and 323-355 (discussing Nero at various points as a focal point of early apocalyptic accounts of a coming Antichrist).

99. There was a substantial non-Christian Roman legend to this effect. Since Nero committed suicide and there were few witnesses to this event, there were doubts that he had really died. Rumor swept Rome several times in the latter first century that Nero had actually fled to the East and would return at the head of an army to retake Rome. See Bernard McGinn, *Antichrist: Two Thousand Years of the Human Fascination With Evil* (New York: Columbia University Press, 2000), p. 46. On the other hand, among contemporary Greeks, upon whom Nero had bestowed a variety of favors, there was a belief that a beneficent Nero might return and usher in a time of favor toward Greek as opposed to Roman civilization. See M.P. Charlesworth, "Nero: Some Aspects," *Journal of Roman Studies* 40 (1950), pp. 69, 73-76.

100. McGinn, *Antichrist, supra*, pp. 100-102.

101. Suetonius's work, *The Lives of the Caesars* (*Vitae Caesarum*), appeared around the year 117, the year Hadrian assumed the imperial throne.

102. Suetonius, *Vitae Caeararum*, Book, VI.51.

103. *Id.*

104. The *Oxford Latin Dictionary* offers as definitions of *luxuria*: "Unruly or wilful behaviour . . . . Disregard for moral restraints, licentiousness." *Oxford Latin Dictionary, supra*, p. 1054.

105. Suetonius, *Vitae Caesarum*, Bk. VI.55.

106. Cassius Dio was Greek and wrote in Greek, not Latin. His career consisted of a series of provincial appointments, but late in life, as he became a favorite of the Senators, he found himself unexpectedly holding high office the governorship of Pannonia. Fergus Millar, *A Study of Cassius Dio* (Oxford: At the Clarendon Press, 1964), pp. 23-27.

107. *Dio's Roman History*, Bk. 61. I am here using the Loeb Classical Library edition. See Ernest Cary, tr. *Dio's Roman History* (Cambridge, MA: Harvard University Press, 1961), vol. 8, pp. 40-41.

108. *Id.*

109. *Id.*

110. Rolando Ferri, *Octavia: A Play Attributed to Seneca* (Cambridge, UK: Cambridge University Press, 2003), pp. 1-54 (discussing compositional issues).

111. ". . . corda tyranni.

odit genitos sanguine claro,

spernit superos hominesque simul."

I am here translating from the Latin text reproduced in Ferri, *Octavia, A Play Attributed to Seneca, supra*, p. 88. Ferri sees in the playwright's choice of metaphors— the evil-doer as an enemy of divine and human laws—a form of characterizing the misbehavior of tyrants in antiquity. *Id.*, p. 152.

112. *Octavia*, lines 958-972. Ferri notes that the author of the play is drawing from

a long tradition of courageous heroines who face death without flinching. see Ferri, *Octavia*, p. 400. It is impossible not to think of the Rape of Lucretia in reading these lines.

113. Edward Champlin, *Nero* (Cambridge, MA: Harvard University Press, 2003), pp. 36-52.

114. *Id.*, p. 52.

115. *Id.*

116. *Id.*

117. Tacitus, *Annales*, Bk. XII.66-67.

118. Tacitus, *Annales*, Book XIV.8-9. Summarizing the prevailing view of Nero following his mother's murder, Tacitus wrote that "his savagery exceeded the outcries of everyone" (*cuius inanimitas omnium questus anteibat*). The word *questus* is the most vexing of these terms to translate; it carries simultaneously the meaning of "outcry," in the sense of an expression of popular outrage; the sense of a formal legal complaint; and the cries of grief that follow unexpected death. *Oxford Latin Dictionary, supra*, p. 1547. Tacitus clearly meant to convey a sense of universal horror and disgust in this compactly-written phrase.

119. Tacitus, *Annales*, XIII.15-16.

120. On Seneca's suicide, see Tacitus, *Annales*, Bk. XV.60-64.; on Petronius's suicide, see *Annales*, Bk. XVI.18-19.

121. Tacitus asserts that his sources were divided on the cause of Afranius Burrus's death, some alleging that he was murdered, while others claiming that he died of illness. *Annales*, Bk. XIV.51.

122. A rumor prevailed at Rome among all classes that Nero had set the fire. Certainly, the popular mood held, he was at least complicit in the fire since he was now able to build a large palace in parts of the City where formerly large number of common folk lived. To deflect these rumors, Nero blamed the Christians for setting the fire. His persecution, however, was so brutal that he turned popular opinion from its original anti-Christian sentiment to a fear of the tyrannical savagery of a single individual. *Annales* XV.44 ("*tamquam non utilitate publica, sed in saevitiam unius absumeretur*").

123. *Annales, supra*, XIII.12.

124. *Id.*

125. *Annales*, XIV.1.

126. *Annales*, XIII.25.

127. *Id.*

128. *Annales*, XIII.47.

129. *Annales*, XIV.15.

130. *Annales*, XIV.20.

131. *Annales*, XIV.15.

132. The *Stagnum Agrippae* was "the great artificial lake or pool in the Campus Martius which had been constructed by Agrippa, the right-hand man . . . of Augustus." Champlin, *Nero*, p. 153.

133. Tacitus, *Annales*, XV.37.

134. *Annales*, XV.37. Champlin adds further details, *Nero, supra*, p. 154.

135. *Annales*, XV.37. Champlin, *Nero, supra*, p. 154.

136. *Annales*, XV.37.

137. *Id.*

138. *Id.* I have translated as "contaminated herd" Tacitus's expression *ex illo contaminatorum grege*. The phrase that I have paraphrased as "no outrage unaccomplished save one" reads in Latin as: "*nihil flagitii reliquerat, quo corruptior ageret . . . .*"

139. John Boswell, *Same-Sex Unions in Pre-Modern Europe* (New York: Villard

Books, 1994), pp. 80-81.

140. *Id.*, pp. 80-81, footnote 135. Boswell's citation to Tacitus is also incorrect. He cites to Book XV.370 of the *Annales*. No such chapter exists. He meant to cite to Bk. XV.37.

141. *Supra*, p. —.

142. Tacitus, *Annales*, XV.37.

143. *Id.*

144. *Id.*

145. Tacitus, *Annales*, XV.38.

146. *Id.*

147. *Id.*

148. *Supra*, pp. —. In his study of Tacitus, Ronald Martin calls attention to the relationship between "Nero's unnatural marriage" and the Great Fire. See Ronald Martin, *Tacitus* (Berkeley: University of California Press, 1981), p. 181.

149. A modern commentator has written concerning Tacitus's larger historiographical goals: "[I]f anything, Tacitus was a moralist. His portrait of Nero was not just the portrait of a particular man in power, it was the image of a tyrant, and more precisely, the image of a tyrant in the Roman tradition of public morality." Joan-Pau Rubiés, "Nero in Tacitus and Nero in Tacitism: The Historian's Craft," in Jas Elsner and Jamie Masters, *Reflections of Nero: Culture, History, and Representation* (Chapel Hill: University of North Carolina Press, 1994), pp. 29, 35-36.

150. *Supra* —.

151. Tacitus, *Histories*, Bk. I.16.

152. Patrick Kragelund wishes to confine the meaning of the word *luxuria*, as applied to Nero by Tacitus, to that of financial profligacy. See Patrick Kragelund, "Nero's *Luxuria* in Tacitus and in the *Octavia*," *Classical Quarterly* 50 (2000), pp. 494-515. Such a reading, however, does not take adequate account of the many relationships we have drawn in this paper between Nero's misgovernment and his sexual *luxuria*.

PART III
DOES LEGALIZING SAME-SEX MARRIAGE HARM THE
RELATIONSHIP AND MEANING OF MARRIAGE?

CHAPTER 11
THE MORALITY OF MARRIAGE
AND THE TRANSFORMATIVE POWER OF INCLUSION

Lynn D. Wardle[1]
Brigham Young University

I.   *Introduction: Of Marriage, Morality, and the Moral Consequences of Legalizing Same-Sex Marriage*

The question, "What's the harm?" invites a dramatic, immediate, visible response—such as pointing to a broken bone sticking through the skin or a blood-spurting severed artery. Such images make great impressions. But severe injuries may also be internal, such as clogged coronary arteries and veins, and the damage from a heart attack, or social rather than physical. This chapter describes one such harm from legalizing same-sex marriage—damage to the morality of marriage from legalizing same-sex marriage.

A.   *Matters of the Heart*

Marriage is not merely one of many social institutions, but it is the most important, foundational *moral* institution in any society. Marriage profoundly shapes the morality of a society. The moral influences of marriage are so pervasive, so essential, that most of the time most members of society are as oblivious to them as they are to the beating of their own hearts. We are now becoming aware of them by the cultural equivalent of a heart attack.

There have been many clear symptoms that the health of the heart of the institution of marriage has been deteriorating for some time, and is at great risk. These symptoms include the high rate of divorce that has remained at unprecedented levels for a full generation, the dramatic increase in nonmarital cohabitation, and the consistent rise in the number and percentage of children born out of wedlock.[2] Now, the growing legalization of same-sex marriage, like a severe myocardial infarction, compels us to consider seriously and immediately how important the institution of conjugal marriage is.

Before the twenty-first century, same-sex marriage had never been permitted in any nation in the history of the world. At the end of the twentieth century, a few nations had created another domestic relationship comparable to marriage for same-sex couples, but in each case, the new relationship was distinct from marriage. Since 2000, however, four nations have legalized same-sex marriage,[3] as has one American state.[4] Additionally, at least six American States,[5] and a dozen nations have created marriage-equivalent same-sex domestic relationships with virtually all of the same legal status, rights, and benefits of marriage.[6] Thus, in a very short period of time, since the beginning of the twenty-first century, the movement to legalize same-sex marriage has gone from an intellectual proposal to a growing legal and political reality.

It is hard to overstate the potential impact of legalization of same-sex marriage upon the institution of marriage and on society. Like all social institutions, marriage cultivates and generates a certain morality among those who enter the institution and throughout society in which the institution operates. However, the morality-shaping influence of the institution of marriage is much greater than that of any other social institution. Marriage is a ubiquitous social institution, and the fundamental unit of society. It dominates, shapes and cultivates the core relational values that influence directly and indirectly all children, adults and other social institutions.

There are many possible forms of marriage, and each has its own morality. Each marriage culture cultivates a certain set of moral values, nurtures certain moral principles, and fosters a particular morality that shapes, in no small part, the morality of individuals who enter that form of marriage, and the society in which it is practiced. The moral content of the relationship and the moral message that the existence and operation of the institution of marriage conveys, reflect not only the formal legal definition, requirements, and boundaries of legal relationship, but also the informal, practical, relational behaviors and social expectations about that relationship. The institution of conjugal (male-female) marriage cultivates a morality of commitment, constancy, fidelity and monogamy, which contrasts starkly with the moral characteristics of same-sex relations. Redefining marriage to include relationships that are characterized by different moral qualities could profoundly alter core normative standards of the basic morality-setting institution in society.

B.   The Morality-Transforming Power of Inclusion

This chapter examines the morality of the institution of conjugal marriage, and contrasts it with the morality of same-sex unions. Legalizing same-sex marriage is likely to produce significant changes in the core meaning and essential morality of the social institution of marriage. The profound moral ramifications of those changes would reverberate through and eventually harm virtually all sectors of society.

The major means by which this metamorphosis of the morality of marriage would occur can be called "the transformative power of inclusion." That refers to the impact upon the morality of the institution of marriage that would follow the redefinition of marriage to include same-sex couples. Conservative advocates of same-sex marriage have long argued that legalization of same-sex marriage will positively influence the life-styles of gays and lesbians because the morality of marriage will rub off on and "tame" the behaviors of same-sex couples. The validity of that optimistic claim is certainly debatable.[7] Nevertheless, the transformative effects of inclusion work *both* ways. The moral qualities and characteristics of homosexual unions and lifestyles will have distorting effect upon the existing morality of, marriage. That modification of the morality of marriage to make it more gay-like could seriously harm to society, families, and individuals.

Part II of this chapter sets forth a dichotomy in the morality of institutions that is borrowed from legal anthropology. The morality of relations of kinship and relations of strangers are distinguished, and this dichotomy is utilized in later Parts to contrast the morality of conjugal marriage and same-sex relationships. Part III of this chapter analyzes the role of marriage as a basic social institution, and how such institutions, generally, and the institution of marriage in particular, foster morality. The different ways that marriage powerfully shapes morality in society are examined. Part IV herein discusses the particular moral content nurtured and fostered by the institution of conjugal marriage. Particular attention is given to the impact of the morality of marriage as it relates to standards of sexual behavior. Part V of this chapter examines the morality of homosexual relations. Particular attention is given to the moral standards of sexual behavior by gays and lesbians who practice homosexual relations (including promiscuity, polyamory, and infidelity). Part VI considers the transformative power of inclusion, and how legalizing same-sex marriage would profoundly alter standards of sexual morality and other critical aspects of morality essential to the safety of children, husband and wives, other adults, and society. Part VII concludes by underscoring the importance of protecting the morality of marriage against redefinition of marriage to include same-sex unions.

II.   *The Morality of Kinship Versus the Morality of Strangers*

Legal and cultural anthropologists have noted that many societies (and, at least to some degree perhaps in all societies) distinguish between kinship relationships and relationships. For example, in his classic study of the Siuai, a people in Melanesia, Douglas Oliver, identified one of the "basic premises" underlying Siuai social life: "'Mankind consist of relatives and strangers.' By *strangers*, the Siuai simply mean those who are not kinsmen."[8] Each relationship has its own morality. BYU Anthropology Professor Merlin G. Myers observed:

> There is a sense in which th[is] Siuai premise, *mutatis mutandis*, is relevant to all human societies the only difference being the relative proportion of each, relatives and strangers, making up mankind for a particular people. For the Siuai, relatives outnumber strangers. For modern society, strangers outnumber relatives.
> A social universe comprised of strangers permits the laying aside of those moral axioms of kinships . . . (amity and altruism) and the adoption of a new, less constraining ethic, *individual gain*, which is often euphemized in words like "progress," "prosperity," "enlightenment," and "maximization." . . . As Fortes puts it, "We do not have to

love our kinsfold, but we [do] expect to be able to trust them in ways that are not automatically possible with strangers." . . . This is why . . . legal contract[s] are necessary for entering into, and maintaining, re-lationships of moral and legal validity with people who are strangers. This is . . . the prevailing circumstance[] in the modern world.[9]

Professor Myers suggested that "relationships can be ranked on a conti-nuum on the basis of their moral content,"[10] and that "sacrifice is the ready index to the moral quality of a relationship. If one is willing to sacrifice only a little, morality is small; if much, morality is great. . . ."[11] Thus,

"[i[n a purely technical means-to-end relationship, the failure of the means to achieve the desired end results . . . in a change of means. . . .[S]ome . . . human social relationships are like this. When there is delay or inbalance in the reciprocal aspects of the relationship, it may be terminated. (People are then being dealt with as if they were things.) However, in other kinds of relationships, neither delay nor inbalance terminates the association. . . . [I]t is morality that makes the difference. The demand for an immediate, or for a strictly equiva-lent, return for services or presentations given is tantamount to a denial of any moral relationship between the parties, while the pres-ence of delay and imbalance between gift and counter-gift is syn-onymous with the presence of morality.[12]

Different kinds of marriage relationships "can be ranked on a continuum on the basis of their moral content."[13] If the relationship is characterized by expec-tations of strict or immediate equality in exchange, it can be characterized as a having the marginal morality of *strangers*, who deal with each other in purely contractual, "means-to-end" relationships intolerant of delay and imbalance. *Kinship* relations are built on a deep morality that takes the long view, expects delays in gratification, and is tolerant of periods of imbalance in the return of services or presentations.[14]

Similarly, James Q. Wilson uses the term "kinship" to distinguish the mo-rality of marriage from the moralities of other institutions. He noted that society "embed[s] marriage in an elaborate set of rules. . . . Those rules are largely part of another universal feature of all human societies, the kinship system."[15]

In every community and for as far back in time as we can probe, the family exists and children are expected, without exception, to be raised in one. By a family I mean a lasting *socially enforced obliga-tion* between a man and a woman that authorized sexual congress and the supervision of children.[16]

This chapter employs the *kinship-stranger* dichotomy to identify two con-trasting kinds of relationships with divergent sets of morality. The following sections explain how and why the institution of conjugal marriage is firmly grounded in, indeed is the foundation for, *kinship* relations and morality, whe-reas same-sex relations generally manifest both the morality and relational cha-racteristics of *stranger* relations.

III.   How the Institution of Marriage Shapes Morality in Society

The institution of marriage generates and molds morality in society both generally and particularly, generally as any social institution, and particularly as the foundation of the family. The constitutional legitimacy of defining marriage in such a way as to protect morality—the morality of marriage, is also noted.

A.   The Moral Influences of Marriage Specifically

Marriage is a very important social institution.[17] It "is the foundation of a successful society, because "[m]arriage is an essential institution of a successful society which promotes the interests of children."[18] All important social institution, like marriage, "suppl[y] to the people who participate in [them] what they should aim for, dictates what is acceptable or effective for them to do, and teach[] how they must relate to other members of the institution and to those on the outside.'"[19] Social institutions"'shape what those who participate in them think of themselves and of one another, what they believe to be important, and what they strive to achieve.'"[20] In other words, all social institutions, contain and foster in those who participate in them, and, through those persons, in society generally, a certain morality, a set of moral standards to guide their behaviors.

Marriage is not just another source of moral standards like many other social institutions (such as schools, law, churches, etc.). The institution of marriage is the primary source of the most important moral standards in society.[21] As the Supreme Court noted, marriage"giv[es] character to our whole civil polity."[22] The Court declared that the institution of marriage "is the foundation of the family and of society, without which there would be neither civilization nor progress."[23]

The importance of marriage and of the morality of marriage today have been forgotten or taken for granted. They have become a mere truisms. The challenge of the movement to legalize same-sex marriage, however, compels us to seriously consider the importance of the role of the institution of conjugal marriage as a morality-generating institution. Before that institution is altered, we should consider whether it should be preserved instead of transformed.

Marriage establishes the moral core of the family and the moral baseline and standards for society in a myriad of ways. There are at least ten reasons why the institution of marriage is the most powerful, most important morality-generating institution in any society.

First, it is an ubiquitous social institution, one of the most common social units of any society.[24] "[A]ll societies that survive are built on marriage. Marriage is a society's cultural infrastructure . . . ."[25] For instance, in the United States today, despite the impacts of changes such as high incidence of nonmarital cohabitation, delayed entry into marriage, and high divorce rates, still nearly all adults marry at some time in their life,[26] and most adults are married at any given time.[27]

Second, it is the institution into which most children are born and in which they experience their earliest socialization (including formation of their moral ideals). Again, the United States provides an example; despite rising rates of nonmarital childbearing, most - nearly two-thirds of all - children are born within marriage,[28] so most individuals trace their existence to and have that bonding link with the institution of marriage.

Third, marriage is usually the foundation of (and the most successful and stable foundation of) the family,[29] the social unit in which the earliest human socialization occurs. As most children are born within marriage, their socialization and nurturing occurs from birth within that institutional environment. Even many children who are born outside of marriage are socialized for some part of their childhood in the marriage environment as many of their mothers either marry their fathers after birth,[30] or they marry another man to create a marital home for their child[ren] born previously.[31]

Fourth, in marriage and family, the individual acquires his core kinshp identity, without which he struggles as an outsider in many ways. "[T]o be adequately a person in one's society, one needs . . . to *know* and *show* . . . that one is a member of [the society]."[32] As Dr. Myers suggested,"kinship and family relationships—because of their irrevocability, irreversibility, their unconditional and obligatory nature, together with their power moral attributes—provide the most important basis for establishing and maintaining personal identity."[33] Such identity conveys a sense of moral identity, and the absence of such identity historically has been associated with a lack of socially-responsible moral values.[34]

Fifth, marriage and the family that branches (most successfully) out of marriage is the place where most persons learn the most poignant, most lasting, and for children the earliest lessons about relationships. Learning about the morality of living in relationships is critical for human beings because humans are social creatures. We require connection, association, relationship; we crave the interdependence of belonging.[35] Humanity requires, thrives, and flourishes (or suffers and wilts) within relationships—many kinds of relationships.[36]

Sixth, marriage is the "hub" of most connective experiences in most lives, and also is the hub of the most transformative personal experiences in life for most people, making kin of strangers, and the bridge between generations and genders. Part of the moral-teaching power of marriage derives from its location at the connective cross-roads of human life experience. Marriage is the critical bridge between the world of strangers and the world of relatives. Marriage transforms both the persons and the relationship from one measured and governed by the morality of *strangers*, where contract, exchange, and equality are the moral expectations, and where individual worth is measure in terms of acquisition, power, prestige, productivity, and gain, into one measured by the morality of *kinship*, where the expectations of love, sacrifice, and altruism are the expected standards, and where individual worth is measured in terms of connection, belonging, nurturing, loving, giving, and service.[37] Marriage also is the bridge between generations. Marriage is the foundation in all societies for the optimal, safest, and most beneficial procreation and parenting whereby intergenerational transmission of morality occurs. Marriage also is the bridge between genders, uniting male and female and integrating their complementary differences. Thus, marriage is at the axis of connection between stranger and kinship, between men and women, between one generation and the next—in sum, between the isolated individual and family communities (of in-laws, genders, and generations). Marriage is truly the hub where all of the spokes in the wheel of human life and society are joined together to support and stabilize the wheel as it rolls along. That hub position gives marriage powerful moral influence.

Seventh, marriage is the site (and sometimes the source) of some of the most difficult steps in individuals' moral development. It is within marriage (and in the marital family) that most individuals learn the most about how to balance self-interest with commitment to the welfare of others; how (and when) to sacrifice, how to nurture, give, develop and express love; how to be one with another (who at times seems so different, even hostile, to our interests and goals); how to trust and to forgive breaches of trust; and how to be trust-worthy and respect-worthy. Marriage is the site for the moral education about the most critical virtues that are essential to a republican (liberal democratic) society.[38]

Eighth, marriage is the institution with the greatest connection with one of the most powerful (and today, one of the most heavily and constantly stimulated) human passions—sexual relations—what the reknown historians Will and Ariel called "a river of fire."[39] A large and important part of morality consists of sexual morality because the consequences of sexual behavior are so significant and so long-lasting for individuals and for society. Most societies try to channel sexual relations into marriage, and pre-marital, extra-marital, or other non-marital sexual relations have carried the stigma of immorality in most societies.[40] Marriage is the relationship in which most couples enjoy the most healthy,[41] most enjoyable, most satisfying, most frequent,[42] and most socially-beneficial sexual relations.[43]

Ninth, our laws help to establish the morality of marriage in important ways. The law generally sustains the general morality of the institution of marriage. In the field of family law there are "three powerful norms: sexual behavior is acceptable only in marriage, marriage operates as the core of the 'family,' and marriage and marriage-based families are morally privileged and should be legally privileged as well."[44] Legal support for the morality of marriage is a basic premise of family law. Moreover, the legal status of marriage is a major variable in both state and federal laws. The meaning, definition, behavioral expectations, relational consequences, legal incidents, and regulation of hundreds of areas of social, economic, educational, employment and other areas of human activity are tied to marriage. For example, a Congressional Report in 1996 noted that recognition of same-sex marriage in a state could have profound implications for federal law as well because "[t]he word 'marriage' appears in more than 800 sections of federal statutes and regulations, and the word 'spouse' appears more than 3,100 times."[45] The following year, in an oft-cited report, "the General Accounting Office (GAO) identified 1,049 federal laws 'in which marital status is a factor.' In January 2004, the GAO updated this report, identifying 1,138 incidents of marriage in federal law."[46] "To obtain these numbers, the GAO compiled a list of all [federal] statutes containing words such as *marriage, married, spouse,* and *widow.*"[47] Thus, federal behavior-bending and value-shaping laws incorporating marital status magnify the moral influence of marriage. Similarly, in every state terms like *marriage*, and *spouse* are used in hundreds of state laws covering everything from contracts to torts, from wills to medical treatment, from property to taxes, from parenting to alimony. State government reports have found hundreds of provisions of state law that use those terms.[48] Thus, the laws use marriage to shape individual behavior and social morality.

Tenth, religion and marriage are closely linked, as from earliest times the formation and celebration of marriages in most world cultures has been a matter of great interest to, and often regulated by, religions.[49] Thus, from their formation and celebration, many (historically most) individual marriages are closely linked conceptually, symbolically, practically and often legally, with morality by the direct or indirect influence of religion - the institution whose role is to nurture and guard important matters of morality.

This list is incomplete,[50] but sufficiently makes the point that in many ways the institution of conjugal marriage is the most powerful, most influential, most significant morality-generating institution in society.

B.   The Legitimacy of Protecting the Morality of Marriage

While there are limits upon the state's authority to regulate social morality,[51] the protection of public health, safety, and morality are well-established as legitimate governmental interests and valid legislative objects.[52] As Justice Harlan so eloquently explained is his classic (now well-vindicated) dissent in *Poe v. Ullman*:

> [T]he very inclusion of the category of morality among [legitimate] state [legislative] concerns indicates that society is not limited in its objects only to the physical well-being of the community, but has traditionally concerned itself with the moral soundness of its people as well. Indeed to attempt a line between public behavior and that which is purely consensual or solitary would be to withdraw from community concern a range of subjects with which every society in civilized times has found it necessary to deal. *The laws regarding marriage which provide both when the sexual powers may be used and the legal and societal context in which children are born and brought up, as well as laws forbidding adultery, fornication and homosexual practices which express the negative of the proposition, confining sexuality to lawful marriage, form a pattern so deeply pressed into the substance of our social life that any Constitutional doctrine in this area must build upon that basis.*[53]

Lord Devlin of England has explained the need for preserving a common morality in any civil society. He wrote:

> If men and women try to create a society in which there is no fundamental agreement about good and evil, they will fail; if, having based it on common agreement, the agreement goes, the society will disintegrate. For society is not something that is kept together physically;

it is held by the invisible bonds of common thought. If the bonds were too far relaxed the members would drift apart. *A common morality is part of the bondage. The bondage is part of the price of society; and mankind, which needs society, must pay its price.*

. . . .

There is disintegration when no common morality is observed and history shows that the loosening of moral bonds is often the first stage of disintegration, *so that society is justified in taking the same steps to preserve its moral code* as it does to preserve its government and other essential institutions.[54]

Or, as another British report more recently put it, "[t]here must be some barriers that are not to be crossed, *some* limits fixed, beyond which people must not be allowed to go."[55]

The Supreme Court has repeatedly emphasized the importance of marriage as a moral institution, noting over 125 years ago that "[u]pon it society may be said to be built, and out of its fruits spring social relations and social obligations and duties, with which government is necessarily required to deal."[56] In Murphy v. Ramsey, the Court observed that "the holy estate of matrimony [is] the sure foundation of all that is stable and noble in our civilization; the best guaranty of that reverent morality which is the source of all beneficent progress in social and political movement."[57] In Maynard v. Hill, Justice Field glorified marriage "as creating the most important relation in life, as having more to do with the morals and civilization of a people than any other institution . . . ."[58] Justice Powell explained that marriage laws "represent[] the collective expression of moral aspirations [of a society, and] . . . reflect the widely held values of its people."[59] The Court has repeatedly emphasized the propriety of legislation to protect and regulate marriage to preserve these public moral interests.[60] In *Williams v. North Carolina*,[61] Justice Murphy noted that marriage law "formulat[es] . . . standards of public morality" for the institutions of family and marriage which "have generally been regarded as basic components of our national life . . . ."[62] Indeed, law protecting marriage is the classic example of valid legislation to protect public morality.[63]

Thus, the morality-forming contribution of marriage to our society is essential. The importance of protecting that contribution has frequently been acknowledged, and the validity of laws designed to uphold the morality of marriage has been repeatedly been upheld.

IV.   The Moral Content and Moral Values of the Institution of Conjugal Marriage

There have been and still are many different kinds of marriage, and; each "form of marriage [is] built upon a set of social and moral principles,"[64] which it fosters, and inculcates in its practitioners and throughout society. Consideration of the morality of conjugal marriage reveals the importance of the moral precepts that it generates.

A.   *Eleven Moral Precepts Nurtured by the Institution of Conjugal*
      Marriage

Conjugal marriage fosters and inculcates in individuals and society numerous moral virtues or sets of moral principles. To illustrate, eleven of those moral precepts are identified below.

First, *gender equality* is one powerful moral principle fostered by conjugal marriage. In order to have marriage, in order to enter the most fundamental, most privileged, most important unit of society, one man and one woman is required. Two men or two women are not sufficient. This sends a powerful message about the equal social worth of men and women and the equal contributions they make to society in and through the fundamental social institution of marriage. Conjugal marriage is the oldest equal rights institution recognized by the law.[65] That conveys a powerful message of gender equality to society, and perhaps we have never needed that message more than we do in today's world of radical-feminist-vs-selfish-misogynist gender wars. The message of equality is fostered from the first moment a child opens its eyes and throughout the formative childrearing years if the child is raised in a home founded on the marriage of a husband and a wife.

Second, conjugal marriage fosters most poignantly morality of *fidelity*.[66] The spouses are expected, indeed obligated, to be loyal and faithful to each other. Particularly in matters of sexual relationship, fidelity is the standard for conjugal marriage. Even today, in our "post-sexual revolution" society, most Americans expect spouses to be faithful to each other and consider infidelity a moral wrong and fidelity characterizes most marriage relationships. The best in fidelity estimates indicate that over the course of an entire marriage, only about 20 percent of husbands and approximately half as many wives commit infidelity.[67] Fidelity is a overwhelming norm and ideal. Reciprocal loyalty is the premise upon which all exchange relationships are built. If you cannot trust people to keep their word, you cannot run the risk of entering into relationships with them.

Third, *monogamy, exclusivity* and *sexual self-control* are related moral principles clearly implied in societies in which conjugal monogamy is the rule and also (if to a lesser extent) in polygamous societies. The morality of conjugal marriage for men especially emphasizes rejecting the greed of multiple sexual partners to satisfy wandering eyes that produce sexual arousal. For women, marriage also underscores self-control in emotional as well as sexual attachment. John Adams declared that: "The foundation of national morality must be laid in private families. . . . How is it possible that Children can have any just Sense of the sacred Obligations of Morality or Religion if, from their earliest Infancy, they learn their Mothers live in habitual Infidelity to their fathers, and their fathers in as constant Infidelity to their Mothers?"[68]

Fourth, *interdependence* is fostered by conjugal marriage. The powerful reality that human beings are social beings, that they need other human beings has been recognized by legal philosophers for centuries if not millennia.[69] The important of teaching the virtue of interdependence is extremely important in our society which emphasizes individualism. Indeed, it has been said that Americans fear dependence, and that can extend to the notion of interdependence. Yet recognizing that we depend upon others throughout our lives, from the time of birth when we were totally dependent through the time of our greatest self sufficiency (when our ability to flourish depends in our large part in our post-agrarian society upon provision of services by others in a usually commercial nature), to the time of our aging when we return to greater dependency including home-care, assisted living, nursing homes, and hospitalization. The skill of successful interdependent living is learned first in the family founded on conjugal marriage and in the "graduate school" education of conjugal marriage. Men and women are different in complementary ways and conjugal marriage builds upon the complementarity of gender to bring joy, satisfaction, fulfillment, offspring, etc.

Fifth, the moral principle of *duty* (*commitment, obligation*) is fostered powerfully in conjugal marriage. Social and legal expectations surround marriage. Since married life is not always a bowl of cherries, learning how to successfully be happy with a husband or a wife, even during the rough spells of marriage, depends to large degree upon the ability to keep obligations and fulfill duties. It is difficult sometimes for a woman to live with her husband, and it can be frustrating for a man to live with his wife. Fulfilling moral duties is learned in marriage and in the home. Those lessons learned and modeled in conjugal marriage powerfully engender in society the morality of duty. The founders of the United States had another term for this important moral quality—they called it *virtue*, and they considered a high degree of virtue in people to be essential to the success and survival of any republican form of government—including the government of the United States of American that they established.[70]

Sixth, *altruistim, selflessness* and *service* comprise a set of moral virtues fostered in the relationship of conjugal marriage. For marriage to succeed the husband and wife must become to some degree selfless and other-oriented. Husbands must sacrifice some of their male yearnings and desires, and wives must also subordinate some of their female interests and expectations. Care for the welfare and concerns of the other must be given priority over ones own interests and preferences. The lessons of selflessness learned in marriage filter through marriage and through married individuals into society at large to undergird acts, deeds, and gifts of charity that are essential even in self-oriented, consumeristic, capitalism-driven, self-gain motivated economies. There needs to be some safety net of altruistic selflessness and charity for civilization.

Seventh, the morality of *service* also is cultivated and required in conjugal marriage. The husband and wife serve one another and their family. At common law, the husband had a legal obligation to provide for his wife with the fruits of his labor and the wife had the obligation to serve her husband in a domestic capacity.[71] Equal service of different nature was the standard and expectation. Today these rigid gender-based division-of-labor boundaries of the common law are erased, but the expectation of mutual service (including mutual spousal support) survives in conjugal marriage. Men and women who serve each other and their families in marriage are more able and willing to serve those in need in society as a whole.

Eighth, *kindness* is an important moral principle fostered and inculcated in conjugal marriage. Marriage transforms persons in a relationship of strangers into a relationship of kinship. Marriage turns mere men into loving husbands and fathers, and mere women into devoted wives and mothers. Kinship, including the voluntary kinship of conjugal marriages, historically has been associated with kindness, gentleness and caring. As Professor Merlin Meyer explained, "[t]he domain of kinship predicates a kind of morality characterized by kindness and a predisposition to love and care . . . . The root words, *kindness, kind* and the German word for child, *kind,* all have the same generic root, and all express the moral character of kinship."[72] While other social relationships generally are characterized by exchange and reciprocity, kinship and marriage are characterized by service and altruism. These moral virtues are needed in our society at large, and not just in the home; but if there is not kindness, caring and concern in marriage or marital home, we will look in vain for it in society at large.

Ninth, a delicate but critical and related moral virtue developed in conjugal marriage is *love.* Husbands and wives (and their children) learn how to love and how to act lovingly most effectively in marriage and marital families. Conjugal marriage is the sole institution in which the three classic facets of love can be united—*philos, agape,* and *eros.*[73] In marriage we experience the power of love as altruistic friendship, as sacrificial, ethical interdependence, and as a sexual self-fulfilling relationship. Married couples learn to channel sexual passions, to give without expectation of return, and to have true friendship.

Tenth, the moral principle of *forgiveness* is taught powerfully in conjugal marriage as there are ample opportunities for both husband and wife to exercise forgiveness as well as to seek forgiveness. Living lives solely upon an ethic of exchange, of an eye for and eye and a tooth for a tooth, is guaranteed to bring disaster and disillusion to the marriage. The expansion of heart that comes with forgiving an erring husband or wife, and the humility that comes from seeking and receiving forgiveness from an offended spouse produces a moral development that can come in no other way. The lessons of seeking and giving forgiveness carried from the marital family into society at large makes our society more charitable..

The eleventh set of moral virtues fostered in conjugal marriage are *patience, faith,* and *endurance.* Men and women have different capacities, strengths, pace, thermostats, interests and calibrations; learning to cooperate with and accommodate those gender and individual differences in marriage develops these virtues. In exchange theory, marriage can be explained in terms of the willingness to make long period of investment with little or no immediate return awaiting a greater return that comes at the long period of patiently enduring a disproportionate receipt of the economic or other benefits the relationship. Waiting for a husband or a wife to mature may take many years and require enormous patience. The principle of patience also is critical for marital childrearing as anyone who has children clearly understands. Development of patience in marriage produces great social dividends in employment, the economy, education, etc. Closely related to patience is the moral principle of *faith,* which is clearly required for a successful conjugal marriage. Men and women enter marriage with the faith that the certain intangible (and tangible) blessings and benefits will come. That's especially important for young adults who are in love and who witnessed the break up of their own parents' marriage or who lived in a family based on a dysfunctional, unhappy marriage. Since nearly one-half of all the children raised in America have witnessed the breakup of their parents' marriage. Since there are other socially acceptable alternatives to conjugal marriage, including nonmarital conjugal cohabitation, same-sex cohabitation (or civil union or marriage), a promiscuous "swinging" or "hooking-up" single lifestyles, etc., it takes a leap of faith to enter into a conjugal marriage in a day when marriage seems so prone to painful failure. Lessons of faith learned in that crucible can be carried into educational life, economic endeavors, etc. Likewise, one learns to *endure* differences, disagreements, and disappointments in the course of true love within conjugal marriage. For people living in a consumer-oriented, fast-food, here-and-now generation, the importance to society or people of learning to patiently endure with faith cannot be overstated.

Other forms of marriage may cultivate some of these virtues. However, no other form of marriage has the capacity and potential to foster so many virtues so fully or so well as conjugal marriage. It also is true that there are other institutions in society that can and to some extent do foster these same moralities in individuals and in society. Educational institutions, churches, institutions of government, institutions of the law, for example, can and do foster and reinforce many of these same moral virtues. But the success of other institutions to reinforce these virtues depends to a great degree upon their being successfully implanted and developed within marriage. If such moral principles are not first learned and lived in marriage and the marital family, it is very unlikely that they can be instilled by other institutions of society.

B   *The Morality of Marriage and the Channeling the "River of Fire" of Sexuality*

The morality of marriage is perhaps most directly and recognizably apparent as it relates to setting and maintaining standards of sexual behavior. "[S]ex is a river of fire that must be banked and cooled by a hundred restraints if it is not to consume in chaos both the individual and the group."[74] Safe and socially-beneficial sexual relations has been an important underlying purpose of marriage for many centuries.[75]

> In many ways, the sexual aspect of the relationship is the very cornerstone of marriage. . . . Sex is not merely an incidental feature of marriage but lies at its heart, and the legal imperative to protect marriage—and its sexual nature—is of constitutional import. Not only does marriage give rise to an approved sexual relationship, but also in many societies (including, in some respects, the United States), marriage gives rise to the only legally legitimate sexual relationship.[76]

For example, ancient and modern consanguinity, incest, impotency, and health restrictions reflect concerns about sexual regulation in marriage law and policy today. All states prohibit marriage and sexual relations between close relatives.[77] Creation and protection of a safe-haven free of the strife and competition for sexual favors, and protection of vulnerable dependents from the emotional traumas associated with sexual exploitation are among the major justifications for incest and consanguinity proscriptions. Marriage by persons with venereal disease in a communicable stage, or infected with pulmonary tuberculosis, or with "loathsome disease[s]," have all been statutorily prohibited.[78] Age of marriage requirements are also intended, in part, to prevent the sexual exploitation of minors, especially teen-age girls. All of these reflect the profound public interest in the safety of sexual relations within marriage.

The importance of sexual relations within marriage is also reflected in other laws. Concealment of an intent not to engage in sexual relations has been grounds for nullifying a marriage on the basis of fraud.[79] More directly, for centuries physical or psychological inability to consummate marriage by vaginal intercourse has rendered a marriage voidable.[80] More than a third of the American states still have statutes explicitly providing that a marriage may be annulled for impotency.[81]

The only kind of sexual relations even considered (let alone considered adequate) in marriage law has been heterosexual *vera copula*. The marriage may be of impaired validity may even though one has he ability to procreate some way, and oral or anal sex or other forms of sexual stimulation without vaginal intercourse has never (before Massachusetts legalized same-sex marriage) been sufficient.[82]

In sum, conjugal marriage is the principal social institution designed to channel human sexual urges, yearnings and expression into responsible, socially constructive outlets.[83] Sex between a married man and woman who are (and have been) chaste before marriage and faithful to their marriage vows during marriage is medically the safest and healthiest form of sex, psychologically the most secure and validating form or sex, and emotionally the most fulfilling, enjoyable and satisfying kind of sex, and provides the optimal setting in which children can be conceived, nurtured, born, and raised.

C.   *The Conjugality of the Morality of Marriage.*

The morality of marriage reflects the conjugal nature of the institution of marriage. Over time, the institution of marriage has been customized to fit the conjugal relationship like a well-tailored glove fits a hand—to support, liberate, nurture, enhance, and strengthen that particular kind of relationship. Inserting the entirely different hand of same-sex relationships into that "glove," as it were, and trying to force the customized morality tailored for male-female, chaste, faithful, committed, relationship of conjugal marriage onto the gay or lesbian couples hand of profoundly different dimensions, size, and structure is to invite frustration for same-sex couples, confusion for conjugal couples, and distortion and tearing of the stitching and fabric of the institution of marriage. That is because the moral expectations, norms, and behaviors that characterize ordinary same-sex couples within the gay and lesbian communities are profoundly different from those of ordinary conjugal couples who enter into matrimony.

V.   The Morality of Gay and Lesbian Relations

As to virtually all of the moral expectations of conjugal marriage, the behavior norms and moral standards of gay and lesbian couples diverge significantly. With some truly exceptional deviations, involving rare couples who have succeeded in abandoning the typical "gay" and "lesbian" lifetyle, gay and lesbian relations are not marital in moral content.

The most obvious differences relate to sexuality, but equal profound, if less prominent or obvious differences exist between same-sex and conjugal marital couples with respect to many of the other moral virtues of marriage described in Part III. Conjugal marriages and same-sex relationships differ markedly in at least six areas relating to sexuality: stability, monogamy, infidelity, commitment, safe-sex practices, and domestic violence. More subtle but telling differences also worth exploring are in such areas as contact and involvement with extended family (their parents, siblings, aunts/uncles, cousins, etc.), integration of their financial lives, involvement in religion (a strong correlate of quality of family life) mutual support in times of crisis, commitment and involvement as a couple to civic responsibility, etc.

Promiscuity, fluidity, creative exploration, and sexual variety are the behavioral norms among gay couples (and, to a lesser extent also lesbian couples), rather than monogamy and sexual self-control which are the norms fostered by heterosexual marriages. Multiple partners and infidelity characterize gay and lesbian relationships (especially gay relations). For example, a study by Dutch researchers, published in 2003 in the journal AIDS, reported on the number of partners among Amsterdam's homosexual population.[84] At the time the research began, gay partners could enter into legal "domestic partnerships" with virtually all of the rights and benefits accorded married couples; by the time the study was published, the Dutch parliament had legalized same-sex marriage and that law was already in effect. These gay-friendly researchers in this very gay-supportive environment in the most gay-affirming nation in the world found that

- 86% of new HIV/AIDS infections in gay men were in men who had steady partners.
- Gay men with steady partners engage in more risky sexual behaviors than gays without steady partners.
- Gay men with steady partners had 8 other sex partners ("casual partners") per year, on average.
- Gay men without a steady partner had 22 casual partners per year on average.[85]

Likewise, in their ground-breaking, sympathetic study of homosexual behaviors, Bell and Weinberg reported that 43 percent of white male homosexuals had sex with 500 or more partners, with 28 percent having one thousand or more sex partners.[86] Similarly, researchers in a more recent study of the sexual behaviors of 2,583 older sexually active gay men reported that "the modal range for number of sexual partners ever . . . was 101-500,"while 10.2 percent to 15.7

percent had between 501 and 1,000 partners, and another 10.2 percent to 15.7 percent reported having had more than one thousand sexual partners in their lifetime.[87]

In their important study two decades ago, McWhirter and Mattison (reportedly themselves a gay couple) interviewed 156 male couples and concluded that in these relationships "fidelity is not defined in terms of sexual behavior, but rather by their emotional commitment to one another."[88] Two-thirds of the couples began their relationship with the expectation of sexual exclusivity, but the partners became more permissive with time. They found that all the couples who had been together at least five years had incorporated some provision for outside sexual activity in their relationships. In fact, the authors concluded that "the single most important factor that keeps couples together past the ten-year mark is the lack of possessiveness they feel. Many couples learn very early in their relationship that ownership of each other sexually can become the greatest internal threat to their staying together."[89]

Likewise, Kirk and Madsen acknowledges that "the cheating ratio of 'married' gay males, given enough time, approaches 100%. . . . Many gay lovers, bowing to the inevitable, agree to an 'open relationship,' for which there are as many sets of ground rules as there are couples"[90]

Not only are characteristic gay (and to a lesser degree lesbian) sexual mores promiscuous and unfaithful, but they are disproportionately "unsafe" in terms of social responsibility and public health. Gay male homosexual sex is the primary means of transmission of AIDS disease in the United States. The U.S. Department of Health and Human Services lists thirty-three different categories of exposure to AIDS (methods of transmission), but the one category that dominates and exceeds all other categories is male homosexual activity.[91] If the multiple modes of exposure that include male homosexual behavior are included, male homosexual behavior is the sole or a potential cause of more than sixty percent (60%) of all AIDS cases that have been reported in the United States from the first case through June of 1993.[92]

Homosexual men are at greatest risk of contracting and transmitting AIDS. A summary of HIV seroprevalence data from STD clinics revealed that nationally, the median percentage of men who, since 1978, have had sex with other men who were positive for HIV was 32.4%, compared with only 5.1% of male heterosexual drug injectors who were positive.[93] Other studies report HIV-infection rates among homosexual men ranging from 20% to 50%.[94]

Moreover, AIDS is not the only sexually transmitted disease or public health problem with extremely disproportionate incidence in homosexual men. Doctors who treat homosexual men for diseases now look for at least fifteen *common* afflictions besides HIV/AIDS, that are not common in heterosexual men.[95] One study gave this succinct summary of the situation:

> Throughout the 1970s and early 1980s homosexual men were known to be at high risk of acquiring sexually transmitted diseases (STDs). In the 1980 Annual Summary Report from the Centers for Disease Control, over half of the reported cases of infection syphilis occurred in homosexual men. Gonorrhea, hepatitis A and B, cytomegalovirus

(CMV) infection, and anorectal warts also occurred more commonly in homosexual men than in heterosexual men or women. Intestinal or rectal infections with *Shigella* species, *Entamoeba histolytica*, Giardia lamblia, and other enteric pathogens were hyperendemic among homosexual men in many communities. . . . [Since the discovery of AIDS, the rate] of many of these STDs has declined . . . . Homosexual men are reporting fewer partners and less frequent sexual exposure. Despite these behavior changes and increased counseling about safer sexual practices, STDs remain a major health problem among homosexual men.[96]

Judith Stacey's recent research on sexual behavior of Gay men in Los Angeles corroborates that promiscuity is a major part of the gay lifestyle for many gay men, in and out of partnerships; and that lack of fidelity is a standard feature of gay partnerships.[97] She notes the immediate, physical, "chemistry" (what she calls the "male gaze") that typifies so many gay relationships she studied in and around Los Angeles:

It is not merely a cultural stereotype to observe that many gay men tend to be even more preoccupied than most straight women with their bodies, physical attractiveness, attire, adornment and self-presentation. Advertisements for every conceivable manner of corporeal beautification and modification flood the pages, airwaves, and websites of the gay male press: familiar and exotic cosmetic surgery and body sculpture procedures, including penile, buttock and pec implants; liposuction; laser resurfacing; hair removal or extensions; cosmetic dentistry; personal trainers and gym rat regimens; tattooing and tattoo removal; body piercing; hair coloring and styling; tinted contact lenses; manicures, pedicures and waxing; as well as color, style and fashion consultants and the commodified universe of couture, cosmetics, and personal grooming implements which they serve. . . . Similarly, many gay men . . . . suffer from eating disorders. . . . Arguably, therefore, gay men are even more oppressed than heterosexual women by injurious effects of what feminists termed "sexual objectification" and of the ageism that accompanies an emphasis on visual criteria for intimacy.
. . . . Because gay men operate in a male sexual economy that grants them greater license to pursue animalistic passions, they subject each other to heightened levels of the tyranny (as well as the titillating and serendipitous pleasures) of the male gaze. . . .[98]

Professor Stacey also describes what she calls the "cruising culture" that was prevalent in the Los Angeles gay community culture.

In cruising culture, the gay male sexual sport arena, it's all in the gaze. Erotic attraction and connection occur (or fail) in the blink of an eye. . . . The extraordinary emphasis on the visual at the core of this dynamic imposes painful challenges for gay men seeking eros and intimacy who fall outside desirable standards of beauty and youth.[99]

Additionally, Professor Stacey described what she calls "creativity" and "fluidity" in the nature of sexual relationships among urban gay males.

> [The] cruising culture also fosters, or enables, some creative, expan-
> sive approaches to intimacy and kinship. Because gay men can more
> readily separate physical sex from social attachment, they enjoy
> greater latitude in which to negotiate diverse terms for meeting their
> sexual and social needs within and beyond dyadic couple arrange-
> ments. Not only do some gay men engage in triads. . . . more than a
> few of the committed gay couples I have interviewed allow them-
> selves to indulge in extra-curricular cruising or "f[***]-buddy" lia-
> sons under a variety of rules (in some cases jointly frequenting cruis-
> ing bars, baths, or the internet). . . .Likewise, gay male culture
> rightfully prides itself on greater comfort with the fluidity and ambi-
> guity of boundaries between lover and friend. Former lovers become
> integrated into chosen kin sets more readily than among heterosex-
> uals . . . .[100]

Thus, it should come as no surprise to learn that while one of the most de-finitive studies on sexual attitudes in the United States found that 77% of Americans sampled believed that extramarital sex is always wrong,[101] and disapproval of sexual relations outside of marriage (infidelity) is a global norm,[102] nearly half of all gay men in relationships have agreements with their partners that sex outside the relationship is acceptable.[103]

As Dr. Stacey's research suggests, instability is a major problem in gay and lesbian relationships. The 2003 Dutch study noted above found that the average duration of gay "steady partner" relations was only 1.5 years—in the most gay-affirming, gay-supportive nation on earth, when marriage-equivalent same-sex domestic partnerships were legal, and the full status of same-sex marriage was being implemented.[104] A study published in 2006, of the demographics of mar-riage-equivalent same-sex registered partnerships in Norway and Sweden, noted significant problems with stability of the relationship, and significantly higher rates of breakup.[105] Despite the fact that same-sex couples were considerably older than male-female couples (a factor that generally correlates with greater stability in marriage),[106] and the ratio of partners from higher socio-economic status was up to 50% higher for gay and lesbian couples (another factor that may be associated with greater stability),[107] the divorce-risk levels were about 50% higher for registered gay men partnerships than for comparable heterosexual couples, and controlling for variables, the risk of divorce was twice as high for lesbian couples as it was for gay men couples.[108] Another study of Swedish reg-istered partnerships found that gay male couples were fifty percent more likely to divorce than married heterosexual couples, while lesbian couples were over 150 percent more likely to divorce than heterosexual couples.[109] Controlling for variables, gay couples were 35 percent and lesbian couples 200 percent more likely to divorce than heterosexual couples in that gay-supportive nation.[110]

While between two-thirds and seventy percent of married American con-jugal couples stay together at least ten years, and nearly sixty percent stay together at least twenty years, the 2003-2004 Gay/Lesbian Consumer Online Census survey reporting on the lifestyles of nearly 8,000 homosexuals found only 15% of respondents described their current relationship as having lasted twelve years, and only five percent (5%) as having lasted twenty years.[111] Thus, as distinguished University of Chicago sociologist Edward O. Laumann and his colleagues reported, "typical gay urban men spend most of their adults lives in 'transactional' relationships or short-term commitments of less than six months."[112]

There are many other behavioral and morality-difference-reflecting dissimilarities between conjugal married couples and same-sex couples. A study of nearly 2,500 same-sex couples who registered for civil unions in Vermont, other same-sex couples who did not register, and married heterosexual couples, found that:

> Married heterosexual couples had been together longer, differed on a variety of demographic factors, and had more contact with their family of origin than did both types of same-sex couples [i.e., gays and lesbians]. . . . [T]he results indicated that same-sex couples [registered an unregistered] were similar to each other on demographic and relationship factors when compared with married heterosexual couples.[113]

A Vermont study reported that "over one-half of gay men in both types of couples had had sex outside their primary relationship, whereas only 15.2% of married heterosexual men had done so."[114] Gay men both in and not in civil unions had nearly four times the rate of infidelity (approximately 60%) as married heterosexual men (15.2%), even though married relationships logically would have been on average much longer-lasting (and with more time for infidelity) than the recent civil unions, and the difference in infidelity rates between gay men in a civil union and those not in a civil union was less than three percent (2.8%).[115] In other words, formalizing gay relationships with marriage-like legal status and benefits has virtually no impact on the high infidelity rates of gay couples. Likewise, Lesbian women in civil unions and not in civil unions had much higher rates than women in heterosexual marriages of having had a meaningful extra-relationship affair (4.7% and 3.0% compared to 0.0%).[116] Significantly, there was a dramatic difference in the percentage of couples who had decided that extra-relationship sex was acceptable; for lesbians both in and not in civil unions it was about 50% higher than for conjugally married women (5.3% and 5.0 compared to 3.5%), and for gay men both in civil unions and not in registered unions it was from 1250% to 1400% higher than for men in conjugal marriages (40.3% and 49.5% compared to 3.5%).[117] In other words, the expectation of fidelity that came with the relationship commitment was drastically different for conjugally married men and women that it was for gays and lesbians in formal and non-registered same-sex relationships.

Thus, while conjugal marriage exemplifies many of the best attributes of the morality of kinship relations, same-sex relations (both formal and unformalized) manifest many of the worst attributes of the morality of strangers. Mixing both kinds of relationship into one "marriage" institution could seriously undermine the moral integrity of marriage.

VI.   The Transformative Effect of Inclusion

As Monte Stewart has noted, "just as human societies create and sustain social institutions, a society can change its social institutions,"[118] and by changing them can change the morality they cultivate in society. One argument for legalizing same-sex marriage argues that redefining marriage to include same-sex couples would have a taming transformative effect, making the morality of gays and lesbians (especially their sexual morality) become more like the morality of marriage.[119] Careful examination reveals that this claim is significantly flawed in that it fails to consider in the calculation of social consequences the transformative influence of gay and lesbian morality upon the morality of marriage. In fact, the tide of transformation by legalizing same sex marriage will run strongly toward altering the morality of marriage. On the other hand, it is unlikely that legalizing same-sex marriage will "tame" or "uplift" or morally transform same-sex relationships significantly with regard to the moral values of marriage. As legalizations of gay unions thus far has not had that effect.[120]

Redefining marriage to include gay and lesbian couples will have a profound impact upon sexual morality in society. Sexual standards will change as homosexual relations will be instantly normalized and equated with marital relations. In terms of "unsafe" sexual practices, infidelity, promiscuity, teen sexuality, sexual exploitation of minors and of other vulnerable populations, and human indignity resulting from demeaning sexual demands, the legalization of same-sex marriage (or marriage-equivalent unions) will have very harmful effect upon the morality of marriage, upon many individuals, and upon society.

Legalizing same-sex marriage will instantly transform the meaning of *marriage, spouse, husband, wife, parent, child* in the law. That redefinition will profoundly influence the meaning of public education, school curriculum, civil rights, family, inheritance, intimacy, relations, public behavior, privacy, disclosures, security, accommodation, filings, custody, guardianship, visitation, reasonable conduct, medical treatment, preferences, privileges, rights, duties, etc.

There is a moral order in society.[121] There is a moral content to the law.[122] While the morality of any particular law and the social morality do not always totally coincide, a natural and necessary gravitational pull connects the legal law and the moral order of any society.[123] That connection is especially important in a democratic society; where the people have establish a form of self-government, the law must manifest some significant connection to the moral order of society if the law is to be legitimate. There are limits on the degree or space of separation between law and the basic values of society that can be sustained in a democracy. The authority of the law and of democratic legal institutions depends, ultimately, upon the acceptance and compliance of the citizens. The respect and obedience of society-at-large to laws even when they are unenforceable are essential for the legitimacy of law and of the legal order system. When the gap between the law and the moral order of society becomes too great, and when that separation is sustained for a substantial period of time, not only does the law lose its legitimacy, but the legal system and the institutions of the law also lose legitimacy.[124]

Legalization of same-sex marriage will create a huge gap between the law of marriage and prevailing, strong social morality. [125] Public opinion polls consistently find opposition to same-sex marriage at between sixty and sixty-five percent,[126] and whenever the people have had the opportunity to vote on same-sex marriage bans, as in the twenty-seven states where state marriage amendment have been on the ballots, popular support for them averages nearly seventy percent (70%).[127] But the gap, if sustained over time, will weaken and change the social morality.[128] The law can change our moral values. The judicial legalization of abortion one-third of a century ago illustrates that, as initial popular outrage and objection cooled into tolerance, then acceptance, and eventually modest social support.

Advocates of same sex marriage significantly overstate the transformative power of the inclusion of same-gender couples within marriage to transform the nature of same-sex relationships. Their argument for the transformative effects that would occur on same-sex relationships by calling them marriages is built upon the Kelsen-ian law of legal positivism. That is, it erroneously assumes that by changing the label of a relationship you can change the nature of the relationship.

VII.   Conclusion: To Protect Marriage, Morality and Society We Must Decline to Legalize Same-Sex Marriage

Much is at stake in the debate over whether same-sex marriage should be legalized, for legalization itself connotes morality and legitimacy.[129] Legalizing same-sex marriage will have a great degenerating effect on the moral meaning and moral consequences of marriage. As Maggie Gallagher has written, legalizing

> same-sex marriage will transform our shared, public meaning of the word 'marriage.' It will disconnect marriage from any futher relationships with . . . making the next generation, and connecting those children to both their mothers and fathers. A new unisex language of parenting in the public square will demote the idea that 'children need mothers and fathers' . . . ."
> You can see the beginning of all these changes in Massachusetts, where [same-sex marriage has been legalized, and] the marriage license already reads not "Husband and Wife" but "Party A" and "Party B."[130]

Wherever the institution of marriage has been radically altered and same-sex relations given high social status, or marriage "captured" by political movements, families (especially children) and society in general have experienced traumatic upheaval and great suffering. Throughout most of history most societies have recognized that there is a critical nexus between marriage and the general welfare of the society itself.[131]

Legalizing same-sex marriage would be another notch in what Professor Helen Alvare calls "The turn toward the self in the law of marriage and family."[132] It would encourage gay fluidity, promiscuity, infidelity, and instability in marriage. However, if we want to foster fidelity, monogamy, responsibility, and emotional bonding in marriages, the redefinition of marriage to include same-sex couples would be counter-productive.

Providing clear proof in family law is difficult.[133] Providing empirical proof for the claim of this chapter is not easy, either. As, John Eekelaar and Mavis Maclean properly "caution" that "claims that marriage is *uniquely* capable of producing certain [moral] 'goods'" in human relationships may be questioned because "[t]he picture is more complex."[134] Nevertheless, their survey clearly did not negate the premise of a significant quantitative difference in the scope and influence of morality-producing relationship outcomes between marriage and alternative relationships, albeit the scope was "hard to substantiate."[135] That, of course, is the rub. Eekelaar and Maclean's study illustrates the point made recently by Professor Brian Bix: "The problem with grounding public policy recommendations on consequentialist reasoning . . . is that the approach requires available relevant data . . . . [That data] is often scarce or controversial or both."[136]

Thus, certainly two men or two women may share a deep, meaningful personal relationship with each other, share common interests, be committed to and supportive of each other, and serve each other. But such relationships are not the same as marriages, and never before have they been labeled *marriages.* Throughout history, for millennia, persons in those relationships have been able to find fulfillment in them and to make beneficial contributions to society through them without claiming the legal status of *marriage.* Since giving marital status is not necessary for such socially-beneficial same-gender friendships to flourish, since extending marital status to such relationships is not justified in terms of the purposes of marriage, and since a redefinition of marriage to include same-sex couples would import into the institution of marriage some of the disintegrating moral values of same-sex relations and undermine the institution of marriage at a time when it is in great need of strengthening, the claim that there may be for some gay and lesbian couples and families some positive social benefits from same-gender friendship simply does not justify legalizing same-sex marriage. As Chief Justice Earl Warren noted in another context many years ago, the "profanation of marriage" for reasons of expediency should not be permitted.[137]

The morality of marriage would be the most devastating casualty of the legalization of same-sex marriage. That's one answer to the question of "what's the harm."

Notes

1. The research assistance of Zachary J. Starr, Evie Brinkerhoff and other student assistants was very valuable, and their contribution is appreciatively noted. Parts of this have been published a Lynn D. Wardle, *A Response to the Conservative Case for Same-Sex Marriage,* 22 BYUJ. Pub.L. 309 (2008).

2. *See generally* Lynn D. Wardle, *Is Marriage Obsolete?* 10 Mich. J. Gender & L. 189 (2003) (reviewing increased incidence of cohabitation, childbearing out of wedlock, divorce, etc., but noting that only the incidence and not the kind of marital pathologies had changed.).

3. The Netherlands (effective April, 2001), Belgium (2003), Spain (2005), and Canada (2005). Also, South Africa (2006) adopted a Civil Union bill that grants the same legal rights of marriage to civil unions, and allows same-sex couples to choose to have their union called a "marriage". Republic of South Africa, Civil Union Bill, B 26B—2006.

4. Goodridge v. Department of Public Health, 798 N.E.2d 941 (Mass. 2003).

5. The States are California (2004), Connecticut (2006), New Hampshire, New Jersey (2006), Oregon, and Vermont (2000).

6. *See generally* Elizabeth Kukura, *Finding Family: Considering the Recognition of Same-Sex Families in Human Rights Law and the European Court of Human Rights,* 13 Hum. Rts. Br. 17, 17-18 (Iss. No. 2, Winter 2006).

7. No evidence has been proffered that the troubling sexual behaviors of gays that the same-sex marriage proponents desire to tame by marriage are not a deeply imbedded part of the attraction of that lifestyle to many who practice it. The hope that marriage will transform irresponsible sexual behavior has produced disappointment and sorrow for many heterosexual women who have married sexually promiscuous men thinking that marriage would "tame" the wandering ways of their men.

8. Merlin G. Myers, *The Morality of* Kinship, the Virginia F. Cutler Lecture, Brigham Young University, Provo, Utah, November 15, 1983, in BYU Speeches of the Year, 1983-84, at 52 (hereinafter "Myers").

9. *Id.*

10. *Id.* at 50.

11. *Id.* at 55.

12. *Id.* at 50.

13. *Id.* "[S]acrifice is the ready index to the moral quality of a relationship. If one is willing to sacrifice only a little, morality is small; if much, morality is great. . . ." *Id.* at 55.

14. *Id.*

15. James Q. Wilson, The Marriage Problem: How Our Culture Has Weakened Families 30 (2002), cited in Scott Fitzgibbon, *A City Without Duty, Fault or Shame,* in Reconceiving the Family 28 (2006).

16. *Id.*

17. *See generally, Marriage and the Public Good: Ten Principles,* May 2006 (PRINCETON, NEW JERSEY) (available at http://www.princetonprinciples.org/index.html) (scholarly work reasoning that "[m]arriage protects children, men and women, and the common good"); Institute for American Values, Why Marriage Matters, Second Edition: Twenty-Six Conclusions from the Social Sciences (2005); Barbara Schneider, et al., Family Matters (Alabama Policy Institute 2005); The National Marriage Project, The State of Our Unions 2001 (2001).

18. Judith E. Koons, *Motherhood, Marriage, and Morality: The Pro-Marriage Moral Discourse of American Welfare Policy*, 19 Wis. Women's L.J. 1, 21 (2004), citing the Personal Responsibility and Work Opportunity Reconciliation Act of 1996 ("PRWORA"), § 101, 42 U.S.C. § 601 note foll. (1996).

19. Monte Neil Stewart, *Genderless Marriage, Institutional Realities, and Judicial Elision*, 1 Duke J. Const'l L & Pub. Pol'y 3, 9 (2006).

20. *Id.* at 9-10.

21. *See generally* John Eekelaar & Mavis Maclean, *Marriage and the Moral Basis of Personal Relationships*, 31 J. L. & Society 510 (2004) (discussion of the moral basis of marriage and other intimate associations); Scott Fitzgibbon, *Marriage and the Good Obligation*, 47 Am. J. Jurisprudence 41 (2002) (a "crisis of obligation" and loss of social moral has eroded the institution of marriage); Scott FitzGibbon, *Marriage and the Ethics of Office*, 18 Notre Dame J. L., Ethics, & Pub. Pol'y 89 (2004) (spouses minister to one another and to others under a system of moral rules and principle that impose obligations); George W. Dent, Jr., *Traditional Marriage: Still Worth Defending*, 18 BYU J. Pub. L. 419 (2004) (noting moral or social significance of marriage); Robert P. George, *What's Sex Got to Do with It? Marriage, Morality, and Rationality* in The Meaning of Marriage 142 (Robert P. George & Jean Bethke Elshtain, eds., 2006); Robert P. George, *What's Sex Got To Do with It? Marriage, Morality, and Rationality*, 49 AM. J. JURIS. 63 (2004) (the complementary nature of men and women facilitates the ability to achieve the basic good of marriage).

22. Maynard v. Hill, 125 U.S. 190, 213 (1988).

23. *Id.* at 211. Thus, marriage "is an institution, in the maintenance of which in its purity the public is deeply interested . . . ." *Id.*

24. *See generally* Myers, note 8; Margaret Mead, Male and Female: A Study of the Sexes in a Changing World 188-195 (1969) ("No matter how free divorce, how frequently marriages break up, in most societies there is the assumption of permanent mating, of the idea that the marriage should last as long as both live ... No known society has ever invented a form of marriage strong enough to stick that did not contain the 'till death us do part' assumption."); Bronislaw Malinowski, Sex, Culture and Myth 63 (1963); Bronislaw Malinowski, *The Group and the Individual in Functional Analysis,* 44 The Am. Journal of Soc. Issue 6 (1939); G. Robina Quale, A History of Marriage Systems 1 (1988); for a collection of quotes from various anthropologists about marriage, see: Bill Muehlenberg, *'Innovative' Definitions of 'Family' Flout History,* On Line Opinion: http://www.onlineopinion.com.au/view.asp?article=2788 (Marriage is a basic need that humans must have satisfied, and an important building block of a successful society. Even in the most primitive tribes, marriage is present and is an essential element of the organization of society. "Since *Homo Erectus,* marriage has been a way in which society has organized itself and prospered.") The others basic social units, of course, are parentage and family, both of which usually are linked with and a subset or outgrowth of marriage.

25. David W. Murray, *Poor Suffering Bastards: An Anthropologist Looks at Illegitimacy*, Policy Rev. (Spring, 1994) at 9. ("The history of human society shows that when people stop marrying, their continuity as a culture is in jeopardy."*Id.*).

26. U.S. Census Bureau. United States Census 2000. *Marital Status: 2000 (Census 2000 Brief)*. Washington: Government Printing Office, 2003. (C2KBR-30), *also found at* http://www.census.gov/prod/2003pubs/c2kbr-30.pdf, *and* U.S. Census Bureau. United States Census 2000. *Married Couple and Unmarried Partner Household: 2000 (Census 2000 Special Report),* Washington: Government Printing Office, 2003 (CENSR-5). *Also found at*: http://www.census.gov/prod/2003pubs/censr-5.pdf. The 2000 Census found that

54.4% of persons over the age of 15 were married and 18.5% were widowed, divorced, and/or separated. Thus a great majority (72.9%) of the population over the age of 15 currently are or have been married. (Of course, the actual number of married persons is greater if rarely-married 15-to-17-year-olds were not included in this calculation.)

27. In the year 2000, 58 percent of adult citizens were married, 10 percent were divorced, 7 percent, widowed, 2 percent separated, and 22 percent had never married. *See* Census Bureau, Population Survey, November 2000, Voting and Registration Supplement, cited in Nicholas H. Wolfinger & Raymond E. Wolfinger *Family Structure and Voter Turnout* presented at the 2006 Annual Meeting of the American Political Science Association in Philadelphia, Pennsylvania, at p.6, & Table 1. *See also supra* note __.

28. Statistical Abstract of the United States, 2004, (in 2000, 33.1% of all children were born out of wedlock); The 2000 Census found that "about two thirds of children lived in married-couple family groups." U.S. Census Bureau. United States Census 2000. *Children and the Households They Live In (Census 2000 Special Report),* at 9, (Washington: Government Printing Office, 2004) (CENSR-14), *also found at* http://www.census.gov/prod/2004pubs/censr-14.pdf. In 2000, 62% of persons under the age of eighteen lived with married parents (at least one parent is a biological or adoptive parent of the child), 27% lived in a single parent home, 5% lived with neither parent, and 6% lived with a single parent and a unmarried partner. *Id.*

29. "The family is thought to 'find[] its origin in marriage' and consist of 'husband, wife, and children born in their wedlock.' Although nontraditional family types have emerged more prominently in recent years, traditional conceptions of the family as centered around a married couple remain culturally potent." Note, *Inbred Obscurity: Improving Incest Laws in the Shadow of the "Sexual Family,"*, 119 Harv. L. Rev. 2464, 2466 (2006) (herein "Note, *Inbred*").

30. Statistical Abstract of the United States, 2004, *supra* note 28 (of women who bear children out of wedlock marry the fathers of those children sometime later).

31. *Id.* (of women who bear children out of wedlock later marry someone [or marry a nonfather male]).

32. Myers, *supra* note 8, at 53.

33. *Id.*

34. That is what the law of illegitimacy was all about, *see generally* William Blackstone, Commentaries on the Laws of England, Book 1, chapter 16, p. 442-447 "Of Parent and Child" (discussing the nature, duties toward, and rights and incapacities of illegitimate children).

35. *See* Bruce C. Hafen, *Individualism and Autonomy in Family Law: The Waning of Belonging,* 1991 BYU L. Rev. 1 (1991); Takeo Doi, The Anatomy of Dependence (John Bestor, transla., 1973).

36. Jeremy Waldron, *Minority Cultures and the Cosmopolitan Alternative*, 25 U. Mich. J.L. Reform 751, 767 (1992), cited in Jeffrey G. Sherman, *Prenuptial Agreements: A New Reason to Revive an Old Rule*, 53 Cleve. St. L. Rev. 359, 363 (2005-2006) "Man, said Aristotle, is the least self-sufficient of animals. But the human indivudal is not merely an animal who happens to lack self-sufficiency; he is an animal whose essence it is to lack self-sufficiency. We need each other, and it is Aristotle's task to make, as it were, a virtue of this necessity. The life of belonging to a polis is not ... a grudging dependence, but a positive and essentialist embrace of interdependence."

37. Myers, *supra* note 8, at 54 ("[T]he sexual union of husband and wife is the instrumentality for transposing life from one sphere to another.")

38. *See generally* Lynn D. Wardle, *The Bonds of Matrimony and the Bonds of Constitutional Democracy,* 32 Hofstra L. Rev. 349 (2003)

39. *See generally* Will Durant & Ariel Durant, The Lessons of History 35-36 (1968). *See infra* Part IV.

40. Alan H. Goldman, *Plain Sex,* 6 Philo. And Public Affairs, 267-287 (Spring 1977) (Marriage has been the primary way in which sexual relations have become legitimate and accepted by society.) ; Mary Ann Lamanna and Agnes Riedmann, *Marriages and Families: Making Choices in an Diverse Society,* 208-213 (Thomson Wadsworth, 2006) (throughout history, extra- marital promiscuity has been stigmatized by society); H. Solotaroff, *On the Origin of the Family,* 11 American Anthro. 232, (Aug. 1898) (marriage has been the most basic relationship in which sexual relations and child bearing have been socially acceptable).

41. *See, e.g.,* Linda J. Waite and Maggie Gallagher, The Case for Marriage 47-52. 152=58. 162-65 (2000) (relations of spouses healthier, less domestic violence, less victimization of many kinds).

42. *Id.* at 75-89 (Married couples generally have more sex and enjoy it more, finding it physically satisfying and emotionally satisfying than non-married couples.)

43. *Id.* at 165-68 (husbands and wives both happier than singles; better mental health).

44. Note, *Inbred supra* note 29, at 2466 (2006); *id.* at 2469 (repeating these three "legally enshrined values surrounding sex and the family") .

45. Defense of Marriage Act, Report from the Comm. on the Judiciary of the House of Representatives, H.R. Rep. No. 104-664, 104th Cong., 2d Sess., July 9, 1996, at 10. *See also id.* at 11, no. 40 citing Prepared Statement of Lynn D. Wardle in Defense of Marriage Act, Hearing before the Subcomm. on the Constitu. of the Comm. on Judiciary of the House of Representatives, 104thSess, 2d Sess, on H.R. 3396, May 15, 1996, at 160, 170-74 (listing areas of federal law such as bankruptcy, immigration, federal pensions, federal taxation, etc. where federal law defines marriage for federal program).

46. Joshua K. Baker, *1000 Benefits of Marrriage? An Analysis of the 1997 GAO Report,* iMAPP Public Policy Brief, May 26, 2004, at 1, available at http://www.marriagedebate.com/pdf/iMAPP.GAO.pdf (Seen September 13, 2006) (citing GAO/OGC-97-16 (Jan. 31, 1997), Letter from GAO Associate General Counsel Barry Bedrick to the Hon. Henry Hyde, dated January 31, 1997, and GAO-04-353R, Defense of Marriage Act (January 23, 2004), letter from GAO Associate General Counsel Dayna K. Shah to the Hon. Bill Frist, dated Jan. 23, 2004).

47. Baker, *supra.*note 46, at 5, n.3, citing GAO/OGC-97-16 at pp. 1-2 (Jan. 31, 1997).

48. *See* The Report of the Commission on Sexual Orientation and the Law in Hawaii (Dec. 8, 1995) (the terms marriage, husband, wife, spouse, and family are used extensively in a wide variety of statutes and programs in state law in Hawaii); *id.* at 105-126, App. B (listing over 300 Hawaiian statutory provisions containing references to marriage, husband, wife, spouse, and similar familial terms); Legal Marriage Alliance of Washington RCW Project 2004, available at http://lmaw.org/rcw_project.htm (reporting 423 state statutes which confer benefits or obligations based on marital status); *see generally* Karen M. Doering, *1,500 Reasons Why We Need Marriage Equality,* National Center for Lesbian Rights, January 2004 (available at http://www.nclrights.org/publications/ 1500reasons-0304.htm) (asserting that each state "provides approximately 500" rights, privileges, or obligations to married spouses).

49. *See generally*; John Witte, From Sacrament to Contract: Marriage, Religion, and Law in the Western Tradition 1 (1997) (religion, family, and marriage have long been linked); William V. D'Antonio, William M. Newman, and Stuart A. Wright, *Religion and Family Life: How Social Scientists View the Relationship,* 21 Journal for the Scientific

Study of Religion 218 (Sept. 1982) ("these main blocks of human existence reinforce and complement each other through both social control and social support. Religion supported the family through its monopoly on marriage and controlled society by demanding marriage be the most appropriate way to reproduce. Religion, through the ages, was a main form of social organization and held the monopoly on control social life, mainly through its hold on marriage and government.") *See also* Charles J. Reid, Jr., Power over the Body, Equality in the Family (2004) (history of marriage as a religious concept); Julie Hanlon Rubio, *A Christian Theology of Marriage and Family*, (2003) (exploring marriage and related issues through the lens of the marriage liturgy, the New Testament, and Christian tradition); Charles J. Reid, Jr., *The Unavoidable Influence of Religion Upon the Law of Marriage*, 23 Quinnipiac L. Rev. 493 (2004).

50. For instance, no discussion has been provided of the power of marriage to cultivate civic virtue, a concept very important at the time of the Founding of the American Republic. *See, e.g.,* Lynn D. Wardle, *The Proposed Federal Marriage Amendment and the Risks to Federalism in Family Law*, 2 Univ. St. Thomas L.J. 137 (2004); Lynn D. Wardle, *The Bonds of Matrimony and the Bonds of Constitutional Democracy*, 32 Hofstra L. Rev. 349 (2003).

51. See, e.g., *Lawrence v. Texas*, 539 U.S. 558, 581; *id.* at 585 (O'Connor, J., concurring); "There are limits to the extent to which the presumption of constitutionality can be pressed," [Skinner v. Oklahoma,] 316 U.S. 535, 544 [(1942)] (concurring opinion), and *the mere assertion that the action of the State finds justification in the controversial realm of morals cannot justify alone any and every restriction it imposes.*" Poe v. Ullman, 367 U.S. 497, 545 (1961) (Harlan, J., dissenting) (emphsis added); Alberts v. State of California, 354 U.S. 476 (1957).

52. *See, e.g.,* Lingle v. Chevron USA, 544 U.S. 528, 51 (2005), citing Village of Euclid v. Ambler Realty Co., 272 U.S. 365, 395(1926) (municipal zoning ordinance will survive substantive due process challenge so long as it is not "clearly arbitrary and unreasonable, having no *substantial relation to the public health, safety, morals, or general welfare*") (emphasis in original); Lucas v. South Carolina Coastal Council, 505 U.S. 1003, 1023 (1992), citing Penn Central Transportation Co. v. New York, 438 U.S. 104, 125 (1978) (where State "reasonably conclude[s] that 'the health, safety, morals, or general welfare' would be promoted" it may bar that use of property without compensation); Barnes v. Glen Theatre, Inc., 501 U.S. 560, 569 (1991)("Thus, the public indecency statute furthers a substantial government interest in protecting order and morality."); *See also* Berman v. Parker, 348 U.S. 26, 32 (1954) Thomas v. Collins, 323 U.S. 516, 536 (1945); Chaplinsky v. State of New Hampshire, 315 U.S. 568, 572 (1942) Poe v. Ullman, 367 U.S. 497, 539 (1961) (Harlan, J., dissenting).

53. *Poe* 367 U.S. at 545-56 (Harlan, J., dissenting) (emphasis added).

54. Patrick Devlin, The Enforcement of Morals (1965) 10,13 (emphasis added). *See generally* Michael McConnell, *The Role of Democratic Politics in Transforming Moral Convictions Into Law*, 98 Yale L.J. 1201(1989); Michael Sandel, *Moral Argument and Liberal Toleration: Abortion and Homosexuality*, 77 Calif. L.Rev. 521(1989).

55. M. Warnock (Chairman), Report of the committee of Inquiry into human fertislzation and embryology (The Warnock Report), Cmnd. 9314 (HMSO, London, 1984), para. 5.

56. Reynolds v. United States, 98 U.S. 145, 165 (1878).

57. 114 U.S. 15, 45 (1885). The connection between marriage and morals is illustrated by a long line of polygamy cases in which the Supreme Court of the United States upheld prosecution and conviction for advocating or practicing polygamy, over claims of first amendment religious exercise rights, and other constitutional claims.

58. 125 U.S. 190, 205 (1888). *See also* Meyer v. Nebraska, 262 U.S. 390, 393 (1923); Skinner v. Oklahoma, 316 U.S. 535 (1942); Griswold v. Connecticut, 381 U.S. 479, 484 (1965); and Loving v. Virginia, 388 U.S. 1, 9-12 (1967).

59. Zablocki v. Redhail, 434 U.S. 374, 398 (Powell, J., concurring).

60. Maynard v. Hill, 125 U.S. at 205.

61. 317 U.S. 287 (1942).

62. *Id.* At 308 (Murphy, J., dissentions).

63. Indeed, Aristotle taught that it was the first duty of the wise legislator to enact laws regulating marriage because it is the foundation of family and society. Aristotle, *Politica, Book Seven, part* XVI, in 10 The Works of Aristotle 1334-35 (W. Ross ed. 1921) (also available at http://etext.virginia.edu/ etcbin/toccer-new2?id=AriPoli.xml &images=images/modeng&data=/texts/english/modeng/parsed&tag=public&part=7&div ision=div2).

64. Cleveland v. United States, 329 U.S. 14, 29 (1946) (Murphy, J., dissenting) (("We must recognize, then, that polygyny, like other forms of marriage, is basically a cultural institution rooted deeply in the religious beliefs and social mores of those societies in which it appears. It is equally true that the briefs and mores of the dominant culture of the contemporary world condemn the practice as immoral and substitute monogamy in its place. To those beliefs and mores I subscribe, but that does not alter the fact that polygyny is a form of marriage built upon a set of social and moral principles. It must be recognized and treated as such.").

65. At common law married women suffered many legal disabilities and discriminations in other aspects of the law; for instance, married women did not have equal rights with their husbands in tort law, contract law, property law, procedural law, etc. However, in *marriage law*—the law governing the relationship of marriage—absolute and strict gender equality was required. Two (or more) men or two (or more) women could not form a marriage; only one man and one woman could.

66. For centuries, at least since the time of Augustine, it has been said that the three moral "goods" of marriage were *fides* (fidelity), procreation, and sacramental unity. Charles J. Reid, Jr., *The Augustinian Goods of Marriage: The Disappearing Cornerstone of the American Law of Marriage,* 18 BYU J. Pub. L. 449 (2004); Charles J. Reid, Jr., *Toward An Understanding of Medieval Universal Human Rights: The Marital Rights of Non-Christians in Early Scholastic and Canonistic Writing,* 3 Ave Maria L. Rev. 95, 97 (2005).

67. *See* Lynn D. Wardle, *Parental Infidelity and the "No-Harm" Rule in Custody Litigation,* 52 Cath. U. L. Rev. 81 (2002).

68. John Adams, 4 Diary and Autobiography of John Adams 123 (L.H. Butterfield, et al. eds. 1962).

69. *See* John Locke, Second Treatise of Government, Chapters VII & VIII (1689) (describing parental power and how the political or civil state arose out of family relations); Aristotle, *Nicomachean Ethics,* VII, 1155a, 5 (stating that "without friends no one would choose to live, though he have all other goods"); Plato, *Republic*: Book II 369b-372d (stating: "I think a city comes to be because none of us is self-sufficient, but we need many things").

70. *See generally* Lynn D. Wardle, *The Bonds of Matrimony and the Bonds of Democracy,* 32 Hofstra L. Rev. 349 (2003); Lynn D. Wardle, *The Proposed Federal Marriage Amendment and the Risks to Federalism in Family Law,* 2 Univ. St. Thomas L.J. 137 (2004).

71. Blackstone's Commentaries on the Laws of England *442-445 (consequences and duties of marriage at common law).

72. Myers, supra note 8, at 48.

73. *See generally* Lynn D. Wardle, *All You Need Is Love?* 14 So. Cal. Rev. L. & Wo.'s Studs. 51 (2004).

74. Durant, *supra* note ___, at 35-36.

75. "The connection between marriage and sexual activity has been consistently recognized by state courts in determining whether certain marriages are against that state's public policy." *See generally* Joseph W. Hovermill, *A Conflict of Laws and Morals: The Choice of Law Implications of Hawaii's Recognition of Same-Sex Marriages*, 53 Md. L.Rev. 450, 472, n.153 (1994). "Even assuming that the constitutional protection of the right to marry may not rest upon procreation or regulation of sexual conduct, the general connection between marital status and sexual activity is difficult to separate. *Id.* at 472.

76. Note, *Inbred, supra* note 3, at 2471-72.

77. *See generally* Lynn D. Wardle, *Essay, "Multiply and Replenish": Considering Same-Sex Marriage in Light of State Interests in Marital Procreation*, 771, 778-86 (2001).

78. 1 Contemporary Family Law, at § 2:47 (L. Wardle et al, eds. 1988) (giving cites). *See also* Jill Elaine Hasday, *The Canon of Family Law*, 57 Stanford L. Rev. 825, 864 n. 139 (2004).

79. *See, e.g.*, Jett v. Jett, 221 A.2d 925 (D.C. App. 1966); Bernstein v. Bernstein, 15 Conn. Supp. 239, 201 A.2d 660 (1964); Handley v. Handley, 179 Cal. App. 2d 742, 3 Cal. Rptr. 910 (1962); Hyslop v. Hyslop, 242 Ala. 223, 2 So.2d 443 (1941); *see also* Faustin v. Lewis, 85 N.J. 507, 427 A.2d 1105 (1981). *See generally* Contemporary Family Laws §2:24.

80. *See* Blackstone's Commentaries on the Laws of England *434; 1 Joel Bishop, Bishop's Commentaries onthe Laws of Marriage and Divorce 295 (6th ed. 1881); Stephen Cretney, Principles of Family Law 31, 49 (1979).

81. 1 Contemporary Family Law, *supra* note 78, at § 2:46.

82. *See Dean v. District of Columbia, No. 90-13892 (D.C. Super. Ct. Dec. 30, 1991) (order granting summary judgment), reconsideration granted,* 1992 WL 685364 (D.C. Super. Ct. June 2, 1992), aff'd on other grounds, 653 A.2d 307 (D.C. 1995) (the term "intercourse" could not include oral or anal sex, because the legislature would not have intended that a couple could consummate a marriage by committing the crime of sodomy).

83. Poe v. Ullman, 367 U.S. 497, 553 (1961) (Harlan, J., dissenting) ("Adultery, homosexuality and the like are sexual intimacies which the State forbids . . . but the intimacy of husband and wife is necessarily an essential and accepted feature of the institution of marriage, an institution which the State not only must allow, but which always and in every age it has fostered and protected.").

84. Maria Xiridou, Ronald Geskus, et al., *The contribution of steady and casual partnerships to incidence of HIV infection among homosexual men in Amsterdam*, 17 (7) AIDS 1029 (2 May 2003), available at http://www.aidsonline.com/pt/re/aids/pdfhandler. 00020302003050200012.pdf;jsessionid=FrMF7bsJNJx6Znq8QlqzTFXPQSShnmnLTy 4TG4pmbXlySXPTnyz9!1057067369!-949856144!8091!-1(seen February 20, 2007).

85. *Id.*

86. Martin S. Bell & Alan P. Weinberg, Homosexualities: A Study of Diversity Among Men and Women 308-09 (1978).

87. Paul Van de Ven, et al., *A Comparative Demographic and Sexual Profile of Older Homosexually Active Men,* 34 Journal of Sex Research 354 (1997).

88. David P. McWhirter,& Andrew M. Mattison, *The Male Couple* 252 (1984).

89. Traditional Values Coalition, Special Report, Statistics on the Homosexual Lifestyle, available at http://www.traditionalvalues.org/pdf_files/statistics_on_homosexual_

lifestyle.pdf#search=%22statistics%20comparing%20homosexual%20and%20   hetero-
sexual%20couples%22 (Seen September 14, 2006) (herein "TVC Statistics"). McWhirter
and Mattison's work is summarized in the professional volume, *Textbook of Homosexuality and Mental Health*, ed. Robert P. Cabaj and Terry S. Stein; American Psychiatric
Press, 1996.) *Id.*

90. Marshall Kirk & Hunter Madsen, *After the Ball* 330 (1989). Likewise, Andrew
Sullivan contrasts male-female marriages with same sex relationships and explains,
"there is more likely to be a greater understanding of the need for extramarital outlets
between two men than between a man and a woman." Andrew Sullivan, *Virtually Normal*
202 (1996).

91. U.S. Dep't of Health & Human Services, Public Health Service, Centers for Disease Control and Prevention, HIV/AIDS Surveillance Report, Vol. 5, No. 2 (July 1993) at
14, Table 12 (Fifty-three percent of all AIDS cases reported through June of 1993
(166,023 cases) involved the single mode of exposure of men who have sex with men.

92. U.S. Dep't of Health & Human Services, Public Health Service, Centers for Disease Control and Prevention, HIV/AIDS Surveillance Report, Vol. 5, No. 2 (July 1993) at
14, Table 12.

93. Scott D. Holmberg, *The Estimated Prevalence and Incidence of HIV in 96 Large
US Metropolitan Areas*, 86 Am. J. Pub. Health 642, 644 Table 1 (May 1996) available
online   at   http://www.pubmedcentral.nih.gov/picrender.fcgi?artid=1380471&   blob-
type=pdf (summary of HIV seroprevalence data from sexually transmitted disease clinics
by metropolitan area, exposure category, and sex, 1988-1990).

94. "The estimated level of [HIV] infection among homosexual men ranges from
20% in a Pittsburgh study to 50% in a San Francisco study." Thomas E. Schmidt, Straight
& Narrow 27 (1995) (citing many studies).

95. *Id.* at 21; *see also id.*, n.92).

96. Anne Tompalo & H. Hunter Handsfield, Chapter 1, *Overview of Sexually
Transmitted Diseases in Homosexual Men*, in AIDS and Infections of Homosexual Men,
3 (Pearl Ma and Donald Armstrong eds., 2d ed. 1989).

97. Judith Stacey, The Families of Man: Gay Male Intimacy and Kinship in a Global
Metropolis (2005).

98. *Judith Stacey, Fellow Families? Genre of A Gay Male Intimacy and Kinship in a
Global Metropolis, at __, available at http://www.leeds.ac.uk/CAVA/papers/intseminar
3stacey.htm (seen September 12, 2006) (herein "Stacey, Fellow Families").*

99. *Id.*

100. *Id.*

101. Sondra E. Solomon, et.al., *Money, Housework, Sex, and Conflict: Same-Sex
Couples in Civil Unions, Those Not in Civil Unions, and Heterosexual Married Siblings,*
52 Sex Roles 561, 566-69 (2005).

102. Adrian Blow & Kelley Harnett, *Infidelity in Committed Relationships II: A
Substantive Review*, 31 J. Marital & Fam. Therapy 217 (2005).

103. Solomon, supra note 103.

104. Xiridou, *supra* note 84, at Table 1.

105. Gunnar Andersson, Turid Noack, Ane Sierstad & Harald Weedon-Fekjaer, *The
Demographics of Same-Sex Marriages in Norway and Sweden,* 43 Demography 79
(2006), available at http://muse.jhu.edu/journals/demography/v043/43.1andersson.html
#tab02.

106. *Id.* at 85. On the other hand, the percentage of same-sex partnerships involving
a partner from another country (43-45% of gay men partnerhips) involved a partner from
a foreign country, a factor likely to be associated with less harmony in the marriage.

107. *Id.* at 87-88.

108. *Id.* at 89-90.

109. Maggie Gallagher & Joshua K. Baker, *Same-Sex Unions and Divorce Risk: Data from Sweden*, iMAPP Policy Brief, May 3, 2004 copy in author's possession.

110. *Id.*

111. Timothy J. Dailey, Comparing Lifestyles of Homosexual Couples to Married Couples, Family Research Council, available at available at http://www.frc.org/get.cfm?i =IS04C02 (seen September 14, 2006).

112. Edward O. Laumann, Stephen Ellison, Jenna Mahay & Anthony Paik, The Sexual Organization of the City 16 (2005).

113. Solomon, *supra* note 103, at 566.

114. *Id.*

115. *Id.* at 59.

116. The percentage of infidelity was higher for married women, but factoring in the longer life of those relationships probably would eliminate that, and the authors said there was no significant difference between lesbians and married heterosexual women in infidelity.

117. *Id.* At 566, 69.

118. Stewart, *supra*, note 20, at 10.

119. *See, e.g.,* Andrew Sullivan, Virtually Normal 111 (1996) (marriage is a unique institution that will strengthen love and commitment of gay couples; civil unions as pseudo marriage are detrimental to both heterosexual and homosexual couples); Jonathan Rauch, Gay Marriage: Why It Is Good For Gays Good for Straights, and Good for America 85 (2004) (without marriage protection, the gay relationship stands that much less likely to be a success).

120. *See* Wardle, supra note 1, at 310.

121. *See* Diamond, *The rule of Law Versus the Order of Custom,* 38 Soc. RESEARCH 42 (19710; Schwartz, *Moral Order and Society of Law" Trends, Problems, and Prospects,* 4 ANN. REV. SOC. 577 (1978).

122. Fuller, *Positivism and Fidelity to Law—A Reply to Professor Hart,* 71 HARV. L. REV. 630 (1958); Hart, *Positivism an dthe Separation of Law and Morals,* 71 HARV. L. REV. 593 (1958); *See also* K. LLEWELLYN, THE BRAMBLE BUSH 107-18 (1960).

123. *See* Schwartz, *supra* note 132, at 589.

124. *See* generally Lynn D. Wardle, *The Gap Between Law and Moral Order: An Examination of the Legitimacy of the Supreme Court Abortion Decisions,* 1980 B.Y.U. L. Rev. 811, 811-13.

125 . Gay leaders demonized opponents of same-sex marriage as hateful bigots and homophobes, completely ignoring the religious and social motivations behind the opposition. The reality is that marriage as the union of one man and one woman is our most basic social institution and deeply rooted in our culture.

Even though during the last few thousand years marriage has had some variations that departed from strict monogamy, same-sex combinations have never been one of them. Gay marriage represents such a fundamental change that few can grasp it, let alone support it.

Jeff Gannon, *Gay marriage is a lost cause*, Wash. Blade, Sep. 1, 2006, at __.

126. *See* PollingReport.com (available at http://www.pollingreport.com/civil.htm) (conglomeration of numerous same-sex issue polls conducted within the past two years by various outlets).

127. Lynn D. Wardle & Lincoln C Oliphant, *In Praise of Loving,* 51 How. L. J. 117, 162-64 (2007).

128. As Alexander Pope wrote centuries ago:
Vice is a monster of so frightful mein
As to be hated needs just to be seen.
But seen too oft, familiar with its face,
First we endure, then pity, then embrace.
Alexander Pope, *An Essay on Man,* Epistle II, part V, available at http://www.theotherpages.org/poems/pope-e2.html (seen February 20, 2007).

129. *See generally* Robert M. Cover, *The Folktales of Justice: Tales of Jurisdiction,* 14 Cap. U. L. Rev. 179, 181 (1985) ("The struggle over what is "law" is . . . a struggle over which social patterns can plausibly be coated with a veneer which changes the very nature of that which it covers up. There is not automatic legitimation of an institution by calling it or what it produces 'law,' but the label is a move, the staking out of a position in the complex social game of legitimation."). *See also* Susan P. Koniak, *When the Hurlyburly's Done: The Bar's Struggle with the SEC,* 103 Colum. L. Rev. 1236, 1245 (2003), citing Cover, *supra,* at 179-180 ("[T]he word 'science,' . . . like the word 'law,' is a powerful normative commodity. . . . To label something law or not is at least as normatively charged a naming as proclaiming something science or not.").

130Maggie Gallagher, *(How) Will Gay Marriage Weaken Marriage As A Social Institution: A Reply to Andrew Koppelman,* 2 U. St. Thomas L. J. 33, 69 (2004).

131. David D. Haddock & Daniel D. Polsby, *Family As A Rational Classification,* 74 Wash. U. L. Q. 15 (1996) at 17 citing Lee E. Teitelbaum, *Family History and Family Law,* 1985 Wis.L.Rev. 1135, 1138-44. *See generally* Nancy Cott, Public Vows *Passim* (2002).

132. Helen M. Alvare, *The Turn Toward the Self in the Law of Marriage & Family: Same-Sex Marriage & Its Predecessors,* 16 Stan. L. & Pol'y Rev. 135 (2005).

133. Brian Bix, *Philosophy, Morality, and Parental Priority,* 40 Fam. L. Q. 7, 11 (2006). Moral philosophy is still grappling with the most basic issues, trying to justify conclusions that are entirely taken for granted in policy arguments. . . . [Family law] topics are not frequently discussed within moral philosophy, and what discussion there has been has yielded little consensus."

134. Eekelaar & Maclean, *supra* note 25, at 511: Their study, albeit of very small size and of limited quantitative significance, suggested that some nonmarital relationship saw similar kinds of moral development and fostered similar moral "goods" in the parties' relationship as marriages.

135. *Id.* Eekelaar and Maclean note: "It appears to be true that, statistically, married relationships last longer than unmarried ones. But is also true that, at times when marriage was more widespread than it is now, the marriages of the young, the poor, and the remarried were at much higher risk of breaking up . . . [and] those risk categories may not be being substantially filled by unmarried cohabitants . . . ." *Id.*

136. Bix, *supra* note 133 at 12.

137. Wyatt v. United States, 362 U.S. 525, 531 (1960) ("Morally speaking, this profanation of the marriage relationship adds an element of the utmost depravity to the ugly business . . . .") (referring to marriage of prostitute to the man being prosecuted under the Mann Act for transporting her interstate for the purpose of prostitution; the Court rejected and noted an exception to the common law rule allowing a married party to exclude the adverse testimony of his or her spouse).

CHAPTER 12

THE CASE FOR TREATING SAME-SEX MARRIAGE AS A HUMAN RIGHT AND THE HARM OF DENYING HUMAN DIGNITY[*]

Vincent J. Samar[**]
Chicago-Kent College of Law

Efforts to exclude same-sex couples from marriage, as exhibited in a recent New York Court of Appeals decision, may undermine the value of marriage for everyone. Since the institution of marriage provides a forum for some of the most private and intimate of human actions to occur, perhaps it is not surprising that the private side of the institution should provide the constitutive elements for why the right to marry is a human right. This is the side of the institution of marriage on which I will focus. The perspective I will adopt is from morality and law, but not specifically religion. My argument will defend same-sex marriage as a human right not for any group, but for distinctive individuals.

This chapter will have four principle parts. Part I explains why the right to marry, including same-sex marriage, should be seen as a human right. Part II then explains why the recent New York Court of Appeals case that limits marriage to only its external attributes demeans human dignity. Next, Part III shows how human rights and, in particular, human dignity, are served by focusing on the internal benefits of marriage as a practice. Part IV concludes that denying recognition of a legal right to same-sex marriage is denying a human right.

I. Why the Right to Marry, Including Same-Sex Marriage, Is a Human Right

By a "human right," I mean to reference a right under universal morality that would be applicable everywhere regardless of whether or not it is locally recognized. More specifically, human rights are the rights that all humans have by virtue of being actual, prospective purposive agents.[1] Here agency, in the sense of human voluntariness and purposiveness, plays a foundational role, since all moral theories must presuppose humans have these capacities in order to make prescriptive claims.[2] Characteristically, these rights have been recognized in more specific detail by such documents as the United Nations' Universal Declaration of Human Rights, which recognizes a right to privacy, though not specifically a right to marry.[3]

In American constitutional law, most of what has been said positively on the subject of same-sex marriage starts with marriage being recognized as a fundamental right under the Due Process Clause of the Fourteenth Amendment, as in *Loving v. Virginia*,[4] and then proceeds to challenge any limitation of legal marriage to only opposite-sex couples as a denial of equal protection in furtherance of the dominant heterosexual culture.[5] The U.S. Supreme Court followed this argument in *Loving* to strike down a Virginia statute that limited marriage of white people to only members of their own race as a denial of equal protection because it was designed to foster white supremacy.[6]

Alternatively, on the negative side, it has been argued that marriage is by definition a relationship requiring one man and one woman, and the only equal protection claim that can be raised is whether everyone has the same right to enter into such a marriage so conceived.[7] I want to claim that the issue of marriage doesn't break down quite so simply.[8] Our conception of marriage, especially in regard to the latter view, is too much image-directed and too little criteria-directed. By "image-directed" I mean the view of marriage that is associated more with churches and weddings, gowns and tuxedos, and religious rituals, versus the view of divorce that is associated with courtroom drama and legal debate.[9] In furtherance of my argument, I want to claim that a right to same-sex marriage is difficult for many in our society to recognize because most people conceive of marriage as it appears in popular culture rather than try to understand what legal marriage really is.

So I am not misconstrued on this point: I am not going to argue that marriage has any special metaphysical status, either of a natural kind or as a component to some essentialist claim about human nature.[10] Although I do not hold the view that everything is a social construction, surely marriage is a social construction—of law, culture, and religion.[11] Of course, that does not mean that people do not have a stake in what does or does not constitute marriage. Being a cultural creation does not undermine the investments people have with the particular forms the convention has evolved to take.[12] And although I do not believe that all marriages need to comport to one style—all religiously blessed or all having to be sexually closed relationships—I do believe that there are certain elements forming the concept of marriage that open the door to a more central, normative conception of what marriage is all about.[13] The elements I have in mind form the institution of marriage as a set of socially recognized practices that operate both to define and benefit the participants, and others who are in various ways associated with the participants. While there have been a number of justifications for legal marriage, including preservation of property, rearing of children, and providing a first building block for wider social structures of community, all of these justifications in effect assign to the parties a socially approved dignity to manage their own affairs as a collective entity.[14] Some examples I have in mind are not disinheriting one's spouse, being free of legal restraints on voluntary sex acts performed between partners in private, and participant demands against the society at large for recognition of their unit in the name of law and etiquette.[15]

This dignity suggests the demarcation of a unique class of permissible behaviors that society is excluded from observing too closely, with exceptions for domestic violence and overt exploitation.[16] It also suggests that the core of the legal marriage concept must involve a set of interrelational prerogatives in which the participants can see themselves as advancing their own individual sense of self-worth by setting the relationship first and their more individual interests second.[17] In this sense, marriage can be seen as a dignity-producing institution, just as chess confers a sense of self-esteem to the players of the game, only in a much more substantial way, provided all participants adopt certain rules of behavior, that is, follow the rules of the game.[18] I do not play chess when I merely move my rook, but only when I move my rook in a certain way at my turn in the game.[19] Without rules to define the game, I would not achieve the self-esteem of being able to play chess or the dignity of a chess player. Without marriage, I do not obtain the public respect of being centrally involved in another person's life and well-being, in the sense of being in a publicly recognized relationship in which both participants are committed to each other's mutual, long-term emotional, physical, economic, and social welfare.[20] And so, the question for marriage becomes: What are the necessary conditions for defining a marriage and would these same criteria define a same-sex marriage?

Here history and tradition can be a help, but only if properly understood.[21] Roman marriages were primarily a means to protect property.[22] Such marriages did not serve any internal interest of the parties as a flourishing unit (they did not constitute a "practice" in Alasdair MacIntyre's sense of the term),[23] but only the more external interests of the parties, which always had to be seen as a game of winners and losers. In contrast, in early Jewish marriages and later Christian marriages, the emphasis was on enhancing the collective well-being of the participants in the relationship, and not on maximizing their individual self-interests.[24] In the case of Christian marriages in particular, one emphasis was bringing new life into the world.[25] It is arguable that not all conceptions of what were essentially seen as Christian marriages—at least in the early church—were focused on procreation, however.[26] This doesn't mean that self-interest played no role for these alternative conceptions, but whatever its role at the beginning of a marriage, it was quickly pushed aside for the mutual benefit that the couple as a whole might achieve from the marriage.[27] And so marriage understood in this pre-modern light can be seen as a practice for supporting a mutually thriving human dignity that ranges over the deepest levels of human intimacy and emotion.

Contrary to what most scholars put forth as the bases for marriage—i.e. relational permanency, financial stability, or child-rearing—I want to claim that these are more the external attributes of marriage.[28] I do not claim that these are unimportant attributes, but rather that, like privacy of information and places, they support a deeper internal structure of private relationships, despite the fact that they may be the first things to come to mind when society attempts to define marriage beyond its visual trappings.[29] The more internal structure or "real" stuff of the marriage relationship is its connection to individual human dignity via the opportunity it provides its participants to achieve levels of human self-fulfillment that are wholly unique and otherwise unobtainable.[30] Going back to my chess example, I do not have the freedom to play, or much opportunity to develop skill at the game of chess, if I do not have an opponent willing to operate by the same rules of the game that I operate by.[31] That being said, I want to focus on marriage not as a vehicle to an external group-centered value, where the group in this case is primarily the two spouses cooperating in some form of mutually satisfying activity, or even the betterment of some wider community. Instead, I want to suggest that marriage does something very positive for the participants individually who seek it out, something that, absent a marriage, they cannot do very well and in some instances cannot do at all.[32] I have in mind that while a dedicated partner deprived of marriage can provide for her other half's future well-being through innovative use of contracts, wills and trusts, she cannot replace the benefits marriage provides in respect to social security benefits, the right to bring a wrongful death action, and being freed from summons to testify against one's partner, to name a few examples. Such examples show that individuals cannot very well imitate marriage without marriage itself. Even the resourceful individual is cut off in his "ability to communicate his commitment and goal to constitute himself in a certain way, expressive of a certain (and widely shared) view of the good life, including obligations and opportunities."[33] That is why marriage, in my view, should be understood as a human right.

To say that human rights represent a set of norms that arise from one's own point of view as human, I am asserting what I believe is an internal value that must be inter-subjectively affirmed not on its descriptive content of how the possibility of human actions give rise to legitimate rights-claims, but on its normative, self-reflective content that makes these rights-claims valuable as such.[34] In other words, one might say externally that, because human actions presuppose the generic features of voluntariness and purposiveness, no human being can deny equal rights to freedom and well-being to any other human being without contradicting himself.[35] This would be particularly true when the freedom at stake does not interfere with any other person's right or, if it does, only by some assumption of facts or social conventions that would not justify the freedom being overridden.[36] The argument should also be viewed as providing an external, logical justification for believing all humans have certain rights.[37]

What translates this outside justification specifically to an internal evaluation by the agent of his own worth is the awareness that the rights being so-valued come about only because the agent values his own actions simply because they are his actions.[38] Put another way, the dignity she assigns to her own creative capacity to achieve her aspirations is affirmed when the agent recognizes that it is that very capacity, including its reliance on the canons of deductive and inductive logic that she intuits, that makes such rights-claims possible.[39] In this sense, the agent's pro-attitude towards those actions that reflect her own self-interest becomes a sense of self-respect for her ability as a creative creature to engineer actions which systematically advance the interests of all other humans as well.[40] The latter arises only because the possibility of achieving her self-interest, when logically pruned, is a human interest.[41] The agent thus affirms those goods that benefit humans as such, not because some outside moral principle sets them, but because, from her own understanding of what it is to be human, those goods are constitutive of that understanding.[42]

In saying this, I do not suggest that all human actions need necessarily form a consistent and mutually beneficial practice. The condition of these actions being human and engendering their appeal to self-respect is that they can be undertaken without violating any other human being's rights. In this sense, the attribution of dignity that the agent assigns to her own actions is necessarily supervenient on her being a voluntary, purposive human agent.[43] I use the word "necessarily" here to indicate that the connection between the agent's purpose for acting, her assignment of worth to that purpose, and her assignment of dignity and preservation to herself and all other purposive agents, is logical and not contingent.[44] Still, such actions may serve a more narrow purpose of advancing, without harm to anyone else, more particular idiosyncratic interests of some narrowly defined group—such as doctors, lawyers, teachers, etc.—or even just the individual herself.[45] Especially, or in those situations where a person's actions advance the collective interests of some group without harming others, they may become part of a mutually beneficial practice such as medicine, law, or education, to name just a few.[46] Still, even at this narrower construal of the worth afforded some actions, the freedom and well-being to perform the acts can be seen to advance the interests of all other persons by providing others a precedent for seeking their own self-fulfillment *qua* human.[47]

To say that marriage allows the individual to set the end of his own personhood into the mind and the heart of the other in a singular way, is to suggest that marriage gives rise to a "corporate person" whose interests are not merely the summation of the interests of the parties involved. The interests of the couple *qua* couple are not only the interests of the group constituted by the duo in any given marriage, but also the interests of the group constituted by those committed to a marriage both as a publicly recognized and celebrated institution.[48] Let me explain more fully what I mean. Because part of what I want to say here involves the usual legal bundle of rights and obligations we assign to marriage, it is only natural to focus on these rights and privileges as the primary interests of the parties to the marriage.[49] But in the more fundamental sense, the status of marriage for the individual participants is itself a new creation.[50] After marriage, the couple assumes a new ontological identity, in which the participants see themselves as "us" rather than "me," just as they see their property as "ours" rather than "mine."[51] I do not suggest the creation of just another legal fiction, for the most important feature of marriage is not that the law should treat the parties and their property as a collective, though certainly it should.[52] The most salient feature is that the parties actually come to see themselves as a collective unit operating for their mutual benefit, and also as part of a still larger set of similarly situated persons.[53] This is why, to quote the old song, "[b]reaking up is hard to do."[54] For the language we adopt as a corporate legal couple is a language of the plural; the interests at stake are the couple's interests which are often balanced in various ways to achieve different levels of satisfaction at different times depending on the emotional importance each party attaches to the interests. This is why it is hard—after one has gotten used to seeing oneself as part of a couple—to convert back to a language of self, in which the only inter-est to be primarily concerned with, at least once one's general obligations to society and others are taken into account, is self-interest.[55]

But notice nothing in what I have said has evoked as its starting point the external attributes of permanency, financial stability, or child rearing that society teaches should be sought from marriage.[56] Instead, I have focused solely on the individual self-fulfillment that attends being part of a corporate entity that shares both intimacy and identity. In this sense, society's teaching focus on what *appears* that humans will externally want if given the opportunity, and not what they *really* want internally because they truly understand their own self-interest though the former presupposes the latter. This, more than anything else, is why marriage is important, why it's a human right and not just a utilitarian cost/benefit solution to a certain set of collective, external problems, and further, why same-sex marriage is fundamentally no different from opposite-sex mar-riage. Indeed, it is for just the reason that a unique kind of human self-fulfillment can be achieved by marriage that the claimed right of same-sex couples to marry can be justified as a fundamental human right. Put another way, the right to marry is a unique human right fulfilling a significant route to human self-fulfillment by allowing the parties to the marriage to achieve an identity that significantly adds to their human dignity. Thus, not to recognize this right, even if just in the same-sex context, is to deny an important avenue of human self-fulfillment that is a foundation of human rights in general. This denial of human rights has happened in several recent state court decisions, one of which I will turn to now.[57]

II.   Why Limiting Marriage Only to Its External Attributes De-means Human Dignity

The recent majority decision by New York's high court in *Hernandez v. Robles*[58] illustrates why an external perspective on a right to marriage is de-meaning of human dignity. In that case, petitioners brought suit against the ad-ministrator of the New York City Marriage License Bureau claiming that the law authorizing the clerk to issue marriage licenses either permitted issuance of such licenses to same-sex couples or was unconstitutional as a violation of the due process and equal protection clauses of the New York Constitution.[59]

Like the federal Constitution, New York's constitutional law recognizes marriage, at least between opposite-sex couples, as a fundamental right.[60] In-deed, the New York high court noted that "[i]n general, we have used the same analytical framework as the [U.S.] Supreme Court in considering due process cases, though our analysis may lead to different results."[61] Furthermore, "we have held that our [state] Equal Protection Clause 'is no broader in coverage than the Federal provision.' "[62] In order to first say same-sex marriage was not contemplated by the statute governing issuances of marriage licenses, the court cited provisions in the statute using the terms "husband and wife," " 'the groom' and 'the bride.' "[63]

The court then began its state constitutional analysis noting that for a fundamental right to be founded on the basis of due process, it must have been part of a longstanding tradition and history of the country.[64] However, in order to avoid the challenge that its interpretation of the state's due process clause might be too narrow when focused on just same-sex marriage as opposed to marriage in general, the court had to make an incredible policy argument.[65] The court held that because unexpected pregnancies can result in opposite-sex relationships, the legislature could have found that "unstable relationships between people of the opposite sex present a greater danger that children will be born into or grow up in unstable homes than is the case with same-sex couples . . . ."[66] The court was unable to merely say that marriage was necessary to secure procreation or various protections of children born to opposite-sex couples because, as the court even admitted, many same-sex couples in New York are able to raise children legally either by artificial insemination or adoption.[67] As a result, the court had to suggest, for purposes of New York constitutional law, that the legislature could view opposite-sex couples as too emotionally unstable to handle intimate relationships without the government affording the opposite-sex couple a right to marry, especially when children might be involved.[68]

The New York high court next considered the plaintiffs' equal protection claim. Since the court had already determined that same-sex marriage was not a due process right, this meant that the state denying the right to same-sex couples would not be reviewed with strict scrutiny under an equal protection analysis unless the regulated group itself was a protected class warranting either strict or intermediate scrutiny.[69] The plaintiffs had not argued that strict scrutiny should apply in an equal protection argument, since the plaintiffs did not allege the traditionally protected classifications of race, color, ethnicity, or national origin or offer any new argument for treating same-sex couples as a similarly situated class warranting strict scrutiny protection.[70] And since the court had already rejected the plaintiffs' claim that same-sex marriage was a fundamental right, the only question the court faced was whether intermediate scrutiny applied, either because the marriage statute discriminated based on gender or because sexual orientation itself deserved heightened scrutiny.[71]

Race, color, ethnicity, and national origin are reviewed under a strict scrutiny standard under both federal and New York state constitutional law because such classifications are considered suspect, resulting from historical discrimination and stereotyping based on an immutable or hard-to-remove trait that the group did not have the political power to overcome.[72] Gender and illegitimacy are afforded intermediate scrutiny because while not all forms of discrimination against these groups was thought to be improper, much of the discrimination these groups have suffered was based on stereotyping and prejudice.[73] Since obviously neither race, color, ethnicity, nor religion (also deserving strict scrutiny)[74] were issues in the present case, the court was free to consider the question of gender at the intermediate level of scrutiny once it had determined a fundamental right was not involved.

The *Hernandez* court noted that the marriage statute treated men and women alike in that neither could marry a person of the same sex and that the distinction was not a kind of "sham equality" as was the distinction in *Loving v. Virginia*,[75] where the U.S. Supreme Court struck down miscegenation statutes because the statutes were " 'designed to maintain White Supremacy.' "[76] As for the question of whether sexual orientation itself warranted heightened scrutiny after the New York court's earlier decision in *Under 21 v. City of New York*[77]—where the level of scrutiny question was left open—the court stated: "We resolve this question in this case on the basis of the [U.S.] Supreme Court's observation that no more than rational basis scrutiny is generally appropriate 'where individuals in the group affected by a law have distinguishing characteristics relevant to interests the State has the authority to implement.' "[78] The *Hernandez* court held that the legislature could distinguish between opposite-sex and same-sex couples on the basis of protecting children.[79] In effect, because the court held that same-sex couples were not members of a protected class invoking strict or intermediate scrutiny, the contested government action need only meet rational basis review, a decidedly low hurdle.[80] Consequently, the court only considered whether the statute was rationally related to a legitimate governmental purpose. In effect, this meant that the statute would be upheld, at least so long as the statute was not supported by mere animus against a specific group.

The question of animus arises because in *Romer v. Evans*, the U.S. Supreme Court held that Colorado's constitutional amendment prohibiting the state legislature and its municipalities from granting any protections against discrimination to gays and lesbians was based on mere animus towards the group and was therefore not a legitimate governmental interest.[81] The U.S. Supreme Court implied that, because the Colorado amendment was so overbroad, it constituted on its face a *per se* violation of equal protection.[82] Although the *Hernandez* majority never cited *Romer*, the majority of New York's high court probably had *Romer* in mind when it took the rather odd approach of justifying the legislature's limitation of marriage to only opposite-sex couples to correct an infirmity that supposedly only opposite-sex couples might suffer: an inability to handle the consequences of their intimate relationships.[83]

This is an odd approach because it demeans opposite-sex couples while at the same time affirming their exclusive right to marry. Yet, it bespeaks the extremes to which a court will go to maintain what is in reality an animus by some in society toward lesbian and gay people and their relationships. Moreover, what is particularly insidious about the *Hernandez* decision is its limited account of the equal interests in stability and support that children of same-sex couples have in comparison to their opposite-sex couple counterparts, not to mention the interests of the parties themselves in seeking to marry.[84] The latter is illustrated by the court's disjunctive language of the interests surveyed between opposite-sex and same-sex relationships. The interests of both types of relationships could more easily have been compared along dimensions of dignity and individual commitment to undertake obligations, which constitute a family.

III.   How Human Rights and, in Particular, Human Dignity Are Served by Focusing on the Internal Benefits of Marriage as a Practice

Here I would begin by adopting Alasdair MacIntyre's definition of a practice:

> By a "practice" I am going to mean any coherent and complex form of socially established cooperative human activity through which goods internal to that form of activity are realised in the course of trying to achieve those standards of excellence which are appropriate to, and partially definitive of, that form of activity, with the result that human powers to achieve excellence, and human conceptions of the ends and goods involved, are systematically extended.[85]

Important to the definition is the distinction MacIntyre sets out between internal and external goods. The latter are identified as the property of some person such that the more one has, the less remains available for others.[86] The former are goods arising within the practice whose achievement through competition benefits "the whole community who participate in the practice."[87] Consequently, the internal goods of a practice can be seen as a set of values that enrich the group as a whole without loss or diminishment to anyone else.[88] The goods of marriage fit well within this definition of internal goods.

Marriage can be conceived as a practice in which the individual participants engage in an obviously complex form of socially cooperative human activities in which the aim is to make possible for both spouses opportunities to enhance for each other their non-conflicting mutual benefits and psychological well-being.[89] In this sense, marriage clearly adds to the participants' capacities as agents to participate in each others' mutual benefit. In some cases, this may mean joint cooperation towards achieving certain family, economic, or social goals such as deciding where to live, whether to raise children, what employment opportunities to pursue, how to aid each other's efforts to achieve further formal education, how to develop a family retirement plan, what means should be chosen to provide for family finances, how to oversee and maintain personal and real property, and what methods should be adopted for deciding matters involving ill health or death.[90] In other cases, and these may be related to the more overt economic and social advantages, marriage means providing for each other a sense that each is not alone in confronting life's joys and difficulties on an ongoing, at least semi-permanent, basis, and in knowing that whatever important choices the individual participants face, their importance to the other cannot be without significance.[91] The latter is even more significant when the actions directly or indirectly affect the other, or persons to whom both have obligations, such as the participants' children.[92] It may also matter in the sense that, because one party is so engaged by an action, the other's mere presence provides some solitude and peace of mind that at least everything else is okay.[93]

Obviously, these benefits of marriage are truly internal insofar as their possession by one couple does not limit their availability to others outside that marriage. That is why claims that allowing same-sex couples to marry will under-mine the meaning and significance of marriage for opposite-sex persons are lu-dicrous.[94] Does anybody really expect that their opposite-sex spouse will leave him or her if the same-sex couple down the street gets married? If that were to happen, it would not be because the same-sex couple got married, but because the opposite-sex couple had not obtained or was no longer obtaining enough of the internal rewards of marriage that made the practice worthwhile for them.[95]

In saying this, it is important to recognize a legitimate constraint on what benefits, mutual or not, a society needs to recognize. Just because a practice is claimed to benefit the parties concerned does not in itself mean the practice should be endorsed, especially when it is controversial whether the practice ben-efits the well-being of its participants.[96] For example, while the so-called "drug culture" may, at least when followed to excess, reflect a practice that adversely affects the well-being of both participants and non-participants, some contend that criminal sanctions against users of illegal drugs creates a still-greater harm to all concerned.[97] But what differentiated this cultural practice from other cul-tural practices that might justify imposing sanctions is that the so-called "inter-nal benefits" of the practice are masquerading over what are really just seduc-tions to suffer greater personal or social harms. In contrast, denial of the right to legally marry a same-sex partner, as opposed to its recognition, represents a de-triment to *all* those who would be served by marriage but—because of their sex-ual orientation, over which they have no choice, and law, for which society has choice—cannot participate.[98]

What principle then should govern the choice of which practices to recog-nize or at least tolerate and which not to recognize, when arguably many prac-tices might add to individual self-fulfillment? The answer must be connected to a full disclosure of all known potential risks and assurance that the human rights of others are not violated in the process.[99] In other words, from a human rights point-of-view, practices that add to human self-fulfillment are morally justified when they enhance the mutual dignity of all involved in the practice without denying dignity to those whose relation to the practice is not a matter of choice.[100] Hence, state-mandated racial segregation in public schools would not be justified, even if it were possible to provide equal facilities, because abundant social science research shows that such segregation produces a sense of inferior-ity in members of one race in their relation to the other.[101] A similar sense of inferiority may accompany restricting the marital relationship to only opposite-sex couples, for even the very limited purpose of protecting the children of op-posite-sex couples, if the society reads that validation as legitimating the rela-tionship itself. In that instance, the external justification is likely to bear nega-tively on the internal valuation of the participants themselves.[102]

In contrast, restrictions on arranged marriages or marriages between minors do not encounter the same difficulty. For minors, there is a serious question at what age minors have developed the capacity of choice with sufficient know-ledge of relevant circumstances to be able to enter the marriage relationship. Similarly, in the case of arranged marriages, the parties to the marriage and the beneficiaries of the internal rewards have no real choice. As freedom serves as the foundation of the right to marry, it follows that such marriages violate the human right to freedom that all people have *qua* human.[103] Moreover, arranged marriages may violate the human right to well-being, as emotional concerns may be too personal to be adequately provided in advance, even by well-meaning parents.

This then raises the troubling question of polygamous marriages. The issue is troubling not because the social standard is for two-person marriages, but because where polygamous marriages have been allowed, in the context of opposite-sex relationships, they usually support patriarchic relationships.[104] In instances where, on the one hand, only men are allowed more than one companion or where the economics of the relationship provide an artificial domination by one party (usually a male) over the other parties, the freedom component that must attend any truly universal system of human rights is not satisfied.[105] On the other hand, providing for marriage between same-sex couples in no way diminishes this universal human rights component because the choice to marry is still with the individual and no one is prevented from accessing the institution of marriage provided they meet the essential conditions of voluntariness and purposiveness that such freedom necessarily presupposes (such as the requirement that they not be too closely related by blood) to either negate voluntariness or affect the well-being of offspring.[106]

Still, some might challenge this argument on the ground that it could create too wide an assortment of rights for society to recognize on the basis of self-fulfillment even with the caveat that no one else's freedom or well-being is otherwise impaired. Even assuming that self-fulfillment might be limited to allow only those life aspirations that benefit one's capacity to discover truth, justice, and beauty, whether in one's own life or that of another, this would still create quite a few rights to be recognized. Yet, in most instances, this would not be a problem, since the rights being recognized are handled by the negative privacy right of non-interference with whatever may be the good life sought.[107]

What sets marriage in need of special attention is that the state has already upset the equilibrium established by negative privacy-right claims by recognizing only opposite-sex couples as eligible to marry.[108] This, for reasons already discussed *supra*, ignores the similar capacity fulfillment that same-sex couples would likely obtain if allowed to marry.[109] Thus, the burden on the state to actually do something, as opposed to contraception and abortion rights cases, where the burden is to not interfere, arises only because the state has chosen to arbitrarily afford the special marital status to certain individuals' private actions based on their gender.[110] Were the state to have left marriage unclassified and not attempted its regulation, this issue would not have resulted.[111] But as that is not the case, this argument must deal with the inequity that the state's action has created.

A corollary to the New York high court's decision is the question: Why can the state not just afford special recognition in the name of protecting children that heterosexual couples are able to produce naturally? Here it seems to me that the answer is twofold. First, recognition of marriage involves a much wider traffic of rights and privileges than would be the case if only the interests of children were concerned.[112] Second, no state requires couples to have a child or pledge to have a child in order to have a valid marriage, and many same-sex couples legitimately do have children through various means.[113]

Finally, one might ask why—even if same-sex marriage is part of the human right to marry—should that make it a legal, let alone a constitutional right? The answer is that the Constitution itself needs justification if it is to produce a duty of obedience that is not all together *sui generis* and seemingly without justification. Such a duty comes about only if the Constitution is itself morally justified as laying out a scheme of government that protects fundamental human rights properly understood.[114] To this extent at least, the courts are obliged to interpret the Constitution and the scheme of government it creates so as not to violate universal human rights and to maximize individual self-fulfillment whenever possible.[115] Extending the right to marry to same-sex couples is just one example of how courts can interpret the Constitution to satisfy its justificatory foundation to preserve and maximize individual human rights.

IV.   Conclusion

Our society is in the middle of a debate. But it is not a debate between two different views of reality, but rather between a fiction and a reality. On the one side is the view that marriage must be maintained as a relationship between one man and one woman. On the other side is the view that same-sex couples can marry. Mediating the former view is the idea that the external goods of marriage are necessary for stability and protection of offspring. But this is a fiction unless at the same time one maintains the erroneous assumption that opposite-sex couples are not capable of handling such matters on their own. On the other side of the debate is the argument that the internal goods of marriage are gender neutral but sufficiently self-fulfilling that, when practiced against a background in which individual freedom is protected, all participants to the relationship gain and no one outside the relationship loses. Given that the state already recognizes a right to marry for opposite-sex couples, if this is not a sufficient basis to extend that right to same-sex-couples, I do not know what would be. It is then almost a self-evident truth that same-sex couples ought to be afforded the same legal right to marry in the name of human dignity that is afforded to opposite-sex couples.

Notes

* Originally published as Vincent J. Samar, 68 Montana Law Review 335, *The Honorable James R. Browning Symposium: The Right to Privacy, Privacy and Same-Sex Marriage: The Case for Treating Same-Sex Marriage as a Human Right* (2007).
** The author wishes to thank Professors Martha Minow of the Harvard Law School and Mark Strasser of Capital University School of Law for their helpful comments and suggestions. This Article is dedicated to Mark Strasser and his partner George, living proof of a commitment based in love and dignity.
1. See Alan Gewirth, *Self-Fulfillment* 84 (Princeton U. Press 1998).

2. Moral theories are prescriptive in that they argue for conduct that might otherwise not occur. In this sense, moral theories differ from even such other theories as exist in economics and the social sciences, which take as their object behaviors that are likely to occur and can be predicted given the presence of certain antecedent conditions.

3. Universal Declaration of Human Rights, GA Res. 217(III) art. 12, UN GAOR, 3d Sess., Supp. No. 13, UN Doc. A/810 (1948). It should be noted, however, that the Declaration does not impose obligations by its own force under international law.

4. *Loving v. Va.*, 388 U.S. 1, 12 (1967).

5. *E.g. Hernandez v. Robles*, 855 N.E.2d 1, 22–34 (N.Y. 2006) (Kaye, C.J., dissenting).

6. *Loving*, 388 U.S. at 11–12.

7. *Cf. Goodridge v. Dept. of Pub. Health*, 798 N.E.2d 941, 972–73 (Mass. 2003) (Greaney, J., concurring).

8. Indeed, such arguments have been said to be circular. *E.g. Halpern v. Atty. Gen. of Can.*, 65 O.R. (3d) 161, 181 (Ct. App. Ont. 2003).

9. *E.g.* Bob Thompson, *A Modern Divorce: A Family's Unique Arrangement for Putting the Children First*, Newsday (N.Y.C.) B6 (Jan. 13, 2003) (depicting Americans' image of divorce as "a sharp-edged collage of uncontrolled rage and debilitating pain"). *Contra Good Morning America*'s annual spring wedding broadcast—with all the trappings—from Times Square in New York City; *Good Morning America*, "Happily Ever After: Love in Times Square" (ABC May 18, 2001) (TV broad.).

10. Whether sexual orientation is of a natural kind remains an unresolved scientific issue. *See e.g.* William N. Eskridge, Jr., *From Sexual Liberty to Civilized Commitment: The Case for Same-Sex Marriage* 178 (Simon & Schuster 1996).

11. Vincent J. Samar, *The Right to Privacy: Gays, Lesbians and the Constitution* 68 (Temple U. Press 1991) [hereinafter Samar, *The Right to Privacy*] (noting that the privacy interest in marriage is the individual's basic interest in freedom combined with the social convention of marriage as a means to satisfy that interest); *see also* John Boswell, *The Marriage of Likeness: Same-Sex Unions in Pre-Modern Europe* 28–34 (Fontana Press 1995) (discussing marriage in the Greco-Roman world).

12. The relative status of a group within a social system will affect its attractiveness to actual and prospective members. In this sense, every group operates its own internal prestige market, but each group is also part of a larger market. Although individuals constantly move among different groups and subsystems within society (which is the essence of social mobility), individuals also have strong incentives to remain within a particular subsystem and to insulate that system from external penetration. "One of the noneconomic benefits of remaining within one's neighborhood ethnic group or organization is precisely the avoidance of a free social market, that is, the avoidance of unremitting and full-scale competition in courtship and marriage, friendship groups, social clubs, and general esteem." Because prestige varies across social groups, individuals will be motivated to join higher status groups, but this option will be closed to many who do not have the ability to make such a transition.

Dennis Chong, *Values Versus Interests in the Explanation of Social Conflict*, 144 U. Pa. L. Rev. 2079, 2118–19 (1996) (footnote omitted) (quoting William J. Goode, *The Celebration of Heroes: Prestige as a Social Control Mechanism* 112 (U. Cal. Press 1978)).

13. In his dissent in *Bowers v. Hardwick*, Justice Blackmun wrote,

> The fact that individuals define themselves in a significant way through their intimate sexual relationships with others suggests, in a Nation as diverse as ours, that there may be many "right" ways of

conducting those relationships, and that much of the richness of a relationship will come from the freedom an individual has to *choose*
the form and nature of these intensely personal bonds.

Bowers v. Hardwick, 478 U.S. 186, 205 (1986) (Blackmun, J., dissenting), *over-ruled, Lawrence v. Tex.*, 539 U.S. 558, 578 (2003).

14. *See* Boswell, *supra* n. 11, at 28–34.

15. *Goodridge v. Dept. of Pub. Health*, 798 N.E.2d 941, 955–57 (Mass. 2003) (recit-ing a very long list of legal responsibilities and benefits that go along with marriage, es-pecially, but not exclusively, as these relate to the raising of children).

16. *See generally* Kristine Soulé, *The Prosecution's Choice: Admitting a Non-Testifying Domestic Violence Victim's Statements under* Crawford v. Washington, 12 Tex. Wes. L. Rev. 689 (2006).

17. In *Goodridge*, the court noted, "Civil marriage is at once a deeply personal commitment to another human being and a highly public celebration of the ideals of mu-tuality, companionship, intimacy, fidelity, and family." *Goodridge*, 798 N.E.2d at 954.

18. *See* Jon Edwards, *Chess Is Fun*, http://www.princeton.edu/~jedwards/cif/intro.html (accessed Feb. 9, 2007).

19. *Id.*

20. *See* Marsha Garrison, *Is Consent Necessary? An Evaluation of the Emerging Law of Cohabitant Obligation*, 52 UCLA L. Rev. 815, 896 (2005) (showing what distin-guishes marriage from cohabitation: "Married couples have chosen obligation; cohabi-tants have chosen independence.").

21. Here I follow a view of legal interpretation advanced by Ronald Dworkin that he calls "law as integrity."

> Law as integrity denies that statements of law are either the back-ward-looking factual reports of conventionalism or the forward-looking instrumental programs of legal pragmatism. It insists that le-gal claims are interpretative judgments and therefore combine back-ward- and forward-looking elements; they interpret contemporary le-gal practice seen as an unfolding political narrative. So law as integri-ty rejects as unhelpful the ancient question whether judges find or in-vent law; we understand legal reasoning, it suggests, only by seeing the sense in which they do both and neither.

Ronald Dworkin, *Law's Empire* 225 (Harvard U. Press 1986).

22. Boswell, *supra* n. 11, at 46.

23. Alasdair MacIntyre, *After Virtue: A Study in Moral Theory* 187, 190 (2d ed., U. Notre Dame Press 1987).

24. Boswell, *supra* n. 11, at 136 n. 119.

25. *Id.* at 112.

26. *Id.* at 115, 119–20.

27. *Id.* at 121.

28. *E.g.* Mark Strasser, *The Challenge of Same-Sex Marriage: Federalist Principles and Constitutional Protections* 3 (Praeger Publishers 1999) (discussing the interests of the state in respect to marriage).

29. Samar, *The Right to Privacy, supra* n. 11, at 75 (noting that while legal recogni-tion of a private act was last in time in the order of privacy recognitions that the U.S. Supreme Court had identified, it was prior, logically, to all the others, as it provided the foundation for why the others *ought* to be recognized).

30. *See* Gewirth, *supra* n. 1, at 143 ("[U]nlike baseball teams and other voluntary as-sociations, [marriage] is formed, as reflecting the partners' mutual love, for purposes of

deeply intimate union and extensive mutual concern and support for the participants, purposes that enhance the partners' general abilities of agency and thus contribute to their capacity-fulfillment.").

31. *See* Edwards, *supra* n. 18.

32. The Defense of Marriage Act, 28 U.S.C. § 1738C (2000). The Defense of Marriage Act (DOMA) provides,

> No State, territory, or possession of the United States, or Indian tribe, shall be required to give effect to any public act, record, or judicial proceeding of any other State, territory, possession, or tribe respecting a relationship between persons of the same sex that is treated as a marriage under the laws of such other State, territory, possession, or tribe, or a right or claim arising from such a relationship.

The statute was passed to allow the federal government and the states to opt out of having to recognize same-sex marriages under section 1 of Article IV of the U.S. Constitution, which requires that "Full Faith and Credit shall be given in each State to the public Acts, Records, and judicial Proceedings of every other State." The ground for the statute follows a further provision in section 1 that Congress may "prescribe the Manner in which such Acts, Records and Proceedings shall be proved, and the Effect thereof." U.S. Const. art. IV, § 1. Whether DOMA is constitutional under Article IV or the Fourteenth Amendment's Equal Protection Clause has not yet come before the U.S. Supreme Court for decision. It might be further noted that a number of states have passed "mini-DOMAs" to avoid a similar situation from arising under their state conflict of law rules. Carlos A. Ball, *The Backlash Thesis and Same-Sex Marriage: Learning from* Brown v. Board of Education *and Its Aftermath*, 14 Wm. & Mary Bill Rights J. 1493, 1524 (2006) (noting that thirty-seven states had passed mini-DOMAs and four had amended their state constitutions to prohibit same-sex marriage).

33. E-mail from Martha Minow, Professor at Harvard L. Sch. to Author (September 2006) (copy on file with Author).

34. Here I, like Gewirth, am following in the Kantian tradition that assigns to reason a command authority set by rational requirements of consistency for obtaining universal maxims of action. Gewirth, *supra* n. 1, at 226; *see also* Immanuel Kant, *Foundations of the Metaphysics of Morals and What Is Enlightenment?* §§ 1–2, 9–64 (Lewis White Beck trans., Bobbs-Merrill Co. 1959).

35. *See* Gewirth, *supra* n. 1, at 81–82.

36. *See* Samar, *The Right to Privacy*, *supra* n. 11, at 69, 107–08, 113.

37. Interestingly, though not based specifically on the justification just offered,

> the European Court of Human Rights considered a case . . . [where an] adult male resident in Northern Ireland alleged he was a practicing homosexual who desired to engage in consensual homosexual conduct. The laws of Northern Ireland forbade him that right. He alleged that he had been questioned, his home had been searched, and he feared criminal prosecution. The court held that the laws proscribing the conduct were invalid under the European Convention on Human Rights.

Lawrence v. Tex., 539 U.S. 558, 573 (2003) (citing *Dudgeon v. U.K.*, 45 Eur. Ct. H.R. ¶ 52 (1981)).

38. "Effective possession of the rights to freedom and well-being is an essential part of capacity-fulfillment," which "sit[s] in reasoned judgment over aspiration-fulfillment." Gewirth, *supra* n. 1, at 93, 101.

39. Here it might be claimed that my argument is internally inconsistent if self-fulfillment is viewed as an egoistic-teleological concept whose goal for human action is

to promote personal happiness, while human rights are generally justified on some universal deontological basis that may place restrictions on how personal happiness can be obtained. For example, if I were to gain self-fulfillment from engaging in genocide, human rights may proscribe that I not do so. But this is to suggest an inconsistency where none exists. For by self-fulfillment I do not mean that the agent's values emerge from his idiosyncratic aspirations alone, but rather from his ability to reason through the canons of deductive and inductive logic first to those aspirations he holds *qua* human and only after that to more individual or group-based aspirations (like being a Catholic, for example), provided they also violate no one else's rights. Because the rights-claim the agent asserts is logically the same claim others can assert, there can be no special privilege for the agent's own position. The range of the agent's self-fulfillment is thus not unbounded, but constrained by the very constituting reasons that justify its centrality as a human right. *See id.* at 215–16.

40. "In self-respect what one values is one's moral qualities, including one's dignity as a moral person who is worthy of the respect of other persons." *Id.* at 94.

41. "Since the generic rights are rights had equally by all agents, and since all humans are actual, prospective, or potential agents, the generic rights are now seen to be human rights." *Id.* at 84.

42. In effect, we have a situation analogous to the Prisoner's Dilemma in which two prisoners who cannot communicate with each other are both told by the prosecutor, "if you turn state's witness against the other prisoner, I will let you go free and the other prisoner will receive three years confinement." It also turns out that if both prisoners confess, they each get two years for making the court's job easier. However, if neither confesses, they will only be convicted of a lesser offense and each get one year. Both prisoners are highly motivated to confess to receive the lesser penalty. Yet, if they rationally assess their situation they will see that their best choice in terms of fewer years' confinement would be for neither to confess. *See e.g.* Stanford Ency. of Phil., *Prisoner's Dilemma*, http://plato.stanford.edu/entries/prisoner-dilemma/ (updated Aug. 11, 2003).

43. Gewirth, *supra* n. 1, at 173. "Properties of type *A* are supervenient on properties of type *B* if and only if two objects cannot differ with respect to their *A*-properties without also differing with respect to their *B*-properties." *The Cambridge Dictionary of Philosophy* 778 (Robert Audi ed., 2d ed., Cambridge U. Press 1995). It is only limited by the agent standing in the same shoes as all other prospective purposive agents.

44. Gewirth, *supra* n. 1, at 173.

45. *See id.* at 142.

46. *See infra* nn. 83–86 and accompanying text. Here I am following Alasdair MacIntyre's definition of a practice.

47. The point being that within the constraints of universal morality is the freedom to further restrain oneself to obtain specific goods either systematically as a group (called "particularist morality") like joining a community of ascetic monks or individually (called "personalist morality") like living the austere life of the artist. The only proviso is that the choice must be real or, at least, not coerced by social, political or economic conditions that could otherwise be avoided. When the latter occurs, those who have the power to alleviate the conditions are not following the requirements of universal morality. *See generally* Gewirth, *supra* n. 1, at ch. 4.

48. *See* Robert Justin Lipkin, *The Harm of Same-Sex Marriage: Real or Imagined?* 11 Widener L. Rev. 277, 308 (2005) (arguing that legal recognition of same-sex marriage might harm "those individuals and couples committed *exclusively* to the traditional notion of marriage" as one man and one woman, while at the same time benefiting those seeking

through such deliberative democratic norms as liberty and equality, a place where all minorities obtain full citizenship (emphasis added)).

49. One example of these rights and obligations is found in Vermont's statutes, Vt. Stat. Ann. tit. 15, §§ 1204(e)(1) to 1204(e)(24) (2005), which extend the same legal rights as apply to marriage to the following non-exclusive list of legal areas:

(1) laws relating to title, tenure, descent and distribution, intestate succession, waiver of will, survivorship, or other incidents of the acquisition, ownership, or transfer, inter vivos or at death, of real or personal property, including eligibility to hold real and personal property as tenants by the entirety . . . ;

(2) causes of action related to or dependent upon spousal status, including an action for wrongful death, emotional distress, loss of consortium, dramshop, or other torts or actions under contracts reciting, related to, or dependent upon spousal status;

(3) probate law and procedure, including nonprobate transfer;

(4) adoption law and procedure;

(5) group insurance for state employees . . . and continuing care contracts;

(6) spouse abuse programs . . . ;

(7) prohibitions against discrimination based upon marital status;

(8) victim's compensation rights . . . ;

(9) workers' compensation benefits;

(10) laws relating to emergency and nonemergency medical care and treatment, hospital visitation and notification, including the Patient's Bill of Rights . . . and the Nursing Home Residents' Bill of Rights . . . ;

(11) advance directives . . . ;

(12) family leave benefits . . . ;

(13) public assistance benefits under state law;

(14) laws relating to taxes imposed by the state or a municipality;

(15) laws relating to immunity from compelled testimony and the marital communication privilege;

(16) the homestead rights of a surviving spouse . . . and homestead property tax allowance . . . ;

(17) laws relating to loans to veterans . . . ;

(18) the definition of family farmer . . . ;

(19) laws relating to the making, revoking and objecting to anatomical gifts by others . . . ;

(20) state pay for military service . . . ;

(21) application for earlier voter absentee ballot . . . ;

(22) family landowner rights to fish and hunt . . . ;

(23) legal requirements for assignment of wages . . . ; and

(24) affirmation of relationship.

50. See Joshua K. Baker, *Status, Substance, and Structure: An Interpretative Framework for Understanding the State Marriage Amendments*, 17 Regent U. L. Rev. 221 (2005).

51. Professor Eskridge has noted that any discussion of marriage would be incomplete without a complete understanding of the obligations it entails that do not exist among single people. Eskridge, *supra* n. 10, at 70–74.

52. *See generally* Goutam U. Jois, *Marital Status as Property: Toward a New Jurisprudence for Gay Rights*, 41 Harv. Civ. Rights-Civ. Libs. L. Rev. 509, 509–10 (2006)

(arguing that there is a property right in the status of marriage itself that should be recognized under the Takings Clause).

53. In Plato's *Symposium*, we find the following speech on the mythological origins of love. Originally, human beings were giants composed of four arms and four legs and two sets of genitalia, either two male, or two female, or a combination of male and female. Once the god Zeus cuts them in half to create gay, lesbian and heterosexual persons the following is said,

> [W]hen this boy lover—or any lover, for that matter—is fortunate enough to meet his other half, they are both so intoxicated with affection, with friendship, and with love, that they cannot bear to let each other out of sight for a single instant. It is such reunions as these that impel men to spend their lives together, although they may be hard put to it to say what they really want with one another, and indeed, the purely sexual pleasures of their friendship could hardly account for the huge delight they take in one another's company. The fact is that both their souls are longing for a something else—a something to which they can neither of them put a name, and which they can only give an inkling of in cryptic sayings and prophetic riddles.

Plato, *Symposium*, in *The Collected Dialogues of Plato Including the Letters* 526, 545. (Edith Hamilton & Huntington Cairns eds., Michael Joyce, trans., Princeton U. Press 1980).

54. The Carpenters, *Breaking Up is Hard to Do*, in *A Kind of Hush* (A&M 1976) (33 rpm record) (cover version of Neil Sedaka, *Breaking Up is Hard to Do*, in *Neil Sedaka Sings His Greatest Hits* (RCA 1962) (33 rpm record)).

55. *Supra* n. 29 and accompanying text. Mark Strasser has noted that society could not prevent divorce because it provides the opportunity for one to "be able to meet someone else and eventually have an enduring, fulfilling, successful marriage." Mark Strasser, *Legally Wed: Same-Sex Marriage and the Constitution* 129 (Cornell U. Press 1997).

56. *E.g. Hernandez v. Robles*, 855 N.E.2d 1 (N.Y. 2006).

57. While I will be primarily discussing *Hernandez*, other recent cases also fail to recognize same-sex marriage as a human right. *Andersen v. King Co.*, 138 P.3d 963, 994 (Wash. 2006); *Standhardt v. Super. Ct. ex. rel. Co. of Maricopa*, 77 P.3d 451, 464 (Ariz. App. 2003). *But see Goodridge v. Dept. of Pub. Health*, 798 N.E.2d 941, 954 (Mass. 2003) (holding that individuals have a state right to same-sex marriage under the Massachusetts Constitution's equal protection clause, but not under its due process clause); *Baker v. Vt.*, 744 A.2d 864, 912 (Vt. 1999) (holding that the Vermont Legislature must adopt an equivalence for marriage for same-sex couples under the Vermont Constitution's common benefits clause—Vermont doesn't have an equal protection clause—as opposed to its due process clause). *Cf.* Vincent J. Samar, *Privacy and the Debate over Same-Sex Marriage versus Unions*, 54 DePaul L. Rev. 783, 785 (2005) (arguing that Vermont-styled civil union statutes, while granting all the legal rights and benefits of marriage under state law, still fail to provide true equality insofar as they allow a normative distinction to exist between same-sex unions and opposite-sex marriage).

58. *Hernandez*, 855 N.E.2d 1.

59. *Id.* at 5–6.

60. *Id.* at 14–15.

61. *Id.* at 9.

62. *Id.* (quoting *Under 21, Catholic Home Bur. for Dependent Children v. City of N.Y.*, 482 N.E.2d 1 (N.Y. 1985)).

63. *Id.* at 6; *see also id.* at 13, 15 (Graffeo, J., concurring) (noting that despite "scientific advances in assisted reproduction technology, the fact remains that the vast majority of children are conceived naturally through sexual contact between a woman and a man").

64. *Hernandez*, 855 N.E.2d at 14; *but see id.* at 26 (Kaye, J., dissenting) (noting "[t]he claim that marriage has always had a single and unalterable meaning is a plain distortion of history" (citing Br. of Profs. of History and Fam. Law as Amici Curiae in Support of Pls. at 1–3, *Hernandez*, 855 N.E.2d 1)).

65. In his dissent, Judge Kaye noted that "fundamental rights, once recognized, cannot be denied to particular groups on the ground that these groups have historically been denied those rights. " *Id.* at 22–23 (Kaye, J., dissenting).

66. *Id.* at 7 (majority).

67. *Id.*

68. *Id.*

69. *Id.* at 10; *see also id.* at 19 (Graffeo, J., concurring) (explaining his analysis of the level of scrutiny that applies—strict, intermediate, or rational relation—to the state's marriage classification scheme).

70. *Hernandez*, 855 N.E.2d at 10 (majority). This too is an interesting point because the general criteria traditionally thought to determine when a classification becomes suspect for equal protection purposes were not followed by the court. *See id.* at 23–24 (Kaye, J., dissenting).

71. *Id.* at 11.

72. *Grutter v. Bollinger*, 539 U.S. 306, 308 (2003) (reaffirming that racial and ethnic classifications are subject to strict scrutiny); *San Antonio Indep. Sch. Dist. v. Rodriguez*, 411 U.S. 1, 28 (1973) (identifying what constitutes a suspect class).

73. *U.S. v. Va.*, 518 U.S. 515, 533 (1996) (A statutory scheme that distinguishes between males and females is subject to heightened scrutiny, and must "serv[e] important governmental objectives," and "the discriminatory means employed [must be] substantially related to the achievement of those objectives.").

74. *Corp. of the Presiding Bishop of the Church of Jesus Christ of Latter-Day Sts. v. Amos*, 483 U.S. 327, 339 (1987) (citing *Larson v. Valente*, 456 U.S. 228, 246 (1982)); *Catholic Charities of the Diocese of Albany v. Serio*, 28 A.D.3d 115, 122 (N.Y. App. App. Div. 3d Dept. 2006).

75. *Hernandez*, 855 N.E.2d at 11.

76. *Id.* at 8 (quoting *Loving v. Va.*, 388 U.S. 1, 11 (1967)).

77. *Under 21, Catholic Home Bur. for Dependent Children v. City of N.Y.*, 482 N.E.2d 1 (N.Y. 1985).

78. *Hernandez*, 855 N.E.2d at 11 (quoting *Cleburne v. Cleburne Living Ctr., Inc.*, 473 U.S. 432, 441 (1985)).

79. *Id.*

80. *Id.* at 10.

81. *Romer v. Evans*, 517 U.S. 620, 635 (1996).

82. *Id.*

83. I emphasize the infirmity that the court associates as the legislature's stand towards opposite-sex couples because it seems hard to otherwise understand why a "legitimate" legislative purpose should be framed in this way. *Hernandez*, 855 N.E.2d at 11.

84. *See id.* at 7–8; *see also* Madeline Marzano-Lesnevich & Galit Moskowitz, *In the Interest of Children of Same-Sex Couples*, 19 J. Am. Acad. Matrimonial Laws. 255, 256 (2005) (arguing that "[e]nding the ban on same-sex marriage would be in the best interest of children of same-sex couples both legally and psychologically"); *see also* Justin R.

Pasfield, *Confronting America's Ambivalence towards Same-Sex Marriage: A Legal and Policy Perspective*, 108 W. Va. L. Rev. 267, 299–304 (2005) (arguing that much policy evidence shows that children suffer when same-sex marriage rights are denied). *But see* Brenda Cossman, *Contesting Conservatisms, Family Feuds and the Privatization of Dependency*, 13 Am. U. J. Gender Soc. Policy & L. 415, 499 (2005) (noting that some non-libertarian, social conservatives argue that children's interest in having opposite-sex parents far outweighs the same-sex marriage choice).

85. MacIntyre, *supra* n. 23, at 175.

86. *Id.* at 178.

87. *Id.*

88. MacIntyre noted that one might induce a bright child to develop the analytic and strategic skills (internal goods) associated with chess by initially bribing them with candy bars (an external good) in the hope that the child will eventually take solace in the rewards that skill at the game itself provides. *Id.* at 175.

89. In *Lawrence v. Tex.*, the Court struck down a Texas statute criminalizing same-sex sodomy between consenting adults in private, and held:

> "These matters, involving the most intimate and personal choices a person may make in a lifetime, choices central to personal dignity and autonomy, are central to the liberty protected by the Fourteenth Amendment. At the heart of liberty is the right to define one's own concept of existence, of meaning, of the universe, and of the mystery of human life. Beliefs about these matters could not define the attributes of personhood were they formed under compulsion of the State."

Lawrence v. Tex., 539 U.S. 558, 574 (2003) (quoting *Planned Parenthood of S.E. Pa. v. Casey*, 505 U.S. 833, 851 (1992)).

90. *See* Ryan Nishimoto, *Marriage Makes Cents: How Law & Economics Justifies Same-Sex Marriage*, 23 B.C. Third World L.J. 379, 384–85 (2003).

91. *See* Terry S. Kogan, *Transsexuals, Intersexuals, and Same-Sex Marriage*, 18 BYU J. Pub. L. 371, 417–18 (2004) (arguing that what matters most in producing a committed marriage is whether two people are physically and emotionally attracted to each other).

92. *See e.g.* Edward Egan Smith, *The Criminalization of Belief: When Free Exercise Isn't*, 42 Hastings L.J. 1491 (1991) (discussing a case upholding the criminal conviction of a mother who prayed instead of seeking out medical help when her child suffered for seventeen days with diagnosed meningitis).

93. At its best, love is a deep desire to be unified with the beloved; it includes intense pleasure both in the other's company and in the hope for its continuation and perpetuation. It is strongly concerned with the other's happiness; it is wishing of good for her for her own sake, in a way that goes far beyond general benevolence, for it includes a special feeling of responsibility for the other's fate as linked with your own. Gewirth, *supra* n. 1, at 146.

94. *See e.g.* John Finnis, *The Good of Marriage and the Morality of Sexual Relations: Some Philosophical and Historical Observations*, 42 Am. J. Juris. 97, 100 (1997) (arguing that same-sex marriage diminishes the institution of marriage). For a broader discussion of this topic from a religious perspective *see generally* Michael J. Perry, *Christians, the Bible, and Same-Sex Unions: An Argument for Political Self-Restraint*, 36 Wake Forest L. Rev. 449 (2001).

95. *See e.g.* Karl Augustine, *Reasons for Divorce: What Constitutes Viable Reasons for Thinking about or Wanting a Divorce?* http://www.selfgrowth.com/articles/ Augustine8.html (accessed Feb. 3, 2007).

96. *See* Gewirth, *supra* n. 1, at 154.

97. *Id.; see also* Melissa T. Aoyagi, *Beyond Punitive Prohibition: Liberalizing the Dialogue on International Drug Policy,* 37 N.Y.U. J. Intl. L. & Pol. 555 (2005) (encouraging state opportunities to explore alternatives to criminalization); MaryBeth Lipp, *A New Perspective on the "War on Drugs": Comparing the Consequences of Sentencing Policies in the United States and England,* 37 Loy. L.A. L. Rev. 979 (2004) (questioning whether punitive sentencing creates more social problems than a relatively free market in drugs); Joshua C. LaGrange, *Law, Economics, and Drugs: Problems with Legalization under a Federal System,* 100 Colum. L. Rev. 505, 506–13 (2000) (highlighting economic difficulties applying the neo-classical legalization arguments in a federal system). *See generally* Douglas Husak & Peter de Marneffe, *The Legalization of Drugs* (Cambridge U. Press 2005).

98. In his dissent, Judge Kaye noted: "Solely because of their sexual orientation, however—that is, because of who they love—plaintiffs are denied the rights and responsibilities of civil marriage." *Hernandez v. Robles,* 855 N.E.2d 1, 22 (N.Y. 2006) (Kaye, J., dissenting).

99. [T]hrough the universal right to freedom, persons have rights to form families and to have the concomitant preferential concerns. This justification does not extend to violations of other persons' rights as upheld by universalist morality, and it also prohibits the nepotism whereby a family member who holds an official position, such as judge or teacher, uses it to favor another family member by giving him a lighter sentence or a higher grade than the rules of his position require. For in such cases to act against the impartiality required by the respective rules is to violate the moral rights of other persons upheld by universalist morality.

Gewirth, *supra* n. 1, at 143.

100. [T]wo general normative relations [emerge] between cultural pluralism and the moral universalism of human rights. Negatively, moral universalism sets the outer limits of the legitimacy of the various practices of cultural pluralism. Affirmatively, within these limits moral universalism encourages and upholds the diverse practices of cultural pluralism, the differences between human beings with regard to values and ways of life, as diverse paths to capacity-fulfillment.

Id. at 157.

101. *See Brown v. Bd. of Educ.,* 347 U.S. 483, 495 (1954) (holding that state-mandated, separate-but-equal education violated the Fourteenth Amendment's guarantee of equal protection, as it creates a sense of inferiority in children of minority families that they carry the rest of their lives); *see also U.S. v. Va.,* 518 U.S. 515, 535–46 (1996) (holding that Virginia Military Institute's exclusion of women violated the federal and state constitutional requirement to afford equal protection of the laws). Note the same condition may not be true when a school is established specifically to provide a safe and welcoming environment for young people coming to grips with a homosexual orientation. *See* Louis P. Nappen, *Why Segregated Schools for Gay Students May Pass a "Separate But Equal" Analysis but Fail Other Issues and Concerns,* 12 Wm. & Mary J. Women L. 101 (2005); Nicolyn Harris & Maurice R. Dyson, *Safe Rules or Gays' Schools? The Dilemma of Sexual Orientation Segregation in Public Education,* 7 U. Pa. J. Const. L. 183 (2004).

102. Here the issue is not with the ways in which cultural groups may treat their individual members by violating their human rights, but rather with the ways in which diverse cultural groups may themselves be treated by the state or society at large. . . . What [universal morality] requires here is that cultural pluralism be affirmatively protected: the right to cultural pluralism is an affirmative as well as a negative right. Gewirth, *supra* n. 1, at 155.

103. *Id.* at 143.

104. Joseph Bozzuti, *The Constitutionality of Polygamy Prohibitions after* Lawrence v. Texas: *Is Scalia a Punchline or a Prophet?* 43 Cath. Law. 409, 440–41 (2004); Adrien Katherine Wing, *Polygamy from Southern Africa to Black Britannia to Black America: Global Critical Race Feminism as Legal Reform for the Twenty-First Century,* 11 J. Contemp. Leg. Issues 811, 861 (2001). *But see* Maura I. Strassberg, *The Challenge of Post-Modern Polygamy: Considering Polyamory,* 31 Cap. U. L. Rev. 439, 440–44 (2003).

105. It may not always be easy to draw the line between [universal morality's] mandatory-negative and permissive-affirmative applications to various cultural practices. Especially where the practices are controversial the applications require both detailed empirical scrutiny of the practices in question, including their causal backgrounds and effects, and careful analysis of how [universal morality's] contents bear on these practices.

Gewirth, *supra* n. 1, at 154.

106. All states and most foreign countries that recognize legal marriage do justifiably set conditions of age and mental awareness to guarantee that the parties seeking to marry are truly acting voluntarily. For an example of state differences, *compare* N.M. Stat. Ann. § 40-1-7 (Lexis 2007) ("All marriages between relations and children, including grandfathers and grandchildren of all degrees, between half brothers and sisters, as also of full blood; between uncles and nieces, aunts and nephews, are hereby declared incestuous and absolutely void. This section shall extend to illegitimate as well as to legitimate children.") *with* Ohio Rev. Code Ann. § 3101.01(A) (Lexis 2006) ("Male persons of the age of eighteen years, and female persons of the age of sixteen years, not nearer of kin than second cousins, and not having a husband or wife living, may be joined in marriage.").

107. In *The Right to Privacy: Gays, Lesbians and the Constitution,* I identify the range of the privacy right's protection to encompass all those actions that on examination do not run afoul of a compelling state interest founded on protecting autonomy in general or violate another right that will better foster maximal autonomy in the long run. Samar, *The Right to Privacy, supra* n. 11, at 116–17.

108. *See* Ala. Code § 30-1-19 (West 2006); Alaska Stat. § 25.05.013 (Lexis 2007); Ariz. Rev. Stat. § 25-101 (Lexis 2007); Ark. Code Ann. §§ 9-11-208, 9-11-109 (Lexis 2006); Del. Code Ann. tit. 13 § 101 (Lexis 2006); Fla. Stat. Ann. § 741.212 (2006); Ga. Code Ann. § 19-3-3.1 (2006); Haw. Rev. Stat. Ann. § 572-1 (Lexis 2006); Idaho Code Ann. § 32-209 (Lexis 2006); 750 Ill. Comp. Stat. 5/213.1, 5/212 (2007); Ind. Code Ann. § 31-11-1-1 (Lexis 2006); Ky. Rev. Stat. Ann. §§ 402.005, 402.045, 402.040 (Lexis 2006); La. Civ. Code Ann. art. 89 (2006); 19-A Me. Rev. Stat. Ann. § 701 (2006); Md. Fam. Code Ann. § 2-201 (2006); Mich. Comp. Laws § 551.1 (2006); Minn. Stat. Ann. § 517.03 (West 2005); Miss. Code Ann. § 93-1-1 (Lexis 2006); Mo. Rev. Stat. Ann. § 451.022 (West 2007); Mont. Code Ann. § 40-1-401 (2005); Neb. Const. art. I, § 29; N.C. Gen. Stat. § 51-1.2 (Lexis 2006); N.D. Cent. Code § 14-03-01 (2006); Ohio Rev. Code Ann. § 3101.01 (Lexis 2006); Okla. Stat. tit. 43, § 3.1 (2006); 23 Pa. Consol. Stat. § 1704 (2006); S.C. Code Ann. § 20-1-10 (2006); S.D. Codified Laws § 25-1-38 (2006); Tenn. Code Ann. § 36-3-113 (Lexis 2006); Utah Code Ann. § 30-1-2 (Lexis 2006); Va.

Code Ann. § 20-45.2 (Lexis 2006); Wash. Rev. Code § 26.04.020 (2007); W. Va. Code Ann. § 48-2-603 (Lexis 2006); Wyo. Stat. Ann. § 20-1-101 (2006).

109. *Supra* nn. 89-93 and accompanying text.

110. *Griswold v. Conn.*, 381 U.S. 479, 485–86 (1965) (recognizing a right of married couples to use contraceptives and of doctors to advise in their use); *Eisenstadt v. Baird*, 405 U.S. 438, 454–55 (1972) (extending the right to obtain and use contraceptives to unmarried persons); *Carey v. Population Servs. Intl.*, 431 U.S. 678, 694–96 (1977) (extending the right to obtain and use contraceptives to minors); *Roe v. Wade*, 410 U.S. 113, 164–66 (1973) (upholding a woman's right, within some constraints, to choose abortion); *Planned Parenthood of S.E. Pa. v. Casey*, 505 U.S. 833 (1992) (upholding *Roe's* recognition of a woman's right, within some constraints, to choose abortion but replacing the *Roe* Court's trimester analysis with an undue burden test).

111. Other issues, however, might arise. For example, in *Zablocki v. Redhail*, 434 U.S. 374, 386 (1978), the U.S. Supreme Court noted, "it would make little sense to recognize a right of privacy with respect to other matters of family life and not with respect to the decision to enter the relationship that is the foundation of the family in our society." The argument for extending the right to marry to same-sex couples is bolstered by the Supreme Court's recent decision in *Lawrence v. Tex.*, 539 U.S. 558, 567 (2003), where it struck down a state sodomy statute prohibiting adult consensual sexual relations involving intimate relationships between same-sex persons. This reversal of *Bowers v. Hardwick* after only seventeen years suggests that the comment in *Zablocki* might now be interpreted to include same-sex relationships. *Lawrence*, 539 U.S. at 578 (reversing *Bowers v. Hardwick*, 478 U.S. 186 (1986)). Note Justice Scalia's dissent in *Lawrence*:

> Today's opinion dismantles the structure of constitutional law that has permitted a distinction to be made between heterosexual and homosexual unions, insofar as formal recognition in marriage is concerned. If moral disapprobation of homosexual conduct is "no legitimate state interest" for purposes of proscribing that conduct; and if, as the Court coos (casting aside all pretense of neutrality), "[w]hen sexuality finds overt expression in intimate conduct with another person, the conduct can be but one element in a personal bond that is more enduring;" what justification could there possibly be for denying the benefits of marriage to homosexual couples exercising "[t]he liberty protected by the Constitution"?

Id. at 604–05 (Scalia, J., dissenting) (quoting majority, citations omitted, brackets added by Scalia, J.).

112. In his dissent, Judge Kaye stated:

> The record is replete with examples of the hundreds of ways in which committed same-sex couples and their children are deprived of equal benefits under New York law. Same-sex families are, among other things, denied equal treatment with respect to intestacy, inheritance, tenancy by the entirety, taxes, insurance, health benefits, medical decisionmaking, workers' compensation, the right to sue for wrongful death, and spousal privilege.

Hernandez v. Robles, 855 N.E.2d 1, 27 (N.Y. 2006) (Kaye, J., dissenting); *see also* Vt. Stat. Ann. tit. 15, §§ 1204(e)(1) to (24) (2006) (showing the range of the rights and privileges a state marriage law may engage).

113. Courtney G. Joslin, *The Legal Parentage of Children Born to Same-Sex Couples: Developments in the Law*, 39 Fam. L.Q. 683, 683 (2005) (noting that

"[a]ccording to the 2000 United States Census data, one out of three lesbian couples and one out of five gay couples are raising children in the United States.").

114. By "properly understood" I mean understood as deriving out of the essential conditions of voluntariness and purposiveness that all moral theories must necessarily presuppose. *See* Gewirth, *supra* n. 1, at 79–80.

115. Vincent J. Samar, *Justifying Judgment: Practicing Law and Philosophy* (U. Press of Kan. 1998) (arguing this point extensively; thus I will not belabor the matter here).

CHAPTER 13
EQUALITY OR IDEOLOGY? SAME-SEX UNIONS IN SCANDINAVIA

Allan Carlson*
The Howard Institute and World Congress of Families

I.   Introduction: The Debate

Debate on the Senate floor in June 2006 over the proposed Federal Marriage Amendment to the United States Constitution had a peculiar quality. As Jon Stewart of Comedy Central's "The Daily Show" remarked, the debate seemed to be primarily a battle over obscure Scandinavian statistics. Supporters of the amendment summoned arguments, numbers, and graphs largely developed by anthropologist Stanley Kurtz to show that "[g]ay marriage undermines marriage."[1] Focusing on Denmark, Norway, Sweden, and the Netherlands, Kurtz has argued that the introduction of same-sex registered partnerships in these nations encouraged the substitution of cohabitation for marriage among heterosexuals, drove up the proportion of births occurring outside of wedlock, and raised the divorce rate.[2] Opponents of the marriage amendment summoned arguments and statistics framed by Yale law professor William N. Eskridge, attorney Darren R. Spedale, and Swedish jurist Hans Ytterberg to show that registered partnerships have been perfectly "fine from the perspective of larger (and largely straight) society" in Scandinavia.[3] These authors argue that any trends toward heterosexual cohabitation, divorce, and out-of-wedlock births in the Scandinavian countries pre-date the introduction of same-sex registered partnerships and that Kurtz's statistical correlations do not hold up.

The dispute reached another phase this summer with publication of *Gay Marriage: For Better or Worse? What We've Learned from the Evidence* by Eskridge and Spedale. The authors argue far more forcefully that signs of deterioration in heterosexual marriage are the consequence of strictly hetero innovations, notably the introduction of no-fault divorce and legal recognition of cohabitation as a distinct status. They also summon new statistical evidence to claim "no harm." For example, Lee Badgett has traced the average rise in the proportion of non-marital birth rates among the European nations that recognize same-sex partnership. She finds an increase from 36 percent in 1991 to 44 percent in 2000, an eight point difference. However, the increase in non-marital births among European nation's *not* recognizing same-sex partnerships was *also* eight points (from 15 to 23 percent), a proportionately higher rate of change.[4] Eskridge and Spedale marshal evidence showing that heterosexual marriage statistics are actually *improving* in Scandinavia. In Norway, for example, the heterosexual marriage rate *rose* from 434.6 (per 100,000) in 1993—the year "registered partnerships" were introduced—to 564.6 in 2000 before declining again to 486.8 in 2004, yet still eight percent *above* the base. In Sweden, the heterosexual marriage rate climbed from 380.7 in 1995—again, the year that registered partnerships became law—to 478.1 in 2004, a surprising 26 percent increase. At the same time, the Swedish divorce rate *fell* by 12 percent over the same years. Meanwhile, the proportion of births out-of-wedlock climbed only three percentage points—to 56 percent—a much *slower* rate of increase than during the prior equivalent time period.[5] "Where's the harm?" Eskridge and Spedale ask.

Kurtz responds by attributing increases in heterosexual marriage rates to the behavior of older couples and argues that the key Swedish date should be 1987, not 1995; the prior year saw enactment of measures granting certain legal claims on shared property to cohabiting couples, both hetero- *and* homosexual. He also suggests that his best case for finding harm is actually in the Netherlands, a non-Scandinavian country.[6]

As I will explain later, both sides of the dispute make valid arguments. However, it is my contention that this debate over the minutiae of Scandinavian demography misses the real, and larger transformation that has occurred in these nations. Eskridge and Spedale see the Scandinavians pursuing equality and steadily "discovering the value of lesbian and gay relationships."[7] Kurtz sees same-sex marriage upending traditional marriage, and so building acceptance for "a host of other mutually reinforcing changes...that only serve to weaken marriage."[8] Both largely ignore the deeper driving force: the triumph in Scandinavian four decades ago of a distinct ideology which seeks to dismantle the autonomous home and to socialize all human life. The lead example of this change is Sweden; the vehicle, Sweden's Social Democratic Labor Party.

This ideology rests on a unique blend of conventional socialism with feminism and neo-Malthusianism. Pursuing a perennial socialist goal, it lifts up the state as a substitute for the family. It embraces sex education, contraception, and abortion as tools of liberation, the vehicles for gaining only "wanted" children. It deliberately undermines gender roles, even those conditioned by nature. Androgyny becomes a specific goal. This ideology transfers the costs and cares of rearing children from the natural couple to the state. Children born in and out of wedlock are treated exactly the same, for all are in essence children of the collective. Equality is gained as husbands are no longer dependent on wives, nor wives on husbands, nor children on parents, nor parents on children. All are equally dependent on the largesse of the welfare state.

This ideology specifically targets marriage for diminution, for it recognizes the truth of G.K. Chesterton's claim that the "institution of the home is the one anarchist institution...[I]t is older than any law, and stands outside the State."[9] Or as Chesterton put it in another tract:

> The ideal for which [marriage] stands in the state is liberty. It stands
> for liberty for the very simple reason...[that] it is the on-
> ly...institution that is at once necessary and voluntary. It is the only

check on the state that is bound to renew itself as eternally as the
state, and more naturally than the state.[10]

From a socialist perspective, such a rival cannot be allowed to stand. In the
new Social Democratic dispensation, marriage would be redefined, expanded,
and deconstructed all at once. Stripped of any meaningful functions, it could be
endlessly reshaped around varied relationships. No longer bearing any authority,
what did it matter?

Legal reforms toward this end explain the Scandinavian experience over the
last four decades. The legalization of same-sex partnerships was not the cause of
this change. Rather, it was a step in the process, useful mainly for underscoring
the severing of marriage from procreation. Perhaps with some level of awareness, or perhaps unwittingly, Sweden's same-sex marriage advocates have been
useful tools in the larger ideological project. The real "harm" of legalizing same-
sex partnerships lies here, in the political sphere that defines liberty.

II.   The Swedish Experiment

A.   Socialism Through The Home

The theory behind the larger project dates from the early 1930's, when a declining marriage rate and a sharply falling fertility rate led to calls for radical
changes in the Swedish home. In 1932, the young socialist intellectual Alva
Myrdal generated a furor by advocating "collectivized homes" for Swedish
families, where young mothers would join fathers in the full time labor force,
with infants and toddlers cared for in common nurseries and with meals prepared in collectivized kitchens. With husband Gunnar Myrdal, she co-authored
in 1934 the book *Kris i befolkningsfrågan* ("Crisis in the Population Question").
They argued that raising the perilously low Swedish birthrate required radical
changes in the natures of marriage and family. Fathers should be freed from
their distinctive "breadwinner" role; mothers freed from "homemaking." All
adults should work, and massive new state welfare benefits funded by a "bachelor tax"—including clothing allowances, daycare subsidies, universal health
care, meals at school, and low interest "marriage loans"—should pay the costs
of parenthood.

On the surface, the Myrdals appeared to elevate the public importance of
marriage. At a deeper level, though, they sought its diminution. The marital
home, under their scheme, would largely cease to be a significant economic unit.
As the feminist historian Yvonne Hirdman explains, the Myrdals adopted here
"a successful Trojan horse tactic": they would "smuggle socialist forms into the
capitalist society" at its most vulnerable spot, "the home." This turn to population policy "set the stage for the politicization of private life" by radically altering "everyday life."[11]

Neo-Malthusian ideas formed another key aspect of the project. Early and
universal sex education, freely available contraceptives, and liberalized abortion
would insure that all children in the new order would be *wanted* children. In

seeking an end to Sweden's ban on the sale of contraceptives, the Myrdals implicitly embraced another new concept: the right of married couples *not* to procreate, which subtly untied the bond of marriage to procreation. [12]

Working through The Royal Population Commission of 1935 and the Swedish Parliament's Women's Work Committee, the Myrdals enjoyed a remarkable influence for the balance of the decade. Notably, Parliament legalized contraceptives, inaugurated sex education, gave new legal protections to working women, and expanded state welfare programs.

By 1940, however, the Myrdals' ideas were in retreat. The onset of World War II and Sweden's perilous position as a "neutral" nation surrounded by Nazi German conquests encouraged a conservative nationalism. Relative to the family, an alternate worldview found in the labor unions—namely that "women were to be liberated *from* the labor market rather than liberated to participate *in* it" and that men deserved to earn a living "family wage"—regained popularity. Sometimes called "maternalism," this attitude saw Alva Myrdal's egalitarian feminism as part of the problem, not the solution. Capitalists, this older socialist claim went, should not be allowed to control the mothers, wives, and daughters of the working class. The labor unions, collectively organized as the LO [Lans organization], negotiated with employers in 1938 the historic *Saltsjöbaden* agreement, which crystallized job segregation by gender, reserving the better industrial jobs and the higher wages for the unions' male members. [13]

Some feminist analysts label the consequent 1940-67 period as "the era of the Socialist housewife." Public policy encouraged the full-time care of small children at home. Instruction in modern homemaking and child care became mandatory for all Swedish girls. The marriage rate climbed, while the average age at first marriage fell. Fertility also rose: Sweden's mini-Baby Boom. As late as 1965, only *three* percent of all Swedish preschool children were in some form of non-parental day care. The "traditional Swedish family" seemed solid. [14] Indeed, feminist historians quietly acknowledge that as late as the mid-1960's there was no pressure for change coming from young Swedish housewives and mothers. [15]

B.   Forms of Cohabitation

All this changed during the 1960's. Radical outbursts—the Red Brigades in West Germany and Italy, the New Left riots in France, "Eurocommunism"—dominated the news. At the same time, Europeans launched a values revolution. The Christian principles of "responsibility, sacrifice, altruism and the sanctity of long-term commitments" gave way across Western Europe to "secular individualism" focused on the needs of the self. [16]

Sweden entered into what Yvonne Hirdman calls its "Red Years," 1967-1976. [17] At their core was a massive "gender turn" that required the radical transformation of marriage. A joint report prepared in 1968 by the Social Democratic Party and the LO abandoned the "family wage" ideal and concluded that "there are...strong reasons for making the two breadwinner family the norm in planning long-term changes within the social insurance system." [18] Alva Myrdal chaired a major panel at this time, "On Equality," for the Social Democrats. Its highly influential 1969 report concluded that "[i]n the society of the future,…the point of departure must be that every adult is responsible for his/her own support. Benefits previously inherit in married status should be eliminated." "Natural" differences between women and men, the report argued, should not pose a barrier to reform. Interventions by the state would make such innate distinctions unimportant. *On Equality* also demanded a tax policy based on individual earnings. This would mean no preference for *any* "form of cohabitation," which was Alva Myrdal's deflating new term for conventional marriage, as well as its emerging rivals.[19]

The Swedish government moved to alter its marriage law. A Committee of Experts formed under the Justice Ministry, and the Minister of Justice issued detailed Directives. At the outset, the Committee was to consider whether there was still even a need for marriage law and, if so, how it should be reconfigured. The Minister pointed to the "clearly anachronistic" nature of community property, based as it was on the now-to-be-discarded Christian notion of "one flesh." He directed the Committee also to consider the shrinking importance of marital status in Sweden, the growing pursuit of "personal fulfillment," the swelling demand for divorce, falling public interest in material property in favor of public pensions and other benefits of the welfare state, and the new place of gender equality as the cornerstone of Swedish social policy. In addition, the State's provision of Social Security should be accepted "as a fact" and this system should *not* face competition from dependency obligations between family members.[20]

Showing the same spirit, Sweden's Parliament approved in 1971 a fundamental reform of the income tax. At the philosophical level, this seemingly minor change ended the tax treatment of marriage as an economic union, a material expression of the "one flesh" ideal. As historian Christina Florin summarizes, "the household as an economic unit with the father as family provider" lost its functional identity under this change, to be replaced by "two free-standing economic individuals." Also lost was the family's position as a distinct legal unit, with its own claims and authority. Significantly, Florin reveals how socialists elites in the media and government strove to keep the real questions involved in this change "away from the people."[21]

Technically, the measure abolished the taxation of households through the joint income tax return premised on "income splitting" by married couples. In the future, all Swedes would be taxed as individuals, without attention to marital status, dependents, or income of a spouse. Sweden would now have the most "fully individualized taxation system" in the developed world. In the context of high marginal tax rates, this change—by intent—strongly aided the two-income household, while penalizing the traditional one-income breadwinner.[22]

Scholars of this era are nearly unanimous in viewing this shift from "joint" to "individual" taxation as the most sweeping social change in Sweden over the last 40 years. Anne Lise Ellingsaeter reports that the male providers role was "more or less eradicated."[23] Sven Steinmo calls it the most "radical" change marking the turbulent 1970's, because "it meant that the Swedish tax system would ignore family circumstances" in imposing tax burden.[24] Maude Edwards calls the turn to equal taxation "the most important step in promoting equality between women and men."[25] Annika Baude, a leading Swedish feminist, concludes: "If I were to choose one reform which has...done the most to promote equality between the sexes, I would point to the introduction of individual income taxation."[26]

Further steps toward the new order followed. A 1972 report from the Family Law Experts Committee urged complete neutrality toward forms of heterosexual cohabitation. This meant that marriage could hardly "be maintained as a special legal institution."[27] A year later, Parliament approved a new measure governing marriage and divorce. Access to marriage actually expanded. Paradoxically, though, this actually meant that the special status and importance of marriage diminished. Parliament abolished most impediments to heterosexual marriage, including a narrowing of the definition of incest. In the future, half-brothers and half-sisters, aunts and nephews, uncles and nieces, and first cousins all could marry. Only siblings and persons related by blood in unilinear descent faced prohibition; bigamy and polygamy remained banned. The minimum marriage age for both spouses would be 18.

The same measure embraced "no fault" divorce. Premised on the idea of marriage as a voluntary union, it was—in one advocate's words—"only natural that if one of the spouses is dissatisfied, he or she may demand a divorce." In practice, this 1973 law meant that the community or state no longer had significant interests in the preservation of a marriage. "Fault" would no longer be considered in divorce proceedings, nor would marital misconduct have any bearing on the division of property. This also meant the elimination of "adultery" and "fidelity" from marriage's institutional construct. If both husband and wife agreed to the divorce, it would be immediately granted. If one spouse objected or if there was at least one child under age 16 in the home, the new law fixed a mandatory reconsideration period of six months. In addition, "separation" no longer had legal status. The measure assumed adult self-support and largely ended the concept of alimony (except in limited cases where "maintenance" payments for a set time might be required).[28]

The result was large. In the words of jurist Jacob W. F. Sundberg, the 1973 reform succeeded in achieving "a goal perfectly analogous to that which loomed before the [Russian] Bolsheviks in 1918: carry socialism to its logical conclusion in the field of family law."[29] Also adapting a principle of ancient Roman law, *libertas matrimonii*, Swedish jurisprudence now implicitly held—again, in Sundberg's words—"that free marriage is only tolerable if marriage is deprived of most of its legal consequences."[30]

C.   Woman's Work

In 1972 a new Social Democratic prime minister came to power, Olof Palme. Alva Myrdal served in his cabinet with the portfolios of Disarmament and Church Affairs. Openly under her influence, Palme addressed the women of the Party that year, declaring an end to the socialist housewife. "In this society," he said, "it is only natural for both parents to work. In this society it is evident that man and woman [i.e., not "husband and wife"] should take the same responsibility for the care of the home and the children." Underscoring the socialist imperative, he added that "[i]n this society...the care of these future generations is just as naturally the responsibility of us all."[31]

Palme launched a true revolution. The Party abolished its Women's League, the enclave of the homemakers.[32] Women would now become "real members" of the Party, he said, dealing with "common issues" alone. New policies made employment nearly mandatory for all women in their twenties and thirties. Surviving homemakers would pay dearly through heightened marginal taxes on their husbands. Small children now moved massively into daycare: 460,000 held places in 1995, compared to only 23,000 three decades earlier.[33]

Hirdman ably underscores the sweep and the novelty of change here. Women's work in this new Swedish had on a remarkable quality. The number of employed women actually declined in the fields of agriculture and forestry, while in private industry it grew only modestly. However, in the heavily governmental service sector, the number of employed women rose from 269,000 in 1950 to 819,000 by 1990; in the education, day care, and health care sectors (exclusively governmental), the number of employed women rose nearly three fold, from 282,000 in 1950 to slightly over 1 million by 1990. For a nation of eight million people, these were enormous changes.

In short, marriage and family policy had been used as a lever to achieve something "truly revolutionary": the shriveling of private homes resting on marriage and a massive expansion of the state sector. In short, socialism had been smuggled in through marriage and home. Women were now largely doing the same work they had done in private homes before, but now they worked for the state in specialized tasks of day care, elder care, institutionalized cooking, and other "services." Private patriarchy had given way to the public patriarchy inherent in the socialist model. Pointing specifically to the experience of Alva Myrdal, Hirdman explains the sweep of change affecting marriage:

> New ideas of gender replaced old-fashioned ideas about the couple. We witness [here] the birth of the androgynous individual (and I speak about the explicit ideal) and the death of the provider and his housewife. We thus witness old ideas popping up, ideas that had been buried for decades—but ideas that very quickly found their advocates and became developed: people, men and women, eager to speak the new tongue of gender.[34]

In a related development, the Social Welfare Act of 1980 greatly enhanced the power of state social workers to take custody of children away from their natural parents. No detrimental effects had to be shown; judgments about the parents' mental character and "personal disposition" were sufficient. One subsequent case of some notoriety, *Ulla Widen v. Sweden,* involved charges that the mother was simply a poor house cleaner.[35] The number of children in state custody grew sharply, as did the cadre of social workers and the compensation paid to state foster parents. Again, these were logical consequences of a system consciously designed to diminish marriage and the home and to enhance the central state.[36]

D.   Family Form Neutrality

Sweden's Parliament further codified this social revolution in two 1987 laws. Focused on property and inheritance questions, the new Marriage Code weakened again the concept of marriage as an economic partnership. On the surface, this was not immediately clear. Despite pressure for a more individualistic formulation, the new law did retain the concept of "deferred community property" first codified in 1920. In principle, a spouse remained entitled to a half share in marital property at the time of divorce or death. The Courts gained more power to set aside pre-nuptial contracts establishing separate property. Surviving spouses also won greater control over marital property relative to children and other heirs. While appearing to raise the claims of marriage, this latter change actually represented the "amputation of the blood line" in Sweden, the deliberate severing of children's economic bonds to their parents.[37]

Other, more representative provisions gave spouses increased independence. One ended the obligation that each person had to manage and preserve matrimonial property. Joint liability for debts acquired by household expenditures or children's education also disappeared. And the 1987 Code ended the husband's special responsibility to support the family.[38] In one commentator's words, the new Code reflected "the increasing focus in the law itself on *termination* of marriage, rather than on its preservation."[39]   The Parliament also approved The Joint Homes Act in 1987. This new measure governing "relationships similar to marriage" rested on "the principle of neutrality toward family form." As legal analyst Ulla Björnberg explains:

> The principle states that individuals are free to develop their personal lives at their own will, to choose a living arrangement and ethical norms for their family life. The role of family law is restricted to providing solutions to practical problems and to formulate rules of a kind that can be accepted by almost all individuals.[40]

Still, the Joint Homes Act did not quite equate "cohabitation" with "marriage." Specifically, cohabitators did not gain the equivalence of "marital property rights" in inheritance or a right to claim "maintenance" after separation. Rather, the rules in this measure applied only to the equal splitting of a dwelling and household goods acquired while living together. All the same, the measure did affirm that parenthood in consensual unions would involve rights and responsibilities equal to those in marriage. Unmarried fathers must register with the state. Joint custody of children after separation would be the assumption for both cohabitating and married couples.

A novel aspect of the 1987 reform, attracting relatively little attention at the time, was that rules for unmarried cohabitation applied to both heterosexual *and* homosexual couples.[41] I would underscore that this latter innovation came near the end of the radical revision of marriage, not at its beginning.

In 1995, the Swedish Parliament expanded on this change and—adapting a policy already developed by Denmark (1989) and Norway (1993)—approved a law granting same-sex couples the ability to form a "registered partnership." This represented a civil contract providing rights and responsibilities nearly identical to those of conventional marriage. For example, "registered partners" gained claim to "deferred community property." The legal rights not granted to "registered parents" were adoption, the joint custody of children, and publicly funded artificial insemination.

E.   The Relationship State

In their 1934 book, *Kris I befolkningsfrågan*, Alva and Gunnar Myrdal summarized their vision of the "new family':

> In the new family,...the wife will stand as a comrade by her husband's side in productive work ....During working hours,...the family will be split to adapt to an industrialized society's broader division of labor: the adult working people must be at their jobs; the children must play, eat, sleep, and go to school. Common shelter, common free time, as well as *that elusive, subtle, personal relationship* that is, we believe, a constituent element of the family, *will remain. Maintaining a private household, individualistic parental responsibility, and the wife's home-centered life, however, will not remain.* These must be driven out of the picture as an adaptation to social evolution.[42]

At this time, the Myrdals still felt it necessary to retain an indirect reference to marriage—the words "wife" and "husband"—in their portrait. However, 35 years later, in her report *On Equality*, Alva Myrdal no longer felt so constrained. If one subtracts marriage from the above vision, what remains is a "new family" where the collectivist state has supplanted the home, where the function-rich household has been supplanted by "elusive, subtle, personal relationship[s]," and where the caring and nurturing work of women has been socialized. While Yvonne Hirdman, a self-labelled radical feminist, and Jacob Sundberg, a conservative jurist and scholar, are worlds apart in political philosophy, they agree that this change constitutes a profound revolution.[43]

III. Conclusion: Transformation and Reclamation

Granting certain property claims to cohabiting gays and lesbians in 1987 and extending "registered partnerships" to the same groups in 1995 were part of this historic transition: from the family as an autonomous institution focused on the bearing and rearing of children to the "new family," socialist in form, understood as an ever-changing network of relationships dependent on the state. Relative to the autonomous family, the principle "harm" done by marriage-like "registered partnerships" was to amplify the dissolution of the once vital bond between marriage and procreation. Sterile by definition, the very concept of

same-sex marriage strips the heart out of the traditional institution, to the confusion and disorientation of society as a whole, and of the young in particular. If
honest in their claims that they want to strengthen marriage, same-sex marriage
advocates let themselves be used here as tools in a larger project to scuttle the
institution of marriage.

In truth, though, the bond of procreation and marriage was already seriously
weakened by the prior legal embrace of contraception within marriage, by the
intentionally childless marriage, by elimination of "illegitimacy" as a legal category, and by recognition in law of heterosexual cohabitation.[44] Indeed, Eskridge,
Spedale, and Ytterberg make a powerful rejoinder that "[i]f the chief concern of
family law should be the creation of a stable family structure for the rearing of
children, then most of the hetero-liberalization of the last generation—no-fault
divorce, cohabitation, rights for non-marital children—has been a mistake. Marriage in America has been compromised in ways that should be reclaimed."
They add that any traditionalist defense of marriage that "leaves no-fault divorce
and cohabitation untouched" has already embraced a radical redefinition of marriage, one that has done much more measurable harm to children and society
than same-sex marriage.[45] On empirical grounds, it appears, here they are correct.

Notes

---

*Allan Carlson is President of The Howard Center for Family, Religion & Society in
Rockford, Illinois. He holds his Ph.D. in Modern European History from The Ohio University. His books include The Swedish Experiment in Family Politics: The Myrdals and
the Interwar Population Crisis (Transaction 1990) and Conjugal America: On the Public
Purposes of Marriage (Transaction 2006).

1. Stanley Kurtz, "Zombie Killers: A.K.A., 'Queering the Social,'" National Review
Online (25 May 2006): 1.

2. See: Stanley Kurtz, "The End of Marriage in Scandinavia," The Weekly Standard
9 (2 February 20004); Found at: http://www.weeklystandard.com/utilities/printer_ pre-
view.asp?idArticle=3660&R=EDED22... (9/8/06).

3. William N. Eskridge, Darren R. Spedale, and Hans Ytterberg, "Nordic Bliss?
Scandinavian Registered Partnerships and the Same Sex Marriage Debate," Issues in
Legal Scholarship (Article 4 2004): 42.

4. M.V. Lee Badgett, "Did Gay Marriage Destroy Heterosexual Marriage in Scandi-
navia?" Slate (20 May 2004), at www.slate.msn.com/id/2100884; cited in William N.
Eskridge, Jr., and Darren R. Spedale, Gay Marriage: For Better or Worse? What We've
Learned from the Evidence (New York: Oxford University Press, 2006): 196.

5. Eskridge and Spedale, Gay Marriage, pp. 275-79.

6. Stanley Kurtz, "No Nordic Bliss," National Review Online (28 February 2006); at
http://www.nationalreview.com/script/printpage.p?ref=/kurtz/kurtz200602280810.asp
(9/8/2006).

7. Eskridge, Spedale, and Ytterberg, "Nordic Bliss?," p. 42.

8. Kurtz, "Zombie Killers," p. 1.

9. G.K. Chesterton, Collected Works. Volume IV: Family, Society, Politics (San
Francisco: Ignatius Press, 1987): 67-68.

10. Chesterton, *Collected Works, Vol. IV*, p. 256.

11. Yvonne Hirdman, "Utopia in the Home," *International Journal of Political Economy* 22 (Summer 1992): 28-29.

12. Alva and Gunnar Myrdal, *Kris i befolkningsfrågan* (Stockholm: Bonniers, 1934); and more broadly: Allan Carlson, *The Swedish Experiment in Family Politics: The Myrdals and the Interwar Population Crisis* (New Brunswick, NJ: Transaction, 1990): chapters 3-5.

13. See: Yvonne Hirdman, *Den socialistiska hemmafru och andra kvinnohistorier* (Göteborg: Carlssons, 1992): 36-112; and Nancy Eriksson, *Bara en hemmafru: Ett Debattinlägg om kvinnan I familjen* (Stockholm: Forum, 1964): 19-38.

14. Yvonne Hirdman, "The Importance of Gender in the Swedish Labor Movement, Or: A Swedish Dilemma." Paper prepared for the Swedish National Institute of Working Life, 2002: 3-5; and Ann-Katrin Hatje, *Befolkningsfrågan och välfärden: debatten om familjepolitik och nativitetsökning under 1930-och 1940-talen* (Stockholm: Allmänna förlaget, 1974): 47-110.

15. Dorothy McBride Stetson and Amy Maxur, eds., *Comparative State Feminisms* (Thousand Oaks, CA: Sage Publications, 1995): 241.

16. Ron Lesthaeghe, "A Century of Demographic and Cultural Change in Western Europe: An Exploration of Underlying Dimensions," *Population and Development Review* 9 (1983): 429.

17. Hirdman, "The Importance of Gender in the Swedish Labor Movement."

18. From: Jane Lewis and Gertrude Åström, "Equality, Difference, and State Welfare: Labor Market and Family Politics in Sweden," *Feminist Studies* 18 (Spring 1992): 67.

19. Alva Myrdal, et al., *Toward Equality: The Alva Myrdal Report to the Swedish Social Democratic Party* (Stockholm: Prisma, 1972 [1969]): 17, 38, 64, 82-84.

20. Fariborz Nozari, "The 1987 Swedish Family Law Reform," *International Journal of Legal Information* 17 (1989): 219-20; D. Bradley, "Marriage, Family, Property and Inheritance in Swedish Law," *International and Comparative Law Quarterly* 39 (April 1990): 378-81; and Jacob W. F. Sundberg, "Recent Changes in Swedish Family Law: Experiment Repeated," *American Journal of Comparative Law* 23 (#1, 1975): 43.

21. Christina Florin, "Skaten som befriar," in Christina Florin, Lena Sommestad, and Ulla Wikander, *Kvinnor mot kvinnor: Om Systerskapets svårigheter* (Stockholm: Norstedts, 1999): 109, 113, 124.

22. Irene Dingledey, "International Comparison of Tax Systems and Their Impact on the Work-Family Balancing," at http://www.latge.de/ak tuellveroeff/am/dinge100b.pdf (11/05/2003).

23. Anne Lise Ellingsaeter, "Dual Breadwinner Societies: Provider Models in the Scandinavian Welfare States," *Acta Sociologica* 41 (#1, 1998): 66.

24. Sven Steinmo, "Social Democracy v. Socialism: Goal Adaptation in Social Democratic Sweden," *Politics & Society* 16 (Dec. 1988): 430.

25. Maud L. Edwards, "Toward a Third Way: Women's Politics and Welfare Policies in Sweden," *Social Research* 58 (Fall 1991): 681-82.

26. Annika Baude, "Public Policy and Changing Family Patterns in Sweden, 1930-1977," in Jean Lipman-Blumen and Jessie Bernard, eds., *Sex Roles and Social Policy: A Complex Social Equation* (Beverly Hills: SAGE, 1979): 171.

27. *Familj och äktenskap. Betänkande avgivet av Familje lagssakkuniga.* Social Offentliga Utredningen [SOU] 1972: 41, p. 91.

28. Michael Bogdan and Eva Ryrstedt, "Marriage in Swedish Family Law," *Family Law Quarterly* 29 (Fall 1995): 678-79; Nozari, "The 1987 Swedish Family Law Reform," pp. 220-23.

29. Sundberg, "Recent Changes in Swedish Family Law," p. 42.

30. Jacob W. F. Sundberg, "Marriage or No Marriage: The Directives for the Revision of Swedish Family Law," *The International and Comparative Law Quarterly* 20 (April 1971): 235.

31. *SAP Congress Minutes, 1972,* p. 759; in Hirdman, "The Importance of Gender in the Swedish Labor Movement," p. 6.

32. See: Ylva Waldermarson, "Att föra kvinnors talan: Lo:s Kvinnorad 1947-67," in Florin, et al., *Kvinnor mot kvinnor*, pp. 75-105.

33. Anita Myberg, "From Foster Mothers to Child Care Center: A History of Working Mothers and Child Care in Sweden," *Feminist Economics* 6 (No.1, 2000): 15-16.

34. Hirdman, "The Importance of Gender in the Swedish Labor Movement," p. 10.

35. *Ulla Widen* v. *Sweden*, 8 EHRR 79.

36. Jacob W. F. Sundberg, *'The Trip to Nowhere': Family Policy in the Swedish Welfare State Analyzed by Means of the Comparative Law Method Immanent in the European Convention on Human Rights, No. 106* (Stockholm: The Stockholm Institute of Public and International Law, 1995): 3-7, 28-29.

37. Quotation in Bradley, "Marriage, Family, Property and Inheritance in Swedish Law," p. 384.

38. Nozari, "The 1987 Swedish Family Law Reform, p. 223-26; and Åke Saldeen, "Sweden: Reforms of Marriage, Inheritance and Cohabitation Proposed," *Journal of Family Law* 26 (1987-88): 197-205.

39. Ibid., p. 383.

40. Ulla Björnberg, "Cohabitation and Marriage in Sweden—Does Family Form Matter?" *International Journal of Law, Policy and the Family* 15 (2001): 352-53. Emphasis added.

41. Björnberg, "Cohabitation and Marriage in Sweden," pp. 350-62.

42. Myrdal and Myrdal, *Kris I befolkningsfrågan* (Stockholm: Koupertiva förbundet, 1944): 75.

43. While developments in Denmark and Norway each followed a distinctive course, the general direction and the end result have been about the same as in Sweden. For example, Danish and Norwegian translations of Alva and Gunnar Myrdal's 1934 book *Crisis in the Population Question* appeared quickly, and both nations created "population commissions" that closely followed the Myrdal line. In the late 1930's, and again in the late 1960's and 1970's, Social Democratic governments in both lands implemented turns toward the "new family" model that closely resembled developments in Sweden. See Chapter VIII: "The Swedish Line Outside Sweden, 1935-73," in Allan Carlson, *The Roles of Alva and Gunnar Myrdal in the Development of a Social Democratic Response to Europe's 'Population Crisis', 1929-38*. Doctoral Dissertation (Grand Rapids, MI: University Microfilms, 1979): pp. 415-42.

44. Allan Carlson, *Conjugal America: On the Public Purposes of Marriage* (New Brunswick, NJ: Transaction, 2006): Ch. 1.

45. Eskridge, et al., "Nordic Bliss?," pp. 40-41.

CHAPTER 14

SAME-SEX "MARRIAGE" AS VERBICIDE: REAFFIRMING
THE LINGUISTIC AND CULTURAL HERITAGE THAT ONCE
MADE "MARRIAGE" A VIBRANT WORD OF SUBSTANCE
AND HOPE

Bryce Christensen
Southern Utah University

I.   *A New Lexicon*

Headlines do not usually send ordinary Americans scrambling for a dictionary. However, recent years have brought a series of news stories that have refused to fit within a traditional lexicon. Certainly, more than a few Americans may have rubbed their eyes and looked for a dictionary when in 1993 the Supreme Court for the state of Hawaii appeared on the verge of making that state the first jurisdiction on earth to allow two homosexuals to receive a *wedding* license permitting them to *marry*. Nor did the semantic confusion end when Aloha State legislators politically outflanked the court by securing a constitutional amendment allowing them to "reserve marriage to opposite-sex couples."[1] For soon homosexual couples were petitioning judges in Vermont and Massachusetts for the right to marry.

At least some vestiges of traditional semantics inhered in a 1999 Vermont high court ruling that compelled the state to give homosexual couples the same rights as married couples by allowing these homosexual couples to form officially recognized civil partnerships, but did not require the state to issue wedding licenses permitting them to marry. But lexical order was thoroughly scrambled by a 2003 ruling of the supreme court of the state of Massachusetts requiring the state to issue wedding licenses permitting homosexual couples to marry. Indeed, the Massachusetts jurists took over both the legislators' and the lexicographers' roles by officially re-defining "civil marriage to mean the voluntary union of two persons as spouses, to the exclusion of all others." In re-defining *marriage* in this radically innovative way, the Massachusetts justices recognized that they were "mak[ing] a significant change in the definition of marriage as it has been inherited from the common law, and understood by many societies for centuries."[2]

Nonetheless, the shrewd Massachusetts jurists cleverly diverted attention away from their dubious remaking of one lexical entry (namely, *marriage*) by resorting to a similarly dubious redefinition of another word. In characterizing their decision as one that ended a putative state "ban on same-sex marriage," the jurists deployed the word *ban* in a deliberately disorienting way. For state authorities can only ban acts or entities of a real and recognizable character—such as incest or spouse abuse. Massachusetts state legislators had never *banned* same-sex *marriage* any more than they had ever *banned* faster-than-light travel. The state lawmakers whose work the high court undid were, as the jurists conceded simply using the "everyday meaning of 'marriage.'" That is, the state lawmakers had framed the law using the only lexicon comprehensible to the people of the state. They were not trying to *ban* something that had never existed.[3]

However, thanks in large measure to the lexical legerdemain of the Massachusetts jurist, by mid-2004 ceremonies officially represented as *marriages* were taking place not only in Massachusetts (where the state's high court had given its blessing) but also in cities in Oregon, New York, and California, where no court had lent its authority to the legal and lexical revolution.[4] Americans across the country have consequently found themselves enmeshed in a bewildering debate over the meaning of the once-familiar words *marriage* and *wedding*. In this debate, reliance on traditional lexicons—even the very best ones— intensifies rather than dispels confusion. The *Oxford English Dictionary* or *OED*, for instance, does little to ratify the lexical status of homosexuals who claim they are marrying, for this esteemed reference gives as its chief definition of *marriage* "the condition of being a husband or wife," clearly signaling a heterosexual union. That heterosexual lexical substance therefore logically inheres in the *OED*'s definition of wedding as "the action of marrying; marriage, espousal."[5]

II.   Verbicide

Just how lexically disorienting the debate over marriage has become is frankly acknowledged by *Washington Post* journalist David von Drehle, who comments that when "courts in Hawaii, Vermont, and Massachusetts [have] overturned the traditional understanding of 'marriage'—a word most people thought they already understood quite clearly—the decisions seemed to drop from an empty sky."[6] Even Alan Duncan, a homosexual British observer sympathetic to the cause of homosexual partnerships, understands why this debate has been lexically confusing for many ordinary people. "To so many people," Duncan has written, "the word 'marriage' has a clear and limited meaning—and I hate to see politicians [and he might have added "jurists"] and would-be opinion formers trying to take away from people the ordinary meaning of words. . . . Words belong to the whole people."[7]

But popular ownership of the language is anathema to those pressing for what they persist in calling homosexual *marriage*. These activists are claiming a politically and culturally perilous right to define a word by judicial or political fiat, even if doing so destroys the traditional meaning of that word. Indeed, their lexical behavior is precisely that which the British literary scholar and Christian apologist C.S. Lewis called "verbicide, the murder of a word."[8]

No doubt some Americans consider verbicide a relatively minor offense. Why worry about mere words? Curiously, even two of the justices who dissented from the majority decision in the Massachusetts Supreme Court's ruling on homosexual marriage confessed that they could see no substantive issue in the "squabble over the name to be used" in denominating the union of homosexuals and deplored the court's involvement in "a pitched battle over who gets to use the 'm' word."[9] As much as the dissenters were justified in questioning the court's involvement in sorting out a lexical question, they erred greatly in discounting that question as one of little importance. Much depends on the lexical integrity of words. Indeed, as grievously as they overstepped their legitimate role in their ruling on homosexual marriage, the justices writing for the majority in the Massachusetts homosexual marriage case were right to recognize that a "message is conveyed by eschewing the word 'marriage' and replacing it with 'civil union."[10]

Legal theorist Christopher Stone notes rightly that "the way we employ morally significant words embeds cues to right conduct."[11] Lexical cues that point to marital and family responsibilities fade when a word such as *marriage* loses lexical identity. In the same fashion, semantic cues that long guided men and women toward moral responsibilities when journalistic and academic verbicidists explicitly reject "blood, legal ties, adoption, [and] marriage" as essential to the meaning of *family* and proceed to re-define the word as a label for "two or more persons who share resources, share responsibility for decisions, share values and goals, and have commitment to one another over time."[12] Moral guidance rapidly disappears from a lexicon that obscures rather than illuminates the distinctions between married heterosexual couples united in an ancient social institution and homosexual couples united by radical new theories and that erases the differences between a fertile intergenerational family unit made up of father, mother, and children and a sterile and short-lived social unit made up of roommates, cohabiting lovers, or friends. As novelist and political commentator George Orwell famously warned, vague and confusing words are dangerous because "the slovenliness of our language makes it easier for us to have foolish thoughts."[13]

Centuries before Orwell, however, Socrates recognized the peril of slippery language. In a profound investigation of the nature of language, the Socrates of Plato's *Cratylus* disputes the Protagorean view that "all is convention" and "relative to individuals" in the use of words. Socrates declares that "things have a permanent essence of their own" and that proper linguistic labels must therefore be given "according to a natural process . . . and not at our pleasure." Words show themselves "false," Socrates explains, if they do not help us "distinguish natures, as the shuttle . . . distinguish[es] threads of the web." In his search for words that will help him distinguish natures, Socrates emphasizes the importance of the "original meaning" of words, reasoning that it is "the ancient form" of words that most clearly bears the imprint of "the minds of gods, or of men, or of both."[14]

Anyone who shares Socrates' desire for lexical order can only be distressed by a verbicide that kills the original meaning of *marriage* by lethally combining it with a radically new one in a way that confounds rather than distinguishes natures. The Massachusetts jurists intent on killing *marriage* acknowledge that the heterosexual capacity for "procreation" constitutes "the one unbridgeable difference" between heterosexual couples and homosexual ones. But they reason that clinging to a meaning of *marriage* that requires this "single trait" will serve chiefly as a justification for "the invidious quality of . . . discrimination" and for policies that "deny [homosexual couples] protection across the board." What is more, the Massachusetts jurists warned that such adherence to the procreation-focused traditional definition of *marriage* would result in the state's "confer[ring] an official stamp of approval on the destructive stereotype that same-sex relationships are inherently unstable."[15] Fearful that the persistence of the traditional meaning of *marriage* will also mean the persistence of negative stereotypes of homosexual couples, the jurists intend to kill the offending word through a judicial fiat that will remove its power to "distinguish natures."

But even if jurists' lexical ambitions can kill a word's power to distinguish natures, they still cannot erase the differences in nature that the word previously signaled. Though verbicidists in Sweden and Norway were years ahead of the Massachusetts in killing the traditional meaning of *marriage* by conferring it on homosexual unions, that lexical murder hardly killed the perception that "same-sex relationships are inherently unstable." Indeed, social scientists reported in a 2006 study that although remarkably few homosexual couples had actually been married in these two Scandinavian countries, the divorce rate among these homosexual couples has run far higher than among heterosexual couples.[16] It even appears that in the Massachusetts jurists' verbicidal attempt to smash the popular stereotype of "same-sex relationships [as] inherently unstable," they unintentionally put the public spotlight on the break-up of the Goodridges, the homosexual couple who gave their name to the ruling in which the Massachusetts committed their lethal lexical assault against *marriage*.[17] Unfortunately, the Goodridge breakup did not reverse the Supreme Court's ruling or undo the jurists' act of verbicide.

As a scholar who recognizes the cultural harm that can result from verbicide committed against the traditional vocabulary of family and sex roles, L.B. Cebik warns of the perils of arbitrary lexical novelty. "From Aristotle onward," Cebik writes, "we took language to be a fixed entity whose nature we sought as one seeks the analysis of a rock. Then . . . we reversed our field and definitions became arbitrary. . . . By stipulation we could make a concept mean whatever we wanted it to mean. The result has been chaos." Cebik sees particular peril in linguistic shifts in the vocabulary of home and family life. "When we attempt to alter concepts [in this cultural sphere]," he cautions, "we do so without investigating the consequences of either the old or the new meanings. . . . This sort of short-sightedness can spell . . . a well-intentioned disaster."[18]

Those who doubt that cultural chaos and disaster may follow from that linguistically murderous abuse of the word *marriage* ought to consider philosopher William Barrett's warning against infinite semantic flexibility:

If you abandon the notion of substance—that there are definite things and that language at least in some of its uses, can and does clearly refer to them—then you begin to float in a sea of indefiniteness, where anything goes. To have meanings at all does require a certain degree of fixity—of persistent identity in the objects of discourse.[19]

The real possibility that the word *marriage* will drown in "a sea of indefiniteness" may be inferred from the cultural history of a word of even greater semantic weight. Literary scholars have plausibly suggested that it was the promiscuous use of the word *God* by nineteenth-century pantheists such as Thomas Carlyle, Percy Bysshe Shelley, and Ralph Waldo Emerson that helped create a culture receptive to atheism. As critic Philip Rosenberg has argued, a pantheism that licensed the application of the word *God* to everything helped open a cultural path between traditional Christianity and an atheistic naturalism.[20] It appears that when a word becomes so elastic as to be applicable to everything—when it utterly ceases to "distinguish natures"—people soon cease to care if the word simply disappears from use. Hence, a society that applies the word *marriage* to all kinds of social relationships is fast becoming a society entirely without marriage, just as a society that applies the word *God* to all kinds of diverse spiritual entities is a society fast becoming atheist.

Anything but an innocent shift in social nomenclature, the verbicide that would kill the word *marriage* thus constitutes a profound threat to American society. That verbicide is already well underway, but it is not yet complete. The great lexicographer Samuel Johnson (whose pioneering 1755 *Dictionary of the English Language* defined marriage as "the act of uniting a man and a woman for life") acknowledged that "tongues, like governments, have a natural tendency to degeneration." Nonetheless, he challenged English speakers to "make some struggles for our language."[21] Those who today accept Johnson's summons to such struggles might begin by fighting to prevent the completion of the attempted verbicide that would kill *marriage*. To prevent the completion of that verbicide, defenders of *marriage* might do well to do precisely what detectives do when dealing with other killings. That is, the first step in preventing the completion of the verbicide of marriage is that of ferreting out the facts concerning the *identity* of the would-be perpetrators and investigating their *motives, methods*, and *opportunities* for committing this lexical murder.

The perpetrators of this verbicide certainly include the homosexual couples who have petitioned the courts for the right to marry. One motive of such couples is quite transparent: these couples want to claim the cultural legitimacy attaching to the word *marriage*. These couples profess a deep desire for the "stamp of societal approval" that comes with that word.[22] However, beneath homosexuals' understandable desire to culturally legitimate their own relationships lies a second motive: homosexuals wish to undermine the morally normative status of heterosexuals' marriages. Homosexual activists have themselves scorned the prospect of a "mere 'aping'" of heterosexual marriage: they want homosexual marriage to "destabilize marriage's gendered definition by disrupting the link between gender and marriage." They thus value the homosexual wedding ceremony in part because of the disruptive "transformation that it makes on the people around us."[23]

III.   Aiding and Abetting Verbicide

Whatever their motives, however, homosexual couples alone could never kill the word *marriage*. They must have help. But they have not lacked for willing accomplices in what historian James Billington has aptly termed the "university-media complex."[24] Nor have journalists and academics been coy about their motives for assisting in the verbicide of *marriage*. By standing up for homosexuals wanting to marry, reporters and professors have burnished their identity as courageous champions of civil rights. Without ever leaving the comfort of their offices and classrooms, the liberal-leftists of the university-media complex have reprised the heady days of "the civil rights movement of forty years ago," hailing gay marriages in Oregon, New York, and California as acts of "civil disobedience" comparable to those of the Sixties-era Blacks who defied the Southern segregation laws denying them the right to eat at public lunch counters or to ride in the front seats of public buses.[25]

A.   Media

By rallying around gay couples demanding the right to marry, progressive journalists and academics thus cast themselves as a new generation of heroes bravely standing up to this century's incarnations of oppression, homophobia's own Lester "Ax Handle" Madduxes and Eugene "Bull" Connors. At times, the media and academic accomplices of the homosexual couples trying to kill *marriage* denounce the "bigotry" of their opponents with the fervor of those who once faced fire hoses and German shepherds. Atlanta journalist Cynthia Tucker, for instance, accused fellow Georgians of "enshrining bigotry in the state constitution" by supporting an amendment defining marriage as heterosexual.[26] Editorialists for Portland's *Oregonian* detect in opposition to homosexual marriage the "retrograde" impulses of "gay-bashers."[27] Likewise, Kenyon College historian Joan Cadden has seen in opposition to homosexuals' appropriation of the word *marriage* "homophobic denial—alive, angry, and . . . caus[ing] serious harm."[28]

In the on-going verbicide of *marriage*, it does not much disturb the university-media accomplices that even some African Americans who generally support homosexual rights object to their deployment of Sixties-era Civil Rights rhetoric. They simply are not listening when African American editorialist Joseph H. Brown, for instance, complains that "you can't compare the struggle for homosexual rights with black America's civil rights movement. The two are not the same. Gay people were not enslaved or forced to live under Jim Crow laws. . . . Sexual orientation can be concealed, skin color can't."[29]

But a closer look at the media verbicidists reveals that in helping to kill the word *marriage* they are doing far more than assigning themselves flattering roles in a misleading 21st-century Civil Rights melodrama. They are also fattening their checkbooks. As the cultural historian Christopher Lasch realizes, journalists maximize their profits by finding new ways to increase the supply of—and the demand for—their product: news. Modern consumer capitalism, in Lasch's compelling analysis, is driven by "the need for novelty and fresh stimulation," a need that amounts to a kind of "addiction." Lasch accuses journalists of profiting by taking advantage of this addiction: "The value of news," he writes, "like that of any other commodity [in the modern consumer market], consists primarily of its novelty, only secondarily of its informational value."[30] Profit-seeking journalists can only view homosexual marriage—a radical novelty—as a golden opportunity.

B.   Academics

Though academic verbicidists do not sell their services to the public in quite the same way that journalistic ones do, they are like journalists in that they too advance their professional interests and lengthen their CVs by focusing on the novel, the cutting-edge, the revolutionary, to the neglect of the proverbial and the traditional. It is therefore quite understandable that sociologist Lewis A. Croser would detect in the academy a pervasive "*neophilia* . . . , that is, the one-sided value emphasis on what is new."[31] For academic neophiliacs, the semantic preservation of the traditional meaning of *marriage* holds far less professional promise than the lexical innovation of *marriage* as a label applicable to the union of homosexual couples.

As university-media professionals who share a vested interest in novelty, journalists and academics alike generally resist cultural influences that reinforce traditional perspectives, including those perspectives preserved in a historically rooted lexicon of *family* and *marriage*. Together, journalists and academics have advanced a liberalism that historian Joyce Appleby indicts for "turning [the nation's] collective life into a kind of perpetual adolescence." Appleby blames "liberalism [for] forcefully project[ing] its optimistic vision of the possible onto the future" in a way that has "denigrated both past and present."[32] The journalists and academics of the university-media complex involved in the verbicidal assault on *marriage* are surely the sort of "modern people" that the distinguished scholar of rhetoric Richard Weaver has said are "prone to resent the past and seek to deny its substance . . . [because] it inhibits them."[33] And as these modern verbacidalists remove the inhibitions of the past by killing a word with deep historical roots, they move society ever further from "the community of language" that Weaver believes can only be founded on an appreciation of "language . . . as a great storehouse of universal memory."[34]

C.   Religion

Because of its deep ties not only to human memory of the past but also to divine revelations of eternity, religion counts for very little within the university-media complex. Pervaded as they are by an anti-religious, (and especially) anti-Catholic bias, the media—in the judgment of columnist William E. Simon—

simply do not regard religion as "a matter of importance in contemporary American life."[35] But then journalists learn their trade in universities where, as historian George Marsden remarks, "antireligious assumptions are . . . deeply ingrained in the very definitions of the subjects" studied.[36] Such antireligious assumptions have become so ubiquitous on campus that Marsden sees in contemporary American universities "the virtual establishment of nonbelief, or the near exclusion of religious perspectives from dominant academic life."[37] Endorsing Marsden's perspective, Louisiana State political scientist James R. Stone, Jr. has decried a "secularization of the university" so complete that "on campus, or at least on the faculty, the theological voice is absent or barely audible."[38]

Curiously, however, by attacking religion rooted in the past and in scriptural revelations, university-media professionals are actually laying claim to a new kind of sacerdotal authority. As literary critic J. Hillis Miller has observed, the disappearance of traditional faith in the transcendent God of scripture "bring[s] into existence a society which generates its own immanent basis for meaning."[39] In other words, Society replaces God as the ground of meaning and itself becomes a kind of surrogate Deity.

That writers become a new kind of priests when Society replaces God was remarkably clear to the great Victorian unbeliever Thomas Carlyle. Dismissing traditional Christianity as merely "the dead Letter of Religion," Carlyle hailed as the central new religious reality "that wonder of wonders, Society," declaring that "every conceivable Society, past and present," constituted "properly and wholly a Church." But Carlyle recognized a Church within the Church, and within this *inner* Church, writers exercise special prerogatives. "The true Church," Carlyle remarked, "is the Guild of Authors." And this Guild—which today populates the university-media complex—does now what prophets and apostles once did. "Every man that writes," Carlyle explained, "is writing a new Bible; or a new Apocrypha; to last for a week, or for a thousand years."[40]

Writing a new Bible allows the priest-writers of the university-media church to elide the old biblical texts that define *marriage* and *family* (cf. Gen. 1:28; 2:18-25; 3:16-19; Eph. 5:28-33; 6:1-4) and replace them with expansive new texts. Social abandonment of the truths of the old Bible greatly distressed Fyodor Dostoevsky, who famously expressed his fears through his character Ivan Karamazov: "Without God and immortal life . . . all things are lawful."[41] But many journalists and academics welcome the permissiveness of a Society answerable only to itself, a permissiveness that permits them to kill the old meaning of *marriage* as they promulgate a radically new one.

Of course, relatively few ordinary journalists consciously think of themselves as quasi-priests writing surrogate scripture for the surrogate deity Society. But particularly in the way they have applauded and actively joined in verbicidal assaults against *marriage*, many journalists have gravitated toward a sociocentric metaphysics that grants them a gratifyingly large and rewarding cultural role. Indeed, although few journalists have made a systematic study of it, many now share the assumptions of the prominent academics who have articulated the professionally potent philosophy labeled "Social Constructivism." In this philosophy—now widely accepted among academic theorists—all of "reality" is whatever "we bring forth in a community of observers" as the "praxis of living" enmeshes us in "the happening of being human, in the languaging of language."[42] For Social Constructivists, "truth" (usually in quotation marks among the theoretically sophisticated) shifts whenever social attitudes shift, for social-constructivist "truth" rests on nothing more than "consensus among [those] who find the proposition credible."[43] Social Constructivists thus maintain that it is Society that dictates the content of reality and truth, including moral truth. That is, Social Constructivists ascribe to Society—their surrogate Deity—something of the omnipotence and omniscience that inheres in God the Father in Christian orthodoxy.

The spirit—if not always the doctrinal letter—of a social-constructivist worship of Society inheres in a great deal of journalistic and academic writing, where readers learn that it is Society—not Nature or Nature's God—that dictates gender roles, group identity, moral virtues, and even supposedly religious doctrines.[44] But no group wields more quasi-priestly authority on behalf of the surrogate deity Society than do jurists, including the four black-robed verbicidists who wrote the same-sex marriage decision for the Massachusetts Supreme Court. It is entirely predictable that the most candid of the Massachusetts verbicidists ultimately defended the Court's radical re-definition of *marriage* not by invoking the clear text of law or the state's constitution but rather by asserting a heightened social awareness. This verbicidal jurist called on Massachusetts citizens to embrace the Court's decision as a measure that would incorporate homosexual couples into "our community" and would afford official recognition that "we [all] share a common humanity and participate in the social contract that is the foundation of our Commonwealth."[45] One of the outvoted dissenters in the Massachusetts same-sex case well understood that in re-defining *marriage* his colleagues on the bench were doing more than examining law; they were attempting to make "a tremendous step toward a more just society" and so leave their mark on "social history"[46]

D.   Utopians

And even as Social Constructivism furnishes the quasi-priests in academe, the judiciary, and the media with a quasi-theology that justifies their labors in generating new meanings for words such as *marriage* and *family*, those meanings have often coalesced in the form of distinctly utopian ambitions. For as they embrace Society as a surrogate deity and the quasi-divine new ground of meaning, the jurists, academics, and journalists most deeply implicated in verbicidal assaults on *marriage* and *family* are hard at work making this deity more perfect, more worthy of their adoration.

The dream of making a perfect Society has, of course, beguiled intellectuals at least since Plato wrote *The Republic* more than two millennia ago. But as Nobel laureate Peter Medawar has pointed out, the utopian impulse has manifest itself as a strongly "audacious and irreverent" cultural force since the 15th century, as Renaissance thinking and modern science have enlarged the scope of human powers and as secular regimes have displaced ecclesiastical authority.[47]

Though his 16th-century book *Utopia* lent its name to the entire genre of works about perfect societies, Thomas More actually depicts an ideal society that differs markedly from those described by most other utopian societies. More depicts an ideal society that is deeply religious and is firmly rooted on marriage and family. In this ideal society, "matrymoneie is . . . never broken, but by death" and "husbandes chastise theire wyfes, and the parents their children."[48]

In contrast, what the authors of most utopian blueprints depict are societies in which religion, marriage, and family life are all weak or absent. In works such as Tommaso Campanella's *City of the Sun*, Dom Léger-Marie Deschamps's *Le Vrai Système* (1761), Edward Bellamy's *Looking Backward: 2000-1887* (1888), William Morris's *News from Nowhere* (1891), H. G. Wells's *A Modern Utopia* (1905), Charlotte Perkins Gilman's *Moving the Mountain* (1911), and B.F. Skinner's *Walden Two* (1948), utopian theorists have laid out blueprints for ideal societies in which religion and family count for little. As sociologist Robert Nisbet has pointed out, utopian thinkers have typically regarded the secular Society created within an ideal "political community" as the proper "successor to the Church in its inclusion of all human needs, desires and hopes."[49] And utopians typically intend to satisfy those needs, desires, and hopes in part by erasing or at least attenuating the traditional social meaning of marriage and family life.[50]

Gender equality will also grow in utopia as "practice makes women suitable for war and other duties."[51] The gender equality that prevails in utopia ensures that "wives are in no way dependent on their husbands for maintenance."[52] Utopians not only eviscerate marriage as an economic tie between husband and wife, but they also weaken—if not altogether abolish—the legal significance of wedlock. When utopians do permit marriage to survive, they still end up weakening it; consequently, "families are held together by no bond of coercion, legal or social, but by mutual liking and affection, and everyone is free to come or go as he or she pleases."[53]

No longer a merely literary fantasy, utopian thinking has firmly established itself among progressive journalists, academics, and jurists of the sort now involved in verbicidal attacks on *family* and *marriage*. Writing more than forty years ago, political analyst George Kateb remarked that although "a sufficient anti-utopian case could be made to rest on the sanctity of the family," progressives had pushed so many utopian ideas into reality that "antiutopian positions on the nature of government" were "out of touch with what already had become part of the political life of the United States."[54] And since Kateb wrote, the United States has moved a good deal further away from the sanctity of the family and a good deal closer toward utopia, as more and more young children have become wards of tax-subsidized day-care centers, as paid employment (often in non-traditional fields) has made more and more women independent of their husbands' incomes, and as liberalized divorce laws have weakened wedlock.

This half-century movement away from the sanctity of family and toward utopia very much deserves the attention of those now trying to understand the verbicidal assault against *marriage*. For regardless of their motives and regardless of their methods, those trying to perpetrate this lexical murder could never have succeeded in their crime—would not even have attempted it—had this broad social and cultural movement not given them their opportunity. Homosexual couples would not have conspired with journalists, academics, and jurists to launch a verbicidal assault against *marriage* in the 21st century if wedding vows had not already been seriously compromised among *heterosexual* Americans in the late 20th century.[55]

E.   Courts

During the last three decades of the 20th century, record numbers of heterosexual Americans began heading for the divorce courts, where revolutionary no-fault divorce made it remarkable easy to give the lie to Samuel Johnson's 18th-century definition of marriage as "the act of uniting a man and a woman *for life*."[56] In part because of fear of divorce, many heterosexuals began delaying or avoiding wedlock altogether.[57] Defying the religious doctrines restricting legitimate sexual expression to marriage (cf. Heb. 13: 4), many heterosexual couples began to live in cohabiting unions without entering wedding vows—or simply pursued sexual satisfaction through random and short-lived trysts.[58]

Even among heterosexual couples who did marry and did stay married, marriage ceased to define the foundation for a fertile, child-rich family or the basis for productive home-based labors.[59] As homosexual activists witnessed these dramatic changes in the marital conduct of heterosexuals, they recognized a prime opportunity for verbicide. Andrew Sullivan plausibly remarks, "it was heterosexuals in the 1970s who changed marriage into something . . . like a partnership between equals, with both partners often working and gender roles less rigid than in the past. All homosexuals are saying, three decades later, is that, under the current definition, there's no reason to exclude us. If you want to return straight marriage to the 1950s, go ahead. But until you do, the exclusion of gays is simply an anomaly."[60] In the same vein, historian Stephanie Coontz writes, "Heterosexuals were the upstarts who turned marriage into a voluntary love relationship rather than a mandatory economic and political institution. . . . [H]eterosexuals subverted the long-standing rule that every marriage had to have a husband who played one role in the family and a wife who played a completely different one. Gays and lesbians simply looked at the revolution heterosexuals had wrought and noticed that, with its new norms, marriage could work for them, too."[61]

Like homosexual activists, Massachusetts' high court recognized that it was the revolution in heterosexual marriage that had given them a prime opportunity for verbicide. These jurists situated their lexical assault in the context of "the changing realities of the American family," changing realities that had produced "the modern family in its many variations."[62] In the same way, when a Superior Court jurist for King County, Washington, handed down a verbicidal decision in 2004 in favor of homosexual marriage (later overturned on appeal), he justified his act of lexical murder by referring to the way "the shape of marriage has drastically changed over the years." This would-be Washington verbicidalist noted in particular that because of the upsurge in non-marital childbearing, "the link between civil marriage and procreation is not what it was" back in the days when "love, marriage and baby carriage would come in a predictable sequence"[63]

The "changing realities" and shifting "shape of marriage" that have given verbicidal jurists their pretext for committing lexical murder can only dismay those who care about marriage as the foundation of family life. For across the country, the marriage rate has plummeted in recent decades. Between 1970 and 2000, the marriage rate for women ages 15 to 44 in the United States plummeted more than 40 percent—and is apparently still dropping. The marriage rate in Massachusetts has likewise tumbled. In 2000, the marriage rate for Massachusetts stood at just 6.0 per 1000 state residents, well below the national marriage rate of 8.3 per 1000 Americans and well below the state's own previous marriage rate of 8.3 marriages per 1000 state residents in 1970.[64] (Given the increased longevity of the population, it seems likely that the drop in Massachusetts's marriage rate has been even more pronounced among women ages 15 to 44, the prime marrying years. State-by-state data, however, are not available for this age group.) And though divorce rates have moderated in Massachusetts and the nation as a whole in recent years, they remain high by historical standards. In other words, the verbicide utopian-minded jurists have tried to commit looks disturbingly like a coup de grace. Yet Massachusetts's verbicidal jurists shrewdly diverted attention away from the sorry state of the institution they were lexically assaulting. "Marriage," the Massachusetts high court jurists misleadingly affirmed, "has survived all of [its] transformations and . . . will continue to be a vibrant and revered institution."[65]

Past masters of deceptive rhetoric about the vibrancy of the institution whose label they wish to lexically murder, the Massachusetts jurists blithely asserted universal acquiescence in the earlier verbicide that—for many progressives—has emptied the word *family* of its traditional marital content. "*No one,*" the jurists declared, "disputes that the [homosexual] plaintiff couples are families."[66] Apparently, these Massachusetts jurists assumed that the same cultural and legal opening that permitted them to commit verbicidal assault on *marriage* also allowed them to simply write out of existence those who still refuse to distort the lexicon by applying the word *family* to homosexual households.[67]

F.   Anti-Utopian Warnings

A much more honest user of the language than the verbicidalists who sit on Massachusetts high court, novelist Aldous Huxley remarked more than 50 years ago that the increasing prevalence of divorce in America meant that "Utopia [has become] far closer than anyone, only 15 years ago, could have predicted." As the author of a powerful novel (*Brave New World* [1932]) depicting the way Utopia destroys marriage and family life, Huxley gloomily predicted that "in a few years, marriage licenses will be sold like dog licenses, good for a period of twelve months, with no law against changing dogs or keeping more than one around at a time."[68] Nor was Huxley alone in sounding the alarm about the utopian threat to marriage and family. A number of other prominent 20th-century authors also penned powerful warnings against the dehumanizing threat of uto-pian projects that would deny men and women the comfort and protection of marriage and family. These authors included Yevgeny Zamyatin (author of *We* [1924]), George Orwell (author of *1984* [1948]), and Anthony Burgess (author of *The Wanting Seed* [1963]).

The anti-utopian novels by this brilliant quartet differ in important ways, but they come together as a powerful warning that much is lost when utopia attacks the family and the vocabulary used to identify family ties. Huxley de-picts a world where an all-powerful utopian government uses psychological pro-gramming and drugs to reduce men and women to a pleasure-seeking conformi-ty in which they remain "infants where feeling and desire are concerned."[69] To keep everyone in this state of infantile docility, the masters of Huxley's imagi-nary utopia have abolished the family: constantly cared for by the state, the resi-dents of this utopia live their entire lives "with no mothers or fathers . . . no wives or children . . . to feel strongly about."[70] Readers encounter the same uto-pian abolition of family ties in Zamyatin's utopian state, where the protagonist D-503 lacks even the kind of name that a family can bestow. "If I had mother," D-503 yearns, "like the ancients: mine—yes precisely *my* mother. To whom I would be . . . not number D-503, and not a molecule of the *One* State, but a sim-ple human being—a piece of herself."[71]

In contrast with Huxley and Zamyatin—who depict utopias that entirely dissolve family life in state-sanctioned promiscuity—Orwell and Burgess por-tray utopias that permit family life but dictate its forms. In Orwell's antiutopian masterpiece, the Party officials firmly control the marital choices of all men and women, denying couples the right to marry if their union is judged out of har-mony with state policies. In Burgess's prescient novel, the utopian state prevents population growth by denying married couples the right to have a second child, by orchestrating real and bloody gender warfare, and by bombarding the popu-lace with "mechanical stories about good people not having children . . . [and] homo[sexual]s in love with each other."[72] (Burgess's utopian bureaucrats could have written much of the verbicidal decision handed down by the Massachusetts Supreme Court. In the spirit of the propaganda stories Burgess describes, the Massachusetts decision evinces contempt rather respect for those who believe that "marriage is procreation" and manifests extraordinarily warm appreciation for homosexuals as "volunteer[s] in our schools [and] as woship[pers] in our churches" and expresses deep affection for homosexuals as "our neighbors, our coworkers, our friends."[73])

The state-sponsored and family-less licentiousness of Zamyatin's and Hux-ley's utopias might seem to be very far from the rigid state regulation of family and marriage in Orwell's and Burgess's utopias. However, the common thread running through all four antiutopian novels emerges in Orwell's explanation that in his utopia government officials avoid the "forming loyalties which [the uto-pian government] might not be able to control" by systematically denying couples permission to marry if they give "the impression of being physically attracted to one another."[74] Utopia may license random fornication or it may allow marriage but dictate its form and meaning. But utopia cannot allow marriage and family life to exercise any moral or social authority which it "might not be able to control."

One of the most important ways utopia-builders prevent family and marriage from creating autonomous and uncontrollable social forces is by controlling the language that labels and describes marital and family behavior. Zamyatin depicts government officials hard at work ensuring that all words—even those found in poetry—are "tamed and harnessed" to utopian purposes.[75] Orwell likewise highlights the importance of language control in utopia, where government experts have perfected verbicide as a strategy for replacing the words in the traditional lexicon with the politically engineered vocabulary of utopian Newspeak. These utopian experts love "the beauty of the destruction of words" because that destruction advances "the whole aim of Newspeak [, which] is to narrow the range of thought." Newspeak prevents men and women from expressing—or even thinking—ideas that offend against utopian orthodoxy. Because the promulgation of Newspeak causes the meanings of old words to be "rubbed out and forgotten," it leaves rebels who wish to say something unacceptable to utopian leaders with "no words in which to express it."[76]

G.   New Masters

Though old words haven't entirely disappeared from the utopia Huxley depicts, "propaganda technicians" have been so successful in their "campaign against the past" that the traditional vocabulary of family life induces shame and confusion. The word *mother*, for instance, has become "a pornographic impropriety," while anyone trying to explain how people in one remote area still "get married" by "mak[ing] a promise to live together for always" can expect utopian listeners to be "genuinely shocked."[77]

In their verbicidal assault on words, as in their manipulation of the family life such words can describe, the would-be engineers of a utopian society never stop trying to erase "loyalties [they] they might not be able to control." Though generally hidden by utopian rhetoric, a deep craving for control emerges as one of the most powerful and persistent motives for verbicide among progressive journalists, academics, and jurists. Few of these verbicidalists frankly acknowledge their desire to control their fellow citizens. But Lewis Carroll (author of *Through the Looking Glass*) depicts that desire in the simple but revealing episode in which a bewildered Alice tries to grapple with the strange way Humpty Dumpty uses the word *glory*:

> "I don't know what you mean by 'glory,'" Alice said.
> Humpty Dumpty smiled contemptuously. "Of course you don't—till I tell you. I meant 'there's a nice knock-down argument for you!'"
> "But 'glory' doesn't mean 'a nice knock-down argument,'" Alice objected.
> When I use a word," Humpty Dumpty said, in rather a scornful tone, "it means just what I choose it to mean—neither more nor less."
> "The question is," said Alice, "whether you *can* make words mean so many different things."

"The question is," said Humpty Dumpty, "which is to be master—that's all."[78]

That a deep desire for mastery—a simple lust for power—motivates those now trying to commit verbicide against *marriage* has been suggested by jurists who witnessed an attempted lexical assault up-close in July 2006. In handing down their 5-4 decision affirming the constitutionality of Washington's law defining marriage as the union of a man and a woman, two of the state supreme court judges in the majority saw in the four dissenters' attempt to overturn that law "a claim of raw judicial power to redefine public institutions such as marriage."[79]

The Washington jurists' characterization of the minority's position as an attempt to claim "raw judicial power" echoes Justice Byron White's famous 1973 criticism of the majority ruling in *Roe* v. *Wade*.[80] The exercise of "raw judicial power" that White discerned in the landmark 1973 abortion decision constituted a judicial usurpation of specific legislative prerogatives. In contrast, the "raw judicial power" which the Washington jurists sought to exercise—and which their colleagues who wrote for the majority in Massachusetts' same-sex marriage case did in fact successfully exercise—constituted a verbicidal usurpation of the broad cultural prerogatives of the entire population. As even an observer sympathetic to the homosexual cause has acknowledged, "Words belong to the whole people."[81] And though a wide range of journalists and academics, advertisers and propagandists do try to murder words for their own purposes, the verbicidalists who assault words from the bench evince a singularly inflated arrogance and a uniquely swollen lust for dictatorial cultural power in committing their lexical crimes.

Unlike the advertisers, sloganeers, and propagandists who rely on a confused public to kill a word slowly by inflicting a million petty lexical wounds, the jurists now trying to kill *marriage* by one official and sacerdotal court decree expect nothing but submission from the general public. Like the Aztec priests who expected the masses to watch in reverent awe as they tore the hearts out of sacrificial victims, the high priests of judicial verbicide expect the American public to watch with deferential passivity as they eviscerate the word *marriage* on their juridical altars to advance their divine vision of a utopian Society

The Newspeak verbicidalists assaulting *marriage* deny that they are seeking power over society as a whole. They insist that allowing homosexual couples to make legal claim to the word *marriage* will "not require anyone to change their [sic] beliefs or adopt behaviors that fall outside their [sic] religious tradition."[82] But verbicide by legal fiat does in fact compel a great many people to do things they do not wish to do. Consider, for example, how the verbicidal assault on *marriage* has already licensed coercive action against conscience and conduct in Massachusetts, where the Catholic social agency handling adoptions has been forced to terminate their operations or violate Church teaching by placing children with putatively-married homosexual couples.[83] And the same government coercion that translated the verbicide of *marriage* into the closure of a religious social-service agency will operate in scores of other settings to compel men and women either to endorse (or at least passively acquiesce in) the lexical violence the high court has wrought—or to absent themselves from the public sphere.

IV. Conclusion

For those who would resist verbicide and the statist coercion it engenders, the need has never been greater to heed Samuel Johnson's summons to "make some struggles for our language." But for the foreseeable future the would-be perpetrators of verbicide against *marriage* will continue to find personal, financial, political and professional advantage in lethally assaulting the word. Verbicide against *marriage* will continue to satisfy the imperatives of the sociocentric metaphysics that foster utopian aspirations. In other words, those who would protect from *marriage* from verbicide can do little to reduce the number of potential perpetrators with substantial motives for committing lexical murder.

Those who would protect *marriage* can try to disrupt verbicidal assaults against the word. They can make sure that their elected representatives know that they still cherish the traditional meaning of *marriage*. Unfortunately, however, those verbicidally assaulting *marriage* have done much of their mischief in the courts, relatively insulated from democratic pressures.

But even in the courts, verbicidists move forward with their lexical crimes only when they see a cultural opening to do so. Logically, then, those who oppose verbicidal attacks against *marriage* should focus their long-term efforts on closing the cultural opening for such attacks. Closing that opening will mean restoring social and legal substance to wedlock. It will mean reaffirmation of wedlock as the lifelong commitment that creates the proper context for sexual expression and child-bearing. It will mean rediscovery of the domestic economy that makes the married-couple home the center of productive labor. When marriage rates among heterosexuals again climb and divorce rates fall, when the numbers of Americans who cohabit or bear a child out of marriage drop, when married couples again devote themselves to building child-rich families and productive homes, then verbicidists will abandon their murderous designs against *marriage*.

Those who wish to protect *marriage* will understand that they face large cultural and social challenges. But the health of the nation's lexicon, culture, and families depends upon determined efforts to meet those challenges and so renew the linguistic and cultural heritage that once made *marriage* a vibrant word of substance and hope—and can do so again.

Notes

1. Cf. Cynthia M. Davis, "'The Great Divorce' of Government and Marriage: Changing the Nature of the Gay Marriage Debate," *Marquette Law Review* 89 (2006): 799-800.

2. "Full Text of Mass. Gay Marriage Ruling" [*Goodridge et al.* v *Department of Public Health, et al.* 44 Mass. 309 SJC-08860 4 March 2003 - 18 Nov. 2003], MSNBC 20 July 2006 <http://www.msnbc.com/news/995055.asp?cp1=1>.

3. Ibid.

4. Cf. Pam Belluck, "Gay Marriage, State by State," *New York Times* 7 Mar. 2004: Sec. 4, p. 2.

5. Coleridge, Herbert et al., eds. *The Oxford English Dictionary*. Compact ed. 2 vols. New York: Oxford University Press, 1971.

6. David von Drehle, "Take the Issues to the People, Not to the Courts," *The Washington Post* 14 Nov. 2004: B4.

7. Alan Duncan, "Hurrah for the new gay weddings," *The Times* [London] 3 Dec. 2005: 1.

8. C.S. Lewis, *Studies in Words*, 2nd ed. (Cambridge: Cambridge University Press, 1967), 7; cf. Bryce Christensen, "Redefining *Family*: War Over a Word," *Utopia Against the Family: The Problems and Politics of the American Family* (San Francisco: Ignatius, 1990), 35-49.

9. Martha Sousman and Francis X. Spina, "Opinions of the Justices to the Senate," Massachusetts Supreme Judicial Court, 3 Feb. 2004. 17 July 2006. <http://newfindlaw.com/cnn/docs/conlaw/maglmarriage20304.html>.

10. Margaret H. Marshall et al., "Opinions of the Justices to the Senate," op. cit.

11. Christopher Stone, *Earth and Other Ethics: The Case for Moral Pluralism* (New York: Harper & Row, 1987), 219-220.

12. Cf. American Home Economics Association, *A Force for Families* (Washington, D.C.: AHEA, c. 1976), 4; cf. also Allan Carlson, "Treason of the Profesionals: The Case of Home Economics," *The Family in America* August 1987: 1-8.

13. George Orwell, "Politics and the English Language," *'Shooting an Elephant' and Other Essays* (1945; rpt. New York: Brace & World, 1950), 77.

14. Plato, *Cratylus*, 385-388, 414-416, 418, 433, trans. B. Jowett, in *The Dialogues of Plato* (New York: Scribner's, 1889), 1: 623-629, 653-655.

15. "Full Text of Mass. Gay Marriage Ruling" [*Goodridge et al.* v *Department of Public Health, et al.* 44 Mass. 309 SJC-08860 4 March 2003 - 18 Nov. 2003], op. cit.

16. Gunnar Andersson et al., "The Demographics of Same-Sex Marriages in Norway and Sweden," *Demography* 43 (2006): 79-98.

17. Cf. Michael Levenson, "After 2 Years, Same-Sex Marriage Icons Split Up," *Boston Globe* 21 July 2006 22 July 2006 <http://www.boston.com/news/local /articles/2006/07/21/
after_2_years_same_sex_marriage_icons_split_up/?page=2>.

18. L. B. Cebik, "Women's Studies and Home Economics," *Journal of Home Economics* January 1975: 28.

19. William Barrett, *Death of the Soul: From Descartes to the Computer* (Garden City: Doubleday, 1986), 129-130.

20. Philip Rosenberg, *The Seventh Hero: Thomas Carlyle and the Theory of Radical Activism* (Cambridge: Harvard University Press, 1974), 49-50; cf. also James Turner, *Without God, Without Creed: The Origins of Unbelief in America* (Baltimore: Johns Hopkins University Press, 1985), 80.

21. Samuel Johnson, *A Dictionary of the English Language*, 9th ed., corr. and rev. (London: Longman, Hurst, Rees, and Orme, Paternoster-Row, 1805); E.L. McAdam, Jr. and George Milne, eds., *Johnson's Dictionary: A Modern Selection* (New York: Pantheon, 1963), 17.

22. Cf. Cecilia M. Vega, "A Celebration of Gay Hope; Group Reception Seen as an Argument for Legitimacy of Same-Sex Marriage," *The Press Democrat* 23 April 2004: B1.

23. Barbara J. Cox, "A (Personal) Essay on Same-Sex Marriage," *National Journal of Sexual Orientation Law* 1.1 (1995): 88-89.

24. James Billington et al., "Europe and America," *Bergedorfer Round Table* 69 21 July 2006 <http:/ /www.koerber-stiftung.de/bg/recherche/pdf_protokoll/bnd_69_de.pdf>.

25. Cf., e.g., Jennifer Peter, "Massachusetts' Gay Marriage Debate Taking on Form, Rhetoric of Civil Rights Movement," *Associated Press Worldstream* 15 Jan. 2004; Ellen Goodman, "Center Has Shifted," *South Florida Sun-Sentinel* 21 Feb. 2004: 19A.

26. Cynthia Tucker, "Our Opinion: On Gay Unions, Pandering Rises Above Principles," *The Atlanta Journal-Constitution* 28 May 2006: B6.

27. "Gay Marriage Ban is a Loser," Editorial, *The Oregonian* 15 Feb. 2004: C4.

28. Joan Kadden, Rev. of *Same-Sex Unions in Premodern Europe* by John Boswell *Speculum* 71 (1996): 696.

29. Joseph H. Brown, "Gay Couples Never Knew Jim Crow," *Tampa Tribune* 11 June 2006: 1.

30. Chistopher Lasch, "What's Wrong With the Right?" *Tikkun* 1 (1987): 23-29.

31. Lewis A. Croser, Intro., *The Social Role of the Man of Knowledge* by Florian Znaniecki (New Brunswick: Transaction, 1986), xx.

32. Joyce Appleby, "Liberal Education in a Postliberal World," *Liberal Education* 79.3 (1993): 18-24.

33. Richard Weaver, *Ideas Have Consequences* (1948; rpt. Chicago: University of Chicago Press, 1984), 176.

34. Ibid., 158-159.

35. William E. Simon, "The Last Bigotry: Time for the Media to Shed Anti-Religious, Anti-Catholic Bias," *Washington Post* 10 March 1996: C4.

36. George M. Marsden, "Are Secularists the Threat? Is Religion the Solution?" *Unsecular America*, ed. Richard John Neuhaus (Grand Rapids: Christian University Press, 1984), 114-115.

37. Qtd. in Francis Oakley, Rev. of *The Soul of the American University: From Protestant University to Established Nonbelief* by George Marsden, *Journal for the Scientific Study of Religion* 34 (1995): 276.

38. James R. Stoner, Jr., et al., "Theology as Knowledge: A Symposium," *First Things* may 2006: 21-22.

39. J. Hillis Miller, *The Form of Victorian Fiction* (Notre Dame: University of Notre Dame Press, 1968), 34.

40. *Two Note Books of Thomas Carlyle*, ed. Charles E. Norton (New York: Grolier Club, 1898), 264.

41. Fyodor Dostoevsky, *The Brothers Karamazov* (1879-1880), trans. Constance Garnett, Part IV, Book XI, Chpt. 4, 25 July 2006 <http://classicreader.com>.

42. Cf. Humberto Maturana, "Ontology of Observing," *Chilean School of Biology of Cognition*, ed. Alfred Ruiz. 2005. 15 Aug. 2005 <http://www.inteco.cl/biology/>.

43. Cf. Egon Guba and Yvonna S. Lincoln, *Fourth Generation Evaluation* (Newbury Park: Sage, 1989), 104-105.

44. Cf., e.g., Barbara F. Meltz, "Dads Are No Longer the 'Assistant Parent,'" *Boston Globe* 16 June 2005: H1; Cheryl Hyde, Rev. of *Women, Violence, and Social Change* by R. Emerson Dobash and Russell P. Dobash, *The American Journal of Sociology* 98 (1993): 954-956; David Brooks, "Soft-Core Spirituality in a Psychobabble Nation," *Seat-*

tle Post-Intelligencer 10 Mar. 2004: B8; Ted Anthony, "Sunday 'Just Another Day':
Fast-Paced Society Dictates Change," *Sunday Gazette-Mail* 10 Mar. 2004: A1; A. Ben-
Porat, Rev. of *People As Subject, People As Object: Selfhood and Peoplehood in Contemporary Israel* by Virginia R. Dominguez, *Contemporary Sociology* 20 (1991): 196-
198.

45. "Full Text of Mass. Gay Marriage Ruling" [*Goodridge et al.* v *Department of
Public Health, et al.,* J. Greaney, concurring, 44 Mass. 309 SJC-08860 4 March 2003 - 18
Nov. 2003], op. cit.

46. "Full Text of Mass. Gay Marriage Ruling" [*Goodridge et al.* v *Department of
Public Health, et al.,* J. Sosman, dissenting, 44 Mass. 309 SJC-08860 4 March 2003 - 18
Nov. 2003], op. cit.

47. Peter Medawar, *The Threat and the Glory*, ed. David Pyke (New York: Harper
& Row, 1989), 39.

48. Thomas More, *Utopia* (1516), trans. Ralphe Robinson, in *Three Renaissance
Classics* (New York: Scribner's, 1953), 202-203, 238.

49. Robert Nisbet, *The Quest for Community: A Study in the Ethics of Order &
Freedom* (1953; rpt. San Francisco: Institute for Contemporary Studies, 1990), 138-147.

50. Cf. Bryce Christensen, "The Family in Utopia," *Renascence* 44 (1991): 31-44.

51. Thomas Campanella, *City of the Sun*, trans. Thomas W. Halliday, in *Ideal Com-
monwealths*, rev. ed. (Port Washington: Kennikat, 1968), 147-159.

52. Edward Bellamy, *Looking Backward: 2000-1887* (1888; rpt. New York: Random House, 1951), 210-212.

53. William Morris, *News from Nowhere: Or an Epoch of Rest* (Boston: Roberts
Brothers, 1891), 83, 112-113.

54. George Kateb, *Utopia and Its Enemies* (London: Free Press, 1963), 209,232.

55. Cf. Bryce Christensen, "Queer Demand? Why Homosexuals Began Demanding
What Marriage Had Become," *Divided We Fall: Family Discord and the Fracturing of
America* (New Brunswick: Transaction, 2005), 91-108.

56. Johnson, op. cit., emphasis added; cf. Herbert Jacob, *Silent Revolution: The
Transformation of Divorce Law in the United States* (Chicago: University of Chicago
Press, 1988), 56-59, 150-151.

57. Cf. Robert Schoen, "The Continuing Retreat from Marriage: Figures from 1983
U.S. Marital Status Life Tables," *Sociology and Social Research* 71 (1987): 108-109;
Jeffrey Jensen Arnett, "Learning to Stand Alone: The Contemporary American Transition
to Adulthood in Cultural and Historical Context," *Human Development* 41 (1998): 295-
315.

58. Cf. Ira Robinson et al., "Twenty Years of the Sexual Revolution, 1965-1985: An
Update," *Journal of Marriage and the Family* 53 (1991): 216-220; Patricia A. Gwartney-
Gibbs, "The Institutionalization of Premarital Cohabitation: Estimates from Marriage
License Applications, 1970 and 1980," *Journal of Marriage and the Family* 48 (1986):
423-434.

59. Cf. Ben J. Wattenberg, *The Birth Dearth* (New York: Pharos, 1987), 127-130.
Lynn White and Stacy J. Rogers, "Economic Circumstances and Family Outcomes: A
Review of the 1990s," *Journal of Marriage and the Family* 62 (2002): 1035-1051; Wen-
dell Berry, *What Are People For?* (San Francisco: North Point, 1990), 180-181.

60. Andrew Sullivan, "TRB: Unveiled," *New Republic* 13 August 2001: 6 ; cf. Stephen Baskerville, "The Real Danger of Same-Sex Marriage," *The Family in America*
May/June 2006: 1-8.

61. Stephenie Coontz, "The Heterosexual Revolution," *New York Times*, 5 July
2005: A17.

62. "Full Text of Mass. Gay Marriage Ruling" [*Goodridge et al.* v *Department of Public Health, et al.* 44 Mass. 309 SJC-08860 4 March 2003 - 18 Nov. 2003], op. cit.

63. William L. Downing, Superior Court of the State of Washington for King County, *Heather Anderson and Leslie Christian et al.* v. *King County* BNo. 04-2-04964-4 SEA 4 Aug. 2004 8 Aug. 2006 <http:seattletimes.nwsource.com/news/local/gaymarriage /downing_opinion.pdf.>.

64. Cf. U.S. Bureau of the Census, Statistical *Abstract of the United States:2002*, Table 117; *Statistical Abstract of the United States: 2004-2005*, Table 113; *Statistical Abstract of the United States:1974*, Table 95 9 Aug. 2006 <http://www.census.gov/ compendia/statab/past_years.html>.

65. "Full Text of Mass. Gay Marriage Ruling" [*Goodridge et al.* v *Department of Public Health, et al.* 44 Mass. 309 SJC-08860 4 March 2003 - 18 Nov. 2003], op. cit.

66. Ibid., emphasis added.

67. Cf. Christensen, "Redefining *Family*: War Over a Word," op. cit.

68. Aldous Huxley, Foreword (1946), *Brave New World* (1932; rpt. New York: Harper & Row, 1969), xiii.

69. Ibid., 94.

70. Ibid., 226.

71. Yevgeny Zamyatin, *We*[1924], trans. Mirra Ginsburg (New York: Viking, 1972), 14, 40, 107, 189.

72. Anthony Burgess, *The Wanting Seed* {New York: W.W. Norton, 1963), 184.

73. "Full Text of Mass. Gay Marriage Ruling" [*Goodridge et al.* v *Department of Public Health, et al.* 44 Mass. 309 SJC-08860 4 March 2003 - 18 Nov. 2003], op. cit.

74. George Orwell, *1984* (1949; rpt. New York: Harcourt Brace Jovanovich, 1961), 57.

75. Zamyatin, op. cit., 60-61.

76. Orwll, op. cit., 46.

77. Huxley, op. cit., 57, 187, 195.

78. Lewis Carroll, *Through the Looking Glass*, in *Alice in Wonderland*, ed. Donald J. Gray (New York: W. W. Norton, 1971), 163.

79. Supreme Court of the State of Washington, *Heather Anderson et al.* v. *King County* No. 75934-1 (concol. w/75956-1), 26 July 2006, J. Johnson with R. Sanders, concurring. 9 Aug. 2006 <http://www.courts.wa.gov/newsinfo/content/pdf/759341 co2pdf>.

80. U.S. Supreme Court, *Doe* v. *Bolton*, 410 U. S. 179 (1973), B. White with W. Rehnquist, dissenting. 9 Aug. 2006 <http://caselaw.lp.findlaw.com/scripts/getcase.pl? court=US&vol=410&involv=179>.

81. Duncan, op. cit.

82. Connie P. Sternberg, "The Right Relationship," *Hartford Courant* 24 Oct. 2004: 7.

83. Cf. Chuck Colbert, "Catholic Agency to Halt Adoption Work," *National Catholic Reporter* 24 Mar. 2006: 6.

PART IV
DOES LEGALIZING SAME-SEX MARRIAGE HARM BASIC HUMAN FREEDOMS AND INSTITUTIONS?

CHAPTER 15
THE EROSION OF MARRIAGE: A PYRRHIC VICTORY?

Seana Sugrue
Ave Maria University

The institution of marriage, understood as the enduring union of man and woman with the responsibility of rearing the children begotten from their sexual coupling, is the cornerstone of civilization. Not only does it provide stability for the family unit, and serve to educate the young who will eventually grow to maturity and replace their parents, it also supports other civic institutions of society and the overarching political order as well. Given its indispensable nature, one might surmise that it would be guarded jealously by the state and other institutions that are dependent upon marriage for their strength and long-term sustenance. The fact that marriage is currently being undermined by those very institutions that depend upon it is indicative of the extent to which advanced industrial societies have forgotten the fundamentals of their own success and vitality. As this occurs, it is children, growing into adulthood, who suffer the most.

I. The Nature of Institutions and their Interdependence

To understand why the erosion of marriage should be expected to contribute to the erosion of other institutions of society requires that one understand, on the one hand, the nature of a social institution, and on the other hand, the interdependence of institutions, especially those which are most essential to social order. An understanding of the nature of an institution serves to explain why marriage cannot be redefined without imperiling its very existence. An understanding of the interdependence of institutions explains how the erosion of marriage poses a threat to other institutions of civil society and to republican governance.

An institution, in its simplest form, is a convention or a norm of behavior serving a coordinative function[1] that is transmitted from one generation to the next.[2] In complex institutions, such as marriage, the institution consists of an interlocking set of norms that are internalized both by those who are participants, that is by a husband and a wife, as well as by those outside of the institution who reinforce and uphold marriage's core norms.[3] The norms of the institution are manifested in the behavior, expectations and moral judgments of a critical mass of society's members.[4] Where these norms are widely regarded as legitimate, they are also supported by other institutions, with religious institutions and the state being among the most significant in the case of marriage.

The norms that constitute marriage are universally known and have existed within societies in virtually all times and places. These universal features of marriage include the recognition of the interdependence of men and women, procreation, and the support of father and mother in rearing their children.[5] To these can be added norms of marriage that have been widely accepted within Western civilization until relatively recently. Among these are the expectation of permanence, sexual fidelity, and the mutual care of husband and wife.

The institution of marriage is embodied in the men and women who consciously enter the institution through a public ceremony to recognize their acceptance of its core norms, which are to define their relationship to one another.[6] Of course, those who marry also have the capacity to shape it to some degree to suit their particular wants, needs and individuality. They are, after all, agents capable of exercising reason and choice.[7] Hence, couples are at liberty to redefine many of the traditions that their parents imparted to them, including how they will solemnize their union, how they will divide responsibilities of care, and how they will raise their children. None of these changes, however, affect the defining norms of the institution of marriage.

The institutional nature of marriage can be changed, however, when its core norms are repudiated or challenged by other institutions. To understand how one institution, like the state, can affect another, like marriage, requires reference to relevant social theory. One of the most helpful anthropological approaches to conceptualize how one institution can affect another has been articulated by Sally Falk Moore, who proposes the paradigm of the "semi-autonomous social field." Moore explains:

> The approach proposed here is that the small field observable to an anthropologist be chosen and studied in terms of its semi-autonomy—the fact that it can generate rules and customs and symbols internally, but that it is also vulnerable to rules and decisions and other forces emanating from the larger world by which it is surrounded. The semi-autonomous social field has rule-making capacities, and the means to induce or coerce compliance; but it is simultaneously set in a larger social matrix which can, and does, affect and invade it, sometimes at the invitation of persons inside it, sometimes at its own instance. The analytic problem of fields of autonomy exists in tribal society, but it is an even more central analytic issue in the social anthropology of complex societies. All the nation-states of the world, new and old, are complex societies in that sense. The analytic problem is ubiquitous. [8]

Marriage, understood as a semi-autonomous social field, is an entity with its own set of rules and processes of self-regulation. At the same time, it is affected by other semi-autonomous social fields, especially by laws decreed by the state. Marriage is shaped by the state, sometimes at the behest of husbands and wives, sometimes against their will. The relationship between marriage and the state need not be symbiotic; it can be competitive or destructive. While these institutions often do cooperate in upholding communal norms, they may also compete with one another or, more rarely, one may eradicate another. Accordingly, the interdependence of institutions can be understood both in terms of their normative interchange as well as their relations of power.

Relations among institutions are arguably of greater political and social significance than the relationship of the individual to the institution, yet institutional interdependence is not usually paid adequate scholarly attention; the analytic foci of scholars tends to be either the individual or the state.[9] Moreover, non-state institutions, especially marriage and the family, are too often short-changed and are not treated as important topics of scholarly analysis. This may be in part because of the growing tendency to treat marriage as merely based upon individual desires.[10] It may also result from the fact that marriage and family are too often viewed as "soft" areas, of concern to women and feminists, but not terribly important or prestigious as it relates to a domain of social life lacking in "hard" power.[11] While it is unfair to label marriage as a "women's issue" as its intrinsic goods and its burdens are shared by both sexes, there is a sense in which it is fair to say marriage is a "soft" domain. Like civic institutions, it tends to lack the power to coerce compliance; instead, it relies almost entirely upon recognition of the legitimacy of its norms, and the authority of mothers and fathers over their children.[12]

The "soft" nature of marriage puts it at a distinct disadvantage when its norms are challenged by the state.[13] The state, within advanced industrial societies, is the most far-reaching and powerful institution for a number of reasons. First, it alone has the ability to exert hard power to directly regulate other institutions. It has a monopoly on the legitimate use of force as well as the capacity to implement economic sanctions. Second, the state has the capacity to redefine the norms of other institutions systematically, either by refusing to enforce their norms or by using a variety of incentives to change the behavior of the institution's agents. Third, and quite significantly, the state possesses its own soft power. Its laws serve an educative function within advanced industrial societies insofar as such societies are deeply dependent upon their people's respect for the rule of law. A society's whose citizens are law-abiding tend to judge right and wrong conduct as being closely aligned with legal or illegal conduct. Moreover, the language of rights, rooted in the principles of equality and liberty, is the *lingua franca* of inter-institutional mediation, which is itself a largely normative enterprise. As the language of rights is the native language of the liberal state, and as the state increasingly claims the power to define rights, it tends to set the terms of inter-institutional mediation.

The institution of marriage, while it is pre-political and not created by the state,[14] nonetheless depends upon the state for its own vitality. Where the state upholds marriage's norms, these institutions enjoy a symbiotic relationship. When the state does not uphold marriage's constitutive norms, it does serious damage to marriage's vitality and long-term viability. What is less well appreciated, however, is that the relationship works both ways: marriage's constitutive norms also serve to uphold other forms of social order, including state order, especially republican political order. Hence, the demise of marriage can be expected to weaken the norms of other institutions, including the state. The de-

mise of marriage may well prove to be a lose-lose proposition for other fundamental institutions of our society.

II.   What's the Harm: A Normative Analysis

The harm incurred by the demise of marriage is best appreciated as operating on two levels. First, harm is done to individuals, particularly to children.
Secondly, harm is done to other institutions, which are dependent upon the institution of marriage for their proper functioning. Both of these harms occur because of the erosion of the norms that constitute the institution of marriage.

A.   Harm to Children

The source of the harm done to children by the demise of marriage can be
summed up in two words: antinomian hedonism. [15] Antinomian hedonism is
what results from the demise of traditional marriage and its replacement by
"companionate marriage," which is premised upon the belief that unions exist to
fulfill the desires and emotional needs of those who wish to enter into them.
Antinomian hedonism regards as good anything that is consistent with human
desire; hence, "marriage" can be whatever you want it to be. That which is
"right" is acting according to one's desires; that which is "wrong" is acting contrary to desire, or being unauthentic. To the extent that there is any normative
constraint, it is simply that there must be consent on the part of those who are
engaged in the union, or the "marriage". The "goodness" of desire and self gratification, limited only by the need for consent, is the fragile normative underpin-
ning of companionate marriage.[16] Antinomian hedonism transforms "liberty"
into a vehicle by which to legitimate libido.

Marriage and family serve vital and indispensable educative functions for
children. The importance of primary socialization, or the socialization of children, which typically occurs within the family, is succinctly stated in Berger and
Luckmann, *The Social Construction of Reality*:

> It is at once evident that primary socialization is usually the most im-
> portant one for an individual, and that the basic structure of all sec-
> ondary socialization has to resemble that of primary socialization.
> Every individual is born into an objective social structure within
> which he encounters the significant others who are in charge of his
> socialization. These significant others are imposed upon him. Their
> definitions of his situation are posited for him as objective reality.
> ...The child takes on the significant others' roles and attitudes, that
> is, internalizes them and makes them his own. And by this identifica-
> tion with significant others the child becomes capable of identifying
> himself, of acquiring a subjectively coherent and plausible identity.
> In other words, the self is a reflected entity, reflecting the attitudes
> first taken by significant others toward it; the individual becomes
> what he is addressed as by his significant others.[17]

The norms constituting marriage and family life provide a child with his or her first sense of self worth, and powerfully shape that child's sense of the worth of others in relations to the self. Marriage is instructive; it is a school of values and virtues. Changes in the underlying norms of marriage must be expected to fundamentally alter a child's moral compass. It follows, then, that if one accepts antinomian hedonism as the legitimate normative basis for marriage and human sexuality, then one is committed to accepting it as the guiding ethos for children's sexuality as well. If that which constitutes being an adult whose decisions are worthy of respect is not growth in moral judgment as one becomes fully socialized into institutional norms, but rather the capacity to have desires, including sexual desires, and to choose to act upon these, then there is no reason why children should not fulfill their desires, too. Minors, especially those who are teens, have sexual desires; to have these suppressed because of "outdated" morals is wrong, in this view. According to its logic, minors should be able to decide for themselves questions relating to their own sexuality; they do not need society to protect them against themselves. [18] Moreover, there are no legitimate sexual norms into which minors are to be socialized. They, like adults, should be liberated to realize their desires. Hence, the sexualization of minors is among the significant negative effects resulting from societal acceptance of antinomian hedonism in the form of companionate marriage.

This point is crucial: the sexualization of children that occurs as the companionate view of marriage takes hold should not be blamed upon homosexuals or any other sexual minority. Individuals are culpable only where they recruit children into sexual activity. Rather, the sexualization of children occurs because of the erosion of the sexual norms constituting traditional marriage and their replacement by the companionate view, which is founded upon an ethos of antinomian hedonism. In this view, there can be no distinction between the desires of children and those of adults as long as consent can be established on the part of children. The ethos of antinomian hedonism is a great equalizer: it renders adults infantile, and children mature. Societal acceptance of antinomian hedonism enables and stimulates movements to lower the age of consent among adolescents. [19]

Traditional sexual norms, upon which the institution of marriage is founded, prohibit the sexualization of children from being an acceptable outcome. Traditional sexual norms demand extensive socialization in self-restraint. Hence, children are not viewed as capable of handling their sexuality as completely as adults because they have not yet been fully socialized, they have lesser impulse control, and they are much more influenced in their judgments by their need for approval, especially among their peer group, than are adults. [20] The ethos of antinomian hedonism underlying companionate marriage, on the other hand, gives these differences between minors and adults little weight since it regards sexual norms generally as illegitimate. Hence, the very idea that children ought to be socialized with traditional sexual norms is anathema. If adults are free to reject them, and they are the role models for children who will grow to adulthood, then why should minors be constrained? To constrain the sexual activity of minors would only serve to perpetuate a matrix of traditional sexual norms that adherents of the companionate view regard as archaic, harmful, repressive.

Children learn much more from companionate marriage than merely that it is laudable to gratify sexual desires, and all of these lessons are highly damaging to their own wellbeing and the wellbeing of others. Children also learn from the normative underpinnings of companionate marriage that only beings capable of expressing and manifesting desires have value. This means that children themselves do not have intrinsic desire until they, like their parents, are capable of self gratification. This lesson is imparted by the fact that companionate marriage teaches that children are not central to marriage; they are appendages that may or may not be elected. Children are optional. The value of children, in the first instance at least, is contingent upon being wanted by adults; their value is not absolute or intrinsic, at least not until they, too, qualify as having desires that can be manifested by acts of will.

Companionate marriage thus differs from traditional marriage, which is "child-centered." Traditional marriage solemnizes the union of a man and woman with the expectation that they are very likely to reproduce and, once they do, they will be transformed into mothers and fathers who are responsible for rearing their children. If children are begotten, the mother and father are expected to fulfill their duty to care by educating and nurturing their children to adulthood. This does not always happen, of course; husbands and wives do not always reproduce and, if they do, they do not always fulfill their duties to their children. However, the norms of traditional marriage provide the basis for recognizing that marriage is created out of the sexual complementary of men and women and that those who become parents are responsible for caring and educating their children. Mothers and fathers owe duties to children, and their first obligation is to advance the best interest of the child in protecting the child's wellbeing and preparing that child to accept the responsibilities of adulthood.

Companionate marriage, unlike traditional marriage, is premised upon the necessity to render children optional. Of course, this justifies birth control and abortion, but it does not end there. When taken to its logical extreme, companionate marriage teaches that it is permissible to abandon an unwanted child or otherwise shed parental responsibilities. This unsavory conclusion follows from the conception of human person underlying companionate marriage: "persons" are beings willing the fulfillment of their desires. If this is accepted, then the parent-child relationship is reduced to adult desires clashing with children's desires. In this clash, adult desires win because: 1. there is no objective basis by which to measure the relative value of these desires; 2. adult desires can be articulated more forcefully; and 3. adults are powerful and de facto make the decisions for children.

When parents are permitted to view as normative only those things which they desire, the "best interest of the child" becomes synonymous with the lifestyle choices of adults. In the optimistic conception of human nature that makes freedom the *summum bonum*, children are regarded as almost infinitely malleable, whether this is true or not. As parents change their lifestyles or their sexual preferences, children are to adapt. As parents change their partners, children are to make the necessary psychological adjustment. As parents abandon their children, children are to regard support payments, if they are lucky enough to receive any, as the equivalent of parental care.

The triumph of adult desires over the needs of children is not a hypothetical proposition. It is consistent with the Supreme Court's privacy jurisprudence, which has turned constitutionally guaranteed liberties into devices for fostering the self-actualization of adults. [21] If, as it appears, the right to marry entails a right of adults to "reproduce" or to have children,[22] it is adult desire, and not the needs of children for a mother and father, that determines who can be parents. If same-sex "marriage" is legalized and comes to entail the right to have children, as it has in Canada, biological mothers and fathers will be further absolved from having lasting obligations to their biological children. This occurs as "mother" and "father" are rendered obsolete legal concepts that are replaced by generic legal parenthood, as is the case in Canada. [23] The severance of sex, procreation and parenthood becomes complete, and with it, the expectation that biological parents owe duties of care to their biological children will be dealt a mortal blow.

Children socialized to accept the norms of companionate marriage are not merely harmed by being raised within an ethos that sexualizes them at a young age and that sacrifices their need for guidance and security upon the altar of adult self actualization. They are also harmed as they are taught extreme self-centeredness from the norms of companionate marriage that inhibits the development of conscience. As children, they may quite accurately infer that no one else can be trusted to care for them; they must put themselves first and care for their own needs and desires. Narcissism, distrust and selfishness are qualities of character that are apt to characterize the children of companionate marriage, just as the norms of companionate marriage encourage such characteristics in their parents.[24] Children socialized to accept antinomian hedonism may also conclude that there are no limits or boundaries in interpersonal relationships except those which others are willing to accept. Hence, as these children grow to adulthood, they are likely to infer that others do not have value except where they are capable of exerting power, for only those with power can set limits or consent. Those incapable of setting limits, those who are powerless, those who cannot consent, don't matter. They do not have intrinsic value, unless, of course, they are wanted by someone who does. Moreover, children raised into a society in which antinomian hedonism prevails will have good reason for drawing the conclusion that "right" and "wrong" are arbitrary conventions. Morality, for such children, is apt to be reducible to relations of power;[25] those with power call the shots, while those without it are vulnerable to the whims of those with power. Hence, children raised within a culture of antinomian hedonism would be justified in surmising that it is important to become powerful because relations of power pose the only meaningful constraint on human behavior. Otherwise, they could once more be made vulnerable to those who cannot be trusted.

These conclusions concerning the harm done to children by companionate marriage are drawn by inferring what its normative underpinnings, or relative lack thereof, teaches children. Of course, there is ample empirical evidence that children raised in unstable unions do not tend to thrive as well as their peers, and this evidence also tends to support the conclusion that companionate marriage harms children.[26] However, the conclusions here drawn about the harms companionate marriage inflict upon children are premised upon the observation that marriage is profoundly instructive to children, and what children learn from companionate marriage is a morally corrupt and spiritually bankrupt worldview. Lipstick might be applied to make companionate marriage more attractive by euphemistically or naively professing that it is really about allowing people freely and authentically to "love" (or "bond" with) others, and that this "love" (or "bond") does no harm to others.[27] But this "love" is devoid of normative content, being utterly dependent upon variable human emotions and desires.[28] Hence, in practice, it amounts to gratifying desire. Altruism, compassion, self sacrifice, self restraint are sacrificed to the idols of self realization, and these value choices have consequences that affect children most acutely.

One further remark about how marital norms shape children is in order. The argument being put forth is not premised upon a deterministic view of human nature such that human beings are mere automata that passively internalize conditioning. Human beings have the capacity for critical reflection, especially as they mature, and their unique experiences and reason may lead them to accept or reject much of the normative framework with which they were raised. Hence, even those adults who were raised as children without the benefit of being fully socialized in legitimate norms remain culpable for their actions contrary to these norms, although they are less culpable than those who were properly socialized, but act defiantly. Conversely, some of those children raised within a home environment that is premised upon antinomian hedonism may grow, as adults, to reject its frail normative structure and may embrace traditional marriage. Nurture is not destiny, but it is profoundly and undeniably influential.

B.   Harm to Religion, the Market and Republican Governance

Children harmed when young, yet who regard their upbringing as normal, should not be expected to serve well the society that did not protect them when they were most vulnerable. A society that guts marriage of its ethical content, and thereby accepts the rise of generations of citizens who are not properly socialized, is one that deludes itself about its own invincibility, and that frivolously undermines its own sustainability. To understand why this is so requires an analysis of the dependence and indebtedness of other institutions upon the existence of robust traditional marital norms that socialize children to exercise restraint over their desires and to serve others.

Marriage, as a "semi-autonomous social field," is interdependent with religious institutions, the economic order, and political order of a society. Hence the weakening of traditional marriage, and its transformation into companionate marriage, premised on antinomian hedonism, is a systemic alteration that should be expected to have far-reaching consequences. This is all the more true since the family is not just any institution: it is the bedrock institution of society.[29] It is within marriage and family that the socialization and education of the next generation occurs.

To transform traditional marriage, an institution with solid and defensible normative content and a proven track record of empirical success, into companionate marriage, an institution that is an empirical experiment and a normative abomination, is the height of societal hubris. For if children do not learn from a young age, by the example of their parents and otherwise, that there are some boundaries that should not be transgressed, that others matter just because they are human beings, that some reasons are legitimate and others are not, they cannot be expected to accept readily the demands of other institutions which require respect for boundaries, respect for others, and self sacrifice. This is bad news for all fundamental institutions of society as we know it.

The crux of the inter-institutional crisis created by the erosion of traditional marriage is that it creates a systemic legitimacy crisis. As Francis Fukuyama has noted, in echoing Václav Havel, legitimacy is "the power of the powerless."[30] The family's capacity to support secondary institutions, such as the state, depends in large measure upon its ability to create a reserve of "soft power" in the form of shared norms that foster cooperative behavior, a sense of a common good, and an ability to resolve differences on the basis of reasons rooted upon a common set of premises. Antinomian hedonism is perhaps the worst possible foundation for a shared sense of institutional legitimacy to take root. It teaches that there are no firm boundaries except for those you create yourself, that there is no right and wrong, just what feels good to me, that there is no objective moral truth, just relations of power. This is a most unpromising ethical foundation for the development of a shared sense of legitimacy or for authority to be sustained. Without a healthy reserve of soft power, a society has only hard power to enforce compliance with its norms, but that tends to lead to the emergence of a Hobbesian Leviathan state.[31] The societal costs are high as soft power is weakened since compliance with norms of behavior must increasingly be extracted with the use of hard power in a context in which that power is not regarded as legitimate. Hence, while it is true that soft power is dependent upon hard power, it is equally true that hard power depends upon soft power for its long-term sustainability.

A comprehensive discussion of the inter-institutional conflicts between marriage and family, premised upon antinomian hedonism, and secondary institutions of society, especially religious institutions, the economic order, and political order, are beyond the scope of a short paper. However, it is possible to develop a thumbnail sketch of the respects in which the erosion of the former works to the detriment of the latter. Such brief depictions shall ensue.

Most traditional western religions premise their norms upon their knowledge of what God, as the source of all objective, normative reality, expects of human beings. Hence, traditional religions are typically antithetical to antinomian hedonism, for the normative foundation of traditional religious institutions is not based upon individual desires and self gratification as the measure of right and wrong. Traditional religions rebuke the view of social reality that adherents of companionate marriage endorse.

Hence, the redefinition of marriage as companionate is a source of considerable tension and potential conflict between adherents of traditional religions and adherents of companionate marriage. Whereas traditional marriage and traditional religions serve to strengthen one another's normative foundations as they are premised upon acceptance of a belief in the goodness of objective normative order independent of human will or desire, the norms of companionate marriage are antithetical to traditional religions and vice versa. Indeed, the profoundly symbiotic interdependence of traditional marriage and religion is such that any effort to undermine the norms of either traditional marriage or religion tends to result in the erosion of both. Traditional religions reinforce the norms of marriage and assist spouses in abiding by these norms in difficult times; parents in marriages, in turn, tend to raise their children in the faith that sustains their marriage. Hence, the weakening of marriage serves to weaken traditional religions as the children of companionate marriage should be expected to be raised within such institutions.[32] But this is not the only way in which traditional religions are undermined.

Religions also become increasingly susceptible to normative challenges from within by their own authority figures and other members who come to accept the ethos of antinomian hedonism as legitimate. As companionate marriage becomes socially acceptable, antinomian hedonism gains acceptance within traditional religions as its members are profoundly influenced by the larger society of which they are also a part. As it is possible to acquire authority within many traditional religions without feeling bound by the religion's norms, religions become increasingly vulnerable from within their own ranks. Hence, the growing prevalence of antinomian hedonism affects not only marriage; it also infiltrates religions through members who no longer believe in norms that are inconsistent with the ethos of antinomian hedonism.

Add to these challenges to religion the fact that the state, in exercising its power to erode traditional marriage, commits itself to the principles of antinomian hedonism underlying companionate marriage. If consistency in the application of principle guides its decisions, the state can be expected to uphold its precedents in the face of challenges by other institutions to companionate marriage. This makes it entirely likely that where conflicts arise between the norms governing traditional religions and those governing companionate marriage, companionate marriage will win, and the coercive power of the state will be invoked to ensure the triumph of antinomian hedonism.

For these reasons, the erosion of traditional marriage should be expected to coincide with the weakening of religions that reject antinomian hedonism. Religions, too, undergo normative assault as traditional marriage is undermined. Two intermediate institutions of society standing between the individual and the state are imperiled by antinomian hedonism as the governing ethos within the domain of marriage and family.

Of all the forms of social order, the economic order in advanced industrial societies might be thought to be most consonant with antinomian hedonism. After all, is not that which constitutes a market simply an amalgam of contracts, based on the consent of individuals acting in their self interest? While there is an element of truth to this characterization of the market insofar as the economic order satisfies materials wants and needs, it is one that overlooks that the market itself is an institution that is dependent upon marriage and family, on the one hand, and the state, on the other, for its very existence. This deep interdependence was expressed by Hegel who observed: "the sanctity of marriage, along with the institutions wherein civil society appears as ethical, constitute the stability of the whole."[33] Traditionally, the family has been regarded as the basic unit of society as the material needs of dependents, who by definition cannot be direct participants in the market, are necessarily met by the economic production of others; the recognition that dependents are best cared for by a society that protects private property is among the firmest justifications for a free market economy.[34] Economics emerges in the first instance out of the economic needs of a family unit, which is why Marx sought to abolish marriage and family at the same time as he sought the abolition of private property; he understood that the traditional family reproduced not just children, but also an economic system of private property and market capitalism.[35] Without private property, traditional marriage and family are unsustainable; without marriage and family, property belongs either to the individual or the state, and the individual in this contest over ownership is at a distinct disadvantage.

The dependence of an economic order upon marriage and family life extends beyond the fact that the latter legitimates a market-based economic system. The economic realm is also dependent in an immediate and practical way upon the socialization that occurs within the family. No advanced industrial society thrives solely with exchange of goods procured by individuals acting on their own. The provision of anything but the most basic good or service requires the cooperative action of numerous people, typically within corporate structures. Moreover, the very basis of contract law, which is at the heart of the market's norms, is the reliance interest.[36] The reliance interest is based upon the premise that it is reasonable for those entering into an exchange to trust that others are going to fulfill their promises or obligations. Market activity thrives within a society that upholds norms that are not strictly economic, such as beliefs in the rule of law and in fiduciary duties owed by those in positions of authority to serve those who rely upon them. [37]

Hence, markets in advanced industrial societies cannot accurately be described as being premised upon antinomian hedonism. They require social capital as much as financial capital. While individuals pursue their self interest, they do so within the context of economic relationship that are founded upon relations of trust, of duty, and of cooperative action within firms that produce of goods and services. Moreover, their smooth functioning depends upon a people who are not corrupt, who tend to obey the rule of law, and who are supported in their adherence to norms by the state that stands willing to enforce these where norms are abused or violated. [38] Self interest and the common good tend to merge in sustainable market activity. [39]

The erosion of soft power within the realm of the family should be expected to undermine the soft power that makes markets work without invoking the heavy hand of the state. The existence of the state, and the threat or actuality of coercion, helps to ensure that flagrant violations of market norms will be deterred or punished. However, the coercive power of the state is not particularly effective in increasing a people's propensity to demonstrate commitment, productivity, good will, or trustworthiness. The threat of state power serves to inhibit Oliver Wendell Holmes' "bad man" who acts simply to avoid sanctions,[40] but it does not produce "good men" who go the extra mile for the sake of maintaining standards or who have a sense of decency.

The relationship between markets and marriage is far more complex than the symbiotic elements stressed here. The demands of economics can, and do, prove to be a strain upon marriage and family life. This is especially true as societies make the transition to industrialization.[41] At the same time, it appears that those societies that are capable of adapting without destroying marriage and other civic institutions are also more successful at industrializing on the whole. Examples of market economies that are being instigated in the absence of robust civil society exist in post Soviet Russia and in much of post colonial Africa. Unlike China, a culture that continues to cultivate deep respect for authority, especially for elders, and which has maintained the existence of extended clan structures fostering some measure of cooperative behavior,[42] post Soviet Russia and much of post colonial Africa have experienced the virtual decimation of traditional familial relations as they attempt to become part of an industrialized world, and their economic transitions are disappointing for their own people. Plagued by corruption and the breakdown of civil society, the normative foundations for a market-based economy are not in place.[43] This serves as a dramatic example of the interdependence of institutions of social order upon one another. It also suggests that antinomian hedonism, unformed by socialization in institutions that cultivate respect for soft power, does not suffice to create a market economy.

Republican order requires a people who exercise their liberty with a view to the common good. This proposition has been a core American belief since its founding. As George Washington warned his countrymen, long before the establishment of the U.S. Constitution: "arbitrary power is most easily established on the ruins of liberty abused to licentiousness."[44] In this context, Washington made the case that the states must make sufficient concessions and be willing to grant such material aid to make the union feasible. Washington's advice is equally applicable, however, to citizens today, who must recognize that their immediate wants must sometimes be subordinated to promote causes that are in everyone's long-term interests.

This appeal falls upon deaf ears if one accepts antinomian hedonism, and this is why hedonism is inconsistent with sustainable republican governance. Both experience and theory suggest that the prospects of maintaining republican governance absent a robust civil society are slim. Republican governance has been the exception, not the rule, historically. From Aristotle to Machiavelli to Rousseau, scholars who have closely studied constitutional governments understand that they are prone to fail from their own excesses.[45] Among these excesses is the tendency of peoples to mistake liberty for license, or to lose a sense of a common good as citizens become absorbed with their own private concerns.[46] Antinomian hedonism, which purports to empower individuals to do as they please so long as others are consenting, is inconsistent with the demands of republican governance requires self sacrifice, including the commitment of its people to defend their freedom from external threats, to give of their resources of time and money, and to otherwise assume responsibility for their actions. Republican governance should be expected to be weakened by the ethos of antinomian hedonism implicit in companionate marriage.

The question remains, however, whether *any* form of government is consistent with antinomian hedonism. In fact, a number of corrupted forms of government may be compatible with it in the short-term, but the long-term prospects of a society imbued with such an ethos are dismal. At best, a society might sustain a form of soft despotism described by Tocqueville, in which people trade to a somewhat benign state their liberty for the license to do as they please.[47] At worst, a virtual collapse of viable forms of social order between the individual and the state could give rise to a totalitarian government in which a leader controls virtually every dimension of the lives of an undifferentiated mass.[48] Whatever the corrupted form of government, its days are numbered not simply because of the illegitimacy of the government that arises in the eyes of the people,[49] but more fundamentally because antinomian hedonism erodes virtually all sources of a state's hard power. Primary among a state's sources of hard power are: its economy, premised upon its advanced industrial capacities, its military or police forces, and its population.[50] These instruments of power tend to be enervated by antinomian hedonism.

In the first instance, a people who accept antinomian hedonism should not be expected to readily serve in the military or otherwise make sacrifices of their blood and treasure. The temptation to use hard power would suggest that a state, faced with this quandary, might require compulsory military service. Yet it is unlikely that this would prove to be a viable solution, as those who are not willing to make sacrifices voluntarily are not usually good soldiers.[51] The effete products of antinomian hedonism are not apt to defend their country well, if at all. Their best hope rests in technological innovation, which may have military applications, and in their industrial economy.

Technological innovations and entrepreneurship are fostered by having a highly motivated, disciplined and educated population,[52] qualities that can be undermined by the self-centeredness of antinomian hedonism. Moreover, inventiveness and self-direction have usually flourished in political orders that have robust civil societies nurtured by republican government,[53] but republican governance and civil society are also undermined by antinomian hedonism. As the mutually supportive relationship between family, civil society, and republican governance is eroded, the technological advantages of currently advanced industrial societies may suffer as well. Indeed, there is significant evidence that the economic advantages that advanced industrial economies of the west have enjoyed during the twentieth century are waning in any event, due largely to the growing diffusion of technological abilities among peoples of the world.[54] These economic difficulties can only be exacerbated by the demands of a people for expensive state entitlements, which also serve to further erode their liberty.[55]

The temptation to use the heavy hand of the state to rectify problems associated with economic stagnation is not apt to work well, given that states that stay on top in a global, competitive environment tend to have peoples with a healthy work ethic,[56] an ethic imparted through families that are also eroded by antinomian hedonism.

Finally, the state is apt to find, as advanced industrial societies are already discovering,[57] that its stock of manpower is shrinking and aging. As marriage becomes a matter of putting adult needs first, fewer and fewer children are had.[58] State subsidies encouraging reproduction are an obvious solution; however, they do not tend to work well.[59] Children remain a cost, not a benefit. Immigration might work for a time, but it may prove to be unattractive to immigrate to those states that need it most, especially if immigrants are expected to support existing welfare entitlements of an aging population. The temptation to use hard power might suggest that entitlements would be revoked, but this would not address the problem that the state, with its stock of hard power, has been weakened overall.

In conclusion, the erosion of society's stock of soft power, which is primarily generated and maintained through the socialization of children in marriage and family, tends to erode its hard power. Much as the institution of marriage is dependent upon the state's hard power, it is also the case that the state and other vital secondary institutions are dependent upon the soft power of marriage and family for their continued vitality. States, like all institutions, do not exist long without power. The enervating effects of antinomian hedonism upon a society's sources of power should not be dismissed lightly.

III.   Conclusion: A Pyrrhic Victory?

Two final observations are in order. First, the argument that the weakening of traditional marriage has a tendency to weaken civil society as well as the state is not a prediction of what the future holds. The unfolding of social events or movements tends to result from multiple causes, and the interaction of these causes does not lend itself readily to prediction about the future. The claim being made here is a more modest one. It is that the erosion of marriage has a tendency to erode other institutions. For this reason, it is reasonable to believe that the erosion of marriage does not serve the long-term interest of advanced industrial societies, and may very well do irreparable harm.

Secondly, there is good reason to believe that antinomian hedonism will not exert its fully destructive systemic effects. Antinomian hedonism can only thoroughly enervate a society if a critical mass accepts it as legitimate and is willing to act consistently with its corrupting ethos. Fortunately, there is little reason to believe that the corruption will be quite so thorough-going. Even in spite of the state's folly in endorsing a companionate view of marriage, there remain robust pockets of resistance among persons and institutions that are equally committed to defending the norms of traditional marriage, as well as husbands and wives who continue to live within traditional marriages. Just as there has never been a pure example of totalitarian government, so too there is unlikely ever to be a perfect example of an utterly hedonistic society. Those whose socialization or strength of character is sufficiently developed continue to resist the rise of companionate marriage, with some effect.

It remains to be seen, however, whether the forces resisting the siren call of antinomian hedonism are sufficient to counterbalance a markedly growing societal trend to embrace companionate marriage. We must pray that companionate marriage does not triumph, for its victory promises to be pyrrhic, and children raised within its corrupting ethos have and will suffer the most.

Notes

1. Mary Douglas, *How Institutions Think* (Syracuse, NY: Syracuse University Press, 1986), 46. A complementary definition depicts institutions as standardized modes of behavior. Anthony Giddens, *Central Problems in Social Theory* (Berkeley and Los Angeles: University of California Press, 1979), 96.

2. Peter Berger and Thomas Luckmann, *The Social Construction of Reality* (New York: Anchor Books, 1966), 60-61.

3. Talcott Parsons, *Sociological Theory and Modern Society* (New York: Free Press, 1967),11.

4. H.L.A. Hart, *The Concept of Law* (Oxford: Clarendon Press, 1961), 55-56 concerning "social rules". According to Hart at 56, "What is necessary is that there should be a critical reflective attitude to certain patterns of behaviour as a common standard, and that this should display itself in criticism (including self-criticism), demands for conformity, and in acknowledgements that such criticism and demands are justified".

5. See Katherine K. Young and Paul Nathanson, "The Future of an Experiment" in Daniel Cere and Douglas Farrow, eds., *Divorcing Marriage* (Montreal & Kingston, McGill-Queen's University Press, 2004), 41-62 at 45.

6. According to Simmel, the institution of marriage is one which is accepted or rejected, but its core norms are not changed by those who participate in it. Georg Simmel, *The Sociology of Georg Simmel*, trans. Kurt H. Wolff (New York: The Free Press, 1950), 130.

7. On the relationship between agents and social structures, see Anthony Giddens, *Central Problems in Social Theory* (Berkeley & Los Angeles, Univesity of Berkeley Press: 1979), 49-95.

8. Sally Falk Moore, "Law and Social Change: The Semi-Autonomous Social Field as an Appropriate Subject of Study," Law and Society Review 7 (1973): 719-746 at 720. For a fuller exploration of Moore's analytic paradigm, see Sally Falk Moore, *Law as Social Process: An Anthropological Approach* (1978) Classics in African Anthropology (Munster: Lit Verlag, 2001). Moore's approach has been influential to "legal pluralism" theory. See John Griffiths, "What is Legal Pluralism?" Journal of Legal Pluralism and Unofficial Law 24 (1986): 1.

9. A third level of analysis which is also fairly common is the systemic level, which may be global or international in scope. Marxism furnishes one such systemic perspective; realism within international relations furnishes another.

10. See, for example, Law Commission of Canada, "The Legal Organization of Personal Relationships," in *Beyond Conjugality: Recognizing and Supporting Close Personal Relationships* (Ottawa, CA: LCC, 2001), c. 4. Retrieved from http://www.lcc.gc.ca/about/conjugality_toc-en.asp. "Marriage, from the point of view of the secular state authority, is a means of facilitating in an orderly fashion the voluntary

assumption of mutual rights and obligations by adults committed to each other's well-being."

11. For a trenchant criticism from a liberal perspective of the neglect of the family as a subject of serious scholarly study, see generally, Susan Moller Okin, *Justice, Gender, and the Family* (New York: Basic Books, 1989).

12. See, for example, John Locke's account of paternal power, which is premised upon duty, in John Locke, *Second Treatise of Government* (1690) (Indianapolis: Hackett, 1980), 30-42.

13. The term "soft power" is typically associated with the work of Joseph S. Nye, Jr., who depicts it as "the ability to attract". Joseph S. Nye, Jr., *Soft Power: The Means to Success in World Politics* (USA: Public Affairs, 2004), 5-6. Whereas Nye focuses upon the point of view of individuals or states seeking to advance their wills, the term "soft power" here refers to institutional glue, or that which holds an institution together absent coercion; it is independent of the will of individuals or states.

14. John Locke, *Second Treatise of Government* (1690) (Indianapolis: Hackett Publishing, 1980), 42; Seana Sugrue, "Soft Despotism and Same-Sex Marriage" in R.P. George and J.B. Elshtain, eds., *The Meaning of Marriage* (Dallas: Spence, 2006), 172-196.

15. Antinomian hedonism presumes that morals are founded upon emotion and desire. David Hume did much to lay the foundation for this understanding of morals in the modern age. "Morals excite passions, and produce or prevent actions. Reason of itself is utterly impotent in this particular. The rules of morality, therefore, are not conclusions of our reason." David Hume, *A Treatise of Human Nature*, 2nd rep'd ed. (London: Oxford University Press, 1981), 457.

16. Daniel Cere, *The Future of Family Law: Law and the Marriage Crisis in North America* (New York: Institute for American Values, 2005).

17. Peter L. Berger and Thomas Luckmann, *The Social Construction of Reality* (New York: Anchor Books, 1967), 131-132.

18. It is disturbing to note that the Supreme Court has established precedents that may be viewed as consistent with the ethos of antinomian hedonism. See for example *Bellotti v. Baird*, 443 U.S. 622 (1979), 643-644: "A pregnant minor is entitled in such a [judicial bypass] proceeding to show either: (1) that she is mature enough and well enough informed to make her abortion decision, in consultation with her physician, independently of her parents' wishes; or (2) that even if she is not able to make this decision independently, the desired abortion would be in her best interest." Note that the first reason to allow the minor to make the decision to abort is that she is deemed to possess adult capacities; the second is that she is deemed too immature to make a decision, from which it would presumably follow that she would be too immature to have a child. Yet she is presumably mature enough to forgo parental care and guidance during an invasive and ethically consequential medical procedure.

19. At the forefront of this movement is the North American Man/Boy Love Association (NAMBLA), whose freedom of speech is of concern to the American Civil Liberties Union (ACLU). See "ACLU Statement on Defending Free Speech of Unpopular Organizations," August 31, 2000. http:www.aclu.org/freespeech/protest/11289prs 20000831.html (accessed August 21, 2006). Bills have also been proposed to lower the age of consent as a means of furthering gender neutrality. Ruth Bader Ginsberg, currently a Justice of the U.S. Supreme Court, cites one such bill with approval in a report she co-authored on gender-biased language in federal legislation, without explaining why lowering the age of consent would be relevant to the goal of promoting gender neutrality. See Ruth Bader Ginsberg et al., *Report of Columbia Law School Equal Rights Advocacy*

Project: The Legal Status of Women Under Federal Law (New York: Columbia University, 1974), 70-71 available online at: www.eppc.org/docLib/20050608_Ginsberg2.pdf
(accessed August 21, 2006): "The 1973 Senate bill, S. 1400, §1631, provides a definition
of rape that, in substance, conforms to the equality principle. It states: 'A person is guilty
in an offense if he engages in a sexual act with another person, not his spouse, and: ... (3)
the other person is less than twelve years of age.'"

   20. Frank E. Zimring, "Toward a Jurisprudence of Youth Violence" 24 Crime and
Justice 477 (1998): "Three dimensions of adolescent diminished responsibility stand
out—incomplete comprehension of moral duty, deficient capacity to manage impulses,
and the vulnerability to peer pressure that is the hallmark of adolescent law violation."

   21. *Planned Parenthood of Southeastern Pa. v. Casey*, 505 U.S. 833 (1992), 851 "At
the heart of liberty is the right to define one's own concept of existence, of meaning, of
the universe, and of the mystery of human life. Beliefs about these matters could not
define the attributes of personhood were they formed under compulsion by the State."

   22. "It is settled now, as it was when the Court heard arguments in *Roe v. Wade*, that
the Constitution places limits on a State's right to interfere with a person's most basic
decisions about family and parenthood." *Planned Parenthood of Southeastern Pa. v.
Casey*, 505 U.S. 833 (1992), 849. See also page 851: "Our law affords constitutional
protection to personal decisions relating to marriage, procreation, contraception, family
relationships, child rearing, and education...".

   23. *Civil Marriage Act*, S.C. 2005, c. 33, s. 10-12.

   24. See generally, Christopher Lasch, *The Culture of Narcissism: American Life in
an Age of Diminishing Expectations* (USA: W.W. Norton, 1991).

   25. For an influential account of human sexual relations as social constructions
formed by relations of power, see the works of Michel Foucault. Examples include: Michel Foucault, *The History of Sexuality: An Introduction* (USA: Random House, 1990);
Michel Foucault, *Power/Knowledge: Selected Interviews and Other Writings, 1972-1977*
(USA: The Harvester Press, 1980).

   26. This conclusion has been forcefully made by Maggie Gallagher, "(How) Does
Marriage Protect Child Well-Being?" in R.P. George and J.B. Elshtain, eds., *The Meaning of Marriage: Family, State, Market, & Morals* (Spence, 2006), 198: "In the last thirty
years, thousands of studies evaluating the consequences of marriage for children and
society have been conducted in various disciplines... In virtually every way that social
scientists know how to measure, children do better, on average, when their parents get
and stay married (provided those marriages are not high-conflict or violent). By contrast,
every major social pathology that can trouble an American child happens more often
when his or her parents are not joined by marriage: more poverty, dependency, child
abuse, domestic violence, substance abuse, suicide, depression, mental illness, infant
morality, physical illness, education failure, high school dropouts, sexually transmitted
diseases, and early unwed childbearing (and later) divorce." Among the well known
sources Dr. Gallagher cites are: Paul Amato and Alan Booth, *A Generation At Risk:
Growing Up in an Era of Family Upheaval* (Cambridge, MA: Harvard University Press,
1997); Linda J. Waite and Maggie Gallagher, *The Case for Marriage: Why Married
People are Happier, Healthier and Better-Off Financially* (USA: Doubleday, 2000); Sara
McLanahan and Gary Sandefur, *Growing Up with a Single Parent: What Hurts, What
Helps* (Cambridge, MA: Harvard University Press, 1994); William J. Doherty, et al., *Why
Marriage Matters: Twenty-One Conclusions from the Social Sciences* (U.S.A.: Institute
for American Values, 2002). Among the conclusions that social scientists have reached
about how children thrive when raised in marriages between their biological parents are
the following: Children raised with their married biological parents spend more time with

their fathers, and receive more affection and warmth from them than do those living with a cohabiting father figure or a stepfather. Sandra L. Hofferth and Kermyt G. Anderson, "Are All Dads Equal? Biology Versus Marriage as a Basis for Parental Investment," *Journal of Marriage and Family* 65 (February 2003): 213-232; Adolescents living with their biological parents are the least likely to use illicit drugs. John P. Hoffmann and Robert A. Johnson, "A National Portrait of Family Structure and Adolescent Drug Use," *Journal of Marriage and the Family* 60 (August 1998): 633-645. Adolescents living with their married biological parents are less likely to engage in delinquent behavior than are their peers in stepfamilies. Wendy D. Manning and Kathleen A. Lamb, "Adolescent Well-Being in Cohabiting, Married, and Single-Parent Families," *Journal of Marriage and Family* 65 (November 2003): 876-893. Children living in stepfamilies are at higher risk of physical abuse than those living with their biological parents. Jean Giles-Sims, "Current Knowledge About Child Abuse in Stepfamilies," *Marriage and Family Review* 25 (March/April 1997): 215-229.

27. The majority opinion of the Supreme Court in *Lawrence v. Texas* endorsed this euphemistic understanding of the value of adult sexual relations in overturning a state criminal sodomy law. According to Justice Kennedy, writing for the majority: "When sexuality finds overt expression in intimate conduct with another person, the conduct can be but one element in a personal bond that is more enduring. The liberty protected by the Constitution allows ... persons the right to make this choice." *Lawrence v. Texas*, 539 U.S. 558 (2003), 567.

28. Hegel's rejoinder to the argument that marriage is merely about intimacy is as follows: "'Such an opinion pretentiously claims to afford the highest concept of freedom, intimacy, and perfection of love; but in fact it denies what is ethical in love, the higher restraining and subordinating of the merely natural drive." G.W.F. Hegel, *The Philosophy of Right* (1820), trans. Alan White (Newburyport, MA: Focus Publishing, 2002), 136.

29. Plato was so convinced of the powerfully educative function of marriage and family that he sought to abolish it entirely to create a utopian society. His fear was that traditional marriage and family teaches children partiality to their kin, which is contrary to the common good. Plato, however, came to accept that his views in the *Republic* were erroneous at the end of his life, and endorsed in *Laws* a traditional monogamous family structure as best suited to advance the interests of the polity: "I say it is the law's simple duty to go straight on its way and tell our citizens that it is not for them to behave worse than birds and many other creatures which flock together in large bodies. Until the age for procreation these creatures live in continence and unspotted virginity; when they have reached that age, they pair together, the male with the female and the female with the male their preference dictates, and they live thereafter in piety and justice, steadfastly true to their contract of first love. Surely you, we shall say, ought to be better than the beasts." Edith Hamilton and Huntington Cairns, *Plato: Collected Dialogues*, trans. A.E. Taylor (Princeton, Princeton University Press, 1961), 1405. Since Plato, many of the best authors of the western intellectual tradition have endorsed the view that marriage precedes political order and political order is dependent upon it. See for example, Aristotle, *Politics*, trans. Benjamin Jowett, in Richard McKeon, ed., *Introduction to Aristotle* (Chicago: University of Chicago Press, 1973), 595-598; John Locke, *Second Treatise of Government* (1690) (Indianapolis: Hackett Publishing, 1980), 42; G.W.F. Hegel, *The Philosophy of Right* (1820), trans. Alan White (Newburyport, MA: Focus Publishing, 2002), 197.

30. Francis Fukuyama, *The End of History and the Last Man* (U.S.A.: Perennial, 1992), 258.

31. Hobbes wrote his classic work on the absolute power of the state in a context of civil war. Hence, perhaps it is not surprising that his state of nature, which gives rise to

the need for the state, is a state of war. See Thomas Hobbes, *Leviathan*, rep. ed. (Oxford: Oxford University Press, 1998), 111-115.

32. A similar argument is made in Seana Sugrue, "Soft Despotism and Same-Sex Marriage," in R.P. George and J.B. Elshtain, eds., *The Meaning of Marriage: Family, State, Market, & Morals* (Dallas: Spence Books, 2006), 172-196 at 191-195. See also Seana Sugrue, "Canadian Marriage Policy: A Tragedy for Children," IMFC Review No. 1 (May 31, 2006) 1-11 at 10-11. http:www.imfcanada.org/events/sugrue/060526-SugruePaper.pdf.

33. G.W.F. Hegel, *The Philosophy of Right* (1820), trans. Alan White (Newburyport, MA: Focus Publishing, 2002), 197.

34. Aristotle, *Politics*, trans. Benjamin Jowett, in Richard McKeon, ed., *Introduction to Aristotle* (Chicago: University of Chicago Press, 1973), 600; John Locke, *Second Treatise of Government* (1690) (Indianapolis: Hackett Publishing, 1980), 37-38.

35. Karl Marx, *Communist Manifesto* (1848): "On what foundation is the present family, the bourgeois family, based? On capital, on private gain."

36. Lon L. Fuller and William R. Perdue, "The Reliance Interest in Contract Damages: 1" Yale Law Journal 46 (1936): 52-96; Lon L. Fuller and William R. Perdue, "The Reliance Interest in Contract Damages: 2" Yale Law Journal 46 (1937): 373-420. The theoretical framework established in these works continues to be highly influential in the field of contract law. See for example, Randy E. Barnett, *Perspectives on Contract Law*, 3rd ed. (USA: Aspen Publisher, 2005) 3-21, Victor P. Goldberg, ed., *Readings in the Economics of Contract Law*, rep. ed. (Cambridge, UK: Cambridge University Press, 1993), 77-79.

37. For a discussion of norms that shape interpretations of contract law, see Charles Fried, *Contract as Promise: A Theory of Contractual Obligations* (Cambridge, MA: Harvard University Press, 1981), 77-111.

38. See generally Deidre N. McCloskey, *The Bourgeois Virtues: Ethics for an Age of Commerce* (Chicago: University of Chicago Press, 2006).

39. Alexis de Tocqueville, *Democracy in America*, trans. George Lawrence (New York: Doubleday, 1969), 525-528.

40. Oliver Wendell Holmes, Jr., "The Path of the Law" Harvard Law Review 10 (1897): 457.

41. Indeed, the process of industrializing has typically put enormous strain on many aspects of social life as well as on the environment. See, for example, Alan Brinkley, *American History: A Survey*, 11th ed. (New York: McGraw-Hill, 2003), 508-515.

42. John K. Fairbank et al., *East Asia: Tradition & Transformation*, rev'd ed. (Boston: Houghton Mifflin Co., 1989), 14-16 and 984-985.

43. See Robert D. Kaplan, *The Coming Anarchy* (New York: Vintage Books, 2000), 9-14 and 30-34 wherein he draws the contrast between life in the slums of Turkey, which is well ordered, with life in the slums of Ivory Coast, which is not. Kaplan notes that one of the reasons for the misery and privation in West Africa is the breakdown of civil society. However, his view of humans as consumers that devastate the environment, rather than as resources in their own right, is shortsighted. Humans have the capacity to be either destructive or constructive; their socialization, which shapes their worldview, does much to direct them.

44. George Washington, "Circular to the States" (8 June 1783) in Philip B. Kurland and Ralph Lerner, eds. *The Founders' Constitution*, vol. 1 (Chicago: University of Chicago Press, 1987), 218-220 available online at http://press-pubs.uchicago.edu/founders/documents/v1ch5s5.html.

45. Aristotle, *The Politics of Aristotle*, trans. Ernest Baker (Oxford: Oxford University Press, 1981), 164-169 (1290b-1292a) and 257-267 (1317a-1319b); Niccolo Machiavelli, "Discourses on the First Ten Books of Titus Livius" in *The Prince and the Discourses* (New York: The Modern Library, 1950), 103-540 at 167-171 and 246-250; Jean-Jacques Rousseau, "The Social Contract" in *The Social Contract* and *The First and Second Discourses* (New Haven: Yale University Press, 2002), 149-254 at 214-216.

46. Aristotole, *ibid.*, 234 (1310a): "The democrat starts by assuming that justice consists in equality: he proceeds to identify equality with the sovereignty of the will of the masses; he ends with the view that 'liberty and equality' consist in 'doing what one likes'. The result of such a view is that, in these extreme democracies, each man lives as he likes—or, as Euripides says, 'For any end he chances to desire.' This is a mean conception of liberty." Niccoló Machiavelli, *ibid.*, 226: "...[W]e should notice also how easily men are corrupted and become wicked, although originally good and well educated." Jean-Jacques Rousseau, *ibid.*, 216-217: "The body politic, as well as the human body, begins to die from its birth, and contains in itself the causes of its own destruction."

47. Alexis de Tocqueville, *Democracy in America*, trans. George Lawrence (New York: Doubleday Anchor, 1969), 690-695.

48. Hannah Arendt, *The Origins of Totalitarianism* (New York: Harcourt Brace Jovanovich, Inc, 1973), 308.

49. Francis Fukuyama, *The End of History and the Last Man* (U.S.A.: Perennial, 1992), 13-38.

50. Karen A. Mingst, *Essentials of International Relations*, 3rd ed. (New York: W.W. Norton, 2004), 108-110. Note that Mingst also includes territory and natural resources as a source of potential power. This is correct, yet its use is dependent upon the ability of people to employ it productively. For an analysis of how the west's sources of hard power, including its military, economic output, and population, have declined over the past century, see generally Samuel Huntington, *The Clash of Civilizations* (New York: Simon & Schuster, 1997), 81-91.

51. Niccolo Machiavelli, *The Prince and the Discourses* (New York: The Modern Library, 1950), 49-53 and 384-388.

52. Francis Fukuyama, *The End of History and the Last Man* (U.S.A.: Perennial, 1992),109-125.

53. Alexis de Tocqueville, *Democracy in America*, trans. George Lawrence (New York: Doubleday Anchor, 1969), 308 and 509-513; Michael Novak, *The Universal Hunger for Liberty* (New York: Basic Books, 2004), 61: "*Culture and politics are prior to economics and supply necessary preconditions for it.*" [italics in original].

54. Samuel P. Huntington, *The Clash of Civilizations: Remaking of World Order* (New York: Touchstone, 1997), 86-88.

55. See generally, F.A. Hayek, *The Road to Serfdom*, rep. ed. (Chicago: University of Chicago Press, 1994).

56. Francis Fukuyama, *The End of History and the Last Man* (U.S.A.: Perennial, 1992), 223-234,

57. See generally, Ben J. Wattenberg, *Fewer: How the New Demography of Depopulation Will Shape Our Future* (Chicago: Ivan R. Dee Publisher, 2004).

58. There are several hypotheses as to why fertility rates in advanced industrial societies have dipped below replacement rate. The decline in fertility is believed to have a number of causes, including urbanization, which renders children more of a cost than a benefit to parents, easy access to contraception, legalized abortion, and increasing numbers of women in the workforce, among other causes. All of these, in different ways, have also eroded the institution of traditional, child-centered marriage. In the first and last

instance, marriage is placed in competition with economic considerations, in the other instances, procreation is made separable from marriage. See *ibid.*, 94-109.

59. Mark Fritz, "Cash Incentives Aren't Enough to Lift Fertility," *Wall Street Journal*, August 17, 2006, B1&B6.

CHAPTER 16
THE UNCONSERVATIVE CONSEQUENCES OF CONSERVATIVE OPPOSITION TO GAY MARRIAGE

Dale Carpenter[1]
University of Minnesota

I.   Introduction: The Unconservative Harms

The point of this chapter is not to argue same sex marriage. The point, instead, is fairly simple. It is that conservative opposition to same sex is having unconservative, harmful effects. Conservative opposition to gay marriage is unintentionally pushing the boundaries of family law into new territory that challenges the primacy of marriage itself. By opposing marriage, conservatives are forcing gay families to seek refuge through untraditional means that undermine marriage itself or destabilize family concepts in ways that gay marriage itself would not and in ways that would and should concern conservatives.

In this chapter, I will do four things. First, I will explain briefly what I mean by "conservative." Second, I will discuss the phenomenon of gay families. Third, I will present some areas in which opposition to same sex marriage is producing unconservative effects. Finally, I will offer some brief concluding thoughts.

II.   Conservativism Defined

What do I mean first by conservative? I mean a particular school of conservatism often called traditionalism, or Burkeanism, after the Eighteenth Century British statesman Edmund Burke.[2] It is not libertarianism. It is not economic conservatism. It is not neo-conservatism. It is not religious conservatism. It is not my aim here to argue normatively for this perspective, although I do, myself, to a very large extent share it.

Burkean conservatism is basically the idea that we should respect tradition and history. We should, in general terms, prefer stability to change, continuity to experiment, and the tried to the untried. Burke himself was not opposed to all changes in his society's practices, traditions, and values. That would not be conservatism, but stupidity. Instead, he counseled deliberation and patience in reform. He wanted what he called a slow, but well sustained progress. In other words, he supported incremental change, and opposed the sort of convulsive changes he saw in events like the French Revolution. .

III.   The Reality of Gay Families

One of the things that is gradually changing in our society is family. In particular, we have seen in recent decades the growth of the gay family. Consider the dimensions of the issue that we are talking about. There are nine or perhaps ten million gay people in the United States today. Most surveys put the number of homosexuals in the range of 3-4% of the population and that's probably a good low baseline figure. A 2005 federal government estimate revealed that perhaps about 777,000 same-sex couple households in the United States. They live in every county in the United States. These are things that the government did not even count two decades ago. It is something we just didn't know about until fairly recently, although of course, the development of these families precedes government counting of them.

It is a lot of people who will never have the prospect of marriage. It denies to these people the most powerful legal and social institution we have for encouraging commitment, fidelity, and monogamy, all values that traditionalists hold dear. Now, maybe that denial is justified. Maybe there are powerful reasons not to make marriage available to these people, but at least we have to recognize that there is some trade off.

According to a 2000 census, about 20% of all male couple households in the United States and about one-third of all female couple households in the United States are raising children. Overall, at least a million children in this country are being raised by gay parents, either single or in a couple. None of these children have the protections and benefits marriage would provide for them.

Again, until very recently, although these families existed, we had no idea how large the phenomenon was. So it was easy to ignore the growth of these families. But the question really is, now that we know, what do we do? Up to now, for the most part, the opponents of gay marriage had nothing to say in response to that question except, "No, no to marriage. Perhaps no to civil unions, perhaps no to other forms of recognition." Here I want to point out that just saying no has consequences conservatives should not welcome.

It is not enough—if you are an opponent of same sex marriage—to simply pass a state constitutional amendment banning gay marriage. If you think you have eliminated the phenomenon of gay families, or the growth of those families, or the legal problems that will arise from the existence of those families, let me suggest that you are mistaken. They will continue to exist and continue to have needs that have to be met in one way or another.

IV.   Some Unconservative Harm Caused by Barring Same-Sex Marriage

There are several areas where simply saying no to same-sex marriage is having unconservative consequences on family law.

One of them is that we have seen in the last few decades the growth of what a lot of people are calling "marriage-lite," that is, the creation of domestic partnerships or civil unions that offer some alternative status to same sex couples. The theory is that if you won't let same-sex couples marry they will have to create alternative forms of recognition, with alternative responsibilities and rights.

We have seen this develop in three different areas. First, it is happening in private companies around the country that are offering health benefits to same sex domestic partners. That is increasing. Second, municipalities and counties around the country offer domestic partnership registration and even some benefits. Finally, and most importantly, we have seen an increasing number of states offer statewide domestic partnerships or civil union statuses to same sex couples. The states that are doing that now include California, Connecticut, New Jersey, Oregon, New Hampshire, Washington, and Vermont. About one-sixth of the people in the United States are now living in a state in which there is nearly complete recognition of same sex couples on a par with marriage. These marriage alternatives have three basic purposes. One is to grant recognition to the couples. A second is to give them benefits. A third is to impose responsibilities for caring and commitment upon the couples.

How might the growth of these alternatives be considered unconservative? The basic answer is that they potentially represent a challenge to the primacy of marriage itself. Jonathan Rauch has suggested that because of the growth of these alternatives to marriage, marriage itself is in danger of no longer being the gold standard for committed couples. And, in fact, where these statuses are available to both opposite and same sex couples, available to both, they are overwhelmingly chosen more often by opposite sex couples than by same sex couples. The opposite-sex couples don't have to choose to marry. They have an alternative and therefore they have less incentive to marry. Exit from these statuses is often easier than it is for marriage. Sometimes it involves nothing more than notice to the other partner and other relevant third parties and there is not a waiting period.

I think that there is something to this concern and I think it is something that conservatives who want to keep marriage as the gold standard should be worried about, although I do feel that its force can be blunted in a couple of ways. First, the harm can be minimized if the alternative statuses are limited to same sex couples—as all the state laws are so far, but not all the city, county, and private party policies are. Second, the alternative statuses should end when same sex couples are finally allowed to marry. The alternative statuses have tended to end in Massachusetts, for example, with private companies requiring that same sex couples get married now that the option is available to them. But nevertheless, it is something conservatives should be concerned about.

A second consequence of the fact that same sex marriage is not available is the growth of what are often called second parent adoptions. When married couples adopt, both spouses become the legal parents of the child. Traditionally, only one member of an unmarried couple could adopt a child. Among other things, that rule has encouraged people to get married because it would provide the child with two legal parents. Now gay couples who, of course, can't marry, must find other ways to protect their children. Starting in early 1980s, the National Center for Lesbian Rights pioneered the concept of second parent adoptions, by which two unmarried people could both be legal parents. Over time, that concept has been embraced by courts or by statutes in at least some jurisdictions in about half of the states. So far so good: there is now at least some legal protection for the children in these gay families.

But from a conservative perspective, here's the problem: second parent adoptions have also become available to unmarried heterosexual couples. So a legal reform that was intended to compensate the unavailability of marriage to same sex couples has been seized on by those who can marry, but who choose not to. That reduces the incentive to marry and means effectively that more children will be raised out of wedlock.

The third development, "triple parenting," is another unconservative consequence of the ban on gay marriage. It is illustrated by a recent court decision in Pennsylvania. The case involved a lesbian couple who enlisted a male friend to act as a sperm donor. The donor relationship resulted in the birth of two children to one of the women. Although the children were raised by two women, the biological father, who was known to them, visited them and helped to support them financially. When the lesbian couple split up, each of the women sought primary custody of these two children. The trial court found that they were both good parents, but that the best interests of the children would be served by living primarily with the biological mother. The other woman was given partial custody and was ordered to pay child support. The biological father, the sperm donor, was allowed to have his two children one weekend per month, but was not ordered to pay child support. The appellate court upheld the decision to give primary custody to the biological mother. It also accepted the argument that the sperm donor/biological father should help with child support. And it did so on the basis of court created equitable estoppel principles since the state legislature has done nothing by statute to deal with these issues. The state legislature in Pennsylvania is busying itself trying to protect marriage from gay families by passing a state constitutional amendment banning gay marriage rather than by dealing with the reality of family life in the state.

Obviously, the issues raised by involving three parents in children's lives are not unique to gay couples. Change the sex of one of the members of the unmarried couple in this case and nothing in the legal analysis changes. In fact, gay and straight couples were using assisted reproduction—including surrogates—long before gay marriage became a national issue and they are going to continue to do so regardless of what we decide to do about the gay marriage issue.

The idea of gay marriage has arisen as an answer to the problems faced by precisely this sort of couple and other couples who have children, especially same sex couples. These families exist whether conservatives like it or not and whether we recognize gay marriage or not. The question is whether we can simplify their lives and consolidate their legal obligations to one another by letting them marry. The lesbian couple in the case that I just mentioned obviously couldn't get married in Pennsylvania, but consider that marriage exists in part to help clarify the legal lines of responsibility for children, giving everyone some assurance about who has responsibility for them. If gay couples could marry, as straight couples under the same circumstances could, they might be more likely to push for exclusive parental rights because of the additional security marriage would give them. Sperm donors and surrogate mothers, for their part, would be more likely to surrender their parental rights to the couple since they would be reassured that the child would live in a family fully protected by the law.

Many lesbian couples opt for sperm donations from a close friend rather than going to a sperm bank for an anonymous donation precisely because they face discrimination at sperm banks. If they could get married, they would face less discrimination and thus might be less inclined to involve a friend in their decision to have a child—a friend who might later demand some role in the child's upbringing. While gay marriage won't eliminate all these scenarios in which you have multiple adults vying for children—just as marriage hasn't eliminated these scenarios for opposite sex couples—it would make them somewhat more rare. So the absence of gay marriage is opening the door wider to the very trends that conservatives believe are destabilizing to families.

Gay families are, of course, just one part of a much larger series of developments that are changing family life in this country. Those living outside of marriage, whether they are opposite sex couples or same sex couples, are understandably going to try to find creative ways to protect their loved ones. Left leaning legal reformers would regard many or all of the innovations that I have just described as good. In fact, they are championing them. They are happy to knock marriage off its pedestal. They are happy to bend long standing traditions in family law to meet the needs of families of choice.

Conservatives, on the other hand, should regard these developments suspiciously because they bring with them the potential to undermine marriage and traditional parental forms and presumptions. Because these alternative arrangements and creative solutions for unmarried families are almost always made available to opposite sex couples each of them reduces in its own way the incentive to marry – a consequence which can hardly be considered conservative in the Burkean sense of respecting longstanding traditions. So ironically, in an effort to protect marriage, conservatives are contributing unwittingly to the very cultural, political, and legal trends that are undermining it. Trying to bolster traditional family life, they are helping to erode it.

So what is a conservative to do?

I have an idea. How about letting gay couples get married? Gay marriage would relieve some of the intense hydraulic pressure to concoct some of these alternatives.

Now if you don't like that idea because you think gay marriage itself is more harmful to tradition and traditional families than all of these other trends put together, I suppose you could try to block each of them. The problem with that approach is that it is almost impossible to block all of the alternative arrangements because families in need and judges who face real crises will always find creative ways to get around any roadblocks. Additionally, it's simply no longer acceptable morally or politically to shut our eyes to the reality of gay families and the problems they confront in everyday life.

V.   Conclusion: A Rising River

Let me end with a metaphor. Think of it this way: gay families are a rising river, stretching across the country. Conservative opposition to gay marriage is a dam blocking the way. Impeded in its natural course, the river does not dry up. Its flow is simply redirected into a hundred rivulets and low pastures all around the countryside. The result is a flood, with damage spread across the land.

Many conservatives may think that the collateral damage that is being done by the opposition to gay marriage is worth it in the end. But at least they have to recognize—before family law is further inundated—that there are some unconservative consequences to that opposition.

Notes

1. This paper was presented initially at the Symposium on Same-Sex Marriage and Gay Adoption: Inclusion, Compromise, Protection and Consequences, held at Brigham Young University, J. Reuben Clark Law School, on November 2, 2007.

2. Edmund Burke, Reflections on the Revolution in France 53 (1790) available at http://www.constitution.org/eb/rev_fran.htm (seen 29 October 2007).

CHAPTER 17

OR FOR POORER? HOW SAME-SEX MARRIAGE THREATENS
RELIGIOUS LIBERTY[†]

Roger T. Severino[*]

*"[T]HE RIGHT TO SAME-SEX MARRIAGE CONFERRED BY THE PROPOSED LEGISLATION
MAY POTENTIALLY CONFLICT WITH THE RIGHT TO FREEDOM OF RELIGION . . . ."*
—SUPREME COURT OF CANADA, DECEMBER 9, 2004.[1]

I.   Introduction

On May 17, 2004, Massachusetts began issuing marriage licenses without
regard to sex of the applicants. By order of the Massachusetts Supreme
Judicial Court, same-sex marriage became a reality in America and triggered a
wave of litigation and church-state conflict that has only just begun. In
Goodridge v. Department of Public Health,[2] the Massachusetts high court
decreed that the definition of marriage as the exclusive union of husbands and
wives discriminates against gays and lesbians so invidiously that it violated
the state's Equal Protection guarantees.[3] Although the decision carried with it
profound implications for religious liberty,[4] the *Goodridge* court dismissed
any religious freedom concerns with the following conclusory footnote:

> Our decision in no way limits the rights of individuals to refuse to
> marry persons of the same sex for religious or any other reasons. It in
> no way limits the personal freedom to disapprove of, or to encourage
> others to disapprove of, same-sex marriage.[5]

Simply put, the Massachusetts Supreme Judicial Court's confidence is mis-
placed. The movement for same-sex marriage is on a collision course with religious liberty. This Article explores the coming clash.

The conflict between gay rights and religious liberty over marriage seems
inevitable because of four concurrent phenomena. First, marriage, as a uniform
concept, pervades the law;[6] second, religious institutions are regulated, both
directly and indirectly, by a multitude of laws that turn on the definition of marriage; third, religious institutions care deeply about marriage and many (if not
most) cannot in good conscience accept same-sex unions as morally equivalent
to husband-wife marriage; and fourth, same-sex marriage proponents are similarly resistant to compromise since many believe, with the *Goodridge* concur-

rence, that "[s]imple principles of decency dictate that we extend to [same-sex couples], and to their new status, full acceptance, tolerance, and respect."[7]

Although it is difficult to predict with certainty the long-term effects of this profound change in the law, it is clear that the effects will be far-reaching. The legal definition of marriage does not exist in isolation; changing it alters many areas of the law. For example, the definition of marriage plays an important role in the law of adoption, education, employee benefits, health care, employment discrimination, government contracts and subsidies, taxation, tort law, and trusts and estates. In turn, these legal regimes directly govern the ongoing daily operations of religious organizations of all stripes, including parishes, schools, temples, hospitals, orphanages, retreat centers, soup kitchens, and universities. Moreover, current law provides no room for non-uniform definitions of marriage within a state, it is all or nothing. But even across states it is difficult to countenance variable definitions across states because of difficult questions like child custody.[8] The high stakes reinforce the uncompromising posture of the contending sides.

Changes in marriage law impact religious institutions disproportionately because their role is so deeply intertwined with the public concept of marriage. Indeed, religious institutions have been regulating marriage since time immemorial[9] so that civil and common law marriage in the West evolved through adopting and accommodating religious conventions not *vice-versa*.[10] This history is reflected today; a solid majority of *civil* marriages are still legally solemnized by *religious* institutions.[11] Because of the undeniable centrality of marriage to civic and religious life, conflicts will inevitably arise where the legal definition of marriage differs dramatically from the religious definition. As this Article explains, recent trends in gay rights and anti-discrimination law make it anything but clear that this conflict will be resolved in favor of religious liberty.

The specific consequences that will likely flow from legalizing same-sex marriage include both government compulsion of religious institutions to provide financial or other support for same-sex married couples and government withdrawal of public benefits from those institutions that oppose same-sex marriage. In other words, wherever religious institutions provide preferential treatment to husband-wife couples, state laws will likely require them to either extend identical benefits to same-sex couples or withdraw the benefits altogether. Correspondingly, as courts elevate same-sex marriage in the hierarchy of constitutional rights, state actors will be induced if not required to treat opposition to same-sex marriage as "invidious discrimination," "irrational," or "motivated by animus." Thus, religious bodies retaining such "discriminatory" beliefs will be subject to a wide range of legal impediments precisely because their policies reflect those beliefs.[12] In short, governments would be prone to punish uncooperative religious institutions directly, by imposing outright civil liability, and indirectly, by excluding the institutions from government programs and benefits both high and petty.

To be sure, religious institutions will be able to assert a wide range of First Amendment defenses against these kinds of sanctions.[13] But it remains difficult to predict the ultimate effectiveness of these defenses given several years of Supreme Court precedents eroding religious liberty.[14] Not surprisingly, lower courts have followed the high court's lead and have been increasingly hostile to claims under the Free Exercise Clause. But just as protections for religious freedom were diminishing, courts became increasingly sympathetic to the notion of gay rights, even as a claim that could override other constitutionally important concerns.[15] Indeed, the movement towards same-sex marriage has been driven overwhelmingly by courts, not legislatures, and courts have been demonstrably willing to set aside even substantial precedent in this context.

For its part, the Supreme Court has cast doubt on the survivability of *any* statute that appears to put homosexual relationships on less than equal footing with heterosexual ones[16]—making the Defense of Marriage Act ("DOMA") particularly vulnerable to attack.[17]

But no matter what the ultimate constitutional balancing of rights, religious institutions will in the meantime face serious legal risks that include the substantial possibility of civil liability and targeted exclusion from government benefits. Whether that risk translates into legal penalties will depend upon the outcome of a whole cascade of litigation; this Article aims merely to point out the contours of the emerging conflicts rather than predict the prevailing parties in each particular case.

But, after much careful study of the question of legalized same-sex marriage, three results seem certain. First, wherever same-sex marriage spreads, lawsuits and revocations of government benefit to religious institutions will follow. Second, no side will be able to claim complete or near-complete victory in the litigation to come. Finally, numerous lawsuits will impose costs and uncertainty that will substantially chill religious expression and represent, by themselves, a form of church-state conflict.

II.   The Evolution of Same-Sex Marriage in Law

A.   The Campaign to Change the Definition of Marriage by Lawsuit Failed for Decades, then Suddenly, Success

Efforts to redefine marriage through direct legal challenge began as far back as 1971 and kicked off an over two decades-long string of complete failures in court.[18] Even oblique attempts to recognize same-sex marriage by litigants who underwent hormonal and surgical "sex change" procedures were routinely rebuffed.[19] Judicial trends, however, have shifted. Beginning with Hawaii in 1993,[20] courts began to question the states' universal definition of marriage and reinterpreted state constitutional protections to strike marriage laws down.[21] The Hawaii court was followed first by Alaska in 1998[22] and then Vermont in 1999[23] in overturning marriage statutes.

Hawaii's judicial imposition of same-sex marriage caused widespread alarm and uncertainty around the country, prompting the federal government to adopt DOMA and motivating states to amend their constitutions to preserve the definition of marriage. The fear centered on two issues. First, as to the federal government, people feared that a drastic state redefinition of marriage would effectively redefine marriage for federal purposes as well since the government traditionally deferred questions of marriage and family law to the states.[24] Second, people feared the Constitution's Full Faith and Credit Clause[25] would require their home states to honor marriage licenses issued same-sex couples married out of state.[26] Attempting to cure these twin risks, Congress passed DOMA in 1996, providing that states need not recognize same-sex marriages entered into under the laws of sister states, and defining "marriage" and "spouse" to mean a union of one man and one woman for federal purposes.[27] The reaction was similarly swift at the state level, as Hawaii and then Alaska citizens quickly amended their constitutions to restore the original marriage definition and preserve it from further judicial attack.[28]

The Vermont case differs from the experience in Hawaii and Alaska in one key respect. Although the Vermont courts forced the state legislature to confer all the substantive privileges of marriage to same-sex couples, it left the legislature the option to choose its own *name* for the arrangement.[29] The Vermont legislature complied with the order and exercised its option by dubbing these newly legally-sanctioned same-sex unions "civil unions," thereby effectively preserving the name (if not the substance) of "marriage."[30] As expected, much confusion and litigation has resulted over what marriage-like obligations and benefits if any attach to persons who enter Vermont civil unions and permanently relocate to other states.[31] Yet as controversial as the Vermont experiment was, it proved merely a preview of things to come.

B.   *The* Goodridge *Decision Firmly Established Same-Sex Marriage in Law and Opened the Floodgates for Copycat Litigation*

On November 18, 2003, the Massachusetts Supreme Judicial Court released the remaining genie in the bottle in *Goodridge v. Department of Public Health.* The *Goodridge* court held that Vermont's nominal distinction between same-sex civil unions and traditional marriage was irrational at best and invidious discrimination at worst.[32] Only opening marriage in substance *and* name to same-sex partners would satisfy the court. Activists, emboldened by *Goodridge,* quickly challenged marriage laws in California,[33] Connecticut,[34] Florida,[35] Indiana,[36] Iowa,[37] Louisiana,[38] Maryland,[39] Michigan,[40] Nebraska,[41] New Jersey,[42] New York,[43] Oklahoma,[44] Oregon,[45] Rhode Island,[46] Washington,[47] federal bankruptcy court,[48] and even on tribal lands.[49] This flurry of litigation resulted in something really quite remarkable. After decades of abject failure, arguments for same-sex marriage are not only being taken seriously, they are winning in court. Although only two out of the seventeen lawsuits mentioned above represent gay rights victories that have survived appeal, this figure is misleading. More important than the raw number of victories is where they have taken place: California, and New Jersey.

The New Jersey Supreme Court's decision in *Lewis v. Harris* is likely the most significant gay rights case since *Goodridge,* largely because it was decided by the supreme court of a major state. In *Lewis,* the court gave the state legislature 180 days either to allow same-sex couples to legally marry, or provide for full marriage equivalents by some other name, such as civil union. But as significant a decision as *Lewis* was, it may soon be eclipsed by a pending ruling by the California Supreme Court on same-sex marriage. With a population of over 36 million people and its status as one of the states most sympathetic to gay rights, California is poised to hand down a watershed same-sex marriage decision in terms of cultural impact. To put this scenario in perspective, if California adopts same-sex marriage, approximately 14% of the American population will be living in same-sex marriage states.[50] When one includes the population of states with same-sex marriage equivalents such as New Jersey, Vermont, and Connecticut,[51] the total figure rises to 18.6% of the population.[52]

In addition to California, same-sex marriage challenges await resolution before the Connecticut and Iowa high courts.[53] As described *infra* Part II.C., the absence of many lower court cases reflects a general slowing of same-sex marriage litigation, but this is likely only temporary. At bottom, same-sex marriage litigation is driven by long-term legal trends that are difficult to reverse since they have been shaped in significant part by firmly-established precedents expanding gay rights at the U.S. Supreme Court[54] and in foreign jurisdictions.[55]

C. Popular Backlash and the Federal Defense of Marriage Act Have Slowed the Spread of Same-Sex Marriage, For Now

Some same-sex marriage advocates, fearing a backlash from moving too quickly, preferred an indirect or "incremental strategy" for overcoming traditional marriage laws piece by piece through targeted litigation[56] and lobbying state and municipal legislative bodies.[57] This approach, however, was sidelined by the Hawaii Supreme Court decision, the Vermont civil union controversy, and the *Goodridge* case. Finally, the spectacle of municipal officials across the country issuing same-sex marriage licenses in defiance of state law signaled the death knell of the incrementalist strategy.[58] The response from legislatures and voters to these successive events has been impressive and swift. As of this writing, 44 states have protected the definition of marriage by state statute, state constitutional amendment, or both. Of these 44 states, 26 have adopted constitutional amendments reserving marriage exclusively to opposite-sex couples, while 17 states took the extra step of banning civil unions or domestic partnerships as well.[59]

The federal government responded quickly in the wake of the Hawaii Supreme Court's 1993 legalization of same-sex marriage with DOMA in 1996. With DOMA, the federal government abandoned its traditional deference to the states on marriage questions and explicitly defined marriage for federal purposes as follows:

> In determining the meaning of any Act of Congress, or of any ruling, regulation, or interpretation of the various administrative bureaus and agencies of the United States, the word "marriage" means only a legal union between one man and one woman as husband and wife, and

the word "spouse" refers only to a person of the opposite sex who is a husband or a wife.[60]

DOMA also sought to protect the states from a court-led imposition of same-sex marriage through expansive judicial interpretations of the Constitution's Full Faith and Credit Clause:[61]

> No State, territory, or possession of the United States, or Indian tribe, shall be required to give effect to any public act, record, or judicial proceeding of any other State, territory, possession, or tribe respecting a relationship between persons of the same sex that is treated as a marriage under the laws of such other State, territory, possession, or tribe, or a right or claim arising from such relationship.[62]

Although DOMA on its face appears to shield states from an undemocratic proliferation of same-sex marriage,[63] its long-term viability is in doubt.[64] Still, DOMA has survived its first court challenges[65] and same-sex marriage advocates have been forced to reconsider waging an immediate frontal assault on the Act. The focus of same-sex marriage litigation has therefore shifted to first redefining marriage state by state and then, after reaching a critical mass of success, finally taking on DOMA.[66]

As discussed in Part II.B., these advocates have been surprisingly successful in spreading the *Goodridge* precedent around the country through the lower state courts. If high courts follow Massachusetts' lead and firmly establish same-sex marriage in various parts of the nation—especially in large states like California—gay rights advocates will more plausibly argue that striking down DOMA would merely work an incremental change.[67]

In addition, the emigration of married same-sex couples from Massachusetts, or any future same-sex marriage state, will force courts around the country to make new and tough decisions in a politically charged environment.[68] Under these conditions, it is highly unlikely that every court considering the issue will uphold state provisions preserving husband-wife marriage.[69] But even if one ignores the potential for more states to join Massachusetts, the U.S. Supreme Court will eventually decide the constitutionality of federal and state same-sex marriage bans if for no other reason than the issue's national prominence. Few doubt that, once review is granted, *Lawrence v. Texas* will be the controlling precedent. It may be several years, however, before this federal question is resolved because gay rights advocates have shrewdly shifted litigation efforts exclusively to the state court system, while at the same time steadfastly refusing to add federal claims.

The Supreme Court's dramatic expansion of homosexual rights in *Lawrence v. Texas*,[70] acutely calls DOMA's constitutionality into question. In *Lawrence*, the Court held that the Due Process Clause of the Constitution protects the autonomy of individuals to engage in private homosexual sex acts, and struck down Texas's anti-sodomy laws.[71] Although the *Lawrence* Court expressly disclaimed implicating the legality of traditional marriage statutes, Justice Scalia noted in dissent:

Do not believe it. More illuminating than [the Court's] bald, unreasoned disclaimer is the [Court's] progression of thought . . . . Today's opinion dismantles the structure of constitutional law that has permitted a distinction to be made between heterosexual and homosexual unions, insofar as formal recognition in marriage is concerned. . . . This case "does not involve" the issue of homosexual marriage only if one entertains the belief that principle and logic have nothing to do with the decisions of this Court.[72]

It is no coincidence that the Massachusetts Supreme Judicial Court in *Goodridge* chose *Lawrence* as its first and primary citation to authority.[73] The sweeping pronouncements of the *Lawrence* opinion are difficult, if not outright impossible to limit to homosexual sodomy statutes.[74] Specifically, the *Lawrence* Court invited constitutional challenge of DOMA when it held that individual decisions "concerning the intimacies of . . . physical relationship[s], even when not intended to produce offspring, are a form of 'liberty' protected by the Due Process Clause. Moreover, this protection extends to intimate choices by unmarried as well as married persons."[75] Of course, by "unmarried persons," the Court in this instance was referring to unmarried persons *of the same sex*. Furthermore, the Court revealed its beliefs about the social benefit of same-sex relations by characterizing them as "but one element in a personal bond that is more enduring."[76]

Anyone seeking to strike down DOMA and establish same-sex marriage nationwide will find plenty of ammunition in *Lawrence*.

The foregoing analysis of the legal history, litigation strategy, and general trajectory of same-sex marriage marks how thoroughly the definition of marriage is likely to change and the extent to which religious institutions might someday fall within same-sex marriage jurisdictions. Building on this foundation, we can now examine the several ways in which the ascension of same-sex marriage specifically threatens religious liberty.

III.   The Legalization of Same-Sex Marriage Is Generating a Multitude of Serious Risks for Religious Institutions

A.   Religious Institutions that Refuse to Treat Legally Married Same-Sex Couples as Morally Equivalent to Married Men and Women Risk Civil Liability

Threats to religious liberty, as with all threats, can come both directly and indirectly. The following Sections explore the most direct of legal threats—the prospect of a court ordered injunction or fine in retaliation for following one's religious beliefs. Here I refer specifically to punishment for violating antidiscrimination laws in employment, housing, public accommodations, or even with regard to speech, due to an organization following its conscience on same-sex marriage. This is not to say that religious institutions cannot live with antidiscrimination laws; they can and do. Rather, antidiscrimination regulations that would attend the widespread recognition of same-sex marriage threaten to erode the traditional deference to religious sensibilities in a uniquely confrontational way, thus creating traction for such lawsuits.

If current trends persist, religious institutions that oppose same-sex marriage will soon confront situations where one of their employees enters into a legal same-sex marriage in defiance of religious teaching. For many religious institutions, such an act would be tantamount to a public repudiation of the institution's core religious beliefs.[77] In certain contexts—e.g., in religious elementary schools—these employers may seek to terminate employees who reject their moral and religious teachings in such an open and enduring way, either because they sincerely believe they must for the good of the religious community, for the ultimate good of the same-sex couple, or both.[78] For their part, terminated employees might respond with a federal or state employment discrimination lawsuit relying on any of at least four theories.

First, and probably least likely to succeed, an employee may allege discrimination based on *religion* by arguing that the dismissal was due to the employee expressing a protected personal religious belief that happens to differ from or contradict the institution's faith teachings. Second, an employee may allege discrimination based on *sexual orientation*. Federal employment discrimination law currently does not provide a cause of action for sexual orientation discrimination[79] but at least seventeen states do.[80] Third, an employee may allege *sex* discrimination under state or federal law on the theory that the employee would not have been fired for marrying the person of their choice had the employee been a member of the opposite sex.[81] Fourth, an employee may allege discrimination based on *marital status*. Although federal employment discrimination law currently does not provide a cause of action for marital status discrimination, at least twenty states do.[82] Similarly, at least twenty-three states ban marital status discrimination in housing.[83] At first blush, this would appear to be the strongest type of discrimination claim, as the employee will have been fired precisely for obtaining a legal marriage.

The principal weakness of the first potential claim is that both federal and state law specifically exempt religious institutions from prohibitions on religious discrimination. Thus religiously-affiliated employers are free to take religion into account in hiring, firing, and other employment decisions.[84] Although this form of statutory protection is the most common, other, broader exemptions exist which may provide some protection from all four types of employment discrimination claims mentioned above.[85] Thus, in many states the Roman Catholic Church may for religious reasons continue to employ *only* Catholic, celibate, unmarried males as priests and still qualify for statutory exemptions from employment discrimination suits.[86] But because these protections are statutory, they vary by state and can be revised or revoked by legislatures at their pleasure.[87] As state legislatures increasingly grant protection for sexual orientation through anti-discrimination laws, these traditional religious exemptions may be modified or omitted by legislatures[88] or narrowed by courts to the point of vanishing.[89]

Employees who legally marry their same-sex partners will likely request that their employers extend all available spousal health and retirement benefits to their legal "spouses" as well, whether or not the employer is religiously affiliated or a religious institution. Of course, some religious employers may accept or overlook an employee's same-sex marriage, but others may refuse on religious grounds to treat it as the equivalent of traditional marriage, much less subsidize it. Before *Goodridge*, courts generally did not require employers to extend benefits to same-sex partners absent specific language in state and municipal anti-discrimination statutes. But the reasoning of these cases suggests that the results are likely to change with the redefinition of marriage.

For example, in *Lilly v. City of Minneapolis*,[90] a lesbian couple alleged that they were impermissibly discriminated against by the city's failure to provide health benefits to same-sex domestic partners.[91] Although the court found that the extension of such benefits was not required under the relevant anti-discrimination statutes, it noted that the question of marriage was at the heart of the dispute:

> Employers are particularly interested in whether the protection against [sexual orientation] discrimination in the workplace would change the marital status classification. Such a change would have a great impact on employer benefit plans, which might have to cover homosexual partners.[92]

Put another way, the legal determinant of whether benefits may be denied is keyed to the *current definition* of marriage. Thus, wherever the definition of marriage changes to include same-sex couples, employers may *automatically* be required to provide insurance and benefits to all legal "spouses"—both traditional and same-sex—to comply with state and municipal anti-discrimination laws.

Since *Goodridge*, courts have become increasingly likely to entertain claims of unlawful discrimination concerning employee benefits for same-sex couples, even in states that ban same-sex marriage. For example, in 2005 the Alaska high court found that same-sex couples are entitled to identical "spousal" benefits under the state constitution, despite the state's marriage amendment.[93] Similarly, the California Supreme Court in 2005 held that denying spousal benefits to registered domestic partners in a *private club* amounted to marital status discrimination, despite the state's DOMA defining marriage as between one man and one woman.[94] Most troublingly for religious liberty, a federal court in Maine in 2004 found that certain anti-discrimination laws required even religious institutions to provide identical health and employee benefits to registered same-sex couples as traditionally married spouses *notwithstanding* any religious freedom objections.[95]

In short, before *Goodridge*, employers were largely free to withhold benefits from same-sex couples and could justify their actions by merely relying on state marriage statutes. However, with the arrival of legal same-sex marriage, courts are increasingly likely to hold that equal protection principles and anti-discrimination statutes require *every* employer to extend spousal benefits to same-sex couples if they provide spousal benefits at all.

Just as same-sex couples will likely seek employee spousal benefits from their religious employers, they will seek spousal benefits from religious institutions in other contexts as well, such as housing. Religious colleges and universities frequently provide student housing and often give special priority, benefits or subsidies to husband and wife couples. Conflict looms at those religious schools that oppose same-sex sexual conduct and that would refuse in conscience to subsidize or condone homosexual cohabitation on their campuses. These schools seek the freedom to refuse to extend housing benefits and services to same-sex couples, regardless of the legal status of their unions.

But in a handful of states, courts have forced landlords to facilitate the cohabitation of their unmarried tenants over strong religious objections.[96] If *unmarried* couples enjoy legal protection from marital status discrimination, legally *married* couples would have comparatively stronger protection as public policy tend to favor and subsidize marriage as an institution.

But one need not argue by analogy to see what lies in store for religious schools that will not accept homosexual cohabitation. The New York Court of Appeals decision in *Levin v. Yeshiva University* addressed the issue directly. In *Levin* the court held that two lesbian students had stated a valid "disparate impact" claim of sexual-orientation discrimination after the university refused to provide married-student housing benefits to unmarried same-sex couples.[97]

Thus, the right of religious universities to implement their beliefs—in particular, to support and favor husband-wife marriage—was already being challenged as illegally discriminatory before *Goodridge*, any court that follows *Goodridge* will be all the more likely to use state anti-discrimination laws to require religious schools to subsidize or otherwise facilitate homosexual cohabitation.[98]

From hospitals, to schools, to counseling, to marriage services, religious institutions provide a broad array of services and facilities to their members and to the general public. And religious institutions have historically enjoyed wide latitude in choosing both what religiously-motivated services and facilities to provide and to whom they will be provided. However, changing the legal definition of marriage may require a reassessment of that understanding for two reasons. First, more states are adding sexual orientation as a protected category in anti-discrimination laws. Second, religious institutions and their related ministries are facing increased risk of being declared places of public accommodation—thus being subject to legal regimes designed to regulate secular businesses. These two facts, when coupled with legalized same-sex marriage, would subject to widespread liability those ministries that refuse, for religious reasons, to provide identical services to married same-sex couples.

Although nearly all states ban discrimination by non-state actors in public accommodations in some form, a growing minority of states (currently 15) have included prohibitions on sexual orientation discrimination.[99] While some states exempt religious organizations from their anti-discrimination statutes generally, more limit that exemption to only certain kinds of accommodations, or to only certain categories of discrimination.[100] Several states provide no religious exemptions at all to one or more of their anti-discrimination statutes.[101] Furthermore, any protection granted by statute can be revoked by statute, and the current trend is to grant greater protection to sexual orientation.

The risk of being regulated by public accommodations laws is especially acute for those religious institutions that have very open membership and service provision policies. Specifically, the more the service or facility can be separated away from "religious worship," and the more a service or facility is made available to persons without regard to religion, the greater the risk that the non-profit religious institution will be regulated like a for-profit business.

Some of the many religiously-motivated services that potentially fall under this rubric include marriage counseling, family counseling, job training programs, health care services, child care, gyms and day camps, education,[102] adoption services,[103] and even the use of wedding reception facilities.[104] Of the innumerable religious organizations that minister to the public in one or more of the ways mentioned above, many simply want to avoid the appearance (and reality) of condoning or subsidizing same-sex marriage through their "family-based" services.[105] Yet, it is possible that none of these institutions would be able to voice their religious objections to same-sex marriage in this way, because they risk being designated a public accommodation barred from discriminating on the basis of sex, marital status, or sexual orientation.

The experience of the Boy Scouts of America is a prominent example of how private organizations which appear "open to the public" can run into trouble.

In *Dale v. Boy Scouts*, the New Jersey Supreme opined that "when an entity invites the public to join, attend, or participate in some way, that entity is a public accommodation . . . ."[106] The court then reflected on the fact that the Boy Scout troops "take part in perhaps the most powerful invitation of all, albeit an implied one: the symbolic invitation extended by a Boy Scout each time he wears his uniform in public."[107] As a result of this broad based solicitation, the court found that the Boy Scouts were a place of public accommodation subject to New Jersey anti-discrimination statutes and ordered them to accept homosexual members. Although the U.S. Supreme Court later prevented New Jersey from interfering with the Boy Scouts' membership policies in this way on appeal,[108] the court left New Jersey's *designation* of the Boy Scouts as a place of public accommodation untouched. And New Jersey is not the only state to have found the Boy Scouts to be a place of public accommodation.[109]

The critical question, of course, is which restrictions might be imposed once the public accommodation label attaches. Forced inclusion of homosexuals, married or otherwise, in positions of organizational leadership is clearly foreclosed by the Supreme Court's decision in *Boy Scouts v. Dale*. But once exposed as a place of public accommodation, religious institutions could face a flood of litigation attempting to regulate any *services or facilities* deemed "open to the public," so long as the organization's membership policies and core associational rights are not implicated in the regulation.[110]

An example of this risk is furnished by *Gay Rights Coalition of Georgetown University Law Center v. Georgetown University*.[111] In that case, the D.C. Court of Appeals held that D.C.'s public accommodations statute required Georgetown to provide a gay rights student group the same access to university facilities as recognized groups.[112] Although the university objected to being forced to use its property to subsidize speech repugnant to its religious beliefs, the court dismissed these concerns by finding that the goal of "eradicating sexual orientation discrimination" represented a more important government interest than protecting religious liberty.[113]

Other courts may hesitate to make such a blatant choice of gay rights over religious freedom and may sidestep the problem by simply declaring that religious entity is not religious enough to merit protection.

A recent example of this phenomenon occurred in the case of *Catholic Charities of Sacramento v. Superior Court*.[114] There, the California Supreme Court found that Catholic Charities of Sacramento, a social service arm of the Catholic Church, did not qualify for a religious exemption as a "religious employer" under the Women's Contraceptive Equity Act ("WCEA") which required the church to provide contraceptive coverage to its female employees contrary to its beliefs. The court analyzed and disposed of the issue by stating that

> The [WCEA] defines a "religious employer" as "an entity for which each of the following is true:" (A) The inculcation of religious values is the purpose of the entity. (B) The entity primarily employs persons who share the religious tenets of the entity. (C) The entity serves primarily persons who share the religious tenets of the entity. (D) The entity is a nonprofit organization . . . ." Catholic Charities does not qualify as a "religious employer" under the WCEA because it does not meet any of the definition's four criteria.[115]

According to the California Supreme Court, Catholic Charities was simply not religious enough.

But the California Supreme Court took pains to add that *even granting that* Catholic Charities' religious exercise would be substantially burdened by the regulation, the hardship would be fully justified by "the compelling state interest of eliminating gender discrimination."[116] The court thus put the church to the Hobson's choice: "We do not doubt Catholic Charities' assertion that to offer insurance coverage for prescription contraceptives to its employees would be religiously unacceptable . . . . Catholic Charities may, however, avoid this conflict with its religious beliefs simply by not offering coverage for prescription drugs."[117]

If other courts follow Massachusetts' and declare a right to same-sex marriage,[118] laws prohibiting discrimination based on sexual orientation or marital status will have new power. Courts will be much more likely to find severe burdens on religious expression justified by a new compelling reason—the eliminating of sexual orientation discrimination. It will then be much more likely that religious institutions will be required by law to extend many of the programs, facilities, and services listed above to homosexual "spouses," or lose the ability to provide them at all.

Suits under increasingly numerous state hate-crimes laws are also potential avenues of civil or criminal liability for religious institutions that actively preach against same-sex marriage. General hate-crime statutes exist in at least 45 states.[119] Of those, currently 32 states have hate crimes laws referencing sexual orientation.[120] Ministers and preachers could face conspiracy or incitement suits under these laws if, after hearing a preacher's strongly-worded (but non-violent) sermon against same-sex marriage, a congregant commits a hate crime against a person or business. The possibility of suit alone may chill controversial religious expression on the topic of same-sex marriage.

Some states have already taken the next step and banned sexual-orientation related hate speech *directly*, as in Massachusetts and Pennsylvania.[121] In fact, religious speakers have already been arrested in Pennsylvania for the "hate crime" of peacefully opposing gay rights in public. In 2004, an organized group of Christians was arrested for "ethnic intimidation" under Pennsylvania hate crimes laws for nonviolently protesting at a Philadelphia gay pride event, even though the event was open to the public and held on city streets and sidewalks. Although the criminal hate-crime charges against the protesters were eventually dropped, the protesters' subsequent lawsuit against the city for violations of their civil rights over the wrongful arrest was dismissed.[122]

Even without statutory hate-speech prohibitions, suits over quintessentially religious speech opposing same-sex marriage are no longer conjectural in America.[123] The day is fast approaching when religiously-motivated speech against gay and lesbian conduct that is deemed "hateful" or otherwise offensive may not be tolerated in law.[124]

B. *Legalizing Same-Sex Marriage Will Induce Governments to Strip Benefits from Religious Institutions That Refuse to Treat Legally Married Same-Sex Couples as Morally Equivalent to Married Men and Women*

As discussed above, legalizing same-sex marriage would generate extensive litigation over state anti-discrimination statutes that directly regulate religious institutions' marriage-related policies. But another battleground awaits over whether governments may withdraw funding or access to government benefits to religious organizations they label as "discriminators" because of their opposition to same-sex marriage. Governments are already arguing that law or public policy prevents them from providing government services to, or even associating with, such discriminatory religious organizations.

Many government-funded programs require that recipients be organized "for the public good" or that they not act "contrary to public policy." Religious institutions that refuse to approve, subsidize, or perform state-sanctioned same-sex marriages could well be found to violate such general standards, and thereby lose their access to public fora, government funding, or tax-exempt status. In states where courts and legislatures cannot force religious groups to accept same-sex marriage norms outright, revocation of otherwise generally available government benefits and accommodations may prove equally effective. The amount of government benefits at risk is enormous, and, in light of the increasing cooperation between faith-based organizations and state and federal government programs, only stands to grow, as well as the controversy.[125]

Religious institutions that refuse to treat same-sex spouses as equivalent to husband-wife marriages may face staggering financial losses if state or federal authorities revoke their tax exemption because of their religious principles and policies. Such a case is not unprecedented. In *Bob Jones University v. United States*, a religious university that banned interracial dating and interracial marriage as part of its admissions policy lost its tax exemption, even though the policy stemmed directly from sincerely held religious beliefs.[126] In affirming the IRS decision, the Supreme Court reasoned that

> [T]he Government has a *fundamental*, overriding interest in eradicating racial *discrimination* in education—discrimination that prevailed, with official approval, for the first 165 years of this Nation's *history*. That governmental interest substantially outweighs whatever burden denial of tax benefits places on petitioners' exercise of their religious beliefs.[127]

The *Goodridge* court's language and reasoning were strikingly similar:

> In this case, as in *Perez* and *Loving* [which overturned interracial marriage bans], a statute deprives individuals of access to an institution of *fundamental* legal, personal, and social significance—the institution of marriage—because of a single trait: skin color in *Perez* and *Loving,* sexual orientation here. As it did in *Perez* and *Loving, history* must yield to a more fully developed understanding of the invidious quality of the *discrimination*.[128]

These similarities cannot be ignored. The *Goodridge* court's choice of similar words and analysis is too striking to be mere coincidence. The court equated sexual orientation discrimination with racial discrimination as "demean[ing] basic human dignity,"[129] but, unlike *Gay Rights Coalition v. Georgetown University* or *Catholic Charities of Sacramento v. Superior Court* (discussed *supra* § III.A.3), it did not specifically endorse the government's power and obligation to eradicate sexual orientation discrimination even when at the price of substantially burdening religious exercise.[130]

Since the issue was not squarely before the court, it may simply be a matter of time before the it, or another court, finds dissenting religious institutions "so at odds with the common community conscience as to undermine any public benefit that might otherwise be conferred," and must, like Bob Jones University, have their tax exemptions revoked.[131]

State and federal taxing authorities, of course, need not necessarily take overt action. In many cases, the mere threat of losing tax-exempt status may force religious institutions to conform to government anti-discrimination mandates rather than risk losing their ability to provide desperately needed social and spiritual services.

These risks are not theoretical. Already, a Methodist institution in Ocean Grove, New Jersey, has lost its real-estate tax exemption for refusing to perform civil unions on its outdoor wedding pavilion[132] and more are likely to follow.[133]

Even where houses of worship are not targeted as such, their closely affiliated social service organizations could be. As it stands, religious universities, charities, and hospitals receive significant government funding, but that funding may one day be stripped away through lawsuits or the decisions of aggressive regulatory bodies.

For example, In *Grove City College v. Bell*, a religious college was denied all federal student financial aid for failing to comply with Title IX's written anti-discrimination affirmation requirements, even though there was no evidence of actual discrimination.[134] Religious universities that reject same-sex marriage are open to similar funding attacks from state education agencies that choose to adopt an expansive view of state anti-discrimination law.

A related concern exists for religious institutions in the adoption context. Will state governments force religious institutions to place orphan children under the care of same-sex couples? It has already happened. In Massachusetts, Boston Catholic Charities, a large religious social-service organization, was pushed out of the adoption business because it was forced to choose between placing foster children with homosexual couples (and violating its religious convictions) or losing its state adoption agency license altogether.[135] In California, a lower court recently found religiously-motivated administrators of an Arizona adoption facilitation website subject to California's public accommodations statute because they refused to post profiles of same-sex couples as potential adoptive parents. As a result, the adoption site can no longer accept profiles from any California resident.[136]

Finally, the Young Men's Christian Association (YMCA) in Iowa was forced to recognize gay and lesbian unions as "families" for membership purposes or lose government support for the YMCA's community programs. Originally, the Des Moines Human Rights Commission found the YMCA in violation of local public accommodations laws because it refused to extend "family membership" privileges to a lesbian couple which had entered a civil union in Vermont.[137] Although the YMCA fully addressed this concern by creating a new membership class providing gay and lesbian couples identical benefits as "family" members, the city council was not satisfied. It demanded full equality of recognition, not just equality of benefits, and subsequently forced the YMCA to change their internal definition of "family" to include gay and lesbian couples or lose $102,000 government funding.[138]

Similarly, gay rights advocates have used municipal laws that forbid outsourced government service providers from discriminating based on sexual orientation to pressure religious organizations to abandon certain positions on sexual morality.[139] Thus, government agencies—that cooperate with or provide services through houses of worship, religious hospitals, or religious schools—

may run afoul of these local anti-discrimination laws if their religiously-affiliated partners can be cast as government "contractors."

Religious institutions will likely face challenges to their equal right to a diverse array of public subsidies on the one hand, and access to fora where they may freely discuss their religious beliefs on the other. Again, the Boy Scouts of America provide an illuminating example in the retaliation they have faced in response to their morality-based membership criteria. The Boy Scouts' unwavering requirement—that members believe in God and not advocate for or engage in homosexual conduct—has resulted in numerous lawsuits by activists and municipalities seeking to deny the Boy Scouts any access to state benefits and public fora. For example, the Boy Scouts had to fight to regain equal access to public after-school facilities,[140] and use of military resources for their annual Jamboree.[141] And they appear to have permanently lost long-standing leases to city campgrounds,[142] access to public marina berths reserved for public interest groups,[143] equal access to public after-school facilities,[144] the right to participate in state charitable fundraising programs[145] and access to a Boy Scouts regional headquarters building.[146] Government ostracism of the Boy Scouts is merely a foretaste of what awaits religious organizations that persist in their theology-based opposition to same-sex marriage, especially in jurisdictions where same-sex marriage is legal. These religious organizations will be forced to either change their beliefs and messages concerning same-sex marriage or risk an avalanche of lawsuits and municipal ordinances seeking their targeted exclusion from public privileges and benefits.[147]

A lawsuit requesting that a court directly order an unwilling religious institution to perform a same-sex marriage would almost certainly fail under the Free Exercise Clause. But this immunity is not the end of the story (and, in light of the other dangers discussed in this entire Article, it is not even the beginning). Religious institutions may still soon face a very stark choice: either abandon their religious principles regarding marriage or be deprived of the ability to perform legally recognized ones. As courts push the civil definition of marriage into greater conflict with its historical religious definition, controversy will inevitably grow over both *how* a civil marriage is solemnized and *who* can do the solemnizing.

The *Goodridge* court facilitated this dilemma by doing a very curious and wholly unnecessary thing in its decision: it stated that religion has nothing at all to do with civil marriage.[148] But, the *Goodridge* opinion notwithstanding, American clergy exercise the legal authority to solemnize civil marriages *through purely religious ceremonies* everywhere and all the time, that is, through weddings.[149] This practice reflects the historical understanding of marriage as primarily a religious union that is also worthy of the highest civil recognition.[150] Even though that understanding has been weakened over time, purely non-religious marriage solemnization is still the exception to the rule.[151] But this may change if the *Goodridge* court's hyper-secularized view of the meaning of civil marriage gains currency.

Thus, if clergy act in the place of civil servants when legally marrying couples, they may soon be regulated just like any other civil servant.[152] Vermont has already held that that the Free Exercise rights of its town clerks are not violated if, for religious reasons, they refuse to participate in the issuance of civil union licenses to same-sex couples and are fired as a result.[153] Already, at least twelve dissenting Massachusetts justices of the peace have been forced to resign for refusing to perform same-sex marriages, despite their willingness to continue solemnizing husband-wife marriages.[154] Since clergy fulfill an important government function when solemnizing marriages, there may be a strong movement to strip all non-conforming clergy of their authority to perform that civil function, notwithstanding any Free Exercise objections.

Indeed, some state regulations already prohibit officiants who solemnize civilly-recognized marriages from discriminating in certain ways. The Texas Family Code, for example, forbids persons authorized to conduct a marriage ceremony—including clergy—"from discriminating on the basis of race."[155] Other state marriage codes could easily be amended to follow the Texas model and, with a simple addition, could also include a prohibition on discrimination based on sex or sexual orientation when solemnizing civil marriages.

Alternatively, some commentators advocate a complete separation between the civil and religious aspects of marriage.[156] But in either case, clergy that object to same-sex marriage would no longer be allowed to solemnize marriages according to their religious practices and retain any legal effect.

IV.   Conclusion

Religious institutions face a variety of grave risks in the wake of legalized same-sex marriage. Some exposure to liability is almost certain to arise, some may never materialize, and some may be blunted by constitutional defenses. The risk alone exerts a chilling effect on religious liberty as religious institutions may feel forced to compromise their principles on same-sex marriage simply to avoid a costly and divisive fight in court, even if such a fight would ultimately prove successful. But since this Article has shown that many of the risks have *already* been realized, it is reasonable to presume that this pattern will continue if or when same-sex marriage spreads further across America. This will put tremendous pressure on religious institutions to compromise their beliefs, especially when faced with losing equal access to a wide array of government benefit programs and licensing regimes that further their religious missions.

What remains then is the question of accommodation. The American legal tradition of accommodating diverse religious beliefs and expression has proven remarkably successful at ensuring both peace and liberty. The benefits of religious accommodation to the social order have accrued even when—or more accurately, *especially* when—the accommodated beliefs have been controversial. Thus, when weighing the benefits and cost of adopting as fundamental social change as same-sex marriage, particularly close consideration must be given to its impact on religious freedom.[157] This Article has attempted to illuminate that special piece of the equation and has found that the likely cost to religious liberty is a high one indeed.

APPENDIX A: TABLE OF UNSUCCESSFUL MARRIAGE CHALLENGES
PREDATING THE GOODRIDGE DECISION

Baker v. Nelson, 191 N.W.2d 185 (Minn. 1971).
Jones v. Hallahan, 501 S.W.2d 588, 590 (Ky. 1973).
Singer v. Hara, 522 P.2d 1187 (Wash. Ct. App. 1974).
Adams v. Howerton, 673 F.2d 1036 (9th Cir. 1982).
De Santo v. Barnsley, 476 A.2d 952 (Pa. Super. Ct. 1984).
In re Estate of Cooper, 564 N.Y.S.2d 684 (N.Y. Surr. Ct. 1990).
Lilly v. City of Minneapolis, No. MC 93-21375, 1994 WL
    315620 (Minn. Dist. Ct. June 3, 1994).
Dean v. District of Columbia, 653 A.2d 307 (D.C. 1995).
Storrs v. Holcomb, 645 N.Y.S.2d 286 (N.Y. Sup. Ct. 1996).
Rutgers Council of AAUP Chapters v. Rutgers Univ., 689
    A.2d 828 (N.J. Super. Ct. App. Div. 1997).
In re Estate of Hall, 707 N.E.2d 201 (Ill. App. Ct. 1998).
Standhardt v. Super. Ct., 77 P.3d 451 (Ariz. Ct. App. 2003).

APPENDIX B: SELECT STATE ANTI-DISCRIMINATION
STATUTES THAT DO NOT EXEMPT RELIGIOUS INSTITUTIONS

Alaska: ALASKA STAT. § 18.80.230 (2006)
California: CAL. CIV. CODE § 51 (Deering Supp. 2007)
Colorado: COLO. REV. STAT. § 24-34-601 (2006)
Delaware: DEL. CODE ANN. tit. 6, § 4502 (1999)
District of Columbia: D.C. CODE § 2-1402.31 (Supp. 2006)
Florida: FLA. STAT. § 760.07 (2006)
Hawaii: HAW. REV. STAT. § 489-2 (1993)
Illinois: 775 ILL. COMP. STAT. 5/5-103 (2004)
Kentucky: KY. REV. STAT. ANN. § 344.130 (West 2006)
Maryland: MD. CODE ANN., Human Relations Commission
    § 5 (LexisNexis 2003)
Massachusetts: MASS. GEN. LAWS ch. 272, §§ 92(A), 98 (2004)
Montana: MONT. CODE ANN. § 49-2-101(20) (2005)
Nevada: NEV. REV. STAT. § 651.050(2) (2005)
North Dakota: N.D. CENTURY CODE § 14-02.4.-14 (2004)
Ohio: OHIO REV. CODE ANN. § 4112.02(G) (West Supp. 2006)
Oklahoma: OKLA. STAT. tit. 25, § 1401 (2001)
Oregon: OR. REV. STAT. § 659A.403 (2005)
Pennsylvania: 43 PA. CONS. STAT. ANN. § 954(l) (West Supp. 2006)
Rhode Island: R.I. GEN. LAWS § 11-24-3 (2002)
South Carolina: S.C. CODE ANN. § 45-9-10 (Supp. 2006)
South Dakota: S.D. CODIFIED LAWS § 20-13-1(12) (1995)
Tennessee: TENN. CODE ANN. § 4-21-102(15) (2005)
Vermont: VT. STAT. ANN. tit. 9, § 4501(8) (1993)
West Virginia: W. VA. CODE ANN. § 5-11-3(j) (2006)
Wyoming: WYO. STAT. ANN. § 6-9-101 (2005)

Notes

† This Chapter is a lightly updated version of one originally published in the Harvard Journal of Law & Public Policy (Vol. 30, No.3 at p.939) (2007) and is used with permission from the publisher.

* The author wass legal counsel for the Becket Fund for Religious Liberty, a public-interest law firm and NGO dedicated to protecting the free expression of all religious traditions. The Becket Fund has represented Agnostics, Buddhists, Christians, Hindus, Jews, Muslims, Native Americans, Sikhs, Unitarians, Zoroastrians, and others. Some of the Becket Fund's clients support both theological and legal recognition of same-sex marriage, while others oppose such recognition. This chapter does not represent the views of any organization with which the author was or is affiliated.

1. Reference re Same-Sex Marriage, [2004] S.C.R. 698, 700 (holding proposed national same-sex marriage legislation consistent with *Canadian Charter of Rights and Freedoms*).

2. 798 N.E.2d 941, 967-70 (Mass. 2003) (ordering the Massachusetts state legislature to amend its marriage statutes to provide for full same-sex marriage).

3. *See id.* at 961 ("[W]e conclude that the marriage ban does not meet the rational basis test for either due process or equal protection.").

4. *See infra* Part III.

5. *Goodridge*, 798 N.E.2d. at 965 n.29.

6. *See, e.g.,* Memorandum from Barry R. Bedrick, Assoc. Gen. Counsel, Gen. Accounting Office, to Hon. Henry J. Hyde, Chairman, H. Comm. on the Judiciary (Jan. 31, 1997), *available at* http://www.lmaw.org/freedom/docs/GAORept-1,049FederalLaws.pdf (citing 1,049 federal laws that are contingent on marital status).

7. *See Goodridge*, 798 N.E.2d at 973 (Greaney, J., concurring).

8. *See, e.g.,* Miller-Jenkins v. Miller-Jenkins, 637 S.E.2d 330, 337-38 (Va. Ct. App. 2006) (full faith and credit must be given to the custody and visitation orders of the Vermont court), *recognizing* Miller-Jenkins v. Miller-Jenkins, 912 A.2d 951, 956 (Vt. 2006) (ruling that a former partner in a Vermont civil union entitled to "parent-child" contact and visitation rights over child in Virginia notwithstanding lack of biological parentage).

9. *See Leviticus* 18:6-18 (setting forth requirements for valid marriages).

10. *See* Marriage Act, 32 Hen. 8 c. 38 (Eng.) ("No Reservation or Prohibition, God's law except, shall trouble or impeach any Marriage without the Levitical Degrees.") (recognizing as lawful all marriages not prohibited by consanguinity rules specified by the Book of Leviticus); *see also* Clandestine Marriages Act, 1753, 26 Geo. 2. c. 33 (Eng.) (abolishing English common law marriage and requiring civil marriages "be solemnized in . . . Parish Churches or Chapels . . . and in no other Place whatsoever"). Even Henry VIII recognized that he could not turn to civil law for a divorce once the Catholic Church found that his marriage to Catherine of Aragon was valid and thereby indissoluble. He instead achieved his goal by changing the state religion.

11. Daniel DeVise, *More Couples Choose to Wed Their Way*, WASH. POST, July 2, 2006, at C1 (noting that "clergy still perform most weddings," rather than purely secular civil authorities, although the gap has narrowed since the 1970s). For example, in 2005, 84.7% of marriages in the District of Columbia and 56.4% of marriages in Maryland were solemnized in religious rather than civil ceremonies. *Id.*

12. It is no answer to say that *personal* freedom of belief is preserved if one cannot reflect those beliefs through his religious institution's policies. For millions of Americans, faith is far more than an internal mental exercise—it is an overarching guide for proper living in private, group, and public life.

13. To be sure, there are many constitutional and statutory defenses for religious liberty, and these defenses are based on substantial legal precedents, but an in-depth analysis of the this body of law is beyond the scope of this Article.

14. Employment Div. v. Smith, 494 U.S. 872 (1990) (finding government-imposed "substantial burdens" on religious expression need not be justified by compelling interests if arising from "neutral" and "generally applicable" laws). *See also* Locke v. Davey, 540 U.S. 712 (2004) (holding that the state's targeted exclusion of devotional theology majors from an otherwise inclusive scholarship program does not violate the Constitution).

15. *See infra* Part II.B.

16. Lawrence v. Texas, 539 U.S. 558 (2003).

17. Defense of Marriage Act of 1996, Pub. L. No. 104-199, § 3a, 110 Stat. 2419, (codified at 1 U.S.C. § 7 (2000) and 28 U.S.C. § 1738C (2000)). DOMA defines marriage for federal purposes as being between only one man and one woman; it seeks to prevent the automatic spread of same-sex marriage to unwilling states by way of "married" same-sex couples moving to another state and then seeking legal recognition of their union under the Constitution's Full Faith and Credit Clause. *See* 28 U.S.C. § 1738C (2000).

18. *See infra* Appendix A.

19. *See, e.g.,* Anonymous v. Anonymous, 325 N.Y.S.2d 499, 500-01 (N.Y. Sup. Ct. 1971) (finding a marriage between two males null, notwithstanding that one male partner believed the other was a female at time of ceremony and that "she" subsequently had a sex-change operation); *In re* Estate of Gardiner, 42 P.3d 120, 136-37 (Kan. 2002) (holding that a marriage between a post-operative male-to-female transsexual and a man is void as against public policy). *But see* M.T. v. J.T., 355 A.2d 204, 211 (N.J. Super. Ct. App. Div. 1976) (holding as valid a marriage between a male and a transsexual who had surgically changed his external sexual anatomy from male to female).

20. *See* Baehr v. Lewin, 852 P.2d 44, 67 (Haw. 1993) (concluding that a marriage statute implicated Hawaii Constitution's Equal Protection Clause), *remanded sub nom.* Baehr v. Miike, No. 91-1394, 1996 WL 694235, at *18 (Haw. Cir. Ct. 1996) ("The sex-based classification in [Hawaii's marriage statute], on its face and as applied, is unconstitutional and in violation of the Equal Protection Clause of article I, section 5 of the Hawaii Constitution."), *aff'd,* 950 P.2d 1234 (Haw. 1997), *superseded by constitutional amendment,* HAW. CONST. art. I, § 23 (amended 1998).

21. *See infra* Part II.B.

22. *See* Brause v. Bureau of Vital Statistics, No. 3AN-95-6562 CI, 1998 WL 88743, at *4 (Alaska Super. Ct. Feb. 27, 1998) (concluding opposite-sex marriage statute violated right to privacy provision in Alaska Constitution), *superseded by constitutional amendment,* ALASKA CONST. art. I, § 25 (amended 1999).

23. *See* Baker v. State, 744 A.2d 864, 867 (Vt. 1999) (concluding opposite-sex marriage statute violated the Vermont Constitution's Common Benefits Clause).

24. *See, e.g.,* THE JUDGE ADVOCATE GENS. SCH., U.S. ARMY, 263, LEGAL ASSISTANCE FAMILY LAW GUIDE ch.1 at 3-4 (1998) ("[T]he [military] generally follow[s] the [Department of Defense] practice of recognizing a marriage that is valid under the laws of the jurisdiction where it was contracted. Ceremonial marriages are presumed valid . . . . [T]he military will defer to state law on whether a valid marriage exists . . . .").

25. U.S. CONST. art. IV, § 1 ("Full Faith and Credit shall be given in each State to the public Acts, Records, and judicial Proceedings of every other State.").

26. Conceptual problems with this state of affairs are legion. Consider the case where a same-sex spouse dies in a car accident after moving to a traditional marriage state; can the surviving same-sex partner claim the body and inheritance rights? If the accident was due to negligence, can the surviving partner sue for loss of consortium? Conversely, consider the case of a same-sex partner who moves to a traditional marriage state, not to claim marriage benefits, but to *avoid* marital obligations after a separation. Will that former spouse be required to pay alimony? Will that former spouse be required to pay child support if she is not the biological mother of a child of a same-sex marriage?

27. *See* 28 U.S.C. § 1738C (2000); 1 U.S.C. § 7 (2000).

28. *See* HAW. CONST. art. I, § 23 (amended 1998) ("The legislature shall have the power to reserve marriage to opposite-sex couples."); ALASKA CONST. art. I, § 25 (amended 1999) ("To be valid or recognized in this State, a marriage may exist only between one man and one woman.").

29. *See Baker*, 744 A.2d at 224-25 ("We do not purport to infringe upon the prerogatives of the Legislature to craft an appropriate means of addressing this constitutional mandate.").

30. An Act Relating to Civil Unions, Pub. Act No. 91, § 3 (2000), Vt. Acts and Resolves 72 (codified as amended at VT. STAT. ANN. tit. 15, §§ 1201-1207 (2001)).

31. Litigation stemming from Vermont's early experiences with civil unions (and civil dissolutions) should be illustrative of the litigation to come. *See, e.g.*, Miller-Jenkins v. Miller-Jenkins, 912 A.2d 951 (Vt. 2006) (described *supra* note 8); *see also* Rosengarten v. Downes, 802 A.2d 170, 184 (Conn. App. Ct. 2002) (finding that because Connecticut did not recognize civil unions from Vermont, it had no authority to dissolve one); Langan v. St. Vincent's Hosp. of N.Y., 765 N.Y.S.2d 411, 413, 422 (Sup. Ct. 2003) (allowing surviving member of a same-sex couple to sue for wrongful death because they had "lived together as spouses . . . and were joined legally as lawful spouses" through a civil union in Vermont).

32. *See Goodridge*, 798 N.E.2d at 968 ("The marriage ban works a deep and scarring hardship on a very real segment of the community for no rational reason."); *id.* at 958 ("[H]istory must yield to a more fully developed understanding of the invidious quality of the discrimination.").

33. *See In re Marriage Cases*, JCCP No. 4365, 2005 WL 583129 (Cal. Super. Ct. 2005) (striking down California's marriage definition as violating Equal Protection), *aff'd in part, rev'd in part*, 49 Cal. Rptr. 3d 675 (Cal. Ct. App. 2006), *cert. granted*, 149 P.3d 737 (Cal. 2006).

34. *See* Kerrigan v. State, 49 Conn. Supp. 644 (Conn. Super. Ct. 2006) (upholding Connecticut's marriage laws), *appeal pending*, No. S.C. 17716.

35. *See* Wilson v. Ake, 354 F. Supp. 2d 1298, 1309 (M.D. Fla. 2005) (upholding Florida's marriage laws and the federal DOMA).

36. *See* Morrison v. Sadler, 821 N.E.2d 15, 35 (Ind. App. 2005) ("[T]he Indiana Constitution does not require the governmental recognition of same-sex marriage.").

37. *See* Varnum v. Brien, No. CV5965 (Iowa Dist. Ct. Aug. 30, 2007) (striking down Iowa's marriage laws), *appeal to Supreme Court pending*, No. 07-1499.

38. *See* Forum for Equality PAC v. McKeithen, 893 So.2d 715, 716 (La. 2005) (upholding state constitution's "Defense of Marriage" amendment).

39. *See* Conaway v. Deane, 401 Md. 219 (Md. 2007) (reversing lower court and upholding Maryland's marriage statute).

40. *See* Nat'l Pride at Work, Inc. v. Governor of Mich., 274 Mich. App. 147 (Mich. App. 2007) (holding state marriage amendment precluded public employers from extending same-sex domestic partnership benefits), *on appeal*, 478 Mich. 862, No. 133554 (Mich. May 23, 2007).

41. *See* Citizens for Equal Prot., Inc. v. Bruning, 368 F. Supp. 2d 980, 995, 1002 (D. Neb. 2005) (holding that Nebraska's marriage amendment "imposes significant burdens on both the expressive and intimate associational rights of plaintiffs' members . . . [and] has no rational relationship to any legitimate state interest"), *rev'd*, 455 F.3d 859 (8th Cir. 2006).

42. Lewis v. Harris, 908 A.2d 196 (N.J. 2006) (finding that New Jersey's marriage laws violate the equal protection guarantee of the New Jersey Constitution and ordering same-sex marriage or its equivalent within 180 days). The New Jersey legislature subsequently adopted Vermont-style "civil unions," stopping short of calling the arrangement marriage. N.J. STAT. ANN. § 37:1-31 (West 2007). The *Lewis* court, however, had already signaled that this option may yet be found unconstitutional in a subsequent suit. *See Lewis*, 908 A.2d at 221.

43. *See* Hernandez v. Robles, 794 N.Y.S.2d 579, 604 (Sup. Ct. 2005) (finding "no legitimate State purpose that is rationally served by a bar to same-sex marriage"), *rev'd*, 805 N.Y.S.2d 354 (App. Div. 2005), *aff'd*, Hernandez v. Robles, 7 N.Y.3d 338 (N.Y. 2006).

44. *See* Bishop v. Oklahoma, 447 F. Supp. 2d 1239, 1258-59 (N.D. Okla. 2006) (ruling that plaintiffs lack standing to challenge certain provisions of DOMA and Oklahoma marriage amendment, though equal protection and substantive due process challenges were permitted to go forward to summary judgment stage).

45. *See* Li v. State, No. 0403-03057, 2004 WL 1258167, at *10 (Or. Cir. Ct. Apr. 20, 2004) (holding that Oregon's opposite-sex marriage statutes violate the Rights and Privileges Clause of the Oregon Constitution and that "all [same-sex] marriages that have been performed must be recorded" (emphasis omitted)), *rev'd*, 110 P.3d 91 (Or. 2005).

46. *See* Chambers v. Ormiston, 935 A.2d 956 (R.I. 2007) (rejecting divorce petition of same-sex couple who legally married in Massachusetts.)

47. *See* Andersen v. King County, 138 P.3d 963 (Wash. 2006) (upholding Washington marriage laws and reversing lower courts).

48. *See In re* Kandu, 315 B.R. 123, 148 (Bankr. W.D. Wash. 2004) (dismissing same-sex couple's petition in bankruptcy and holding that "DOMA does not violate the principles of comity, or the Fourth, Fifth, or Tenth Amendments to the U.S. Constitution").

49. *See* Anglen v. McKinley, No. JAT-05-11, (Jud. App. Trib. Cherokee Nation 2005), *available at* http://www.lmaw.org/freedom/docs/US%20-%20CherkeeDismissal.pdf (finding that private citizens had no standing to void a same-sex marriage license issued by clerk but not registered by the tribal court).

50. *See* U.S. Census Bureau, Population Division, "Table 1: Annual Estimates of the Population for the United States, Regions, and States and for Puerto Rico: April 1, 2000 to July 1, 2006 (NST-EST2006-01)," http://www.census.gov/popest/states/NST-ann-est.html. The population estimates show California's population as approximately 12.18% of the national population; adding Massachusetts with 2.15% of the national population yields a total of 14.33%.

51. Connecticut was the first state to create the functional equivalent of marriage through civil unions without judicial intervention, *see* CONN. GEN. STAT. §§ 46b-38aa-gg

(2005), and remains the only state to do so. Even so, Connecticut still faces a same-sex marriage challenge. *See supra* note 34.

52. *See* U.S. Census Bureau, *supra* note 50.

53. *See supra* notes 34, 37.

54. The *Goodridge* court relied most heavily on *Lawrence v. Texas*, 539 U.S. 558 (2003) (striking down all laws criminalizing homosexual sodomy for lack of rational justification). *See also* Romer v. Evans, 517 U.S. 620 (1996) (striking down state constitutional amendment prohibiting the definition of a specially-protected class based on sexual orientation as a violation of equal protection).

55. The Netherlands, Belgium, Spain, Canada, and South Africa have legalized same-sex marriage, while Croatia, Denmark, England, Finland, France, Germany, Hungary, Iceland, New Zealand, Norway, Portugal, Scotland, Sweden, and Wales provide the functional equivalent of marriage to same-sex couples. *See* Int'l Gay & Lesbian Human Rights Commission, Where You Can Marry: Global Summary of Registered Partnership, Domestic Partnership, and Marriage Laws (Nov. 2003), http://www.iglhrc.org/site/iglhrc/content.php?type=1&id=91. *But see French High Court Rejects Gay Marriage*, GUARDIAN UNLIMITED (London), Mar. 14, 2007, *available at* http://www.guardian.co.uk/worldlatest/story/0,,-6478741,00.html.

56. Same-sex marriage incrementalists have used a variety of approaches to erode resistance to same-sex marriage. Most notably, they have petitioned for legal recognition of their unions as legal "families" fully equivalent to heterosexual ones. *See, e.g., In re* the Parentage of L.B., 122 P.3d 161, 177 (Wash. 2005) ("[H]enceforth in Washington, a de facto [same-sex] parent stands in legal parity with an otherwise legal parent, whether biological, adoptive or otherwise.").

57. Legislatively, incrementalists have lobbied municipal and state government to provide an array of partner benefits approaching marriage through "domestic partner" laws which grant, for example, government employee health insurance benefits and inheritance rights. The most notable examples are Connecticut, which grants full civil union status, and California, which granted domestic partners all the benefits of marriage excepting joint tax filing and state solemnizing of partnerships. *See* CAL. FAMILY CODE § 297.5a (Deering 2006).

58. *See* Lockyer v. City and County of San Francisco, 95 P.3d 459 (Cal. 2004) (preventing San Francisco's mayor from issuing same-sex marriage licenses and voiding 4,000 already issued); Hebel v. West, 803 N.Y.S.2d 242 (App. Div. 2005) (enjoining mayor of New Paltz, New York from issuing any additional marriage licenses to homosexual partners); Li v. State, 110 P.3d 91 (Or. 2005) (holding that officials in Multnomah County, Oregon, did not have the authority to issue marriage licenses for 3,000 same-sex couples).

59. For a continuously updated catalog of same-sex marriage laws by state, see The Heritage Foundation, Marriage in the 50 States, http://www.heritage.org/Research/Family/Marriage50States.cfm (visited on Apr. 21, 2008); *see also* State Policies on Same-Sex Marriage, http://www.stateline.org/.

60. 1 U.S.C. § 7 (1996).

61. Congress fears that judges will find that the U.S. Constitution's Full Faith and Credit Clause requires states to recognize same-sex marriages contracted out of state even if such marriages cannot be contracted in state. *Cf. generally* RESTATEMENT (SECOND) OF CONFLICT OF LAWS § 283(2) (1971) ("A marriage which satisfies the requirements of the state where the marriage was contracted will everywhere be recognized as valid unless it

violates the strong public policy of another state which had the most significant relationship to the spouses and the marriage . . . .").

62. 28 U.S.C. § 1738C (1996).

63. *See, e.g.*, Hennefeld v. Twp. of Montclair, 22 N.J. Tax 166, 187 (Tax Ct. 2005)
("New Jersey cannot be mandated to accept more of another state's law [Vermont], with
regard to same-sex relationships, than New Jersey's Legislature intended. To hold otherwise would offend the spirit, intent, and substance of DOMA.").

64. *See, e.g.*, LAURENCE H. TRIBE, 1 AMERICAN CONSTITUTIONAL LAW 1247 n.49 (3d
ed. 2000) (arguing that DOMA violates the Full Faith and Credit Clause).

65. *See In re* Kandu, 315 B.R. 123 (Bankr. W.D. Wash. 2004) (upholding DOMA);
Wilson v. Ake, 354 F. Supp. 2d 1298 (M.D. Fla. 2005) (finding DOMA "constitutionally
valid"); Smelt v. County of Orange, 374 F. Supp. 2d 861, 880 (C.D. Cal. 2005)
("Upholding DOMA), *aff'd in part, rev'd in part*, 447 F.3d 673 (9th Cir. 2006).

66. Elaine Silvestrini, *Appeals Dropped On Gay Marriage*, TAMPA TRIB., Jan 26,
2005, at 1 (noting voluntary dismissals of challenges to the federal DOMA and quoting
an activist as saying, "We are all trying to avoid being in federal court . . . . Now does
that mean forever? No . . . we've got to do the work to get ready for a case to be a
win . . . .").

67. Anti-death penalty advocates successfully followed an analogous "states first"
strategy which recently culminated in a significant victory against the juvenile death penalty. *See* Roper v. Simmons, 543 U.S. 551, 564-67 (2005). In examining the new
"trend" against the juvenile death penalty, the *Roper* Court opined that "it is not so much
the number of these States that is significant, but the consistency of the direction of
change." *Id.* at 566.

68. *See supra* note 31 (discussing several such "hard cases").

69. Indeed, there may be no limit to a court's creativity on this issue if it seeks a particular result. *See, e.g.*, United States v. Costigan, 2000 WL 898455, at *4 n.10 (D. Me.
June 16, 2000) ("Through the passage of the Defense of Marriage Act ('DOMA'), Congress has defined the term spouse to refer only to persons of the opposite sex. Thus, a gay
partner is not a 'spouse or former spouse.' However, Congress' definition does not clearly foreclose the finding that a member of a same sex couple may be cohabiting '*as a
spouse.*'") (citations omitted) (emphasis added).

70. 539 U.S. 558 (2003); *see also* Romer v. Evans, 517 U.S. 620, 634 (1996) (using
the Equal Protection Clause to strike down a state constitutional amendment deemed
"born of animosity" for prospectively removing homosexuality as a protected class under
state law).

71. *Lawrence*, 539 U.S. at 578-79. Interestingly, the Court hesitated to establish a
fundamental right to homosexual conduct, but instead struck down the statute for failing
rational basis review. *See id.* at 586 (Scalia, J., dissenting) ("[N]owhere does the Court's
opinion declare that homosexual sodomy is a 'fundamental right . . . .'").

72. *Id.* at 604-05 (Scalia, J., dissenting) (citations omitted).

73. *See Goodridge*, 798 N.E.2d at 948.

74. *See, e.g.*, *Lawrence*, 539 U.S. at 574 ("At the heart of liberty is the right to define one's own concept of existence, of meaning, of the universe, and of the mystery of
human life.") (*quoting* Planned Parenthood v. Casey, 505 U.S. 833, 851 (1992)).

75. *Id.* at 577 (quoting Bowers v. Hardwick, 478 U.S. 186, 216 (1986) (Stevens, J.,
dissenting)).

76. *Id.* at 567.

77. *See, e.g.*, United States Conference of Catholic Bishops, Between Man and Woman: Questions and Answers About Marriage and Same-Sex Unions (Nov. 12, 2003), http://www.nccbuscc.org/laity/manandwoman.shtml ("Marriage, whose nature and purposes are established by God, can only be the union of a man and a woman and must remain such in law.").

78. *See id.* ("To uphold God's intent for marriage, in which sexual relations have their proper and exclusive place, is not to offend the dignity of homosexual persons. Christians must give witness to the whole moral truth and oppose as immoral both homosexual acts and unjust discrimination against homosexual persons.").

79. Proposals to ban such sexual orientation discrimination under Title VII have been rejected by Congress repeatedly. *See* Employment Non-Discrimination Act of 2001, S. 1284, 107th Cong., 1st Sess. (2002); Employment Non-Discrimination Act of 1994, S. 2238, 103d Cong., 2d Sess. (1994); Civil Rights Amendments, H.R. 5452, 94th Cong., 1st Sess. (1975).

80. *See* HUMAN RIGHTS CAMPAIGN, STATE OF THE WORKPLACE REPORT 2005-2006, at 12 (2006), *available at* http://www.hrc.org/Template.cfm?Section=Get_Informed2&CONTENTID=32936&TEMPLATE=/ContentManagement/ContentDisplay.cfm.

81. The argument, put simply, is that if Cindy and Bill both seek to marry Jane, only Cindy would face dismissal for actually marrying her on account of Cindy's sex. *Cf.* Barnes v. City of Cincinnati, 401 F.3d 729 (6th Cir. 2005) (finding that the city police department violated a homosexual transvestite officer's rights under Title VII by demoting officer on the basis of "sexual stereotyping"; the city was ordered to pay the employee $320,000 in addition to $550,000 in attorney fees and costs), *cert. denied*, 126 S. Ct. 624 (2005).

82. For citations to all 20 statutes, see Unmarried America, State StatutesProhibiting Marital Status Discrimination in Employment, http://www.unmarriedamerica.org/ms-employment-laws.htm (last visited Mar. 15, 2007).

83. *See id.*

84. *See* 42 U.S.C. § 2000e-1(a) (2000) (creating a statutory exemption to Title VII permitting religious organizations to define their religious character through their employment practices). This exemption was upheld in Lown v. Salvation Army, 393 F. Supp. 2d 223, 246 (S.D.N.Y. 2005) ("The broad language of the federal exception bars all of plaintiffs' Title VII claims. The narrower language of the state and city exceptions precludes plaintiffs' discrimination claims, but not their retaliation claims. Application of none of the exceptions runs afoul of the Constitution.").

85. *See, e.g.*, MASS. GEN. LAWS ch. 151B § 1(5) (2004) ("[N]othing [in these anti-discrimination laws] shall be construed to bar any religious or denominational institution or organization . . . from giving preference in hiring or employment to members of the same religion or from taking any action with respect to matters of employment, discipline, faith, [or] internal organization . . . which [is] calculated by such organization to promote the religious principles for which it is established or maintained."); N.Y. EXEC. LAW § 296(11) (McKinney 2005) (same).

86. For a comprehensive list of state-by-state employment anti-discrimination statutes and their applicable religious exemptions, see Religious Institutions Practice Group, Sidley Austin Brown & Wood, Religious Employer Exemptions: A State by State Guide, http://www.sidley.com/db30/cgi-bin/pubs/final_religious%20institutions%20practice%20group.pdf (last visited Mar. 15, 2007).

87. Of course, state legislatures cannot repeal federal constitutional protections for religious freedom; but, as stated earlier, a full analysis of federal constitutional law is beyond the scope of this Article.

88. For example North Carolina and Virginia have no religious exemptions to their anti-discrimination statutes at all. *See* Equal Employment Practices Act (codified at N.C. GEN. STAT. §§ 143-416.1-422.2 (2006)); Virginia Human Rights Act (codified at VA. CODE ANN. § 2.2-2639 (2006)).

89. *See, e.g.*, McClure v. Sports & Health Club, 370 N.W.2d 844 (Minn. 1985) (holding employer liable for marital status discrimination for refusing, due to sincere religious beliefs, to hire cohabiting job applicants despite statutory religious exemption).

90. No. MC 93-21375, 1994 WL 315620 (Minn. Dist. Ct. June 3, 1994), *aff'd* 527 N.W.2d 107 (Minn. Ct. App. 1995).

91. *Id.* at *5.

92. *Id.* at *9.

93. Alaska Civil Liberties Union v. State, 122 P.3d 781 (Alaska 2005) (holding that a state employer's exclusion of same-sex couples from "spousal" health insurance benefits violates Alaska's Equal Protection Clause despite that 1998 marriage amendment); *see also* Tumeo v. Univ. of Alaska, No. 4FA-94-43 Cir., 1995 WL 238359 (Alaska Super. Ct. Jan. 11, 1995) (finding "marital status discrimination" in university's denial of health insurance coverage for same-sex partners), *aff'd sub nom* Univ. of Alaska v. Tumeo, 933 P.2d 1147 (Alaska 1997).

94. Koebke v. Bernardo Heights Country Club, 115 P.3d 1212 (Cal. 2005).

95. Catholic Charities of Maine, Inc. v. City of Portland, 304 F. Supp. 2d 77 (D. Me. 2004) (forcing religious charity to extend employee spousal benefit programs not preempted by ERISA to registered same-sex couples or else lose access to all city housing and community development funds).

96. *See* Smith v. Fair Employment & Housing Comm'n, 913 P.2d 909 (Cal. 1996) (finding no substantial burden on religion in forcing landlord to rent to unmarried couples despite sincere religious objections because the landlord could avoid the burden by exiting the rental business); *See also* Swanner v. Anchorage Equal Rights Comm'n, 874 P.2d 274, 282 (Alaska 1994). *But see* State by Cooper v. French, 460 N.W.2d 2 (Minn. 1990) (holding state constitutional protection of religious conscience exempted landlord from ban against marital status discrimination in housing).

97. 96 N.Y.2d 484 (N.Y. 2001). Yeshiva did not make its religious affiliations an issue in the appeal. *Id.* at 489.

98. *Cf.* Swanner v. Anchorage Equal Rights Comm'n., 513 U.S. 979, 981 (1994) (Thomas, J., dissenting from denial of cert.) ("[T]he federal Fair Housing Act does not prohibit people from making housing decisions based on marital status.").

99. The minority includes California, Connecticut, Illinois, Maine, Maryland, Massachusetts, Minnesota, New Hampshire, New Jersey, New Mexico, New York, Rhode Island, Vermont, Washington, Wisconsin, and the District of Columbia. *See* Human Rights Campaign Foundation, Non-Discrimination Laws: State by State, http://www.hrc.org/Template.cfm?Section=Get_In-formed2&Template=/ TaggedPage/TaggedPageDisplay.cfm&TPLID=66&ContentID=20650 (last visited Mar. 20, 2007).

100. For a comprehensive list of state-by-state employment anti-discrimination statutes and their applicable religious exemptions, see SIDLEY AUSTIN BROWN & WOOD, *supra* note 86.

101. *See infra* Appendix B.

102. *See* Gay Rights Coalition of Georgetown University Law Ctr. v. Georgetown University., 536 A.2d 1 (D.C. Ct. App. 1987) (*en banc*) (holding that while the D.C. public accommodations statute did not require a Catholic university to give homosexual groups university "recognition," it nevertheless required the university to allow them equivalent access to all university facilities.).

103. *See* Butler v. Adoption Media, 486 F.Supp.2d 1022 (N.D. Cal. 2007) (religiously-motivated administrators of Arizona adoption facilitation website held subject to California's public accommodations statute because they refused, to post profiles of same-sex couples as potential adoptive parents).

104. *See* Harriet Bernstein et al., v. Ocean Grove Camp Meeting Assoc., No. PN34XB-03008 (NJ Dep't. of Law and Public Safety, filed June 19, 2007) (seeking damages and injunction against religious organization that denied complainants use of wedding pavilion for civil union ceremony); *see also* Smith and Chymyshyn v. Knights of Columbus, 2005 BCHRT 544 (British Columbia Human Rights Tribunal 2005) (fining Knights of Columbus for refusing to rent a hall for use for a same-sex couple's wedding reception).

See also World Net Daily, *Lesbians Target Innkeeper Over Same-sex Wedding* (June 30, 2005), http://worldnetdaily.com/news/article.asp?ARTICLE_ID=45073 (noting lesbian couple's suit against owners of a small Vermont inn that refused, on religious grounds, to host a same-sex civil union ceremony.).

105. *See Consider Us Family, Lesbians Tell YMCA*, DES MOINES REGISTER, June 22, 2007, at 1A (noting Des Moines human rights commission's finding of "probable cause" that YMCA violated city anti-discrimination ordinance for denying lesbian couple "family membership" benefits).

106. 734 A.2d 1196, 1210 (N.J. 1999), *rev'd on other grounds*, Boy Scouts of Am. v. Dale, 530 U.S. 640 (2000).

107. *Id.* at 1211.

108. *See* Boy Scouts of Am. v. Dale, 530 U.S. 640 (2000).

109. *See* Chicago Area Council of Boy Scouts of Am.v. City of Chicago Comm'n on Human Relations, 748 N.E.2d 759, 769 (Ill. App. Ct. 2001) (finding that narrowly tailored injunction based on public accommodations law may issue if applicants are denied "nonexpressive" positions in the Boy Scouts because of homosexuality). *But see* Welsh v. Boy Scouts of Am., 993 F.2d 1267 (7th Cir. 1993) (holding that the Boy Scouts are *not* a place of public accommodation); Curran v. Mount Diablo Council of the Boy Scouts of Am., 952 P.2d 218 (Cal. 1998) (same).

110. *Cf.* Nathanson v. MCAD, 16 Mass. L. Rptr. 761, 765 (Super. Ct. 2003) (holding that an ostensibly "private" law firm fell under public accommodations regulations notwithstanding the firm's free speech concerns); *Cf.* Villegas v. City of Gilroy, 484 F.3d 1136 (9th Cir. 2007) (Motorcycle club, similar to Hell's Angels, not considered an expressive association).

111. 536 A.2d 1 (D.C. 1987) (en banc).

112. *See id.* at 39.

113. *See id.* at 38.

114. 85 P.3d 67 (Cal. 2004) (denying a religious charity a "religious employer" exemption from employment discrimination laws).

115. *Id.* at 292 (quoting CAL. HEALTH & SAFETY CODE § 1367.25(b)).

116. *Id.* at 313.

117. *Id.* at 312.

118. *Goodridge*, 798 N.E.2d at 959-69.

119. *See* Christopher Chorba, *The Danger of Federalizing Hate Crimes*, 87 U. VA. L. REV. 319, 347-48 nn.130-32 (cataloging hate crimes statutes and penalty enhancements in 46 states).

120. *See* Human Rights Campaign, State Hate Crimes Laws, http://www.hrc.org/documents/hate_crime_laws.pdf (visited on Apr. 21, 2008).

121. Pennsylvania's hate crimes statute, 18 PA. CONS. STAT. § 2710, bans "ethnic intimidation" (*i.e.*, hate speech) on the basis of sexual orientation if the message is "motivated by hatred;" Massachusetts' hate speech law, MASS. GEN. LAWS 151B § 4(4)(A), makes it unlawful to "intimidate" another person in their right to be free from sexual orientation discrimination in employment and housing, but currently exempts religious institutions. *See* MASS. GEN. LAWS 151B §§ 1(5), 4(18).

122. *See* Startzell v. City of Philadelphia, No. 05-05287, 2007 WL 172400, at *6 (E.D. Pa. Jan. 18, 2007).

123. In Bryce v. Episcopal Church in the Diocese of Colorado., 289 F.3d 648 (10th Cir. 2002), a church discovered that its youth minister had just had a civil commitment ceremony with her homosexual partner and responded by a series of parish discussions condemning the relationship as being incompatible with Scripture. The youth minister responded by suing her church for sexual harassment.

124. *See e.g.*, Harper v. Poway Unified Sch. Dist., 445 F.3d 1166, 1179-80 (2006) (holding that a student's religious speech opposing school support of homosexuality could be banned as such "injurious remarks" "intrude[] upon . . . the rights of other students"), *appeal dismissed as moot and decision vacated by* 2007 WL 632768 (U.S. Mar. 5, 2007).

125. *Cf.* Lambda Legal, The Continuing Push to Give Tax Dollars to Religious Organizations: Why It's So Dangerous (May 3, 2004), http://www.lambdalegal.org/our-work/publications/facts-backgrounds/page.jsp?itemID=31989074 (visited on Apr. 21, 2008).

126. 461 U.S. 574 (1983).

127. *Id.* at 604 (emphasis added).

128. *Goodridge*, 798 N.E.2d at 958 (emphasis added).

129. *See id.* at 958 n.17.

130. This omission is unsurprising since this precise question was not before the *Goodridge* court.

131. *See Bob Jones Univ.*, 461 U.S. at 592; *cf.* Branch Ministries v. Rossotti, 211 F.3d 137 (D.C. Cir. 2000) (affirming the IRS's revocation of a church's tax exempt status due to intervention in a political campaign through paid newspaper advertising).

132. *See* Harriet Bernstein et al., v. Ocean Grove Camp Meeting Assoc., No. PN34XB-03008 (NJ Dep't. of Law and Public Safety, filed June 19, 2007) (seeking damages and injunction against religious organization that denied complainants use of wedding pavilion for civil union ceremony). *See also Group Loses Tax Break Over Gay Union Issue*, NEW YORK TIMES, September 18, 2007.

133. *See* Richard A. Epstein, Letter to the Editor, *Same-Sex Union Dispute: Right Now Mirrors Left*, WALL ST. J., July 28, 2004 at A13 ("[P]rivate churches losing their tax exemptions for their opposition to homosexual marriages . . . are among the very dangers from the left against which I warned.").

134. 465 U.S. 555 (1984).

135. *See* Patricia Wen, *Archdiocesan Agency Aids in Adoptions by Gays; Says it's Bound by Antibias Laws*, BOSTON GLOBE, Oct. 22, 2005 (reporting on Catholic Charities having to "choose between its mission of helping the maximum number of foster children

possible [hundreds of adoptions] and conforming to the Vatican's position on homosexuality.").

136. *See* Butler v. Adoption Media, 486 F.Supp.2d 1022 (N.D. Cal. 2007); *see also* http://www.alliancedefensefund.org/news/pressrelease.aspx?cid= 4128 (visited on Apr. 21, 2008).

137. *See Consider Us Family, Lesbians Tell YMCA*, DES MOINES REGISTER, June 22, 2007, at 1A (noting Des Moines human rights commission's finding of "probable cause" that YMCA violated city anti-discrimination ordinance for denying lesbian couple "family membership" benefits).

138. *See YMCA Rewrites Rules for Lesbian Couples*, DES MOINES REGISTER, Aug. 6, 2007 (despite YMCA's compliance with the commission's ruling in creating equivalent category for same-sex couples, City forced YMCA to change "family" definition or lose government grant); *Lesbians Reject YMCA Agreement*, DES MOINES REGISTER, Aug. 7, 2007 (noting lesbian couples rejection of settlement agreement with YMCA due to inclusion of confidentiality clause).

139. *See* Under 21 v. New York, 126 Misc. 2d 629 (N.Y. Spec. Term 1984) (noting that funds cannot be used to support or encourage discrimination on the basis of sexual orientation committed by others in the context of private providers of government services.).

140. *See* Boy Scouts of America v. Till, 136 F. Supp. 2d 1295 (S.D. Fla. 2001) (preliminarily enjoining a school board from continuing to exclude the Boy Scouts from school facilities based on their negative views of homosexual conduct).

141. *See* Winkler v. Gates, 481 F.3d 977 (7th Cir. 2007) (vacating lower court Establishment Clause decision banning military loans of land and logistics for annual Scout Jamboree due to insufficient standing).

142. *See* Barnes-Wallace v. Boy Scouts of America, 275 F. Supp. 2d 1259 (S.D. Cal. 2003) (renewal of lease of public parkland would violate the Establishment Clause in light of the Scouts' required belief in God).

143. *See* Evans v. City of Berkeley, 129 P.3d 394 (Cal. 2006) (affirming revocation of a boat berth subsidy at public marina due to Scouts' exclusion of atheists and openly gay members).

144. *See* Boy Scouts of Am., S. Fla. Council v. Till, 136 F. Supp. 2d 1295 (S.D. Fla. 2001) (preliminarily enjoining a school board from continuing to exclude the Boy Scouts from school facilities based on their anti-gay viewpoint).

145. *See* Boy Scouts of Am. v. Wyman, 335 F.3d 80 (2d Cir. 2003) (holding that the Boy Scouts may be excluded from the state's workplace charitable contributions campaign for denying membership to the openly gay).

146. *See* Joseph A. Slobodzian, *Council Votes to End City Lease with Boy Scouts*, PHILADELPHIA INQUIRER, June 1, 2007 at B1 (noting city decision to evict Boy Scouts from their city-owned headquarters of 79 years due to their policy of excluding openly gay members).

147. *See, e.g.*, Catholic Charities of Maine v. City of Portland, 304 F. Supp. 2d 77 (D. Me. 2004) (upholding ordinance forcing religious charity to either extend employee spousal benefit programs to registered same-sex couples or lose access to all city housing and community development funds).

148. "We begin by considering the nature of civil marriage itself. Simply put, the government creates civil marriage . . . a wholly secular institution." *Goodridge*, 798 N.E.2d at 954. According to the court, "there are three partners to every civil marriage: two willing spouses and an approving State." *Id.* "In short, for all the joy and solemnity

that normally attend a marriage, governing entrance to marriage, is a *licensing law.*" *Id.* at 952 (emphasis added and internal citations omitted).

149. *See, e.g.*, MASS. GEN. LAWS ch. 207 § 45 (2004) ("The record of a marriage made and kept as provided by law by the person by whom the marriage was solemnized, . . . shall be prima facie evidence of such marriage."); MASS. GEN. LAWS ch. 207 § 38 (2004) (requiring that civil marriage be solemnized only by priests, deacons, rabbis, imams, ministers of the Gospel, various other religious officiants, and justices of the peace).

150. *See, e.g.*, Gould v. Gould, 61 A. 604, 610 (Conn. 1905) (Hammersley, J., concurring) (recognizing that clergymen were authorized to join persons in marriage for civil law purposes in Connecticut as far back as 1694 and that the policy had remained unchanged).

151. *See* wedding statistics *supra* n.11.

152. Some state legislation prohibits officials conducting marriage ceremonies from discriminating in certain ways. The Texas Family Code, for example, forbids persons authorized to conduct a marriage ceremony—including religious officials—"from discriminating on the basis of race, religion, or national origin." *See* TEX. FAM. CODE ANN. § 2.205 (2006). Marriage codes such as Texas' could easily be amended to include a prohibition on discrimination based on sex or sexual orientation and made to apply to *all* persons authorized to solemnize civil marriage.

153. *See* Brady v. Dean, 790 A.2d 428, 435 (Vt. 2001).

154. *See* Pam Belluck, Massachusetts Arrives at Moment for Same-Sex Marriage, N.Y. TIMES, May 17, 2004, at A16.

155. *See* TEX. FAM. CODE § 2.205. *Cf.* CAL. FAM. CODE § 354(d) ("Applicants for a marriage license shall not be required to state, for any purpose, their race or color").

156. *See* Alan Dershowitz, *To Fix Gay Dilemma, Government Should Quit the Marriage Business*, L.A. TIMES, Dec. 3, 2003, at B15 (advocating complete separation of civil and religious aspects of marriage).

157. "This generation does not have a monopoly on either knowledge or wisdom. Before abandoning fundamental values and institutions, we must pause and take stock of our present social order." State by Cooper v. French, 460 N.W.2d 2, 11 (Minn. 1990).

CHAPTER 18
SAME-SEX MARRIAGE AND PUBLIC SCHOOL CURRICULA: REFLECTIONS ON PRESERVING THE RIGHTS OF PARENTS TO DIRECT THE EDUCATION OF THEIR CHILDREN

Charles J. Russo[1]
University of Dayton

"Therefore a man shall leave his father and his mother and be joined to his wife, and the two shall become one flesh."[2]

Since the earliest days of the Judaeo-Christian era, with Judaism leading the way as the first major religion to include monogamy as a fundamental tenet,[3] marriage has been defined as a union between one man and one woman.[4] Moreover, even though polygamy, polyandry, and open marriage have occasionally been in vogue,[5] until recently, there has been little serious discussion of the possibility of marriage between two members of the same sex, commonly referred to as same-sex marriage. Yet, spurred by social and judicial[6] activists, talk of same-sex marriage has been wide-spread in recent years, especially in academic journals, the popular press, and media.

At the outset, it is important to address two delimitations. First, in supporting what is now euphemistically referred to as "traditional" marriage, thereby distinguishing it from unions between members of the same sex, this chapter is not intended as a personal criticism of those who support the adoption of, or practice, the radical societal transformation referred to as "same-sex marriage." Rather, since he sees no reason to modify marriage as it has been lived through the ages as the basis of civil society, the author respects those whose ideas differ, but disagrees with their point of view. Further, the author believes that while all persons are entitled to respect and dignity regardless of their sexual orientations, it is something altogether different to espouse the view that relationships between two persons of the same sex should be accorded the legal status of marriage. Second, this chapter does not follow the same line of inquiry as those who have written legal histories[7] and addressed related aspects in support of[8] or who question the validity of[9] same-sex marriage. Instead, by touching on these topics only as they impact on its major theme, this chapter focuses primarily on the effect that gay-friendly curricular changes in public schools, meant to include instruction on same-sex marriage, might have on the right of parents to direct the educational upbringing of their children.

This chapter supports traditional marriage in defending the long-recognized parental right to direct the education of their children.[10] This chapter upholds the rights of parents in response to educators in public schools who, spurred on by activists, over-step their authority by attempting to implement major social transformation through the introduction of teaching that borders on proselytizing in support of the acceptability of same-sex marriage, as part of a larger gay-friendly agenda, to unsuspecting, impressionable children. Additionally, in defending the right of parents to object to curricular initiatives in public schools with which they disagree, the author expresses his serious concern about the approach that proponents of single-sex marriage have adopted in attempting to enact a radical metamorphosis of the institution of marriage that, however imperfect, has stood the test of time. It should be troubling to all that proponents of same-sex marriage have relied on "the least democratic of the branches,"[11] the courts, albeit with mixed results,[12] to accomplish goals that they could not achieve through the political process.

As reflected in litigation in Massachusetts,[13] the only jurisdiction to recognize same-sex marriage, albeit via judicial fiat, the inability of its advocates to rely on political, rather than judicial,[14] activism is clear in the fact that through mid-2006, at least forty-five states restrict marriage to a relationship between one man and one woman.[15] Of the states that have rejected calls to treat same-sex living arrangements as marriages, nineteen adopted constitutional amendments while the remaining twenty-six enacted statutes restricting marriage to one man and one woman.[16]

In a related concern, one can only wonder why many supporters of same-sex marriage simultaneously demonstrate overt hostility to all things Christian. The antipathy of proponents of same-sex marriage may aptly be referred to as Christophobia,[17] at least to the extent that many of its supporters seek to remove references to Christianity and its underlying values, including marriage, from the public marketplace of ideas. Such behavior by proponents of same-sex marriage clearly reveals an attitude that "bristles with hostility to all things religious in public life."[18] These activists rely on essentially anti-Christian, if not bigoted,[19] sentiment in wishing to impose their world-view on society writ large due in substantial part to their bias against, and perhaps even hatred toward, the underlying values that Christianity represents in many areas, not the least of which is marriage.

The remainder of this chapter primarily reflects on the right of parents to direct the education of their children. The first part briefly highlights the ways in which marriage uniquely benefits society with an eye toward school-aged children since education serves as the focus of the second section of the chapter. Undoubtedly, supporters of same-sex marriage are likely to respond that concerns over reconceptualizing marriage are specious in the face of the apparent breakdown in traditional marriage as witnessed by increased divorce rates,[20] the growing rate number of shared living arrangements,[21] and the dramatic rise in single-parent families, most of which are headed by women.[22] The chapter parries objections of proponents of same-sex marriage by pointing out that as regrettable as developments with regard to marriage and alternative living arrangements are, they are still, by-and-large, taking place within the context of heterosexual, rather than homosexual, liaisons.

The second part of the chapter examines ways in which the benefits that marriage offers to society can be harmed by a shift to permitting unchallenged instruction on same-sex marriages in public school. More specifically, the chapter suggests that permitting educators to introduce a regimen of unfettered instruction supporting a gay rights agenda and same-sex marriage can have a profoundly negative impact on the right of parents to direct the educational upbringing of their children by exposing them to ideas that are best discussed at home.

The chapter rounds out with a brief reflection on where this debate on same-sex marriage may be headed in the near future. While respectfully disagreeing with proponents of same-sex marriage, the chapter concludes that insofar as words have meaning, calling a relationship between two members of the same sex does not make it a one because a marriage is, and should retain its original meaning as, a union between one man and one woman. At the same time, it is important to note that although this chapter describes marriage as a word, the author fully recognizes that marriage is a concept or a vocation, a state in life between one man and one woman that is meant to be permanent.

I.   Beneficial Effects of Marriage

Over the millennia, marriage has helped to preserve the moral and social order through ensuring a stable environment within which children can grow, defining and promoting legitimacy (if this has not already been rendered, in effect, an archaic concept in light of the growth of out-of-wedlock births in the United States), and providing a form of population control by placing limits on the ability of some to procreate without consequence. In the face of research that reviews these points in detail,[23] this section briefly reflects on one major point that most directly impact the right of parents to direct the education of their children.

From the perspective of those who are interested in education, point 4 in the Princeton Principles, that "[m]arriage protects and promotes the well-being of children,"[24] is an excellent departure point from which to consider the impact that curricular changes to include gay-friendly instruction on same-sex marriage might have on public school curricula, let alone families. As discussed in greater deal in the following section, the Supreme Court, in *Pierce v. Society of Sisters*,[25] recognized the right of parents to direct the education of their children. Yet, tension has arisen as courts have increasingly stood *Pierce's* notion that the "the child is not the mere creature of the state"[26] on its head in granting school officials almost unfettered curricular discretion when conflicts arise with parents over teaching about same-sex marriage and gay-friendly initiatives.

There can be no doubt that "education is perhaps the most important function of state and local governments,"[27] and that states have plenary power, that they delegate to local school boards, to set curricular content and a host of other educational matters. Even so, despite the authority of states to regulate public education, significant disagreements emerge when school officials overstep their boundaries by intruding on parental prerogatives over values formation by implementing curricula that instruct children about same-sex marriage from a gay-friendly perspective. Insofar as parents have the duty to ensure that their children are educated, a task that is of even greater significance than ever before in an increasingly technological, information-aged based society, the next part of the chapter addresses issues related to control over the vehicle of instruction, public school curricula.

II.   Potential Harm to Society In Light of Same-Sex Marriage: Same-Sex Marriage and School Curricula

In discussing the potential deleterious ramifications of same-sex marriage on families and the schooling of young children, this chapter concomitantly examines legal developments dealing with sexuality education and gay-friendly initiatives in pre-K-12 schools because of the symbiotic relationship that these political agendas share. This review is limited to an analysis of the impact of curricular developments in pre-K-12 schooling, rather than higher education, since state laws require children to attend schools, typically between the ages of six and seventeen or eighteen.[28] As such, this chapter, in part, discusses whether permitting teachers, often spurred on by their unions,[29] and educational administrators to serve as the vanguard of "[s]ocial experiments on other people's children"[30] is ultimately a form of *ultra vires* when they exceed the boundaries of their authority.

Educators act as purported harbingers of radical social change when teaching, if not proselytizing, impressionable young minds in pre-K-12 settings who, due to compulsory attendance laws, constitute essentially a captive audience barraged with the unchallenged proposition that same-sex marriage is an acceptable alternative lifestyle. The chapter does not examine developments in higher education because, as the courts have recognized,[31] students in colleges and universities are free not to attend either classes or graduation ceremonies at which prayer might occur and with which they may have significant differences of opinion. Insofar as students in higher education should have the intellectual and emotional maturity to make their own judgments about controversial topics, even in the midst of fears of political correctness that many individual faculty members and administrators have imposed on campuses in higher education,[32] they should not be as subject to professorial and peer pressure as young children.

At the heart of debate over who should control the content of curricula in public schools is the tension of how a democratic society can safeguard the rights of both the majority and minority. In other words, consistent with Justice O'Connor's salient observation that "we do not count heads before enforcing [constitutional rights],"[33] it is imperative to balance the interests of the minority who advocate same-sex marriage as a right and the rights of parents (and others) who do not wish their children, especially during their tender years, to be subject involuntarily to concepts about family and human sexuality at the hands of public school officials.

Tension flares as a small number of activists attempt to change the nature and meaning of marriage while supporters in the educational establishment subject a captive audience of children to be taught forcibly about same-sex marriage in public schools. Unfortunately, in addressing the rights of increasingly vocal proponents of same-sex marriage, the judiciary has not steered a clear path in avoiding what can best be described as the tyranny of the minority which, led by various public interest groups, seek to impose a kind of "heckler's veto."[34] The judicial lack of clarity can permit small groups of activists to, in effect, drown out the wishes of the majority, even as one keeps in mind that constitutional rights and personal freedom neither are, nor should be, subject to a majority vote.

Aware of unresolved tension over the control of public school curricula, should proponents of same-sex marriage succeed in implementing their radical agenda, then pre-K-12 curricula will undoubtedly undergo significant modifications. Curricular changes in this arena have already led angry parents to initiate litigation[35] and are likely to leave children confused, especially as some advocates of same sex-marriage wish to begin presenting gay-friendly programming for children as young as in pre-schools, at a time when human sexuality is most certainly well beyond their developmental needs or grasp.[36]

Young children who are exposed to state-mandated, gay-friendly teaching that essentially legitimizes same-sex marriage by presenting it as one of an array of familial alternatives will probably suffer from confusion to the extent that they may well be exposed to ideas in school that they cannot fully comprehend. Further, ideas that children encounter in schools about same-sex marriage may well conflict with the values that they are taught at home, especially at a time when they are beginning to explore their own nascent sexuality. Of course, the author is not advocating that all revolutionary or unpopular ideas be presented or ignored in classes. Rather, as discussed in greater detail below, while believing that the better course of events is for educators to think about deferring to reasonable parental requests on sensitive issues, school officials should develop responsible programs that take parental input into consideration.

Purportedly for fear of permitting adults to exert undue influence in shaping the ideas of children, the judiciary has refused to permit school officials to invite a rabbi to pray at a graduation ceremony[37] or a teacher to read privately, and silently, a Bible in class while students were doing their own work.[38] If courts are truly concerned about the potential for unduly influencing children, then one can only wonder why school officials should be regarded as any less capable of shaping the attitudes of students when providing unchallenged gay-friendly instruction on same-sex marriage to impressionable young minds which may not even grasp the import, or impact, of what they are being taught.

When reviewing the role of educators who expose children to ideas that might be considered controversial, they and the courts have adopted an uneven approach. For example, in *Lee v. Weisman*,[39] the Supreme Court prohibited prayer at public school graduation ceremonies insofar as the state, through school officials, played a pervasive role in the process not only by selecting who would offer the prayer but also by directing the content of prayer. The Court also feared that governmental activity could have resulted in psychological coercion of students where individuals constituted members of a captive audience that may have been forced, against their own wishes, to participate in ceremonies that they were not genuinely free to be excused from attending.

If the courts are genuinely concerned about the coercive authority of school officials, it is unclear why they would permit educators to create learning environments that leave children susceptible to the same kinds of peer pressure from students who adopt contrary perspectives and who are capable of ostracizing those with whom they disagree with regard to same-sex marriage. While admittedly dealing with religion rather than marriage and human sexuality, in *Engel v. Vitale*, its first ever prayer case, the Supreme Court reasoned that even absent overt pressure, placing the power, privilege, and support of the government *qua* school public systems behind particular points of view that might have been presented in prayer ran the risk of asserting indirect coercion on those who refused to conform to the official position.[40] Given the Court's espoused concern that the state not be viewed as promoting a particular point of view, there should be no less reason to believe that fears about subtly influencing or indoctrinating, if not coercing, young children to adopt a particular perspective on same sex-marriage is any less warranted in the present day.

Any discussion over who should control the curriculum must begin[41] with *Pierce v. Society of the Sisters of the Holy Names of Jesus and Mary (Pierce)*,[42] In *Pierce,* the Supreme Court struck down a compulsory attendance law from Oregon which would have required parents to compel their children, other than those needing what today would be described as special education, between the ages of eight and sixteen, to attend public schools. *Pierce* was filed by officials in two non-public schools, one religiously-affiliated and the other a non-sectarian military academy, who sought to avoid having their institutions forced out of business by asserting their property rights under the Fourteenth Amendment.

Ruling in favor of the non-public schools in the primary issue in *Pierce*, the Court held that the statute violated their due process rights by, in effect, trying to force them out of business. In addition, and more importantly for the focus of this chapter, the Court found that since parents had the right to decide where their children would attend school, state officials could not "unreasonably interfere with the liberty of parents and guardians to direct the upbringing and education of children under their control."[43] In determining that parents could satisfy the compulsory attendance law by enrolling their children in the non-public schools of their choice, the court unequivocally declared that "the child is not the mere creature of the state; those who nurture him and direct his destiny have the right, coupled with the high duty, to recognize and prepare him for additional obligations."[44]

Unfortunately, since neither *Pierce* nor later case law on parental rights created a bright-line test that the judiciary or school officials could use when evaluating when, or how seriously, parental concerns should be weighed in curricular challenges, both have adopted what can be best described as an almost ad hoc "I know it when I see it"[45] approach. At the same time, it may be that setting a mechanistic standard in this challenging area could create more problems than it would solve for schools officials and the courts. Put another way, complications could arise as some parents might object to inappropriate material such as teaching young children about same-sex marriage while others might criticize instruction that does not comply with their politically correct positions on topics including environmental policy, politics, and history, especially as teachers depict war. The difficulty with creating such a standard notwithstanding, school officials should respectfully consider reasonable parental concerns, especially when they involve potential conflicts involving matters that have traditionally been left to the realm of child-rearing, while the courts should seek to create meaningful guidelines for educators.

Piece takes on heightened significance in light of nascent conflicts as parents who do not support same-sex marriage and overly explicit teaching about human sexuality raise legitimate objections over having their children exposed to curricular materials that are not consistent with the values that are held in their homes. Of course, some educators and proponents of same-sex marriage might argue that in the state's role as *parens patria*, literally "father of the country," under which legislatures have the plenary authority to enact reasonable laws for the welfare of their residents, school officials have the sole duty to direct the curriculum, refusing to consider, let alone defer, to parental wishes. However, almost fifty years after *Pierce*, in *Wisconsin v. Yoder*,[46] the Supreme Court rejected *parens patriae* in deciding that Amish parents were free not to send their children to public schools beyond eighth grade because they would learn all that they needed in their home communities. In refusing to apply *parens patriae* to compulsory attendance, the Court did uphold the general principle that the state has the authority to regulate education.

One of the concerns about having same-sex marriage taught in public schools is that including material on it in curricula may tear at the fabric of society by causing inter-generational rifts as children are indoctrinated on points-of-view that are not consonant with the values of their parents. One of the most dramatic examples of inter-generational change, if not potential conflict, is reflected in the types of reading materials that children are exposed to in schools.

Initially published in 1990, *Heather Has Two Mommies*,[47] with its discussion of how the birth mother was artificially inseminated by an anonymous donor in its original edition, has engendered both controversy and similar works.[48] Two other gay-friendly books, *Daddy's Roommate*,[49] which depicts gay relationships, and *King & King*,[50] which tells the story about the marriage of two princes, also fostered significant controversy in their portrayals of gay, lesbian, bi-sexual, and transgendered (LGBT) lifestyles. In fact, after school officials in Massachusetts continued to use *King & King* in classes, parents of second grade[51] and kindergarten-aged[52] children challenged their doing so. The First Circuit ultimately affirmed a grant of the school system's motion to dismiss the parents claim on the basis that the parents failed to demonstrate that the use of the books burdened their parental rights to due process in the upbringing of their children or their rights to the free exercise of religion; the court also affirmed that educators did not violated the free exercise rights of the children.[53]

As well-intentioned authors of books such as *Heather Has Two Mommies,*
Daddy's Roommate, and *King & King* and proponents of same-sex marriage and
LGBT lifestyles may be, since these activists are presenting issues on diversity
of living arrangements, one can only imagine the confusion that runs through the
minds of young children. Children in pre-schools and early primary grades may
be most susceptible to being confused because they are being exposed to materials that discuss as intimate, and possibly medically complicated, a topic as
artificial insemination, let alone sexual intercourse, often times without parental
consent or input. In fact, since it is virtually inconceivable that young students
can comprehend the process of artificial insemination, one must wonder why
educators, in their quest to impose their values on a captive audience, cannot
recognize that parents might have legitimate concerns about the types of issues
that their children are being taught in public schools.

Heather Has Two Mommies, Daddy's Roommate, and *King & King* could
not be more different than the idyllic, if unrealistic and uncomplicated, depiction
of marriage and family life that many baby-boomers experienced in their formative years in the *Dick and Jane*[54] series readers. As conflict arises over parame-
ters that should be placed on sexuality education in public schools, the courts
have aided educators in giving a radical new meaning to the common law concept *in loco parentis,* "literally, in place of the parent," a legal construct that is
based on presumed voluntary parental consent.[55] These conflicts have been
heightened by judicial deference to school officials in the face of overly explicit,
if not inappropriate, sexuality instruction[56] and surveys[57] in public schools, even
when educators failed to comply with applicable school policy requiring written
parental consent before students could be exposed to explicit sexual material.[58]

In debates over the place, if any, of religion in public school curricula,
courts have prohibited public readings from the Bible,[59] reached mixed results in
disputes over elective courses on the Bible,[60] allowed students to organize religious clubs,[61] and prohibited prayer at graduation[62] and extra-curricular activities.[63] In these cases, critics typically claim that religion has no place in a public
school curricula or activities because it involves both alleged violations of the
Establishment Clause and might include teaching of (Christian) values whether
directly or indirectly. Yet, nothing in the American legal tradition prohibits the
teaching about religion,[64] or for that matter, by extension, religious values as
long as the instruction is an objective presentation "about" rather than subjective
inculcation "of" particular religious points of view.[65]

Considering the content of books such as *Heather Has Two Mommies,*
Daddy's Roommate, and *King & King,* it is disingenuous at best to claim that
they are value-free. If anything, the subject-matter of such gay-friendly books is
every bit as value-laden as teaching that "Jesus Loves Me, The Bible Tells Me
So."[66] Clearly, the debate is not so much about challenges to the teaching of
values as it is over whose values should prevail, those of parents or activist
groups. Moreover, an argument can be made that the use of books such as
Heather Has Two Mommies, Daddy's Roommate, and *King & King* is truly insidious because they seek to exert subtle influences over unsuspecting children,
often without parental knowledge or consent, while purportedly acting under the

guise of teaching about diversity and openness, even though many proponents of same-sex marriage demonstrate anything but when dealing with individuals and religious groups such as the Catholic Church[67] with which they disagree.

Litigation over the rights of parents has addressed whether limits should be placed on public school officials in their capacity to act *in loco parentis* or whether they have used their positions to usurp parental authority, imposing their collective wills on children and their families. These disputes also give rise to concerns about the continuing viability of *in loco parentis* in light of compulsory attendance laws which require parents to send their children to school at the risk of punishment for noncompliance.[68] However, rather than engage in a discussion about the viability of *in loco parentis*, suffice it to say that this is a question in need of discussion at another time. Even so, when school officials implement highly sensitive material, they ought to take parental perspectives into consideration. In implementing curricular changes on sensitive topics such as same-sex marriage, since they need to be mindful of respecting the parental right to direct the upbringing of their children, educators may wish to consider the following four points.[69]

First, school officials should resist pressure from political action groups that are not part of school communities. Put another way, insofar as outside groups lack what can be described as analogous to the legal concept of standing to the extent that they neither have children in nor are taxpayers in local school systems, educators should focus on input from their real stakeholders, parents and community members.

Second, in recognizing the paramount stake that parents have in the education of their children, school officials should engage in some form of consultation, whether individually or through parent-teacher organizations, in order to afford them the opportunity to express their opinions. This is a particularly significant point because at a time when educators often decry the lack of parental involvement in the education of their children, when it comes to the topic of human sexuality, these same officials suddenly seem to take the inexplicable approach that parental input is at best superfluous. While certainly not suggesting that parents should have the final say over the content of school curricula, one wonders how much educators can hope to accomplish if they ignore legitimate parental concerns about the nature and content of the instruction that their children receive about same-sex marriage and other sensitive topics.

Third, even in conceding that material about artificial insemination was removed from the second edition of *Heather Has Two Mommies*, educators that are determined to proceed with instruction on same-sex marriage should develop age-appropriate materials. While some discussion of same-sex marriage is undoubtedly inevitable, and perhaps desirable, in courses on human sexuality, inappropriate discussions may cause more harm than good, especially if they lead to misperceptions about sexuality in the minds of young, impressionable students. In addition, considering that children, especially those in pre-schools and early primary grades, may not understand material about same sex-marriage and human sexuality, prudence dictates that educators present them with subject

matter that they can comprehend and in a manner that respects legitimate parental concerns.

Fourth, educators should consider permitting parents to opt-out based on religious, and perhaps other, grounds.[70] Alternatively, officials that are determined
to proceed with instruction in the face of opposition to teaching about same-sex-
marriage might offer programs that covering the material in a less controversial
format or that permits other perspectives to be voiced. Treating parents as partners may not only generate additional support for the aims of public schools but
may also translate into increased student achievement by ensuring that parents
are more actively involved in the education of their children. While readily conceding that decision-making must remain in the hands of educational leaders,
and that there is no guarantee that they will eliminate all risk of controversy with
parents, it would be a significant step in the direction of conflict avoidance if
educators responded appropriately to legitimate parental concerns.

In the midst of controversy over what can, or should, be taught in classes on
sexuality education, including subject matter on same-sex marriage, parents may
well be "talking with their feet," placing their children in educational environments that are consonant with their beliefs. This movement is reflected in significant growth of Christian schools, which, as part of the non-public school network in the United States, has outpaced enrollment gains in public schools since
1989[71] and is expected to continue to do so through 2014.[72] This growth does
not take into account the more than one million children who are home school-
ed, often due to parental concerns over the treatment of religion and issues and
associated with values formation in public schools.[73] The large increase of
Christian, mostly Evangelical, schools is replenishing, if not replacing, the
strong, albeit diminished, presence of Roman Catholic schools in the religiously-
affiliated non-public school community.[74]

As a sign of the growing tension and dissatisfaction with the direction of
public education, some Evangelical Christian leaders are encouraging parents to
remove their children from public schools over issues such as the use gay-
friendly curricular materials.[75] Considering how long and well public education
has served the United States, developments of this type, coupled with the national data in the previous paragraph, should give educational leaders, policy
makers, and politicians reason to pause in recognition of the fact that many parents are both vocally expressing their dissatisfaction with curricular modifications that support gay-friendly programming and same-sex marriage while also
taking steps to act on the courage of their convictions..

In a final point in addressing curricular control and same-sex marriage, perhaps the most highly visible example of how proponents of GLBT lifestyles are
seeking to influence the education of children,[76] admittedly through the legislative rather than judicial process, played itself out in California late in the summer of 2006. After amending an earlier version of a bill that would have required public school curricula to reflect the contributions that gays and lesbians
made to American society in the face of significant opposition and the threat of a
gubernatorial veto,[77] a later version of the bill,[78] which forbade discrimination
that might have adversely reflected on people because of their sexual orienta-

tion, passed both chambers of the California legislature.[79] Following Governor Arnold Schwarzenegger's making good on his promise to veto the bill, because it "attempt[ed] to offer vague protection when current law already provides clear protection against discrimination in our schools based on sexual orientation),"[80] it will be interesting to observe whether its sponsor acts on her plan to pursue future legislative action. However, Governor Schwarzenegger signed the California Student Civil Rights Act, a law mandating nondiscrimination against "disability, gender, nationality, race or ethnicity, religion, sexual orientation, as well as other characteristics."[81]

III.   Conclusion

While it is not yet inevitable, it appears that absent swift legislative action, coupled with voter initiatives, to blunt an expected onslaught of judicial activism, same-sex marriage may soon become a reality. It is one thing to share in the American ideal that all persons are entitled to basic respect and dignity as persons regardless of their sexual orientations. However, it is something altogether different to espouse the view that a relationship between two persons of the same sex be accorded the legal status of marriage.

When deliberating the propriety of recognizing same-sex unions as marriages, a story attributed to President Lincoln over the fact that words have meaning is instructive. Amid debate, and his own concerns over his authority to emancipate slaves under the War power, "he used to liken the case to that of the boy who, when asked how many legs his calf would have if he called its tail a leg, replied 'five,' to which the prompt response was made that calling the tail a leg would not make it a leg."[81] Analogously, while advocates may wish to describe gay unions as marriage, since they do not fit the traditional definition as a union between one man and one woman calling such arrangements marriages simply does not make them so.

Notes

1. B.A., 1972, St. John's University; M. Div., 1978, Seminary of the Immaculate Conception; J.D., 1983, St. John's University; Ed.D., 1989, St. John's University. Panzer Chair in Education and Adjunct Professor of Law, University of Dayton.

The author would like to express his thanks to Drs. David Dolph, Rev. Dr. Joseph Massucci, and A. William Place at the University of Dayton, Dr. Ralph Sharp at East Central (OK) University, Rev. Dr. Paul Babie at the University of Adelaide, Australia, Dr./ Frank Brown at the University of North Carolina at Chapel Hill, and Mr. William E. Thro, Solicitor General, Commonwealth of Virginia for the useful and insightful comments on drafts of this manuscript. An expanded version of this paper was published as Charles J. Russo, *Same-Sex Marriage and Public School Curricula: Preserving Parental Rights to Direct the Education of their Children*, 32 U. Dayton L. Rev. 361 (2007).

2. Genesis 2.24. The same quote also appears at Matthew 19.5-6, Mark 10.7-8, and Ephesians 5.31. A similar version can be found at 1 Cor. 6.16.

3. *See, e.g.*, the Seventh (or Sixth, depending on the version that is used) and Ten Commandments, respectively: "Thou shalt not commit adultery." "Thou shalt not covet

thy neighbor's house, thou shalt not covet thy neighbor's wife, nor his manservant, nor his maidservant, nor his ox, nor his ass, nor any thing that is thy neighbor's." Exodus 20.1-7; Deuteronomy 5.1-22.

4. *See, e.g.*, the OXFORD ENGLISH DICTIONARY where sample use 1.a. reads: "The condition of being a husband or wife; the relation between persons married to each other; matrimony." www.oed.com

5. For a discussion of some of these issues, *see, e.g.*, Larry Catá Backer, *Religion as the Language of Discourse of Same Sex Marriage*, 30 CAP. U. L. REV. 221 (2002); Judith E. Koons, *"Just" Married?: Same-Sex Marriage and a History of Family Plurality*, 12 MICH. J. GENDER & L. 1 (2005); Cheshire Calhoun, *Who's Afraid of Polygamous Marriage? Lessons for Same Sex Marriage Advocacy from the History of Polygamy*, 42 SAN DIEGO L. REV. 1023 (2005).

6. *See, e.g., Goodridge v. Department of Pub. Health*, 798 N.E.2d 941 (Mass. 2003) (holding that limiting the protections, benefits, and obligations of marriage to individuals of opposite sexes lacked a rational basis in violation of the commonwealth's equal protection principles); *In Re Same-Sex Marriage*, 2004 WL 2749380 (Canada 2004), 2004 SCC 79, [2005] (finding that the federal government's proposed act to accord same-sex couples the ability to marry was both within Parliament's exclusive legislative competence and consistent with the Canadian Charter of Rights and Freedoms). *See also Lawrence v. Texas*, 539 U.S. 558 (2003) (interpreting a statute that made it a crime for two persons of the same sex to engage in specified intimate sexual conduct as unconstitutional as applied to adult males who participated in a consensual act of sodomy in the privacy of their home).

But see Hernandez v. Robles, 2006 WL 1835429 (N.Y. 2006) (rejecting arguments from gay and lesbian plaintiffs that their inability to obtain marriage licenses violated their rights); *Perdue v. O'Kelley*, 632 S.E.2d 110 (Ga. 2006) (ruling that a state constitutional amendment adopted by voters, barring the recognition of same-sex marriages, did not violate the constitutional prohibition of multiple subjects in proposed constitutional amendments submitted to voters).

7. For histories and the background on same-sex marriage, *see, e.g.*, Katherine M. Franke, *The Politics of Same-Sex Marriage*, 15 COLUM. J. GENDER & L. 236 (2006); Charles P. Kindregan, *Same-Sex Marriage: The Cultural Wars and Lessons of Legal History*, 38 FAM. L. Q. 427 (2004); William N. Eskridge, *A History of Same-Sex Marriage*, 79 VA. L. REV. 1419 (1993);.

8. *See, e.g.*, Jeremiah H. Russell, *The Religious Liberty Argument for Same-Sex Marriage and its Effects Upon Legal Recognition*, 7 RUTGERS J. L. & RELIGION 4 (2005); Richard D. Mohr, *The Case for Gay Marriage*, 9 NOTRE DAME J.L. ETHICS & PUB. POL'Y 215 (1995).

9. *See, e.g.*, Richard F. Duncan, *Homosexual Marriage and the Myth of Tolerance: Is Cardinal O'Connor a "Homophobe?"* 10 NOTRE DAME J.L. ETHICS & PUB. POL'Y 587 (1996); Gerald V. Bradley, *Same-Sex Marriage: Our Final Answer?* 14 NOTRE DAME J.L. ETHICS & PUB. POL'Y 729 (2000); Lynn D. Wardle, *Multiply and Replenish:" Considering Same-Sex Marriage in Light of State Interests in Marital Procreation*, 24 HARV. J.L. & PUB. POL'Y 771 (2001); Kevin J. Worthen, *Who Decides and What Difference Does it Make: Defining Marriage in "Our Democratic Federal Republic,"* 18 BYU J. PUB. L. 273 (2004); Joshua K. Baker, *Status, Benefits, and Recognition: Current Controversies in the Marriage Debate*, 18 BYU J. PUB. L. 569 (2004).

10. The seminal case in this area is *Pierce v. Society of Sisters (Pierce)*, 268 U.S. 510 (1925). For a more detailed discussion of *Pierce*, *see* note 41 *infra* and accompanying text.

11. In FEDERALIST NO. 78, at 465 (Clinton Rossiter, ed., 1962), Alexander Hamilton wrote that "the judiciary, from the nature of its functions, will always be the least dangerous to the political rights of the Constitution; because it will be least in a capacity to annoy or injure . . . because it has neither FORCE NOR WILL [sic] but merely judgment . . . ."

    For a discussion of the role of the court as the least democratic branch, see ALEXANDER M. BICKEL, THE LEAST DANGEROUS BRANCH: THE SUPREME COURT AT THE BAR OF POLITICS (2d ed 1986).

12. Cf., e.g., the recent results from Massachusetts with those from New York and Georgia, supra note 6.

13. Goodridge v. Department of Pub. Health, 798 N.E.2d 941 (Mass. 2003). In July 2006 the lead couple in this suit announced that they separated. Elizabeth Mehren, Couple in Massachusetts Gay Marriage Case Split Up, L.A. TIMES, July 21, 2006 Pagination unavailable on line), 2006 WLNR 12584995.

14. For a brief discussion of judicial activism generally, especially as it relates to education, see Charles J. Russo, In the Eye of the Beholder: The Supreme Court, Judicial Activism, and Judicial Restraint. SCHOOL BUSINESS AFFAIRS, October 2005, at 47-50.

15. Massachusetts is the only jurisdiction that grants marriage licenses to same-sex couples. Four other states, New Jersey, New Mexico, New York, and Rhode Island, as well as the District of Columbia, have no explicit laws prohibiting same sex marriages.

    Human Rights Campaign, Statewide Marriage Laws, http://www.hrc.org/Template. cfm?Section=Your_Community&Template=/ContentManagement/ContentDisplay.cfm &ContentID=19449 This web-site has not required an update since July 2006.

16. Id.

17. For a discussion of Christophobia, see GEORGE WEIGEL, THE CUBE AND THE CATHEDRAL: EUROPE, AMERICA, AND POLITICS WITHOUT GOD (2006, paperback edition), at 19, 72-77.

18. Santa Fe Indep. Sch, Dist. v. Doe, 530 U.S. 290, 318 (2000) (Rehnquist, C.J., dissenting) (striking down student-led prayer prior to the start of a high school football game).

19. In a particularly egregious example of antipathy for Christian, specifically Roman Catholic, beliefs and sensitivities, on December. 10, 1989, members of the radical gay group ACT-UP chained themselves to pews in St. Patrick's Cathedral and shouted down Cardinal O'Connor at a Sunday Mass before others "received" the Eucharist but spat it out and desecrated the Sacrament by stepping on the hosts. One can only wonder what kind of outrage this behavior might have stirred had it occurred in a house of worship of some other faith. See Mike Dorning, Animosity Over Gays Threatens St. Pat Parade: New York's Irish March will go on, But Sexual Minority Plans a Protest, CHICAGO TRIBUNE, March 15, 1993, at 1, 1993 WLNR 4062014. Interestingly, the purported "newspaper of record" in New York City, the Times, did not report on this highly insensitive incident. See, e.g., Bruce Weber, Tangle of Issues in St. Patrick's Brouhaha, N.Y. TIMES, March 16, 1992, at B3, 1992 WLNR 3351573; Sam Roberts, One More Time, With Turmoil: True to Tradition. St. Patrick's Marchers Face Controversy, N.Y. TIMES, March 17, 1993, at B1, 1993 WLNR 3367862.

    Situations such as these bring to mind the notion that anti-Catholicism, or if modified to fit today's circumstances to include anti-Christianity, is the anti-Semitism of the intellectuals. The original quote was that "Catholic-baiting is the anti-Semitism of the liberals." PETER VIERECK, SHAME AND GLORY OF THE INTELLECTUALS 45 (1953). Although Viereck is misquoted regularly, the spirit of his comment remains true.

20. Keeping in mind the dicta from Mark Twain, who was quoting Benjamin Disraeli, that "there are three kinds of lies: lies, damned lies, and statistics," MARK TWAIN, AU-

TOBIOGRAPHY 246 (1924), the data are revealing. After increasingly rapidly during the 1970s and 1980s the rate of divorce in the United States stabilized in the 1990s but remains at roughly 50% BUREAU OF THE CENSUS, U.S. DEP'T OF COMMERCE, CURRENT POPULATION REPORTS, AMERICA'S FAMILIES AND LIVING ARRANGEMENTS: 2003, at 5, 10 (2004). For links to these statistical reports and other sources, *see* http://www.divorcereform.org/rates.html *See also* U.S. DEPARTMENT OF HEALTH AND HUMAN SERVICES, CENTERS FOR DISEASE CONTROL AND PREVENTION, NATIONAL VITAL STATISTICS REPORTS, Vol. 52, No. 22 (June 10, 2004), http://www.cdc.gov/nchs/ data/nvsr/nvsr52/nvsr52_22.pdf. (reporting that since the marriage rate in 2003 was 7.5 per 1,000 and the divorce rate was 3.8 per 1,000, there was almost one divorce for every two as marriages in the United States; this is consistent with the two previous years, 2001 and 2002, which reported the marriage and divorce rates as 7.8 and 8.2 marriages and 4.0 and 4.0 divorces respectively). For a comprehensive report on this topic, relying on date from 1995, *see* U.S. DEP'T OF HEALTH & HUMAN SERV., COHABITATION, MARRIAGE, DIVORCE, AND REMARRIAGE IN THE UNITED STATES, VITAL AND HEALTH STATISTICS, July 2002, at 1, 22, available at http://purl.access.gpo.gov/GPO/LPS22381.

21. The federal government has made data available on cohabitation since 1995 and in its statistical tables since 1996. BUREAU OF THE CENSUS, U.S. DEP'T OF COMMERCE, CURRENT POPULATION REPORTS, AMERICA'S FAMILIES AND LIVING ARRANGEMENTS: 2003 at 12 (2004).

22. BUREAU OF THE CENSUS, U.S. DEP'T OF COMMERCE, CURRENT POPULATION REPORTS, AMERICA'S FAMILIES AND LIVING ARRANGEMENTS: 2003 at 7 (noting that the number of single-mother families increased from 3,000,000 in 1970 to 10,000,000 in 2003 while the number of families headed by single fathers in the same time frame increased from less than a half of a million to 2,000,000).

23. *See, e.g.*, Wardle, *supra* note 9; Teresa Stanton Collett, *Civil Unions in Vermont: Where to go from Here? A Symposium Addressing the Impact of Civil Unions*, 11 WIDENER J. PUB. L. 379 (2002); MARRIAGE AND THE PUBLIC GOOD: TEN PRINCIPLES (2006). This study, also known as the Princeton Report, the result of scholarly discussions initiated by the Witherspoon Institute in 2004. Available at www.princeton principles.org

24. MARRIAGE AND THE PUBLIC GOOD: TEN PRINCIPLES (2006) at 12.

25. 268 U.S. 510 (1925). For a more detailed discussion of *Pierce, see* note 41 *infra* and accompanying text.

26. *Id.* at 535.

27. *Brown v. Board of Educ.*, 347 U.S. 483, 493 (1954) (striking down racial segregation in public education).

28. *See, e.g.*, ALA. CODE ANN. § 16–28–7; CAL. EDUC. CODE § 48200; DEL. CODE ANN. tit. 14 § 2702; GA. CODE ANN. § 20–2–690.1; 105 ILL. COMP. STAT. ANN. 5/26–1; KY. REV. STAT. ANN. § 159.010; MD. CODE ANN., EDUC. § 7–301; MASS. GEN. LAWS ch. 76, § 1; N.J. STAT. ANN. § 18A:38–25; N.Y. EDUC. LAW § 3205; OHIO REV. CODE ANN. § 3321.01; OKLA. STAT. ANN. tit. 70, § 10–105; 24 PA. CONSOL. STAT. ANN. § 13–1327; TEX. EDUC. CODE ANN. § 25.085; WIS. STAT. ANN. § 118.15.

29. Despite some differences as opinion as to why, the National Education Association (NEA), the largest union of public school teachers in the United States, did not endorse same-sex marriage. *See* Ginger Tinney, *Teachers union fails members*, OKLAHOMAN, Aug. 11, 2006, at 13A, 2006 WLNR 14045762 (noting that the NEA "back[ed] off endorsing same sex marriage at its July convention in Orlando, Fla. However, a resolution did encourage tolerance of homosexual lifestyles in civil unions and marriages (in states that have approved it). The intent is clear. OEA/ NEA focuses on spreading gay marriage instead of finding ways to improve our schools."). *But see* John W. Sparks,

Teachers group offers faith help for classroom, Memphis Commercial Appeal (TN), July 15, 2006, at A1, 2006 WLNR 12306518 (reporting that "The NEA said in a statement that it "has no plans to endorse same sex marriage and never did.".

30. *Grutter v. Bollinger*, 539 U.S. 206, 372 (2003) (Thomas, J., dissenting) (upholding racial preferences in law school admissions).

31. The courts have recognized distinctions between students in pre-K-12 and higher education. *Compare Lee v. Weisman*, 505 U.S. 577 (1992) (striking down prayer at graduation since the state, through school officials, played a major role in the by selecting who would pray and by directing the content of prayer). *with Tanford v. Brand*, 104 F.3d 982 (7th Cir. 1997), *cert. denied*, 522 U.S. 814 (1997); *Chaudhuri v. State of Tenn.*, 130 F.3d 232 (6th Cir. 1997), *cert. denied*, 523 U.S. 1024 (1998) (upholding graduation prayers at universities because they did not involve young students and attendance in higher education is voluntary).

32. For an interesting examination of selected faculty members and administrators over the extent to which political correctness has overtaken many campuses, *see* DAVID HOROWITZ, THE PROFESSORS: THE 100 MOST DANGEROUS ACADEMICS IN AMERICA (2006).

33. *McCreary County, Kentucky v. American Civil Liberties Union of Kentucky*, 125 S. Ct. 2722, 2747 (2005) (striking down a public display of the Ten Commandments at a courthouse) (O'Connor, J., concurring). The full quote reads "we do not count heads before enforcing the First Amendment."

34. In *Good News Club v. Milford Cent. Sch.*, 533 U.S. 98, 118 (2001) (Thomas, J., dissenting) (permitting a religious group to use public school facilities), Justice Thomas made this point in warning that the Court is unwilling " . . . to employ Establishment Clause jurisprudence using a modified heckler's veto, in which a group's religious activity can be proscribed on the basis of what . . . members of the audience might misperceive.").

35. Jeff Vaznis, *Lawsuit Invokes Religious Freedom: Parents Say Beliefs Ignored by School*, BOSTON GLOBE, May 4, 2006, at 1, 2006 WLNR 7704418 (reporting that parents sued the school system alleging that including discussions about homosexuality violated their religious beliefs that homosexual behavior is immoral).

36. *Educators say the pre-school set needs straight talk on gay issues*. BAY WINDOWS, NEW ENGLAND'S LARGEST LGBT NEWSPAPER. June 22, 2006 (calling for the creation of age and developmentally appropriate instruction on gay, lesbian, bi-sexual, and transgendered issues). Available at http://www.baywindows.com/ME2/dirmod.asp?sid=&nm=&type=Publishing&mod=Publications::Article&mid=8F3A7027421841978F18BE895F87F791&tier=4&id=BDF1272D78F344BE8CD79B483A72D327

37. *Lee v. Weisman*, 505 U.S. 577 (1992).

38. *Roberts v. Madigan*, 921 F.2d 1047 (10th Cir.1990), *cert. denied*, 505 U.S. 1218 (1992).

39. 505 U.S. 577, 593 (1992). The Court maintained that

> "Research in psychology supports the common assumption that adolescents are often susceptible to pressure from their peers towards conformity, and that the influence is strongest in matters of social convention." (internal citations omitted).

40. *See Engel v. Vitale*, 370 U.S. 421, 431 (1962) (striking down prayer at the start of the school day) ("When the power, prestige and financial support of government is placed behind a particular religious belief, the indirect coercive pressure upon religious minorities to conform to the prevailing officially approved religion is plain. But the purposes underlying the Establishment Clause go much further than that.").

41. Two years earlier, in *Meyer v. Nebraska*, 262 U.S. 390 (1923), the Supreme Court invalidated a prohibition against teaching a foreign language in grades lower than ninth under which a teacher in a non-public school was convicted of teaching German. The Court rejected the statute's purported goal of promoting civic development by "inhibiting training and education of the immature in foreign tongues and ideals before they could learn English and acquire American ideals, and 'that the English language should be and become the mother tongue of all children reared in this state.'" *Id.* at 401.

42. 268 U.S. 510 (1925).

43. *Id.*, at 534-535.

44. *Id.* at 535.

45. In *Jacobellis v. State of Ohio*, 378 U.S. 184, 197 (1964) (Stewart, J., concurring), a case dealing with hard-core-pornography, Justice Potter Stewart wrote: "I shall not today attempt further to define the kinds of material I understand to be embraced within that shorthand description; and perhaps I could never succeed in intelligibly doing so. But I know it when I see it, and the motion picture involved in this case is not that."

46. 406 U.S. 205 (1972).

47. LESLEA NEWMAN, HEATHER HAS TWO MOMMIES (1990) (telling the story of a pre-school child with two "mothers" who discovers that some of her friends have different sorts of families). *See also Editorial, Teaching About Gays and Tolerance*, N.Y. TIMES, Sept. 27 1992, 1992 WLNR 3292103 (reporting that *Heather Has Two Mommies* was included in the curriculum for first graders in New York City's public schools).

For a more detailed account of the controversy in New York City, *see* Josh Barbanel, *Under 'Rainbow,' a War: When Politics, Morals and Learning Mix*, N.Y. TIMES, Dec. 27, 1992, 1992 WLNR 3296006 (detailing how one local board in New York City refused to allow gay and lesbian relationships to be discussed in classes).

48. For the only reported case involving a challenge to *Heather Has Two Mommies* and *Daddy's Roommate* in a public library, albeit in a non-school context, *see Sund v. City of Wichita Falls, Tex.*, 121 F. Supp.2d 530 (N.D. Tex. 2000) (enjoining enforcement of a city resolution that granted card holders of a public library the right to have these books moved from the children's area to the adult section on the basis that it violated patrons' First Amendment rights to receive information, the library was a "limited public forum," the resolution was an improper delegation of governmental authority to private citizens under state law, and the patrons' First Amendment right to receive information would have been irreparably injured if they were denied the permanent injunction).

49. MICHAEL WILLHOITE, DADDY'S ROOMMATE (1990).

50. KING & KING, LINDA DE HAAN & STERN NIJLAND (2002). This book led to a sequel, KING & KING & FAMILY, LINDA DE HAAN, STERN MIJLAND, & STERN NIJLAND (2004).

51. Tracy Jan, *Parents Rip School Over Gay Storybook*, BOSTON GLOBE, April 20, 2006, at B1, 2006 WLNR 6606392 (reporting that parents of a second-grade child protested after his teacher read a fairy tale about gay marriage to the class without giving them advanced notice). *See also Boy Allegedly Beaten Over Gay Rights Issue*, BOSTON GLOBE, June 15, 2006, at B2, 2006 WLNR 10303728 (reporting that the one of the parents who filed a federal suit against his local public schools over classes in which homosexuality was discussed claimed that his first-grade son was beaten up during recess by a group of eight to ten pupils on the second anniversary of the legalization of same-sex marriages in Massachusetts). *But see* Maria Sacchetti, *Official Says Father's View of Gays Didn't Spark Fight*, BOSTON GLOBE, June 20, 2006, at B 2, 2006 WLNR 10665659 (reporting that school officials denied assertions that the child was beaten because of his father's views, claiming that it was over where students would sit in the school's cafeteria).

52. *NEWS in Brief; Dad dodges school rap in flap over gay topic.* BOSTON GLOBE, Oct. 21, 2005, at 14, available on line, 2005 WLNR 17089605 (reporting that prosecutors agreed to drop the charges against a father who refused to leave school after demanding that officials notify him before any discussion of homosexuality in his son's kindergarten class).

53. *Parker v. Hurley*, 514 F.3d 87 (1st Cir. 2008).

54. For representative discussions of this series, *see, e.g.*, Allan Luke, *Making Dick and Jane: Historical Genesis of the Modern Basal Readers*, 89 TEACHERS COLLEGE RECORD 91-116 (1987); Richard L. Mandel, *Children's Books: Mirrors of Social Development*, 64 ELEMENTARY SCH. J. 190-199 (1964).

55. *State ex rel. Burpee v. Burton*, 45 Wis. 150 (Wis.1878).

56. *Brown v. Hot, Sexy and Safer Productions*, 68 F.3d 525, 529 (1st Cir.1995), *cert. denied*, 516 U.S. 1159 (1996) (refusing to prohibit a highly explicit program in a high school as shocking to the conscience even where a school policy required written parental consent for their children to receive such instruction)

57. *Fields v. Palmdale Sch. Dist.*, 427 F.3d 1197, 1202, n. 3 (9th Cir. 2005), *cert. petition filed*, 75 U.S.L.W. 3095 (Aug 28, 2006) (No. 06-300) (parents unsuccessfully challenged educators who distributed surveys to first, third, and fifth grade students which asked such questions as whether they engaged in "8. Touching my private parts too much; 17. Thinking about having sex; 22. Thinking about touching other people's private parts; 23. Thinking about sex when I don't want to; 44. Having sex feelings in my body; 47. Can't stop thinking about sex."

C.N. v. Ridgewood Bd. of Educ., 430 F.3d 159, 168-169 (3d Cir. 2005) (parents unsuccessfully challenged questionnaires that were distributed to their children in grades seven through twelve that contained questions related to sex, including "have you ever had sexual intercourse ('gone all the way,' 'made love')," . . . and "when you have sex, how often do you and/or your partner use a birth control method such as birth control pills, a condom (rubber), foam, diaphragm, or IUD."

58. *Brown v. Hot, Sexy and Safer Productions*, *supra* note 56.

59. *See, e.g.*, *School District of Abington Township (Abington) v. Schempp* and *Murray v. Curlett*, 374 U.S. 203 (1963) (striking down reading verses from the Bible prior to the start of class on the basis that doing so lacked a secular legislative purpose and a primary effect that advanced religion). *See also Roberts v. Madigan*, 921 F.2d 1047, 1049 (10th Cir.1990), *cert. denied*, 505 U.S. 1218 (1992) (preventing a teacher from silently reading a Bible during class time).

60. *See, e.g., Doe v. Human*, 725 F. Supp. 1503 (W.D. Ark.1989), *aff'd*, 923 F.2d 857 (8th Cir.1990), *cert. denied*, 499 U.S. 922 (1991) (affirming the unconstitutionality of a program that permitted students to leave their regular classrooms to learn about the Bible in voluntary sessions that took place during regular school hours); *Gibson v. Lee County School Bd.*, 1 F. Supp.2d 1426 (M.D. Fla. 1998) (permitting a board to offer a class on the Old Testament but enjoining one on the New Testament based on its belief that the plaintiffs were likely to prevail on the merits of their claim that it violated the Establishment Clause); *Doe v. Porter*, 370 F.3d 558 (6th Cir. 2004) (affirming that a school board's fifty-one year practice of permitting students from a local Christian college to teach weekly religion classes that presented the Christian Bible as religious truth during the regular school day violated the Establishment Clause).

61. *See, e.g., Board of Educ. of Westside Community Schs. v. Mergens*, 496 U.S. 226 (1990) (upholding the constitutionality of the Equal Access Act, a federal statute that permits student organized prayer and Bible study clubs to meet in public schools during non-instructional time).

62. *Lee v. Weisman*, *supra* note 39.

63. *Santa Fe Indep. Sch, Dist. v. Doe, supra* note 18.

64. For an interesting discussion of the intersection between law and religion, *see* HAROLD J. BERMAN, FAITH AND ORDER: THE RECONCILIATION OF LAW AND RELIGION (1993).

65. *See Abington*, 374 U.S. 203, 225 (1963):
"It certainly may be said that the Bible is worthy of study for its literary and historic qualities. Nothing we have said here indicates that such study of the Bible or of religion, when presented objectively as part of a secular program of education, may not be effected consistently with the First Amendment."

66. *See, e.g.*, http://www.cyberhymnal.org/htm/j/e/jesuslme.htm (providing background on the song *Jesus Loves Me*).

67. *See supra* note 19.

68. *See, e.g., Eukers v. State*, 728 N.E.2d 219 (Ind. Ct. App. 2000) (upholding the conviction of a mother for violating a compulsory attendance law where her child exceeded the limit of absences at school).

69. Points two through four in this discussion are adapted from Charles J. Russo & William E. Thro (2006). *Parents, Educators, and the Courts: Who Directs the Education of Students?* SCHOOL BUSINESS AFFAIRS, Aug. 2006, 39-41 (discussing the cases cited in notes 55-57, *supra*).

70. *See, e.g., Ware v. Valley Stream High School Dist.*, 551 N.Y.S.2d 167 (N.Y.1989) (affirming the denial of a board's motion for summary judgment where genuine issues of material fact existed over the burden that exposure to an AIDS curriculum would have had on the religious beliefs of students and their parents).

71. *The Condition of Education 2006, Indicator 4, Trends in Private School Enrollment*. NATIONAL CENTER FOR EDUCATION STATISTICS, 2006. Also available at http://nces.ed.gov/programs/coe/2006/pdf/04_2006.pdf

72. *Projections of Education Statistics to 2014. Appendix A: Projection Methodology: Enrollment*. NATIONAL CENTER FOR EDUCATION STATISTICS 2006.
http://nces.ed.gov/programs/projections/app_a1.asp
See also http://nces.ed.gov/fastfacts/display.asp?id=65 ("Public secondary enrollment is projected to rise through 2007, and then decline. Overall, school enrollment is projected to set new records every year from 2006 until at least 2014, the last year for which NCES has projected school enrollment.")

73. *The Condition of Education 2006, Indicator 4, Trends in Private School Enrollment*. NATIONAL CENTER FOR EDUCATION STATISTICS 2006. Also available at http://nces.ed.gov/programs/coe/2005/pdf/03_2005.pdf

74. *Private School Enrollment: Percentage distribution of private school students in kindergarten through grade 12, by school type: 1989–90 and 2003–04*, NATIONAL CENTER FOR EDUCATION STATISTICS 2006
http://nces.ed.gov/programs/coe/2006/charts/chart04.asp?popup=true

75. David Crary, *Public Schools Take Heat*, DESERET NEWS, Sept. 5, 2006, at CO2, 2006 WLNR 15373867.

76. *See, e.g.*, Wyatt Buchanan, *Bill would include gays in public school tests: Plan will reignite debate over who controls curricula.* SAN FRANCISCO CHRONICLE (CA), April 16, 2006, at B1, 2006 WLNR 637270.

77. *See, e.g.*, Jim Sanders, *Kuehl guts her gay education bill: Veto threat forced an overhaul, but senator sees progress on rights.* SACRAMENTO BEE (CA), Aug. 8, 2006, at A3, 2006 WLNR 1374512. Andy Furillo & Judy Lin, *Gay school bill in trouble: Spokesman says the governor plans to veto curriculum measure, but Kuehl insists it can still pass*, SACRAMENTO BEE (CA), May 25, 2006, at A3, 2006 WLNR 9047698.

78. 2005 Cal. S.B. 1437; 2005 Cal. A.B. 606.

79. The Assembly approved the bill by a 47 to 31 vote on August 21, 2006 while the Senate did the same, by a margin of 22 to 15 on August 29, 2006. 2005 AS S.B. 1437 (NS). Jim Sanders, *Controversial gay-rights bill OK'd: Measure would ban demeaning actions in public schools*, SACRAMENTO BEE (CA), Aug. 22, 2006, at A3, 2006 WLNR 14555020; Mike Zapler, *Bill banning anti-gay speech in schools advances Assembly, unsure of Schwarzenegger's stance on measure, shows approval with 46-31 vote along partisan lines*, CONTRA COSTA TIMES (WALNUT CREEK, CA), Aug. 22, 2006, at F4, 2006 WLNR 14507103; Judy Lin, *Gay equality bill advances*, SACRAMENTO BEE (CA), Aug. 30, 2006, page unavailable on-line, 2006 WLNR 15039852.

80. Judy Lin, *The governor says current law prohibits bias based on sexual orientation, but the bill's author says the battle's not over: School measure on gays vetoed.* SACRAMENTO BEE (CA), Sept. 7, 2006, at A3, 2006 WLNR 15555087. *See also* Greg Lucas, *Sacramento: Governor vetoes gay teaching measure He says current laws guard against discrimination*, SAN FRANCISCO CHRONICLE (CA), Sept. 7, 2006, at B4, 2006 WLNR 15481301).

81. Cal. S.B. 777, codified at Cal. Educ. Code § 220 (West 2007). *See also* sections 200, 212.6, and 219.

82. COL. ALEXANDER K. MCCLURE, LINCOLN'S YARNS AND STORIES (1980) at 323. Another version of this story has Lincoln speaking about a dog rather than a calf. *See, e.g.,* John Thorn, http://thornpricks.blogspot.com/ Dec. 2, 2005 "What's in a Name?"

CHAPTER 19
REDEFINITION OF MARRIAGE AND THE RULE OF LAW

William C. Duncan[1]
Marriage Law Foundation

"How the desire for reforms took precedence of the desire for freedom."[2]

The unprecedented legal and political debate over the definition of marriage threatens to detract from the integrity of constitutional principles and our commitment to the rule of law that under girds them. The redefinition movement is accelerating and/or inaugurating trends that are likely to prove harmful to our form of government.

The potential threats posed by the redefinition movement to our governmental system go much deeper than the question of who is to decide what the law will say about what marriage is. It threatens core governmental concepts: (1) limitations on government jurisdiction, (2) separation of powers, (3) predictability and consistency in lawmaking, and (4) avoidance of official intolerance of citizens' deeply-held beliefs.

I.   Jurisdiction

Implicit in the American ideal of government is the principle that government has only a limited jurisdiction. Thus the U.S. Constitution's First Amendment wording, "Congress *shall make no law* respecting, and the Ninth and Tenth Amendments putting some subjects off-limits for government control or manipulation. Even where the state is empowered to legislate, there are jurisdictional limits like the system of federalism whereby the national government's jurisdiction is limited *vis a vis* the governments of the states and *vice versa*. If these kinds of constitutional boundaries are ignored by "those intended to be restrained . . . [t]he distinction[] between a government with limited and unlimited powers is abolished."[3]

The redefinition movement threatens this concept of limited jurisdiction, generally and as embodied in federalism.

A.   Substantive Limitations

As regards the family, the principle of limited jurisdiction is manifest in ve-
nerable legal principles such as the presumption that parents act in the best interests of their children, the hesitancy of the law to address disputes within intact
families and the presumption that a mother's husband is the baby's father to
avoid disrupting an intact family. [4]

These longstanding doctrines are under girded by the powerful ideal that
"[t]he rights inherent in family relationships—husband-wife, parent-child, and
sibling—are the most obvious example of rights retained by the people. They
are 'natural,' 'intrinsic,' or 'prior' in the sense that our Constitutions presuppose
them, as they presuppose the right to own and dispose of property."[5] The U.S.
Supreme Court has recognized that parents can do for children what the state
cannot do, so its past decisions generally "have respected the private realm of
family life which the state cannot enter."[6] Thus "[t]he family interposes a significant legal entity between the individual and the state, where it performs its mediating and value-generating function."[7] Following from this:

> [i]t remains fundamental to democratic theory that parents, through
> this institutional role of the family, control the heart of the value-
> transmission process. As that crucial process is dispersed pluralisti-
> cally, the power of government is limited. It is characteristic of totali-
> tarian societies, by contrast, to centralize the transmission of values.
> Our system thus fully expects parents to interact with their children in
> ways we would not tolerate from the state—namely, through the ex-
> plicit inculcation of intensely personal convictions about life and its
> meaning.[8]

An early Twentieth Century case specifically rejected theories that children
and families are creatures of the state, noting these "ideas touching the relation
between the individual and the State were wholly different from those upon
which our institutions rest; and it hardly will be affirmed that any legislature
could impose such restrictions upon the people of a State without doing violence
to both letter and spirit of the Constitution."[9] Robert Nisbet notes the idea of
family autonomy is linked to individual freedom, pointing to "conservative ide-
ologists" who have seen "individual freedom as an inextricable aspect of a kind
of social pluralism, one rich in autonomous or semi-autonomous groups, communities, and institutions."[10]

The consequences of a threat to the ideal of limited jurisdiction over the
family are momentous because, when state officials "attempt to put legal norms
in place of social norms" as Roger Scruton notes, "[t]he consequence is a wi-
thering away of community, an undermining of family sentiment and a demora-
lisation of society."[11] This calls to mind Alexis de Tocqueville's famous warning of "an immense tutelary power" that "willingly works for [its subjects'] happiness; *but it wants to be the unique agent and sole arbiter of that.*"[12]

The expansion of state jurisdiction over the family is immediately obvious
in the court decisions holding state constitutions mandate a redefinition of mar-

riage. These decisions baldly assert that marriage is a creature of the state,[13] despite the fact that "[t]he state came to marriage even later than did the Church."[14] The majority in the Massachusetts marriage case said "civil marriage" was created by the state,[15] conveniently failing to note that the definition of marriage in Massachusetts came from an existing tradition that predated the existence of the Commonwealth. These court's assertions of a controlling role for the state in the creation of family life are in sharp distinction to the limited jurisdiction ideal in which the law recognizes preexisting institutions like marriage and the family rather than claiming to call them into being at will.

As the state redefines marriage it inevitably runs into inextricably connected principles like legal parenthood. In the vast majority of cases, for instance, the presumption that a mother's husband is the father of her child makes sense but the presumption cannot possibly extend to a new kind of "marriage" where inherently non-procreative couplings are considered in every way equivalent to male-female pairings. Same-sex couples cannot acquire children without the participation of some third party, so to maintain the fiction of equivalence the state will have to extend the presumption to same-sex partners of biological parents. In doing so, it will automatically extinguish the parental status of at least one of a child's biological parents. When the traditional presumption allowed the law to ignore a potential parent it did so as a way of shrinking from interference in an intact family, not to create a family where there was none before. The new legal fiction of a child with two fathers or two mothers removes from the law any recognition of an organic connection between marriage and parenthood and constitutes a greatly expanded state role: the creator not only of marriage but parenthood.[16]

Most would understandably shrink from a proposal that at birth, a child would have to be adopted by the person who gave birth to him or her regardless of biological connection. The deliberate setting aside of an existing relationship derived from ties of biology and love would be an obvious usurpation. Yet, in the marriage context, courts and legislatures are mulling proposals that would set aside the inherited understanding of the marriage institution in favor of a new version, entirely the product of government will.

B.   Structural Limitations

Federalism typically confines family law matters to State jurisdiction, allowing decisions about core personal relationships to be made closest to those who will be affected by them.

Proponents of redefining marriage have generally pursued their claims in state courts relying state constitutional claims. This allegiance to federalism is, however, tactical rather than principled.[17] As the recent effort to overturn Nebraska's state marriage amendment in federal court has made clear, redefinition advocates are unwilling to forego federal claims when state law would otherwise foreclose them from asserting their position.[18]

The strategic nature of the redefinition movement's commitment to federalism is illustrated by a Ninth Circuit case from where a same-sex couple sued to invalidate California's marriage law based on the federal constitution.[19] Mainstream gay activist groups sought intervention in the appeal in order to *prevent* a decision by the federal court[20] even though they believed the federal Defense of Marriage Act is "unconstitutional and eventually should be held so if an appropriate case is brought." They say DOMA "violates the rights of same-sex couples to due process of law under the United States Constitution; and that Section 3 of DOMA cannot survive even rational basis review under the Fifth Amendment's equal protection guarantee" but that "the District Court should not have reached any of these issues *in this case*."[21] Federalism will clearly not be a barrier for these organizations when, "eventually," a suit is brought, presumably with their representation.

A recent Vermont decision suggests state courts that emphasized state uniqueness in their decisions regarding marriage will have no qualms about overriding the law of other states. In a dispute over child visitation between two women (one of whom was the child's mother) who had come from Virginia to Vermont to contract a civil union, the Vermont Supreme Court held that Virginia law was inapplicable to determining the visitation issue.[22] This decision may be a correct interpretation of the federal law but it highlights an irony: Vermont's civil union law[23] was created by order of the supreme court, purportedly relying entirely on a unique provision of the state constitution,[24] but it now results in a vehicle for circumventing the law of another state.

Rather than evidencing respect for the uniqueness of each state's constitution the effort to secure marriage redefinition in state courts is meant to create (1) persuasive precedent for other states and the federal government, (2) opportunities for litigation in other states regarding interjurisdictional recognition, and (3) a sense that legal redefinition of marriage is inevitable; and, thus, wear away popular opposition.

The authoritative federal decision redefinition advocates seek would be a severe blow to federalism by imposing a national definition of marriage. Thus, the movement creates, at the very least, a potential threat to this structural limitation on government jurisdiction.

II.   *Separation of Powers*

Separation of powers acts constrains the authority of the various departments of government, guarding against the tyranny of one person or group wielding arbitrary power, unchecked. [25] Thus, John Adams' constitution for Massachusetts provides for a strict division of powers among government branches "*to the end it may be a government of laws and not of men*."[26] James Madison made the same link: "The accumulation of all powers, legislative, executive, and judiciary, in the same hands, whether of one, a few, or many, and whether hereditary, self-appointed, or elective, may justly be pronounced the very definition of tyranny."[27]

This principle limits the authority of governmental branches so that each can serve as a check to the ambition or overreaching of another. In many constitutions, provision is also made for citizens, as a body, to act as a de facto branch of government through the amendment process and through initiatives and referendums. The principle of separation of powers also extends to the actions of any branch that would infringe on these citizens' prerogatives.

The following examples, far from comprehensive, illustrate the many instances in which the redefinition movement has prompted incursions by one branch on the authority of others.

A.   Judiciary

In our constitutional system, the power of the judiciary is significantly limited by provisions requiring courts only to rule on "cases" and "controversies" which come before it.[28] As Alexander Hamilton described it, the judiciary has "neither FORCE nor WILL, but merely judgment."[29] In Justice Benjamin Cardozo's words: "The judge, even when he is free, is still not wholly free. He is not to innovate at pleasure. He is not a knight-errant, roaming at will in pursuit of his own ideal of beauty or of goodness."[30] The marriage debate, however, has tempted the inner "knight-errant" in some judges to emerge.

When the Vermont Supreme Court decided the state constitution would be offended if the benefits of marriage were not offered to same-sex couples.[31] The court stayed the effect of its decision for a "reasonable period of time" while the legislature acted on the court's order. To ensure the legislature did not mistakenly believe that the decision was merely a helpful suggestion, the court retained jurisdiction over the case with the threat that "[i]n the event that the benefits and protections in question are not statutorily granted, plaintiffs may petition this Court to order the remedy they originally sought" (ordering marriage licenses for same-sex couples).[32] This minute oversight of legislative action resembles "force" and "will" rather than mere "judgment."

The subsequent Massachusetts decision to redefine marriage employed a similar exercise of judicial "will." There, the court stayed its judgment for 180 days with a nod to the legislature.[33] The legislature, mistakenly believing it had a substantive role, responded with a proposal to create "civil unions" as the Vermont legislature had done. It then came, hat in hand, to the court only to be soundly rebuffed.[34] Why then did the court suggest any legislative role? One commentator plausibly suggests it was an attempt to make "its eventual imposition of same-sex marriage rights more publicly accepted," a strategy this commentator believed was ultimately successful.[35] Accepting this explanation, the court's actions clearly constituted a bald use of strategy to gain political ends.

For some of the justices, the Massachusetts court's exercise of power in these cases presaged an even greater role. When the people of the state put forward a proposal to amend the state constitution to define marriage, the attorneys representing the *Goodridge* plaintiffs sued to prevent a legislative vote on the proposal. In the resulting decision allowing the vote to go forward, two members of the Supreme Judicial Court invited "an appropriate lawsuit" challenging a state marriage amendment since they believed "the *Goodridge* decision may be irreversible."[36] In the famous constitutional "conversation" between the judiciary and the other branches and the citizens, these judge's line is: "Shut up he explained."[37]

B.   Executive

Executives have not been immune from the temptation to expand their power to serve the cause of "marriage equality." The most well known instance of *ultra vires* exercise of authority began with secret meetings between San Francisco city officials and activist organizations, convened at the instigation of the mayor, to plan the issuance of marriage licenses to same-sex couples.[38] The city began issuing the licenses in early February 2004.[39] Despite clear state laws on marriage[40] and the power of municipalities, two judges refused to enjoin the licensing.[41] After more than a week, the governor of California finally asked the state attorney general to take action against the city, though he refused to do so for another week.[42] Just one day short of the month anniversary of the inauguration of San Francisco's media event, the California Supreme Court finally (after 4, 000 licenses had been issued to same-sex couples) ordered a stop to the practice.[43]

This pattern was followed in Multnomah County , Oregon. [44] In New Paltz, New York, the mayor officiated in same-sex marriage ceremonies and the state attorney general refused to intervene leaving the local district attorney to finally file charges to stop the mayor. [45]Shorter-term executive rebellions took place in Asbury Park, New Jersey and Sandoval County, New Mexico.[46]

C.   Legislature

In Massachusetts, the Legislature too overstepped its bounds, usurping the right of the people to propose amendments to the constitution. Previous to the *Goodridge* decision, a citizens group had collected far in excess of the number of signatures needed to propose an amendment defining marriage.[47] The Massachusetts Constitution requires that such an amendment "shall be voted upon" by the legislature acting in constitutional convention and the convention can take action "only by a call of the yeas and nays."[48] Even the Supreme Judicial Court had previously ruled that a vote was required on amendment initiatives brought before the constitutional convention.[49] Notwithstanding only fifty votes were needed in favor of the proposed amendment to preserve it for the next session, the Senate President adjourned the convention without a vote on the amendment.[50] A legislator opponent of the amendment said "I'm proud to have done anything possible to defeat this."[51]

The redefinition movement has already eroded the principle of separation of powers and, ominously, laid the foundation for further usurpation.

III.   Predictability & Consistency

The great historian Forrest McDonald described one sense of the term "rule of law" as "uniform and predictable rules of conduct within a jurisdiction."[52]

Similarly, Professor Robert George describes "constancy over time" and "generality of application" as important elements of the rule of law.[53] Consistency and predictability enhance the ability of citizens to comply with the law and guide lawmakers in their responsibility. The benefits of knowing that one is acting or legislating in accordance with legal principles (and thus not risking prosecution of wasting legislative resources) are obvious.

To prevent the law from reflecting arbitrary and mercurial opinions of individual judges or "[t]o avoid an arbitrary discretion in the courts," Alexander Hamilton said, "it is indispensable that they should be bound down by strict rules and precedents, which serve to define and point out their duty in every particular case that comes before them."[54] When predictability and consistency are missing, the law can create distrust and alienation. As Professor Robert Nagel notes: "Perversely, our legal institutions teach ordinary people the scary lesson that anything can be done with words," thus creating a "fear of indirection, of false assurances, of an agenda pushed heedlessly."[55]

The shifting rationales courts have offered for holding that state constitutions provide a mandate for changing the definition of marriage illustrate the redefinition movement's threats to consistency and predictability in the law.

For instance, courts in Alaska, New York and Washington have relied on theories that those state's constitutions include an unwritten fundamental right to choose one's own definition of marriage.[56] The Hawaii Supreme Court endorsed the same outcome but came to the directly opposite result on the merits of this legal argument.[57]

Similarly, courts in Hawaii, Maryland and California have relied on a unique understanding of sex discrimination in their redefinition decisions[58] but other courts that have mandated redefining marriage have disagreed, including the Vermont Supreme Court which held: "The difficulty here is that the marriage laws are facially neutral; they do not single out men or women as a class for disparate treatment, but rather prohibit men and women equally from marrying a person of the same sex."[59] One redefining court in Oregon said marriage constitutes sexual orientation discrimination but redefining courts in Massachusetts and Hawaii noted that marriage laws are neutral as to the orientation of applicants for marriage licenses.[60]

Some cases do not even bother to identify a specific constitutional violation, instead holding that state marriage laws fail to satisfy even the most lenient form of judicial review, rational basis scrutiny. To these courts, the laws are unconstitutional because they are irrational (and by extension, could only be explained as manifestations of invalid hatred against a disadvantaged minority).[61] Reliance on this justification is highly subjective. As Judge Michael McConnell notes: "If such an approach were applied across the board, it would make the substance of the Constitution essentially irrelevant—replacing its enumeration of powers and rights with a generalized examination of 'reasonableness.'"[62]

Indeed, the moving target of court rationales for invalidating state marriages laws allows the courts "like some lumbering bully, to disrupt social norms and practices at its pleasure."[63]

IV.   Official Intolerance

Beyond constitutional structure and first principles, there is a sound prag-matic reality—that government ought to be very, very hesitant to officially brand segments of those governed as holding opinions that are officially repug-nant. Government can, of course, appropriately distance itself from particularly noxious viewpoints, such as racial hatred or advocacy of violence, but it is as-sumed that such instances will be rare and obvious. This idea is related to Justice Robert H. Jackson's famous dictum: "If there is any fixed star in our constitu-tional constellation it is that no official, high or petty, can prescribe what shall be orthodox in politics, nationalism, religion, or other matters of opinion."[64]

In the context of the definition of marriage, caution is particularly appropri-ate since the proportion of the population that would be labeled outliers by a decision that redefined marriage is the new "orthodoxy" is so large. Indeed, as Maggie Gallagher has noted, a decision to redefine marriage and the resulting characterization of opponents of the change as outside the constitutional main-stream would have serious and broad effects particularly for religious groups and individuals.[65]

The logic of the position that "marriage equality" is a constitutional re-quirement can easily result in the stigmatization of those who have good faith objections to this conclusion.

When the Massachusetts Supreme Judicial Court ruled in favor of a new de-finition of marriage, one judge in concurrence added a slightly patronizing aside: "Simple principles of decency dictate that we extend to the plaintiffs, and to their new status, full acceptance, tolerance, and respect."[66] The rhetoric esca-lated, however, a few months later when the Massachusetts legislature tried to respond to the court's decision by enacting a "civil union" status for same-sex couples. In reviewing this proposed legislation, the majority tarred the proposed legislation with the taint of racism by invoking the segregation cases for the proposition that "[t]he history of our nation has demonstrated that separate is seldom, if ever, equal."[67] The court further accused the legislature of trying to "enshrine in law an invidious discrimination" and "[m]aintain[] a second-class citizen status for same-sex couples."[68] As noted above, the people of the state then proposed an amendment to the state constitution that would define mar-riage. In reviewing this proposal, two justices accused the citizens who proposed the amendment of "purposefully discriminat[ing] against an oppressed and dis-favored minority of our citizens in direct contravention of the principles of liber-ty and equality."[69]

The dissents in two recent cases rejecting the redefinition claims employ similar characterizations. The New York dissent accuses the majority of an "un-fortunate misstep" and of retreating from a "proud tradition of affording equal rights to all New Yorkers."[70] A Washington justice goes further, characterizing the state's marriage law as a "discriminatory enactment" and saying it "amounts to animosity with a nicer name."[71] She characterizes the legislative history of the law as "reveal[ing] that what the proponents intended was to impose religious and moral restrictions on the state regulated civil institution of marriage."[72] She concludes: "Future generations of justices on this court will undoubtedly look back on our holding today with regret and even shame."[73]

These kinds of overblown charges are not confined to the judiciary. They were prominent in the recent Senate debate over a proposed federal marriage amendment. Senator Patrick Leahy of Vermont accused amendment proponents of making "efforts to demonize gay and lesbian Americans."[74] Senator Edward Kennedy of Massachusetts claimed the amendment would be "writing bigotry into the constitution" and engaging in "the politics of prejudice and division at its worst."[75] Senator Mark Dayton of Minnesota said the amendment was "un-American."[76]

When policy debates are framed in terms of a choice between unadulterated goodness and mean-spirited prejudice, it is not surprising that the side of "goodness" will be tempted to engage in inflammatory and accusatory language. The result, however, is deeply harmful to the wise policy of government neutrality on highly debatable issues because it expands the scope of issues on which the government will be willing to treat some of its citizens as holding opinions beyond the pale.

V.   Conclusion

The threats to foundational constitutional principles are not confined to the exploits of "activist judges." Indeed, although courts are prominent in the debate over the definition of marriage, all branches of government at all levels are susceptible to the distorting effect of the redefinition effort.

The examples reviewed above illustrate the inevitability of most of the harms to our system from the marriage redefinition movement. When the fundamental definition of marriage is removed from the social to the state realm, an expansion of government jurisdiction cannot be avoided. Likewise, the logic of a fundamental right to create one's own definition of marriage cannot be restrained from making dissenting states, institutions and individuals legal outliers. The absence of a clear mandate for the redefinition in state and federal charters also makes inevitable the creation of a body of legal justifications that will appear arbitrary and subjective. Perhaps redefinition could be achieved without harm to the principle of separation of powers, but as discussed below, the impetus for the movement makes very likely a strategy that will result in cutting corners in working for the legal change.

None of this is to say that the redefinition movement presents an entirely *sui generis* case. Analogous issues have and will produce similar kinds of distortions of our constitutional fabric. A factor common to these issues and the marriage question is that they are fueled by a perfectionist ideology. Unlike the normal give and take that characterizes the typical political process, a perfectionist ideology requires its demands to be met absolutely. After all, the argument runs, if this is a "right" it cannot be withheld without doing something not merely unwise but deeply wrong, even immoral.

As a result, the adherents of this ideology can be expected to believe that almost any manner of tactic is justifiable because of the self-evident rightness of their position. In this case, adherents of the ideology believe the benefits of a legal regime that treats all freely chosen adult relationships as precisely equal (or rather, the same) are likely to be so great that some restraints are merely nuisances. By extension, they believe that opposition to the effort can reflect nothing other than bad faith animus towards them.

While I am not sanguine about the possibility that actual and potential constitutional harms will motivate a cessation of the fight to appropriate the social capital of the marriage institution, perhaps a realization of the stakes might bolster the resolve of the institution's defenders.

Notes

1. Thanks to Joel Blickenstaff, Scott Paul and Professor Lynn Wardle's research assistant, Todd K. Jenson, for research assistance.

2. John Lukacs, *Alexis de Tocqueville: A Historical Appreciation* 5 LITERATURE OF LIBERTY 7 (Spring 1982).

3. Marbury v. Madison, 5 U.S. 137, 176-177 (1803).

4. *See* William C. Duncan, *State, Society and the Redefinition of Marriage* 19 THE FAMILY IN AMERICA 1 (September 2005).

5. In re J. P., 648 P.2d 1364, 1373 (Utah 1982).

6. Prince v. Massachusetts, 321 U.S. 158, 166 (1944).

7. Bruce C. Hafen, *Law, Custom and Mediating Structures: The Family as a Community of Memory* in LAW AND THE ORDERING OF OUR LIFE TOGETHER 100 (Richard John Neuhaus, ed. 1989).

8. Id.

9. Meyer v. Nebraska, 262 U.S. 390, 402 (1923).

10. ROBERT NISBET, THE QUEST FOR COMMUNITY 25 (1969).

11. Roger Scruton, *Forget ID Cards, This is the Real Big Brother* DAILY MAIL 12 (Aug. 17, 2004).

12. ALEXIS DE TOCQUEVILLE, DEMOCRACY IN AMERICA 663 (Translated by Harvey C. Mansfield & Delba Winthrop, 2000) (emphasis added).

13. *See* Baehr v. Lewin, 852 P.2d 44, 58 (Haw. 1993); Baker v. Vermont, 744 A.2d 864, 885 (Vt. 1999).

14. F.C. DeCoste, *Courting Leviathan: Limited Government and Social Freedom in Reference re Same-Sex Marriage* 42 ALBERTA L. REV. 4, 18 (2005).

15. Goodridge v. Department of Public Health, 798 N.E.2d 941, 954 (Mass. 2003).

16. Versions of this very idea have been advanced in the legal literature, *see* James G. Dwyer, *A Child-Centered Approach to Parentage Law* 14 WM. & MARY BILL RTS. J. 843 (20060; Nancy E. Dowd, *Parentage at Birth: Birthfathers and Social Fatherhood* 14 WM. & MARY BILL RTS. J. 909 (2006).

17. *See* William C. Duncan, *Avoidance Strategy: Same-Sex Marriage Litigation and the Federal Courts* 29 CAMPBELL LAW REVIEW 29 (2006).

18. *See* Citizens for Equal Protection v. Bruning, 455 F.3d 859 (8th Cir. 2006).

19. Smelt v. Orange County, 374 F.Supp.2d 861 (D. Cent. Ca. 2005) affirmed 2006 WL 1194825 (9th Cir. 2006).

20. *See* Wyatt Buchanan, *Going for Broke in Battle Over Gay Vows* S.F. CHRONICLE A1 (Jan. 23, 2006); Phil LaPadula, *Gay Groups Ask Court to Throw Out Suit Against Defense of Marriage Act* N.Y. BLADE (Jan. 25, 2006).

21. *Opening Brief of Proposed Intevenor Equality California*, Smelt v. County of Orange, No. 05-56040 (9th Cir. 2005) at 18-20, notes 7-8.

22. Miller-Jenkins v. Miller-Jenkins, 2006 WL 2192715 (Vt. 2006).

23. 15 Vt. Stat. Ann. §1204.

24. Baker v. State, 744 A.2d 864 (1999).

25. GEORGE W. CAREY, IN DEFENSE OF THE CONSTITUTION 60 (1989).

26. MASS. CONST. Art. XXX.

27. *Federalist 47* in THE FEDERALIST 260 (Michael Lloyd Chadwick, ed., 1987).

28. U.S. CONST., art III, sec. 2.

29. *Federalist 78* in THE FEDERALIST 421 (Michael Lloyd Chadwick, ed., 1987).

30. United Steelworkers of America, AFL-CIO-CLC v. Weber, 443 U.S. 193, 218-219 (1979) (Burger, C.J., dissenting) (quoting BENJAMIN CARDOZO, THE NATURE OF THE JUDICIAL PROCESS 141 (1921)).

31. Baker v. Vermont, 744 A.2d 864 (Vt. 1999).

32. Id. at 887.

33. Goodridge v. Department of Public Health, 798 N.E.2d 941, 970 (Mass. 2003)

34. In re Opinion of the Justices to the Senate, 802 N.E.2d 565 (Mass. 2004).

35. Tonja Jacobi, *Sharing the Love: The Political Powers of Remedial Delay in Same-Sex Marriage Cases* 15 LAW & SEXUALITY 11, 56 (2006).

36. Schulman v. Attorney General, 850 N.E.2d 505, 512 (Mass. 2006) (Greaney, J., concurring). The justices gave no explanation of the source of authority for this proposition.

37. RING W. LARDNER, JR., THE YOUNG IMMIGRUNTS 78 (1920). This also brings to mind Professor Robert Nagel's observation that some court behavior is "suggestive of the sort of self-importance that in private lives precedes public commitment." Robert F. Nagel, *Name-Calling and the Clear Error Rule* 88 NW. U. L. REV. 193, 204 (1993).

38. David Austin, Tom Hallman Jr., & Scott Learn, *The Marriage Brokers*, OREGONIAN A1 (Mar. 7, 2004).

39. Rachel Gordon, *S.F. Defies Law, Marries Gays* S.F. CHRONICLE A1 (Feb. 13, 2004).

40. Cal. Fam. Code §308.5 "Only marriage between a man and a woman is valid or recognized in California.").

41. Lee Romney & Patrick Dillon, *S.F. Judge Won't Halt Marriages* L.A. TIMES A1 (Feb. 18, 2004); Harriet Chiang & Rachel Gordon, *The Weddings Go On, Day in Court: Judges Refuse Immediate Halt to Same-sex Marriages* S.F. CHRONICLE A1 (Feb. 18, 2004).

42. Letter from Arnold Schwarzenegger, California Governor, to California Attorney General Bill Lockyer Regarding Same-Sex Marriage (Feb. 20, 2004) (available at http://www.governor.ca.gov/state/govsite/gov_homepage.jsp); Maura Dolan, *S.F. Gets a Week to Make Case for Gay Marriage* L.A. TIMES A1 (Feb. 28, 2004).

43. Press Release, Judicial Conference of California, Administrative Office of the Courts, California Supreme Court Takes Action in Same-Sex Marriage Cases (Mar. 11, 2004) (available at http://www.courtinfo.ca.gov/presscenter/newsreleases/NR15-04.HTM); Maura Dolan & Lee Romney, *High Court Halts Gay Marriages* L.A. TIMES A1 (Mar. 12, 2004).

44. David Austin, Tom Hallman Jr., & Scott Learn, *The Marriage Brokers* OREGONIAN A1 (Mar. 7, 2004); Attorney General Hardy Myers Opinion to Governor Kulongoski, Mar. 12, 2004 (available at http://www.doj.state.or.us/pdfs/AG_ samesexopinion.pdf); Li v. State, 2004 WL 1258167 (Or. Cir. Ct. 2004).

45. Marc Santora & Thomas Crampton, *Same-Sex Weddings In Upstate Village Test New York Law* N.Y. TIMES A1 (Feb. 28, 2004); Thomas J. Lueck, Al Baker & Thomas Crampton, *Police Charge New Paltz Mayor For Marrying Same-Sex Couples*, N.Y. TIMES B4 (Mar. 3, 2004); Thomas Crampton, *Court Says New Paltz Mayor Can't Hold Gay Weddings* N.Y. TIMES B6 (June 8, 2004).

46. Robert Hanley & Laura Mansnerus, *Asbury Park Deputy Mayor Officiates At A Gay Marriage* N.Y. TIMES B5 (Mar. 9, 2004); Evelyn Nieves, *Calif. Judge Won't Halt Gay Nuptials; New Mexico County Briefly Follows San Francisco's Lead* WASH. POST A1 (Feb. 21, 2004).

47. *See* Wendy J. Herdlein, *Something Old, Something New: Does the Massachusetts Constitution Provide for Same-Sex "Marrriage"?* 12 B.U. PUB. INT. L. J. 137, 178 (2002).

48. MASS. CONST., art 48.

49. LIMITS v. President of the Senate, 604 N.E.2d 1307 (Mass. 1992).

50. Wendy J. Herdlein, *Something Old, Something New: Does the Massachusetts Constitution Provide for Same-Sex "Marrriage"?* 12 B.U. PUB. INT. L. J. 137, 179 (2002).

51. Id. at 180.

52. FORREST MCDONALD, NOVUS ORDO SECLORUM 291 (1985).

53. Robert P. George, *Reason, Freedom, and the Rule of Law: Their Significance in Western Thought* 15 REGENT U. L. REV. 187, 188 (2002-2003) (citing LON FULLER, THE MORALITY OF LAW 39 (1964)).

54. *Federalist 78* in THE FEDERALIST 426 (Michael Lloyd Chadwick, ed., 1987).

55. ROBERT F. NAGEL, THE IMPLOSION OF AMERICAN FEDERALISM 129 (2001).

56. Brause v. Bureau of Vital Statistics, 1998 WL 88743, *4 (Alaska Super. Ct. 1998); Hernandez v. Robles, 794 N.Y.S.2d 579 (N.Y. Sup. 2005) *reversed* 2006 WL 1835429 (N.Y. 2006); Andersen v. King County, 2004 WL 1738447 (Wash. Super. Ct. 2004); Castle v. Washington, 2004 WL 1985215 (Wash. Super. Ct. 2004).

57. Baehr v. Lewin, 852 P.2d 44, 56-57 (Haw. 1993).

58. Baehr v. Lewin, 852 P.2d 44, 67 (Haw. 1993); Deane v. Conaway, 2006 WL 148145 (Md. Cir. Ct. 2005); Consolidated Marriage Cases, 2005 WL 583129, 9-10 (Cal. Super. Ct. 2005).

59. Baker v. Vermont, 744 A.2d 864, 880 note 13 (Vt. 1999).

60. Li v. State, 2004 WL 1258167 (Or. Cir. Ct. 2004); Baehr v. Lewin, 852 P.2d 44, 51 note 11 (Haw. 1993); Goodridge v. Department of Public Health, 798 N.E.2d 941, 953 note 11 (Mass. 2003).

61. *See* Consolidated Marriage Cases, 2005 WL 583129 (Cal. Super. Ct. 2005); Goodridge v. Department of Public Health, 798 N.E.2d 941 (Mass. 2003).

62. Michael W. McConnell, Book Review, *Active Liberty: A Progressive Alternative to Textualism and Originalism?* 119 HARVARD L. REV. 2387, 2410 (2006).

63. Robert F. Nagel, *The Formulaic Constitution* 84 MICH. L. REV. 165, 203 (1985).

64. West Virginia v. Barnette, 319 U.S. 624, 642 (1943).

65. Maggie Gallagher, *Banned in Boston* WEEKLY STANDARD 20 (May 15, 2006).

66. Goodridge v. Department of Public Health, 798 N.E.2d 941, 973 (Mass. 2003) (Greaney, J., concurring).

67. In re Opinion of the Justices to the Senate, 802 N.E.2d 565, 569 (Mass. 2004).

68. Id. at 570-571.

69. Schulman v. Attorney General, 850 N.E.2d 505, 512 (Mass. 2006) (Greaney, J., concurring).

70. Hernandez v. Robles, 2006 WL 1835429 (N.Y. 2006) (Kaye, C.J., dissenting).

71. Andersen v. King County, 138 P.3d 963, 1032 &1036 (Wash. 2006) (Bridge, J., dissenting).

72. Id. at 1034.

73. Id. at 1040.

74. Congressional Record—Senate, S5407 (June 5, 2006).

75. Congressional Record—Senate, S5465 (June 6, 2006).

76. Id. at S5466.

ABOUT THE CONTRIBUTORS

Martha Bailey, LL.B. (U of Toronto), LL.M. (Queen's), D.Phil. (Oxford), is a professor in the Faculty of Law of Queen's University. She teaches Family Law, Conflict of Laws, and Comparative Legal Traditions. Her research focuses on transnational family law, religious diversity and legal pluralism. During 2006-2007, she was a research visitor at NALSAR University of Law in India, Melbourne University in Australia, and Emory University in Atlanta, Georgia.

A. Dean Byrd, Ph.D. M.B.A., M.P.H., is Adjunct Clinical Professor, University of Utah School of Medicine with appointments in the Department of Family and Preventive Medicine, the Department of Psychiatry as well as an adjunct appointment in the Department of Family Studies, also at the University of Utah. He received his academic training at Spartanburg Methodist College, Brigham Young University, Virginia Commonwealth University and Medical College of Virginia, Loyola University and the University of Utah. He is the author of 4 books and more than 100 journal articles, book chapters, book reviews and opinion editorials.

Allan Carlson is President of The Howard Center for Family, Religion & Society in Rockford, Illinois. He holds his Ph.D. in Modern European History from the Ohio University. He is the editor of The Family in America monograph series and a contributing editor to Touchstone magazine. His books include The Swedish Experiment in Family Politics: The Myrdals and the Interwar Population Crisis (1990), Fractured Generations: Crafting a Family Policy for Twenty-first Century America (2005), and Conjugal America: On the Public Purposes of Marriage (forthcoming in September 2006).

Dale Carpenter is the Earl R. Larson Professor of Civil Rights and Civil Liberties Law at the University of Minnesota Law School. He teaches and writes in the areas of constitutional law, the First Amendment, sexual orientation and the law, and commercial law. Professor Carpenter was chosen the Stanley V. Kinyon Teacher of Year for 2003-04 and 2005-06 and was the Tenured Teacher of the Year for 2006-07. He was the Julius E. Davis Professor of Law for 2006-07 and the Vance K. Opperman Research Scholar for 2003-04. Since 2004, he has served as an editor of *Constitutional Commentary*. He received his B.A. degree in history, *magna cum laude*, from Yale College in 1989. He received his J.D., with honors, from the University of Chicago Law School in 1992, where he was Editor-in-Chief of the *University of Chicago Law Review*. He received both the D. Francis Bustin Prize for excellence in legal scholarship and the John M.

Olin Foundation Scholarship for Law & Economics. He clerked for The Honorable Edith H. Jones of the United States Court of Appeals for the Fifth Circuit, and practiced law in Houston and in San Francisco.

Jason S. Carroll received his B.S. (Family Science) and M.S. (Marriage and Family Therapy) degrees from Brigham Young Univeristy, and his Ph.D. from theUniversity of Minnesota (Family Social Science). He teaches in the School of Family Life at Brigham Young University. He has published empirical and qualitative research dealing with premarital education, prediction of marital quality, prediction of marital breakup, marital negotiation, marriage theory, family process and family relations. In 2001 he was recognized for the best manuscript by a professional in training family process.

Bryce Christensen earned his Ph.D. at Marquette University in Milwaukee, Wisconsin. The founding editor of The Family in America published by the Howard Center (Rockford, Illinois), Dr. Christensen has since 2001 been a member of SUU's English department, where he is assistant professor of composition. Author of Utopia Against the Family (Ignatius, 1990) and Divided We Fall: Family Discord and the Fracturing of America (Transaction, 2005), Dr. Christensen has published articles in Philosophy and Literature, Christianity and Literature, Renascence, Modern Age, and other journals. He and his wife are the parents of three sons.

Louis DeSerres B.A., M.B.A., is involved on the front lines of the marriage debate in Canada, participating in efforts to reverse current legislation allowing same-sex marriage. He is co-founder and director of Preserve Marriage - Protect Children's Rights (www.preservemarriage.ca). He also serves as Québec Regional Director for Vote Marriage Canada, a non-partisan organization lobbying in favor of man-woman marriage in Canada. He testified at the Judiciary Committee of the Massachusetts Legislature on the Marriage Amendment: "How heterosexual marriage protects children's rights and best interests – Does marriage need a constitutional definition?"

David C. Dollahite is a Professor of Family Life in the School of Family Life at Brigham Young University. His research has focused on fathering, families and religion, family conflict resolution, and strengthening families. He is the author or co-author of scores of scholarly and professional publications, and author or editor several academic and professional books. In 2003 he was the recipient of the (2-year) Eliza R. Snow University Fellowship.

William C. Duncan formerly served as acting director of the Marriage Law Project at the Catholic University of America's Columbus School of Law and as executive director of the Marriage and Family Law Research Grant at J. Reuben Clark Law School, Brigham Young University, where he also was a visiting professor. He has published numerous articles on constitutional and family law issues in a variety of legal journals.

Scott FitzGibbon Professor at Boston College Law School. J.D. from Harvard, B.C.L. from Oxford. Member of the Massachusetts Bar. Professor FitzGibbon has published extensively on the jurisprudential issues in family law generally and regarding same-sex marriage.

Edwin E. Gantt is an Associate Professor of Psychology at Brigham Young University in Provo, Utah. He received his doctorate in psychology at Duquesne University in 1998. He is the author of numerous peer-reviewed articles and invited chapters examining the assumptions of egoism, determinism, and reductionism in contemporary psychological theory and practice. In particular, his work has addressed some of the ways in which these assumptions render psychological theory and therapeutic practice unable to adequately account for empathy, altruism, moral agency and meaning. His is also coauthor (with Richard N. Williams) of the book Psychology-for-the-Other: Levinas, Ethics, and the Practice of Psychology. He and his wife have been married for 19 years and are the proud parents of four sons.

Marianne M. Jennings is a professor of legal and ethical studies in the W.P Carey School of Business at Arizona State University. She has taught there since 1977. She has served as a consultant to companies, government agencies and educational institutions. She writes a weekly column that is syndicated around the country. She is the author of Business Ethics: Case Studies and Readings (4th edition) as well as the forthcoming *A Business Tale: A Story of Choices, Success, Ethics and A Very Large Rabbit.*

Lynne Marie Kohm (B.A. Albany, 1980, J.D. Syracuse, 1988) is the John Brown McCarty Professor of Family Law at Regent University School of Law. She has been licensed to practice law in NY, MA, VA, DC and FL after serving as a partner in the New York general practice firm of Webster & Kohm. Professor Kohm has taught Family Law at Regent University's law school since 1994, at William and Mary School of Law in 2000, and guest lectured at Cornell University in the 1990s. Her work has focused on legal research and scholarship on marriage, women's issues, children, and family issues, for which she received the Chancellor's Award at Regent University in 2005. She teaches courses in family law, bioethics, human life & death, and elder law. Her professional service includes the Virginia State Bar Family Law Section Board of Governors, the Virginia Bar Association Domestic Relations Council, the Chief Justice's Task Force on the Family Court in Virginia, and the Governor's Advisory Committee on Child Abuse and Neglect.

Charles J. Reid, Jr. was born in Milwaukee, Wisconsin. He graduated from the University of Wisconsin-Milwaukee, where he majored in Latin, Classics, and History. Reid then attended the Catholic University of America, where he earned J.D. and J.C.L. (license in canon law) degrees. Reid then attended Cornell University, where he earned a Ph.D. in the history of medieval law under the supervision of Brian Tierney. His thesis at Cornell was on the Christian, medieval origins of the western concept of individual rights. In 1991, Reid was appointed research associate in law and history at the Emory University School of Law, where he has worked closely with Harold Berman on the history of western law. Reid has also pursued a research agenda involving scholarship on the history of western notions of individual rights; the history of liberty of conscience in America; and the natural-law foundations of the jurisprudence of Judge John Noonan.

Charles J. Russo, M.Div., J.D., Ed. D., is the Joseph Panzer Chair in Education in the School of Education and Allied Professions and Adjunct Professor in the School of Law at the University of Dayton. The 1998-99 President of the Education Law Association, he authored or co-authored more than 170 articles in peer-reviewed journals, authored, co-authored, edited, or co-edited twenty-two books, and almost 600 publications. Dr. Russo speaks extensively on issues in Education Law in the United States and has lectured in nineteen other countries on six continents. He has also taught summer courses in England and Spain and served as a Visiting Professor at Queensland University of Technology in Brisbane, Australia; the University of Sarajevo, Bosnia; South East European University, Macedonia; and the Potchefstroom Campus of Northwest University in Potchefstroom, South Africa.

Vincent J. Samar is an Adjunct Professor of Law at Illinois Institute of Technology, Chicago-Kent College of Law, and an Adjunct Professor of Philosophy at both Loyola University Chicago and Oakton Community College. He is the author of Justifying Judgment: Practicing Law and Philosophy (University Press of Kansas, 1998), The Right to Privacy: Gays, Lesbians and the Constitution (Temple University Press, 1991), and editor of New York Times, 20th Century in Review: Gay Rights Movement (2001), along with also having published numerous articles and review articles in law, philosophy, same-sex marriage, and gay rights as human rights.

Roger Severino is Legal Counsel for the Becket Fund for Religious Liberty, an interfaith public-interest law firm based in Washington D.C. After graduating from Harvard Law School, Mr. Severino joined the Becket Fund in 2003 where he has worked on religious freedom cases under immigration, landuse, free speech, and international law. In addition to radio and television appearances, Mr. Severino has contributed articles on church and state for the Wall Street Journal, the New Republic Online, and Jewish World Review and has been quoted by the Chicago Tribune, World Magazine and the Weekly Standard. Before law school he received a Master's Degree in Public Policy with highest distinction from Carnegie Mellon University and a Bachelor's in Business Administration with honors from USC.

Mark Strasser is Trustees Professor of Law at Capital University Law School in Columbus, Ohio. He teaches and writes in family and constitutional law, among other areas. Much of his writing focuses on the recognition of families involving sexual minorities, whether as a matter of state or of federal law.

Seana Sugrue is Associate Professor of Politics and Chairman of the Department of Politics at Ave Maria University. She came to Ave Maria University from Princeton University, where she was the Associate Director of the James Madison Program in American Ideals and Institutions. Her research interests include civil liberties and constitutional governance, the role of law in the formation of a just society, civic institutions such as the family, and pro-life concerns. She teaches courses in Constitutional Law, American Civilization, International Relations, and Public Policy, among others. Dr. Sugrue holds the degrees of B.B.A. from Bishop's University, LL.B. from the University of Ottawa, and both LL.M. and D.C.L. from McGill University. She has taught at Princeton and McGill.

Lynn D. Wardle is the Bruce C. Hafen Professor of Law at the J. Reuben Clark Law School at Brigham Young University in Provo, Utah. He teaches law and directs the Marriage & Family Law Research Project there. His major areas of research and writing have been family law, biomedical law, conflicts of laws, and US legal history. He is the author, editor, or co-author/editor of nine books or treatises and more than one hundred articles, chapters in monographs, and other publications. He served as Secretary-General (1994-2000) and President (2000-2002) of the International Society of Family Law, now serves on the ISFL Executive Council, and is a member of the American Law Institute. He had taught at law schools Japan, Australia, China, Scotland and the United States, and lectured in universities or academic conferences in fifteen other nations. He has given expert testimony to legislative committees of the U.S. Congress and of several state legislatures on a variety of issues concerning family law. He and his wife, Marian, are the proud parents of two children and four grandchildren.